Mastering
Poetry

WITHDRAWN

D1346779

Palgrave Master Series

Accounting
Accounting Skills
Advanced English Language
Advanced Pure Mathematics
Arabic
Basic Management
Biology
British Politics
Business Communication
Business Environment
C Programming
C++ Programming
Chemistry
COBOL Programming
Communication
Computing
Counselling Skills
Counselling Theory
Customer Relations
Database Design
Delphi Programming
Desktop Publishing
e-Business
Economic and Social History
Economics
Electrical Engineering
Electronics
Employee Development
English Grammar
English Language
English Literature
Fashion Buying and Merchandising
    Management
Fashion Marketing
Fashion Styling
Financial Management
Geography
Global Information Systems

Globalization of Business
Human Resource Management
Information Technology
International Trade
Internet
Java
Language of Literature
Management Skills
Marketing Management
Mathematics
Microsoft Office
Microsoft Windows, Novell Netware
    and UNIX
Modern British History
Modern European History
Modern United States History
Modern World History
Networks
Novels of Jane Austen
Organisational Behaviour
Pascal and Delphi Programming
Philosophy
Physics
Poetry
Practical Criticism
Psychology
Public Relations
Shakespeare
Social Welfare
Sociology
Spanish
Statistics
Strategic Management
Systems Analysis and Design
Team Leadership
Theology
Twentieth-Century Russian History
Visual Basic
World Religions

www.palgravemasterseries.com

Palgrave Master Series
Series Standing Order ISBN 0–333–69343–4
(outside North America only)

You can receive future titles in this series as they are published by placing a standing order. Please contact your bookseller or, in case of difficulty, write to us at the address below with your name and address, the title of the series and the ISBN quoted above.

Customer Services Department, Macmillan Distribution Ltd
Houndmills, Basingstoke, Hampshire RG21 6XS, England

Mastering
Poetry

Sara Thorne

First published 2006 by
PALGRAVE MACMILLAN
Houndmills, Basingstoke, Hampshire RG21 6XS and
175 Fifth Avenue, New York, N.Y. 10010
Companies and representatives throughout the world

PALGRAVE MACMILLAN is the global academic imprint of the Palgrave
Macmillan division of St. Martin's Press, LLC and of Palgrave Macmillan Ltd.
Macmillan® is a registered trademark in the United States, United Kingdom
and other countries. Palgrave is a registered trademark in the European
Union and other countries.

ISBN-13: 978–0–333–69875–4
ISBN-10: 0–333–69875–4

This book is printed on paper suitable for recycling and
made from fully managed and sustained forest sources.

A catalogue record for this book is available from the British Library.

10	9	8	7	6	5	4	3	2	1
15	14	13	12	11	10	09	08	07	06

Printed and bound in China

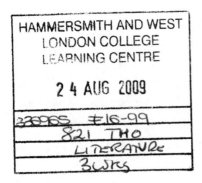

▣ ⍦ Contents

PART II   KEY POETS

Hughes's approach to poetry.   Hughes, nature and the inner life.
Content and themes.   Images and symbols.   Poetic form.   Style.
Ted Hughes and the English poetic tradition.   *Activity 13.8 'Red'.*
Women poets 1960–90: The emergence of a strong women's
tradition.   Single-gender anthologies.   The groundbreakers.   Sylvia
Plath (1932–63).   Women poets of the 1970s and 1980s.   The
search for an appropriate voice.   The dramatic monologue.
Content and themes.   Language, style and tone.   Women poets
and the English poetic tradition.   *Activity 13.9 'Because She Has
Come', Grace Nichols.*

▼ Acknowledgements

The author and publishers wish to thank the following for permission to use copyright material: Bloodaxe Books for Frances Horovitz, 'January' from *Collected Poems* by Frances Horovitz, ed. Roger Garfitt (1985); Carcanet Press Ltd for Gillian Clarke, 'RS: For R. S. Thomas' from *Collected Poems* by Gillian Clarke (1997); Curtis Brown, London, on behalf of the author for Grace Nichols, 'Epilogue' from *I is a Long-Memoried Woman* by Grace Nichols, Karnak House (1983). Copyright © Grace Nichols 1983; and Grace Nichols, 'Because She Has Come' from *Lazy Thoughts of a Lazy Woman* by Grace Nichols, Virago (1989). Copyright © Grace Nichols 1989; Faber and Faber Ltd for Ted Hughes, 'A Kill' from *Crow* by Ted Hughes (1970) and 'Red' from *Birthday Letters* by Ted Hughes (1998); Ezra Pound, 'In a station of the metro' from *Collected Shorter Poems* by Ezra Pound (1968); Seamus Heaney, 'Seeing the Sick' from *Electric Light* by Seamus Heaney (2001); and extracts from T. S. Eliot, 'The Love Song of J. Alfred Prufrock' and 'The Waste Land' from *Collected Poems 1909–1962* by T. S. Eliot (1963); Farrar, Straus and Giroux, LLC for Elizabeth Bishop, 'One Art' from *Complete Poems 1927–1979* by Elizabeth Bishop. Copyright © 1979, 1983, by Alice Helen Methfessel; The Gallery Press and the author for Paula Mehan, 'You Open Your Hands to Me' from *The Man who was Marked by Winter* by Paula Meehan (1991); Harvard University Press and the Trustees of Amherst College for Emily Dickinson, 'If I shouldn't be alive' from *The Poems of Emily Dickinson*, ed. Thomas H. Johnson, J254, The Belknap Press of Harvard University Press. Copyright © 1951, 1955, 1979, 1983 by the President and Fellows of Harvard College; David Higham Associates on behalf of the Estate of the author for Dylan Thomas, 'Fern Hill' from *Collected Poems* by Dylan Thomas, J. M. Dent (1977); Houghton Mifflin Company for material from *The Works of Geoffrey Chaucer*, ed. F. N. Robinson. Copyright © 1957 by Houghton Mifflin Company; Brian Keeble, Literary Executor of the Estate of the author, for Katherine Raine, 'Invocation' from *The Collected Poems of Kathleen Raine*, Hamish Hamilton (1956); Tom Leonard for his poem, 'right inuff' from *Intimate Voices* by Tom Leonard, Etruscan Books (2003). Copyright © 2003 Tom Leonard; The Orion Publishing Group for material from William Langland, *The Vision of Piers Plowman*, ed. A. V. C. Schmidt, J. M. Dent (1978); Oxford University Press for Gerard Manley Hopkins, 'God's Grandeur' and 'The Windhover' from *Poems of Gerard Manley Hopkins*, 4th edition, ed. W. H. Gardner and N. H. MacKenzie (1970); and material from Edmund Spenser, *Faerie Queene*, ed. J. C. Smith, Oxford English Texts (1909); Pan Macmillan for Carol Ann Duffy, 'White Writing' from *Feminine Gospels* by Carol Ann Duffy, Picador (2002); and Kathleen Jamie, 'Ultrasound' from *Jizzen* by Kathleen Jamie, Picador (1999); Penguin Books Ltd for material from *Beowulf*, ed. Michael Alexander, Penguin Classics (1996). Copyright © Michael Alexander 1995; Peterloo Poets for Elma Mitchell, 'Country Life' from *People Etcetera* by Elma Mitchell (1987); PFD on behalf of the authors for Andrew Motion, 'Regime Change' read on Radio 4, Today programme (2003). Copyright © Andrew Motion 2003; Roger McGough, 'Everyday Eclipses' from *Everyday Eclipses* by Roger McGough, Viking (2002). Copyright © Roger McGough 2002; Jane Ross for an extract from Alan Ross, 'Embankment Before Snow' from *To Whom it May Concern: Poems 1952–7* by Alan Ross, Hamish Hamilton (1958); University of Kansas Libraries on behalf of William Terry for John Gould Fletcher, 'The Skaters'; A. P. Watt Ltd on behalf of Michael B. Yeats for W. B. Yeats, 'Meru' from *A Full Moon in March* by W. B. Yeats (1935). Every effort has been made to trace the copyright holders but if any have been inadvertently overlooked the publishers will be pleased to make the necessary arrangement at the first opportunity.

The author would like to thank all the people who have helped at each stage in the preparation of this book.

◼ ⅄ Preface

This book explores a wide range of poetry, introducing you to examples from the earliest Old English verse to poems of the twenty-first century. It also provides you with practical guidelines for reading and analysing poetry, encouraging you to look at the ways in which language, structure and style work together to create meaning.

Poetry is an intensely personal genre, in terms both of the poet's creation and the reader's response. This book, therefore, offers its explorations of verse not as comprehensive interpretations, but as the foundations of discussion and understanding. The aim is to nurture a fascination with the genre that will take readers far beyond the confines of the contents here.

In order to help you approach what can seem a difficult genre, this book is divided into two distinct areas: approaches to poetry; and key poets. Part I draws together the main features of poetry that you will need to recognise and understand. It is important to become familiar with the terminology used so that you can enhance your critical skills. Part II explores the work and context of significant poets in the English literary tradition, tracing the development of their work, the major influences on them, and the literary movements that were to shape their writing.

Each part is divided into clearly defined chapters that focus on a key topic. General information provides definitions and explanations; a wide range of texts broadens your experience of poetry; activities test your understanding; and commentaries suggest possible readings and demonstrate the ways in which linguistic and literary approaches can be used. For those requiring additional support, there is also a structured framework to guide you through the process of analysis.

Mastering Poetry provides an introduction to the skills and knowledge needed to read poetry effectively. It has been designed to enable you to get the most out of your study. Using the contents list and index, you can learn about specific literary and linguistic features of poetry, find out about particular literary movements, understand the chronology of a poet's work, or explore the ways in which a poet's linguistic and structural choices affect the way we read and respond to a poem. Whether developing personal interests, supporting work covered in school or college, or revising, this book will help you to feel confident in your ability to read any poem.

Readers are often wary of poetry – disconcerted by its apparent obscurity, its personal and sometimes unfamiliar way of seeing the world, and its tendency to play fast and loose with the rules of language. I hope that this book will encourage you to overcome any fears you may have because poetry is, above all, something that we can enjoy.

Part I

Approaches to poetry

▓ ⚙ | Introduction

Poetry is perhaps the most distinctive literary genre in terms of its presentation on the page, its structural conventions, and its often unexpected approach to language and syntax. For these very reasons it is both challenging and exciting. This book aims to help you unravel the complexities so that you can enjoy your experience of poetry whether you are reading it for pleasure or as part of an examination syllabus.

Reading a poem

On first reading, we respond to a poem at a personal level. We may engage with the ideas, empathise with the poet's attitudes, relish the sound of the words, or be fascinated by the lexical choice – we may even be bewildered. All of these are valid first responses, but where do we go from this starting point? Poems are complex texts that merit closer reading. They are 'products' created by a poet who wishes, perhaps, to explore universal feelings and attitudes, or to express a personal response to a particular event, place or occasion. They are 'products' in the sense that poems, on the whole, do not just 'happen' – they are crafted, consciously composed from words, grammatical structures, poetic devices and forms. The poet makes decisions and each of these decisions will have an effect on the final work.

This book will help you to look at a poet's decisions, moving beyond your first response to an analytical assessment that will enhance your understanding. You will become an active reader, able to look more closely at the techniques a poet uses and the effects they create.

The approach of the book

Beginning with the assumption that **how** a poet says something is as important as **what** he or she says, this book aims to use close reading techniques to explore the ways in which poets communicate with their readers. Words may be chosen according to their sound, their meaning, their function or their relationship with the words around them. They are used within syntactical structures and, on a larger scale, within the conventions of poetic form. It would therefore seem logical that, once we have familiarised ourselves with the general ideas of a poem, we must look more closely at the language and structure.

By combining the benefits of language study with traditional literary approaches, you will be able to explore the relationship between poets and their material, words and their effects, meaning and structure. You will move beyond first impressions to considered opinions that can be supported by reference to the text. This kind of analysis does not have to preclude pleasure in the 'being-ness' of a poem – its sound, images, ideas and textures. Instead, it encourages us to ask questions, a process that helps us to move towards an understanding of the multiple possibilities of poetry.

It is important to remember that poems are polysemic – different readers interpret them in different ways. What this book offers is a wide range of texts with commentaries that suggest a possible reading based on the literary and linguistic features. The hope is that you will become an active reader, using the discussions as a starting point and coming to your own conclusions based on evidence that supports your point of view.

The organisation of the book

The first part of this book is designed to make you think about poetry in general terms. It addresses key areas that are relevant to the genre whether you are tackling a single poem, a key poet, or a period or movement. Explanations, examples and commentaries are used to help you understand the terminology and its relevance to a particular poem.

Part II tackles a selection of poets who have made a significant contribution to the development of a distinctive English poetic tradition. Poets are set within their literary and historical context, and their work is considered under key headings that will enable you to discuss their poetry in a focused and analytical way. The selection of poets is clearly not exhaustive, but offers an introduction to the development of English poetry.

Finally, the book will conclude with a glossary that will explain the terminology used in the book for those who wish to develop or reinforce their knowledge of key literary and linguistic concepts. Definitions, examples and explanations will demonstrate how each concept works in context.

Above all, I hope that this book will overcome general fears about the difficulty of poetry by encouraging you to look closely at the words on the page. Enjoy exploring the physical properties of poetry and benefit from the pleasure at seeing the layers of meaning unfold.

▼ 2 What is poetry?

Each reader of this book will have a different experience of poetry. You may not have read a poem for a long time; you may be haunted by fears of 'not understanding'; you may be about to embark on a study of a particular poet. Whatever your experience, this book will help you to engage with poetry in an enjoyable and productive way.

A starting point

Most people have read some poetry and have some knowledge of the features that make it distinctive. As a starting point, it is useful to think about what poetry means to you and what particular features you would associate with it. No doubt you can identify some of the distinctive features of poetry; you will have some idea about the kinds of things poets write about; and you will have personal opinions about poetry as a genre.

Activity 2.1

> **What do you already know about poetry?**
> **Jot down your thoughts on the mind map below. Some ideas have been included to get you started.**

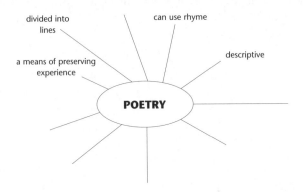

Commentary

Each reader's response to this activity will have been different, but inevitably there will be some common ideas. You may have identified the visual element that poetry shares with painting – its words paint pictures for the reader. The importance of the words may also have featured in your jottings. Like other writers, poets choose language carefully to convey powerful feelings, recreate a moment in time, or to address difficult issues. The words they choose can stir our emotions and our intellect, enabling us to feel and experience something about the world or ourselves. You may also have noted the eloquence and musical qualities of poetry – its origins can be traced back to the earliest oral traditions in which rhythmic chants accompanied by a simple drum beat were used to recall the memorable and significant events of life.

In addressing its meaning, you may see poetry as a means of coming to terms with life, or a means of bringing order to a chaotic world. As an elevated written form, poetry is used to mark public occasions such as weddings and funerals; it can also remember events that have a relevance to us all (the Paddington train crash, 5 October 1999; the terrorist attack on the Twin Towers, 11 September 2001; the Asian Tsunami, 26 December 2004). You may have noted the way in which poetry can make familiar things seem unfamiliar, presenting everyday things in a new light – equally, you may have recognised the way in which some poets make the unfamiliar familiar. You may find it comforting, threatening, or exciting.

Technically, you may have identified the distinctive visual impact of a poem on the page with its variations of line and stanza length; the often individual use of language; the inversion of standard word order and the condensed, elliptical style; or the importance of rhythm. You may have made a note of the descriptive diction, the concentrated imagery, or heightened tone.

All your observations demonstrate that you already know a great deal about poetry as a distinctive literary genre. What this book will do is underpin your personal knowledge with a critical terminology and approach. It will define features of poetic form and devices, content and style so that you are able to discuss the effects created in a poem in a focused and analytical way.

What the writers say

We can learn a great deal about poetry from what poets and other writers say about it as a genre. It can help us to understand the nature of the things poets write about, the poetic forms they choose, and the stylistic features they draw on. The views of poets and literary critics can complement our own thoughts and experiences.

Activity 2.2

The following quotations offer a variety of views about poetry. They include statements from different periods and different perspectives. Read through the list and think about the points being made in each quotation.

What do we learn about poetry from the following statements?
Do you agree or disagree with the different points
of view expressed?

EXTRACT 1 – ROBERT FROST (1874–1963), American lyric poet

'Poetry is a way of taking life by the throat.'

EXTRACT 2 – HORACE (65–8BC), Roman lyric poet and satirist

'Poetry is like painting.'

EXTRACT 3 – SUSAN WICKS (1947–), English poet and novelist

'The poet's first and most important tool is syntax: the challenge is to make it do what you want it to invisibly . . .'

EXTRACT 4 – EAVAN BOLAND (1944–), Irish poet and critic

'Poetry is defined by its energies and its eloquence . . .'

EXTRACT 5 – WILLIAM WORDSWORTH (1770–1850), English Romantic poet

'Poetry is the spontaneous overflow of powerful feelings . . .'

EXTRACT 6 – I. A. RICHARDS (1893–1979), English literary critic, linguist, poet and teacher

'[Poetry] is a perfectly possible means of overcoming chaos.'

EXTRACT 7 – GUSTAV FLAUBERT (1821–80), French realist novelist

'Poetry is as exact a science as geometry.'

EXTRACT 8 – R. S. THOMAS (1913–2000), a Welsh poet and clergyman

'A rich background is essential in the making of a poem of substance . . .'

EXTRACT 9 – PERCY BYSSHE SHELLEY (1792–1822), English Romantic poet and dramatist

'[Poetry] lifts the veil from the hidden beauty of the world, and makes familiar objects be as if they were not familiar . . .'

EXTRACT 10 – ANDREW MOTION (1952–), Poet Laureate, novelist and biographer

'There is some primitive connection between poetry and significant events or crises in our lives.'

EXTRACT 11 – SAMUEL TAYLOR COLERIDGE (1772–1834), English Romantic poet, philosopher and critic

'. . . prose = words in their best order; poetry = the best words in the best order.'

EXTRACT 12 – PHILIP LARKIN (1922–85), English poet and novelist

'[a poem] is a verbal device that would preserve an experience indefinitely by reproducing it in whoever read the poem.'

EXTRACT 13 – J. S. MILL (1806–73), English philosopher, economist, reformer and politician

'Poetry is feeling, confessing itself to itself in moments of solitude.'

EXTRACT 14 – ANNE STEVENSON (1933–), English poet and biographer

'. . . rhythm [is] the unconscious engine of poetry, the pulse or muscle that governs it and has its physical source in walking, breathing and heartbeat.'

EXTRACT 15 – JEREMY BENTHAM (1748–1832), English writer and philosopher

'Prose is when all the lines except the last go on to the end. Poetry is when some of them fall short of it.'

EXTRACT 16 – SIR PHILIP SIDNEY (1554–86), English poet and patron

'Poetry is a speaking picture, with this end, to teach and delight.'

EXTRACT 17 – MATTHEW ARNOLD (1822–88), English poet and critic

'. . . poetry is at bottom a criticism of life . . .'

Commentary

From these quotations, we can see that poets use their own **experiences and context** as a source for their ideas – they *take life by the throat* and face its complexities. Personal, local, national and international events or crises can provide them with material that can be worked into a poem. They draw on a vivid background, powerful feelings, or a desire to make the reader reconsider things that are taken for granted. They aim to preserve a particular experience, commenting on, interpreting or questioning what has happened in order to engage the reader in their search for meaning. Often underlying the focus of the poem, there will be an implicit or explicit criticism of life as the poet seeks to find meaning in chaos.

The **style** will be distinctive because the poem is ultimately a *verbal device*, a composition in which language and structure are manipulated to create specific effects. The energy of poetry comes from its condensed syntax, the eloquence and musicality of its diction, and the importance of word order. Poets paint pictures for us with their words, freezing time so that we can see what they see.

Poetic form is almost scientific because of the precision required of the poet. Variations in line length, stanza structure, rhyme and rhythm provide constraints – the poet chooses a framework within which to explore ideas and this is often directly linked to the meaning. Poetic form can bring order to the chaos of modern life, or structure to an overwhelming sense of grief; it can focus our attention and contain powerful feelings. Often when we read a poem, we identify with the feelings or ideas expressed – although we have not articulated them ourselves, we have been in a similar situation or experienced the same emotions.

Above all, we need to recognise that poetry can both *teach* and *delight* – it is both instructional and entertaining; we can read it as part of a programme of study or for pleasure. Poets do not just exist in the past as names we recognise, but as living, contemporary commentators on life. We can read their work in class or at home, but we can also hear them read it themselves and this can be when we truly recognise the power of poetry to move us.

Poetry versus prose

Poetry is usually far more concentrated and intense than prose because of the restrictions created by its form, line length, rhythm, rhyme and a tendency towards a telegraphic or elliptical style. Poetic language is also heightened and intensified as the poet strives to recreate experience.

Ezra Pound (1855–1972), an American poet, wrote about the way in which a poet reduces experience into an intense and concentrated form.

> Three years ago in Paris I got out of a 'Metro' train at La Concorde, and saw suddenly a beautiful face, and then another and another, and a beautiful child's face, and then another beautiful woman, and I tried all that day to find words for what this had meant to me, and I could not find any words that seemed to me worthy, or as lovely as that sudden emotion . . .
>
> I wrote a thirty-line poem, and destroyed it because it was what we call work 'of second intensity'. Six months later I made a poem half that length; a year later I made the following . . . sentence:
> **The apparition of these faces in the crowd:**
> **Petals on a wet black bough.**
> I daresay it is meaningless unless one has drifted into a certain vein of thought. In a poem of this sort one is trying to record the precise instant when a thing outward and objective transforms itself, or darts into a thing inward and subjective.

Pound's poem is tightly structured and clearly conveys his experience in a very visual way. It is quite unlike his narrative account of what took place on that day in Paris. Where the prose version is rambling and loosely structured, the poem is made up of two post-modified noun phrases; the concrete language and the repetition of the prose is replaced by an abstract noun (*apparition*) that encompasses all that he saw. The image of the *petals* reinforces and familiarises the abstract noun with a concrete visual picture – one with which most readers can associate. In addition, traditionally poetic features like end rhyme (*crowd/bough*) and internal rhyme (*petals/wet*), and the recurring plosives (*black/bough*) intensify the effect of the lexical choice. The poem is a powerful and condensed visual representation of a personal experience.

What makes a poem?

When you look at any literature, you can expect an individual and personal use of language. Writers choose words for their descriptive, connotative, or figurative possibilities, and literary texts therefore tend to have a heightened tone in which every word is charged with significance. Imagery is crucial to the way in which writers build up a particular world view – it gives literature its visual quality and is often used to underpin the themes or ideas a writer wishes to address. The arrangement of words and clause elements allows writers to stress the significance of particular lexical items or grammatical structures that are important in terms of the meaning. By manipulating standard word order and moving words/clause elements to unexpected positions, the writer can draw attention to particular parts of the text.

The distinctive features of poetry, however, lie in the form, rhythm, rhyme and the often elliptical style. We can see immediately the variation in line lengths and the division into stanzas, and such visual features have an effect on the meaning. Poets divide their ideas into logical units and we can often chart the development of a poem's ideas through the stanza structure; by placing semantically important words and phrases at the beginning and end of lines poets can draw attention to them. Sound and rhythm enhance the overall effect of a poem, bringing it together as a semantic unit, reminding us of the poem as a text to be read aloud, and controlling the expression of ideas. The style is often condensed and intensified because the poet is capturing an experience or moment in time within the tightness of a prescribed form. Conforming to a particular rhythmical pattern or rhyme scheme, or changing word order for semantic effect can make the style elliptical – grammatical function words are omitted and this is one of the reasons poetry gains its reputation for being difficult to understand.

Yet we have been surrounded by poetry from an early age – nursery rhymes and playground chants, songs and advertising jingles. We enjoy what we hear because the patterns are memorable and they appeal to something instinctive in us. In almost all societies, poetry appeared before prose. The rhythmic patterns and repeated sounds made poetry suitable for oral cultures in which songs and ballads were the means of keeping history alive. The principles are the same in the poetry we read or study: we must recognise the music of the words and the poet's ability to help us to understand our own experiences.

Read to enjoy! Do not let initial difficulties of structure, language and syntax overwhelm you. Despite these challenges, close reading of poetry is rewarding. In exploring the words on the page, we find meaning and, when we stop being afraid and begin to enjoy the experience, the poem will sing.

Activity 2.3

Which features of the poems on page 10 are 'literary' and could be found in other types of literature, and which features are distinctive to poetry?
Comment on the effects created by the features you identify.

You may like to think about: the content, the language, the grammatical and rhetorical features and the layout.

Sonnet 43: How Do I Love Thee?

1   How do I love thee? Let me count the ways.
I love thee to the depth and breadth and height
My soul can reach, when feeling out of sight
For the ends of Being and ideal Grace.
5   I love thee to the level of everyday's
Most quiet need, by sun and candlelight.
I love thee freely, as men strive for Right;
I love thee purely, as they turn from Praise.
I love thee with the passion put to use
10   In my old griefs, and with my childhood's faith.
I love thee with a love I seemed to lose
With my lost saints, – I love thee with the breath,
Smiles, tears, of all my life! – and, if God choose,
I shall but love thee better after death.

The Eagle

1   He clasps the crag with crooked hands;
Close to the sun in lonely lands,
Ring'd with the azure world, he stands.

The wrinkled sea beneath him crawls;
5   He watches from his mountain walls,
And like a thunderbolt he falls.

Commentary

The **content** of the Elizabeth Barrett Browning sonnet is a traditional focus for literature of all kinds – not just poetry. Her treatment of love is personal and she attempts to qualify the extent of her feelings for her lover, Robert Browning. Where the meaning of Barrett Browning's sonnet is literal, Tennyson's treatment of the eagle can be seen as both literal and symbolic. He is writing of a bird and its mastery of its environment, but also, perhaps, symbolically of a human ruler who conquers and reigns supreme in his kingdom. The opening simple clause creates an immediate and dramatic image, but we are dependent on the anaphoric reference back to *The Eagle* of the title to understand the significance of the pronoun *He* (l.1). This ambiguity of reference underpins the reader's feeling that the poem is doing more than literally describing a bird. This kind of semantic layering is not exclusive to poetry, but the condensed form is suited to the intensity of its expression.

The **diction** of each poem also demonstrates many features that are typical of any literary writing. Barrett Browning's poem is dominated by abstract nouns (*soul* l.3, *passion* l.9, *faith* l.10, *love* l.11) because the subject itself is abstract. The language develops a contrast between extremes in order to represent the limits of her love – antithetical references to *sun/candlelight* (l.6), *smiles/tears* (l.13) and *life/death* (ll.13–14) help us to understand Barrett Browning's protestation of love in terms of ordinary and familiar things. Similarly, the lexis reminds us that this state of being is new, emphasising the power of love to transform life. Modifiers like *old*, *childhood's* (l.10) and *lost* (l.12), and the verb *lose* (l.11) draw attention to the present and her love for Browning by contrasting it with the past.

For Tennyson, the lexical choice is directly linked to a physical environment. The concrete nouns *crag* (l.1), *lands* (l.2), *sea* (l.4) and *mountain* (l.5) give the reader a sense of the terrain over which the eagle flies. Modifiers are important because they develop our sense of perspective: both literally in terms of height, but also symbolically in terms of the eagle's distance from others. The intensity of the blue sky surrounding the eagle is indicated by the modifier *azure* (l.3) – it symbolically represents the height of the eagle's perch because he appears to be above the cloud, literally in a world of his own. This is reinforced by the verb modifier *wrinkled* (l.4) that reduces the powerful sea to something insignificant. The selection of *crooked* (l.1) and *lonely* (l.2) create a different sort of perspective: Tennyson's eagle is personified and this is reinforced by the choice of *hands* (l.1) rather than 'claws', and the reference to *walls* (l.5) with its connotations of man-made constructs. This kind of heightened language use is common in other kinds of literature, so although typical of poetry, it is not distinctive to the genre.

Grammatical features can also be used to create particular effects. In the sonnet, for instance, changes in grammatical mood are used to focus our attention: the opening interrogative *How do I love thee?* introduces the topic and is answered with the imperative *Let me count the ways*; the declarative mood then allows Barrett Browning to list the extent of her love.

While Tennyson uses the declarative mood throughout the poem, his manipulation of word order is an important means of guiding and influencing the reader. The delayed second main clause *he stands* (l.3) draws attention to the fronted adverbials *Close to the Sun . . .* (l.2) and *Ring'd with the azure world . . .* (l.3) that begin to characterise the bird/ruler in terms of elevation, isolation and entrapment. A similar pattern is created in the final line of the poem in which the simile *like a thunderbolt* (l.6) precedes the main clause *he falls*. The delay heightens our sense of the power in the bird's action as it drops down to strike its prey, or the ruler's meting out of punishment. The simile conjures up images of both the natural and the god-like with its allusions to the Greek Zeus, all-powerful father of the gods and ruler of the sky, and the Scandinavian thunder-god Thor.

Form and meaning are also combined in Tennyson's use of the adverbial *beneath him* (l.4) in the medial position. By delaying the main verb *crawls*, Tennyson reinforces the power of the bird/ruler – the connotations of the words, their order and the possible symbolic reading of the 'sea' as the ruler's subjects suggest an unforgiving and potentially cruel tyrant alongside the literal description of the instinctive bird.

Rhetorical features are used by Barrett Browning to intensify her declaration of love. Repetition of the subject-predicator-object clause *I love thee . . .* establishes a link to the poet's desire to *count* the different ways in which she loves. Other patterning can be seen in the parallel use of adverbs (*freely/purely*, ll.7–8), the syndetic listing of *depth and breadth and height* (l.2), the asyndetic listing of *the breath,/Smiles, tears* (ll.12–13), and in the parenthesis highlighted by dashes (ll.12–13) and commas (l.13). These kinds of techniques are persuasive, allowing the poet to argue her case emphatically. They are not distinctive to poetry, but they are used where a writer wishes to create a dramatic effect – they are suggestive of a conscious writing process where words and structures are manipulated in order to influence the reader or listener.

But what makes these two texts 'poetry'? When we first see them on the page, we know that they are poems – the **layout** is distinctive. Poems can be recognised by their division into stanzas rather than paragraphs; their irregular line lengths; the relationship between the lines in terms of sound or rhythm. Syntactical structures do not necessarily relate to the patterning of the lines: while the end of some may be marked by punctuation, others clearly run over. Because poems are often shorter than other kinds of literary genres, the lexical choice tends to be more intense – every word has been chosen for a purpose, and grammatical function words are often omitted.

In the Barrett Browning poem, the **form** is distinctive: it is a sonnet divided into an octave rhyming abbaabba and a sestet rhyming cdcdcd. The patterning of the end rhyme is reinforced by internal rhyme (*depth/breadth*; *Being/ideal*; *level/everyday's*; *thee/freely*) which enhances our sense of the poem as a complete unit. Ten-syllable lines are typical of the traditional sonnet and here the regularity of the rhythm underpins the poem's logical attempt to explain the extent of Barrett Browning's love. Form and meaning are inextricably linked – the tightness of the poetic form orders and limits the poet's love, making it possible for her to express it in a lucid and controlled way.

Tennyson uses two 3-lined stanzas, or tercets, linked by end rhyme to order his ideas, dealing first with the eagle's location and then with his power. Internal rhyme (*Close/lonely*; *sea/beneath*), the regular octosyllabic (8-syllable) rhythm, and the importance of end-stopped lines where the final words are given extra weighting contribute to the overall effect of the poem. The tightness of the form emphasises the power of the bird/ruler and reinforces the sense of entrapment created by the verb *Ring'd*.

▶ 3 Distinctive features of poetry

It is useful to recognise the distinctive features of poetry because they have an effect on the way in which poets create meaning. Identifying them is only a starting point – of most importance is an exploration of the effects that are created and the way these influence the reader.

End-stopped and run-on lines

We have already recognised that the length of lines is a significant feature of verse, but it is also important to look at the end of each line to see whether the poet has used punctuation or not, and to consider the effect this has on the meaning of the poem.

End-stopped lines

Where the end of a line of verse is marked by punctuation, we describe the line as being **end-stopped**. It marks a natural pause in the grammatical structure. A full stop or a semicolon marks a strong pause; a comma or a colon creates a less prominent break in the flow of the verse.

Activity 3.1

How does Jonathan Swift (1667–1745) influence our response to the General in this extract from 'A Satirical Elegy on the Death of a Late Famous General'?

You may like to think about: the title, the language and tone, the use of end-stopped lines, the sentence type and structure.

A Satirical Elegy on the Death of a Late Famous General

1	His Grace! impossible! what, dead!
	Of old age too, and in his bed!
	And could that mighty warrior fall,
	And so inglorious, after all?
5	Well, since he's gone, no matter how,
	The last loud trump must wake him now;

And, trust me, as the noise grows stronger,
He'd wish to sleep a little longer.

Commentary

The title of the poem prepares us for the tone – this is a satire, not a traditional elegy. We can expect not grief and mourning, but a biting attack on the dead *Famous General*. The end-stopped lines help Swift to create an informal, conversational tone. This is reinforced by the sequence of exclamatory minor sentences that expresses a mood of disbelief and allows Swift to begin his process of undermining a man of authority. The elliptical style draws attention to his ironic tone.

Satire allows the writer to treat his or her subject with ridicule. Swift here undermines the General by juxtaposing our expectations of the great soldier with the reality of an old man dying in his bed. The antithesis of the modifiers *mighty* (l.3) and *so inglorious* (l.4) draws attention to Swift's dissatisfaction with the social hierarchy: society honours the leaders who live long enough to get old, while ordinary soldiers, who have to face danger, die young. The conversational *Well* and the parenthetical *no matter how* (l.5) with their apparently dismissive tone are examples of Swift's ironic stance. Similarly, the reference to *The last loud trump* (l.6) works on two levels: as a crude colloquialism that further undermines the General's status as a great man; and perhaps as a metaphor for the Day of Judgement – the time when the General will wish he could *sleep a little longer* (l.8) to avoid facing the reality of his life.

The emphatic end-stopped lines and the stress on each final word create pauses in which Swift's ironic stance is clear – a traditional poetic lament is transformed into an attack on the social order.

Run-on lines

Run-on lines are not marked by punctuation because the grammatical structures are not completed within one line of verse. The meaning is continued across line boundaries and the reader must therefore read on in order to understand what a poet is saying. You may also see the French term **enjambement** used to describe run-on lines.

This approach was common in sixteenth- and seventeenth-century poetry, but was used far less frequently by eighteenth-century poets. In the nineteenth century, the Romantic poets were reacting against the restrictive rules governing eighteenth-century verse. They aimed to use everyday language and the rhythms of speech; run-on lines were a natural extension of this principle.

Activity 3.2

Explore the way D. H. Lawrence (1885–1930) presents the workers in his poem 'Morning Work'.

You may like to think about: the language, imagery, sound patterning and the use of run-on lines.

Morning work

1   A gang of labourers on the piled wet timber
    That shines blood-red beside the railway siding
    Seem to be making out of the blue of the morning
    Something faery and fine, the shuttles sliding.

5   The red-gold spools of their hands and their faces swinging
    Hither and thither across the high crystalline frame
    Of day: trolls at the cave of ringing cerulean mining
    And laughing with labour, living their work like a game.

Commentary

In this poem, Lawrence is recreating an image of some men he has seen at work. The run-on lines enhance the activity of the men, but also the feeling of enchantment that Lawrence creates through his language and the metaphor of the trolls.

The long noun phrase of the opening two lines provides the reader with much concentrated description. While some of the modifiers are factual (*piled, wet, railway*), Lawrence's use of *blood-red* and the verb *shines* begins to lift the vision of a *gang of labourers* beyond the everyday. The reader is driven on towards the end of the stanza where the literal becomes figurative: the everyday work is transformed into something *faery and fine* (l.4). The soft fricatives are unexpected in a poem about railway workers, yet Lawrence has prepared us for this transformation by his use of the verb *Seem* (l.3) with its connotations of uncertainty and mystery.

Although the two stanzas are divided by an end-stopped line, the final image of the *shuttles* in the first stanza is developed in the second where the workers' hands become *spools* (ll.4–5). The connotations of weaving build upon the suggestion that they are *making . . ./Something faery and fine*. Traditional images of the coarseness of labouring have been replaced with a sense of creativity. This is enhanced by Lawrence's concentration on rich colours that intensify the otherworldly atmosphere (*blood-red, red-gold, crystalline, cerulean*).

The present participle *swinging* and the adverbial *hither and thither* (ll.5–6) draw attention to the movements of the men. Framed against the sky, they are reduced to their parts – *hands* and *faces* – almost like elements of a machine. The final two lines, like the first, are made up of a complex noun phrase that makes explicit the comparison between the men and the fairy world. The soft repeated lateral sounds (*laughing, labour, living, like*), like the earlier fricatives, contrast the rough labourers with the vision Lawrence sees. The patterning of the present participles, the internal rhyme (*labour/game*), and the alliterative sounds enhance this morning vision.

Lawrence has used enjambement to intensify the effect of his poem. It provides cohesion by mirroring the movement of the men and driving the reader forward to the final metaphor. He does not present us with a typical image of men at work, but transforms the mundanity and indignity of physical labour into something magical.

Metre

In poetry, rhythm is very important: it affects the way we say the poem aloud, and it allows the poet to make important words stand out. All words have a natural rhythm that can be identified by counting the number of syllables. For instance, 'deep' has one syllable; 'morning' has two (MOR - NING); 'blundering' has three (BLUN - DE - RING); and 'harmonious' has four (HAR - MON - I - OUS).

Each syllable does not always have equal weight – words are made up of weak and strong syllables. A strong syllable places more emphasis on one syllable than on another and is therefore stressed; a weak syllable is unstressed. When we speak, we instinctively stress certain syllables. For instance, we say 'MOR - ning' rather than 'mor – NING', 'EM – pha – sis' rather than 'em – PHA – sis', and 'TEA – cher' rather than 'tea – CHER'. In a sentence, lexical or meaning words usually bear the stress, while grammatical function words are unstressed.

In poetry, this kind of natural patterning is intensified. Poets often consciously arrange the words to create a regular and recurring pattern of stressed and unstressed syllables. We refer to this kind of rhythmic patterning as **metre**. The metre may vary from line to line; the poet may use a complicated metrical pattern that extends over several lines or stanzas and is then repeated; or, as in many modern poems, there may be no recognisable recurring pattern. The choices a poet makes about the metre are important because in creating a particular rhythmic pattern, the poet can influence the way in which we read and understand a text. Variations in a pattern, for instance, may mark changes in the mood or the poet's attitude.

The study of metre can be very technical, but it is possible to recognise basic rhythmic patterns and comment on their effects without becoming overwhelmed by the complexities. An awareness of these patterns can help you to understand how a poem achieves its effects.

Stressed and unstressed syllables

First, it is important to think about the pattern of **stressed and unstressed syllables**. In the examples above, we marked stressed syllables by using capitals – in poetry, it is customary to place / (or sometimes ¯) over the stressed word or syllable.

/   /   /
Hick o ry dick o ry dock

Unstressed syllables are marked with ˘.

Hick ŏ rў dick ŏ rў dock

There are five basic patterns of stressed and unstressed syllables in English poetry and it is useful to be able to recognise them.

IAMBIC: one unstressed syllable is followed by one stressed syllable (dĕ-líght, ă-bóut).

TROCHAIC: one stressed syllable is followed by one unstressed syllable (gá-thĕr, féel-iňg).

DACTYLIC: one stressed syllable is followed by two unstressed syllables (há-pĭ-nĕss, sén-tĭ-mĕnt).

ANAPAESTIC: two unstressed syllables are followed by one stressed syllable (ĭn-tĕ-rrúpt, dĭs-ă-ppéar).

SPONDEE: two stressed syllables (héart-bréak, wíne-gláss).

The most common rhythm in English poetry is the **iambic** weak-strong pattern because it fits the natural rhythm of the English language. It can be seen in the extract below from 'Virtue', a poem by George Herbert (1593–1633) – only the opening noun phrase and the closing verb phrase alter the weak-strong rhythm.

> Sweet day, so cool, so calm, so bright!
> The bridal of the earth and sky –
> The dew shall weep thy fall to-night;
> For thou must die.

The iambic regularity of Herbert's poem is suitable for his contemplation of virtue. In this opening stanza of the poem, he considers the transience of the day's beauty. The patterning of the first line (*sŏ cóol, sŏ cálm, sŏ bríght*) illustrates the freshness and pureness of the early morning, building to a climax in the bridal image (l.2). In line 3, however, the positive tone is undermined by lexis with negative connotations. The verbs *weep* and *fall*, as well as the certainty implied by the modal *shall*, prepare us for the final line with its explicit *must die*.

Herbert's use of technical devices also highlights the importance of this final line. Visually, it is shorter than the previous lines, but perhaps more importantly, the use of a **spondee** emphasises the semantic significance of the verb phrase *múst díe*. With its two consecutive stressed syllables, the spondee can be used to slow the rhythm of a line, making it heavier and therefore more noticeable. By altering the rhythm in this way, Herbert is able to draw attention to the impor-tance of the phrase, developing a contrast between mortality and the sense of life created in the description of the day.

A similar technique is used in the opening noun phrase *Swéet dáy*: the two stressed syllables create a pause before the lilting iambics carry the reader forward to the final emphatic reference to death. The metrical pattern of the poem there-fore directly ties the opening and closing phrases of the stanza together – the reader needs to recognise the relationship between these antithetical references because they are central to Herbert's theme. In the following two stanzas of 'Virtue', the pattern is repeated; in the final stanza, however, Herbert changes the metre because here he directly addresses the nature of virtue and its permanence in a transient world.

*   *   *

Iambic and **anapaestic** metres are known as rising rhythms because they move from unstressed to stressed sounds, throwing the movement of the line forward towards the stress. It was traditionally used in popular verse before the eighteenth century, but poets such as Scott and Byron in the nineteenth century used the anapaest in serious verse. It creates the effect of speed and is therefore often used to push the pace of a poem onwards.

The **trochee**, on the other hand, is a falling rhythm because after an initial stress, the words die away. This is not the natural rhythm of spoken English and it therefore creates a noticeable change in sound patterns. The trochee was not common in English poetry before the sixteenth century, but became an important means of varying the traditional iambic metre of blank verse. It is rare to find a poem written exclusively in trochees, although Longfellow's narrative poem 'Hiawatha' (1855) uses an unrhymed trochaic metre throughout. As the dominant metre, the trochee can seem monotonous, but as a variation to other metrical patterns it can have dramatic effects.

Like trochees, **dactyls** create a falling rhythm. While they were often used in Classical verse, they were not common in English poetry until the nineteenth century when Scott, Byron, Tennyson and Browning experimented with them.

In addition to these five basic patterns, poets can use an **amphibrach**, a metrical foot consisting of a stressed syllable with a unstressed syllable before and after it. Although not common in English poetry and rarely occurring as a dominant metre, the amphibrach can occur alongside other metrical feet. A poet may also sometimes need to add an additional unstressed beat to a line to complete it – this does not affect the overall pattern.

Metrical feet

Having identified the pattern of weak and strong syllables, each line of poetry can then be divided into **metrical feet** – groups of syllables forming a recognisable poetic unit. Each foot consists of a stressed syllable and any unstressed syllables that accompany it. The foot will therefore be iambic, trochaic, anapaestic, dactylic or spondaic. It is customary to mark each separate foot with I. To identify the number of feet in a line, you need to count the number of stressed syllables, remembering that a spondee is made up of two consecutive stresses which constitute one metrical foot.

If there is one foot (one stress) in the line, we call it monometer; 2 feet (two stresses) – dimeter; 3 feet (three stresses) – trimeter; 4 feet (four stresses) – tetrameter; 5 feet (five stresses) – pentameter; 6 feet (six stresses) – hexameter; 7 feet (seven stresses) – heptameter; 8 feet (eight stresses) – octameter.

1	2	3	4	5 IAMBIC PENTAMETER
Ĭ lóve I	thĕe tó I	thĕ dépth I	ănd bréadth I	ănd héight

If we look back to the extract from 'Virtue', we can identify the metre by counting the number of main stresses in each line. Herbert uses iambic tetrameter in the first three lines: the iambic weak-strong stress pattern dominates and there are four stresses in each line. The final line has only two stresses, and Herbert is drawing attention here to his theme by changing the iambic tetrameter to iambic dimeter.

Although novelists can also manipulate the rhythm of prose by choosing words for their pattern of weak and strong syllables, this kind of patterning is distinctive to poetry. In order to conform to their chosen metre, poets select words not just for their meaning, but also for their sound quality and internal rhythm. They may also invert the word order or elide words, shortening grammatical function words or polysyllabic words to fit the rhythm. For example, 'whoever' becomes *whoe'er*, 'over' becomes *o'er*, 'it was' becomes *'twas*, 'beneath' becomes *'neath*.

If poets want to mimic the rhythms of informal conversation, they choose iambic pentameter because the pattern of stressed and unstressed syllables is closer to that of spontaneous speech. Variations from this most common metre enable poets to draw attention to key words, change the pace and mood, and underpin meaning.

Scanning a poem is not an exact science and readers can sometimes see different patterns according to the way in which they believe a line should sound. For some, perhaps the opening foot in the extract of 'Virtue' is not a spondee, but another iamb. Thus *Sweet day* does not slow the pace of the line, but drives the reader on through the listed adjective phrases to the image in the second line. Most important of all is to be able to link metre to meaning: think about the effects created and the relationship between the movement of the verse and its themes. You are unlikely to need to scan every single line, but it is useful to be able to see where the poet varies a pattern to underpin meaning, change tone, or develop a counterpoint.

If you wish to scan a line of poetry, it is useful first to decide on the **pattern of stressed and unstressed syllables** so that you can see whether the poet is using iambic, trochaic, anapaestic, dactylic, or spondaic feet. Next, count the **number of stressed syllables** so that you know how many feet there are in a line – remember that two consecutive stresses, the spondee, make up one foot. Finally, combine your findings to describe the metre in terms of the pattern of stressed-unstressed syllables and the number of stresses.

Caesura

We have seen that the rhythm of poetry is very important because poets make conscious choices about the kind of metre they wish to use depending upon the content, tone, theme and style of their poems. Of equal importance is the use of a **pause**, or **caesura**, to break or interrupt the rhythm. Often a pause will be directly linked to the grammatical structure of a line and it will be marked by punctuation. In Herbert's 'Virtue', for instance, the opening line is balanced by the grammatical pauses. To mark a pause on a text, critics use ‖.

Sweet day, ‖ so cool, ‖ so calm, ‖ so bright!

The pauses work with the initial spondee, the alliterative 's' and the long vowel sounds (*Sweet, day, cool, calm, bright*) to create a languorous mood that will be destroyed by the harshness of the final line with its lack of pauses and its fast-moving dimeter.

The most common caesura is the **medial** – a pause dividing a line of poetry into two at the middle. Poets can also use the **initial** caesura near the beginning of a line, or the **terminal** caesura near the end. In Old English verse, the medial caesura was used with little variation to divide the two halves of the alliterative poetic line. By Chaucer's time, the movement away from alliterative verse and the use of an iambic stress pattern meant that the caesura could be used in a more flexible way. Shakespeare's blank verse offered even wider possibilities as poetry became less stylised and closer to the rhythms of speech. In modern verse, the caesura is used in a variety of places depending upon the kind of effect the poet wishes to create.

In the first lines of Swift's poem, 'A Satirical Elegy' (see Activity 3.1), for instance, the caesura is used to underpin the exclamative, satiric tone. The pauses divide the first line in three places, which draws attention to the fact that this will not be a traditional elegiac poem.

> His Grace! ‖ Impossible! ‖ What, ‖ dead!

While the second line is balanced elegantly around a medial caesura, its effect is undermined by the dismissive tone. Similarly, the medial caesura in line 5 is thrown off balance by the initial caesura after the conversational *Well*.

> Well, ‖ since he's gone, ‖ no matter how

Swift's use of pauses thus reinforces the effects he creates through language, style and structure.

The caesura is used to achieve a degree of variety in the metre: it can make verse formal and stylised; or it can relax rigid metrical patterns and mimic the rhythms of speech. Some lines of poetry will have no caesura.

Activity 3.3

> **Explore the effects created by each poet's use of metre and the caesura in the poems below.**
>
> You may like to think about: the content, the language and imagery, the metrical patterns, any changes in pace, and the use of the caesura

EXTRACT 1 – ANONYMOUS (seventeenth century)

Binnorie

1   There was twa sisters in a bow'r°,   bower
      Binnorie, O Binnorie:
      There cam° a knight to be their wooer,   came
      By the bonnie mill-dams o'Binnorie.

He courted the eldest wi' glove and ring;
5 He courted the eldest wi' glove and ring;
    Binnorie, O Binnorie:
But he lov'd the youngest abune a'thing°.   above everything
    By the bonnie mill-dams o'Binnorie.

        He courted the eldest wi' brotch° an° knife;   brooch/and
           Binnorie, O Binnorie:
10   But lov'd the youngest as his life.
           By the bonnie mill-dams o'Binnorie.

EXTRACT 2 – ROBERT BROWNING (1812–89)

The Lost Leader

1 Just for a handful of silver he left us,
    Just for a riband to stick in his coat –
Found the one gift of which fortune bereft us,
    Lost all the others she lets us devote;
5 They, with the gold to give, doled him out silver,
    So much was theirs who so little allowed . . .
We that had loved him so, followed him, honoured him,
    Lived in his mild and magnificent eye,
Learned his great language, caught his clear accents,
10   Made him our pattern to live and to die!

Commentary

'Binnorie' is a ballad from the oral tradition that exists in a number of slightly different versions. It tells the tale of two sisters in love with the same man and has a typically tragic ending. Ballads traditionally use the iambic metre because of its close relationship with the rhythms of speech and this is the dominant metre in the first and third line of the first stanza.

There was | twa sis | ters in | a bow'r

In the second and third stanzas (ll.5, 7, 9, 11), however, the poet moves between iambs and anapaests.

He cour | ted the el | dest wi' glove | and ring; . . .
But he lov'd | the youn | gest abune | a'thing.

Although some readers may scan this differently, substituting amphibrachs for the anapaests (*He courted* | *the eldest*), it is significant that in both cases the tension of the love-triangle is intensified by the change in metre. Where the pace of the 'running' rhythm is jaunty, the mood is ominous: the juxtaposition of the verbs *courted* and *lov'd* alerts us to the underlying conflict.

    The regularity of the first and third lines with their consistent rising rhythm gives the verse a musical quality typical of the ballad form. This is, however, set against the refrain (ll.2/4). The recurring final line of each stanza begins with an anapaest and an iamb, but it ends with a trochaic rhythm mirroring the second line – it moves from a strong to a weak beat.

Binnŏ | ríe, Ŏ | Bínnŏ | ríe: . . .
Bў thĕ bó | nňie mǐll- | dáms ŏ' | Bínnŏ | ríe.

The inversion of the traditional lilting iambic rhythms in the trochaic feet and the extra stressed syllable at the end of each line create a sense of unease. The harsh stressed plosives and the medial caesura before the plaintive interjection *O* add to this feeling, drawing attention to the inevitably tragic ending of the ballad where the youngest sister is drowned in the Binnorie mill-dams.

'The Lost Leader' is a poem written in 1834 on Wordsworth's acceptance of the title Poet Laureate. The Victorian poet Browning saw this as evidence that his predecessor had abandoned the radical beliefs of his younger years and betrayed the principles that Browning and many of his contemporaries had followed – for them, the next generation of poets, Wordsworth had been a poetic and political inspiration. Browning's personal disappointment is conveyed in the sardonic references to *a handful of silver*, with its implicit reference to the biblical Judas, and *a riband to stick in his coat*.

Poems composed entirely of dactyls are rare, but 'The Lost Leader' is dominated by the strong-weak-weak metre.   In the extract here, the falling rhythm is created by dactyls with trochees at the end of some lines (ll.1, 3, 5, 7).

Jŭst fŏr ă | hándfŭl ŏf | sílvĕr hĕ | léft ŭs,
Jŭst fŏr ă | ríbănd tŏ | stíck ĭn hĭs | cóat –

While dactyls are common in light verse, they are used here to express a deep-felt and serious state of affairs. The regularity of the four-stress line with its inverted pattern underpins the gravity of the verse, but the neatness of the structure is at odds with the disruption caused by what Browning sees as Wordsworth's betrayal.

The use of an initial caesura after the dismissive third person pronoun *They* (l.5) emphasises that Wordsworth has changed allegiances. His acceptance of the publicly acclaimed role of Poet Laureate is further undermined by Browning's use of a medial caesura in the same line – the verb (*give*) and the noun (*gold*) of the parenthetical phrase are set against the reductive connotations of *doled . . . out* and *silver*. The caesuras that divide the sequence of verb phrases expressing Browning's admiration (*loved . . ., followed . . ., honoured . . .*, l.7) slow the pace and throw additional weight onto these initially stressed words. Similarly, the medial caesura (l.9) balances the noun phrases *his great language* and *his clear accents* as the extract builds to a climax in the noun phrase *our pattern to live and to die* (l.10).

■ ⩔ **4** Poetic form

As we have already seen, it is poetic form that most clearly distinguishes between poetry and other literary genres. A poem can be recognised immediately by its distinctive appearance on the page and we now need to think more precisely about the different kinds of poetic conventions poets can draw on when they shape and structure their work.

End rhyme, blank verse and free verse

At the most basic level, it is useful to distinguish between poetry that uses a rhyme at the end of the line, poetry that has a regular rhythm and constant 10-syllable pattern, and poetry that tends not to use either end rhyme or a regular syllabic pattern.

End rhyme

If the poet uses **rhyme** at the end of the line, try to identify a pattern and think about the connections created between the words by the use of recurring sounds. It is important to remember that there will usually be a connection between the meaning of the poem and the kind of poetic structures the poet chooses. Full rhyme, for instance, often suggests a sense of harmony and order by creating an underlying cohesion that underpins the meaning. If the rhyme is imperfect or incomplete (half rhyme – e.g. up/step), or if the pattern is disrupted, on the other hand, the poet creates a sense of discord.

T.S. Eliot (1888–1965) uses end rhyme in 'The Love Song of J. Alfred Prufrock' to underpin the meaning. Moving away from the nature poetry of the Romantics and the traditional narrative poetry of the Victorians, he creates a protagonist, Prufrock, who is unheroic and self-conscious. The poem represents his failure to communicate or achieve anything.

The Love Song of J. Alfred Prufrock

1   Let us go then, you and I,
When the evening is spread out against the sky
Like a patient etherised upon a table;
Let us go, through certain half-deserted streets,
5   The muttering retreats
Of restless nights in one-night cheap hotels
And sawdust restaurants with oyster-shells:

> Streets that follow like a tedious argument
> Of insidious intent
> 10   To lead you to an overwhelming question . . .
> Oh, do not ask, 'What is it?'
> Let us go and make our visit.
>
> In the room the women come and go
> Talking of Michelangelo.

In this extract from the opening of the poem, the rhyme scheme falls into couplets, but the pattern is not complete: while lines 1–2, 4–5, 6–7, 8–9 and 11–12 rhyme, the final sound in lines 3 (*table*) and 10 (*question*) is left hanging. This draws attention to the lines and ensures that the reader recognises their significance in terms of the meaning of the poem as a whole. The image of the anaesthetised patient is dramatic and quite unlike the imagery of nineteenth-century poetry. In addition, it tells us about Prufrock's state of mind – it is indicative of his emotional paralysis and inertia. In the second unrhymed line, the sense of incompleteness is heightened by the use of continuation marks (. . .). This creates suspense because we do not know what Prufrock's question will be – the tension is soon undermined, however, by the dismissive interjection (*Oh*) and the rejection of any attempt to reveal his question (l.11).

A further distinction can be drawn between the kinds of rhyme used and the meaning of the poem. Masculine rhymes link single syllable words like *I/sky*; or words of more than one syllable where the same sound occurs in a final stressed syllable (*streets/retreats*; *hotels/shells*; *argument/intent*). These rhymes have a sense of completeness that further isolates the unrhymed lines. The final couplet of the first stanza uses a different sort of rhyme – a feminine rhyme in which a rhymed stressed syllable is followed by one or more rhymed unstressed syllables (*is it/visit*). This changes the tone of the poem: Prufrock's weary commentary on his urban environment is brought to an end by the almost flippant rejection of any kind of communication. The feminine rhyme is emphatically conclusive and prevents any continuation of the subject.

The final couplet of the extract (ll.13–14) is isolated in a stanza of its own. It represents an imagined room in which, as a detached observer, Prufrock sees the women chattering. The almost trite masculine rhyme (*go/Michelangelo*) emphasises the trivial nature of the conversation and further distances the unheroic Prufrock from the real world.

Blank verse

If there is no rhyme, but a disciplined 10-syllable iambic (weak-strong) 5-stress line, then the poet is using **blank verse**. While the majority of eighteenth-century poets used the tightly structured heroic couplet, blank verse was used extensively by the Romantic poets in their longer poems.

Blank verse is considered to be close to the rhythms of everyday speech, but it is recognisably more stylised than speech or prose. It is often used in verse dramas, and in long narrative poems and reflective poems where the poet can explore ideas without having to fit them into traditional stanza and rhyme patterns.

Although it appears to be less consciously structured than a poem that rhymes, the regularity of the verse often implies a search for order.

In some cases, a wider definition is used so that any unrhymed regular poetry is classified as blank verse. In 'Hiawatha', for instance, Henry Wadsworth Longfellow (1807–82) uses a strong-weak (trochaic) stress pattern in an 8-syllable line. Despite this variation from the traditional weak-strong 10-syllable line, the regularity of the verse and its lack of rhyme link it to other examples of blank verse.

Wordsworth uses blank verse in his long autobiographical poem *The Prelude*, begun in 1798–9 and finished in 1805. He composed his poems aloud as he walked, later dictating them to his sister Dorothy and wife Mary. This method allowed him to concentrate on the music and rhythm of the verse – he believed that *the apt arrangement of pauses and cadences, and the sweep of whole paragraphs* were essential to the creation of blank verse. Its flexibility enabled him to develop a sense of the spoken voice directly addressing the reader.

In the extract below (Book II, ll.181–93), he describes the effect of the natural world on him after an account of playing games on the bowling green of an inn on the shores of Lake Windermere with school friends. As is typical of *The Prelude*, after the excitement and noise comes quiet reflection as Wordsworth retrospectively recognises the link he has always had with nature.

> 1   Thus daily were my sympathies enlarged,
>   And thus the common range of visible things
>   Grew dear to me: already I began
>   To love the sun, a Boy I lov'd the sun,
> 5   Not as I since have lov'd him, as a pledge
>   And surety of our earthly life, a light
>   Which while we view we feel we are alive;
>   But, for this cause, that I had seen him lay
>   His beauty on the morning hills, had seen
> 10   The western mountain touch his setting orb,
>   In many a thoughtless hour, when, from excess
>   Of happiness, my blood appear'd to flow
>   With its own pleasure, and I breath'd with joy.

Wordsworth is reflecting on his reaction to the sun and the natural world – both as a boy and as an adult. The opening lines represent the mature voice of the poet summarising his childhood as a time of learning. The regularity of the blank verse helps to create a reasoned and reflective tone that is reinforced by the lexical choice. Contrasts between the child and the adult are developed through the adverbs *Thus* (ll.1–2) and *since* (l.5) that distinguish between the time of writing and the experience itself; while the child's awareness of the environment is represented by concrete nouns (*hills, mountain*) and familiar abstract nouns (*beauty, pleasure, joy* ll.9–10), the adult poet uses more complicated concepts (*pledge, surety, life* ll.5–6).

The 13 lines consist of one sentence made up of numerous clauses. The absence of end rhyme and the many run-on lines drive the reader on through the extract to the end of the grammatical unit. This creates a fluency and rhythm that is reminiscent of the spoken voice, giving an almost conversational feel to the verse. Blank verse can deviate from strict metrical regularity without affecting the overall rhythmic feel – in line 2, for instance, the extra syllable does not disrupt the movement of the line into the emphatic monosyllabic *Gréw déar tŏ mé*. Variations allow poets room for manoeuvre, but also enable them to personalise the style and draw attention to important lines. The change in the traditional weak-strong stress pattern on the opening of line 3 emphasises the importance of the two words. Both *Grew* and *dear* have a strong stress (a spondee), drawing attention to the young Wordsworth's empathy with the natural world. The usual weak-strong iambic pattern is resumed in the rest of the line and this reinforces the importance of the change.

Free verse

If a poem is written in irregular lines without any regular metre or noticeable pattern of stressed and unstressed syllables, the poet is using **free verse** (*vers libre*). In this kind of poetry, rhythm can be created through repetition, the arrangement of words on the page or variations in line length. Occasionally rhyme may be used in free verse, but it tends to be irregular.

Sometimes the term **open form** is used in place of free verse to avoid the impression that this kind of poetry lacks shape and organisation. Although it may not draw on traditional poetic forms and structures, free verse is consciously crafted – poets create their own ordering principles, directly linking form and structure to meaning.

This kind of verse produces a very individual response, allowing poets to explore their subject matter in a distinctive way. Often, the visual element of the poem's appearance on the page will be as important as the lexical, syntactical and structural choices the poet makes. Twentieth-century poets often choose this form as an appropriate medium to present the complexity and disorder of the modern world. Free verse challenges preconceptions and refuses to conform to traditional expectations.

Frances Horovitz (1938–83) uses free verse to explore her experience of the natural world in 'January'. The form allows her to explore details of the landscape in an apparently random way. Lines vary in length; there is no regular pattern of stressed and unstressed syllables; there is no end-rhyme. While the poem seems to move indiscriminately from element to element, however, the language and structure guide our response.

January

1	A sealed stillness
	– only the stream moves,
	tremor and furl of water
	under the dead leaves.
5	In silence
	the wood declares itself:
	angles and arabesques of darkness,
	branch, bramble,
	tussocks of ghost grass
10	– under my heel
	ice shivers
	frail blue as sky
	between the runes of trees.

<pre>
                    Far up
    15   rooks, crows
             flail home.
</pre>

The poem's appearance on the page immediately demonstrates that Horovitz has not used a traditional poetic form or measured syllabic count. Instead, she has opted for a layout and structure that mirror her experience. There is, however, clear evidence that the poem is tightly organised.

Each stanza focuses on a specific feature of the natural landscape: the stream, the wood, and finally the birds. In each, a simple sentence is embedded within a sequence of phrases that draw attention to specific elements of the scene. The emphasis is on a recognition of the life that lurks beneath the surface deadness of winter. The opening noun phrase *A sealed stillness* epitomises this in its suggestion that an unknown 'something' is waiting to break out of its confines.

To reinforce this sense of a temporary stasis, the poet describes a scene in which movement is minimal. The dynamic present tense verb *moves* (l.2), for instance, is diminished by the post-modified noun phrase that follows it. The connotations of the nouns *tremor* and *furl* (l.3), along with the prepositional phrase *under dead leaves* (l.4), reduce the stream's potency as the traditional symbolic life-giver. Yet the dominance of winter is not secure – January is represented as a month in which, despite the desolation of the natural world, there is a confidence that the end is in sight. The adjective phrase *frail blue* (l.12) describing the tentative hold of the ice and the connotations of the verb *shivers* (l.11) can be set against the confidence of the stative verb *declares* (l.6). Although lacking any sense of movement, the verb and the reflexive pronoun that follows it become a strong statement of self, asserting the power of the wood amongst the *stillness* (l.1) and *silence* (l.5) of the scene.

The description of the wood is given an added importance by the use of consecutively end-stopped lines which slow the pace of the verse and focus attention on the details the poet observes. The images she uses reinforce its dominance of the winter scene. References to the mathematical *angles*, the balletic *arabesques* (l.7) and the literary *runes* (l.13) give it a dignity that befits its emphatic statement of self. The poem freezes a moment in time, recreating the poet's experience so that we too are able to participate in her awe.

Activity 4.1

Explore the way in which the verse form underpins the meaning in each of these poems.

You may like to think about: the content, layout, language, tone, grammatical structure and the imagery.

Ulysses

1   It little profits that an idle king,
By this still hearth, among these barren crags,
Matched with an agéd wife, I mete and dole
Unequal laws unto a savage race,
5   That hoard, and sleep, and feed, and know not me.
I cannot rest from travel; I will drink
Life to the lees. All times I have enjoyed
Greatly, have suffered greatly, both with those
That loved me, and alone; on shore, and when
10   Through scudding drifts the rainy Hyades
Vext the dim sea. I am become a name;
For always roaming with a hungry heart
Much have I seen and known, – cities of men
And manners, climates, councils, governments,
15   Myself not least, but honoured of them all;
And drunk delight of battle with my peers,
Far on the ringing plains of windy Troy.

TEXT 2 – STEPHEN CRANE (1871–1900)

A Man Said to the Universe

1   A man said to the universe:
'Sir, I exist!'
'However,' replied the universe,
'The fact has not created in me
5   'A sense of obligation.'

TEXT 3 – GEORGE GORDON, LORD BYRON (1788–1824)

We'll Go No More A-Roving

1   So, we'll go no more a-roving
So late into the night,
Though the heart be still as loving,
And the moon be still as bright.

5   For the sword outwears its sheath,
And the soul wears out the breast,
And the heart must pause to breathe,
And love itself have rest.

Though the night was made for loving,
10   And the day returns too soon,
Yet we'll go no more a-roving
By the light of the moon.

Commentary

The content of each poem here is very different: Tennyson is using a first person narrative to tell Ulysses' story; Crane is reflecting on the meaning of life and man's position in the universe; and Byron is telling his lover their relationship is over. Because the focus of the poems is so varied, we can expect each poet to choose a different verse form.

The layout immediately justifies this because the poems look so different on the page. Tennyson uses quite long lines of very similar lengths – the syllabic pattern is identical in each case. He does not divide the extract here into smaller units and uses no end rhyme. Byron, on the other hand, uses quatrains (4-lined stanzas) to separate his ideas, and the second and fourth lines in each stanza are inset. He creates a rhythmic quality to the poem by patterning the syllables: the longer lines are mostly made up of 8 syllables, while the shorter lines contain 6 or 7. The link between alternate lines is intensified by the use of alternating end rhyme. Crane chooses lines of varying lengths, dividing them according to grammatical units rather than poetic convention. The syllabic pattern in each line is different and there is no patterned end rhyme.

From these observations, it is possible to identify the verse forms used by each poet: Tennyson chooses **blank verse** which is an appropriate medium for a narrative poem because of its flexibility; Byron uses **end rhyme** to create a lyrical verse form that is reminiscent of a song; and Crane adopts **free verse** as a structural reminder of the fragmentation and detachment of life at the turn of the century. The verse form chosen in each case reinforces the meaning.

For Tennyson, 'Ulysses' was a response to the death of his good friend Arthur Hallam in 1833. He described the poem as *written under a sense of loss and that all had gone by, but that still life must be fought out to the end.* The blank verse provided him with a framework that could control his personal grief, while offering opportunities for variation. The mood of the opening is marked by dissatisfaction and impatience. The modifiers *idle* (l.1), *still, barren* (l.2) and *agéd* (l.3) reflect the speaker's state of mind – Ulysses is unhappy with his life. The traditional positive connotations of *king* have been undermined by the dismissive tone. The co-ordinated verbs *mete and dole* make the king's role seem unimportant; this is intensified by the use of the modifiers *Unequal* and *savage*.

The classical Ulysses is an heroic figure: brave, resourceful and eager for new experiences. He is a wanderer searching for truth and the nature of his own identity. We can therefore understand the feelings of entrapment and disillusion at the beginning of Tennyson's poem. The syndetic listing of verbs (l.5) emphasises the mundanity of the king's life; the repetition of the conjunction structurally represents his entrapment. The final clause of the list, *and know not me*, brings the opening five lines together – the great Ulysses, whose quest is for knowledge of himself, has been worn down by the pointlessness of everyday events. The regular 10-syllable lines have been crafted to mirror the ennui of the king, balancing noun phrases with monosyllabic verbs.

The tone changes, however, in the next line. Weariness is replaced by energy as Ulysses reveals his true nature – he is the man of purpose and action. The modal verbs reflect the king's self-awareness: *cannot* emphasises his inability to stop travelling, and *will* his certainty that life must be lived to the full. The change in tone is reinforced by the run-on lines that force the reader on (ll.6–11), mirroring Ulysses' excitement as he speaks of travel and adventure. The syndetic listing (l.5) is replaced with asyndetic listing (ll.14–15) and the effect is one of breathlessness as Ulysses remembers the things he has seen and known. The modifiers now set the scene in places far away: *scudding, rainy* (l.10), *dim* (l.11), *ringing, windy* (l.17). Despite their negative connotations, however, Ulysses' tone is not weary since they represent challenges to be overcome. This sense of the heroic Ulysses of the past is reinforced by the noun phrase *hungry heart* (l.12) in which the modifier represents a physical desire that is as yet unfulfilled.

The extract presents a character reflecting on life: his dissatisfaction with the present and his recollections of youthful adventure and achievement. The blank verse creates a regularity of rhythm that Tennyson can use to frame both Ulysses' and his own fears of the pointlessness of life. For the most part, the traditional weak-strong stress pattern of blank verse predominates; where Tennyson changes it, there is a significant reason. At the beginning of line 7, for instance, he uses a strong-weak trochaic rhythm, inverting the stress pattern to draw attention to *Life*. Added emphasis is placed upon this noun by the preceding run-on line because Tennyson wants the reader to notice Ulysses' changed tone, and to see the thematic significance of life to a man who feels trapped by a pointless routine.

Stephen Crane's poem challenges man's innate belief that he is of importance. It is a typically modern poem in that it rejects traditional poetic structures and language, opting instead for a free verse form and mundane, everyday words. The tone is one of detachment, reducing man's self-importance by emphasising his insignificance.

The poem takes the form of a dialogue in which the participants are a man and the universe. Despite the fact that it is the man who opens the discourse, Crane's use of determiners immediately establishes the relationship. The indefinite determiner *a* undermines the apparent confidence of the man's opening statement – he is 'Everyman', a universal figure with no individuality.

The emphatic statement *I exist* (l.2) is preceded by the vocative *Sir*, reflecting on the man's respect for the universe. The universe, however, fails to address the man directly and this reinforces the reader's sense that the man is insignificant. His short statement can also be contrasted with the longer speech turn taken up by the universe – in discourse analysis, the speaker with the longest turns is seen to be the dominant participant. The formality of the language in the last three lines adds to our feeling that the universe is in control of this exchange.

Crane has used free verse to manipulate our response to the speakers. The variations in line length and rhythm, the lack of end rhyme, and the matter-of-fact language allow him to question the meaning of life in the modern age. The tone is ironic – Crane is challenging traditional beliefs at a time when the work of the naturalist Charles Darwin had brought doubt into a society previously governed by faith and an egocentric belief in the importance of man. Written in 1899, it is an experimental poem that is quite different from the work of contemporary Victorian poets.

Byron's poem is a lyric, using alternate end rhyme, a syllabic pattern and the traditional 4-lined stanza. It is song-like in its approach and yet the content is quite unlike the traditional love song. Byron was renowned as a lady's man who revelled in a debauched lifestyle. In this poem, the speaker is ending a relationship with his lover and the jaunty rhythm and full rhymes are set in opposition to the nature of the content.

The tone is conversational and the reader almost feels as if they are overhearing part of a conversation that began before the opening of the poem. The use of the informal conjunction *So* (l.1) suggests that the speaker's argument is about to reach its climax. He gives the jilted lover no opportunity to intervene and the certainty of his decision is conveyed by the elided modal verb 'will' (ll.1/11). A similar effect is created by the use of *must* (l.7) with its connotations of obligation.

In the opening stanza, Byron's use of the subjunctive *Though . . . be* (ll.3–4) structure is significant since it suggests an ambiguity between appearance and reality – the subjunctive suggests an unreal or hypothetical meaning. Had he used the present tense 'is', the final lines of stanza 1 would have constituted an emphatic declaration of love. As it stands, Byron's apparently positive statement – that they must give up their relationship even though he still loves her – is undermined. When Byron chooses the past tense *Though . . . was* (ll.9–10) in the final stanza, on the other hand, he explicitly states something that he sees as real and true – while he cannot say his heart is still *as loving*, he can say that night is for lovers and that it is always too short. The contrast between these two types of grammatical structure reinforces our sense of the poem's speaker as a breaker of hearts, a true Byronic hero.

The imagery is traditional for a love poem with references to *the night* (ll.2, 9), *the heart* (ll.2, 7) *the moon* (ll. 4, 12) and the *soul* (l.6). Because Byron is ending rather than glorifying love, however, he also uses an unexpected image of *the sword* (l.5). It creates a striking effect at the beginning of the second stanza – its connotations of violence and possibly of physical sexuality are juxtaposed with the romantic bright moon of the first stanza. The language of the stanza is negative and the repetition (*outwears/wears out, pause/rest*) enhances our sense of the speaker's ennui. The stanza begins with *For*, used here as a conjunction ('because'), and each of the following lines then begin with *And* in the initial position. The speaker is providing reasons for leaving and the emphatic positioning of the conjunctions adds force to his argument. His reasons are, however, figurative rather than literal, allowing him once again to avoid the reality of what he is doing.

The neatness and harmony of the end rhymes is set in opposition to the negative content, and Byron has used the poetic, lexical and grammatical features of a song to ameliorate the harshness of what he is doing. He has made the love-song into a medium for rejection by adapting traditional conventions.

Form

As well as identifying the kind of verse used, it is useful to be able to recognise distinctive types of poem. By looking at the content, the number and length of lines, the stanza structure, and other key features it is possible to pinpoint particular types of poetry. An understanding of poetic form and its links to meaning can help us to read poetry more effectively.

Some poetic forms can be recognised by a distinctive stanza structure, line pattern, rhyme scheme or rhythm – these are known as 'fixed forms'. Although poets may vary the traditional structure to achieve certain effects, the underlying principles will always be recognisable.

Other poetic forms are distinguished by their content and diction rather than by structural patterns. Poets can chose to approach a particular subject in a way that will link their poem to a recognisable poetic tradition, choosing language that will establish a tone appropriate to the form.

The sonnet

If the poem has 14 lines with a distinctive rhyming pattern, it is a **sonnet**. It will often use iambic pentameter. There are three basic sonnet forms.

If there is an octave (an 8-line stanza) rhyming abbaabba and a sestet (a 6-line stanza) rhyming cdecde, cdcdcd, or cdccdc, it is an **Italian** or **Petrarchan** sonnet. There may be variations in the rhyme scheme of the sestet, but there will never be a couplet. This is probably the most common sonnet form. The octave develops one thought; there is a turn or volta, and the sestet develops from the octave, varying and completing the original thought. Often, the octave presents a problem, situation or attitude and the sestet is used to comment upon or resolve it. The volta acts as a pivot on which the two sections are balanced.

If there are three quatrains (4-lined stanzas) and a couplet, rhyming abab bcbc cdcd ee, it is a **Spenserian** sonnet. If there are three quatrains and a couplet, rhyming abab cdcd efef gg, it is a **Shakespearean** sonnet. These sonnets are often called English sonnets. They develop a different idea in each quatrain, concluding the argument with an ingenious final couplet that rounds off the argument and resolves the tension created.

The content of sonnets tends to deal with love, the problems of life, disorder and other complex issues of relevance to the poet. The rigidity of the form forces poets to concentrate on their topic in a very focused way. Sometimes the structural restraints bring order to the disorder of life as the poet reaches understanding of the topic he or she is exploring. Other sonnets juxtapose an ideal with the harsh reality of life, placing the neatness of the sonnet's form in opposition to an awareness that life does not itself conform to an ordered pattern.

In Shakespeare's Sonnet LXXIII, the form is typical: the rhyme scheme conforms to the usual pattern of abab cdcd efef gg and the content is divided into three quatrains and a couplet.

Sonnet LXXIII

1   That time of year thou may'st in me behold
     When yellow leaves, or none, or few, do hang
     Upon those boughs which shake against the cold,
     Bare ruin'd choirs, where late the sweet birds sang.
5   In me thou see'st the twilight of such day
     As after sunset fadeth in the west,
     Which by and by black night doth take away,
     Death's second self, that seals up all in rest.
     In me thou see'st the glowing of such fire,
10   That on the ashes of his youth doth lie,
     As the death-bed whereon it must expire,
     Consum'd with that which it was nourish'd by.

> This thou perceiv'st, which makes thy love more strong,
> To love that well which thou must leave ere long.

The poem literally describes autumn (ll.1–4), the end of a day (ll.5–8) and a dying fire (ll.9–12). On a figurative level, however, the poet is facing his own declining years – the tone is one of sadness because of the poet's awareness of things coming to an end.

The metaphors clearly reflect the poet's feelings and prepare the reader for the final couplet. The description of autumn draws attention to the end of natural things: modifiers like *yellow*, *Bare* and *ruin'd* mirror changes that the poet sees in himself; references to night as *death's second self*, to *the ashes of . . . youth* and to the *deathbed* then highlight the concept of death in a more human way. Euphemistically, descriptions of *twilight*, *sunset* and the *black night* are also synonymous with death. The treatment of death is not gloomy, however. By presenting night that *seals up all in rest* as death's parallel, Shakespeare implies that death, like sleep, is something to be accepted rather than feared.

What Shakespeare considers in this sonnet, however, is not just the inevitability of death. The couplet provides the change of direction which puts the previous stanzas in context – the focus in the final lines is on time's effect on human relationships and on the way the poet's lover will value him more as his death approaches.

The style is formal and Shakespeare uses iambic pentameter in most lines.

That time | of year | thou may'st | in me | behold

However, there are also examples where the rhythm is changed in order to draw attention to key points. In line 4, the pattern of stresses is used to reflect the slowing down of life.

Bare ru | in'd choirs, | where late | the sweet | birds sang

The use of a spondee at the beginning and end of the line affects the pace of the poem and clearly also has a thematic function.

The sonnet form has been used to describe the approach to death vividly through striking metaphors. The 14 lines are divided in such a way that the reader is forced to consider one aspect at a time. In the final couplet, all the ideas are drawn together: knowing that life is coming to an end makes love more valuable.

The sonnet form demands compression of ideas and thus the central issue is intensified. Here the relationship between death and love is personalised through Shakespeare's cohesive references to himself (ll.1, 5, 9). By using metaphors that are embedded in the real world, Shakespeare forces the reader to face the reality of death, mirroring its inevitability in his use of the modal verb *must*. Despite the tone of sadness, the sonnet ends on a positive rather than a negative note, stressing the strength of love which death can inspire rather than the sense of loss with which death is traditionally associated.

Activity 4.2

Explore the relationship between form and content in the sonnets below.

You may like to think about: the language, tone, imagery and structure.

TEXT 1 – EDMUND SPENSER (C.1552–99)

Amoretti LXXIX: Men Call You Fair

1   Men call you fair, and you do credit it,
For that your self ye daily such do see:
But the true fair, that is the gentle wit,
And virtuous mind, is much more prais'd of me.
5   For all the rest, how ever fair it be,
Shall turn to naught and lose that glorious hue:
But only that is permanent and free
From frail corruption, that doth flesh ensue.
That is true beauty: that doth argue you
10   To be divine, and born of heavenly seed:
Deriv'd from that fair Spirit, from whom all true
And perfect beauty did at first proceed.
He only fair, and what he fair hath made,
All other fair, like flowers untimely fade.

TEXT 2 – JOHN KEATS (1795–1821)

On First Looking into Chapman's Homer°

1   Much have I travelled in the realms of gold
And many goodly states and kingdoms seen;
Round many western islands have I been
Which bards in fealty to Apollo hold.
5   Oft of one wide expanse had I been told
That deep-browed Homer ruled as his demesne;
Yet did I never breathe its pure serene
Till I heard Chapman speak out loud and bold:
Then felt I like some watcher of the skies
10   When a new planet swims into his ken;
Or like stout Cortez when with eagle eyes
He stared at the Pacific – and all his men
Looked at each other with a wild surmise –
Silent, upon a peak in Darien.

° a C17th translation of the Greek poet Homer by George Chapman (?1559–1634)

Commentary

Although each poem is a sonnet in form, there are variations in the structure. 'Amoretti' is a Spenserian or English sonnet in which the octave is made up of three quatrains rhyming abab bcbc cdcd and a final couplet. Keats adopts the

Italian or Petrarchan model with an octave made up of two quatrains rhyming abba and a sestet rhyming cdcdcd.

The content and the development of ideas are directly linked to the kind of sonnet chosen. Spenser's poem is part of a sonnet sequence recording his courtship with his second wife Elizabeth Boyle. The content is therefore traditional – he addresses the nature of love. In each quatrain, he develops a different idea. His first premise is that inner beauty (*the gentle wit* and *virtuous mind*, ll.3–4) is more important than physical beauty; he then explores the nature of impermanence; and finally asserts that God is the source of this true beauty.

'On First Looking into Chapman's Homer' chooses a different topic – Keats is writing not about love, but about his discovery of Chapman's translation of the Greek poet Homer. His personal experience becomes a symbol for the imaginative possibilities of all literature and he uses the metaphor of travel and exploration to convey his excitement to the reader. The first quatrain of the octave focuses on physical journeys, but by the end of the second quatrain the symbolic link to reading is clear. The turning point occurs at the start of the sestet where Keats begins to focus on the effect reading Chapman has had on him. Images of exploration are replaced by images of discovery; the tone of elevated description changes to one of wonder.

The language is an important means of conveying ideas. Repetition of *fair* (ll.1, 2, 5, 13–14) establishes the theme: Spenser is using ordinary language to draw a contrast between the beauty that other men can see, that you can see in a reflection, and *true beauty* (l.9) that is *born of heavenly seed* (l.10). The positive connotations of *glorious hue* (l.6) – physical beauty – are undermined by the noun *naught* (l.6) and the reductive reference to *flesh* (l.8). Inner beauty, on the other hand, is elevated by the adjective phrases *permanent* and *free/From frail corruption* (ll.7–8), and its association with the divine. The religious words (*divine, heavenly* l.10, *that fair Spirit* l.11) reinforce the difference between external and inner beauty – between something worldly and something spiritual, between *the true fair* (inner beauty) and *All other fair* (physical beauty).

Spenser's argument does not depend upon imagery, but in the final line the simile of the transient *flowers* becomes a powerful symbol for his case against physical beauty. The theme of impermanence contrasts a love that is dependent upon appearance with one that aspires to higher things.

Keats's language is more elevated and allusive. The archaic *goodly* (l.2), *fealty* (l.4) and *demesne* (l.6) enhance the poetic atmosphere created by the allusion to El Dorado (*the realms of gold* l.1) and the description of being immersed in the atmosphere of Homer (l.7). While concrete nouns *states, kingdoms* (l.2), *islands* (l.3), *demesne* (l.6) create the physical image of a journey, references to *bards* (poets), *Apollo* (the Greek god of poetry), *That deep-browed Homer* (author of two early Greek epics), and *Chapman* (an Elizabethan poet and dramatist who translated Homer) remind us that reading takes us on a metaphorical journey.

The sonnet's turning point is marked by the volta after *bold* (l.8) and a change in tone. The adverbial *Then* at the beginning of the sestet ensures that we notice the new mood. The formal dispassionate tone of the octave with its predominantly regular weak-strong stress pattern and end-stopped lines indicates its reflective quality. In the sestet, Keats's excitement is mirrored by a far less predictable stress pattern and the driving force of the run-on lines. The similes also convey his wonder and excitement: he is like an astronomer seeing a new planet (1.9); and Cortés, the Spanish sixteenth-century explorer, seeing the Pacific Ocean having not known of its existence. The weight of this image is important – it extends over the final four lines of the poem. After the pause marked by the dash (1.13), the emphasis on *Silent* in the initial position indicates the power of this experience. The image draws a parallel between the explorer who can now contemplate further discoveries and the poet for whom reading can open new worlds.

The link between form and meaning in these sonnets is clear: Keats is containing his excitement within the disciplined structure, while Spenser is arguing his case for the pre-eminence of inner beauty, concluding emphatically in the couplet with a reminder of the impermanence of all but love and God. In each case, the poet is exploring a personal experience that becomes a universal truth.

The villanelle

The **villanelle** is a complex fixed form. It consists of 19 lines of any length divided into six stanzas with only two rhymes throughout. The five tercets rhyme aba and the concluding quatrain rhymes abaa. In addition, line 1 is repeated in lines 6, 12 and 18; and line 3 in lines 9, 15 and 19.

The form was originally used for pastoral subjects, but in the twentieth century, it has been used in a variety of ways. Dylan Thomas's villanelle 'Do not go gentle into that good night' uses the repeated lines and recurring rhymes to create a haunting plea to his father in the face of death. William Earnest Henley adopts a lighter tone in his poem 'Villanelle' as he addresses the possibilities of the form itself.

Activity 4.3

Explore the ways in which Elizabeth Bishop (1911–79) uses the villanelle to develop her argument in 'One Art'.

You may like to think about: the title, the structure and any alterations to the traditional form, the ideas, the language and the tone.

One Art

1   The art of losing isn't hard to master;
    so many things seem filled with the intent
    to be lost that their loss is no disaster.

    Lose something every day. Accept the fluster
5   of lost door keys, the hour badly spent.
    The art of losing isn't hard to master.

Then practice losing farther, losing faster:
places, and names, and where it was you meant
to travel. None of these will bring disaster.

10   I lost my mother's watch. And look! my last, or
next-to-last, of three loved houses went.
The art of losing isn't hard to master.

I lost two cities, lovely ones. And, vaster,
some realms I owned, two rivers, a continent.
15   I miss them, but it wasn't a disaster.

– Even losing you (the joking voice, a gesture
I love) I shan't have lied. It's evident
the art of losing's not too hard to master
though it may look like (*Write* it!) like disaster.

Commentary

We can immediately see that the poem conforms to the division of stanzas into
five tercets and a final quatrain. In addition, there are only two rhymes and a
repetition of the key words *master* and *disaster*. Bishop does not, however, follow
the repeating pattern of lines.

While line 1, *The art of losing isn't hard to master*, recurs exactly in lines 6 and
12, it becomes slightly less emphatic in line 18 – *the art of losing's not too hard to
master*. The addition of the adverb of degree *too* undermines the confident tone of
the other stanzas in which the poet is able to 'master' everyday losses of *door keys*
(ll.4–5), *places, and names* (ll.8–9) her *mother's watch* (l.10) and so on. The loss in
the final quatrain is different – it is emotional rather than physical and the poet
therefore feels it more intensely. The tone of bravado or assumed confidence is an
attempt to conceal her true response.

The third line establishes the central idea that loss is not a 'disaster'. Although
Bishop does not repeat this line exactly as is traditional of the form, the sentiments are echoed in lines 9, 15 and 19, and each ends with the abstract noun
disaster. Again, the variation in the quatrain is more noticeable. The dash marking
the start of the stanza makes it appear like an afterthought, and yet the focus here
is crucial to our understanding of the poem as a whole.

The tentative modal verb *may* (l.19) suggests that the poet is not convinced by
her argument in this final instance of loss. Our sense of this is reinforced by the
parenthesis and the repetition of the preposition *like*. The poet appears to be
struggling to complete the line – as though she is trying to convince herself that
losing her lover is just as unimportant as losing the other things she has listed.
The change in grammatical mood from declarative to imperative and the use of
italics in the parenthesis draw our attention to the underlying dilemma.

Bishop has used the structure of the villanelle to develop an argument. The
title initiates the idea of an 'art' – something that can be learnt and practised with
guiding principles – and the opening noun phrase of stanza 1 qualifies this art.
Each tercet then relates the 'art of losing' to a particular object or concept, growing in significance until we have moved beyond the personal to *cities, realms, two*

rivers and *a continent* (ll.12–13). Having reached what would seem to be the pinnacle of the argument, the final quatrain changes direction, revealing a loss that seems to be harder to 'master'. This time, the reader is not quite convinced by the poet's argument. The delay in the completion of the simile (*like . . . like disaster*) mirrors the poet's hesitation, suggesting that in this instance the loss is a disaster.

Haiku

Haiku is a form of syllabic poetry in which the three lines must be made up of 5–7–5 syllables respectively. The original haiku were written by Japanese Zen Buddhists in the sixteenth century. The haiku (or hokku as it was called before the nineteenth century) was the opening verse in a linked cycle of poems. It was seen as an object of meditation, revealing some essential truth about life.

A single idea, image or feeling forms the focus of the three lines. The poet's exploration of his topic leads to an epiphany in which something significant is understood. The simplicity, naturalness and directness of the form is juxtaposed with a profundity of meaning.

The strict syllabic pattern makes haiku concise. Despite this, the poetry is challenging for the reader because of the wider associations that arise from the words on the page. Traditional haiku focus on something in the real world as their starting point; the poet then meditates on his object until he is able to penetrate the surface; in this state of enlightenment, he finds universal truth.

Although most of the translations of traditional haiku lose the original syllabic pattern, they still convey the connections the poet is making between the object before him and the essential truth he wishes to reveal. In the following example by Issa (1763–1827), the sound of the natural world around the poet encourages him to think of the inevitability of death. The physicality conveyed by the verb modifier *creeping* with its suggestions of ongoing activity is contrasted with the connotations of the abstract noun *transience*. The poet has moved from the concrete to the abstract, drawing on the symbolism of the bell tolling to mark the end of life.

> Listen,
> all creeping things –
> the bell of transience

The form has been used in English by Ezra Pound and the Imagist poets who found the visual qualities and intensity of the form fulfilled their poetic principles. Other poets such as W. B. Yeats (1865–1939) and Robert Frost (1874–1963) have also written haiku. The English versions do not always develop the spiritual intensity of the original Japanese poets.

Elegy

If the poem has been written on the death of a specific person, it is an **elegy**. It will both praise and mourn the individual in an attempt to come to terms with the death. Serious meditative poems in which the poet conveys melancholy thoughts are also described as elegies. Before the sixteenth century, elegies were also written on other subjects like war, love and similar themes. Traditional elegies draw on the pastoral tradition, using a rural scene and representing the poet and the person mourned as shepherds. Elegies allow the poet to meditate on the problem of death, working though a personal experience and moving towards acceptance.

The poet Edmund Spenser used the pastoral conventions in 'Astrophel', an elegy for Sir Philip Sidney; Thomas Gray (1716–71) wrote 'Elegy written in a Country Church-yard' lamenting not the death of an individual, but the passing of a way of life.

Lyric

If the poem is song-like and the poet is writing about his or her thoughts and feelings in a subjective and personal way, it is a **lyric**. Lyric poems can deal with love, death, nature, religion or social/political issues. The poet confronts a particular aspect of experience and tries to organise his thoughts and feelings. Lyric poems will either present an ordered view of the world, or will focus on the disorder and chaos of life. The term 'lyric' is also used generally to include all poems (e.g. sonnets, odes and elegies) in which the poet is responding to life. Narrative poems, poems that tell stories, are excluded from this category.

The Renaissance period was the great age of the lyric with Sir Thomas Wyatt (1503–42) and Henry Howard, Earl of Surrey (1517–47), beginning the English lyric tradition. In the nineteenth century, there was a revival with the Romantic and Victorian poets writing poems such as 'The Daffodils' (Wordsworth), 'When We Two Parted' (Byron), 'Blow, Bugle, Blow' (Tennyson) and 'In a Gondola' (Robert Browning).

Ode

If the poem addresses a person, thing or abstraction and extends over several stanzas with elaborate and elevated language, and a marked formal and stately tone, the poem is an **ode**. Some odes are public, celebrating ceremonial occasions like funerals, birthdays and state events; others are private, dealing with intense, personal moments and subjective experiences. In its most basic form, an ode praises its subject, but it can also be more philosophical and reflective.

The Romantic poets moved away from an exclusively celebratory tone, and the ode became a vehicle for a contemplation of life's problems. While the elevated language heightens the significance of the subject, contradictory images convey a sense of reality.

The great odes of the Augustan age were written by William Collins (1721–59) and Thomas Gray. It was also a form popular with the Romantic poets: Samuel Taylor Coleridge wrote 'France' and 'Dejection'; William Wordsworth wrote 'Ode on Intimations of Mortality' and 'Ode to Duty'; and John Keats wrote 'On Melancholy' and 'To Pysche'.

Pastoral

If the poem focuses on rural life, particularly the life of shepherds, it is a **pastoral** poem in which the poet describes a peaceful world far removed from the corruption of contemporary life. Such poems celebrate the idealised classical country of Arcadia, offering it as an image of escape, a perfect world. The implicit contrast between this innocent world and harsh reality allows the poet to highlight the true nature of society. The language and form of pastoral poems are artificial, signalling to the reader that it should not be taken at face value. Often there is an underlying moral, political or religious point being made about the state of society.

Early English pastoral can be seen in Spenser's *Shepheardes Calender* and then in Michael Drayton's (1563–1631) 'Daffodil' and 'The Muses' Elysium'. Later examples can be seen in the work of Alexander Pope (1688–1744) and John Gay (1685–1732). In Book VIII of *The Prelude*, Wordsworth charted the whole history of pastoral, contrasting the original idea of the idyllic shepherd's life with harsh reality.

Narrative

If the poem tells a story, it is a **narrative** poem. The three main kinds are epic, metrical romance and ballad, but some narrative poems do not fall neatly into these categories. While the story itself is important, the underlying ideas and experiences, and the poet's means of presenting them are central to our understanding of the poem.

If the poem is an **epic**, it will present the deeds of an heroic character as a means of revealing something about human experience. Traditional epic poems are very long and use classical references to make the story universal.

If the poem is a **ballad**, it is a song that tells a story, originally with a musical accompaniment. Ballads date back to the oral tradition of the late Middle Ages. The beginning is often abrupt; the focus is on a single event; the story is told through action and dialogue; the theme is often tragic. There is minimal background description and the imagery is sparse and simple. Dialect is often used, helping to create a vivid sense of time and place. The tone of the narrator is impersonal and the underlying ideas therefore emerge implicitly from the text. As a part of the oral tradition, ballads use simple language and repetition, and there is often a refrain. Such features contribute to the immediacy and intensity of the form.

If the poem is a **metrical romance**, it will be a story of adventure, love and chivalry. There is often an element of mystery and the supernatural.

Narrative verse has been written in English since the eighth-century *Beowulf*. Other great narrative poems include Geoffrey Chaucer's *Canterbury Tales* (c.1387), Edmund Spenser's *The Faerie Queene* (1589, 1596), John Milton's *Paradise Lost* (1667), Pope's *The Rape of the Lock* (1712, 1714), Coleridge's *The Rime of the Ancient Mariner* (1798), Keats's *The Eve of St. Agnes* (1819), Robert Browning's 'Fra Lippo Lippi' (1855) and the ballads of Rudyard Kipling (1865–1936). More recent examples can be found in 'Journey of the Magi' (T.S. Eliot, 1888–1965), 'The Ballad of the Mari Lwyd' (Vernon Watkins, 1906–67), 'The Age of Anxiety' (W.H.Auden, 1907–73) and 'Whitsun Weddings' (Philip Larkin, 1922–85).

Activity 4.4

> **Identify the form of each poem below and explore the poet's use of that form to communicate his or her feelings, or relate an experience.**
>
> You may like to think about: the content and underlying ideas, the language and tone, the grammatical features, and the links between form and meaning.

TEXT 1 – EMILY BRONTË (1818–48)

Spellbound

1   The night is darkening round me,
        The wild winds coldly blow;
    But a tyrant spell has bound me,
        And I cannot, cannot go.

5   The giant trees are bending
        Their bare boughs weighed with snow;
    The storm is fast descending,
        And yet I cannot go.

    Clouds beyond clouds above me,
10   Wastes beyond wastes below;
    But nothing drear can move me:
        I will not, cannot go.

TEXT 2 – ALFRED LORD TENNYSON (1809–92)

Break, Break, Break

1   Break, break, break,
        On thy cold gray stones, O Sea!
    And I would that my tongue could utter
        The thoughts that arise in me.

5   O, well for the fisherman's boy,
        That he shouts with his sister at play!
    O, well for the sailor lad,
        That he sings in his boat on the bay!

    And the stately ships go on
10   To their haven under the hill;
    But O for the touch of a vanish'd hand,
        And the sound of a voice that is still!

    Break, break, break
        At the foot of thy crags, O Sea!
15   But the tender grace of a day that is dead
        Will never come back to me.

The Twa Corbies°   ravens/crows

1   As I was walking all alane,
     I heard twa corbies making a mane;
     The tane unto t'other say,
     'Where sall we gang and dine to-day?'

5   'In behint yon auld fail° dyke°,   turf/ditch
     I wot there lies a new slain knight;
     And naebody kens° that he lies there,   knows
     But his hawk, his hound, and lady fair.

     'His hound is to the hunting gane,
10   His hawk to fetch the wild-fowl hame;
     His lady's ta'en another mate,
     So we may make our dinner sweet.

     'Ye'll sit on his white hause-bane°,   collar bone
     And I'll pike out his bonny blue een°;   eyes
15   Wi' ae lock o'his gowden hair,
     We'll theek° our nest when it grows bare.   thatch

     'Mony° a one for him makes mane,   many
     But nane sall° ken where he is gane;   shall
     Oer his white banes°, when they are bare,   bones
20   The wind sall blaw for evermair.'

To Autumn (an extract)

1   Season of mists and mellow fruitfulness!
     Close bosom-friend of the maturing sun;
     Conspiring with him how to load and bless
     With fruit the vines that round the thatch-eaves run;
5   To bend with apples the moss'd cottage-trees,
     And fill all fruit with ripeness to the core;
     To swell the gourd, and plump the hazel shells
     With a sweet kernel; to set budding more,
     And still more, later flowers for the bees,
10   Until they think warm days will never cease,
     For Summer has o'erbrimm'd their clammy cells.

The Passionate Shepherd to his Love

1   Come live with me and be my Love,
     And we will all the pleasures prove,
     That hills and valleys, dales and fields,
     Or woods or steepy mountain yields.

5   And we will sit upon the rocks,
     And see the shepherd feed their flocks
     By shallow rivers, to whose falls
     Melodious birds sing madrigals.

<pre>
            And I will make thee beds of roses,
   10   And a thousand fragrant posies;
            A cap of flowers and a kirtle
            Embroider'd all with leaves of myrtle.

            A gown made of the finest wool,
            Which from our pretty lambs we pull;
   15   Fair-lined slippers for the cold,
            With buckles of the purest gold.

            A belt of straw and ivy-buds
            With coral clasps and amber studs;
            And if these pleasures may thee move,
   20   Come live with me and be my Love.

            The shepherd swains shall dance and sing
            For they delight each May morning:
            If these delights thy mind may move,
            Then live with me and be my Love.
</pre>

Commentary

Forms like the sonnet and villanelle can be recognised by their fixed features. The poems here fall into different categories not because of their structural patterns, but according to their content and diction. Tennyson may use quatrains with the second and fourth lines rhyming, but of more significance is his attempt to come to terms with the death of his friend. Brontë uses quatrains in which alternate lines rhyme, but it is her expression of thoughts and feelings as she confronts a particular experience that helps us to identify her poem. Both Marlowe and the anonymous poet of 'The Twa Corbies' choose quatrains made up of rhyming couplets, but while Marlowe creates a rural, idealised world, 'The Twa Corbies' tells a story. Keats, on the other hand, praises autumn – the structure and rhyme scheme are complex, and the lines are longer.

In each case, while it is useful to be able to comment on the structural features and link them to meaning, it is the topic and the language used to discuss it that helps us to classify the kind of poem we are reading. It is sometimes helpful to know if a poet is drawing on a particular tradition because this can help us to understand what we are reading.

'Spellbound' is a **lyric**, recognisable for its emphasis on the personal, and its attempts to make sense of a particular experience. The quatrains with their alternate rhyming lines are reminiscent of song, although the mood here is not joyful.

The style is simple and the language ordinary, but Brontë creates a powerful atmosphere through her lexical and grammatical choices. The use of the present progressive (*is darkening* l.1, *are bending* l.5, *is . . . descending* l.7) immediately transports the reader to the scene. The action of the verbs is ongoing, suggesting something inescapable and without end. Modifiers such as *wild* (l.2), *giant* (l.5) and *bare* (l.6) convey the sense of a brooding, inhospitable environment reminiscent of the moors of Brontë's childhood and the backdrop to her novel, *Wuthering Heights*.

The poet seems insignificant and vulnerable within this landscape. This is reinforced by the metaphorical *tyrant's spell* (l.3) that restricts and traps the poet, and by the repeated use of the modal verb *cannot* (ll. 4, 8). The description in the opening of stanza 3 further emphasises her diminutive presence. The patterning of the words and the prepositional phrases (ll.9–10) mirrors the poet's entrapment – there is no escape.

There is a change, however. The contrastive conjunction *But* in the initial position suggests a turning point. In earlier stanzas, the co-ordinating conjunctions (*And* l.4, *And yet* l.8) have created an accumulative effect, emphasising the impossibility of escaping. Now we sense the poet's refusal to move and this is underpinned by the emphatic modal verb *will not* (l.12). Used alongside *cannot* it creates ambiguity – the poet is both unwillingly held captive by the storm, and yet relishes her presence in it.

For some critics, the literal storm becomes a symbolic representation of the dominant and restrictive male hierarchy that was typical of Victorian society. The poem can then be read as a declaration of the impossibility of independence for women in a male-orientated world. For others, it is an autobiographical poem in which images of death (*night is darkening*) and entrapment reflect Brontë's attitude to life.

'Break, Break, Break' is an **elegy** even though Tennyson has not directly referred to the death of his friend, Arthur Hallam. Instead, he portrays his state of mind and contrasts it with the world around him. The only references to death are symbolic, emphasising the poet's sense of loss. The longing expressed by the interjection *0* (l.11) and the contrastive conjunction that precedes it mark a turning point. The poet moves away from the physical world and attempts to express his feelings, *the thoughts that arise in [him]*.

The poet becomes an outsider, detached from what is happening around him. The dynamic verbs *shouts* and *sings* (ll.6,8) reflect a world that is going on, unaffected by death. Similarly, the ships can go to a *haven under the hill* (l.10), but there is no solace for the poet. His loss is conveyed by the complex noun phrases *the touch of a vanish'd hand* (l.11), *the sound of a voice that is still* (l.12) and *the tender grace of a day that is dead* (l.15). The things he yearns for are not physical as the abstract nouns here (*touch, sound, grace*) indicate. The focus on abstract concepts is in direct contrast to the concrete lexis of the earlier stanzas. It reflects that the poet has moved beyond his physical location and his inability to communicate his feelings, to a point at which he can put his loss into words.

The repetition of the dynamic verbs in the opening line sets the tone. The strong plosives suggest Tennyson's anger at the death of his friend, and this is reinforced by the hard consonants in line 2 (*cold grey stones*). The interjections of stanza 2 (ll.5, 7) moderate Tennyson's anger to bitterness and this is finally replaced by a tone of acceptance in the final stanza. The hypothetical *would* (l.3) has become *will* (l.16) with its connotations of certainty as the poet faces the reality of his friend's death.

The inevitability of the sea's cycle establishes the framework for the poem – we begin and end with the breaking waves. Within this framework, however, the tone changes. The anger of the opening line and the negative modifiers *cold* and *gray* (l.2) are replaced by the resignation of the final stanza; the harsh rhythm of *cold gray stones* with its sequence of stressed syllables is replaced by the lilting *the foot of thy crags*. The symbolism of the sea breaking on the shore is crucial to our understanding of the poem: as it breaks on the shore it is a parallel to Tennyson's breaking heart; and yet its cyclical pattern of ebb-and-flow moves the poet towards an acceptance that life will go on.

The ballad, 'The Twa Corbies', is a **narrative**, telling a story in a direct and unsentimental way. It is stark and realistic in its treatment of its subject: the death of a knight. The first two lines frame the narrative, introducing an impersonal narrator who overhears a conversation between two ravens, and reports it with no interpretative comment. The opening is abrupt so that the poet can move immediately to the focus of the poem – the two ravens debating their hunger and the possibilities of dining on the newly slain knight. As is traditional, this single event forms the basis for the dialogue with the theme emerging in the final stanza.

The background is real, but description is minimal. This is reminiscent of the oral roots from which this kind of poem evolved where monosyllabic, everyday language was used economically. We know enough to set a scene: we are made aware of the isolation of the landscape and of its one key feature (*yon auld fail dyke*, l.5) in the first stanza; the final stanza creates the atmosphere with its bleak description of the wind.

The matter-of-fact tone is achieved through the kind of language chosen. Noun phrases (*his hawk, his hound*) tend to be simple. Because there are few modifiers, those that are included are inevitably significant. The compound *new-slain* is emotive because of its emphasis on the recent past – we are hearing about a topical event, not something consigned to history. This draws attention to the indifference of the *hawk, hound* and *lady*, who we would expect to be grieving. The contrast developed between the *white hause-bane*, the *bonny blue een* and the *gowden hair* juxtaposes the bleakness of the abandoned body stripped of its flesh with the traditional image of the blue-eyed golden-haired hero. Ironically, in this bleak world, his heroic good looks are worthless.

The poem deals with death in a realistic and simplistic way. The birds describe precisely what they will do (ll.13–16), eating the eyes and thatching their nests with the hair. The detachment is reflected in the direct, mainly monosyllabic words. Language is used literally rather than figuratively, but that does not prevent the poet from exploring ideas. The final image of the wind blowing over the stripped bones becomes a symbol for man's mortality. Its bleakness reminds the reader of the betrayal lying at the heart of the poem – the hawk, hound and lady are the only ones who know about the knight's death other than the ravens. This suggestion of guilt is reinforced by the dispassionate reference to the lady taking *another mate* (l.11).

The poem is written in a Scottish dialect, which helps to create a sense of place despite the fact that there is little physical description. Most words are recognisable even though the spellings have been altered to reflect pronunciation (*alane* – alone, *behint* – behind, *naebody* – nobody); others may be quite unfamiliar (*corbies, fail, theek, hause-bane, ken*). The sound qualities created by these features are part of the traditional oral qualities of ballads – poems written to be read aloud or sung.

The style in the extract from '**To Autumn**' is heightened, and Keats is using language in a more obviously descriptive way than Tennyson and Brontë. The tone is formal and stately, the language is elevated, and the poem is addressing an abstraction – autumn. Keats is using the **ode** as a form in which he can contemplate life. Although it is known from Keats's letters that the poem was based on personal experience (a walk in the fields near Winchester), he does not use a first person narrative as Tennyson and Brontë do. Instead, he adopts a detached tone that allows him to explore the experience in a more universal way.

The elliptical style of this extract intensifies the reader's experience. Stanza 1 is made up of a sequence of increasingly complex noun phrases, each providing a detailed snapshot of autumn. The opening noun phrase, *Season of mists and mellow fruitfulness*, sets the tone with its melodious sounds: sibilance and the gentle bilabials (*mists*, *mellow*) and fricatives (*of*, *fruitfulness*).

The following noun phrases (ll.2–11) personify autumn as the *Close-bosom friend of the maturing sun*. The connotations of *Conspiring* here are positive rather than negative – the ageing sun, reaching its peak before dying away for winter, plots with autumn to bring the natural world to ripeness. The diction is rich, suggesting the fertility and abundance of nature. Concrete nouns bring the physical elements of the scene to prominence (*fruit, vines, apples, gourd, hazel shells, kernel*); dynamic verbs (*load, bless, bend, fill, swell, plump*) convey the energy of autumn; compound nouns (*thatch-eves, cottage-trees*) provide concentrated description; modifiers (*sweet, warm*) create the atmosphere. The intensity of the writing elevates the scene – this is more than just a natural description. Keats is praising the richness of autumn by evoking sights, sounds and smells that we can all recognise.

The structure of the stanza is complex. The rhyme scheme creates intricate links between lines and ideas: the alternate rhymes of the first quatrain (abab) are neatly resolved, establishing a direct link between autumn and the summer sun. The next seven lines use a less obvious pattern (cdedcce). The stanza ends with a couplet followed by a rhyme echoing line 7, a delay that gives the stanza a wistful tone. This is enhanced by the internal rhyme (*mossed cottage-trees, swell/shell*) and the long vowel sounds.

In addition to the cohesion provided by the sound patterns, the complex grammatical structure contributes to the intensity of the description. There are no standard main clauses – the non-finite verb *Conspiring* is post-modifying the *Close bosom-friend* of line 2, and each subsequent non-finite clause (*to load and bless, To bend, And fill* and so on) is dependent on *Conspiring with him how to. . . .* The elliptical style intensifies the effect of the ode. Grammatical function words are omitted, leaving only those of semantic importance. Keats creates a cinematic scene, freeze-framing moments of symbolic significance.

This stanza emphasises the fertility and life of autumn – a season often linked to the deadness of winter. There is an implicit suggestion in the final three lines, however, that this perfection is momentary. The use of *think* (l.10) suggests that the bees have been deceived by this burst of life, and this is reinforced by the connotations of excess suggested by *o'er-brimmed* and the modifier *clammy*. Keats recognises the transience of the moment he records, but there is no sense of regret because he knows that the natural process is cyclical, an idea which is developed in the rest of the ode from which this extract has been taken. The ode form allows Keats to praise the richness of autumn, but also to reflect on the nature of life and death.

Marlowe's poem, 'The Passionate Shepherd to his love' is a pastoral because of the ideal world it presents and his traditional use of shepherds. He is using a rural backdrop to frame his appeal, offering his love an escape from the corruption of everyday life to a place of idyllic innocence.

It is a persuasive poem in which Marlowe is trying to communicate his undying love and worthiness. The repetition of the modal *will* with its suggestions of potential future action reminds us that the poet is petitioning his lover. The opening imperative is a direct appeal that is substantiated by the things the poet offers in the following stanzas: the beauty of the natural world is combined with the riches of the town. This is indicative of the idealistic rather than realistic tone of the poem. The language and style are consciously crafted, reminding us that we should not be taking things at face value. The poet is making a figurative rather than literal offer to his lover – he is seeking to move her *mind* (l.27).

The use of first person pronouns (*me, we, I*) emphasises the personal tone of the poem. This is also demonstrated in the use of familiar second person pronouns (*thee, thy*). The poet is engaging his love, fantasising about a simple life in which they can be passive observers. The use of the verb *see* distances them from the activity of the shepherds feeding their flocks; the passive *Shall . . . be/Prepared* places the action of preparing meals with someone else. Theirs will be a life of leisure with no responsibilities.

The only active verb linked to the poet (*make*, l.9) is creative. It indicates the gifts he will forge to demonstrate his love: *beds of roses, posies, cap, kirtle, gown, slippers, buckles, belt*. The integration of natural things with symbols of court life is indicative of the way in which the poet is trying to persuade his lover. Marlowe uses post-modified noun phrases to place the two worlds in opposition: *A cap of flowers, a kirtle/. . . with leaves of myrtle, A gown . . . of the finest wool, A belt of straw and ivy buds*. In each case, the prepositional phrase brings the reader back to the natural world.

Because the poem is a pastoral, the language is firmly rooted in nature and concrete nouns are crucial in setting the scene (*hills, valleys, dale, field, rocks* and so on). It is an idyllic world, however, and Marlowe uses emotive modifiers. Superlatives (*finest/purest*, ll.13, 16), excessive quantifiers (*thousand*, l.10), and nouns suggesting wealth and luxury (*coral, amber* l.17, *silver* l.21, *ivory* l.23) are used to develop his argument. He is not presenting a real picture, but fantasising about a simple life.

The simplicity of the quatrain structure with its rhyming couplets reinforces the power of Marlowe's vision. Internal rhyme (*me/be*), the soft labial (*mind may move*) and lateral (*will all*) sounds, and the iambic weak-strong stress pattern create a melodious mood, softening the repeated imperative (ll.1, 20, 28). In celebrating his love, Marlowe is also celebrating the beauty of the natural world and the joy of living for the moment. The pastoral form allows him to do this because in the rural idyll he creates, he can distance himself from the harsh realities and responsibilities of life.

■ ᵛ 5 Style

Whether you are reading a poem, a novel, or a drama text, the style will usually be more intense than in other non-literary contexts. The words will have been chosen carefully to convey a certain mood, situation or character; the grammar will often be formal or consciously crafted to suggest informality; the sound of words will have been purposefully considered; the images will be developed and cohesive; and rhetorical techniques will be used to guide reader response.

In poetry, these features will be particularly noticeable because of the restrictions that poetic form and structure place upon the poet. The traditional format of certain types of poetry, line length, metre and a tendency towards a telegraphic style all contribute to the distinctive nature of the genre. It is immediately recognisable by its visual effect upon the page, but diction, grammar, sound patterning, imagery and rhetorical devices are also an integral part of the ways in which poetry works.

Some of the terminology used in this section may be new to you. If so, use the glossary at the end of the book to learn about any unfamiliar concepts.

Diction

The visual effect of a poem on the page may be the feature we notice first, but it is the words that lead us towards the poet's ideas. Because poems are usually significantly shorter than other literary forms, the **diction** plays an important part in creating the overall effect.

Although poetic language is often more intense than ordinary speech, the diction is not necessarily different from words we use on a day-to-day basis. During the eighteenth century, poets did choose elevated or consciously poetic language, distancing poetry from everyday speech. The nineteenth century, however, marked a turning point. The Romantic poets wanted to avoid an artificial distinction between the language of poetry and the language of ordinary people, and they began the movement away from the very formal diction of their predecessors. In modern poetry, poets have a limitless choice – the diction of a poem is linked directly to the kind of effects a poet wishes to create, the social, regional and cultural context in which it is written, and the themes and ideas the poet is exploring.

Tone

The **tone** of a poem reflects the poet's attitude towards the subject or ideas she or he is exploring. It can be identified by looking at the kind of words the poet chooses. If the diction is formal and the poet has chosen consciously poetic or elevated words that are not in common usage, the tone will probably be detached and impersonal. At the other end of the scale, where the diction is informal, using colloquial or non-standard words, a conversational tone is created.

The poet's choices inevitably affect the kind of relationship created between reader and poet – it may be formal, polite and impersonal; informal, familiar and personal; or somewhere between the two extremes. Because traditional poetry tends to use intense and heightened language, the relationship with the reader is usually formal; in modern poetry, the less formal and more personal use of language tends to create a more informal relationship.

The tone will not always be the same throughout a poem, but can change depending upon the kinds of words chosen. Changes in tone can indicate that the poet is looking at the subject from a different angle, has altered an initial personal viewpoint, or has changed subjects.

Activity 5.1

How do the speaker's attitude and tone change in 'If I shouldn't be alive' by Emily Dickinson (1830–86)?

You may like to think about: the subject matter, the poet's attitude, the diction and the structure.

If I shouldn't be alive

1   If I shouldn't be alive
When the Robins come,
Give the one in Red Cravat,
A Memorial crumb.

5   If I couldn't thank you,
Being fast asleep,
You will know I'm trying
With my Granite lip!

Commentary

The title and first line of the poem use a hypothetical negative (*If I shouldn't . . .*), allowing Dickinson to avoid the harsh realities of her subject – death. The end position of the adjective *alive* seems to place the emphasis upon life rather than death. This is reinforced by Dickinson's use of enjambement (ll.1–2), which pushes the reader on towards the cheerful image of the robin with its almost picture-book quality. While these features of the diction seem to counteract the stasis and finality of death, Dickinson's figurative use of the modifier *Memorial* (l.4) hints at the underlying nature of her subject. Although the tone may be calm and almost playful, the choice of a single word can alter our perception.

The same pattern is repeated in the second stanza. Although the euphemism of *Being fast asleep* (l.6) undermines the horror of death, the modifier in the final line suggests the reality. Dickinson's use of *Granite* reflects a shift in attitude – the easy platitudes are replaced by an image of inanimate and cold stone that reminds the reader of the lifelessness of a dead body.

The poet's attitude to death is conveyed by the diction and the tone. It is represented as something ordinary, something inevitable that takes place while the rest of life goes on. The apparently easy acceptance, however, is qualified by the harshness of the noun modifier *Granite*. Recognised for her ability to see beyond the surface of everyday life, Dickinson perhaps reflects in this poem her own shifting attitude to death.

The connotations of words

Words have meaning. If we look up something in a dictionary, we are given its literal meaning or **denotation**. When we read a poem, however, we do not just rely on the dictionary definition of a word to understand what the poet is telling us. Words also have **connotations** – that is, associations and implications that go beyond a word's literal meaning. The connotations of a word derive from the ways in which it has been used, the contexts in which it is used, and the associations people make with it.

In the dictionary, the denotation of the word *bird* is quite technical:

a general name for a feathered animal (orig. applied to the young)

The connotations, however, are much wider. We might think about a bird's vulnerability and fragility, its grace, beauty or potential for freedom. In a poem, the poet can draw on any or all of these wider ideas to develop the theme. In addition, references to particular birds can draw on connotations that have evolved over time: the swan has connotations of grace and beauty; the robin is homely and domestic; the eagle savage and powerful; the turkey ungainly; the owl wise.

These kinds of associations are often entrenched within a culture, and people with a different physical location or cultural background may make quite different associations. When poets draw upon the connotations of words, however, they usually rely upon associations that have been experienced by many people. This means that most readers will recognise the wider ideas that the poet is using to enhance the meaning. Poetry can sometimes be difficult to understand because the poet has developed a personal view of the world, drawing on connotations that are not immediately accessible to the reader. W.B. Yeats, for instance, created his own complex view of the relationship between the spiritual and the physical world as two interlocking cones called 'Gyres' and this underpins much of his imagery. Only by studying a poem and becoming familiar with a poet's world view can we begin to see the significance of the wider associations.

The economy of poetic form means that poets have to be selective in their choice of words. Drawing on connotative meanings enables them to develop complex associations using a minimum number of words. Emotions, attitudes and states of mind can be woven into the language through the associations that the diction evokes.

Word classes

Just as it is important to think about the tone of the diction and the connotations of key words, it can also be useful to identify the kinds of words being chosen. Different subjects require different kinds of words and sometimes the poet will tend towards words of a certain **grammatical class**.

Nouns enable us to classify and label people, places and things. If a poem is about a particular place, concrete nouns may dominate. They will help to create a sense of reality, enabling the reader to visualise the setting. Abstract nouns, on the other hand, can help a poet to develop a more reflective approach to the subject matter. They refer to ideas, qualities and processes, and thus convey emotions and states of mind.

Modifiers provide extra information, refining a noun's range of meaning. Adjectives, nouns or verbs can fulfil the function of a modifier. It can be useful to recognise the form of a modifier because poets can create distinctive effects according to the kind of word they choose. Present participle modifiers (*verb + ing*), for instance, can create a sense of movement within the noun phrase.

Modifiers can be used to describe people or places in detail; to arouse the reader's emotions; or to evaluate and judge. Poets use them to convey their attitudes and to influence their readers.

The kinds of actions or processes the **verbs** describe and the form they take can also tell the reader something about the message the poet wishes to convey. Descriptive passages use stative verbs that express states of being or processes in which there is no obvious action. The stative verb 'to be' (*am, is, are, was, were*) allows poets to describe a place or person as they are; others like 'appear' or 'seem' suggest that there is a difference between appearance and reality. Dynamic verbs, on the other hand, express a wide range of actions and poets can use them to convey a sense of activity and movement.

Adverbs are also modifying words: they tell us 'how' a verb is carried out and give us information about time and place (circumstance adverbs); they can modify adjectives and other adverbs (degree adverbs); and express attitudes or values (sentence adverbs).

Activity 5.2

What kind of words does Sara Teasdale (1884–1933) use in 'Song Making' and what effect do they have?

You may like to think about: the word classes of specific words and their connotations, the ways in which the lexical choices help the poet to develop her ideas, the imagery and the structure.

Song Making

1   My heart cries like a beaten child,
      Ceaselessly, all night long;
    And I must take my own heart cries
      And thread them neatly into a song.

5   My heart cries like a beaten child,
      And I must listen, stark and terse,
    Dry-eyed and critical, to see
      What I can turn into a verse.

    This was a sob at the hour of three,
10   And this when the first cock crew –
    I wove them into a dainty song,
      But no-one thought it true!

Commentary

This is a poem about writing, about turning painful personal experience into the subject matter of verse. The language therefore reflects both the detachment of the creative process and the intensity of an individual's emotional response to a particular event. It is the opposition created between these two attitudes that lies at the heart of the poem.

The concrete noun *heart* functions figuratively and its repetition is a haunting reminder of the feeling underpinning the poem. Linked to the verb *cries* (ll.1/5), the plural noun *cries* (l.3) and the emotive image of the *beaten child*, it emphasises the emotional tone. The repetition of the possessive determiner *my* and the use of the adjective *own* create an intensely personal field of reference in which both subject and object can be traced back to the poet. This enhances the mood of entrapment that pervades the poem, reinforced by the adverb *Ceaselessly* and the phrase *all night long* (l.2) – the poet can escape only when she has contained her emotions within the pattern of a verse.

While the immediacy of the present tense verbs (*cries*) epitomises an emotional state, the emphatic modal *must* represents the certainty of the writer. The foregrounded conjunctions (*And*) reinforce this since they represent the poet's attempt to take control. Similarly, where the repeated image of the suffering child is emotive and disturbing, the adjectives (*stark, terse, Dry-eyed, critical*) suggest detachment. Developing this contrast between instinctive emotion and conscious discipline, the verbs *thread* and *turn*, and the adverb *neatly* (ll.4/8) suggest something of the creative process as the poet curbs her feelings.

The structure of the poem's neat quatrains reflects the movement towards control. In the first stanza, there is a balance between the subjectivity of feeling and the objectivity of the writing process, with two lines focusing on the poet's emotional state and two representing her need for constraint. The second stanza restricts personal emotion to one line, leaving three lines to describe the detachment of the writer. This process is brought to its conclusion in the third stanza, where the change of tense suggests that the poet has achieved her goal: she is now able to talk in a detached way about her emotions. The possessive determiner *my* has been replaced by the indefinite article *a* (l.9); the heartfelt plural noun *cries* has been replaced by the less emotive singular noun *sob* (l.9); the infinite reference to time (l.2) is contained by specific references (*at the hour of three, when the first cock crew*, ll.9–10).

Picking up on the connotations of *thread* in the first stanza, Teasdale uses the past tense *wove* to describe the completed creative process that has taken a painful personal experience and transformed it into *a dainty* song (l.11). The lexical link forces us to remember the emotional opening lines, and the juxtaposition of the adjective *dainty*, with its connotations of something delicate and neat, with the disturbing image of the beaten child reinforces this.

The poem reaches its climax in the final line. The dismissive use of the conjunction *But* (l.12) and the exclamative tone draw attention to the distance that exists between the poet, her subject matter and the reader. The neatness of the poem's structure with its masculine rhymes and the pleasant connotations of the title are set against the reality of the experience that lies behind the poem.

Unusual words

Although the diction can be elevated and the tone heightened by the use of consciously poetic language, poets do not always choose to use Standard English words. Poetry, perhaps more than other literary genres, is a very personal medium, and poets sometimes choose to write in a form of English that is distinctive and reflects their individual purpose.

Dialect words can be used to create a certain social or regional atmosphere, or to make a point about culture and language. **Archaisms** can heighten the dignity and solemnity of the language, reminding the reader of the poetic and cultural traditions on which poetry draws. Poets can equally make their lexis very modern by using **neologisms** (invented words) or **colloquialisms** which give their writing an immediacy and contemporaneity. Sometimes words can seem incongruous – poets borrow words from non-poetic registers in order to disrupt reader expectations, or change the usual word class of a word. **Collocations** (set phrases) can be disrupted as poets experiment, throwing new light on familiar things and forcing readers to reconsider things they had previously taken for granted.

Activity 5.3

How does Tom Leonard (1944–) use language in this extract from *Ghostie Men* to underpin his theme?

You may like to think about: the content, the diction, the tone and the poetic form.

1   right inuff
    ma language is disgraceful

ma maw tellt mi
ma teacher tellt mi
5   thi doactir tellt mi
thi priest tellt mi

ma boss tellt mi
ma landlady in carrington strett tellt mi
thi lassie ah tried tay get aff way in 1969 tellt mi
10   sum wee smout thit thoat ah hudny read chomsky tellt mi
a calvinistic communist thit thoat ah wuz revisionist tellt mi

po-faced literati kerryin thi burden a thi past tellt mi
po-faced literati grimly kerryin thi burden a thi future tellt mi
ma wife tellt mi jist-tay-get-inty-this-poem tellt mi
15   ma wainz came home fray school an tellt mi
jist aboot ivry book ah oapnd tellt mi
even thi introduction tay thi Scottish National Dictionary tellt mi
ach well
all livin language is sacred
20   fuck thi lohta thim

Commentary

This is clearly a 'poem' because it is written in lines, uses stanzas to divide the poet's ideas, and is rhythmic. It does not, however, adopt the poetic language or metrical patterns of traditional poetry. Leonard is consciously choosing a form of English that will reflect his physical location, background and culture – his poem is dealing with the political issues of language, status and identity and he therefore chooses a tone and diction that are fitting.

The heightened tone and elevated diction of traditional poetry are directly linked to the formality of written language. By contrast, Leonard draws on the spoken voice, using the less rigid structural patterns and colloquialisms of informal conversation. Expressions like *right inuff* (l.1) and the taboo expletive *fuck* (l.20) are indicative of this. In addition, the lack of written conventions such as punctuation and capitalisation for proper nouns both reinforces our sense of the spoken voice, and marks the poet's disenchantment with a society that makes artificial judgements about people based on the way in which they express themselves.

Leonard's regional identity is crucial to the meaning of the poem and he therefore mixes dialect words with Standard English. *Lassie* (l.9) is the ordinary Scots word for girl; *wee* – the adjective for tiny; *smout* (l.10) – a small person or child; *wainz* (l.15) – children. Where Leonard uses Standard English words, many have a non-standard spelling that reflects the poet's Scottish accent. He uses *mi* (l.3) for me; *ma* (l.2) for my; *inuff* for enough; and *ivry* (l.16) for every. By combining dialect words with Standard English words and non-standard spellings, Leonard is able to convey his message in a powerful way. He both gives Scots prestige by using it in a poem, and ensures that his message will be widely understood by not alienating his readers.

Leonard draws attention to the way in which society makes judgements about language in this poem. By using a non-standard form of English to discuss the issue, he dramatises an abstract theoretical debate. His use of dialect does not obscure meaning and he is therefore able to prove in a concrete way that language cannot simply be judged as 'right' or 'wrong'.

In the first stanza, Leonard introduces the idea of a judgemental attitude towards the Glaswegian dialect with his use of the adjective *disgraceful*, apparently agreeing with society's viewpoint. The negative connotations of the word establish a self-deprecating tone, and yet the fact that the poem is written in this supposedly 'disgraceful' dialect immediately challenges the attitude.

The repetitive structure of the poem allows Leonard to address the attitudes of society directly. Domestic personal responses are made by the speaker's *maw* (l.3), *wife* (l.14) and *wainz* (l.15); impersonal judgements are made by authoritative, social institutions like the Church (*priest*, l.6), education (*teacher*, l.4), the literary elite (*the po-faced literati*, ll.12–13), *ivry book* (l.16), and the *introduction to the Scottish National Dictionary* (l.17); and social, educational judgements by employers (*boss*, l.7). The listing of various people and groups who think a Scots dialect is unacceptable, and the repetition of *tellt mi* reinforce the all-pervading disparaging attitude to non-standard English as the poet sees it.

The poet's choice of the modifier *sacred* (l.19) ensures that the poem ends in a very different tone to the self-deprecation of the opening stanza. The religious connotations suggest that linguistic variation is something to be valued and preserved – it is far removed from the derogatory and sinful connotations of *disgraceful*. The informality of the last lines reflects the confidence of the speaker who refuses to accept the artificial judgements of society. The final stanza, therefore, offers an alternative view – Scots English is a colourful variation to the standard; it is evidence that English is a living language, adapting to the demands of its users.

The use of language that is unexpected and unfamiliar allows poets to challenge preconceptions, create a strong sense of place and individuality, directly link their ideas to the medium in which they write, engage the reader in a very personal way, and experiment with language and the effects that can be created. For Leonard, the choice of diction and tone is integral to the meaning of the poem; it allows him to undermine preconceived ideas about language and identity.

Grammar

Poetic licence allows poets to manipulate language structures – they may need to meet the requirements of traditional poetic forms, or may want to create distinctive effects. This means that the grammar of poetry can be complicated. The omission of grammatical function words, the use of minor sentences, extended phrases and complex sentence structures, which may run over a number of lines, all contribute to the complexity associated with the genre. These kinds of grammatical features as well as a compression of thought can make poetry seem obscure, and readers sometimes have to work hard to trace the development of ideas within a poem.

An understanding of grammatical features can help you to discover what a poem is about. By identifying interesting structures and exploring the effects they have, you will be able to see how the poet has created meaning. Some of the terminology may be new to you – if you would like additional explanations, use the glossary.

Phrases

Sentences are made up of groups of words that do different jobs. We call these groups of words **phrases**. It is useful to be able to recognise the phrases in a sentence because it can help the reader to understand how the poet is creating meaning. Noun phrases and verb phrases are the most frequently occurring phrases in English.

A **noun phrase** can be made up of a single noun (the head word), or it can have words before it (determiners and modifiers) and words after it (post-modifiers). Poets use noun phrases extensively in poetry because they can contain a lot of information in a compact form. In some poems, noun phrases dominate and there are almost no complete grammatical sentences. This creates a cinematic effect because the poet focuses our attention on a sequence of images. The emphasis is on creating a sense of place or atmosphere rather than on describing events.

An **adjective phrase** can be made up of a single adjective (head word), or it can have words before it (another adjective or an adverb) and words after it (a prepositional phrase or a post-modifying clause).

Poets can choose to include descriptive detail embedded within the noun phrase – adjectives that are found before the head noun of a noun phrase are called attributive adjectives (e.g. *My **dull** and **careful** life*). In this position, adjectives are described grammatically as pre-modifiers. It is also possible, however, to place adjectives after verbs like *to be, seem, appear, become* (e.g. *My life is **dull** and **careful***). In this position, the adjective is described as the head word in an adjective phrase. They are called predicative adjectives because they come after the verb or predicator.

By selecting one position rather than another, a poet can change the emphasis created: predicative adjectives carry more weight since they are a distinctive grammatical unit rather than an element of another structure. By choosing some predicative and some attributive adjectives, it is also possible to guide the reader's attention to key words and to provide a richness of texture to the poem.

The following extract is from the opening of a poem by Alan Ross (1922–2001). It is made up of a sequence of noun and adjective phrases designed to create a strong visual image of a particular place. There are no present or past tense verbs so the poem creates the effect of a moment frozen in time as we wait for the snow to fall.

Embankment Before Snow

1   A zinc afternoon. The barges black,
    And black the funnels of tugs nosing
    Phlegm-coloured waves slap slapping
    Stone wharves. A smell of sacking
5   And soot. Grey chimneys, and statues
    Grey with cold, and grey life-belts.

The only verbs used here are the non-finite present participles *nosing* and *slapping* which function as post-modifiers, providing extra information in the long noun phrase *The **funnels** of tugs nosing/Phlegm-coloured waves slap slapping/Stone wharves* (head word in bold). Both verbs help the poet to create a sense of movement through description rather than through direct action and this enhances the feeling of lethargy and stagnation.

Concrete nouns dominate the extract because the poet is recreating a particular place for his readers. The industrial scene is created through an appeal to our senses: we 'see' the *barges*, *tugs*, *wharves* and *chimneys*; we 'hear' the *waves*; we 'smell' the *sacking* and *soot*. The pre- and post-modification provides the detail that makes this portrait of the embankment atmospheric – strong images are conveyed through the noun phrases, many of which are long and complex.

Some of the modification is factual, like the noun modifier *Stone*, but in most cases words are chosen in order to generate an emotive response in the reader. The negative connotations of the compound modifier *phlegm-coloured* ensure that the reader can have no romantic visions – this scene is bleak, dirty and undesirable. The repetition of the simple predicative adjective phrases *black* and *grey*, and the omission of the stative verb intensify this mood. Yet the opening noun phrase with its unusual noun modifier *zinc* suggests something distinctive. As a metallic element, it fits comfortably with the industrial theme; its bluish-white colouring vividly conveys the strange light quality that often precedes the fall of snow.

The feeling of anticipation created by the title dominates the poem. Its telegraphic style intensifies the effect: the verb 'to be' is omitted in a number of places (e.g. *The barges [are/were] black* . . .), leaving only the semantically important words. With no finite (tensed) verbs, the reader is left waiting for something to happen, waiting for the greyness to be obliterated by the whiteness of snow. The transformation that is about to take place may conceal the landscape's urban bleakness, but it will be transitory – the scene is characterised by its industrial nature and the diction emphasises this.

The poet's use of noun and adjective phrases is dramatic because time seems to have been suspended as we wait for the snow to fall. There are no complete grammatical sentences and this intensifies the sense of anticipation. In moving from one element of the scene to another, the poet uses a cinematic approach – he guides the reader just as a camera may pan across a scene to focus on particular features. We focus on a sequence of images that create a sense of place and atmosphere rather than movement. The result is an intensely visualised moment in which we experience the sights, sounds and smells of the embankment one winter afternoon.

*　*　*

A **verb phrase** can be made up of a single verb – a lexical verb that conveys the meaning of the phrase; or one or more auxiliary verbs followed by a lexical verb. The primary auxiliary verbs (*be*, *have*, *do*) help to construct different time scales, questions and negatives. A progressive verb phrase (*be* + *present participle*) indicates that the action of the verb is incomplete and still in progress; a perfective verb phrase (*have* + *past participle*) indicates an action that is complete. The modal auxiliaries (*can, could, shall, should, will, would, may, must, might, ought to*) convey shades of meaning such as possibility (*could*), probability (*should*), obligation (*must*), necessity (*ought to*) and so on.

Where noun phrases convey the descriptive information, verb phrases provide references to tense, time scale, modality. The use of present tense, past tense, or references to future time can affect the way we relate to a poem. The spontaneity of present tense creates a sense of immediacy, while past tense verbs suggest something complete, something final. The progressive (*be + present participle*) implies that an activity is ongoing and is probably not complete.

The **voice** of the verb is also important. Most sentences are written in the active voice, which directly links the action of the verb to the person or thing carrying out the action.

The crumbling walls shattered the winged statue.

The passive voice changes the focus of the sentence by reordering the elements. The object (the person or thing receiving the action of the verb) is moved to the front of the sentence; the subject (the person or thing doing the verb) is moved to the end of the sentence after 'by'; and the verb is changed into the past participle form and placed after the verb 'to be'.

The winged statue was shattered (by the crumbling wall).

Using the passive voice can create suspense by delaying the subject; it can alter the balance of the sentence by putting more emphasis on the object; or it can completely exclude the person or thing responsible for the action of the verb by omitting 'by + actor'.

The grammatical **mood** of a sentence can also influence the way we read a poem. There are three moods: the declarative is used to make statements; the interrogative to ask questions; and the imperative to express a command. Changes in grammatical mood can affect the relationship between the poet and reader, or the poet and the subject matter.

An **adverb phrase** can be made up of a single adverb (head word), or it can have words before it (an adverb) and words after it (a prepositional phrase or a post-modifying clause). Adverb phrases provide extra information about the verb phrase – they describe how the action of the verb is being carried out.

Activity 5.4

What kind of phrases does Elma Mitchell (1919–2000) use to present her ideas in 'Country Life', and what effect do they have?

You may like to think about: the content, the diction, the types of phrases and the effects they create, and the structure.

Country Life

1 Within half-a-mile, to my knowledge,
 Two solitary alcoholics,
 A divorce in progress,
 Homes crumbling under nettles.

5 Badgers, nocturnally ambling,
 The fox caught red-muzzled,
 The owls hanging up night in inverted commas,
 Molework. The moon's partners.

 Swamp waiting in patience
10 To suck down plough, or be ripped open.
 Trees prevented from falling
 Only by trees. The furze-defended common.

 Barbed-wire entanglement of stars. The river's
 Gradual grovelling infiltration.
15 Like a farm dog edging into the living-room.
 And men. And women.

Commentary

Mitchell uses noun phrases in this poem to create a vivid image of life in the country that is at odds with the traditional romantic vision of the rural idyll. There are no tensed verbs, only present participles (*crumbling, ambling, hanging*) and past participles (*caught, prevented*) functioning as post-modifiers. This creates a sense of stasis that is in keeping with the scene the poet creates.

While the noun phrase of the title suggests that the poem will offer us a representative view of country life, the prepositional phrases of the opening line suggest a narrower frame of reference. We are presented with a specific area (*Within half-a-mile*) and a subjective viewpoint (*to my knowledge*). The picture that emerges, therefore, reflects something of the time in which the poem was written and the views of the poet: rather than a pastoral scene, we experience something of the reality of the country in the twentieth century.

Mitchell immediately sets people and the natural rhythms of the world she recreates at odds. The noun phrases describing the human inhabitants in the first stanza have negative connotations – even the potentially positive reference to *Homes* (l.4) is undermined by the post-modifying non-finite clause (*crumbling under nettles*). The use of the present participle draws attention to the ongoing process of deterioration that seems to characterise the first stanza.

The tone changes, however, in the second stanza where the natural inhabitants are presented through post-modified noun phrases that reflect their instinctive nature. Each animal is characterised through an image of activity that emphasises their difference from the sterile portraits of people in the first stanza. Where the people are isolated, the second stanza reaches its climax in the possessive pre-modified noun phrase *The moon's partners* (l.8), with its connotations of rightful belonging.

This inherent sense of connection is continued in the third stanza through the description of the *swamp* (l.9) and the *trees* (l.11). Despite the potentially destructive connotations of the post-modifying clauses (*waiting in patience . . ., prevented from falling . . .*), the mood is positive; unlike the crumbling homes of the first stanza, everything here is in its place and fulfilling its essential nature. As in the second stanza, the final noun phrase (*The furze-defended common*, l.12) is set apart to mark the climax. The compound pre-modifier becomes a symbol of the separation between man and the natural world, which is reinforced by the pre-modifier *barbed-wire* in the fourth stanza.

With the long pre-modified noun phrase *The river's/Gradual grovelling infiltration* (l.14) and the simile of the *farm dog* (l.15) insinuating itself into the human domain (*the living-room*), the poet introduces the idea of intrusion – and the intruders are the people of the opening and closing lines of the poem. The dismissive noun phrases describing humanity (ll.2–3) become the reductive simple noun phrases of the final line (*men, women*). In a poem that has been made up of complicated pre- and post-modification, this form of reference is significant. The redundancy of human life within the context of this natural scene is reinforced by the almost accidental way in which they are tagged onto the end of the poem. The use of the co-ordinating conjunction in the initial position makes their inclusion seem like an afterthought.

Elma Mitchell has composed this poem using phrases rather than grammatically complete sentences. By eliminating tensed verbs, she freezes each moment in time and creates a sequence of images that become representative of the natural world. There is, however, still a strong sense of movement because she embeds natural activity within the very structure of the noun phrases, using non-finite clauses as post-modifiers. The effect is both cinematic and symbolic, immersing us in the physical elements of the scene and encouraging us to see their underlying significance.

Sentence types

Phrases are combined to make sentences and there are four main types: simple, compound, complex, and compound-complex. By varying the sentence type, poets can change the pace of a poem, draw attention to key elements of the content, create different moods, or develop contrasts and parallels. You will not need to analyse all the sentences in a poem, but it can be useful to recognise sentence types if the poet is using them distinctively.

A **simple** sentence will be made up of one main clause with only one verb phrase, and it will make sense on its own. It will contain a subject (the person or thing doing the action of the verb) and a predicator (the most important clause element). The subject site will be filled by a noun phrase and the predicator by a verb phrase. There are also other optional elements that may be included:

- an object: the person or thing receiving the action of the verb;
- a complement: extra information about the subject or object following a verb like 'be', 'appear', 'become' or 'seem';
- an adverbial: extra information about time (when?), manner (how?) and place (where?).

The object site will be filled by a noun phrase; the complement site by a noun phrase or adjective phrase; and the adverbial site by an adverb phrase, a prepositional phrase, or a noun phrase.

Simple sentences enable poets to create interesting effects by altering the pace, mood or focus of a poetic line. It is important to remember that they may not always be short – even a simple sentence can contain a number of grammatical elements. They will usually, however, be emphatic, drawing attention to important semantic information or highlighting a turning point. A sequence of short simple sentences may make a poem seem disjointed, or the poet's viewpoint simplistic; they can suggest an innocence or naïvety of style.

A **compound** sentence will contain two or more simple sentences linked by a co-ordinating conjunction such as 'and', 'or', 'but'. Each part of a compound sentence carries equal weight and makes sense on its own. Long strings of co-ordinated clauses are common in speech and in the extended monologues of young children. Sometimes poets use repeated co-ordination to create a sense of the spoken voice or to capture the breathless excitement of a child's-eye view of the world.

Complex sentences combine clauses that do not have equal value. One is a main clause, and the one or more other clauses are subordinate or dependent clauses that do not make sense by themselves. A subordinate clause may take the form of:

- a **noun clause**: begins with 'that' or 'what' and acts as a subject or object; it can post-modify noun or adjective phrases

  $\quad$ S $\qquad$ P $\qquad\qquad$ O
  e.g. (We) (must obey) (what is written in the law).
  $\qquad$ SCl - NCl

- an **adverbial clause**: begins with a subordinating conjunction such as 'if', 'while', 'because', 'before' and provides information about time (when?), manner (how?), place (where?) and reason (why?)

  $\qquad\qquad$ A $\qquad\qquad$ S $\quad$ P $\qquad$ O $\qquad$ A
  e.g. (If the storm does not break) (we) (will cross) (the moor) (safely).
  $\qquad$ SCl - ACl

- a **relative clause**: begins with 'who', 'which', 'that' or 'whose' and post-modifies noun phrases

  $\qquad\qquad$ S $\qquad\qquad$ P $\qquad$ O
  e.g. (The man who wanders on the shore) (has lost) (his home).
  $\qquad$ SCl - RelCl

- a **non-finite clause**: begins with a non-finite-verb and post-modifies noun or adjective phrases; it functions as a subject, object, complement or adverbial.

  $\qquad\qquad$ S $\quad$ P $\qquad$ A $\qquad\qquad\qquad$ A
  e.g. (The sea) (writhed) (beneath the bows), (twisting and turning like a serpent). $\qquad$ SCl - NFCl

Complex sentences will often suggest an intensity of thought. They can be difficult to understand because they often contain a lot of information. It is useful to identify the main clause as a starting point; then decide what kind of information is being provided in the accompanying subordinate clauses. Think about the order in which the clauses occur, and the effect this has on the meaning – complex sentences can withhold information until a certain point in the sentence, or subordinate some ideas to others that are more important to the poet.

Compound-complex sentences contain both co-ordination and subordination. They can be used to convey the complexity of a poet's worldview, situation, or theme.

Minor sentences do not follow expected patterns, although they will probably start with a capital letter and end with a full stop. They omit important clause elements and cannot be easily analysed. Formulae used in social situations ('hello', 'thanks'), interjections ('well!', 'who'd have thought!'), abbreviated forms and exclamations ('Taxi!', 'hey, you!') can all be described as minor sentences. We use them in informal situations, but they are often found in poetry because of their concise form.

A poet's grammatical choices inevitably affect the meaning because they influence the way in which we encounter the poem's ideas. If you can identify something significant in the grammatical structure, explore the effects created and consider the relationship between the structure and the meaning. Literary criticism is not about naming features, but about considering how meaning is conveyed.

Activity 5.5

How do the poets use style and structure to develop their ideas and convey their attitudes in the poems below?

You may like to think about: the language, grammatical structure, and poetic form.

TEXT 1 – D. H. LAWRENCE (1885–1930)

Work

1   There is no point in work
unless it absorbs you
like an absorbing game.

If it doesn't absorb you
5   if it's never any fun,
don't do it.

When a man goes out into his work
He is alive like a tree in spring,
He is living, not merely working.

It's Coming

1   It's Coming – the postponeless Creature –
It gains the Block – and now – it gains the Door –
Chooses its latch, from all the other fastenings –
Enters – with a 'You know Me – Sir?'

5   Simple Salute – and Certain Recognition –
Bold – were it Enemy – Brief – were it friend –
Dresses each House in Crape, and Icicle –
And Carries one – out of it – to God –

Commentary

Lawrence and Dickinson have chosen very different styles in which to develop their ideas. Lawrence's poem is reflective, addressing the nature of work and our relationship with it. In the first two stanzas, he chooses to address us directly, using the second person pronoun *you* (ll.2, 4) and the imperative mood (l.6). He thus engages the reader personally with his theme, before moving towards a more aphoristic approach in the final stanza where he uses the generic term *man* (l.7). Dickinson, on the other hand, chooses a more oblique approach in which to write about her theme, death. The impersonal terms of address (*It* ll.1–3, 6; *one* l.8) enhance the poem's sinister mood and generalise the experience. The reader is forced to recognise that the death described in the poem is not a specific account of the death of a particular person, but a universal one. Dickinson is describing a universal process as she perceives it.

The style of each poem is equally different. Lawrence's poem is reflective – it uses complex sentences to explore the meaning of work. Dickinson's is descriptive. It is a narrative account that uses simple and compound sentences to create a mood of urgency.

In 'Work', each stanza is made up of a single sentence with a number of related clauses: the first emphatic negative main clause *There is no point in work* is qualified by the conditional *unless . . .* (ll.2–3); the second *don't do it* (l.6) is delayed, coming after two conditional subordinate clauses *If . . .* (ll.4–5). This pattern clearly establishes the argumentative nature of the poem. For Lawrence, work is not merely a means of earning an income, but an integral part of who we are. The repetition of *absorbs/absorbing/absorb* emphasises the importance it should have in our lives. The positive connotations of the verb are in direct contrast to the negatives that dominate the first two stanzas (*no* l.1, *doesn't* l.4, *never* l.5, *don't* l.6). Thus although the poem may initially seem to be an attack on work, it is in fact a declaration of the enlivening possibilities of the right kind of work.

The final stanza reinforces this positive concept in an explicit declaration of the power of work to enhance our lives. The tone has changed and the language reflects this. The natural simile, *like a tree in spring*, with its connotations of growth and new life, provides a strong visual image for this change in tone. Stylistically, Lawrence replaces the familiar phrase 'go to work' with a more emotive *goes out into his work* with its connotations of conscious choice and personal engagement. He uses the adjective *alive* predicatively (after the verb 'to be') and the progressive verb phrase *is living* to emphasise the power of constructive work to animate us. The words are stressed, allowing Lawrence to add weight to his argument. The adverb phrase *merely* in the final line is a stern reminder of the deadening influence of the wrong kind of work.

Dickinson's poem tackles the theme of death obliquely – where the title of Lawrence's poem explicitly addresses the central issue, Dickinson's enhances the mystery: the undefined third person pronoun *It* has no clear field of reference, and the reader will automatically associate it with a non-human being; the progressive verb phrase *[i]s Coming* suggests an ongoing movement forwards that is, as yet, incomplete. The repetition of the title in the first line clearly establishes the mood of apprehension that hangs over the poem, and the following noun phrase intensifies this. The head noun *Creature* confirms our feeling that the non-human being advancing is indeed something monstrous, while the adjective modifier *postponeless* introduces the theme of inevitability. There is no escape from the encounter that is about to take place and the reader is, like the poet, trapped.

Dickinson's use of the present tense (*gains, Chooses, Enters*) gives the poem a feeling of immediacy, and her use of simple clauses separated by dashes intensifies this. There are no clear stopping points – the reader is driven on through this inevitable process towards an inescapable conclusion. The staccato effect of the punctuation mirrors a breathlessness as the creature moves from a distant point (*the Block*) to a familiar one (*the Door* 1.2). The process of selection implied by the verb *Chooses* and the prepositional phrase *from all the other fastenings* (1.3) intensifies the atmosphere because this is no random process. Although the reader may be bewildered by the world in which the poem immerses them, the nameless creature is purposeful.

The use of direct speech in the final line of the first stanza changes the balance: these are not the words of a monster. The tone is formal and, as a conversation opener, the statement is appropriate. The opening of the second stanza recognises this. While the noun phrases *Simple Salute* and *Certain Recognition* emphasise the normality of the words, there is still a sense that this is not an ordinary exchange between friends. The adjective phrases *Bold* and *Brief* with their qualifying subjunctive clauses (*were it Enemy . . . were it friend*) draw attention to the strangeness of the context. This *It* is neither enemy nor friend – yet nor is it a monster.

The mystery created by the consciously oblique language and approach is resolved in the final lines of the poem, but Dickinson still refrains from explicit references. We know that she is talking about a personified 'Death' only through the imagery – the symbolism of *Crape* (1.7) and the figurative use of *Icicle* through the connotations of the verb phrase *Carries out* and the reference to *God*. These ensure that we understand the end of this process where we did not understand the beginning.

Throughout the poem, Dickinson uses only simple and compound phrases and sentences. The dashes, which further divide the clauses, emphasise the sense of movement and the breathlessness with which we await the arrival of the unnamed creature. Modifiers are used sparsely and therefore have a powerful effect, working on our emotions and intensifying the mood.

Both poets use a different style to tackle their topic and, in each case, the effect is dramatic. Equally, both are dealing with a theme that recurs in their work in a style that is integral to the communication of meaning.

For Lawrence, the industrial age was threatening the very integrity of the individual. He believed that mechanised work, bad physical working conditions and the disintegration of social order were forcing people into a life of apathy. The poem asserts the power of fulfilling work in which people are not passive instruments, but active participants. Lawrence uses the style of his poem to emphasise this, balancing sequences of clauses, repeating key words and grammatical structures, and replacing negatives with an emphatic statement of what work should be.

For Dickinson, the inevitability of death is a recurring theme – her writing is full of the fear hidden in the corners of ordinary rooms. Although here the unnamed individual is carried out to God, the feeling of isolation, emptiness and lack of control is typical of her darkest poems about death. Only seven of her poems were published during her lifetime and these were heavily edited to smooth out what was seen as erratic punctuation. It is now recognised, however, that her originality lies in her defiance of the poetic conventions of the time. Her use of dashes, her elliptical style and the intensity of her imagery make this poem a unique vision of death.

Word order

The **order of words and phrases** in poetry can influence the way we respond to the content. Sometimes words will be changed around in order to fulfil the requirements of a rhyme scheme or a metrical pattern, but equally poets can manipulate word order to draw attention to key concepts.

English is a word order language – rather than using word endings to indicate the role of a particular clause element, we put them in a prescribed order. For instance, 'the dog ate the bone' means something quite different from 'the bone ate the dog'. In a traditional declarative sentence, the subject (*the dog*) comes first and is followed by the verb phrase (*ate*) and any other clauses elements that are necessary to convey the meaning (objects, complements, adverbials).

Whatever comes first or last is given prominence and sometimes poets change the focus of a sentence in order to throw emphasis on something other than the subject. This can be achieved in a number of ways.

The **passive voice** changes the focus of a sentence by bringing the object forward to the beginning and delaying the subject until the end of the sentence after 'by'. This allows the poet to place more emphasis upon the person or thing receiving the action of the verb, rather than the person or thing responsible for the action of the verb.

Some complete clause elements can be moved to the front of a sentence, replacing the usual thematic subject. This is called **foregrounding** or **fronting**. Adverbials are the most flexible clause elements and therefore thematic adverbials are most common. The clause element that has replaced the subject in the initial position is called a **marked theme**. Poets can use marked themes to draw attention to time and place references, the mood, and the reasons for things happening.

New information can also be put at the end of a sentence to give it prominence. This is described as **end focus**. By delaying the subject, for instance, the poet can create suspense, or build to a climax.

Activity 5.6

Published in 1972, *Crow* is a collection of poems in which Ted Hughes explores the nature of twentieth-century life. The central protagonist is an anthropomorphic Crow who struggles to understand the world around him. The following poem appears near the beginning of the collection.

Explore the stylistic techniques Ted Hughes (1930–98) uses to describe Crow's experience in 'A Kill'.

You may like to think about: the title, the form, the sentence type, the ordering of clause elements, and the diction.

A Kill

1 Flogged lame with legs
 Shot through the head with balled brains
 Shot blind with eyes
 Nailed down by his own ribs
5 Strangled just short of his last gasp
 By his own windpipe
 Clubbed unconscious by his own heart

 Seeing his life stab through him, a dream flash
 As he drowned in his own blood

10 Dragged under by the weight of his guts

 Uttering a bowel-emptying cry which was his roots tearing out

 Of the bedrock atom
 Gaping his mouth and letting the cry rip through him as at a distance

 And smashed into the rubbish of the ground

15 He managed to hear, faint and far – 'It's a boy!'

 Then everything went black

Commentary

On first reading, the title and the content of the poem suggest we are reading about a violent and horrific experience. Only in the penultimate line when Crow hears *'It's a boy!'* do we recognise that this is a poem about birth. Hughes has adopted a non-traditional approach, replacing a romantic and idealistic view of birth with a realistic and brutal one. This immediately prepares the reader for the poet's relationship with his subject matter – he intends to challenge preconceived ideas, forcing the reader to look more closely at experiences that have become shrouded by myth.

The grammatical structure is interesting: the poem is made up of just two sentences. The first runs from lines 1–15 and the second makes up the final line. Hughes delays the main clause (*He managed . . .*) in the first sentence for 14 lines, forcing the reader on towards the end. After the original and untraditional descriptions, the cliché '*It's a boy!*' is unexpected. It forces the reader to reconsider the sequence of foregrounded adverbials (ll.1–14) – we realise that they describe not gang warfare, but the birth process.

Hughes has conveyed the birth experience from the point of view of the baby's journey down the birth canal and the violent language suggests something of the stress and fear this journey may create. Because the main clause is delayed, the poem creates a feeling of suspended animation; the reader is immersed in a violent process from which there seems to be no escape. In these circumstances, the clichéd '*It's a boy!*' becomes a meaningless response – it fails to take account of the physical experience that has just taken place. Crow is distant from the world into which he has burst and the words are *faint and far* away from him. Birth is an anticlimax and the final line reinforces this as Crow loses consciousness.

The diction is chosen to represent the experience of birth. Concrete nouns like *legs* (l.1), *head*, *brains* (l.2), *eyes* (l.3) remind us that this is a physical experience. Dynamic verbs like *Flogged* (l.1), *Shot through* (ll.2–3), *Nailed* (l.4), *Strangled* (l.5) and *Clubbed* (l.7) have connotations of violence and death – hence the title of the poem. They suggest what birth is like for Crow and it is far from the romantic image of creation and celebration. Instead, it is an experience in which pain is more dominant than pleasure.

In challenging traditional attitudes, Hughes also disrupts recognisable sayings: he takes the idea of life flashing before you at death and adapts it for a new context. Now, as he undergoes birth, Crow, who has experienced nothing, sees *his life stab through him* (l.8); because he does not yet have a life to flash before his eyes, he sees *a dream flash* as he *drown(s) in his own blood* (ll.8–9). The use of present participles (*uttering, tearing* l.11, *gaping, letting* l.13) intensifies the experience because it makes it seem never-ending. Crow becomes the victim of a terrible crime, which ultimately delivers him into *the rubbish of the ground* (l.14). He is already experiencing the basic cruelty of life and, as everything goes *black* (l.16), Hughes reinforces the sense of both life and birth as brutal.

Like the content and diction, the form of the poem does not follow any traditional verse structure: stanza and line lengths are irregular; there is no end rhyme; and syllabic patterning is not used. Hughes has chosen to write free verse because he wishes to make the reader reconsider the idea of birth and build up an impression of the individuality of his main protagonist. By using an irregular form, Hughes reflects the originality of his thought in the structure as well as the content.

The style and approach of the poet prevent the reader falling into a false sense of security. The reader must feel slightly uncomfortable in order to reassess things that society takes for granted. Yet Hughes needs us to be able to relate to Crow, and thus he is anthropomorphised, not born from an egg, but as a human baby. He is both bird and human and as such he challenges our preconceptions about life. We are encouraged to see Crow as a victim – he has been tortured in birth and is born into a life of pain and meaninglessness. Although the poem is specifically about Crow, it also deals with universal themes and this is what makes it powerful.

Manipulating the grammatical structure influences the way in which we receive information, and Hughes has used foregrounding here to great effect. It allows him to delay any explicit reference to the central focus of the poem, and to undermine our expectations by denying us the climax we anticipate.

6 Literary and rhetorical devices

Literature is marked by its evocative use of language – even where a writer chooses to use everyday words and structures, the end result is crafted and conscious. The effect is intensified by the use of **literary and rhetorical devices** that enrich and heighten the power of the words on the page.

Poetry draws on a rich source of language and the use of literary and rhetorical devices enables poets to intensify the effect of their words on the reader. Sound patterning can be used to underpin the meaning; figurative language can help to convey a vivid personal vision; images can make abstract ideas concrete; rhetorical patterning can focus attention on key words.

Sound patterning

Poetry is a genre in which sound is often just as important as the written word. Sometimes a poem that seems difficult on the page will come alive when it is read aloud – poetry is, after all, directly linked to the earliest oral traditions. The connection between poetry and music has been made by many people: Edgar Allan Poe (1809–49), for instance, described poetry as *music . . . combined with a pleasurable idea*. The music created can be pleasant to the ear and smooth (**euphony**) or discordant and jarring (**cacophony**).

There are two ways in which poets can create a musical quality in their verse: through the choice and arrangement of sounds, and in the pattern of stressed and unstressed syllables. We have already considered the effects created by metrical pattern in Chapter 3; in this section we will look at some of the literary devices that can be used to create sound patterns and the effects they have.

Alliteration is the close repetition of consonant sounds usually at the beginning of words. Nearly all Old English poetry uses alliterative patterning extensively to provide cohesion in the standard 2-part line, with either two or three stressed syllables in each line alliterating. Interest in alliterative verse was revived in the nineteenth century when Gerard Manley Hopkins experimented with alliterative patterning.

Alliteration is based on sound rather than spelling and it is therefore important to think about the sound of words rather than just their initial letter. For instance, *car* and *city* are not alliterative because the **c** sound in each case is quite different. Equally, *shine* and *sin* are not alliterative because the **s** in *shine* is bound up with the **h** – the sound is therefore **sh** rather than **s**.

Poets can choose to pattern the sounds of their words in order to underpin the meaning. Plosives like **b**, **d**, **k** and **p** can be used where a hard sound is required; the fricatives **f**, **v**, **th** and the lateral **l** create a softer sound quality; the sibilant **s** can seem harsh and hissing, or soft and murmuring depending upon the context in which it is used.

Assonance is the close repetition of similar vowel sounds, usually in stressed syllables (*free/easy; time/mind*). **Consonance** is the close repetition of identical consonant sounds before and after different vowels (*flip/flop*). Some writers accept as consonance the repetition of consonant sounds at the ends of words only (*east/west; hid/bed*).

Onomatopoeia is the use of words whose sounds seem to express or reinforce their meanings (*hiss, bang, buzz*). The sound and sense of such words is closely related. It is the most direct way in which poets can create a sense of sound in the words they choose.

Rhyme is the repetition of similar sounds, usually the final syllable of words at the end of lines. It is one of the features most commonly associated with poetry, but poems do not have to employ rhyme – John Milton (1608–74) spoke against its use, and many modern poets choose to avoid it. At its worst, rhyme is a frivolous decoration that is dull and predictable: some greetings cards and advertising slogans provide examples of rhyme in its weakest form. Used skilfully, however, it can enhance the musical qualities of a poem, provide a complex framework for the poet's ideas, and make lines memorable.

Rhyme draws attention to the sound quality of words, and, in the best poetry, will play a significant role in conveying meaning. It also functions as a signal for the end of a rhythmical unit or stanza.

Some rhyme can be recognised by its position: **end rhyme** occurs at the end of the line; **internal rhyme** occurs within the line or stanza. Other rhyme is notable for its sound quality: **full rhyme** repeats the final accented vowels of the rhyming words and all succeeding sounds (*pick/stick*); **masculine rhyme** repeats only a single end syllable (*cat/hat*); **feminine rhyme** repeats a rhyme over two or more syllables (*flower/power*). Where rhymes extend over three or more syllables, the effect is often humorous (*clerical/hysterical*). Other kinds of rhyme can also be used: **eye rhymes** depend upon spelling rather than sound (*through/though*); **near or imperfect rhymes** repeat close rather than exact sounds (*mate/sweet*); **identical rhyme** or rime riche uses two words which have exactly the same sound but different spelling and meanings (homophones like *flower/flour*), or two identical words (homographs).

Rhyme has metrical and rhetorical functions. Structurally, it marks the metrical ends of lines and links them in couplets or stanzas; it can also establish connections within a line, linking one metrical foot with another. In this sense it is a rhythmical device that intensifies the meaning by drawing attention to the way in which the poet's ideas are organised. As a rhetorical device, rhyme enhances the musical qualities of verse, encourages the reader to see connections between words, and concentrates meaning.

Old English poetry used structural alliteration as its main poetic device because the Germanic language was less suited to rhyme. As English was influenced by French and the Romance languages in the Middle Ages, rhyme became easier and the verse of the Medieval period is dominated by rhyme. Changes in pronunciation during the sixteenth to eighteenth centuries made rhyme straightforward and this can be seen in the popularity of forms like the sonnet that use restrictive rhyme to structure the content.

Activity 6.1

How does Gerard Manley Hopkins (1844–89) use sound and rhythm to underpin meaning in 'God's Grandeur'?

You may like to think about: the poetic form, language, sound patterning and metre.

God's Grandeur

1 The world is charged with the grandeur of God.
It will flame out, like shining from shook foil;
It gathers to a greatness, like the ooze of oil
Crushed. Why do men then now not reck his rod?
5 Generations have trod, have trod, have trod;
And all is seared with trade; bleared, smeared with toil;
And wears man's smudge and shares man's smell: the soil
Is bare now, nor can foot feel, being shod.

And for all this, nature is never spent;
10 There lives the dearest freshness deep down things;
And though the last lights off the black West went
Oh, morning, at the brown brink eastward, springs –
Because the Holy Ghost over the bent
World broods with warm breast and with ah! bright wings.

Commentary

This poem focuses on the distance between man, God and the natural world, which, for Hopkins, is the reason for man's machine-like existence in an industrial society. He is looking beneath the surface detail of nature to a visionary and ecstatic recognition of God's presence in the world, and man's ignorance of it.

The end rhyme organises Hopkins's ideas, allowing him to control and develop his theme through the tightness of the Italian or Petrarchan sonnet form. The four recurring end rhymes (abbaabba cdcdcd) provide cohesion: the octave describes man's destruction of nature and his disregard for God; the volta creates a turning point, and the sestet then focuses on God's power. It concludes with an image of protection that celebrates the redemptive nature of God's love. The full rhymes create a strong cohesive sound and add to the hymn-like quality of the poem.

The rhythm created by the metrical pattern also contributes to the sound quality of the poem. Hopkins moves away from what he called 'running rhythm' – the alternating weak/strong stress pattern of the traditional iambic metre – using instead a less predictable rhythm in which a fixed number of stresses are accompanied by a varying number of weak syllables. Although the length of the lines is varied, the fixed number of stresses gives a sense of balance.

Metrical variations are used to emphasise key words and to challenge the reader's complacency. In the opening line, for instance, Hopkins sets the lilting rhythm of the first two iambic feet against a weak pyrrhic foot (two unstressed syllables) and an accented trochaic foot:

Thĕ world | ĭs chargéd | wĭth thĕ | grandeŭr | ŏf God.

The substitution prepares us for a counterpoint – the unstressed foot leads us straight to the harder trochaic foot, forcing the reader to recognise that this will not be a traditional Romantic poem in which the natural world is represented as a retreat from industrialisation. A similar technique is used in line 5, where the trochaic opening is juxtaposed with the tedium of the repeated iambic foot.

Genĕ | ratiońs | hăve trod, | hăve trod, | hăve trod;

The metrical change here, as well as the monosyllabic words and recurring short vowel sounds, emphasises the world-weariness of the people who have lost sight of their God.

Hopkins's use of the spondee also demonstrates how metrical pattern can underpin meaning. The consecutive stresses in *bleáred, smeáred* (l.6), *mán's smúdge . . . mán's smell* (l.7) and *bright wings* (l.14) draw attention to key ideas. The first three examples emphasise man's distance from God, while the final one is an emphatic recognition of the power of God despite man's abandonment of Him. By changing the metrical pattern, Hopkins is able to highlight important lexical items. Read aloud, the sounds of the stressed syllables guide readers, helping them to feel their way through the complexity of the style.

Perhaps most important of all in creating the intensity of this poem is the density of sounds Hopkins creates. As listeners we are struck by the power of the music. The harshness of the octave is modified by the softness of the sestet as Hopkins moves towards his celebratory final lines. Alliteration of the soft fricatives in *shining shook* (l.2) is juxtaposed with harsher sounds like the plosives in *grandeur, God* (l.1), *gathers, greatness* (l.3) and *Crushed* (l.4). Similarly, long vowel sounds like *foil/oil, ooze* and *now* (ll.2–4) can be contrasted with the harsher assonance created by the pure vowels in *men then . . . reck* (l.4). The contrast of these sounds reflects the two sides of God: His gentleness – represented by the protective image in the final lines; and his power – conveyed in the image of His *rod* (l.4).

For Hopkins, the sound is an integral part of the meaning: it enhances the poem's ideas and helps the reader to understand by working on our emotions. The internal rhyme in *seared . . . bleared . . . smeared* (l.6) and the alliteration of *smeared . . . smudge . . . smell* (ll.6–7) mirror the repetitive nature of industrial life. The connotations of the words and our emotional response to the sounds affect the way in which we engage with the text. In the sestet, however, the effects created are different. The soft alliteration of *last lights* and *West went* (l.11) creates a soothing tone that is quite different to the roughness of the octave. Hopkins marks the strength of nature to go on in spite of man's failures – it is the quiet moment before the dynamic return of morning, which is evidence of God's *grandeur*. The assonance of *Holy Ghost over* (l.13) and the alliteration of **broods** . . . **breast** . . . **bright** (l.14) draw attention to the poem's climax. The reassuring tone of the long vowels is heightened by the upbeat monosyllabic alliterative words: the positive connotations of the words and the sound patterning create an inclusive feel to the final lines.

Imagery

In general terms, **imagery** refers to a descriptive use of language to represent people, things, places, actions, experiences. Images appeal to our senses – most frequently recreating a visual experience through words. As well as portraying a literal picture based on physical sensations, they can also convey emotions and suggest ideas.

Literal images

In some poems, the poet's predominant interest is in creating a physical representation of a particular place, person, or experience. The diction is chosen in order to communicate the details that are important to the poet. In this case, the images may be literal – they draw on the senses, using words that can be understood at a literal rather than a metaphorical level. The reader needs to respond by visualising rather than by exploring layers of meaning.

Activity 6.2

Explore the way in which Robert Bridges (1844–1930) presents the scene in the extract from 'London Snow'.
You may like to think about:
the language, images and grammatical structure.

from **London Snow**
1   When men were all asleep the snow came flying,
    In large white flakes falling on the city brown,
    Stealthily and perpetually settling and loosely lying.
      Hushing the latest traffic of the drowsy town;
5   Deadening, muffling, stifling its murmurs failing;
    Lazily and incessantly floating down and down:
      Silently sifting and veiling road, roof and railing;
    Hiding difference, making unevenness even,
    Into angles and crevices softly drifting and sailing.

Commentary

The language of the poem is effective in creating a strong visual image of London as a layer of snow changes it. The poet uses modified noun phrases to establish a sense of contrast: the *large white flakes* and *the city brown* (l.2); *the latest traffic* and *the drowsy town* (l.4). While these give the reader a sense of time and place, it is the adverbs and verbs that communicate the poet's vision most powerfully.

This extract is made up of one compound-complex sentence: the main clause *the snow came flying/In large white flakes* (ll.1–2) introduces the theme; the foregrounded adverbial clause *When men were all asleep* sets the time scale; and the non-finite present participle clauses describe the poet's observations as a transformation of the city takes place. While some of the verbs describe the process (*falling* l.2, *settling*, *lying* l.2, *floating* l.6, *drifting*, *sailing* l.9), others describe the effects of the snow (*Hushing* l.4, *Deadening*, *muffling*, *stifling*, *failing* l.5, *sifting*, *veiling* l.7, *Hiding* l.8). These are basically synonyms that intensify our response to the scene the poet describes – our senses are heightened and we are drawn into this new world where sound is muted and the details of the landscape obscured.

The use of adverb phrases to modify these non-finite verbs enhances our experience. They too fulfil different semantic functions: *Silently* (l.7) and *softly* (l.9) work accumulatively with the verbs describing the muting of sound; *perpetually* (l.3) and *incessantly* (l.6) convey a sense of the time scale; and *Stealthily* (l.3) and *Lazily* (l.6) begin to suggest a more figurative use of language. These two adverbs almost personify the snow, endowing it with human-like qualities that suggest a consciousness in its process.

Bridges creates strong visual and sound images to give the reader a physical experience of the scene he is recreating. He appeals to our senses through the language he chooses and the sound patterns he creates. The feminine end rhyme, the internal rhyme (*When men* l.1, *drowsy town* l.4, *veiling/railing* l.7), and the alliteration (*Silently sifting . . . road, roof and railing* l.7) intensify the experience by drawing us into the scene.

The imagery here can be described as predominantly literal because the poet is describing the scene in such a way that it will physically be recreated in the reader's mind. The emphasis is on communicating a sense of the process of transformation.

Figurative language

Figurative language requires the reader to work harder because the poet uses language in a more complex way: the words on the page mean something in addition to their literal meaning. Recognising these embedded layers of meaning will help the reader to understand a poem as a whole, since they will inevitably be related to the poet's themes and ideas.

Figures of speech enable the poet to say one thing in terms of something else. They bring together two things that are both similar and different – and it is in the relationship between them that the poet finds meaning. Figurative language thus enriches the semantic possibilities of a poem because the images created can communicate on two levels: they represent physical experience and simultaneously function as a thematic signpost.

There are many ways of saying one thing and meaning another, but the most common figurative devices used by poets are metaphors, similes and personification.

A **simile** takes two things that are essentially unlike and makes an explicit comparison between them by using words such as *like, as, than*.

A **metaphor** takes two things that are unlike and makes an implicit comparison: the figurative term is substituted for or identified with the literal term. The link between the two things may be signalled by the use of the verb 'to be'. In Shakespeare's *Life's but a walking shadow* (*Macbeth*), for instance, both the literal term *Life* and the figurative term *shadow* are named. In other examples, the literal term is not named and the original idea is replaced by the metaphorical concept. We see an example of this in the octave of Shakespeare's Sonnet 146: *Poor soul, the centre of my sinful earth*. Here the metaphor develops an implied link between the body and the earth: the literal concept (body) is not named but implied by the associations the reader makes with *soul*. Where a poet develops a metaphor or a sequence of related metaphors over a number of lines it is described as an extended metaphor.

We use metaphors in everyday speech, but because the expressions become familiar, they lack the vitality they once had. Where it was once dramatic to say that 'no stone will be left unturned' in an investigation, or that someone had 'burnt his boats', such expressions have now lost their unique quality. We call these dead metaphors because we no longer recognise the metaphorical relationship between the literal and figurative terms.

Metaphors will often form the central organising principle for a poem because they are not merely decorative, but an integral part of the semantic and poetic structure. They work by association – the links between the literal and figurative terms, and the resonance created by the diction extending the metaphor intensify the poet's vision. The effectiveness and originality of the comparison, and the connotative richness of the language govern the success of a metaphor. Where a poet can surprise readers and encourage them to look at things in a new way, the effect is dramatic.

Personification is a figure of speech that gives inanimate objects or abstract ideas human qualities and actions. In Stephen Crane's poem 'A Man Said to the Universe', the universe is personified; in Ted Hughes's poem 'Thistles', the thistles are given human qualities and relationships.

Closely related to personification is **apostrophe**, although this is not always used figuratively. It consists of an address to someone absent or dead or something non-human as if that person or thing were present and alive, and could reply to what is being said. Apostrophe provides an opportunity for the speaker of a poem to think aloud, and often the thoughts are expressed in a formal tone. The interjection *O* can be used as a signal of the intense emotions that underpin an apostrophe.

Apostrophe can create a powerful and immediate voice in a poem, but when used extravagantly the effects can be comic. Modern poets are less likely to use apostrophe than their predecessors because they see it as an overtly self-conscious figure that is theatrical rather than sincere.

Activity 6.3

> **How does the figurative language in the following poem enable Robert Burns (1759–96) to convey his emotions in 'A Red, Red Rose'?**
>
> You may like to think about: the tone, the use of dialect, the imagery, and the structure.

A Red, Red Rose

1   O my Luve's like a red, red rose
       That's newly sprung in June:
    O my Luve's like the melodie
       That's sweetly play'd in tune!

5   As fair art thou, my bonnie lass,
       So deep in luve am I:
    And I will luve thee still, my dear,
       Till a' the seas gang dry:

    Till a' the seas gang dry, my dear,
10   And the rocks melt wi' the sun;
    I will luve thee still, my dear,
       While the sands o' life shall run.

    And fare thee weel, my only Luve,
       And fare thee weel a while!
15   And I will come again, my Luve,
       Tho' it were ten thousand mile.

Commentary

Burns wrote verse in both eighteenth-century Standard English and his native Scottish dialect. The fact that he chose to write of love using Scots words (*gang* ll.8–9) and spellings that reflect pronunciation (*Luve*; *a'* for 'all'; *weel* for 'well') make the tone of this poem seem particularly personal and familiar. This feeling is reinforced by the familiar use of the second person pronoun *thou* and the terms of address. Noun phrases like *my Luve* (ll.1, 3, 15), *my bonnie lass* (l.5), *my dear* (ll.7, 9, 11) emphasise the speaker's emotional attachment and build to a climax in the premodified noun phrase *My only Luve* (l.13), where the adjective implies the exclusivity of his love.

The weight of the speaker's emotions, however, is conveyed in the comparisons the poet makes. In the first stanza, the similes link traditional romantic images explicitly with the speaker's love: the *red rose* (l.1) and the *melodie* (l.3). In each case, the head word occurs at the end of a line where it is given prominence and then post-modified by a relative clause that intensifies the image. The rose is *newly sprung in June* and thus symbolic of all that is fresh, beautiful and perfect; the melody is *sweetly play'd in tune* and thus symbolic of harmony and togetherness.

The adverbs *newly* and *sweetly* enhance the positive connotations of the traditional images, but also make them more distinctive.

In the second and third stanzas, the poet uses metaphor to emphasise the extent of the love he feels. The descriptions of the seas becoming dry (ll.8–9) and the rocks melting in the sun (l.10) are not meant to be understood literally – they represent a figurative use of language in which the speaker tries to convey the limitlessness of his love. Burns uses two unlikely events to create a sense of timelessness, thus intensifying the abstract concept of love through physical images. While these metaphors are direct, the reference to *the sands o' life* (l.12) is implied. The metaphor suggests the visual image of a sandglass, an instrument used for measuring passing time by the running out of sand, to convey the longevity of this love. We make links between the noun *sand* and the verb *run* as we read, and the associations enhance the speaker's declaration of love.

While the first three stanzas build to a climax, the final stanza changes the mood – this declaration of love has been brought about by an imminent separation. The metaphorical reference to a distance of *ten thousand mile* (l.16) and the subjunctive *Tho' it were* emphasises that physical distance is no object to the speaker's love. The certainty of the repeated modal verb *will* and the adverb phrase *still* (ll.7, 11), however, now take on a slightly different timbre.

The figurative language has allowed Burns to convey his love effectively in concrete terms of beauty, harmony and geological extremity. The images make the abstraction concrete and thus add depth to the declaration. Burns has avoided cliché by qualifying the traditional red rose and melody in ways that re-remind his reader of their essential and relevant qualities.

* * *

Symbolism is related to devices such as simile, metaphor and personification because it is a means of saying more than just the sum total of the literal words on the page. It does not, however, depend upon actual likeness since associations as well as sensory resemblance play a part in the creation of a symbol. References to objects and people, descriptions of places, events and actions, the expression of ideas can assume a symbolic significance that resonates through a poem.

While an image will function as a sense-based representation of a particular place or experience, a symbol moves beyond this sensory level. It is a vehicle for two things at once: it functions as a literal image, but simultaneously suggests a wider, more abstract field of meaning. It is this dual purpose that helps us to recognise a symbol – when a literal interpretation seems insufficient, and there appears to be an underlying significance, an image probably has a symbolic function.

The context in which a symbol occurs, and the associations commonly linked to it, will help us to interpret its significance. In some poems, the symbols will be recognisable because they have universal relevance: climbing a mountain or other high place will often symbolically represent a spiritual quest for higher things. Symbols with a historical, cultural or mythical background exist outside the context of a specific poem and are therefore also more accessible to the reader. While some poets are content to use natural, religious and mythical symbols that are part of a common heritage, other poets create symbols that have a personal significance. Because of their private nature, these symbols will often be less straightforward.

Image, metaphor and symbol overlap in terms of their effect, and are sometimes difficult to distinguish. In general, however, an image means only what it is; a metaphor means something other than what it is; and a symbol means what it is and something more in addition. Images are at the heart of metaphors and symbols because in using these literary devices, the poet is trying to create a sensory impression through the words he chooses. In considering the visual and sensory effect of Robert Frost's poem 'The Road Not Taken', for instance, we would discuss the two leaf-covered roads in the yellow wood as an image; in addressing the significance of the poem, we would talk about the symbolic effect of the image as a symbol for life's choices.

Activity 6.4

Explore the symbolism of the extract from 'You Open Your Hands to Me', a poem by Paula Meehan (1955–).

You may like to think about: the images, the language, the tone and the structure.

You Open Your Hands to Me

1   They hold nothing
    They are calloused
    Earth under the fingernails
    The heart line strong and sure
5   As any river crazy for the sea

    These hands hold nothing
    They are the hands of a worker
    They are the hands of one who has no job

    They have tucked a whole city up at night
10   And in the morning cast it adrift

    These hands could pack everything they value
    In a minute or less

    From a burning building
    They would save what is living
15   Not what is Art

Commentary

When an image seems to mean more than just a literal representation of the thing described, the poet has probably used a symbol. In this poem, Meehan focuses on images of hands, but, as the poem develops, we are aware that she is interested in more than just physical description. An apparently straightforward poem, therefore, has an underlying significance: the hands have a symbolic value that affects the way we read the poem.

The first five lines provide us with physical information: the language draws attention to certain features that help us to build up a literal picture. The simple sentence *They are calloused* (l.2), with its suggestion of use and age, is followed by isolated phrases. The elliptical style directs our gaze as we move from the callouses to the *Earth under the fingernails*, and finally to the *heart line strong and sure* (ll.3–4). Where these details are physical, the simile moves towards a more figurative use of language. The image of the *river* (l.5), symbolic of fertility and perpetual motion, begins to suggest something of the person to whom these detached hands belong.

In the next stanzas, the poet moves away from the physical individuality of the hands described in the first five lines, and it is at this point that we become explicitly aware of the wider symbolic significance of the central image. The opposition created between the noun phrases in the second stanza (*the hands of a worker . . . the hands of one who has no job*, ll.7–8) suggests two quite different physical images, and yet both are united in the image of motherhood created in the third stanza. In bringing together the expansive noun phrase *a whole city* and the comfortable domestic verb phrase *tucked . . . up* (l.9), Meehan emphasises the symbolic value of her poem – while it may be a tribute to her own mother, it is also a poem in praise of motherhood.

The repetition of the noun *nothing* is ironic within the context of 'value' that is at the heart of the poem. While the hands may be physically empty, their potential is emphasised in a variety of ways. Stanza 3 draws attention to their maternal function; stanza 4 suggests their practical ability. By juxtaposing the noun clauses *what is living* and *what is Art* (ll.14–15), however, Meehan again moves into the realm of symbolism: the hands become representations of what it means to be a mother. We become aware of not only the jobs that these hands do, but of the psychological and emotional judgements lying behind the physical activity.

The symbolism of hands is complex and appears in a wide range of cultures through the ages: in the Middle East and India, brides' hands are decorated with complex patterns of red henna for luck; the Jewish 'Hand of God' is a symbol of strength and power; gestures can signify blessing, protection, anger, affection, greeting. Meehan draws on this traditional symbolism in her poem. The simple sentence of the title is both a literal action and a symbolic gesture in which the mother offers herself to her child. Open hands are representative of humility, vulnerability, directness and, in the context of the poem, giving. The poem thus represents an exploration of the symbolic gifts given by the parent to the child: the hands may be physically empty, but the gesture is a symbol of love.

Rhetorical devices

Rhetoric is the art of persuasive writing and speaking. It is used in everyday life to persuade people to do or to believe things: politicians use the devices in their speeches to persuade us to vote for them; advertising jingles and slogans depend upon them to convince us that we need the product they are promoting. In literature, rhetoric can help readers to engage with and believe in the world presented in the story, poem or play; the devices can be used to draw attention to key ideas or words.

Rhetorical devices allow writers to consciously pattern and structure their work, thus heightening its effect – ordinary experiences are intensified by the way in which the poet realises them on the page. Lexical and grammatical choices can manipulate us, guiding and controlling our responses; rhetorical patterning can highlight important elements through repetition, listing and parallelism. It is, of course, important to remember that identification of a device is only the first stage – with no evaluative comment considering the effects created, the naming of devices becomes no more than feature-spotting.

Repetition, tripling and parallelism

Repetition of words, phrases, clauses or sentence structures can draw attention to key ideas. The recurrence of a lexical or grammatical item, for instance, can highlight the poet's theme; create a sense of entrapment; develop a comforting rhythmical pattern that underpins the meaning; or establish a haunting, indignant, or passionate tone. Having identified an example of repetition in a poem, it is important to think about the context in which it has occurred and its relationship with the meaning.

In **tripling**, similar structures or words are repeated in patterns of threes to draw attention to key concepts. A poet may use three words, phrases, or clauses to emphasise the importance of a particular experience, place or idea – the repetitions may not be exact, but the reader will be able to see an underlying similarity or relationship between the linked elements.

Parallelism patterns linguistic and grammatical structures so that a recognisable balance is created between two related elements. Links established between phrases, lines or stanzas can reinforce the musical, rhythmical and semantic qualities of a poem. The device can be used to create a strong sense of logic and balance, to reflect passion and emotion, or to develop a lyric, song-like refrain.

The exact nature of the parallels varies: the structures may be the same, where the second line reinforces the first by repeating the thought; they may be antithetical, where the second line denies or contrasts the first; or they may be accumulative, where each repetition of the pattern supplements and develops the first, often moving towards some kind of climax.

Activity 6.5

How do the poets use stylistic features and rhetorical patterning to convey their ideas in the poems below?

You may like to think about: the language, the tone, the images and the structure.

Forgetfulness

1   Forgetfulness is like a song
    That, freed from beat and measure, wanders.
    Forgetfulness is like a bird whose wings are reconciled,
    Outspread and motionless, –
5   A bird that coasts the wind unwearyingly.

    Forgetfulness is rain at night,
    Or an old house in a forest, – or a child.
    Forgetfulness is white, – white as a blasted tree,
    And it may stun the sybil into prophecy,
10   Or bury the Gods.

    I can remember much forgetfulness.

TEXT 2 – GRACE NICHOLS (1950–)

Epilogue

1   I have crossed an ocean
    I have lost my tongue
    from the root of the old one
    a new one has sprung

TEXT 3 – CHRISTINA ROSSETTI (1830–94)

A Birthday

1   My heart is like a singing bird
      Whose nest is in a water'd shoot;
    My heart is like an apple-tree
      Whose boughs are bent with thickset fruit;
5   My heart is like a rainbow shell
      That paddles in a halcyon sea;
    My heart is gladder than all these
      Because my love is come to me.

    Raise me a dais of silk and down;
10   Hang it with vair° and purple dyes;   vair – a kind of squirrel
    Carve it in doves and pomegranates,   fur, bluish-grey and
      And peacocks with a hundred eyes;   white in colour
    Work it in gold and silver grapes,
      In leaves and silver fleurs-de-lys;
15   Because the birthday of my life
      Is come, my love is come to me.

Commentary

Each poet uses rhetorical patterning to draw attention to the ideas: Hart Crane repeats his key word, the abstract noun *Forgetfulness*, and draws attention to its qualities through similes (stanza 1) and metaphors (stanza 2); Grace Nichols creates a parallel between a physical journey and its psychological effect by repeating the opening of the clause and varying its end; and Christina Rossetti emphasises her excitement through a repeated pattern that builds to a climax at the end of each stanza.

Hart Crane takes an abstract quality and gives it a concrete presence through the comparisons he makes. The images represent forgetfulness as a state of freedom and perfect balance in which we no longer need to be bound by the conventions and expectations of day-to-day life. An adjective phrase like *freed from beat and measure* (l.2), verbs like *wanders* (l.2), *reconciled* (l.3) and *coasts* (l.5), and the adverb *unwearyingly* (l.5) suggest that Crane is approaching forgetfulness from an untraditional angle. For him, it seems to be representative of a life without stress or responsibility, where everything can be lost in the sound of rain, the isolation of the forest, or the innocence of a child who is not bound by the rules of the adult world. It is a state of exultation, rather than an impairment.

The patterning of the stanzas is effective because it provides a sequence of images that counter the connotations of forgetfulness as a 'failure', or as 'neglectfulness'. The repetition of the key word *Forgetfulness* in the initial position (ll.1, 3, 6, 8) followed by *is like* or *is . . ./Or . . . or* creates a balanced structure that draws us into the poet's vision. The richness of the images appeals to our senses and develops a positive rather than negative context for the poet's theme. They build to a climax in the description of forgetfulness as *white* with its connotations of purity and blankness. This is not an obviously negative image – it seems to develop the positive associations of the metaphors in the previous lines. The post-modified adjective phrase *white as a blasted tree* (l.8), however, seems to alter the tone: as a symbol of lifelessness, the dead tree perhaps offers another view of forgetfulness. It is an absence from life; it represents a detachment from the world of the living.

The final lines of the second stanza capture the paradox: while forgetfulness can *stun the sybil into prophecy*, unexpectedly revealing life's secrets, it can also *bury the Gods*, leaving the individual disconnected and remote. The poet's use of the modal verb *may* emphasises the unpredictability of *forgetfulness*.

The main body of the poem offers a detached view of *forgetfulness*, but the last line introduces a more personal element. The use of the first person pronoun *I* makes the poem a statement about a particular individual's experience of life. It is left to stand alone, as a reflective overview. The juxtaposition of *remember* and *forgetfulness* is not illogical, but a recognition of a life that is notable for its periods of blankness. The tone is neither nostalgic, nor regretful – the speaker has experienced both the freedom and state of balance created by *forgetfulness*, and the sterile detachment from life.

Hart Crane's poem is structured around the repetition of the key word *forgetfulness*, the patterning of the similes and metaphors, and the recognition of the paradoxical nature of his theme. Grace Nichols's short poem 'Epilogue' also uses rhetorical patterning to underpin a central antithesis. As a poet interested in the relationship between language, culture and identity, she addresses the experience of an immigrant. The repetition of the personal pronoun *I* and the use of the possessive determiner *my* suggests that this is a poem with a particular resonance for Nichols – we know she has herself experienced such a physical and cultural relocation.

The patterning of the first two lines creates a direct contrast between the physical journey from one country to another and the emotional effect this has. In each line, the grammatical structure is identical: subject (*I*) predicator (*have crossed/have lost*) object (*an ocean/my tongue*). This creates an explicit link between the journey and the poet's changing sense of self – the nouns (*ocean* and *tongue*) become symbols of the poet's separation from her homeland and her native language.

Despite this sense of loss, the tone is exuberant rather than nostalgic. The lack of punctuation drives the reader forward; the foregrounding of the prepositional phrase (l.3) delays the final main clause (l.4) and thus places added emphasis upon it; and the poem ends with the dynamic verb *sprung* with its connotations of energy and spontaneous creativity. In addition, the image of growth represents the experience as a fruitful one. The fact that the poet's new language is 'rooted' in her old one means that she has not completely detached herself from her native language and culture.

For poets, language is crucial to the way in which an understanding of the world can be expressed – in losing your *tongue*, you lose your ability to comment on the world around you. For Nichols, however, the experience gives her an additional language, and she now writes in both Creole and Standard English.

The final poem is more obviously patterned, using repeated words and clause structures to convey the poet's emotional state. In stanza 1, lines 1–6 repeat the noun phrase *My heart* followed by *is* and a simile made up of a complex noun phrase; lines 7–8 replace the simile with a post-modified comparative adjective phrase (*gladder than all these*) and an adverbial clause of reason explaining the poet's state of mind. In stanza 2, lines 9–14 consist of a sequence of imperatives, concluding in lines 15–16 with a second adverbial clause of reason that provides the motivation for everything the poet wants done.

Rossetti's poem is a passionate declaration of love in which the arrival of her lover is perceived as the best birthday present she could be given. The language is rich, full of elaborate natural images and extravagant luxuries. Although the modifiers *singing* (l.1), *thickset* (4), *rainbow* (l.5) and *halcyon* (l.6) create a positive mood, the patterning of the poem drives the reader onto the comparative phrase that portrays the poet's heart as more ecstatic than any of the comparisons made in the similes.

The exuberance of the first stanza is then replaced by the emphatic imperatives of the second: *Raise, Carve, Work*. The natural images of the *bird*, the *apple-tree* and the *shell* become bound up with the creation of a *dais* raised in honour of the lover. The diction is ornate with references to opulent materials (*silk and down, vair, gold and silver*), emblematic birds and flowers (*doves, peacocks, fleurs-de-lys*), and rich colours (*purple dyes*). The visual image is sumptuous and the poet creates a fitting tribute to her lover.

The climax is reached in the emphatic repetition of the final lines, where the title and final line of stanza 1 come together in a euphoric statement of justification. By using the verb phrase *is come*, Rossetti creates an interesting intensity – there is an emphasis on the realisation of the poet's dream. From the usual structure of English verb phrases, we would expect either 'is coming' (progressive) or 'has come' (perfective). By combining the two patterns, Rossetti has created a sense of immediacy that encompasses both the process of arriving and its completion.

The result is a present tense form that emphasises the moment of arrival and the poet's ecstatic state of being.

Listing, climax and anticlimax, antithesis

Poets will often pattern their language by creating links between the words – they may list modifiers, nouns or verbs; they may build to a high point, or unexpectedly undermine our expectations by not providing a climax; they may develop contrasts by placing words, phrases and ideas in opposition. Using these kinds of devices enables them to affect the way their readers respond to the subject matter and ideas of a poem.

Different approaches to **listing** can change the pace of a poem, the tone, and the way the reader relates to the content. If conjunctions are used to co-ordinate the elements of a list, it is said to be syndetic listing; if commas are used instead and there is no co-ordinating conjunction, the list is said to be asyndetic. The semantic effect in each case is quite different: an asyndetic list can suggest breathless excitement, chaotic confusion, or an overwhelming sense of infinite possibilities; a syndetic list can suggest reason and logic, something that can be controlled and managed, or a predictable and comforting context. Listing always has an accumulative effect and it enables poets to create a range of impressions. We would normally expect a list to build to a **climax**, but a poet can defy our expectations by concluding with an **anticlimax**.

By drawing on opposites, a poet can intensify the ideas at the heart of a poem. We call this **antithesis**. It can be used to draw a contrast between places, attitudes to life, people or events. The poet may choose words that are directly opposed, or may develop contrasts through the grammatical structures or literary language.

Activity 6.6

> **What kinds of linguistic, stylistic and rhetorical patterning does Wordsworth use to describe London in 'Composed Upon Westminster Bridge'?**
>
> You may like to think about: the form, language, imagery, metre, and rhetorical devices

Composed Upon Westminster Bridge, September 3, 1802

1   Earth has not anything to show more fair:
       Dull would he be of soul who could pass by
       A sight so touching in its majesty:
       The City now doth, like a garment, wear
5   The beauty of the morning; silent, bare,
       Ships, towers, domes, theatres, and temples lie
       Open unto the fields, and to the sky;
       All bright and glittering in the smokeless air.

Never did sun more beautifully steep
10 In his first splendour, valley, rock, or hill;
Ne'er saw I, never felt, a calm so deep!
The river glideth at his own sweet will:
Dear God! the very houses seem asleep;
And all that mighty heart is lying still!

Commentary

Wordsworth's poem is firmly rooted in time and place – the title immediately establishes a very specific location (*Westminster Bridge*) and precise date (*September 3, 1802*). The use of the personal pronoun *I* (l.11) suggests that this is a poem with a particular relevance for the poet, and in Dorothy Wordsworth's journal there is an entry for this day in which she describes the scene that lay before them as they crossed the bridge.

The patterning Wordsworth uses to describe the city is explicit in a number of ways: the tightness of the Petrarchan sonnet form; the lexical sets of words relating to the natural and urban worlds; the rhetorical listing; the figurative language; and the challenge to reader expectations. Wordsworth uses the various forms of patterning to frame his response to the city, representing not the vision of industrialisation that we expect, but the beauty he saw on that particular September morning. The structures he chooses give the poem a sense of balance that complements the harmonious vision he describes.

The sonnet form is framed by its rhyme structure. It allows the poet to explore a central thought or experience and then, after a turning point, to address another element that varies or completes the original focus. Here, the octave (abbaabba) praises the city's beauty, personifying it as a majestic figure, while the sestet (cdcdcd) compares the city to the natural world and marvels at its unexpected tranquillity. Sonnets are traditionally used to praise or express love for a woman, but Wordsworth here uses the form to express his overwhelming feelings for the sleeping city. The dirt and noise of nineteenth-century London are replaced by Wordsworth's vision of a new creation, and there is an almost spiritual devotion in the words he uses to describe the city. The balance and harmony of the form become synonymous with the perfection Wordsworth sees before him.

In keeping with the visionary quality of the sonnet and its peaceful mood, the long vowels at the end of lines (*fair/wear/bare/air, by/lie/sky*) and the internal assonance (*seem/asleep, mighty/lying*) are gentle, appropriate for the hushed sleeping city Wordsworth observes. Where stronger sounds are used, they express the poet's surprise and amazement at the sight that lies before him. Plosives in phrases like *a calm so deep* (l.11) and *Dear God!* (l.13) carry the weight of the poet's emotional response – this is not the city he was expecting to see. This patterning of long soft vowels and hard plosives allows Wordsworth to convey both the peacefulness of the scene and his ecstatic response to it.

Traditionally, the sonnet form uses the iambic pentameter rhythm. This predominates in Wordsworth's sonnet, but there are notable points at which a trochaic foot is used to change the focus. In the first two lines, for instance, the first words are stressed – *Earth* and *Dull* are given extra importance both by the stress and by the fact that *Dull* is foregrounded. This helps Wordsworth to emphasise the unique nature of this experience. He also uses a spondee at the beginning of some lines to draw attention to elements of the landscape (l.6), or to express his wonder.

The structural patterning is mirrored in the lexical patterning. While concrete nouns represent the physical details of the scene (l.6), emotive words like the modifiers *fair* (l.1), *bright, glittering* (l.8), *calm* (l.9), *sweet* (l.12) and abstract nouns like *beauty* (l.5), *majesty* (l.3) and *splendour* (l.10) convey the distinctive nature of this particular morning. There is an almost spiritual mood suggested by the reference to *soul* (l.2), the post-modifying present participle *touching* (l.3), and the ecstatic interjection *Dear God!* (l.13). Similarly, the use of archaic verb forms (*doth* l.4, *glideth* l.12) and prepositions (*unto*, l.7) have a biblical ring, contributing to the feeling that this is a vision of an untainted and innocent world. Wordsworth's experience on Westminster Bridge thus becomes an epiphany – he does not just record the outward beauty he sees, but conveys his state of mind on experiencing that beauty.

The all-embracing generic *Earth* of the opening line draws both natural and industrial together, emphasising that there is nothing more beautiful than the scene before the poet's eyes. The expected antithesis of rural and urban is never quite fulfilled because the poet is overwhelmed by the unexpected beauty he finds in the sun-drenched city. References to the urban (*Ships, towers, domes, theatres, temples, houses*) and the natural (*valley, rock, hill*) are brought together in the sun's redeeming light.

Rhetorical patterns work alongside the lexical and structural frameworks – devices such as listing and parallelism add to the balance and harmony of the poem as a whole. The syndetic listing of concrete nouns (l.6) is expansive, conveying the panoramic view Wordsworth has from the bridge. Equally important is the range of reference of these nouns – they address the industrial (*Ships, towers*), the cultural (*theatres*) and the religious (*temples*). The fact that each of these is a plural noun intensifies our sense of the city's variety.

Wordsworth uses rhetorical parallels to link his key ideas structurally. The parallel syndetic listing of *valley, rock, or hill* (l.10), for instance, forces the reader to recognise the central link between industrial and natural. This is reinforced by the parallel created between *Never did . . .* (l.9) and *Ne'er saw . . .* (l.11) which emphasises that these two very different environments can both be *steep[ed]/In [the sun's] first splendour*.

The personification of the city plays an important part in Wordsworth's vision. While the simile *like a garment* (l.4) gives a physical quality to the city's *majesty*, the metaphor of its *mighty heart* (l.14) suggests it is the source of all life. By describing the river as having its *own sweet will* and the houses as being *asleep*, Wordsworth pushes his personification of the city further. It is given a conscious life quite distinct from its human inhabitants.

This poem surprises us as readers because we do not find what we expect: Wordsworth the observer of nature is here the observer of an urban scene; the city is beautiful rather than grime-ridden and dreary; it is as much the source of life as the natural world. We are aware, however, that this vision is temporary – the simile of *The beauty of the morning* as a *garment* suggests that its beauty will be thrown off at the start of the working day, and the stative verb *seem* indicates an opposition between appearance and reality. This is reinforced by the modifier *smokeless* since we know that when work begins, London will once again be clouded in a haze of smog.

Wordsworth's poem observes individual details of the city landscape, but it also records his emotional response to the scene before him. The patterning he uses to organise his subject matter helps him to move beyond an exact representation to something more intense. J. S. Mill (1806–73), the philosopher and social reformer, described Wordsworth's verse as expressing *not mere outward beauty, but states of feeling, and of thought coloured by feeling, under the excitement of beauty*. This is what we experience in this poem: not just the visual elements of the landscape, but the breathtaking awe that Wordsworth felt as he paused on his journey across the bridge.

▪ ⊻ **7** How to read a poem

Reading poems can be illuminating, frustrating or downright terrifying. Each poet presents us with an individual vision of the world and we can, sometimes, feel that there is so much distance between ourselves and the poet that we will never understand what we are reading. As the American poet Robert Frost said: *Poetry provides the one permissible way of saying one thing and meaning another*. This can cause problems for the reader because the words on the page are rarely significant on a literal level alone – we need to be able to draw on the literary context in which the poet was writing, on the connotations of words, on the bank of symbols and images built up in a particular period or culture, and sometimes on the poet's own background.

In most cases, a knowledge of poetic approaches and devices will help us to overcome our difficulties. Being able to recognise specific features and understand the effects created will set us on the path to constructive discussion. And from our reading will come a moment of recognition in which we identify with the poet and his or her vision.

It is important, above all, to remember that poems work on a number of levels: we can immerse ourselves in the sound of the words, empathise with the sentiments, or marvel at the technical expertise. Each of these is a perfectly valid response to poetry, but as a critical reader, we need to combine all three. This first section of the book has introduced you to some key concepts: distinctive poetic features, poetic form, diction, grammatical structure, and literary and rhetorical devices. By considering these in relation to any poem you are reading and by developing an awareness of the poet's context, you will be able to move towards a critical understanding.

Readers will inevitably find their own way of approaching a poem, but the method outlined below provides a logical starting point.

On first reading, do not try to ponder the meaning of every word – instead, try to get a feeling for the poem as a whole. Read it aloud and feel the natural rhythms of the lines, paying attention to those that are marked with punctuation at the end and those that drive you on to the next line.

Try to decide what the poet is describing by identifying the concrete or actual references. This kind of approach will help you to get a basic feeling for the **content**, the literal focus of the poem, and its sound qualities.

Next consider what lies beneath the concrete references – what is the poet asking us to think about? You need to trace the abstract ideas represented by the content. Ask yourself what connections the poet wants you to make – what kinds of underlying **ideas** or **themes** are being introduced?

Look at the layout of the poem on the page and try to identify any notable features of **poetic form**. Think about the way in which the features you note seem to underpin the literal content and the themes.

Finally, it is necessary to explore the **style**, the words on the page and their organisation. Identify and comment on the specific linguistic and structural elements of the poem, and the literary and rhetorical devices. You need to consider the effects created by the features you see, and to understand how they influence the reader. Look at the ways in which layers of meaning are built up.

This kind of approach encourages you to consider the range of responses that make up a critical appreciation. Personal engagement is an important element of poetry because it is such a private experience; when we need to analyse texts, however, it is necessary to combine the personal with an objective assessment of the ways in which literary and linguistic approaches are used to convey meaning.

A guide to analysis

Some people may find it useful to have a more specific guide to tackling a poem. The following framework suggests the kind of questions you can ask yourself as you read. Use it as a method for taking notes after first reading the poem through to familiarise yourself with the content.

CONTEXT
(a) Are there any significant historical, cultural or contemporary events that may have influenced the poet or his or her attitudes to the subject matter?
(b) How do the literary influences of the period affect the poet's writing? – genre? content? structure? language? style?
(c) What is significant about the kind of English in which the poem is written? – period in which it is written? vocabulary? spelling? grammar? pronunciation? regional variation? personal variation?
(d) How does the poem fit into the chronology of the poet's work? – sources? content? form? style? structure?

CONTENT AND IDEAS
(a) What does the title tell us about the poem? – literal? symbolic? its relationship to the content?
(b) What is the literal subject matter of the poem? – a person? a place? an event? a particular occasion? ordinary experiences? social comment? emotions? the nature of art and the artist? something else?
(c) What viewpoint are we given? – the poet's? a character's? a subjective or objective narrator? changing viewpoints?
(d) What are the underlying ideas/themes? – childhood? love? nature? religion? death? society and its values? imagination? change? doubt? social comment? or something else?

FORM

(a) How does the poem look on the page? – its shape? the use of stanzas? the length and number of lines? any other typographical features?

(b) What kind of verse form does the poet use? – end rhyme? blank verse? free verse?

(c) Does the poem have a conventional poetic form? – sonnet? haiku? villanelle? elegy? lyric? ode? pastoral? narrative?

(d) Is there anything noticeable about the presentation of the content? – building towards a climax or anticlimax? narrative structure and development? dramatic interaction? developing an argument?

(e) How do the poem's physical structure and form affect the reader? – the link between form and meaning?

DISTINCTIVE FEATURES

(a) Is there any evidence of influence from particular literary genres?

(b) Does the poet use end of line punctuation? – end-stopped lines? run-on lines?

(c) What kind of rhythm does the poet create? – stressed and unstressed syllables? metrical feet? pauses?

(d) How do the poetic features you have identified underpin the meaning?

STYLE: DICTION

(a) What kind of tone does the poet develop? – the poet's attitude to his/her material? the relationship between poet/reader? modifiers used to develop the atmosphere or mood?

(b) What kind of words does the poet choose? – formal/informal? colloquial? descriptive? evaluative? reflective? elevated? subject specific? or a mixture?

(c) Are any words of particular significance? – the connotations of words? lexical sets? subject specific words? terms of address/naming?

(d) Does any particular word class play an important part in the poem? – concrete/abstract/proper nouns? pronouns? noun/adjective/verb modifiers? stative/dynamic/active/modal/passive verbs?

(e) Are there any unusual words? – collocations? disrupted collocations? dialect? neologisms? archaic or obsolete words?

(f) How does the diction influence the reader's response to the poem?

STYLE: GRAMMAR

(a) Are the phrase structures interesting? – noun phrases? verb phrases? adjective or adverb phrases?

(b) What is the time scale? – present/past? progressive? future time?

(c) What kinds of sentences does the poet use? – simple/compound/complex? minor? finite/non-finite? mood?

(d) How are the sentences organised? – foregrounding? end focus? inversion? initial position conjunction? predicative phrases? ellipsis? parenthesis?

(e) How do the grammatical features help the poet to communicate the poem's meaning?

LITERARY AND RHETORICAL DEVICES

(a) What kind of sound patterning does the poet use? – alliteration? assonance? consonance? onomatopoeia? rhyme? plosives? fricatives? sibilance?

(b) What kind of imagery does the poet create? – literal? figurative?

(c) What devices does the poet use to develop the figurative imagery? – simile? metaphor? personification? symbolism?

(d) What kind of rhetorical patterning does the poet use? – repetition? tripling? parallelism? listing? antithesis?

(e) How do the literary and rhetorical devices underpin the poem's meaning?

* * *

This framework should be used with sensitivity – if a particular poem does not use certain approaches or devices, you do not need to consider them. Be discriminating and decide which sections are relevant to the text you are studying. Feature spotting, identifying approaches and techniques without commenting on their function, is meaningless. Saying that the poet has used particular techniques without discussing the effects created will make your writing list-like and will not enable you to demonstrate understanding. In order to show that you have a real appreciation of a poem, you must comment on the effects created by the literary and linguistic features you identify, showing how these help the poet to communicate meaning.

It is important to use the STATEMENT-EVIDENCE-ANALYSIS approach when making notes, writing essays or discussing your ideas. Be prepared to start with a statement that expresses a relevant point, provide an appropriate example from the text to support your point, and then analyse the effects. This will ensure that your understanding of poetry is complete – it will demonstrate your ability to recognise key poetic features and show how these help the poet to convey meaning.

Getting started

Whether reading for pleasure, tackling a set text, or preparing for an unseen practical criticism examination, it is important to remember that none of the areas listed above work in isolation. When a poet writes a poem, or you read it, poetic form and structure, diction and grammar, rhetorical and literary devices are all an integral part of the overall effect. The poet has made choices in order to best communicate the poem's ideas and it is your job to try and understand how this process of communication takes place. While addressing each area separately in the process of studying a poem, ultimately your aim is to understand how the approaches and techniques come together in the final product.

Poetry takes the material of everyday life and creates from it a means by which we can understand ourselves and our world more fully. It encourages us to see things and feel things in a way that both intensifies and reveals experience. As the American writer Maya Angelou (1928–) says: *Poetry can tell us what human beings are. It can tell us why we stumble and fall and how, miraculously, we can stand up.* In your reading, try to enjoy the experience poetry gives us – feel your way through the words to the meaning; explore the structure to understand the poetic process; and immerse yourself in the sounds and images that convey the poet's vision.

Part II

Key poets

Introduction: English poets and the English poetic tradition

Having considered the decisions a poet can make about the content, language, style and form of a poem, it is useful to understand how poets develop a personal style or approach to writing poetry, how they are influenced by a particular period or literary movement, and how the poetry they compose relates to their contemporaries. Part II will address these areas, looking at some of the poets who have made a significant contribution to the development of a distinctive English poetic tradition.

Inevitably, the male-dominated traditional literary canon does not show the complete picture, but the poets discussed in Part II represent those most commonly occurring in anthologies and on examination syllabuses. The aim is to introduce the general reader to some of the important figures in English poetry, and to give those studying an English Literature course a critical approach to some of the poets they will be asked to read. The focus is on language and style, and the way in which poets create meaning.

You may not always agree with the readings of particular poems in this book, but they are offered as a starting point for discussion. Each reader brings a different set of experiences and knowledge to a text and this means that we all have a distinctive personal relationship with what we read. Poets recognise this themselves: for W.B. Yeats, meaning was different for everyone and he avoided interpreting his poems because he didn't want to limit what they suggested to individual readers.

Reading poetry is an active process and, as we engage with the text, we may see meanings and make connections of which the poet was not consciously aware as she or he wrote. What you must remember is that the key to effective literary criticism lies in your ability to support your argument with reference to the text's language, structure and style. Sometimes you may be clinging to meaning by the skin of your teeth, but that is part of the excitement – and when you do find understanding, recognise a familiar experience, or feel 'that's just what I think', when you do see how a poet has communicated meaning, then you will appreciate the power of poetry to move us emotionally and engage us intellectually.

You can approach Part II in a number of ways. You may be reading a particular poem and want some help in interpreting it; you may wish to gain an understanding of an individual poet; you may require some background information on a specific period or literary movement; or you may wish to develop a general picture of the way in which English poetry has evolved.

The contents list and index will help you to find your way around the book. Use them to support your wider reading of poetry and literary criticism. The background information can help you to develop your knowledge of the social, historical and cultural context in which poets were writing, while the activities can help you to refine your analytical approach to poetry. Use the framework suggested in Chapter 7, 'A guide to analysis', to make notes on the poems in the activities before tackling the question. This will help you to become familiar with the source material and will ensure that you develop effective critical skills. The aim is to apply the practical information of Part I within a broader context in order to understand how different poets communicate with their readers.

▼ 8 The beginnings of the English poetic tradition

From the arrival of the Romans in 55BC to the eleventh century, Britain was invaded over and over again. It was a time dominated by change and confusion – the invaders brought with them their own languages, laws, customs and religions and this inevitably affected life in Britain. Cultural, linguistic, legal and religious practices were changed or modified by the new settlers, contributing to the rich diversity of the English language and its culture today.

The literary context

It is against this background of invasion, and cultural and linguistic blending that the first written tradition of English poetry emerges. After a 'dark age' in which there are only a handful of scattered inscriptions, Old English manuscripts began to appear alongside Latin religious texts – translations and paraphrases of books of the Old and New Testaments, legends of saints, and devotional and didactic pieces.

The arrival of the Roman missionaries led by Augustine in 597 marked the beginning of the literary age in Britain. The growth of Christianity had significant effects: it played a part in establishing a unified state and introduced book art to the Anglo-Saxons. Texts such as the Lindisfarne Gospels (AD698) and the Book of Kells (AD810) clearly demonstrate the influence of both the Mediterranean (the Roman source of the texts' Christianity) and the Celtic (their Irish origins).

Great libraries at Wearmouth-Jarrow, Hexham, Malmesbury and Canterbury collected and housed fine manuscripts covering a range of subjects: historical, moral and religious. Initially, the historical texts tended to record sagas of legendary heroes, but later they became an authentic record of key events like *The Anglo-Saxon Chronicle* (AD891–1154). Writings such as *The Catholic Homilies* (AD990) and *The Lives of the Saints* (AD991) by Archbishop Alfric and a translation of Boethius' *Consolation of Philosophy* (AD878) by King Alfred provided a moral outlook on life, while Cædmon's *Song of Creation* (AD670) paraphrased the scriptures in verse.

Anglo-Saxon literature was also rich in a poetry that was pagan in origin, but often overlaid with Christian sentiments. Much of the surviving verse has a religious or didactic focus, but so much was destroyed during invasions, that we can only guess at its original range. In the four surviving tenth-century manuscripts, biblical subjects, heroic ideals and a concern with the transience of life are recurring themes; the tone is often tragic, with religious hope offered as a means of overcoming the struggle of life.

Skilled poets probably composed Anglo-Saxon poetry spontaneously for public performance, using well-known material, formulaic patterns and stock language. Linguistic and structural features made the verse memorable, but in some cases written versions were ultimately made of the original oral poetry. From these we can identify a number of structural features: each line is divided into two halves, each consisting of two stressed and a varying number of unstressed syllables. Although separated by a space, each half is linked by alliteration of the stressed syllables. In later poems, rhyme is used as an additional decoration.

Lexical patterns work alongside the structural patterns, contributing to the dignified and rhetorical effect of Old English verse. The two half-lines are often linked semantically, so that the second half paraphrases the meaning of the first. Synonyms are used, avoiding repetition and meeting the demands of the alliterative patterning. Because poets drew on a stock of metrical and linguistic units, the same line can occur in different poems. Words and phrases are often used figuratively, adding to the richness of the poetic vocabulary, and it is this that makes the poetry so important. Prose works like the *Anglo-Saxon Chronicle* can tell us about significant events, and the grammar and general word stock of the time, but it is in the poetry that we see a more personal and vivid insight into the Anglo-Saxon way of seeing the world.

In the medieval period, literary traditions were mainly oral and communal. Much literature was communicated by word of mouth, changing as it was passed from one region to another, and across time, with individual authors having little or no influence. People did not read alone, but enjoyed social 'performances' of literature – in a medieval context, the word 'read' actually meant 'to read aloud'. There is evidence that many stories, plays and songs were never recorded in written form, but were part of the repertoire of travelling professional entertainers or resident amateurs.

After the alliterative and metrical poems of the Old English period, the earliest poets of the twelfth and thirteenth centuries composed religious and didactic verse. Using French models, poets replaced the Old English tradition with simple stanzas of short rhyming couplets, 8 or 6 syllable lines and internal rhyme. The beginning of the fourteenth century saw poems of romance and secular society – instead of spiritual reflection, poets focused on stories of courtly love, of saints and sinners with examples and digressions exploring contemporary notions of astronomy and geography as well as religious ideals.

With the dominance of French verse, there was a gap in the English poetic tradition. By the middle of the fourteenth century, however, foreign and English literary features had been brought together in a new distinctive English verse tradition. It combined the Old English free stress alliterative half-lines with the French model of syllabic rhyming couplets, and poets began to compose works in an English that more closely resembled contemporary manners of speech and thought.

Two distinct types of verse can be identified during the second half of the fourteenth century. In the West Midlands, poems like *Gawayne and the Green Knight* and *Piers Plowman* adopted an unrhymed alliterative form. In the South, a separate poetic culture emerged with Chaucer (1343–1400) as its most famous representative. The use of rhyme, a varied syllable line and a five-stress couplet (a form of blank verse) distinguish Chaucer's verse from that written in the West Midlands. By this time, the literary centre had returned to London and Chaucer's writing added prestige to the emerging standard form of the English language.

Religious verse

Religious verse is common throughout the Old English and medieval periods – it provided poets with a means of exploring spiritual and moral concerns through a popular literary form that did not alienate their wide-ranging audience. The message is often conveyed through the character of an ordinary man recounting a particular experience in order to share his newfound understanding with others.

Of the four surviving tenth-century manuscripts, two contain religious verses: *The Junius Book*, written and illuminated in AD994, contains biblical poems; *The Vercelli Book*, compiled in the 980s, is a collection of religious verse including the dramatic monologue *The Dream of the Rood*. Fragments of this lyrical poem have been found inscribed on the Ruthwell Cross, a stone monument dating from about 700, which suggests that either the poem already existed or that the inscription inspired it.

The poem is made up of 156 lines and uses traditional OE half-line divisions and alliterative stress patterns. It is one of the first examples of devotional poetry, a **dream vision**, in which Christ's cross speaks – in many ways, it represents the beginning of the dramatic monologue tradition in English poetry. Some critics believe that it may be the work of the sceop or minstrel Cynewulf, written at some point in the eighth century, recreating the story of his own conversion.

The content of the poem focuses on the poet's dream and its significance. Having introduced the idea of a dream he desires to share, he goes on to describe in detail the wonderful tree of which he has dreamt.

> Hwæt, ic swefna cyst   secgan wylle
> hwæt mē gemætte   tō midre nihte
> syð þan reordberend   reste wunedon
> þūhte mē þæt ic gesāwe   syllicre trēow

Oh, I want to tell of the best dream that I dreamed at midnight when men stayed at rest. I thought that I saw a wonderful tree . . .

He sees it covered with gold and jewels, but as it streams with blood, he is aware of its suffering as well as its beauty and symbolic significance. The tone changes when the tree begins to speak. Its words recreate the Crucifixion and implicitly establish the link between itself and Christ. Only when its status is recognised do men learn to honour it as the link between life on earth and eternal life in heaven. The dream is a vision that must be shared so that others, like the dreamer, understand the importance of the cross. It encourages the poet to reflect on the tree's symbolism, and to long for a reunion with friends who have died.

The language of the poem is rich and the poet seems consciously aware of the stylistic effects he wishes to create. There is little evidence of formulaic linguistic structures or of paraphrase in this particular poem, and this draws attention to its originality. Synonyms do, however, provide variety and show the richness of Old English as a language of poetry: *trēow* (tree), *beam(a)*, *beacen* (beacon) and *sigebeam* (victory-tree), for instance, are all used to represent the 'tree'; and *molde* (earth) and *mære ġesċeaft* (glorious creation) convey a sense of the human world. Superlatives like *cyst* (the best) and *beorhtost* (brightest) are used to emphasise the symbolic significance of the tree; and phrases like *foldan sceatum* (at the earth's corners), *for ġesċeaft* (for all time) and *ofer moldan* (over all the earth) draw attention to the extent of the cross's power. The poet has used such language to reveal not only one man's dream, but its significance to mankind as a whole.

The Dream of the Rood is notable for the simplicity of its devotional narrative, but also for the power of the imagery that is used to dramatise the dream and its message. In describing the tree as a *beacen* and a *sigebeam*, the poet suggests that it has powers beyond those normally associated with natural things. In personifying it, he encourages the reader to see it as a spiritual guide: because Jesus died on the cross, and because the cross suffered as he did, it becomes mankind's link to salvation. The personification of the cross creates a personal voice that engages the audience.

Another strength of *The Dream of the Rood* lies in its range of styles. The tree's description of the crucifixion is stark and dramatic, while the dreamer's introduction and conclusion are more didactic. This represents the dual purpose of the poet who aims both to entertain and to raise the religious concerns of the day.

For a modern reader tackling the poem in the original Old English, the word order is unusual. Because it is an inflected language, word endings rather than word positions indicate the role of each word in a sentence. This means that readers have to rearrange words in order to achieve an understandable contemporary English version. The main alterations come in the relocation of the subject and the verb: in the Old English extract, other phrases often separate these. The position of modifiers is also recognisably different. Many are placed in the final position in phrases like *swefna cyst* (of dream the best) and *beama beorhtost* (of trees brightest).

* * *

Religious verse in the Middle English period often draws on the tradition of the **medieval sermon**. It interweaves the ideas of abstract theology with a satirical attack on society that appealed to the general audience. The fourteenth-century *Piers Plowman* by William Langland, for instance, mixes traditional religious teachings with a vivid picture of contemporary life, exposing what Langland saw as the corruption of the state, the Church and society in general. Starting in the 1360s, Langland continued to revise and add to the poem for the next 25 years.

The content focuses on the central character of Piers, an honest and hardworking peasant. Langland uses him as an Everyman figure, an individual based in a specific time and place who is representative of us all. The use of concrete descriptions, possibly based on Langland's own experience of rural life, gives the poem a physical and visual quality.

The structure establishes a sequence of waking episodes that are separated by the dreams or visions Piers experiences. While the former are grounded in reality and allow Langland to introduce key themes and develop a sense of Piers as a real man, the dream sections create a dramatic contrast. The two strands allow Langland to create an overall narrative framework within which he can develop his poem as an allegory – a story with an underlying meaning in which abstract ideas are often personified.

The poem uses some of the features of Old English verse, but adapts them to meet the demands of the Middle English tradition. The alliterative half-lines find their model in Old English, but Langland creates a balanced contrast between the two halves by building to a climax in the first part and then allowing it to fall away. The dream vision of Old English poetry also reappears, but without the decorative poetic vocabulary. Touches of humour replace the over-riding theme of transience that dominated so much of the Old English verse surviving today.

Activity 8.1

> **How does Langland vary his approach to mirror changes in his purpose in the following extracts from *Piers Plowman*?**
>
> You may like to think about: the language and its connotations, style, imagery and structure.

EXTRACT 1 – PROLOGUE (ll.1–10)

1	In a somer seson, whan softe was the sonne,	One summer season, when the sun was mild,
	I shoop me into shroudes as I a sheep were,	I dressed myself in clothes as if I were a shepherd,
	In habite as an heremite unholy of werkes,	In the habit of a hermit who roams outside his cell,
	Wente wide in this world wondres to here.	Went far and wide in this world to hear wonders.
5	Ac on a May morwenynge on Malverne hilles	But on a May morning on the Malvern Hills,
	Me bifel a ferly, of Fairye me thoghte.	A marvellous thing happened to me, from fairy land I thought.
	I was wery forwandred and wente me to reste	I was tired from my wanderings and went to rest
	Under a brood bank by a bourne syde;	Under a broad bank by the side of a stream;
	And as I lay and lenede and loked on the watres,	And as I lay and leaned over and looked into the water,
10	I slombred into a slepyng, it sweyed so murye.	I fell into a sleep it made so sweet a sound.

Thanne gan I meten a merveillous swevene –	Then I began to dream a marvellous dream
That I was in a wildernesse, wiste I nevere where.	That I was in a wilderness, I never knew where.
Ac as I biheeld into the eest an heigh to the sonne,	But as I looked to the east, high up towards the sun,
I seigh a tour on a toft trieliche ymaked,	I saw a tower splendidly built on a hill,
15 A deep dale bynethe, a dongeon therinne,	A deep valley beneath with a dungeon in it,
With depe diches and derke and dredfulle of sighte.	With deep and dark ditches which were dreadul to see.
A fair feeld ful of folk fond I ther bitwene –	I found a beautiful field full of people between them –
Of alle manere of men, the meene and the riche,	All kinds of men, the poor and the rich,
Werchynge and wandrynge as the world asketh.	Working and wandering as the world requires.

EXTRACT 3 – PASSUS I (ll.1–2, 12–16, 59–64)

20 What this mountaigne bymeneth and the merke dale	What this mountain and dark valley means
And the feld ful of folk, I shal yow faire shewe.	And this field full of people, I shall show you clearly.

. . .

'The tour upon the toft', quod she, 'Truthe is therinne,	'The tower on the hill,' she said, 'Truth is in there,
And wolde that ye wroughte as his word techeth.	And He wishes that you would do as His word taught.
For he is fader of feith and formed yow alle	Because He is the father of faith and created you all
25 Bothe with fel and with face and yaf yow fyve wittes	With both skin and face and gave you five senses
For to worshipe hym therwith while that ye ben here.'	With which to worship Him while you are here.'

. . .

'That dongeon in the dale that dredful is of sighte –	'That dungeon in the valley that looks so dreadful –
What may it bemeene, madame, I yow biseche?'	What does it mean, lady? I beg you to tell me.'
'That is the castel of care – whoso comth therinne	That is the Castle of Sorrow – whoever comes there
30 May banne that he born was to bodi or to soule!	May curse the fact that he was born, body and soul!
Therinne wonyeth a wight that Wrong is yhote,	There dwells a creature called Wrong,
Fader of falshede – and founded it hymselve.	Father of falsehood – and who founded it (the dungeon) himself.

Commentary

In the opening lines of the Prologue to *The Vision of Piers Plowman*, Langland fulfils all the requirements of narrative: he sets the time and place, introduces his main character and establishes the focus of the plot, building up the narrative detail we need to be able to engage with the text. We know the time – it is summer in the month of May and it is warm. The connotations of *somer seson* and *softe* ensure that the tone is positive. References to the natural world then build up a concrete sense of place through the proper noun *Malverne hilles* (l.5) and the phrases *a brood bank by a bourne side* (l.8) and *the waters* (l.9). The tranquillity of the setting is an appropriate backdrop against which Piers can drift into his dream, allowing the poet to explore his moral themes.

Langland uses a first person narrative and this encourages the reader or audience to identify with the poem. We are not given any explicit description of the main character, but references to his clothing indicate something of his position in society and his nature. The concrete nouns *shroudes* (l.2) and *habite* (l.3) suggest that he is clothed in ordinary rather than elegant clothes and this is reinforced by the similes that identify him with a shepherd (*as I a sheep were*, l.2) and a hermit (*as an heremite unholy of werkes*, l.3). The connotations of simplicity and moral integrity associated with these two symbolic figures develop our sense of Piers as a decent, ordinary man. He becomes an Everyman whose experience will have significance for the lives of the readers.

Alongside the concrete imagery of the landscape and the speaker's appearance, Langland also establishes the main movement of the plot. Physical action is going to be kept to a minimum because the dream visions will provide the heart of the poem. In the first section, we see dynamic verbs like *shoop* (dressed, l.2) and *Wente* (l.5) that give an account of the speaker's actions. These lead us towards the less active *Me bifel* (l.6) that removes responsibility for action from the speaker, leaving him as the fortunate recipient of the marvellous thing that takes place. This sense of the speaker's passivity is reinforced by the connotations of the verbs at the end of the passage. Preparing us for the movement from the concrete to the dream world, the verbs *reste* (l.7), *lay, lenede, loked,* and *slombred* (ll.9–10) suggest the speaker's inactivity, and in this state of mind he is open to the experience of his dream.

In form, the alliterative half-lines are reminiscent of the Old English tradition. The patterning of the sounds creates cohesion, and contributes to the general mood of the opening. The poet uses sibilance (ll.1–2, 10), the soft fricatives /h/ (l.3) and /f/ (ll.6–7), and the approximants /w/ (l.4, 7) and /l/ (l.9) to develop a mellow and restful tone that is appropriate to establish the languor in which Piers can drift off into his dream.

The waking episodes are juxtaposed with sleeping episodes where visions introduce the didactic material of the poem, creating a symbolic world in which the poet can explore his moral themes. The concrete world is replaced by an allegorical one in which personified abstract concepts and symbolic figures dominate the dream landscape.

In the next nine lines of the Prologue (ll.11–19), Langland introduces Piers' first dream in which he learns about the Tower of Truth, the Castle of Sorrow –

where Wrong, the Father of Falsehood, lives – and the human world that lies between them.

The May morning is replaced by something more sinister in the beginning of this first dream sequence. Piers is now in a *wildernesse* (l.12) which lacks any of the positive descriptions of the opening lines. There is still a sun, but it is no longer *softe*; where the Malvern Hills were recognisable, this landscape is unfamiliar (*wiste I nevere where*). The concrete nouns (*tour, toft, dale, dongeon, diches*) clearly mark out distinctive features of the scene before Piers, but these are not made to seem pleasant, as the earlier landscape was. The harsh plosives (/d/ and /t/) and the negative connotations of the modifiers linked to these nouns create a very different mood. The tower may be *trieliche* (splendidly, l.14) built, but the dungeons and ditches are described using words with negative connotations like *depe, derke* and *dredfulle*.

The focus of the extract is on what Piers can see before him and the verbs are therefore quite different. The emphasis now is on the fact that the speaker is an observer and verbs like *biheeld* (l.13) and *seigh* (l.14) draw attention to this. The passage is, in effect, an asyndetic list of the landmarks Piers sees (ll.14–17) as his eye roves from the *tour* to the people, *alle manere of men*. The effect is cinematic – we can visualise the scene from the words on the page.

This landscape is one of opposites where the first was harmonious. The juxtaposition of the *toft* and the *dale*, and the *tour* and the *dongeon* (ll.14–15) mark this place out as one of extremes. The antithesis is developed in the description of the people who are *the meene* (poor) and *the riche* (l.18). The use of opposition here prepares the reader for the allegorical significance of the landscape and the people. This is no longer part of the real world, but a symbolic backdrop against which Piers will learn about life.

Where Extract 2 introduces us to a new landscape and prepares us for the lesson that Piers will learn, Extract 3 is didactic. Langland explicitly records the meaning of the allegory through the character of Lady Holy Church, a personification of true faith.

The movement from the descriptive observation of the earlier extracts to explicit instruction is marked by a change in tone. Although drawing on Piers' viewpoint on two occasions (ll. 20–1, 27–8), we are now given a different narrative perspective with the introduction of a new character. The first person narrative is replaced by direct speech, which, although apparently recounted by Piers, has an air of objectivity. It is a detached and authoritative voice and, instead of the surprise and wonderment of Piers, we now experience understanding and knowledge of the landscape and its inhabitants.

Although bound by the physical elements of the landscape, the *tour upon the toft* (l.13) and *the castel* (l.29), the language is now dominated by abstract rather than concrete nouns. The personified *Truthe . . . fader of feith* (ll.22–4) and *Wrong . . . Fader of falshede* (ll.31–2) provide us with the central antithesis at the heart of the extract. They represent the opposition between good and bad crucial to religious teachings, and other antithetical language develops this. References to the physical elements of earthly life (*fel and face* l.25, *bodi* l.30) are balanced by abstract language (*five wittes* l.25, *soule* l.30) as spiritual insight replaces description.

The religious connotations of verbs such as *formed* (l.24) and *to worshipe* (l.26), and the didactic *techeth* (l.23) explicitly draw attention to the instructive nature of this extract. The two symbolic landscapes offer humanity the choice between God and the Devil, between good and evil. In Piers' description of *alle manere of men* (l.18) stranded between the tower and the dungeon, Langland visually represents this choice.

The approach and purpose of each extract is quite distinct. The first has a narrative function, introducing us to the narrative elements of time, place, character and events through a first person account that is firmly based in the physical world. The second is more explicitly descriptive, presenting us, through the structure of a dream vision, with a new landscape that will be given symbolic meaning in the third extract. The allegorical interpretation of what Piers sees by a detached and authoritative character changes the way in which we respond to the text: like Piers, our wonder and bewilderment are replaced by understanding.

Old English heroic verse and medieval romance

Heroic verse and the medieval romance offered a different kind of entertainment. All the verse in this period tends to be both didactic and entertaining, but where the religious verse explicitly explores spiritual themes, these more popular forms had a less blatant didactic content. The unambiguously instructive sections of religious verse are replaced by a moral that emerges as an integral part of the story's denouement. It represents the narrative climax in which the poet's lesson is firmly embedded.

Old English **heroic verse** focuses on the nature of society and its leadership. It uses background physical details to give a sense of reality, and develops a story celebrating the heroic life of an individual and exploring his role in society as a leader. The main protagonist is characterised through his actions and the poem inevitably ends with a heroic death as the climax to the hero's life. The hero's growing self-awareness and his recognition of the nature of the world provide the didactic moral of the poem. We are reminded that while heroic deeds ensure a hero is remembered after death, life must be lived with an awareness of God's will and the afterlife. One of the dominant themes, common to much poetry of the time, is that of mutability – the transience and fickleness of life.

Beowulf is perhaps the most famous remaining heroic poem of the Old English period. It was probably written between 680 and 790, but is preserved in a manuscript made by scribes in about 1000. The main protagonist, Beowulf, the noble Geat subject of the historical king Hygelac, seems to have no basis in reality. Mixing folktales, legends, historical events and Christian beliefs, it tells the story of Beowulf's legendary rise, linking him to heroes of the past. It also provides a commentary on specific historical events, and on the ways in which Beowulf affected the people around him.

The poem is not made up of a continuous narrative, but focuses on Beowulf's three greatest heroic deeds: the killing of the giant Grendel to free the Danes; the pursuit and killing of Grendel's enraged mother after she has raided the Danes' royal hall and killed Æschere in revenge for the death of her son; and the killing of the treasure-guarding dragon who has ravaged the country. It then concludes with an account of Beowulf's death. The three narrative incidents are surrounded by digressions. Some evoke the physical background in a vivid way, or tell us about Old English courtly life, while others mention real international events. Such digressions allow the poet to develop running threads through the 3182 lines of verse.

The triple structure of three fights with three monsters is traditional, and forms the basis for the didactic element of the poem – each incident symbolises a growth in Beowulf's understanding. His initial self-reliance is replaced by doubts about the value and longevity of his physical strength; his self-questioning is then ultimately replaced by a recognition that despite the inevitability of old age, physical weakness and mental despair, God will provide spiritual strength. The final section of the poem is explicitly didactic since it culminates in Hrothgar's, the King of the Danes, sermon.

Because Beowulf's struggles have a moral as well as narrative purpose, places and characters in the poem often have a symbolic significance. The hall, Heorot, for instance, is used as a symbol of heroic society – by protecting it from the marauding mother of Grendel, Beowulf is defending the centre of heroic society from destruction by evil. Grendel is associated with darkness and evil: his home is the antithesis of Heorot. This juxtaposition allows the poet to develop a sequence of contrasts: the court represents the security of community life while Grendel's home is seen as dangerous and solitary; he is a force of evil where the court represents good; Grendel's life is marked by chaos where Heorot is representative of order.

The style is similar to that of other Old English verse: formulaic phrases enable the poet to meet the demands of the strict metrical pattern; synonyms create variety and richness in the vocabulary; and poetic words occurring only in verse are indicators of the distinctive Old English poetic tradition.

Activity 8.2

Explore the style and purpose of the following extracts from Michael Alexander's modern verse translation of *Beowulf*.

You may like to consider: the content and ideas; the use of language; and imagery.

EXTRACT 1 – BEOWULF TELLS THE COURT OF HIS BATTLE WITH GRENDEL'S MOTHER

1   '. . . Not easily did I survive
       the fight under water; I performed this deed
       not without a struggle. Our strife had ended
       at its very beginning if God had not saved me.
5   Nothing could I perform in that fight with Hrunting,
       it had no effect, fine weapon though it be.

But the Guide of mankind granted me the sight
– He often brings aid to the friendless –
of a huge Giant-sword hanging on the wall,
10   ancient and shining – and I snatched up the weapon.
When the hour afforded, in that fight I slew
the keepers of the hall. The coiling-patterned
blade burnt all away, as the blood sprang forth,
the hottest ever shed; the hilt I took from them.
15   So I avenged the violent slaughter
and outrages against the Danes; indeed it was fitting.
Now, I say, you may sleep in Heorot
free from care – (ll.1655–72)

EXTRACT 2 – THE NARRATOR OFFERS ADVICE TO BEOWULF

Beloved Beowulf, best of warriors,
20   resist this deadly taint, take what is better,
your lasting profit. Put away arrogance,
noble fighter! The noon of your strength
shall last for a while now, but in a little time
sickness or a sword will strip it from you:
25   either enfolding flame or a flood's billow
or a knife-stab or the stoop of a spear
or the ugliness of age; or your eyes' brightness
lessens and grows dim. Death shall soon
have beaten you then, O brave warrior!   (ll.1758–68)

Commentary

While the first extract can be identified as coming from one of the **narrative sections** of the poem, the second is explicitly **didactic**, providing both the reader and Beowulf with moral advice. The content of each is therefore quite different. Extract 1 is made up of a formal speech by Beowulf to the assembled court of Heorot. It focuses on the sequence of events making up the fight, on God's role in the victory and on the peace that Beowulf's success has brought to the court. We are aware that order has now replaced chaos. The second extract is quite different since it moralises about the way in which a great warrior like Beowulf should react to his victory. It reminds us that life is transient and that since death is inescapable, it is important to look ahead to what will follow.

The themes are typical of Old English poetry although the narrative and didactic sections approach them in different ways. In lines 1–18, the poet draws on the tradition of the heroic battle and the return of order after disorder. Alongside these human accomplishments lies the recognition of God's role in victory. In lines 19–29, the narrative is underpinned by the recurring themes of the transience of life and the superior values of heaven and the afterlife.

The language of the two extracts is quite different because of the distinct function each serves within the poem as a whole. The first is dominated by the language of battle. The synonyms *weapon* (ll.6, 10), *Giant-sword* (l.9), *blade* (l.13) and *hilt* (l.14), and the nouns *struggle*, *strife* (l.3), *fight* (l.5), *slaughter* (l.15) and *outrages* (l.16) emphasise the scene of conflict and chaos. The second extract, on the other hand, includes phrases like *this deadly taint* (l.20) and *lasting profit* (l.21) and abstract nouns like *arrogance* (l.21) and *strength* (l.22), which are indicative of the philosophical approach of the narrator's voice. In the first extract, the only similar reference comes in Beowulf's recognition of God's part in his victory as *the Guide of mankind* (l.7).

Modifiers in Extract 1 are used to create a dramatic atmosphere by providing physical description. The sword that fails Beowulf is *fine* (l.6), but this particular battle requires something more – the Giant-sword is *huge* (l.9), *ancient and shining* (l.10) and *coiling-patterned* (l.12). The juxtaposition of modifiers like *violent* (l.15) with *free* (l.18) draws attention to the reinstatement of order. In Extract 2, many of the modifiers are used to name Beowulf – he is *Beloved, best* (l.19), *noble* (l.22) and *brave* (l.29). These positive epithets are, however, juxtaposed with his mortality and his ultimate physical weakness.

As may be expected, figurative language is more prominent in the second extract. In conveying its didactic message, metaphors like the *deadly taint* (l.24) to represent the sins of life and *lasting profit* (l.25) to represent eternal life provide the reader with a concrete image to reinforce the abstract message. Death is also given a physical presence since he is personified as a future adversary for Beowulf (ll.28–9) – and in this battle Beowulf will not be victorious. The metaphor of Beowulf at the *noon of* [his] *strength* (l. 22) is ambiguous: while it could be seen as describing him at the height of his powers, it is also indicative of the fact that these powers will wane.

In form, this Modern English version does not follow the strict syllabic pattern of the original Old English verse, but attempts to retain some of the alliterative patterning and the balance of the half-lines. Punctuation often divides lines into distinct halves (ll. 2, 3, 12–14, 19, 27–9), and alliterative patterning provides structural links between the two halves (*struggle/strife* l.3; *blade/blood* l.13); *flame/flood* l.25; *dim/ Death* (l.28). Listing is used rhetorically to emphasise a point: the syndetic list of the images of death (ll.24–8) emphasises human vulnerability – even great men will eventually be subject to *sickness*, or *sword*, or *enfolding flame, a flood's billow* (l.25), *a knife-stab, the stoop of a spear* (l.26) or *the ugliness of age* (l.27–8).

* * *

Romance was a popular form in the Middle Ages and, like heroic verse, any didactic content tended to be incidental. In the twelfth and thirteenth centuries, English writers often used French models. The main focus was an adventure story in which the characters were fictional and the backdrop was the courtly world of heroic deeds, chivalry and gallant love. Many romances used the framework of a knight on a quest – underlying the physical journey was a symbolic one in which the main protagonist had to face a sequence of moral and spiritual tests. The key events often involved supernatural encounters, enabling the writer to emphasise that the world of the poem was remote from the real world.

The most famous romance still surviving in the English tradition is *Sir Gawain and the Green Knight*, written in the fourteenth century in the North-West Midlands dialect. Like *Piers Plowman*, it uses the Old English alliterative metre with 4 stresses and a varied number of unstressed syllables. The first half of the line generally carries the main weight of the meaning, and there may be as many as three alliterating stress-words in it.

Features such as the harsh landscapes, violent events, grim humour and moral seriousness of Anglo-Saxon literature are continued, but the French influence is also evident. The use of stanzas with a refrain made up of 5 short lines (a bob), rhyme and the representation of the court and courtly love are typical of French romance. It is this interweaving of distinctive literary traditions that makes the Gawain poem so rich. We see the spirit of French romance alongside the heroic qualities of a saga; traditional Celtic beliefs overlaid by a Christian consciousness; rich description balanced by dramatic incidents.

Perhaps the most difficult thing about the *Gawain* text for the modern reader is the language in which it is written. It uses the North-West Midlands dialect in which some of the Old English runes appear alongside the Roman alphabet. In addition, the dialect contains many Scandinavian words that were later replaced and this means that a number of words are alien to us because they are now obsolete. The Norse *etaynez* (l.11), for instance, was replaced by 'giant' from the French 'géant'; *wormez* (l.8) was replaced by 'dragon' from the Latin 'draco'. The word order is also unlike contemporary English because inflections (word endings) are used to identify the function of a word in a sentence.

The content focuses on the adventures of Gawain, one of King Arthur's knights. On New Year's Day in the middle of the festivities, the arrival of a green man and his talk of beheading disrupts the harmony of the court. Gawain strikes off his head in a challenge and the severed head then tells Gawain that he must travel to the Green Chapel in one year to receive a return blow. The remainder of the poem focuses on Gawain's travels and on the physical and moral tests which he has to face.

He reaches a castle where he is welcomed by the lord and his young wife. Each day the lord goes out hunting while the lady tempts Gawain. In a bargain between the two men, Gawain has to give what he has received during the day in return for the lord's hunting trophies. However, when the lady gives Gawain a green girdle, which supposedly has the ability to protect him, he fails to declare it. He leaves the castle and journeys to the Green Chapel where the Green Knight draws blood on his third blow – not in return for his earlier beheading, but as payment for Gawain's failure to declare the green girdle. On his return to Arthur's court, Gawain tells his story honestly, recognising his own weaknesses and moral failings. Green girdles are then worn by Arthur's court in commemoration of his adventures: where he sees it as a symbol of his failings as a knight, the court wear it as a badge of honour.

The poem is typical of the romance genre in many ways. The appearance of an intruder who creates disorder is common, and the supernatural elements of the genre can be seen in Gawain's adventures and in the character of the Green Knight himself. He is an ambiguous figure, appearing as a human in his role as the lord of the castle and as a representative of the supernatural in Arthur's court and at the Green Chapel.

Civilised courtly life is juxtaposed with the wild natural background of the Green Knight and the Green Chapel and this creates the central dramatic tension of the poem. It is developed through the recurring theme of conflict in Gawain's adventures and in the links that emerge between the poem's events and the seasonal cycle.

Activity 8.3

How does the Gawain poet use literary and linguistic approaches to create a sense of place and mood?

You may like to think about: the language, style, imagery and structure.

EXTRACT 1 – FIT I (ll.37–49)

1	þis kyng lay at Camylot vpon Krystmasse	This king lay at Camelot at Christmas
	With mony luflych lorde, ledez of þe best –	With many courteous lords, knights of the best –
	Rekenly of þe Rounde Table alle þo rich breþer –	Worthily of the Round Table all those noble brothers –
	With rych reuel ory3t and rechles merþes.	With revelry in proper fashion and carefree amusements.
5	þer tournayed tulkes by tymez ful mony,	There knights rode in tournaments on very many occasions,
	Justed ful jolilé þise gentyle kni3tes,	Jousted very gallantly these noble knights,
	Syþen kayred to þe court, caroles to make;	Then rode to the court to dance and sing;
	For þer þe fest watz iliche ful fiften dayes,	For there the feast was kept up in full for fifteen days,
	With alle þe mete and þe mirþe þat men couþe avyse:	With all the food and merriment that men could devise:
10	Such glaum ande gle glorious to here	Such noise and revelry was glorious to hear
	Dere dyn vpon day, daunsyng on ny3tes –	A pleasant sound of revelry by day, dancing by nights –
	Al watz hap vpon he3e in hallez and chambrez	Everywhere was happiness on high in halls and rooms
	With lordez and ladies, as leuest him þo3t.	Among lords and ladies, most pleasant they thought

EXTRACT 2 – FIT II (ll.713–23)

	Mony klyff he ouerclambe in contrayez straunge.	Many a cliff he climbed over in strange countries.
15	Fer floten fro his frendez, fremedly he rydez.	Flown far from his friends, he rides as a stranger.
	At vche warþe oþer water þer þe wy3e passed	At each ford or stream where the knight passed
	He fonde a foo hym byfore, bot ferly hit were,	He found a foe in front of him, unless it were exceptional,
	And þat so foule and so felle þat fe3t hym byhode.	And that [foe]so ugly and so fierce that he must fight.

So mony meruayl bi mount þer þe mon fyndez

So many marvels among the hills there the man finds

20   Hit were to tore for to telle of þe tenþe dole.

It would be too difficult to tell of the tenth part [of them].

Sumwhyle wyth wormez he werrez and with wolues als,

Sometimes with dragons he fights and also with wolves,

Sumwhyle wyth wodwos þat woned in þe knarrez,

Sometimes with men of the woods who lived in the rocks,

Boþe wyth bullez and berez, and borez oþerquyle,

Both with bulls and bears, and boars at other times,

And etaynez þat hym anelede of þe heȝe felle.

And giants that pursued him about the high hills.

Commentary

The opening descriptions in Extract 1 set the scene at Arthur's court and establish the mood of gaiety and celebration. The proper nouns *Camylot* and *Krystmasse* (l.1) indicate place and time, while *þe Rounde Table* (l.3) is symbolic of the courtly values at the heart of the poem. The synonyms *lorde*, *ledez* (lords, knights l.2), *tulkes* (knights, l.5), *kniȝtes* (l.6) are used to people the scene with noble, chivalrous figures who, at first sight, are very different from the ungainly bizarre figure that is to disturb the court's peace.

The nouns *reuel*, *merþes* (revelry, amusements, l.4), *caroles* (courtly ring dances accompanied by singing, l.7), *fest* (feast, l.8), *mete* and *mirþe* (food, merriment, l.9) create the mood of festivity. Their positive connotations emphasise the harmony of the court and modifiers like *glorious* (l.10) and *Dere* (pleasant, l.11) enhance this. Other modifiers represent the chivalry of the courtly world – *luflych* (courteous, l.2), *Rekenly* (Worthily, l.3), *jolilé* and *gentyle* (gallantly, noble, l.6) describe the knights who are seen to be worthy in every way.

There is also, however, an undercurrent that prepares us for the disruption and testing of Gawain's values. The *glaum* and the *gle* (noise, revelry, l.10) and the *daunsyng* (l.11) by day and night suggest that the court has forgotten its true purpose as the representative of order. The modifier *rechles* (carefree, l.3) reinforces our sense of unease. The mood is one of excess and phrases like *ful mony* (very many, l.5), *ful fifteen dayes* (l.8), *alleþe mete and þe mirþe* (l.9) suggest that knightly values have been lost in the pleasure of celebration. It is the arrival of the Green Knight and his disruption of the celebrations that allows Gawain both to prove his individual bravery and to revive the chivalric values of the court.

The language of the first extract is clearly of the court and as such is representative of order. Similarly, the style also conveys a sense of pattern. The half-lines linked by alliteration, reminiscent of the Old English poetic tradition, create an internal balance: *luflych*, *lorde* and *ledez* (l.2); *kayred*, *court*, *caroles* (l.7). The synonyms are also an example of patterning drawn from the Old English tradition: *ledez* (l.2), *tulkes* (l.5) and *kniȝ tes* (l.6).

In Extract 2, the scene which is created on Gawain's journey establishes a different mood – the natural world is wild where the court is civilised; the inhabitants of the court are elegant and gracious while those of the natural world are ugly and savage; the superficiality of the New Year celebrations is juxtaposed with the dangers Gawain has to face.

The language as well as the content changes in this second extract. Concrete nouns like *klyf* (cliff, l.14), *warþe*, *water* (shore, water l.16), *mount* (hill, l.19), *knarrez* (rocks, l.22) and *felle* (l.24, hills) build up an image of the natural world. This is an untamed wilderness where the inhabitants are classified by the word *foo* (l.17) – juxtaposed with the positive connotations of *frendez* (l.15), it emphasises Gawain's isolation and his distance from the civilised court he has left behind. Some of the alliterative patterns (*to tore, to telle, ten þe* 1.20; *bullez, berez, borez* l.23) use hard consonants to reinforce the mood of hostility.

This is a savage world far from the festivity of Camelot and by listing Gawain's enemies individually the poet draws attention to the perils he has to face: *wormez*, *wolues* (dragons, wolves l.21), *wodwos* (wild men l.22), *bullez, berez, borez* (bulls, bears, boars l.23) and *etaynez* (giants l.24). The negative mood is developed through the modifiers: his foes are *so foule* and *so felle* (ugly, fierce l.18); he travels through *straunge* (strange l.1) lands *fremendly* (as a stranger l.15); he is *fer* (far l.15) from his friends. Synonyms for fighting like *feȝt* (l.18) and *werrez* (l.21) are in direct opposition to the language of celebration and feasting which dominated the first extract.

The Middle English interest in supernatural happenings is found here in Gawain's encounters with dragons, wild men and giants, and in the *mony meruayl* (many marvels l.19) that he sees on his journey. His heroic battles with these representatives of disorder remind the reader of the intruder who appeared at Arthur's court and of the agreement made between Gawain and the Green Knight. The extraordinary things he encounters and the bleak landscapes are integral to the otherworldly atmosphere of Gawain's quest.

Despite the drama of these supernatural attractions, however, they are no more than functions of the plot, entertaining us with Gawain's physical feats of strength and existing as a symbolic contrast to the court. It is Gawain's spiritual strength with which the reader must engage, recognising that he reveals his true self in his willingness to offer his life to save others. This is the moral vision with which the poem ends: Gawain has resisted all temptations except that linked to his love of life; he has proven himself loyal and of good faith. Like the members of King Arthur's court, we can understand and accept his one fault because it emphasises the power of life rather than death.

The beginnings of the English poetic tradition

During this period running from the first to the fourteenth century, the first written tradition of English poetry emerges. Old English verse establishes poetic conventions that were to be central to the development of English poetry. Although changes in the language inevitably affected the tightly structured Old English syllabic patterning, the influence of the alliterative tradition can be seen even into the twentieth century with the poetry of G.M. Hopkins and W.H. Auden.

The content of the extant OE poetry is varied and clearly linked to the lifestyle and concerns of the period. Many of its key themes still have relevance today despite the different social and cultural context in which the poetry is now read. Although the events and characters may seem alien to modern readers, the underlying messages are universal. In addition, the richness of English as a language of poetry, and the energy of the imagery allows us, as twenty-first-century readers, to gain an insight into the way the Anglo-Saxons viewed their world.

Langland, as an educated cleric and Londoner, was able to draw on a wide range of speech traditions. His poem reflects the influence of bawdy French songs, oral ballads, religious discourse, the Scriptures and the vernacular – his skill lies in his ability to move between these different repertoires effortlessly, interweaving a learned riddle with a popular joke, a homily with a social or regional dialect.

While drawing on the Old English tradition, Langland distanced himself from the strict rules of the earlier verse form. He chose a basic approach in which the alliteration was unobtrusive and the style simple. This allowed him to engage his reader directly with the spiritual truth he was exploring – his art was explicitly didactic and his language was shaped to his religious purpose.

The Gawain poet, on the other hand, has a less consciously instructive approach. He develops his central protagonist as a real character, but treats both Gawain and his adventures with an ironic detachment rather than as a model of knightly perfection. The testing of a knight's chivalric code was traditional in romance, but the *Gawain* poet tests Gawain in a real-life situation in the castle as well as in his supernatural encounters with monsters and wild men. The poet's style is also individual: he creates drama through his attention to detail and in his use of conversation. Descriptions of clothing, armour, feasting, hunting and other elements of courtly life provide a concrete backdrop to events, while stylistic variations in the direct speech characterise individuals distinctively. Although there is some explicit moralising, the success of the *Gawain* poet lies in his ability to develop an underlying theme through the associations of the religious and chivalric words he chooses.

▶ **9** Geoffrey Chaucer (c.1343–1400)

Chaucer's work reflects a different and distinctive English tradition that emerged in the Middle Ages. As a man of the court, he used the prestigious dialect of the South and his poems seem far less alien to modern readers than those recorded in the North-West Midlands dialect. He read extensively and, while travelling in his role as a diplomat, possibly met some of the great European writers of his time such as Petrarch (1304–74) and Boccaccio (1313–75). His experiences, however, did not mean that his own verse fell between the English tradition of syllabic freedom and the French tradition of syllabic rigidity – instead he created his own poetic form, making English an accepted literary medium.

Chaucer's world

Chaucer was born in the early 1340s at a time when England, with Edward III on the throne, was more stable and settled than it had been for half a century. The Black Death (1348–9), however, was to eliminate about one-third of Britain's 4 million population, returning on several occasions before the 1400s, and beginning a process of change that was dramatically to alter the social structure of Britain. The shortage of labour created by the plague freed many serfs from their bondage, and enabled merchants' sons, like Chaucer, the opportunity to rise in the King's Service.

Edward was a warrior king – he started the Hundred Years' War with France by claiming the right to rule it – but his court was highly cultured. As a squire to Edward's son Lionel, Chaucer would have heard fashionable French poets reciting their romances, experiencing the splendour and sophistication of the London court at first hand. It was a world where a man of letters and a linguist like Chaucer was held in high regard.

With the death of Edward III, however, in 1377, the court became divided as different factions fought for control of the boy king Richard II. These were uneasy times and when the barons gained the upper hand in 1386, many of those associated with the court were purged. Despite this, Richard was artistic and, when he came of age in 1389, he encouraged court writers such as Chaucer. His uncle John of Gaunt, son of Edward III, was also an invaluable patron to the arts and Chaucer's first major poem, *The Book of the Duchess* (1369), was written as a memorial to Gaunt's wife.

There was evidence of disquiet in society outside the court too. The Peasants'

Revolt (1381) was an indication of a widespread discontent at high taxes, raised to cover the cost of the wars with Scotland and France. With no other means of voicing their concerns in a public arena, a peasant army marched from south and east England to London. There was a general feeling that ordinary people were suffering while greed and corruption in the Church and amongst the nobility were rife.

Many people were also calling for reforms of the Church – one of the most eminent was the Oxford scholar John Wycliffe (1329–84) with his followers, the Lollards. They questioned the amounts of money spent on churches, and they doubted some of the church teachings such as the devotion to saints' bones and other holy relics. Both the nobles and the bishops feared attacks on their wealth, so the Lollards were persecuted, many being burned at the stake around 1405.

This was the world in which Chaucer was writing and we see the influence both of a cultured court and of contemporary medieval life. While he was not a political poet, nor a poet interested in great events or specific social causes, a poem like *The Canterbury Tales* is very much based in the real world of ordinary people and provides an insight into contemporary attitudes to the Church, marriage, materialism and women. Beneath the surface of good humour and geniality, we see a portrait of the Middle Ages as Chaucer wished to represent it, complete with larger than life characters, social inequities, corrupt institutions, and, above all, an understanding of human vulnerabilities.

The literary context

In the military society of the eleventh century, minstrels wandered from court to court, singing popular songs in French to entertain the aristocrats. The subject matter reflected the culture of heroic deeds and great men – the warlords who ruled the courts had little interest in stories of love and romance. These songs were like the French *chansons de geste*, which told stories of earlier historical figures and their great deeds in a simple formulaic style. It was a male environment where love had little place and the women were peripheral.

Minstrels were low down in the social order and were expected to do more than just play music. The word minstrel actually means 'little servant' and there was little distinction drawn between those servants who cooked and served, and those who could write songs and play musical instruments. Minstrels were therefore menials in the household who needed to be able to perform, serve, stand guard, and even go into battle for their lord and master. They performed in the galleries above their masters' halls, where the acoustics ensured that their music could be heard, but, in addition, the minstrels were kept apart from their social superiors.

In the service of a great lord, a minstrel was entitled to wear livery. It was a mark of status and the sign of a regular income. In return, they were expected to be propagandists, promoting their masters and patrons by glorifying their acts in verse. The entertainment they provided was popular and often coarse rather than sophisticated, and the Church had an ambivalent attitude towards them. Their music encouraged dancing and revelry and was quite unlike the heavenly, angelic music of the celestial angels. For some, therefore, the minstrels were the servants of the devil.

The fortunes of the minstrels reached their height in the court of Edward III and they were firmly woven into the fabric of everyday life. While the English nobility were still enjoying tales of battle and heroes, however, a new kind of song was emerging in the south of France. It marked the beginning of a new kind of entertainment created by educated aristocrats rather than professional musicians. These were the troubadours who flourished from the end of the eleventh century until the thirteenth. Guilhem IX (1071–1127), count of Poitiers and duke of Aquitaine, is the first known troubadour, and his court in the twelfth century was the most important cultural centre in France. He was to change the story of minstrels by inventing a new kind of poetry that focused on love rather than war, and used a style that was irreverent and witty.

The poetry of the troubadours was to change the way people thought about themselves and their society – it accorded women a superior status over men; made love a suitable topic for literature; challenged accepted attitudes; and used the everyday language of ordinary people to do so. Up until the twelfth century, all literature had been written in Latin for an aristocratic audience. Using the Occitanian languages of southern France, the troubadours created poetry that everyone could understand. They used the language of the man in the street for intellectual verbal games in which two poets would try to outwit each other, and the *langue d'oc* was spread as they travelled across Provençal with their sophisticated stories and music.

The influence of the troubadours was significant and the fashion for writing poetry in a native language spread across the European courts. As a new breed of court poets emerged, the uneducated minstrels were forced to become wandering minstrels looking for an audience where they could find one. In some ways, this was liberating for the minstrels because they were no longer tied by an allegiance to a master – instead of propagandists for a patron, they became political agitators.

Medieval England was full of political intrigue, factions and court favourites, and it was sometimes dangerous for the minstrels and poets of the court. As detached observers, it was not uncommon for them to be employed as spies, passing on the things that they heard to secondary sources. In 1386, for instance, many of those most closely associated with Richard, John of Gaunt and the Lancastrians were purged – some even going to the block. Chaucer must have felt wary of his own position, associated with the court party and the Lancastrians, and he disappeared from royal service between 1386 and 1389. When Richard came of age and was able to rule in his own right, Chaucer was once again a member of the court, working as Clerk of the Works and supervising the construction and maintenance of many important buildings.

In the 1390s, the arts flourished in Richard's court where an easygoing intellectual atmosphere enabled satire and lampoon to thrive. Chaucer took advantage of the mood to satirise what he saw as the commercialisation of the Church, but a changed mood by the end of the century was to leave him exposed. Richard was overthrown in 1399, imprisoned and probably murdered, and the political scene changed dramatically. A religious crackdown ensued – those who criticised the Church in plain English were threatened with burning; vernacular satires like those written by Chaucer were deemed to be unacceptable.

As a diplomat, civil servant, court poet and an accomplished scholar, Chaucer was one of the most famous men in the kingdom by the end of the fourteenth century and yet there is no record of his death. He disappeared around the time that Henry IV's Archbishop Arundel was trying to limit the use of English vernacular in literature. Modern literary historians question the mystery surrounding his demise, and wonder whether his disappearance at this time was deliberate. Although he was buried in Westminster Abbey at his death – a rare event for a commoner – it was to be another 150 years before a monument was erected to Chaucer in 1555, establishing the precedent for the present 'Poets' Corner'.

Chaucer's work

Some critics divide Chaucer's works into three distinct periods reflecting changes in influence, content and style. These are a convenient way of classifying the various poems, but should be used with caution. In some cases, critics make corresponding judgements about the relative immaturity or maturity of the works according to the period in which they were written. This is, perhaps, less useful since some parts of *The Canterbury Tales* were written before the final period of supposed maturity, and *Troilus and Criseyde* from the middle period is thought by many to be Chaucer's greatest work. The three key periods are, however, a good basic starting point and for a student of Chaucer they do draw attention to the way in which his work evolves.

In the first period, Chaucer wrote *The Book of the Duchess* (1369–70) to commemorate the death of John of Gaunt's first wife, Blanche. It is an idealised romance influenced by French sources. The content focuses on the spiritual side of courtly love, and the style is marked by Chaucer's use of the octosyllabic line and his experimentation with rhyme.

The second period reveals his interest in Italian sources. Works such as *Troilus and Criseyde* (1372–84) and *The Assembly or Parlement of Foules* (c.1384) continue to show Chaucer's interest in courtly love, but his style becomes more decorative and the content more moral. Although he uses many of the contemporary literary devices such as dreams, classical references and digressions, it is in poems like the *Parlement of Foules* that Chaucer's distinctive ironic humour begins to emerge.

By the third period of development, Chaucer uses personal observations of English society and the people around him, and it is the works in this final stage which establish his distinctive 'English' style. Chaucer's most well-known text in this period is *The Canterbury Tales* (1385–1400). The poem is recognised for its skilful use of couplets, the variety of genres it embraces, the sophistication of its characterisation, Chaucer's individual sense of humour and his understanding of people and society.

Another key distinguishing feature of Chaucer's works is his presence in the poems as a narrator. Moving beyond an expression of personal opinions and attitudes conveyed through his lexical choice, Chaucer actually takes up a physical presence in his verse. Critics describe this as the mask or persona of the poet – rather than a literal representation of himself, Chaucer creates a character through which he can voice his thoughts and opinions.

This character is there even in the earliest of his major works, *The Book of the Duchess* (1369) in which he adapts the traditional French dream-allegory to make his work more immediate. Many features of the form are still present (the discussion of sleeplessness, the spring setting, the vision, the personified abstractions), but in Chaucer's hands the poem becomes a dialogue between two real people in a wood one May morning: the sympathetic but somewhat bumbling Chaucer and a knight in black, probably representative of the broken-hearted John of Gaunt. Chaucer uses the traditional love vision as an elegy, creating a poem that is both an eulogy of Blanche and a consolation to John of Gaunt. The sorrow at the heart of the poem is balanced by the narrator's sympathy and the gentle comedy of Chaucer's self-characterisation.

This imperfect, genial and rather naïve persona recurs throughout Chaucer's work. As we read, however, we realise that his apparent innocence is a front concealing a sharp wit and astute understanding. His rambling digressions and ironic asides are evidence of a good-natured and tolerant character.

It is perhaps also useful to remember that Chaucer would have read many of his poems aloud at court. The creation of a poet-narrator figure would have allowed him to engage directly with his audience through a representation of himself. As a slightly humorous and self-deprecating figure, his satirical verse would have been more palatable to the aristocratic audience of the court, and the empathy he offered to his patron in *The Book of the Duchess* more subtle.

The Canterbury Tales

The Canterbury Tales was largely written in Chaucer's later years. It is, however, also made up of writings from his early and middle periods, making it difficult to fit neatly into a chronology of his work as a whole. It is thought, however, that he probably conceived the idea some time around 1386 at the time when he disappeared from court service. While individual sketches of characters are common in medieval French and English literature, no other work now exists in which a framework like Chaucer's *Prologue* draws a wide range of sketches together.

The poem is made up of a narrative that is dominated by description rather than a sequence of events. Chaucer introduces us to a disparate group of people who have been drawn together by their common desire to go on a pilgrimage and who will entertain each other with stories as they proceed on their journey to Canterbury. Each character is described in turn with additional comments scattered through the poem in the interludes that take place before and after each tale. The characterisation is complex: we learn about individuals from their clothes, their occupation, their attitudes and ideas, their behaviour and speech, and from the asides in which the poet points out discrepancies that encourage us to read between the lines.

The portraits are recognised as being far more vivid and animated than others composed at the time. Some critics believe that this is partly due to the fact that Chaucer may have drawn on real people. Despite the fact that the pilgrims of *The Canterbury Tales* exist as credible individuals, however, it is also noticeable that they function as representatives of groups of people, as universal types. Taken together they cover a wide range of life: the court; the clergy and the Church; the learned professions of law and medicine; merchants and craftsmen; sailors; officials of the manor and the common peasant farmer. Chaucer's skill lies both in bringing them to life and in using them as the basis for his satirical treatment of medieval society.

The style is equally important in alerting us to the wider significance of Chaucer's poem. He moves from formal to informal registers, interweaving colloquial language, traditional poetic diction and the flexibility of the spoken voice. He creates humour through the satirical comments of the narrator, and in the juxtaposition of different registers. The language of romance, for instance, may be used to describe the actions of animals in a mock-heroic style. Rhetoric, the art of literary composition, was central to a medieval education and medieval writers used rhetorical devices to structure their stories, manage descriptions, and embellish them according to their purpose and type. Chaucer used such principles traditionally, but he also used them for comic effect, juxtaposing humorous or low-key events with the elevated patterning of rhetorical devices.

While Chaucer's verse resembles contemporary French models in its use of rhyming couplets, he developed the 10-syllable line rather than the 6 or 8 of his French counterparts. Although most of his work is made up of iambic pentameter, which was later to become the most common versification of English poetry, his lines have great freedom and variety. He changes the position of the caesura, and uses a trochaic foot where he wishes to place a particular emphasis. When reading the poems, it is important to remember that Middle English was still an inflected language in which the final –e and other endings were pronounced and are, therefore, essential to the rhythm.

The General Prologue

The Canterbury Tales opens with a prologue that creates the framework within which Chaucer will develop his characters and their tales: a group of pilgrims accompanied by the host of the Tabard Inn at Southwark will entertain each other with two stories on their journey. The motif of the pilgrimage allows Chaucer to draw together a wide range of people from different social, cultural and educational backgrounds bound together only by their common purpose. The Knight, for instance, represents courtly society; the Nun's Priest and the Pardoner represent the religious life; and the Miller and the Man of Law represent the secular world of work.

Activity 9.1

Explore the effect of these lines as an opening to Chaucer's *Canterbury Tales* (*The General Prologue*, ll.1–12, 19–27, 35–41) .

You may like to think about: the content and themes, the language, imagery, structure and purpose.

1	Whan that Aprill with his shoures° soote°	showers; sweet
	The droghte° of March hath perced° to the roote,	drought; pierced
	And bathed every veyne in swich° licour°	such; moisture
	Of which vertu° engendred° is the flour°;	power; given birth to; flower
5	Whan Zephirus° eek° with his sweete breeth°	west wind; also; breath
	Inspired° hath in every holt° and heeth°	breathed upon; plantation; heath
	The tendre° croppes, and the yonge° sonne°	tender; young; sun
	Hath in the Ram° his halve cours° yronne°,	Aries – zodiac sign; course; run
	And smale° foweles° maken melodye°,	small; birds; melody
10	That slepen° al the nyght with open ye°	sleep; eye
	(So priketh° hem° nature in hir° corages°);	incite, rouse; them; their; hearts
	Thanne° longen° folk to goon° on pilgrimages . . .	then; long for, desire; go
	Bifel° that in that seson on a day,	it happened
	In Southwerk at the Tabard as I lay	
15	Redy to wenden° on my pilgrimage	go
	To Caunterbury with ful° devout corage°,	most; heart
	At nyght was come into that hostelrye	
	Wel° nyne and twenty in a compaignye,	fully
	Of sondry folk, by aventure° yfalle°	chance; fallen
20	In felaweshipe, and pilgrimes were they alle,	
	That toward Caunterbury wolden° ryde. . . .	wished
	But nathelees°, whil I have tyme and space,	none the less
	Er° that I ferther° in this tale pace°,	before; further; step
	Me thynketh it acordaunt to resoun°	in line with reason
25	To telle yow al the condicioun°	state of being (inner character as well as external circumstances)
	Of ech of hem°, so as it semed me,	them
	And whiche they weren°, and of what degree°,	which profession they were; rank
	And eek° in what array° that they were inne . . .	also; clothing

Commentary

Chaucer uses the General Prologue to establish the background and traditional narrative details of time, place and character. We begin with a general description of spring, which is followed by a narrowing of the focus as we are introduced to a particular time (*in that seson on a day*, l.13) and place (*In Southwerk at the Tabard*, l.14), and a specific group of characters (the poet, l.14 and *Wel nyne and twenty in a compaignye/Of sundry folk*, ll.18–19). Thematically, the pilgrimage becomes a symbol of the pilgrims' desire for new beginnings just as the season is symbolic of new growth and new life.

The opening description of spring sets the scene and establishes the mood. Juxtapositions of *shoures soote* (l.1), *swich licour* (l.3) and the *sweete breeth* (l.5) of the west wind with the *droghte of March* (l.2) mark a new beginning. The language is positive with modifiers like *soote* (l.1), *sweete* (l.5), *tendre* and *yonge* (l.7) empha-sising the change that accompanies the arrival of spring. Verbs like *Inspired* (l.6) and *priketh* (l.11) reinforce this mood of new beginnings. There is a real sense of energy and growth.

The imagery is concrete with a strong visual representation of the natural world through the many concrete nouns (*shoures* 1.1, *roote* 1.2, *licour* 1.3, *flour* 1.4, *holt and heeth* l.6, *croppes* l.7, *foweles* l.9). This is balanced by the personification of the west wind in the reference to Zephirus, a character taken from Greek mythology. Breathing life into the dead world, he is the herald of spring. The neatness of the rhyming couplets and the regularity of the recurring 10-syllable line add to the harmony and order of this vision of spring.

To convey a sense of excitement in the returning life and new growth, Chaucer uses foregrounded subordinate clauses that drive the reader on towards the adverb of time marking out the main clause (l.12): *When . . . hath perced . . . /And bathed . . . When . . ./Inspired hath . . . /Hath . . . yronne/And . . . maken . . . Thanne*. The emphasis is on a natural order and a sense of process that is comfortably predictable – we can relish the description of spring because we know what it brings. The parenthesis (l.11) describing the effect of spring on the *smale foweles* enhances the mood of anticipation and prepares us for the introduction of the human world (*folk*) in the next line. The foregrounded adverb *Thanne*, the connotations of the verb *longen*, and the end position of the key word *pilgrimages* marks this as the climax of the opening section.

Having established a parallel between the natural world and the humans who long to go on a pilgrimage, Chaucer moves from the general to the specific. The use of proper nouns such as *Southwerk*, the *Tabard* (l.14) and *Caunterbury* (l.21) marks his change of direction. It is the point at which he begins to develop the narrative framework through his role as observer – the use of the first person develops a personal tone and engages the audience directly. The account, therefore, will be subjective.

One of the engaging features of *The Canterbury Tales* is the way in which Chaucer plays with the idea of viewpoint. By juxtaposing the subordinate clause *as it semed to me* (l.26) with the phrase *accordaunt to resoun* (l.24) and the list of categories in which he will consider the pilgrims, he suggests that there will be a logic to his observations in spite of their subjectivity. This encourages us to trust what he tells us about his companions. His observations will address both the internal and external: appearance (*array*, l.28), character (*condicioun*, l.25), their role in society (*whiche they weren*, l.27) and their rank (*degree*, l.27). Each portrait helps to create a sense of the pilgrims' individuality and, at the same time, the poet-narrator's shrewdness. Until the pilgrims speak themselves, however, it is important to remember that we are being given a subjective viewpoint.

As an introduction to the poem, Chaucer achieves an enormous amount in these opening lines. He has created a strong sense of time, place and character; established a framework that will bring all the disparate people and their tales together; developed a persona that will allow him to comment freely on his contemporaries; and engaged his audience directly through his lexical choice and style. The introduction of key themes also sets the tone for the rest of the work. The concept of natural harmony and order will be set against the notion of both heavenly order and earthly disorder. This can be seen here in the juxtaposition of the inn (a worldly place of pleasure and social gratification) and the pilgrimage to Canterbury (a spiritual place of holy reflection and communion with God). The poem will represent a vision of medieval society as Chaucer saw it and the opening section effectively draws us in to this world of *sundry folk* who have come together *by aventure*.

*   *   *

The poem does not include a complete representation of medieval society – the most wealthy and the poorest are absent. We do, however, see a distinctive viewpoint in which Chaucer uses his persona to attack the failings of individuals and institutions in some portraits and offer idealised versions in others. His characterisation is skilful: he creates conflicts between social role and the way some characters live their lives; he reveals human weakness and the ways in which individuals fall short of their ideals; he contrasts what they say with what they do. The pilgrims emerge as complex individuals because of the range of techniques Chaucer uses to characterise them. We learn about them from their appearance, from the things Chaucer says about them, from what they say and do, from our awareness of the tensions existing within them, and from what the other pilgrims say about them.

Although the pilgrims emerge as distinctive individuals, the portraits also allow Chaucer to use them as representatives or types. The knight, for instance, is a complex individual who wears a surcoat spotted with rust, has fought in many specific battles and speaks *as meeke as is a mayde*; he is also an ideal of a pious crusader, a caricature of a 'type'. This duality allows Chaucer to create a narrative, a story about a particular group of people, and to satirise 'types' and their attitudes. The reader is encouraged to judge the pilgrims by recognising them as representatives of noble 'ideals' or a particular social group, as rogues or as hypocrites.

As well as providing detailed portraits of each character and representing them as types, Chaucer also groups them into categories. These loose groupings lead us towards an understanding of the social hierarchy in medieval society and encourage us to set one group against another. The contrasts that emerge are another means of characterisation since we inevitably see features of the group as an indication of the nature of the individuals.

There are five groups. The first, containing the Knight, the Squire, and the Yeoman, a servant, is symbolic of society's best – they are representatives of the world of the court. While the Knight is symbolic of the traditional crusading knight defending his love of God, the Squire, his son, is linked to the contemporary fashion for romance. While one fights for religious ideals, the other wishes to win his lady through a demonstration of his courtly skills.

The second group is made up of members of the religious community: the Prioress, the Monk, the Friar, a nun and three priests. While all united by their religious roles, Chaucer divides them according to their different attitudes. Physical desires for food, sexual pleasure and hunting are balanced against such spiritual values as charity, abstinence and prayer. Judgements against them vary. The Prioress and the Monk are seen to be vulnerable to physical pleasure, but Chaucer is not bitingly satirical about them. His account of these characters does not alienate the reader because we can see their humanity. In the portrait of the Friar, however, Chaucer is less sympathetic. The Friar's worldliness is explicit in his sexual nature rather than implicit, and he has none of the charm of the Prioress, nor the physical health of the Monk.

The third group is represented by the middle class: the merchant, the Clerk, the Lawyer, the Franklin, five guildsmen (a Haberdasher, Dyer, Carpenter, Weaver and Carpet-maker) and their cook, the Shipman, the Doctor, and the Wife of Bath. The fourth group comprises the Parson and the Ploughman, representatives of the lower social orders; and the final group are the rogues – the Reeve, Miller, Manciple, Pardoner and Summoner. In line with Chaucer's ironic and self-deprecating treatment of himself, he is tagged on at the end along with the rogues.

The function of these descriptions is to introduce us to the character from the poet's viewpoint. They prepare us for the prologues and tales in which the characters are given a voice of their own. We hear about the individuals before we meet them and this makes the characterisation more complex – it forces us to be active readers, balancing the poet's viewpoint with our own experience of the characters who reveal themselves to us through their actions, words, attitudes and interactions.

When reading the portraits, always begin with the weight of detail since this helps to create a vivid sense of individuality. Physical description, information about lifestyle and occupation, and suggestions about moral state are all part of Chaucer's vision. It is not just content, however, that enables us to understand his approach to characterisation. The language, style and structure underpin the content, and, in order to fully recognise the complexity of the characters, we need to appreciate the way Chaucer guides our response through his lexical, stylistic and structural choices.

Activity 9.2

How does Chaucer characterise the Franklin and the Miller, and how does he wish us to respond to them in the following extracts (General Prologue ll.331–60; ll.545–64)?

You may like to think about: the content, language, tone, style and structure.

EXTRACT 1 – *THE GENERAL PROLOGUE* (ll.331–60)

1	A Frankeleyn° was in his compaignye.	franklin, a landowner
	Whit° was his berd° as is the dayesye°;	white; beard; daisy
	Of his complexioun° he was sangwyn°.	temperament; blood-red
	Wel loved he by the morwe° a sop in wyn°;	morning; wine
5	To lyven° in delit was evere his wone° . . .	live; custom
	A bettre envyned° man was nowher noon°.	stocked with wine; none
	Withoute bake mete° was nevere his hous	baked meat pies
	Of fissh and flessh, and that so plentevous°,	plentiful
	It snewed° in his hous of mete and drynke,	snowed, abounded
10	Of alle deyntees° that men koude thynke . . .	dainties, delicacies
	His table dormant° in his halle alway°	permanent, fixed; always
	Stood redy covered al the longe day.	

	At sessiouns° ther was he lord and sire;	local courts
	Ful ofte tyme he was knyght of the shire°.	member of Parliament for his county
15	An anlaas° and a gipser° al of silk	anlace, a short two-edged knife; purse
	Heeng° at his girdel°, whit as morne milk.	hung; girdle
	A shirreve° hadde he been, and a contour°.	sheriff; accountant
	Was nowher swich a worthy vavasour°.	substantial landholder

EXTRACT 2 – *THE GENERAL PROLOGUE* (ll.545–64)

	The Millere was a stout carl° for the nones°;	fellow; indeed – an emphatic tag phrase
20	Ful byg he was of brawn, and eke of bones.	
	That proved wel, for over al ther he cam,	
	At wrastlynge° he wolde have alwey the ram.	wrestling
	He was short-sholdred, brood, a thikke knarre°;	sturdy fellow
	Ther was no dore° that he nolde° heve° of harre°,	door; would not; heave; hinge
25	Or breke it at a rennyng with his heed.	
	His berd as any sowe or fox was reed,	
	And therto brood°, as though it were a spade.	broad
	Upon the cop° right of his nose he hade	top
	A werte, and theron stood a toft° of herys°,	tuft; hairs
30	Reed as the brustles° of a sowes erys°;	bristles; ears
	His nosethirles° blake were and wyde.	nostrils
	A swerd and bokeler° bar° he by his syde.	buckler; carried
	His mouth as greet was as a greet forneys°.	furnace
	He was a janglere° and a goliardeys°,	gossip; coarse buffoon
35	And that was moost of synne° and harlotries°.	sin; wickedness
	Wel koude he stelen corn and tollen° thries°;	take his due or payment; thrice
	And yet he hadde a thombe° of gold, pardee°.	thumb; a common oath
	A whit cote and a blew hood wered° he.	wore

Commentary

By using contrasts and parallels, and by consciously arranging the sequence in which the tales occur, Chaucer is able to guide reader response. Having opened with the ideal portrait of the Knight, he proceeds to catalogue a series of individuals who are not what they seem. The Franklin, a wealthy landowner, is self-indulgent, striving to impress his guests with the lavishness of his hospitality. His desire to be like an aristocrat results only in a demonstration of his vulgarity and greed. Where the Knight is noble in deed, the Franklin is merely interested in the appearance of nobility.

The Miller also stands in direct opposition to the values of the Knight: his life does not uphold the codes of chivalry and courtly manners which the Knight represents; he provides comedy where the Knight can be seen as a role model; and he is boorish where the Knight is a gentleman.

On first reading, the Franklin appears to be a man of social importance – he is *lord and sire* (1.13) at the local courts; he is *knyght of the shire* (1.14); he is a *shirreve* and a *contour* (1.17; and he is a *worthy vavasour* (1.18).This suggests that he is a noble and worthwhile member of the community. It is important to recognise, however, that these details of his social position come after Chaucer's account of his extravagant lifestyle. The emphasis on the Franklin as a generous host is undermined by the fact that *To lyven in delit was evere his wone* (l.5). References to *wyn* (l.4), *bake mete* (l.7), *fissh and flessh* (l.8), *mete and drynke* (l.9) and to *alle deyntees that man koude thynke* (l.10) reflect his own self-indulgent interest in physical pleasure.

The irony of the final line of the extract (l.18) is reinforced by Chaucer's use of rhetoric: the kinds of food stocked in the Franklin's house are juxtaposed with his high status professions (ll.17–18); and the whiteness of his beard and his girdle are juxtaposed with the redness of his face. Chaucer also uses figurative language to draw attention to the excessive nature of the Franklin: the simile *as is the dayesye* (l.2) is ironic since it juxtaposes the delicacy of the flower with the gluttony of the man; and the figurative use of the verb *snewed* (l.9) suggests something excessive and unnatural.

Central to Chaucer's satire are the contrasts established between what the individuals appear to be and what they actually are – he uses antithesis to draw attention to the underlying meaning. Although the Franklin appears to be a generous man, Chaucer's use of antithesis draws the reader's attention to his personal interest in a lavish life-style. He holds positions of high social status and yet, because we learn of his extravagance first, we are left with thoughts of his self-gratification rather than his professional achievements. Chaucer wants readers to recognise the Franklin's hypocrisy in pretending that his table *dormant* (l.11) is set for visitors – his household seems vulgar and ostentatious and this inevitably colours our view of the Franklin himself.

This view of the Franklin prepares us for his tale: we need to listen actively in order to distinguish between reality and appearance in his story. In telling his tale, he claims to know nothing of rhetorical devices because he is an unlearned man, when in fact, his tale is taken from Boccaccio (1313–75), a leading Italian writer, and his story is full of rhetoric. As a politician (*knight of the shire*), he is accustomed to persuading people, to presenting the facts in an advantageous way, and to using rhetoric. The description of the Franklin in the Prologue there-fore alerts us to his inner nature – he is a hypocrite more concerned with appear-ance than reality, and, in trying to win the supper for his tale, he aims to please his audience, in particular, those who are most eminent in the party.

Chaucer's description of the Miller concentrates on his physical appearance and strength. The modifiers *stout* (l.19), *ful byg* (l.20), *short-sholdred, brood* and *thikke* (l.23) draw attention to his size, suggesting that he is a larger than life character. This is reinforced by the descriptions of his *berd*, which is *reed* and *brood* (ll. 26–7), the *werte* on his nose with its *toft of herys* (ll.29–30), his *blake* and *wyde* nostrils (l.31), and his *greet* mouth (l.33). The physical description indicates something about his character too – the coarseness of his appearance is paralleled by a coarseness in his personality. He is a *janglere* and a *goliardeys* (l.34), who likes to talk of sin and wicked-ness (l.35); he is a fighter who always wins the prize in wrestling matches (l.22); and he can take any door off its hinges or break it with his head (ll.24–5).

The portrait in *The General Prologue* creates a sense of the Miller as a caricature, presenting him as a representative of his social class as well as an individual. This allows Chaucer to satirise him as loud-mouthed, vulgar, shameless and dishonest with the underlying suggestion that all millers are the same.

By using rhetorical devices and imagery, Chaucer is able to manipulate reader response. In describing the Miller's physical appearance, he uses parallelism: . . . *of brawn . . . of bones* (1.20), *a janglere and a goliardeys* (1.34), *of synne and harlotries* (1.35). The balance given to the lines by such parallel structures persuades the reader of the accuracy of Chaucer's observations. The physical details are presented in an objective manner and this suggests that the implications about the Miller's personality are also grounded in reality. Lists of physical details work in a similar way to build up a precise and carefully observed portrait – *short-shol-dred, brood, a thikke knarre* (1.23), *His berd . . .* (1.26) *. . . A werte . . .* (1.29) *. . . His nosethirles . . .* (1.31). The reader trusts Chaucer's observations because they draw attention to important features that tell us about more than just his appearance – his physical coarseness hints at an underlying boorishness.

The imagery also works on more than just a visual level. Similes – *as any sowe or fox* (1.26), *as though it were a spade* (1.27), *Reed as the brustles of a sowes erys* (1.30), *as greet was as a greet forneys* (1.33) – draw comparisons between the Miller and things which throw light on him as an individual. The references to the *sowe* and *fox* explicitly tell the reader about his colouring. At the same time, however, they suggest that he is like a wild animal – uncivilised and unrefined. The comparison with the furnace develops the colour imagery, while also suggesting something about the Miller's temperament.

The description builds towards an ironic climax. After creating a concrete physical portrait (ll.19–20, 23, 26–31) and after describing the kinds of things the Miller does (ll.22, 24–5), Chaucer summarises his character: the Miller is a gossip who loves to tell vulgar tales; he is a disreputable trader who cheats his customers. This places him in direct contrast with the Knight who is a worthy man charac-terised by words like *chivalrie, trouthe, honour, fredom* and *curteisie*.

Although fairly static with little sense of a developing sequence of action, *The Canterbury Tales* is in many ways like a drama because of the interaction that takes place between the characters before and after each tale is told. The exchanges prior to the telling of a tale provide concrete evidence that the portrait based on Chaucer's observations is accurate. His description of the Miller prepares us for what we later see and hear – the Miller's drunken interruption prior to his tale is typical of the character who emerges from the Prologue. Readers can therefore verify what they have been told at first-hand: the Miller is a *cherl* (a rough fellow) who has no sense of courtesy and who drunkenly insists that his own tale be heard immediately (*The Miller's Prologue*, ll.14–15, 60–1).

The tales

Since the tales are narrated by the pilgrims, it is important to remember that the telling is influenced by the teller – the stories reflect something of the character and opinions of the speaker. As we have seen, the descriptions of each character in the General Prologue and the linking sections between the tales provide a useful framework for character analysis. The poet/narrator's observations (subjec-tive characterisation) and the characters' words and actions (objective characteri-sation) reveal the storyteller and thus enable us to read the tale with an awareness of its wider significance. The characters, themes and style of telling will be indica-tive of the attitudes, experiences and life-style of each individual pilgrim.

The tales can be divided into categories according to their content and style. The main types include the court romance, the fabliau, and the explicitly religious tales. The court romances focus on courtly love, the competition for a woman's favour and on courtly occupations such as hunting, feasting and tournaments. Tales in this category include *The Wife of Bath's Tale*, *The Knight's Tale* and *The Franklin's Tale*. The fabliau is a kind of short story in which characters from the lower social classes are involved in plots and intrigues with a humorous and often indecent content. The style is plain, with a focus on action rather than description or reflection. Tales in this category include *The Miller's Tale*, *The Summoner's Tale* and some sections of *The Wife of Bath's Prologue*. The religious tales contain features typical of medieval religious writing: sermons, moral tracts, confessions in which the speaker reflects on life, and holy lives in which the main protagonists, often women, are holy people who battle against evil for the love of God. In this group, *The Pardoner's Tale* contains a sermon, *The Parson's Tale* a confession, and *The Franklin's Tale* uses elements of the holy life.

Each tale is an extended narrative in which we are introduced to a group of characters and events taking place in a particular time and location; underpinning the narrative are recurring themes that provide cohesion throughout the poem as a whole. Although the pilgrims tell very different stories, together they can be seen as a sequence of debates in which Chaucer is able to satirise medieval society and its attitudes through an exploration of the weaknesses and idiosyncrasies of both people and institutions. Where the didactic content of *Piers Plowman* is explicit and serious, the tone of Chaucer's work is lighter and more humorous. The satire of *The Canterbury Tales* may seem gentle, but beneath its apparent good nature there is a cutting edge.

The Knight, for instance, is presented in the General Prologue as an ideal knight who is modest and pious, *a verray, parfit gentil knight*. He is described first and this implicitly assigns to him a position of rank within the company of pilgrims; he is committed to the crusades; and has come straight from his journey to join the pilgrimage. We do not know, however, whether he fights for his faith or for money, and this creates a complexity within the portrait that adds to his individuality.

He tells a story of courtly romance in which knights and ladies must overcome obstacles and conflicts to their love before marriage brings social harmony. The characters are ideal representations of aristocratic life and yet, just as we recognise a tension in the characterisation of the Knight, so too we see a tension here between the perfect ending and the disorder caused by war, love triangles and arguments amongst the gods.

It is a tale that interweaves medieval courtly life and classic settings. The tone is instructive – its purpose is to explore moral dilemmas of good and evil, fate and free will so that the audience learn from its telling. This is indicative of the teller who is in a position of authority as an experienced crusader and senior member of the group of pilgrims.

Studying a tale

Whichever tale you are reading, it is possible to approach your study in a similar way. Initially, think about the way in which Chaucer describes the storyteller in the General Prologue, and decide what his observations tell us about the character. Then assess the way in which the interactions before and after the tale develop our understanding of the pilgrim. Having established this background information, summarise the type of tale being told (court romance/fabliau/religious), its content (setting/characters/plot), style and underlying ideas. Finally, focus on the relationship between the teller and the tale – identify the tone (e.g. serious, ironic, comic) and the purpose (e.g. to instruct, entertain, impress), and relate these to what you know about the storyteller and his or her relationship with the other pilgrims.

The tale told by the Miller, for instance, reinforces the observations made by Chaucer in the General Prologue. We are aware of him as a man with none of the Knight's social graces. The fact that Chaucer places the *Knight's Tale* immediately before the *Miller's Tale* draws attention to this contrast between them, and the reader is encouraged to recognise the difference in content and narrative style. He moves us away from the courtly ideals of the Knight and towards the harshness of the real world – the Miller's tale is a *cherles tale* of *harlotrie* in which wickedness, lowness and coarseness characterise both the story and the teller.

In a typically self-deprecating style, Chaucer disclaims any responsibility for the tale that is to follow since he has warned us that the Miller is *a cherl* (*The Miller's Prologue*, ll. 74–8). Although subjective, his observations of the Miller will be proven true in the tale that follows, with its coarse humour and bawdy content. Despite this, however, there is more to the tale than just a rude story. Chaucer heightens the comedy by creating a tension between two literary forms: he interweaves the seriousness and dignity of the courtly romance with the slapstick and disorder of the low-life fabliau. A carpenter's wife becomes the courtly lady and her extravagant courtly lovers are a student and a church clerk. Some of the coarser elements of the traditional fabliau are abandoned, but the content of the Miller's tale is clearly in direct contrast to the purity and nobility of *The Knight's Tale*.

The comedy is further enhanced by the Miller's own lack of understanding. He describes his tale as a *noble storie*, a tale *worthy for to drawen to memorie* (ll.3–4, *Prologue*), failing to take account of his audience or their general purpose. An appreciation of Chaucer's satirical tone here intensifies the comedy of the tale that is to follow. We have borne witness to the Miller's rudeness to the Knight and Reeve, and his apparent drunkenness, and yet there is a certain craftsmanship in his telling of the tale that perhaps stands at odds with the character that emerges from the poem. This tension between style and content reminds us that ultimately Chaucer is recounting the story of the pilgrimage for us – while the content is clearly marked as the responsibility of the Miller himself, we can hear the poet's voice in the patterned rhetoric and sophisticated linguistic choices.

The story revolves around a young girl, Alison, who marries an older man at the age of eighteen. Chaucer describes her as *wylde and yong* (*The Miller's Tale*, ll.117), while the carpenter John, her husband, is *sely* (simple, l.493) with a *wit* (mind/understanding) that is *rude* (rough/unlearned, ll.119). Nicholas, a young student and lodger in the carpenter's house, persuades John that a second Noah's flood is coming and that they must all sleep in tubs suspended from the roof to avoid certain death (ll.364–529). This allows Alison and Nicholas the opportunity to make love without interruption.

The comedy of this subterfuge is intensified by a second trick played on Absolon the *parissh clerk* (l.549), an affected fop who also loves Alison. While Nicholas and Alison are in bed, Absolon declares his love outside Alison's window (ll.563–605). He asks for a kiss and is rewarded with one – he only realises afterwards that he has kissed *hir naked ers* (l.626). In a rage, he borrows a red-hot coulter (the iron cutter at the front of a plough) to seek his revenge. This time Nicholas repeats the trick, greeting Absolon with *a fart/As greet as it had been a thonder-dent* (ll.698–9). In return, Absolon is *redy with his iren hoot* (l.701).

In line with Chaucer's satirical tone, the reader feels sympathy not for the old carpenter, but for Alison with her *likerous ye* (lecherous eye) (l.136). The carpenter has failed to learn from books (l.119) and from experience that a man *sholde wedde his simylitude* (l.120). Since this is common sense, Chaucer's underlying criticism is far more cutting than would at first appear – he is not critical of John because he is uneducated, but because he is foolish. Perhaps even worse than making an inappropriate marriage, he keeps Alison *narwe in cage* (l.116), imprisoning her because of his jealousy.

Having made sure that the reader sees John's weaknesses, Chaucer then explicitly draws attention to Alison through his figurative language. She sings like *a swalwe* (swallow, l.150) and skips like *any kyde or calf* (l.152); her mouth is *sweete as bragot or the meeth* (alcoholic drinks containing honey, l.153); and she is skittish like *a joly colt* (l.155). The imagery is positive, yet it focuses on external detail – we have little sense of Alison beyond her appearance and her zest for life. She is, therefore, a 'type' rather than a developed character and Chaucer's use of 'types' is central to our appreciation of the tale. Our interest lies in the interactions between 'pretty young girl', 'foolish husband', 'artful and cocksure student', and 'a dandy'; in the comedy of the plot; and in the thematic oppositions that emerge (learned/unlearned, old/young, physical labour/intellect, love of God/sex, court/country, and so on).

Although the description of Alison is poetic in tone (ll.125–62), *The Miller's Tale* is dominated by everyday language: idioms like *as stille as stoon* (l.364) and *derk . . . as pich, or as the cole* (l.623); references to ordinary objects like *trogh* (l.440), *knedyng tubbes* (l.456) and *breed and chese* (l.520); and the coarse language traditionally associated with low-life characters like *fart* (l.698), *to pisse* (l.690), *ers* (l.626). Where courtly romances present an ideal world, the fabliaux recreate the world as it really is. The language Chaucer chooses, therefore, is linked directly to the language of popular speech.

Equally, the characters are drawn from life – Alison is not the symbolic heroine of courtly romance, she is a living, spontaneous individual who enjoys her crude trick, laughing *Tehee!* (l.632) at the disconcerted Absolon; the *sweete clerk* (l.111), Nicholas, is inventive and a good storyteller, but he must learn his lesson – his knowledge of the future does not protect him from Absolon's revenge. The way in which Alison and Nicholas enjoy life is contrasted with the carpenter's belief that he *moste endure . . . his care* (troubles/burdens, l.124). Such contrasts encourage the reader to make judgements: Alison and Nicholas win reader sympathy because they are vital, while John is no more than a stock figure of fun.

Chaucer's attitudes to his characters are reinforced in the terms of address he uses. Alison is *so gay a popelote* (doll), *swich a wenche* (l.146), *a prymerde* (primrose) and *a piggesyne* (flower, l.160), *a deere lady* (l.253), *a sweete bryd* (l.697). The carpenter is *a riche gnof* (churl) (l.80) and *a sely* (innocent, simple) *jalous housbonde* (l.296). Nicholas is *a poure scoler* (l.82), a *sweete clerk* (l.111) and *hende* (courteous/pleasant, (ll.164, 293, 379, 418). Absolon is *this joly Absolon* (l.240), *this joly lovere* (l.580) and *this sely Absolon* (l.636). In each case, Chaucer's choice of words influences reader response by developing positive or negative associations in relation to each character.

The plot centres on the theme of love and the dramatic conflict between Alison and the rivals for her love. This could form the basis for a courtly romance, but by using low-life characters and by replacing noble acts with coarse ones, Chaucer presents one of his central themes in a different light. By referring to the biblical story of Noah and the flood, he also reminds his readers of another kind of love – the love of God. In spite of its bawdiness therefore, *The Miller's Tale* implicitly reminds us of the world beyond, juxtaposing spiritual love with an earthly, physical love.

Activity 9.3

> ## Discuss Chaucer's presentation of Absolon in this extract (*The Miller's Tale* ll.579–99, 619–38).
>
> You may like to consider: the type of tale, the content and style, imagery, themes, and the relationship between the teller and the tale.

1	Whan that the firste cok hath crowe, anon	
	Up rist° this joly lovere Absolon,	rose
	And hym arraieth° gay°, at poynt-devys°.	dresses; showily dressed; to perfection/precisely
	But first he cheweth greyn° and lycorys,	grain (cardmom)
5	To smellen sweete, er° he hadde kembd° his heer°.	before; combed; hair
	Under his tonge a trewe-love° he beer°,	herb paris, four-leaved plant; kept
	For therby wende° he° to ben° gracious°.	went; himself; be; agreeable/attractive
	He rometh° to the carpenteres hous,	makes his way
	And stille he stant under the shot-wyndowe° –	window with a hinge or bolt
10	Unto his brest it raughte°, it was so lowe –	reached
	And softe he cougheth with a semy° soun:	gentle
	'What do ye°, hony-comb, sweete Alisoun,	what are you doing?
	My faire bryd, my sweete cynamome?	
	Awaketh, lemman°, myn and speketh to me!	lover/sweetheart
15	Wel litel° thynken ye upon my wo°,	little indeed; wretchedness
	That for youre love I swete° ther° I go.	sweat; wherever
	No wonder is thogh that I swelte° and swete;	faint with the heat
	I moorne° as dooth° a lamb after the tete.	mourn/yearn for; does
	Ywis°, lemman, I have swich love-longynge,	certainly
20	That lik a turtel° trewe° is my moornynge°.	turtle dove; true/faithful; yearning

I may nat° ete° na moore than a mayde°.' . . .   *not; eat; girl*
    The wyndow she undoth, and that in haste.
'Have do°,' quod° she,'com of°, and speed the faste°,   *have done; said; hurry up;*
    be quick

    Lest that oure neighebores thee espie.'
25   This Absolon gan wype his mouth ful° drie.   *very*
    Derk was the nyght as pich, or as the cole,
    And at the wyndow out she putte hir hole°,   *hole/backside*
    And Absolon, hym fil no bet ne wers°,   *no better or worse thing happened to him*
    But with his mouth he kiste° hir naked ers°   *kissed; buttocks/arse*
30   Ful savourly°, er he were war of this°.   *eagerly/with relish; before he realised*
    what he was doing

    Abak° he stirte°, and thoughte it was amys°,   *backwards; jumped; something*
    was wrong

    For wel he wiste° a womman hath no berd.   *knew*
    He felte a thyng al rough and long yherd°,   *covered with hair*
    And seyde, 'Fy°! allas! what have I do?'   *expression of contempt*
35   'Tehee!' quod she, and clapte° the wyndow to,   *closed*
    And Absolon gooth forth a sory pas°.   *at a sorrowful pace/dejectedly*
    'A berd! a berd!' quod hende° Nicholas,   *courteous/gentle*
    'By Goddes corpus°, this goth faire° and weel.'   *God's body; successfully*
    This sely° Absolon herde every deel°,   *simple/naive; detail*
40   And on his lippe he gan for anger byte,
    And to himself he seyde, 'I shal thee quyte°.'   *repay*

Commentary

We can immediately see how Chaucer has adapted traditional genres here. The content of the opening lines (ll.1–21) describing Absolon's preparations and his courting of Alison reflect the traditions of courtly romance; the content of the final section (ll.22–41) narrating Alison's trick is directly linked to the fabliau tradition. The juxtaposition of these genres allows Chaucer to develop his distinctive satirical tone – he mocks the affected mood of the court romances while sharpening the comedy of the original fabliaux. The antithesis of the two sections creates a tension between the ideal and the real, the court and the country and between rhetoric and action.

The style Chaucer adopts is directly linked to the genre and content – each section has a distinctive tone and diction to draw attention to Chaucer's satire. The opening focuses on the characterisation of Absolon as a romantic hero. He uses the traditional language of love, calling Alison *hony-comb, sweete Alisoun* (l.12), *faire bryd* and *sweete cynamome* (l.13). These are in direct contrast to the words used earlier in the *Tale* to describe Alison – she is compared with a *wezele*, a *kide or calf* and a *joly colt*. Such descriptions identify her individuality and love of life in a way that Absolon's traditional language does not. The opposition between these two approaches to naming allows Chaucer to mock the superficiality of Absolon's language and undermine the conventional nature of court romance.

The tone of mockery is developed in the details linked to Absolon's preparations (ll.4–6). Everything is done to excess – he dresses *at poynt-devys* (l.3); he chews *greyn and lycorys* in order to *smellen sweete* (l.5). Chaucer draws attention to the triviality of all these acts in his satiric remark that all this is done *er he hadde kembd his heer* (l.5). Throughout the *Tale*, references to Absolon's hair as *Crul* (curled), *gold* and *strouted* (spread out) *as a fanne* and to the fact that he *kembeth* (combs) *his lokkes brode* to make himself look appealing, suggest that he is interested in appearance rather than in more meaningful things. This also enables Chaucer to undermine the ideals of courtly romance represented by Absolon, and promote the values of everyday life represented by Alison and Nicholas.

Chaucer's choice of language reinforces our sense of Absolon as a dandy who cares more about the appearance of things than about the reality of love. The direct speech (ll.12–21) prepares the reader for this. Absolon uses the traditional language and sentiment of courtly love, asking for a favour and saying that Alison should pity his *wo* (l.15) – his melancholy, his love-sickness and his inability to eat. Chaucer's tone is satirical and the rhetorical patterning draws attention to the shallowness of Absolon's words. The listing of epithets for Alison is excessive (ll.12–13); the juxtaposition of his attempts to *smellen sweete* (l.5) and Chaucer's use of *swelte and swete* (l.7) is humorous – particularly since we do not associate any extreme emotion or physical exertion with Absolon. Similarly, the contrast created between *this joly lovere Absolon* (l.2) and words like *wo* (l.15), *moorne* (l.18) and *moornynge* (l.20) suggests a crafted performance on Absolon's part.

Such language draws attention to the differences between Nicholas and Alison's physical passion and the artifice of Absolon's declaration. While Alison and Nicholas plan a consummation of their love, Absolon merely talks. The traditional portrait of an 'ideal' lover is used satirically and Chaucer ensures that the reader recognises this through his lexical and stylistic choices.

The imagery heightens the satire. The simile likening Absolon to a *turtel* (turtle-dove, l.20) may be traditional, but the metaphors of the *lamb* that mourns *after the tete* (l.18) and the *mayde* (l.21) who cannot eat undermine the concept of Absolon the courtly lover. He is instead seen as pathetic – where he has aimed to inspire pity and sympathy, he has instead made himself seem ridiculous. In comparison with the masculine Nicholas, he is presented as weak and inadequate.

Chaucer clearly wants his readers to identify with the young lovers: Absolon is portrayed as an affected fop and the carpenter as a fool for taking a wife who is so unlike him. Absolon may have the courtly manners, the fashionable clothes and the style of a courtly lover, but he lacks Nicholas' practicality and rural directness. The focus on everyday life, and the use of a vernacular form of English is typical of the fabliau genre. Chaucer adds to the comedy of the traditional form, however, by using the conventions associated with courtly romances in a satirical way.

The Miller's narrative does not live up to the standards set up by the Knight's traditional courtly tale – the gentility of the 'ideal' at the heart of the earlier story is replaced here by a reminder of the real world and all its faults. It is indicative of the teller that the tale is a celebration of physicality; it is indicative of Chaucer's approach that, despite his abnegation of responsibility for the content, we see his delight in life's variety. The comic approach is typical of both *The Miller's Tale* and *The Canterbury Tales* as a whole: traditional figures of fun such as tradesmen and scholars are allowed to thrive, while the superficiality of the court is exposed through references to dress, manners and language; contrasts between characters are exaggerated for comic effect; and Chaucer's use of different voices – the crude one of the Miller and his own sophisticated one – guides the reader's response.

Chaucer and the English poetic tradition

During the Middle Ages, the emergence of a standard form of English began the process of fixing the language, and printing made the written word accessible to a wider audience. English gained in prestige and became an acceptable medium for scholarly debate, religious treatises and literature.

Much of the surviving literature still revolves around biblical stories and religious thought, but the content is far more varied than that of the extant Old English manuscripts. Medieval texts reflect the growing interest in secular as well as religious themes. The focus is on everyday life and ordinary people as well as biblical figures, the lives of the saints, heroic knights and supernatural beings. By mixing genres, adapting sources and developing recognisable individual voices, medieval writers established a distinctive English literary tradition.

Chaucer is perhaps the most well known of the Middle English writers and is certainly central to the development of English poetry. He records his observations in balanced and polished verse that still has the directness of everyday language, proving that English could be a successful literary medium. His skill in narrative and characterisation make his work unique, but it is his comic method that distinguishes him from other writers of the time. The ironic tone with which he observes and comments on medieval society and its inhabitants is distinctive. He exploits the conflicts between the real and the ideal in the form, language and structure of his work for comic effect.

In *The Parliament of Fowls*, for instance, Chaucer subverts the ideal of courtly traditions. The lower orders among the birds not only criticise the conventions of courtly love, but also win their mates and can celebrate the coming of summer with a song and dance. The noble eagles, on the other hand, are so entangled in a complex code of behaviour that, having wasted most of the day in pleading their cases, they must wait a year before learning of their mates. The courtly elevated love of *Troilus and Criseyde* is balanced by the practical realism of Pandarus who intervenes to get the lovers into bed together. Finally, with the companionable rather than censorious humour of *The Canterbury Tales*, we see Chaucer both expose the real hypocrisies and failings of his time and exemplify the ideal of nobility where it exists.

Chaucer's reputation dominated fifteenth-century English literature – William Caxton, who introduced printing in 1476, believed that it was not worth publishing any book in English earlier than *The Canterbury Tales*. He was to be praised for his skill in characterisation by the poets John Dryden (1631–1700) and William Blake (1757–1827), and for his *liquid diction, fluid movement, largeness, freedom, shrewdness, benignity* by the poet Matthew Arnold (1822–88). In addition, modern critics recognise the significance of his religious and philosophical themes, the sophistication of his apparently simple language and style, and his understanding of dramatic interaction.

10 Poetry of the sixteenth and seventeenth centuries

As the medieval period came to an end, there was a great explosion of interest in learning and the arts – it was to be known as the Renaissance. The term literally means 'rebirth' and was used to reflect a renewed interest in the writings of the Classical pagan world, and in intellectual and artistic pursuits. Interest in exploration and investigation in the fields of science, geography and maths meant that there was increased understanding of the nature of the universe. Questions were asked about things that had always been accepted and boundaries were broken. This inevitably had an effect on man's relationship with God – it was an age marked by religious doubt. Much of the literature focuses on topics such as the nature of spirituality in an increasingly secular society, faith and doubt, disorder, and moral codes in a time of decadence. The medieval approach to the arts also changed, providing the kind of cultural and intellectual background that was to produce such writers as Christopher Marlowe (1564–93), William Shakespeare (1564–1616), Ben Jonson (1572–1637) and John Milton (1608–74).

Humanism was an important movement at this time since it placed emphasis on personal judgement and individualism, on education and literacy, and on the value of the vernacular for serious writing. It saw classical studies as a central part of education and believed that antiquity should be used as a model or standard for culture. It aimed to produce a society of thinkers, individuals who were able to develop their own judgements and cultural tastes.

Although there were to be no more invasions, the sixteenth and seventeenth centuries were not without conflict. The Reformation of the early sixteenth century saw violent changes in the Church and State. One of the biggest upheavals in English history was when Henry VIII and his Chief Minister Thomas Cromwell broke the 1000-year link with the Catholic Church in Rome after Henry's failure to persuade the Pope to allow his divorce from Catherine of Aragon. Between 1532 and 1534, Henry instituted Acts of Parliament that were to end the Pope's power in England and make the king Supreme Head of the Church. This was followed by the legalised suppression of the monasteries and the seizure of their property, the creation of Protestant churches and a growing interest in the Calvinist tradition.

The seventeenth century was also a time of continuing religious and political conflict. Britain was firmly Protestant, and Roman Catholics and Puritans were persecuted – the Gun Powder Plot of 1605 was intended to undermine Protestant rule. The struggle between Charles I and Parliament over the collecting of state revenue led to unrest in London and it quickly spread to the rest of the country, making civil war inevitable by 1642. When Charles was beheaded in 1649, the monarchy was abolished and England became a 'Commonwealth' led by Oliver Cromwell, the Lord Protector, from 1653 to 1660. After Cromwell's death in 1658, splits emerged in the Commonwealth and negotiations were begun for the restoration of Charles II to the English throne after 11 years with no monarch.

The literary context

The years following Chaucer are often described as a transition period because there were few distinctive individual writers – his continuing influence meant that much of the verse written adopted his style and tone. Poets like Lydgate (c. 1370–1449) and Skelton (1460–1529) imitated him, producing work with romantic tendencies or with a humorous tone, using allegory and realistic narrative.

Skelton's later work is, however, original, recognisable for its satirical tone and individual style. Poems like 'The Tunning of Elinor Ruming' and 'Colin Clout' make humorous attacks on contemporary life. He wrote in short, repeatedly rhyming lines in a vernacular form of English – a style that became known as 'Skeltonics' or 'tumbling verse'. Although similar to doggerel, Skelton's later verse is recognised as a distinctive and respectable development of poetic form.

The Petrarchan sonnets of Sir Thomas Wyatt (1503–42) and Henry Howard, Earl of Surrey (1517–47), written in the style of the Italian school where love is contemplated as a theme for reflection rather than as a passion, also mark a significant development in the English poetic tradition. Wyatt's poems reflect the social concerns of his time, but also record a personal response to events in his life. His focus is on human experience and this means that his work still has relevance for modern readers. The love poems, for instance, focus on the emotions of falling in love, the hurt of rejection and the effects of betrayal. He adopts the traditional conventions of love poetry, but at the same time manages to make his poems a direct personal statement. The style reflects this mix of the conventional and the individual – he mixes conversational everyday English with the formality of a tightly structured poetic form.

Wyatt is an important figure in the development of English poetry because he represents a complete break with the Chaucerian tradition. Rather than developing the loosely structured satiric verse of Skelton, he establishes a new approach and lays the ground for the great age of English poetry that was to follow. As a court poet, he composed verse to entertain his audience, but also made his mark by developing a distinctive personal voice.

The Elizabethan period (1558–1603) marks an exciting departure for English literature in terms of the quantity and quality of the texts produced, the range of thought, the variety of expression, the number of well-known names, and the success achieved in all genres. It saw the increasingly sophisticated use of poetic and dramatic forms, and it was at this time that English literature acquired European fame. For many literary critics, it represents the beginning of the modern literary tradition.

Sometimes seen as a preparation for the development of a distinctive literary prose tradition in the eighteenth century, the Restoration period (1660–1700) is perhaps most well known for its characteristic dramatic comedy. By the end of the century, however, there was a growing interest in culture with biographies, satires, journals and diaries becoming popular forms of writing. More was published by women writers and a distinctive Restoration theatrical style had emerged.

There are many reasons for the flourishing literary tradition of the sixteenth and seventeenth centuries: printing made texts more accessible; the Renaissance revived interest in learning; the reformation of religion placed importance upon individual literacy; and the patronage of the arts by the Court gave artists a more professional role. English literature became a serious medium and no longer needed to imitate the classical and foreign models it had earlier used as its sources.

Elizabethan verse

The Elizabethan age was to mark one of the richest periods in the history of English literature; it was remarkable for the creative activity and range of its output. Although perhaps most well known for its drama, Elizabethan poetry also flourished with poets such as Sir Philip Sidney (1554–86), Edmund Spenser, Sir Walter Ralegh (1554–1618), and later Christopher Marlowe, Shakespeare and Ben Jonson.

None of Sir Philip Sidney's works were published during his lifetime, but his verse set a standard for contemporary poets. His *Defence of Poetry* (1579–80) draws attention to the value of poetry in all cultures, and to its potential for teaching virtue through a representation of the possible rather than the actual. It also includes discussion of the *parts, kinds, or species* of poetry, and Sidney's belief that English is a fitting language for the poet. Sidney's essay was to be the first significant example of English literary criticism.

Sidney was a supporter of the humanist movement with its interest in classical form and its belief in the value of the vernacular as an appropriate language for literature. He experimented with classical metres in English and was influential in shaping the verse of the period both as a literary patron and as a practitioner. His romance *Arcadia* (1581; revised 1583–4) and sonnet sequence *Astrophel and Stella* (1582) – the first sonnet sequence in English – are evidence of his belief that English verse could be metrically and structurally perfect. Although the style is rhetorical, the diction is simple and the range of imagery striking. At his death, volumes of Latin elegies from Oxford, Cambridge and the Continent testified to his political and literary influence.

Edmund Spenser (c. 1552–99)

Spenser is one of the most well-known poets of the Elizabethan period. He was an accomplished scholar and a pupil of the humanist school with a classical background that provided him with inspiration for his writing. He was introduced to Court society by Lord Leicester who became his patron: a contact that gave him access to the political and literary society of his times. When Leicester fell from favour in 1580, the individuals who had been dependent on him were also affected. Spenser was sent to Ireland as a secretary to the Lord Deputy who governed Ireland. He felt as though he had been exiled and much of his poetry indirectly reflects his strong feelings about his exclusion.

In 1579, Spenser's first major work, *The Shepheardes Calender*, was published. It was made up of twelve eclogues (a short poem in the form of a dialogue or soliloquy, often with a pastoral content) – one for each month. The poems were closely modelled on the eclogues of Theocritus (c.308–c.240BC), Virgil (70–19BC) and Mantuan (1448–1516). The collection of poems provided the first evidence of Spenser's distinctive personal approach – he combined allegory and pastoral elegy with a discussion of key issues; he portrayed the everyday experiences of English shepherds alongside the idyllic pastoral world of classical literature; and he demonstrated his technical skills.

The publication of the first three books of *The Faerie Queene* in 1590, followed by books IV–VI in 1596, marks an important point in the English literary tradition. The work can be identified with the Middle English allegorical tradition of *Piers Plowman*, but can also be seen as an English version of the Italian Arthurian epics of Ariosto (1475–1533) and Tasso (1544–95). Spenser wanted to create a Tudor myth to reflect the grand tradition of the British monarchy, however, so he does more than imitate his sources: the Faerie Queene is Queen Elizabeth I – *the most excellent and glorious person of our sovereign Queen*. The work is on a grand scale, covering some 1030 pages. In it, Spenser combines political reality with moral allegory; records details of life in the Court within a framework of epic adventure; and develops a distinctive poetic form.

The Fairie Queene was to have been made up of twelve books, but the text was not completed before Spenser's death; he wrote only six books with some cantos and stanzas for the seventh. The first book provides no explanations but launches straight into the narrative (the overall framework was to have been revealed in the twelfth book). It is *an historicall fiction* which focuses on the history of Arthur before he became king. He is *a braue knight, perfected in the twelue morall vertues*, and a symbolic representation of Magnanimity.

Other characters are also symbolic – each of the twelve knights is associated with a particular virtue: for example, the Red Cross Knight is Holiness, Britomartis is Chastity, Sir Calidore is Courtesy. The poem is made up of the adventures each knight must face as their virtue is tested. After a dream of the Fairy Queen, Gloriana, Arthur decides to search for her and comes across the other knights at a crucial point in their adventures. The book was to end with the marriage of Arthur and Gloriana, although in the six books Spenser completed, Arthur is not a central character and the Fairy Queen does not appear.

The moral allegory, embedded in the personification of the virtues, is underpinned by Spenser's political allegory. As well as representing a moral virtue, the poem's characters are also symbolic of historical figures or institutions: Una personifies Truth in the abstract and the Protestant Church in the concrete; Arthur is Magnanimity and the Earl of Leicester; Orgoglio is the Antichrist and King Philip of Spain. In this way, Spenser could combine contemporary comment with the traditional personification of the morality plays.

As a court poet, Spenser was expected to use the conventions of contemporary verse. He was not content, however, just to adopt the existing poetic traditions. Instead he refined existing literary forms and created a distinctive style of poetry. Spenser devised his own poetic form from Chaucer's 8-lined stanzas. Each stanza is made up of 9 iambic lines; the first 8 have five feet (pentameter), the ninth has six (the Alexandrine or English hexameter). The rhyme follows the pattern of ababbcbcc: a structure that came to be known as the 'Spenserian stanza'.

The language of Spenser's poetry is also distinctive. He drew on Chaucer's vocabulary to create an archaic mood, but also chose words that reflected the reality of the Court and its language. The expression is clear, the style fluent and polished, and the argument well organised. The verse works on different levels – narrative action is combined with description, reflection, and moral or political comment. Although a modern reader may find the world Spenser portrays alien, his work was to influence many poets from Milton to the Romantics of the nineteenth century.

While some disliked Spenser's consciously anachronistic diction and style, no one could deny the ambitious scale and craftsmanship of his verse: *The Faerie Queene* is a significant work in the English poetic tradition. Beneath the fairyland story with its strong visual images lie both a traditional moral allegory and a political commentary. Within the context of the Elizabethan period, some critics see the poem as an ironic comment on the growing difference between the ideal fictional world Spenser created on the page and the harsh reality of what he saw around him.

Other key works include his collection of love sonnets (*Amoretti*, 1595), *Epithalamion* (1595) written in celebration of his second marriage, and *Prothalamion* (1596) written for the double marriage of the Earl of Richmond's daughters. Although Spenser was to fall from favour during the eighteenth century, his influence on English poetry is significant.

Activity 10.1

How do changes in content, language and tone relate to the function of each of the following extracts from Spenser's *The Faerie Queene*?

You may like to think about: the diction, the sound patterning, literary and rhetorical devices, the medieval allegorical tradition, narrative features, personal comments and moral reflection.

EXTRACT 1 – BOOK I, CANTO IX, STANZA 33

1	Ere long they come, where that same wicked wight°	man [Despair]
	His dwelling has, low in an hollow caue°,	cave
	Farre vnderneath a craggie clift ypight°,	placed
	Darke, dolefull, drearie, like a greedie graue°,	grave
5	That still for carrion carcases doth craue°:	crave
	On top whereof aye dwelt the ghastly Owle,	
	Shrieking his balefull note, which euer° draue°	ever; drove
	Farre from that haunt all other chearefull fowle°;	bird
	And all about it wandring ghostes did waile and howle.	

10   The knight much wondred at [Despair's] suddeine wit°,   quick intelligence
        And said, The terme of life is limited,
        Ne may a man prolong, nor shorten it;
        The souldier may not moue from watchfull sted°,   place
        Nor leaue his stand, vntill his Captaine bed.
15   Who life did limit by almightie doome°,   judgement
        (Quoth he) knowes best the termes established;
        And he, that points the Centonell his roome,
        Doth license him depart at sound of morning droome°.   drum

        And him beside rides fierce reuenging° *Wrath*,   revenging
20   Vpon a Lion, loth for to be led;
        And in his hand a burning brond° he hath,   brand/sword
        The which he brandisheth about his hed;
        His eyes did hurle forth sparkles fiery red,
        And stared sterne on all, that him beheld,
25   As ashes pale of hew and seeming ded;
        And on his dagger still his hand he held,
        Trembling through hasty rage, when choler° in him sweld.   anger/wrath

        His ruffin raiment° all was staind with blood,   clothes
        Which he had spilt, and all to rags yrent°,   torn
30   Through vnaduized° rashnesse woxen° wood°;   unadvised; became; mad
        For of his hands he had no gouernement°,   government/control
        Ne car'd for bloud in his auengement°:   vengeance
        But when the furious fit was ouerpast°,   past
        His cruell facts° he often would repent;   deeds
35   Yet wilfull man he neuer would forecast°,   predict
        How many mischieues should ensue° his heedlesse hast°.   follow; haste

        The time was once, in my first prime of yeares,
        When pride of youth forth pricked my desire,
50   That I disdain'd amongst mine equall peares
        To follow sheepe, and shepheards base attire:
        For further fortune then I would inquire.
        And leaung home, to roiall court I sought;
        Where I did sell my selfe for yearly hire,
55   And in the Princes gardin daily wrought:
        There I beheld such vainenesse, as I neuer thought.

Commentary

In Book I, Canto IX, the content focuses on the meeting between the Red Cross Knight and Una's enemy, Despair. On one level, this is a confrontation between two characters, the Red Cross Knight and *A man of hell, that cals himselfe Despaire*; on another level it is a moral discussion about holiness and despair. Within this structure, **Extract 1** fulfils a **narrative function**. Spenser creates a vivid setting in which the encounter between the Red Cross Knight and Despair can take place. Concrete nouns such as *caue* (l2) and *clift* (l.3) give details of the physical background; adverbials of place (*vnderneath*, *On top*, *all about*) add depth to the setting; and modifiers create an appropriate mood for the moral lesson underpinning the narrative. Adjectives such as *hollow* (l.2), *Darke, dolefull* and *drearie* (l.4) describe the cave where Despair lives – the asyndetic listing (l.4) intensifies the atmosphere of gloom. Other modifiers (*ghastly*, l.6; *balefull*, l.7) describe the Owl, the only other inhabitant of this place apart from the *ghostes* (l.9) who *waile and howle*. The atmosphere created by the modifiers is reinforced by the simile (ll.4–5) of the *greedie graue* and the personification implied by the emotive verb *craue*. The sound patterning adds to the eerie mood: alliteration of harsh consonants like *craggie clift* (l.3), *Darke, dolefull, drearie, greedie graue* (l.4) and *carrion carcases* (l.5) mirrors the harshness of the physical environment and its mood.

The literary techniques here create the background for a traditional narrative with brave knights, damsels in distress, giants, dragons, haunted forests and enchanted castles of epic adventure. Embedded within the narrative, however, there is another more meditative layer in which the characters comment on philosophical or spiritual issues. In **Extract 2**, narrative is replaced by **reflection on a moral issue**. Although spoken by a character, the content is now discursive: the Red Cross Knight becomes the spokesman for the traditional Christian belief that God dictates how long we live and when we die. Spenser is paraphrasing the Roman writer Cicero (106–43BC) in *De Senectute* 20.73, describing God as the Captain who will dismiss us from our posts when the time is right.

The style is no longer descriptive, but formal and discursive. Emotive modifiers are replaced with legal diction: *terme* (l.11), *termes, established* (l.16) and *license* (l.18); parallel structures create a sense of balance and logic: *prolong . . . shorten* (l.12); *not moue . . ./Nor leaue* (ll.13–14). The need to create a powerful atmosphere is replaced with the need to convey a spiritual truth and this is achieved through the extended metaphor of the *souldier* (l.13) and his *Captaine* (l.14).

Spenser's description of one of the Seven Deadly Sins in **Extract 3** is directly linked to the **morality play tradition** of the Middle Ages, but he creates a character that has a strong physical presence as well as a moral function. The visual detail helps readers to create a powerful image of Wrath as an individual, and begins to convey something of his temperament. Concrete nouns such as *eyes* (ll.23), *hand* (ll.21, 26), *raiment, blood* (l.28), *rags* (l.29) giving us physical information are balanced by the abstract nouns *rage, choler* (l.27) and *rashnesse* (l.30) that develop the traditional characteristics of the personified sin. The image of Wrath riding on a lion and carrying a burning brand reinforces this in a visual way since the reader associates Wrath with the wildness of the lion and the potential destructiveness of fire.

The modifiers *fierce* (l.19), *sterne* (l.24), *hasty* (l.27) and *cruell* (l.34) characterise Wrath in a negative way, adding to the attributes of his personality already established by the abstract nouns. Other modifiers (*wilfull*, l.35; *heedlesse*, l.36) distance us from Wrath by suggesting that his actions and attitudes are conscious. This is juxtaposed with the repentance which follows each *furious fit* (l.15) – although regretting what he has done, Wrath is not concerned enough to *forecast* (l.17) other occasions, thus preventing future bloodshed. Lexical sets enhance the mood of destruction: references to the *burning brond* (l.21) and the metaphorical *sparkles fiery red* (l.23) which *hurle forth* from his eyes represent his flaring temper; associated words and phrases such as *vnaduized, wood* (l.30), *no gouernement* (l.31) and *fit* (l.33) reflect Wrath's lack of control.

Spenser's portrait of Wrath is successful because visual detail is directly linked to the nature of his character. He has a strong narrative presence and the two stanzas quoted here portray more than just a traditional cameo of one of the Seven Deadly Sins. Instead, the lexical choices persuade readers to see Wrath as an individual as well as a symbolic representation.

By adding a sense of his own time, Spenser enlivens the medieval moral allegorical tradition on which he draws. While the religious symbolism is directly related to the literature of the Middle English period, the comment is often contemporary – some directly related to Spenser's own experiences. In **Extract 4**, the sentiments expressed are thought to reflect **Spenser's feelings about the Court** and his own position within it. An opposition is created between the purity of the simple rural life and the superficiality of the *roiall court*. Phrases with positive connotations (*equall peares*, l.50) represent the honest occupation Spenser left behind, while the negative connotations of *vainenesse* (l.56) highlight his dissatisfaction with court life.

In the opening lines, the reader is shown the potential that the young Spenser could not see in his rural life. By using the adjective *prime* as the head word in a noun phrase, Spenser draws attention to what could have been the best years of his life. Yet the juxtaposition of *pride of youth* and *desire*, with its connotations of physical rather than spiritual longings, prepares us for the lack of fulfilment he will find in the Court. The negative connotations of the verb *disdain'd* and the adjective *base* emphasise the young Spenser's attitude. The certainty and hopeful potential conveyed by the modal verb *would* (l.52), however, will come to nothing.

His tone is self-critical. Words like *sell* and *yearly hire* (l.54) indicate his dislike of the way in which allegiance to the Court affects the independence of the Court poet – he appears to feel compromised by the need to sustain favour. Other words like *pride* (l.49) and *disdain'd* (l.50) suggest that the mature poet considers the actions of his youth to have been ill advised.

In all the extracts here, we see the regularity of the ababbcbcc rhyme and the eight pentameters and final hexameter, or alexandrine (12 syllables), giving the poem its distinctive structure and mood. The addition of the ninth line to the traditional octave changes the pace and thus demands our attention. Tied to the last line of the octave by the creation of a rhyming couplet, the alexandrine brings each stanza to a stately conclusion – a mark of the personal voice Spenser created.

Shakespeare's sonnets

In Elizabethan England, the sonnet was a fashionable pastime and sonneteers flourished. **Shakespeare** (1564–1616) adapted the traditional sonnet, developing and extending the possibilities of the form. In his sequence, the overall narrative structure is not as clearly defined as in other contemporary sequences, but the cohesion developed between the sonnets is more sophisticated.

Shakespeare's *Sonnets* were published in 1609, but there is an ongoing critical debate about the date of their composition. Some critics believe they were written early in Shakespeare's career, around the time of *King Henry VI, Richard III, Titus Andronicus, Love's Labour's Lost, The Two Gentlemen of Verona, The Comedy of Errors* and *The Taming of the Shrew* – that is, before 1594. A more acceptable proposal would suggest that the sonnets were written at different times and then later brought together in an order that consisted of a developing argument with an underlying sense of continuity.

The sequence is marked by similarities in subject matter, theme and style. In terms of the **content**, the poems can be divided as follows: I–CXXVI are addressed to a handsome young man, the poet's patron and social superior; CXXVII–LII are addressed to the 'Dark Lady' of the sonnets who appears to be both perverse and bewitching; CLIII–IV are conventional exercises. Many readers approach the sonnets hoping to find out something about the poet himself and his life, but it is difficult to assess Shakespeare's relationship with the content. There may be hints of autobiographical detail (the poet's love for *a woman colour'd ill*; a stolen mistress; his transcendent love for the man who transforms his whole vision of the world), but the sonnets cannot be seen in the same way as intimate letters. Many appear to draw on universal subjects (the transience of beauty, the destructiveness of time, the immortality of poetry) with none of the dramatic intensity of real life experiences.

Traditional **themes** provide a focus, but Shakespeare looks at these with a new perspective. He presents a contradictory argument and then attempts to reconcile the conflicting ideas. The sonnet form has long been associated with the theme of love and Shakespeare's sequence also uses this as its running thread. He treats the theme broadly, however, dealing with relationships (with his patron: Sonnet CII; his lover: Sonnet XVIII) and analysing the complexity of emotions and attitudes (the nature of love: Sonnet CXVI; the passing of beauty: Sonnet XII; death: Sonnet LXXIII). Many of the sonnets have a bitter tone and these focus on the restrictions time places on all human relationships. In addressing the nature of our mortality, Shakespeare considers ways in which we can defy time through marriage (Sonnet XI), children (Sonnets I and VI), love (Sonnets CXV, CXVI and CXXIII) – even through the sonnets themselves, which will inevitably outlive him (Sonnets LV, LX and LXIII).

The theme of mutability is closely linked to his recognition of the ever-changing processes of life (Sonnet LX). Deceptive appearances, illusions and the unpredictable nature of the imagination all feature in his observations. Underlying everything is an understanding of the instability of life.

The **form** is tightly structured: the division of the 14 lines is directly linked to the organisation of the argument. Unlike Petrarchan sonnets, the Shakespearean sonnet uses three quatrains to build an argument and the final couplet to provide a conclusion which forces the reader to reassess what has just been read. Where the Petrarchan sonnet form provides a logical conclusion to an ordered argument, the Shakespearean form mirrors the poet's attempt to resolve the conflict lying at the heart of his topic.

The rhyme scheme is distinctive:

<pre>
 1   Like as the waves make towards the pebbled shore,
      So do our minutes hasten to their end;
      Each changing place with that which goes before,
      In sequent toil all forwards do contend°.   struggle
 5   Nativity, once in the main of light,
      Crawls to maturity, wherewith being crown'd
      Crooked eclipses 'gainst his glory fight,
      And Time, that gave, doth now his gift confound°.   overthrow
      Time doth transfix° the flourish set on youth,   pierce through
10   And delves° the parallels in beauty's brow;   digs
      Feeds on the rarities of nature's truth,
      And nothing stands but for his scythe to mow:
          And yet to times in hope my verse shall stand,
          Praising thy worth, despite his cruel hand.
                                          (Sonnet LX)
</pre>

The pattern of the rhyme (ababcdcdefefgg) distinguishes the Shakespearean sonnet from the Petrarchan, which uses a different pattern. The rhymes mark out the separate elements of the argument, by providing cohesion in each thought. In Sonnet LX, lines 1–4 establish an analogy by comparing movement in the natural world with the progress of Time in human life; lines 5–8 elaborate the concept of Time by focusing in more detail on the effects it has on people; lines 9–12 return to the parallel between the natural and human worlds, concluding with a recognition of the irresistible process of Time which will inevitably destroy everything. The certainty of that knowledge, however, is replaced in the final couplet with an element of hope – despite the inevitability of mortality, the poem itself cannot be ravaged by Time. The change of direction forces us to reconsider the poem as a whole: the structure is circular; the final lines require readers to reinterpret the apparently logical argument of the previous lines.

The economy of the form means that the **style** is marked by intensity: the language is heightened; the structure is tightly patterned; and metrical rhythms are carefully controlled. The technical rigour of the sonnets means that readers must be active; Shakespeare expects us to make connections, to engage with the argument, and to reassess accepted knowledge in the light of the final couplet.

In Sonnet LX quoted above, the emphasis on time is stressed through the lexical set of words linked to it: *minutes, end, changing, sequent*. These allow Shakespeare to focus on the instability of things in the face of passing time and this moves him logically to the direct effect these have on people. The lexical patterning of the first quatrain clearly identifies the parallel between the natural and human worlds: words such as *waves* and *pebbled shores* are placed alongside the image of *our minutes* moving inevitably towards *their end* where the use of the possessive determiners clearly identifies man's futile attempt to control time.

The suggestion of man's false sense of superiority is continued in the second quatrain through the image of growth from birth (*Nativity*) to adulthood (*maturity*). The verb *Crawls* implies the length of time it takes to reach adulthood, yet this is deceptive since time cannot be trusted – once *crown'd*, the verb suggesting some kind of peak of achievement, time seems to gain authority. Shakespeare reinforces this through his juxtaposition of the abstract noun *glory* and the dynamic verb *fight*, reminding us of man's inability to do anything in the face of passing time. The end position of *fight* and the personification of *Time* in the following line build Shakespeare's argument to a climax: life is but Time's *gift*. The parenthetical phrase *that gave* and the end focus on *confound* emphasise that people cannot control Time; life is a process of change in which we are at the mercy of a greater force. Words such as *toil* and *contend* remind us that life is a struggle, while the use of the predeterminer *all* stresses that no one is exempt from time's power.

In the first quatrain, time's power is implicit in the sense of process (l.3). Although the *crooked eclipses* in the second quatrain are concrete evidence of the passing of time, it is the personification (l.8) which gives Time a physical presence. With the image of his giving and taking of gifts, Shakespeare can suggest his tyrannical domination of the human and natural worlds.

The image of Time as a merciless tyrant is then developed in the final quatrain where dynamic verbs (*transfix*, *delves*, *Feeds*) convey Time's destructive nature. Juxtaposed with the negative verbs are positives: *the flourish set on youth, beauty's brow* and *the rarities of nature*. The fact that none of these are strong enough to withstand the onslaught of Time emphasises the inevitability of the process that will affect both man and Nature. The final line of the quatrain with its stressed co-ordinator in the initial position marks the climax of Shakespeare's argument: the use of *nothing* reinforces the sense that all life is subject to Time's authority; the use of *but for* . . . implies that life is only created so that Time can cut it down. The traditional image of the *scythe* is indicative of the mood at this stage of the sonnet – Time is symbolically associated with death, the natural and inescapable end to all life.

The final couplet changes the tone by suggesting that there is a way to defeat Time. The new direction to the argument is marked by the contrastive *And yet* in the initial position. Although Shakespeare recognises that the process cannot be stopped – hence the use of *despite* – his *verse* will survive. His certainty is conveyed by the modal verb *shall* and the negative mood of the quatrains is replaced with a focus on the positive: Time's *cruel hand* cannot be prevented from its work, but the poet's craft of *Praising* [his lover's] *worth will last for longer*. Attention is drawn to the importance of the last lines in changes to the iambic pattern:

> And yĕt | tŏ times | iň hope | mў verse | shǎll stǎnd,
> Praisiňg | thў worth, | dĕspite | hǐs cru | eľ hǎnd.

The use of the spondee in the first foot of the first line and the trochee in the second disrupts the weak-strong stress pattern just as Shakespeare's verse will defy death. The challenge to Time is highlighted by the grammatical style – readers have to wait for the emphatic main clause *my verse shall stand* because of the sequence of phrases that precede it.

* * *

In Shakespeare's sonnets we see evidence of a mature style: compression of thought, depth of meaning, an expressive use of language, and a combination of logical argument and personal views. He uses the intensity and economy required by the tight structure to create powerful reflections on subjects that are still meaningful to a modern reader. While the Petrarchan sonnet was less common after the 1590s, the English sonnet used by Shakespeare has continued, with John Donne and John Milton as the greatest masters of the form in the seventeenth century.

The Metaphysical poets

As a transitional age, the sixteenth and seventeenth centuries were marked by social disorder and religious breakdown. The general mood of doubt created by the Reformation provided the kind of atmosphere that encouraged scientific exploration and analysis, and this, in its turn, led to questions about man's place in the scheme of things. The poetry of this period is therefore marked by a need to question. The idealism of Spenser's fairytale epic is replaced by a sense of realism in which doubts about human experience, the soul and the world in general are voiced.

The Metaphysical poets took Spenser's creation of a personal voice in a new direction. While using traditional forms such as the sonnet and the lyric, they marked their work with a distinctive tone and style: colloquial language was mixed with formal expression; intellectual argument was combined with an intensely personal world view; satire and irony were used alongside a lyrical and devotional mood. They used 'wit' to encourage an intellectual response to a range of traditional subjects – paradox, antithesis and unexpected associations were used to challenge readers. By disrupting structural patterns, by creating unusual images which reflected the new scientific, mathematical and geographical knowledge of the time, and by treating the traditional topics of religion, love, death and the meaning of life in a stimulating way, they defied reader expectations.

It is important to remember that the term 'metaphysical' was only used to label poets like John Donne, George Herbert, Thomas Carew (1594/5–1640), Henry Vaughan and Andrew Marvell (1621–78) some time after their deaths. Dryden (1631–1700) first coined the word in 1693 and it was later used by Dr Johnson (1709–84) in his *Life of Cowley*. Critics continue to use it as a convenient label because the poetry written by the 'metaphysical' poets does have identifiable characteristics making it quite different from the poetry that came before and after it.

John Donne (1572–1631)

The poetry of **John Donne** reflects the period in which he lived – in a time of scientific exploration and discovery, his experimentation with content and style reflects interest in the new rather than the traditional. He treats poetic subjects such as love and religion in an unconventional way: his poems are full of original ideas and often revolve around a central paradox in which he challenges conventional morality. In a time that valued the individual, his poems clearly establish an idiosyncratic voice speaking about personal experiences and attitudes. Intellectual abstract thought exists alongside the sensual; wit and passion replace the lyrical purity of Elizabethan verse.

It is poetry that reflects an age in transition and Donne's approach to writing is therefore marked by the desire to find new ways of saying things. The traditional language of poetry is used alongside intellectual references to science, maths and geographical discovery; colloquial expressions and the natural rhythms of speech take the place of the poetic conventions of the time.

The content of Donne's poems is wide ranging – although he concentrates on the themes of love and religion, his approach is diverse and often unexpected. The poems from *Songs and Sonnets* deal with common themes: the constancy of love in a world of change; the anguish of physical separation; the falseness of lovers; the celebration of true love. While the *Songs and Sonnets* are probably the best known of Donne's poetry, he was also to write some of the finest English devotional poetry. In the highly personal 'Holy Sonnets', he explores the difficulty of finding true religion, the conflict between sin and the desire for purity, and his paradoxical relationship with God.

Donne's tone ranges from bitter cynicism at the fickleness of his mistress to a serious consideration of the nature of love; from querulous peevishness at God's judgements to resignation and humility. The poems are often addressed to an unseen listener (a lover, the sun, the Holy Trinity, God) and focus on the poet's state of mind. Because of the approach, they have an almost conversational tone.

Despite Donne's use of the language and rhythms of ordinary speech, the poems reflect everyday experience in an ingenious way. In each one, he presents an argument through a sequence of **metaphysical conceits** (an unexpected metaphor in which two disparate things are brought together in a comparison). Through the unusual images he creates, Donne seeks to confront and understand the complexity of the world around him. He links the intellectual and the emotional, the religious and the secular, the scientific and the poetic. The argument will seem to lead the reader in a particular direction, but the conclusion will often be paradoxical – the metaphysical wit provides an ending that is self-consciously clever and surprising.

In a poem like 'A Feaver', Donne adopts a traditional approach to love. On the surface, the content is predictable: while watching his mistress lying ill, the poet considers the possibility of a world without her, saying

> For I had rather owner bee
> Of thee, one houre, than all else ever.   (ll.27–8)

Despite the conventional mood of this sentiment, however, the content is unexpected. Donne portrays his mistress as the *worlds soule* – with her death, the world will become no more than her *carkasse*. Such images are clearly traditional in the sense that they draw attention to the lover's perfection, but they are unusual in the way that Donne links unexpected things. He elevates his mistress by emphasising her worth in comparison with the *fairest woman* and *worthiest men*, who are reduced to no more than a *ghost* and *corrupt wormes*. The negative connotations of the diction, the undermining of the superlatives and the unexpected comparisons allow Donne to express his love in an original way.

The fever that he observes in his mistress is also transformed. Initially associated with death, we are aware of its physical presence through words such as *fire*, *burne, torturing, burning fits*. It becomes symbolic, however, of the apocalyptic biblical fire that will cleanse the world (ll.13–16). The emphatic use of the modal verb *shall* and the dismissive tone of the opening interjection *O*, expressing Donne's disapprobation of the *wrangling* theologians who have failed to appreciate the significance of this *feaver*, elevate his mistress by assigning to her a worldly significance.

As the severity of the fever wears off, Donne's imagery changes. The *burning fits* become no more than *meteors*, shooting stars, *whose matter . . . is soon spent*. With the danger of death safely passed, he can once again contemplate his mistress's beauty, which, unlike the *meteors*, is the *unchangeable firmament*. In personifying the fever (ll.25–6), describing it as temporarily *seising* his lover as though in an embrace, he emphasises the value of his love.

Just as the content combines a traditional expression of love with unexpected images, so too the language combines a very personal address with more formal terms. The poem opens with a direct appeal to his mistress: *Oh doe not die . . .* and this personal note is reinforced through the informal and familiar use of pronouns like *thee* and *thou*. In stanzas 4–5, Donne changes to the third person using *her* and *she* as he tries to dispel his fears about her fever: he distances himself from his lover as though standing back and observing rather than directly addressing her. As he moves towards the climax of his argument, the return to direct address in the final stanzas is therefore made all the more poignant.

Alongside this personal use of language and the traditional language of love in references to *beauty* and *soule*, Donne uses unexpectedly harsh words like *carkasse*, *wormes* and *death*, and scholarly words like *schooles*, *wit*, *knowledge*, *search* and *aspire*. The end result is a poem in which he expresses his love for his mistress through the development of an intellectual argument rather than a traditional love lyric. The argument is framed by phrases like *But yet . . .*, *Or if . . .*, *And yet . . .* which mark out the stages of Donne's intellectual approach to an emotional moment.

This sense of control is reinforced by the rhetorical patterns. The repetition of *die* and associated words and the euphemisms *gone, leave . . . behinde*, and *goe* (ll.1–8) sets the opening tone. In the third stanza, the tripling of *but* (no more than) emphasises the insignificance of everything beside Donne's lover as he considers what a world without her would be like. It is a poem that uses parenthesis to control the pace and to draw attention to key phrases. The emphatic *I know*, for instance, highlights the poet's desperate attempts to convince himself that his lover will recover; the non-finite *seising thee* draws attention to the parallel Donne creates between the fever's embrace and a lover's embrace.

The form of the poem is regular and lyrical, observing a traditional use of quatrains and alternate rhymes. The iambic tetrameter creates a singsong conversational tone that is fitting for a love poem. Where the iambic foot changes, the shift in stress patterns emphasises key ideas. At the end of the second stanza, Donne uses a noun 'vapour' as a verb *vapors* to convey the dramatic effect the death of his mistress would have. As well as the change in grammatical class of the key word, he also changes the metrical pattern: the iambic foot is replaced by a spondee.

$$\text{Th}\breve{\text{e}} \text{ wh}\acute{\text{o}}\text{le} \mid \text{w}\acute{\text{o}}\text{rld v}\breve{\text{a}} \mid \text{p}\breve{\text{o}}\text{rs with} \mid \text{th}\breve{\text{y}} \text{ br}\acute{\text{e}}\text{ath.}$$

In the fifth stanza, Donne uses a trochaic foot to draw attention to his mistress's suffering:

$$\text{N}\breve{\text{o}}\text{r l}\acute{\text{o}}\text{ng} \mid \text{be}\acute{\text{a}}\text{re th}\breve{\text{i}}\text{s} \mid \text{t}\acute{\text{o}}\text{rt}\breve{\text{u}} \mid \text{r}\breve{\text{i}}\text{ng wr}\acute{\text{o}}\text{ng}$$

Such changes are an integral part of the meaning, allowing Donne to express his love through a poem that, while it recognises accepted poetic convention, challenges the idealism and lyricism of contemporary Elizabethan poets.

'A Valediction: Forbidding Mourning' has a similar tension between its language and content. It takes a traditional theme – love is not destroyed by physical absence – but treats it in an unexpected way. The opening focuses on a deathbed scene which seems an unlikely starting point for a love poem. The positive connotations of the lexis, the sibilance and the general mood of tranquillity soften the harshness of the scene as Donne begins to prepare readers for his unexpected comparison – just as there are no tears at the death of a good man, so too will Donne and his wife *melt, and make no noise* when they must part. The opening subordinate clauses (ll.1–4) reduce the importance of the death scene by driving us forward to the main clause in the first line of stanza 2: *So let us melt.*

Donne uses the grammatical structure to place emphasis upon the focus of his poem – the lovers. He then elevates their status through the use of the words *prophanation* and *layetie*. The religious connotations of these exalt the lovers, raising them to the status of saints who do not need superficial external signs as proof of their love as do the *Dull sublunary lovers* of stanza 4. By juxtaposing the physical (*eyes, lips, and hands*) with the psychological (*mind*), Donne draws attention to the ways in which he and his wife are *so much refin'd*. The tone of disparagement conveyed by the contrastive conjunction *But* at the beginning of stanza 5 clearly distances Donne and his lover from those dependent on physical proximity.

As in 'A Feaver', Donne's tone is personal: he directly addresses his wife in an intimate way using inclusive pronouns like *we* and *us*, and determiners like *our*. References to *virtuous men, their sad friends* and *Dull sublunary lovers* establish a sense of the wider world. In their impersonality, however, instead of diluting our sense of the lovers, they succeed in intensifying the microcosm of their inner world. The traditional language of love is private and personal, but here it is intensified as Donne sets his discussion within the context of different dimensions: the emotional and the earthly (*teare–floods/sigh–tempests*); the spiritual and physical (*prophanation of our joyes*). He delights in the sensual, but simultaneously elevates his theme by emphasising that his love can overcome absence.

The intellectual approach is more explicit here than in 'A Feaver'. Having established the nature of physical separation in stanzas 1–5, Donne proceeds to focus on the ways in which he and his wife are spiritually united:

> Our two soules therefore, which are one,
> Though I must goe, endure not yet
> A breach . . . (ll.21–3)

By making us wait for the main verb, *endure,* Donne can draw attention to the key information in parenthesis: their souls are joined; he has to leave her. The end of line focus on the negative *not yet* and the emphatic position of *A breach* adds to the dramatic effect. The negative phrase marks Donne's recognition of the truth: they will, in the end, be divided by death even though his present journey will not separate them. In addition, the use of the verb *endure* implies that they will suffer although there will be no visible signs. This is juxtaposed with the superficiality of other lovers *Whose soule is sense* – dependent on physical proximity to sustain their love, separation is marked by empty gestures. The inclusion of such references is typical of Donne's non-traditional approach. Instead of indulging in typically 'romantic' claims about their love, he places recognition of its strength within the context of the real world.

Donne uses technical images of the malleability of gold and the *stiffe twin compasses* in order to develop his argument. The image of the gold beaten to *ayery thinnesse* reflects the growth and delicacy of their love, while the compass forms the intellectual conceit that runs through the final stanzas. The comparison between the separated lovers and the compass is unexpected and striking. It allows Donne to continue his image of the two lovers as one – they are the circle formed by the compass when

> . . . the fixt foot, makes no show
> To move, but doth, if th'other doe.   (ll. 33–6)

The mathematical image of the compass is personalised with words like *leanes* and *hearkens* which create a sense of the physical and emotional yearnings of the lover who is left at home while *the other far doth rome.* The conceit is made explicit in the final stanza: the compass has drawn a perfect circle and this becomes an analogy for the stability of Donne's wife, who provides the moral centre to which he can return from his journey. These two levels are united in the use of the modifier *just* which refers both to the precision of the metaphorical circle and to the 'rightness' of his return to his wife at the end of his journey.

The poem is not a typical expression of love since Donne avoids commonplace images and seeks to find a means of presenting his feelings in an individual way. He takes disparate images of the deathbed, gold, the compass and circles in order to intellectualise his emotions. The poem is based upon contrasts: Donne and his wife versus the *Dull sublunary lovers*; soul versus body; death versus life; travelling versus staying at home; physical love versus spiritual love. These form the basis of Donne's argument, allowing him to lead the reader through his analogies to an understanding of the experience of being in love. His argument is dramatised because it is presented in the form of a direct address to his wife and this makes it accessible despite the complexity of his approach.

John Donne's love poetry is always grounded in the real world. He replaces the Elizabethan quest for the ideal with a tone and style that reflect the world in which he is living. Where Shakespeare and Spenser saw marriage as the fitting goal of true love, Donne writes of physical desires. Although the style and content can be unexpected, poems like 'A Feaver' and 'A Valediction: Forbidding Mourning' use a traditional basic premise. In 'The Flea', however, Donne adopts a cynical tone and a more disparaging approach to the nature of love: using the metaphysical wit typical of his poems, Donne tries to convince his lover to sacrifice her virginity to him. The poem is often seen as shocking because of its open treatment of physical love and its attitude to women.

'The Flea' begins with the same kind of direct address seen in the other poems: *Marke but this flea*. The focus now, however, is more impersonal as Donne and his lover look at a third party: the flea. The language is crude and physical – where the circle represents the unity of the lovers in 'A Valediction: Forbidding Mourning', in this poem the flea that has sucked blood from each of them performs the same symbolic task. The perfect geometric shape has been replaced by an insignificant insect and this inevitably alters the way Donne perceives the woman he addresses. Here the tone is cold and contemptuous; the woman is seen as no more than a sex object. Verbs linked to the flea (*suck'd*, *sucks*, *pamper'd swells*) describe this in a very concrete, physical way. It is in direct contrast with the abstract language of *sinne*, *shame* and *losse of maidenhead* Donne uses in his argument against his lover's chastity. Such abstractions seem meaningless in the development of his logic – the flea *enjoyes before it wooe*, he argues, so why can't they?

In 'A Valediction: Forbidding Mourning', Donne uses the image of two united as one in the image of *two soules . . . which are one*. Here the beauty of the idea is undermined by the symbol of the flea which *swells with one blood made of two*. The spiritual image used to describe physical love is now replaced by a crude physical image suggesting Donne's disregard for the lover to whom the poem is addressed.

In stanza 2, he elaborates upon his theme. As the woman attempts to kill the flea, Donne argues that in doing so she will kill three people since the flea is *you and I*. He uses religious language to give authority to his argument. The words *temple*, *cloysterd*, *sacrilege* and *sinnes* elevate the physical act he urges upon her to one of spiritual worship: in the mingling of their blood, he sees the marriage ceremony and describes them as *almost, yea more than maryed*.

The paradoxical ending allows Donne to twist the poem in a new direction. The language in the opening lines of stanza 3 marks the woman as a murderer. Modifiers like *Cruell*, *sodaine* and *guilty* and phrases like *blood of innocence* suggest that she has performed a terrible sin. Juxtaposed with Donne's view of what she has done, the use of *triumph'st* reflects the woman's response – she argues that neither of them are weaker for the crushing of the flea, therefore apparently disproving Donne's argument. In his final three lines, however, he turns her triumph to his own ends.

The climax comes in demonstrating how insignificant the loss of her virginity will be. The emphatic imperative *then learne* asserts Donne's position of authority; the euphemism *yeeld'st* undermines the importance of the woman's virginity; and the abstract noun *honor* is set against the reductive phrase *Just so much*. Donne has used the flea as a conceit to give his case a concrete grounding in reality and, in the face of his logic, the woman's resistance becomes meaningless.

The structure of the poem is precise. It is made up of three stanzas in which the final rhyming triplet always brings the point Donne is making to a climax. The language unites the spiritual and the physical in order to prove a point – physical desire is acceptable and the fulfilment of this before marriage is both logical and uncontroversial.

Some critics argue that the poems that appear to be contemptuous of women were written before he met his wife, and that those which celebrate the possibility of lasting love reflect his married life with Anne More, niece to Sir Thomas Egerton, Donne's employer (a secret marriage in 1601 that was to result in Donne's imprisonment and the loss of his job). What all his love poems have in common, however, is their rejection of the traditional lyricism of love poetry in favour of realism and a harsher tone more often associated with satire.

He was born into a Roman Catholic family at a time when Catholics were persecuted, and there is historical evidence that Donne's childhood religion caused the family suffering – his brother died in prison after being charged with concealing a priest. While studying law at the Inns of Court, Donne read widely in theology, trying to make his own decisions about the nature of Catholicism and Anglicanism. It was a tension that was to underpin much of his religious verse, most of which was written between 1607 and 1615. In 1615, he was ordained into the Church of England, King James I having made it clear that he would not gain advancement outside the Church. It is said that Donne's love of Anne More led him towards his love of God, and his interest in religion can clearly be traced back to the 1590s. His conversion and ordination should perhaps therefore not be seen as a cynical ploy to gain worldly advancement, but as an intellectual acceptance of the Anglican tradition by an intelligent man who was, nevertheless, aware of the emotional pull of his childhood Catholicism – his poems are often about the difficulty of finding true religion. He was to write little verse after his ordination, but became known as one of the age's greatest preachers.

Despite the fact that the divine poems deal with a very different subject matter from the love poems, the style and tone are still the same. He uses direct address, speaking passionately and personally to God; the diction is often unexpected; and the approach paradoxical and dramatic. Where Donne chose to distance himself from the courtly love sonnet, he now uses the sonnet form to convey the intensity of his religious dilemmas.

In 'Holy Sonnet XIV', for instance, Donne dramatises his fears as a sinner before God. The language of the octave reflects a battle in which he sees himself as *an usurpt towne* and verbs like *Batter, knocke, breake, blowe* and *burn* with their strong initial plosive establish the tone. Paradoxically, Donne believes that he must be thrown down so that he can *rise and stand* before his God. The sestet replaces the image of battle with one of love – the point of change is marked by the contrastive conjunction *Yet*. Verbs such as *love, loved, betroth'd, divorce* are used to portray his relationship with God in a concrete way – he is married to God's *enemie*, sin, and wishes God to *breake that knot againe*.

The poem ends with Donne's usual paradoxical twist – he can only be *free* if God will *imprison* him; he can only be *chast* if God will *ravish* him. Just as Donne uses spiritual language to describe physical love, so here he uses physical language to describe divine love. 'Sonnet XIV' reinterprets the godhead – although He is still the *three person'd God* of the Scriptures, He is also the hero who will *free* the *usurpt towne*; gentle Jesus meek and mild is replaced by a figure of *force* who can *breake, blowe, burn* sinners.

At the heart of the poem is a request by a sinner to be led back to the right path, but Donne makes it dramatic through his central image of the siege and his direct, personal appeal to God. We see Donne's awareness that the demands of the real world are leading him away from God and harsh initial consonants reflect the mood of conflict. His passionate desire for renewal is found in the heightened style created by the rhetorical effects: listing allows him to intensify his demands (*knocke, breathe, shine, and seeke to mend; breake, blowe, burn, and make me new*); juxtapositions highlight the poem's central tension. By placing passion and reason, God and the devil, divine and sexual love, and marriage and divorce in opposition, Donne can draw attention to the paradox – that only in God's service can he find freedom.

The poems in *Songs and Sonnets* cover a wide range of tones. They may be improper or serious, they may mock convention, or they may challenge our expectations, but the metaphysical approach is always evident. In the divine poems, he deals with quite different themes, but even here the approach is the same. Donne uses remarkable comparisons to shock his readers into reconsidering traditional topics. His style is marked by a conversational mood in the direct address he adopts, and the language is grounded in reality, uniting the spiritual with the physical. The range of references is always wide and the conceits are often striking. Each poem argues a case logically through a progression of associated ideas and ends with a paradoxical twist, forcing the reader to reassess Donne's attitude as a whole.

Activity 10.2

Explore the linguistic and literary techniques that Donne uses to develop his argument in 'Goodfriday, 1613. Riding Westward'.

You may like to think about: the content and tone, the structure, diction, imagery and style.

Goodfriday, 1613, Riding Westward

1 Let mans Soule be a Spheare, and then, in this,
   The intelligence that moves, devotion is,
   And as the other Spheares, by being growne
   Subject to forraigne motions, lose their owne,
5 And being by others hurried every day,
   Scarce in a yeare their naturall forme obey:
   Pleasure or businesse, so, our Soules admit
   For their first mover, and are whirld by it.
   Hence is't, that I am carryed towards the West
10 This day, when my Soules forme bends toward the East.
   There I should see a Sunne, by rising set,
   And by that setting endlesse day beget;
   But that Christ on this Crosse, did rise and fall,
   Sinne had eternally benighted all.
15 Yet dare I'almost be glad, I do not see
   That spectacle of too much weight for mee.

Who sees Gods face, that is selfe life, must dye;
What a death were it then to see God dye?
It made his owne Lieutenant Nature shrinke,
20 It made his footstoole crack, and the Sunne winke.
Could I behold those hands which span the Poles,
And tune all spheares at once, peirc'd with those holes?
Could I behold that endlesse height which is
Zenith to us, and our Antipodes,
25 Humbled below us? or that blood which is
The seat of all our Soules, if not of his,
Made durt of dust, or that flesh which was worne
By God, for his apparell, rag'd, and torne?
If on these things I durst not looke, durst I
30 Upon his miserable mother cast mine eye,
Who was Gods partner here, and furnish'd thus
Halfe of that Sacrifice, which ransom'd us?
Though these things, as I ride, be from mine eye,
They are present yet unto my memory,
35 For that looks towards them; and thou look'st towards mee,
O Saviour, as thou hang'st upon the tree;
I turne my backe to thee, but to receive
Corrections, till thy mercies bid thee leave.
O thinke mee worth thine anger, punish mee,
40 Burne off my rusts, and my deformity,
Restore thine Image, so much, by thy grace,
That thou may'st know mee, and I'll turne my face.

Commentary

This is a poem strongly rooted in an occasion: as Donne rides westwards towards *Pleasure or businesse* (l.7) on Good Friday, he thinks of Christ on the Cross. Although concerned with things of the real world, he is still able to meditate on his relationship with God. At the poem's heart, as in the love poems, is an intellectual argument. We see Donne as the lawyer setting out his proposition – how can man, who wishes to worship God, do so when he is easily distracted by the real world of pleasure and business?

Having established the problem in lines 1–10, Donne elaborates upon his theme, developing a more visual account of the crucifixion itself. He personifies nature as Christ's *owne Lieutenant* (l.19) and draws attention to the physical results of man's inhumanity in failing to recognise Christ. Verbs such as *shrinke* (l.19), *crack* and *winke* (l.20) suggest the devastating effects of the death – a spectacle of *too much weight* (l.16) for Donne. In the process of his argument, he has therefore validated his movements away from the East for he *durst not look* (l.29). His argument becomes a devotion as he pays tribute to the sacrifice God made for man.

In the last ten lines, he returns to his initial position – he is riding towards the West with the relevance of Good Friday and its events *present yet unto* [his] *memory*. In a paradoxical twist, Donne's journey is no longer a rejection of God, but a recognition of man's unworthiness before God. He concludes with an understanding that even while man has become distant from God, he can be received again. While physically moving to the west therefore, Donne is spiritually moving towards the east – his arrogance has become humility, his ignorance knowledge. As we move towards a resolution of the opening problem, he has both justified his journey and paid his devotions to God.

The skill with which Donne controls his argument is impressive: each paradox is resolved; each negative is made a positive. The fact that he is travelling westward becomes not only a symbol of his inability to face the suffering of Jesus on the cross, but also a means of turning his back so that he can be corrected. It does not matter that the poet, an insignificant man, does not look at Christ because Christ looks at him.

Although there is a serious reflective mood to the poem, Donne's terms of address are personal. Just as in the love poems, he uses direct address with familiar second person pronouns such as *thee* (l.37), and *thine* (l.41), *thou* (l.42), and the possessive determiner *thy* (l.38, 41). These mark the climax of Donne's argument – his realisation that even the sinful man who has deviated from the track can be forgiven adds poignancy to his choice of pronouns.

The diction of the poem is unexpected in that Donne combines traditional religious language of *Soule(s)* (ll.1, 7, 10, 26), *Christ on this Crosse* (l.13), *God(s)* (ll.17, 18, 28, 31) and *mercies* (l.38) with scientific references to the *Spheares* (ll.1, 3, 22) and geographical references to *the Poles* and the *Antipodes* (ll.21, 24). The image of the planets (ll.1–6) becomes Donne's metaphysical conceit: just as a planetary body can be subject to the orbital forces of another planet, so too we can be diverted from our true path by the distractions of the real world. It is presented as a general analogy that will lead us towards an understanding of a complex abstract issue.

The formal language of argument represented by words such as *Let . . .* (l.1), *Hence . . .* (l.9), *Yet . . .* (l.15) provides a general framework for the poem. Donne, however, moves from the universal to the personal as he presents his own circumstances for evidence. The repetition of the first person pronoun *I* draws attention to the poet's role in personalising his general point. It allows him to dramatise the situation and engage his readers. This is both the work of a lawyer trying to convince his audience, and an act of private devotion.

In characteristic style, Donne uses rhetorical patterning to underpin his argument. Antithesis mirrors the conflict at the heart of the poem: while his body moves towards the West, his *Soules forme bends* (l.10) to the East. Continuing the juxtaposition of the real world and the divine, he puns on the meaning of *Sunne* which is both the sun and the 'Son of God' who rose (*rising*) on the Cross and in his death (*set*) brought eternal life (*endlesse day*, ll.11–12) – paradoxically, although the sun sets, the afterlife offers man a kind of immortality through Christ's sacrifice. In order to develop the contrast between his own unworthiness and God's holiness, Donne juxtaposes verbs like *punish* and *Burne* with *Restore*, nouns like *rusts* and *deformity* (ll.39–41) with *grace* (ll.40–1). Rather than indicating a rejection of God, his journey now becomes a chance to demonstrate his unworthiness – the poem is a plea to God for correction.

The style is formal, using compound-complex sentences to develop the argument, and changes in grammatical mood to reflect Donne's state of mind. The imperative opening *Let . . .* establishes the tone, but this certainty is not sustained, and with the repetition of the tentative interrogative *Could I behold . . .* (ll.21, 23) we begin to see Donne's movement towards humility. The central section of the poem (ll.15–32) is dominated by questions that reflect Donne's inability to face the suffering of Christ. When we return to the imperative mood in the final lines (*Burne . . . Restore . . .,*), however, the poet has become the supplicant begging for correction.

Sentences are arranged so that key words fall at the beginning or ends of lines, thus gaining extra emphasis. The foregrounding of the object, for instance, allows the thematic phrase *Pleasure or businesse* (l.7) to fill the site at the beginning of the line; the foregrounding of the adverbial *There* (l.11) reinforces the importance of the *East* and its religious connotations; the parenthetical *that is self life* (l.32) delays the emphatic verb phrase *must dye* which is given added importance by its position at the end of the line. The formality of the style acts as a permanent reminder of the importance of Donne's themes: he guides our responses through his organisation of the syntax.

This poem reflects something of the age in which it was written and of its author. In a time marked by religious conflict, scientific experimentation and geographical discovery, Donne's poem draws on a range of experiences and profound thoughts. He was at this time himself suffering from syphilis and thoughts of death and forgiveness will have had a personal resonance. It is a poem in which Donne delights in verbal ambiguity and paradox, yet the message is clear: he is the sinful man who has deviated from the path, but repents. His God is both one of wrath (*anger/punish*) and forgiveness (*grace*) and thus the poem ends on a positive note.

George Herbert (1593–1633) and Henry Vaughan (1621–95)

The other Metaphysical poets owed much to John Donne – **George Herbert** learnt technical approaches from him. He adopted the same strong openings, direct address and colloquial language, and developed the same kind of logical argument that is typical of Donne. Similarly, he too drew on personal experience, using his poetry to express his thoughts on religion. Many of his poems consist of a dialogue with God, which reflects his state of mind. His poetic technique is varied and there are close links between the form and meaning – his experiments with language and verse pattern enhance his message. Concrete images of everyday things such as gardening and day-to-day living are used to develop a logical argument, making abstract religious themes more approachable. Although his imagery is more down-to-earth than that of John Donne, he too links the earthly with the spiritual. While Donne portrays physical love in terms of the spiritual and vice versa, Herbert presents a vision of heaven in earthly terms. His work is clearly influenced by Donne's work, but his poetic voice is distinctive.

Herbert wrote only religious lyrics in which his private experience of religion becomes an opportunity for readers to contemplate God themselves. His anthology of poems, *The Temple. Sacred Poems and Private Ejaculations* (1633) is divided into three distinct sections: 'The Church-Porch' contains one long poem which prepares the reader for entrance into the sanctuary of the church itself. The central section, 'The Church', forms the main body and is made up of poems about the basic principles of Christianity and the conflicts that can arise because of the distance between people and God. The final section looks at the results of Christianity in the world at large. Unity is provided in the distinctive poetic voice: key words like *grief, love, affliction, tears* and *friend* are repeated through the volume; the tone is always down-to-earth and practical; the style is almost conversational in its direct address; and the content focuses on the conflict between the religious and the secular, the worldly and the inner.

This is reflected in a poem such as 'The Collar': it has a rebellious tone as Herbert attempts to break away from an acceptance of his role as priest. The title puns on both a 'collar' as a symbol of religious discipline and on 'choler', the bodily humour that causes anger. This immediately prepares the reader for a poem of defiance. The verse structure is irregular and the language is aggressive to reflect Herbert's mood of restlessness. The verbs such as *struck* and *cry'd* are juxtaposed with *sigh* and *pine* to draw attention to Herbert's dissatisfaction with life. The repetition of *free* and the use of words like *abroad, Loose* and *large* mark out the temptations of secular life – *his lines* (verse) and *life* (distinct from his spiritual calling) could set him free from the restrictions of his religious role. The rest of the poem is marked by similar outcries – he writes of the *cage* and *rope of sands* that restrict him, and of his intention of living *sigh-blown age/On double pleasure*.

The last four lines of the poem, however, replace anger with submission and the language changes – in choosing the words *rav'd, fierce* and *wilde* the poet suggests that his anger has been uncontrolled. He becomes the child who is brought back to calmness by the understanding parent. The short final line therefore mirrors the child's acceptance of correction and of his role.

In 'Virtue', the pattern allows Herbert to create four quatrains with alternately rhyming lines in which he addresses the cycle of life and death in a logical and balanced way. The first three stanzas begin with a phrase allowing the poet to make a direct address: *Sweet day, Sweet rose* and *Sweet spring*. Herbert then proceeds to juxtapose the beauty of day, the rose and spring with their inevitable decline. Antithetical language provides the central opposition of life and death: *cool, calm* and *bright* are contrasted with *weep* and *fall*; *hue angrie and brave* is contrasted with *wipe his eye* and *grave*; *sweet dayes and roses* is contrasted with *closes*. The inescapability of all life coming to an end is reinforced through the repetition of the final refrain in stanzas 1–3: *thou must die* is followed *by all must die*. The fourth stanza provides a contrast – the *sweet and virtuous soul . . . never gives*; while the natural world is mortal, the soul is immortal and lives even though the *whole world turn to coal*.

In a perfectly balanced poem, Herbert addresses the nature of mortality and the soul's hope of immortality. The personification of the rose, and the metaphors of a beautiful day as a marriage of heaven and earth, and spring as a box full of perfumes provide an initial tone of hope. The connotations are positive, but Herbert shows that such hope is transient – the rose's *root* is ever in its *grave*; night will always replace day; and the *box of sweets* will be emptied. The short fourth line in each stanza is emphatic and has an air of finality. The change of direction is marked by the use of *Only* as the opening word of stanza 4. It characterises the soul as unique and sets it apart from God's other creations. The simile of the *season'd timber* develops this by implying that while other natural beauties are ephemeral, the soul, like the wood that has been treated (*season'd*), will last forever.

As a poet, **Henry Vaughan** was influenced by George Herbert – the subtitle of his 1650 collection of verse, *Silex Scintillans – or Sacred Poems and Private Ejaculations*, echoes that of Herbert's *The Temple*. This can also be seen in his poem 'The Match' which is a direct response to Herbert's 'Obedience'. His early poetry is secular, but, as with George Herbert, his literary reputation is based on his religious poetry. Unlike Herbert, however, his interest lay less with this life than with the afterlife. He uses intensely remembered experiences as a means of communing with God and his verse becomes a symbol of what he was searching for in life.

Many of Vaughan's poems use the natural world as a source of meditative reflection. 'I walked the other day' is a poem written on the death of his brother William. It describes a walk during which he digs up the ground to try and discover what has happened to the flower he had seen before winter began. The search becomes symbolic of his need to understand the mysterious cycle of life and death. The first three stanzas focus on the physical activity of digging up the ground. They conclude with the personification of the flower as a *Recluse* who *fresh and green . . . lived . . . unseen*. This leads Vaughan to a meditation on *Many a question intricate and rare* as he contemplates both the natural cycle and the concept of resurrection.

The final three stanzas are addressed to God in an invocation. Vaughan asks God to show him the way in a sequence of commands: *Grant I may so/Thy steps track here Below*; *Show me thy peace,/Thy mercy, love, and ease*; and *Lead me above*. Positive words (*light, joy, leisure, true comfort*) are juxtaposed with negative words (*care, sorrows, pain*) as the poet tries to make sense of the death of his brother. Mourning the disappearance of the flower in the opening stanza is replaced in the final lines with mourning at the *dumb urn* of his brother.

The tone has changed from the mundanity of his usual walk to the intensity of recognising the process of generation, in which life and death are inextricably linked. Just as the flower will be resurrected from its grave in spring, so will the soul of his brother rise from his dead body. The regularity of the poem's structure adds to the gravity of the meditation. Each of the nine stanzas has 7 lines and a rhyme structure that follows the pattern of abbaacc. The alternating short lines help Vaughan to mirror the process in which first the *gallant flower* is revealed in its *other bower*, and then *the truth and light of things* becomes clear. Vaughan uses the flower as a metaphysical conceit – it allows him to move from the real world of his walk to an intense contemplation of the spiritual.

The poetry of Vaughan is very different from that of John Donne and yet many of the metaphysical hallmarks are still there. Vaughan uses ordinary language; he uses powerful imagery to capture unique moments; he develops conceits to mirror his meditative reflections in a concrete way; he questions the role of the poet in an irreligious age. His personal voice can be seen in the intensity of his visions: the intellectuality of the metaphysical wit is replaced by a personal search for God in life.

The Metaphysicals and the English poetic tradition

Although it is recognised that the work of the Metaphysical poets is actually very different, it is possible to identify certain characteristics that set them apart from their contemporaries. Their use of the language and rhythms of the spoken voice, their love of paradox, their unexpected and often incongruous images, and the complexity of their conceits can be seen as distinctive. Although the meaning can seem obscure, the individual style and approach of metaphysical verse marks a significant development in the English poetic tradition. Donne, as the founder of this poetic 'school', is a key figure.

Seventeenth-century poetry could have continued in the reflective tradition of Spenser and the Elizabethan poets, but Donne began to do something quite different. His verse lacks the melodious polish of much Elizabethan poetry, but the harshness of his diction and tone are integral to his poetic voice. The unexpected words and images, the sometimes complicated syntax and the uneven rhythms are what make his poetry so distinctive. Critics struggle to find a precedent for the kind of verse he composed because his approach and style are so original. By the mid-seventeenth century, he was the leading voice in English poetry: more creative than his contemporaries and one of the few poets to really convey a sense of the excitement of the age.

His reputation is primarily based on his secular love poetry, which often challenges traditional poetic responses to lovers and relationships. It is successful because he both dramatises and analyses the experience of love. Other Metaphysical poets including George Herbert and Andrew Marvell drew on the poetic techniques Donne used, but his influence on English poetry went beyond the group labelled 'Metaphysicals' by literary critics.

With the Restoration's love of clarity and dislike of figurative language, however, the Metaphysical poets were to fall from favour – most poets were to be influenced by John Milton in the years to come. It was not until the nineteenth century that Donne's influence was to be seen in the poetry of Gerard Manley Hopkins. Like Donne, Hopkins is innovative, using language and form in unexpected ways to destroy reader expectations. Twentieth-century poets such as T.S. Eliot and W.B. Yeats were later to explore the link Donne established between emotions and ideas, and to use, like him, the language of speech as an appropriate medium for poetry.

John Milton (1608–74)

Milton's verse does not fit neatly into any of the contemporary schools of poetry. In the tradition of Spenser and the Elizabethan poets, he mixes classical, mythological and biblical references; he adopts the elegance of the Elizabethan style; and he uses variations of the Spenserian stanza form. In the tradition of the Metaphysical poets, he sometimes uses the kind of wit associated with their conceits. His work, however, has none of the striking images that enable the reader to see ordinary things as extraordinary, and the content is no longer obviously personal or linked to everyday life. He also moves away from the loose natural rhythms of speech associated with the Metaphysical poets, replacing the spoken voice of their poetry with a more resonant and formal tone.

Milton identified Spenser as his model: like his predecessor, he was interested in the conflict between life and Puritan ideals; in moral truth; and in the Scriptures as a guide to living. Because he saw poetry as a means of instruction which could help people to achieve an understanding of the divine, Milton chose biblical themes as his subjects: the fall of man; the tempting of Christ by Satan; God's vengeance on his enemies.

Classical Latin verse was also to influence Milton: his diction is often stylised with many words derived from Latin; his syntax is complex; and his style is ceremonial and elaborate. Avoiding the distinctive variations in style of the Metaphysical poets, his verse often resembles incantation. *Paradise Lost* and *Paradise Regained* use the classical epic form, mixing pagan classical references with biblical stories. While traditional epics had always been based on heroic individuals and their experiences in the world, however, Milton's longer poems focus on the divine, losing contact with earthly existence.

By combining the approaches of so many predecessors, Milton created a distinctive poetic voice. As a Renaissance scholar, he demonstrated his classical learning and succeeded in promoting the English language and culture; as a Puritan, he recorded his beliefs and promoted the Puritan concept of moral truth; as a writer, he harmonised the medieval, the Puritan and the Renaissance traditions in a unique form.

Milton was a supporter of the parliamentary party in the civil war and during the period 1639–59, he wrote prose rather than poetry. He worked as a pamphleteer, publicising the parliamentary cause – because of his links with Cromwell and his support of the execution of the King, Parliament wanted to arrest Milton just before the Restoration.

His prose work is almost a kind of journalism since it reflects Milton's attempt to get ordinary people involved in public affairs. He wrote about divorce in tracts published in 1643 and 1644 after the failure of his own marriage; *Areopagitica* (1644) addressed the issue of free expression of ideas in print; and other pamphlets focused on regicide after the execution of Charles I. Like his verse, his prose also imitates the classical style, but it tends to be less carefully crafted than his poetry. It is consciously rhetorical in style, marked by long convoluted sentences and Latinate diction.

Milton is most well known now for his poetry, particularly for the sublime epics he wrote at the end of his life. Many of his minor works were produced as occasional poems, marking the death of particular people, including 'Elegia Secunda, in Obitum Praeconis Academici Cantabrigiensis' (Elegy II, on the Death of the Beadle of Cambridge University); others reflected his interest in political events such as 'On the New Forcers of Conscience under the Long Parliament' (1646?), and the public response to his own writing in poems such as 'On the Detraction Which Followed upon My Writing Certain Treatises' (1647). Many of the poems combine public occasions and private feelings in a distinctive way.

Lycidas (1638), for instance, was written as a funeral poem for Edward King, a fellow student from Cambridge who was drowned in the Irish Sea. Although the poem is a public tribute to the young man, it also becomes an occasion for Milton to face personal, private fears. The poem provides an example of the way in which Milton used classical models – *Lycidas* is a pastoral elegy with its roots in Greek and Roman verse. Pastoral poetry usually focuses on shepherds and rural life, implicitly comparing a perfect ideal world with the real corrupt one. Milton, however, adapts the form in order to address the idea of death; he is explicit in illustrating the difference between the real and the ideal.

The traditional form of the pastoral allows Milton both to mourn the death of a friend and to express personal fears about his own life and death. Figuratively, Lycidas represents Edward King, who had intended to enter Holy Orders and would therefore have been, in the biblical sense, a 'shepherd', a priest, caring for his 'flock', the congregation. After the opening references to King, however, much of the poem does not relate to the dead man, instead focusing on Milton himself – his writing, the value of his life and the possibility of his own premature death.

The opening lines (ll.1–14) demonstrate the way in which Milton uses his classical learning within the framework of his poems. The *Laurels* and *Myrtles* are the leaves with which classical poets were traditionally supposed to be crowned; in referring to them, Milton seems to speak of his own poetic inspiration. The question *Who would not sing for Lycidas?* mirrors a similar one in Virgil's *Eclogues, X* and the expression *he knew/Himself to sing . . .* is a Latin idiom. These links to the classical tradition allow Milton to control his expression of grief. They provide a sense of order in a world of disorder by reminding the poet that this is part of the nature of things: the experience of death and the poetic response to it can be traced through literary history. Milton's recognition of this can be seen in the opening phrase *Yet once more* which implies that this is just one of many disruptions forcing him to turn to poetry.

The language of the opening is distinctive. There is no explicit celebration of King and no direct expression of grief. Instead, Milton focuses on his own act of writing – he will *pluck* the metaphorical *Berries* to gain inspiration for the elegy. In describing his fingers as *rude* and in using verbs like *forc'd* and *shatter*, Milton suggests that his verse lacks the sensitivity required for the task ahead of him. This is reinforced by references to the berries as *harsh* and *crude*, suggesting that his writing is 'unripe' and lacking in maturity. The references to *Bitter constraint* and *sad occasion* and the use of the verb *Compels* reflect the kind of circumstances in which Milton is writing – his poem is not spontaneous, but has been composed in response to a particular event. Similarly, the verb *disturb* mirrors the way in which news of King's death has unsettled Milton by replacing order with disorder. This makes the tone distinctive: instead of personal grief and the expected obituary, the poem opens with the sense that things are being done before they are due – King has died prematurely; Milton's verse is not yet mature; the metaphorical *Laurels*, *Myrtles* and *Ivy* are unripe.

Repetition refocuses the poem: the three references to Lycidas establish the real theme of the elegy. The structure is reminiscent of Spenser's pastoral elegy *Astrophel* for Sir Philip Sidney who died at the age of 37. Milton's language draws attention to the untimely nature of King's death. References to age (*Young, ere his prime*) remind the reader of the tragedy the poem is attempting to understand. The parallel structure of line 8, the rhetorical question and the repetition of *dead* all contribute to the formal tone as Milton moves from the metaphor of the opening to the harsh reality of the event he is contemplating.

The repetition of the verb *sing* allows Milton to move from his own purpose in writing the poem to praise of King's own achievements in *lofty rhyme*. References to the *wat'ry bier* and the *parching wind* provide a sense of the real world – they remind us in a concrete way of the reality of death. The harsh consonants of the opening (*pluck*, *Bitter*, *dead*) are replaced with more harmonious sounds (*wat'ry*, *welter*, *meed*, *melodious*) as the anger of the initial section is submerged in the need to remember.

Milton clearly identifies himself with King – he too had considered a vocation in the Church, he too wrote verse, he too was about to make a journey by sea. The anger of the opening is therefore a personal response to what has happened as well as a public tribute. By combining biblical and classical references, Milton searches for a way to understand the event and move beyond a feeling that life is meaningless.

Paradise Lost

In his later work Milton drew on biblical themes, but the tension between public and private is still central. Although using stories from the Scriptures, links can be seen with Milton's own life. *Paradise Lost* (1667) focuses on the rebellion of Satan and his followers from Hell as they seek revenge against God – a parallel can be seen with the rebellion against Charles I organised by the parliamentary party. Just as Adam, Eve and Satan suffer in the biblical story for questioning authority, so Milton had to go into hiding for his support of Cromwell and the Protectorate, only escaping punishment because of the intervention of his friend the poet Andrew Marvell.

Paradise Lost opens with an invocation (Book I, ll.1–26) – a traditional beginning to a public poem. In it, Milton outlines the poem's action and dedicates his poem to God, asking Him to be the muse which will inspire the verse. The tone of the final lines is liturgical. Phrases such as *thou O Spirit*, *eternal providence* and *the ways of God* use traditional biblical language and immediately mark out the religious nature of the lines. The imperative verbs (*Instruct*; *Illumine*, *raise*, *support*) are typical of the supplicant in prayer asking God for His guidance.

The main body of the poem uses narrative description and direct speech to dramatise the subject, and meditative comment to reflect on its significance. The description of Hell (Book I, ll.60–9), for instance, acts as a visual backdrop to the speeches that follow. A central tension is created in the lines by antithetical language and by Milton's use of the contrastive conjunction *yet*, which prepares the reader for the contradictions that follow. Words associated with light (*furnace*, *flamed*, *flames*, *fiery*) are juxtaposed with *No light* and *darkness*; *woe* with *peace* and *rest*; *fed* with *unconsumed*. This immediately establishes Hell in negative terms: it is a place where fire does not give light or warmth and *hope never comes/That comes to all*. The negative mood is also underlined by the repetition of *never* and by the use of words like *No* and *without*, suggesting an absence of something.

Milton's rhetoric is effective since it allows him to create a powerful physical description of the place to which Satan and his followers have been condemned.

The use of tripling in *sights of* **woe**, *Regions of* **sorrow** and **doleful** *shades* reinforces the horror of the situation and the effect is made more dramatic because of the negative connotations of the key words. Other lexical sets remind the reader that hell is a dungeon from which the inhabitants cannot escape – words and phrases such as *ever-burning*, *never comes* and *without end* convey its infinite scale. The use of enjambement and the fact that the whole description is made up of one complex sentence similarly drives the reader on.

Having created the context, Milton proceeds to dramatise the scene he has created. Although this is a story that everyone will know, he makes it distinctive through his characterisation of Satan. From the biblical story, we know that Satan is associated with the serpent that tempted Eve (Satan means 'accuser', 'tempter') and caused the fall of Adam and Eve. He is also known as the leader of the angels who rebelled against God. By choosing Satan as his main protagonist, Milton moves away from his classic models. He replaces the noble heroes of epic with an ambiguous figure in line with the evil heroes of Renaissance drama – Shakespeare's Macbeth and Marlowe's Doctor Faustus.

The characterisation of Satan is skilful. In reading the poem, we are aware of both his strengths and his weaknesses – he is energetic and charismatic, but he is also self-obsessed; he is persuasive, but also obstinate; he is a powerful leader, but will not submit himself to a greater authority. The reader cannot help but have sympathy with him because he is in the same state as humanity – in terms of the Bible, he too has fallen from grace, just like Adam and Eve. The figure of Satan is therefore paradoxical: the reader cannot help admiring him, but within the religious framework of seventeenth-century society, Milton also expected his readers to recognise that Satan is evil and God is good.

Even before starting to read *Paradise Lost*, we know how the plot will end. What Milton does is provide the detail that leads us to that predefined end. To make his epic a success, he needs readers both to sympathise with Satan and simultaneously to condemn him for his challenge to God's absolute autonomy. This paradox lies at the heart of the poem and provides it with its central tension. Milton depends upon the fact that readers will associate with Satan as fellow sinners; that they will identify with his energy and perseverance in the face of disaster; and that they will recognise him as a kind of hero. Milton's poem ultimately upholds the justice of God in an attempt to explain His ways so that his readers can find salvation.

Samson Agonistes

A tension also exists at the heart of *Samson Agonistes* (1671), Milton's last poem. It juxtaposes Samson's despair with the need to accept God's grace: if he despairs, he will be damned; if he accepts God's will, he can be saved. The main protagonist is the biblical Samson whose superhuman strength is embedded in his hair – when he is captured by the Philistines, they shave his head and he loses his power. Milton's epic focuses on the last days of Samson's life in captivity.

The poem recreates a 'real' world rather than the sublime background of *Paradise Lost* and *Paradise Regained* (1671) and its hero is a man rather than a spiritual figure like Christ or Satan. It deals, however, with many of the same themes:

rebellion against authority, man's relationship with God, and the need for self-knowledge. For most of the poem, Samson rebels against his situation: he resents his blindness; he wants to fight against his captivity; he is bitter at Dalila's betrayal; and he wants to boast about his past exploits. The result of this is that he cannot listen to God. The poem, therefore, is a spiritual journey during which he must face himself – self-examination leads him towards acceptance and only then is he ready for salvation.

The poem is closely modelled on classical tragedy with five distinct sections, roughly corresponding to the five acts of a play. Samson receives a sequence of visitors and after each the Chorus comments. Each encounter allows him to discover something about himself, leading to his last heroic act, which is reported in the final speeches of the play.

Samson's opening speech (ll.1–114) immediately portrays his restlessness. The Philistines' solemn Feast to Dagon the Sea-Idol provides him with a break from his labours, but Milton's use of the adverb *unwillingly* makes it clear that the diversion is undesired. Once physical work stops, Samson is forced to confront his inner self.

The juxtaposition of *body* and *mind* introduces the tension – while Samson's body can be rested, his mind cannot find peace. This link between the physical and the mental is developed in the simile where the abstract *thoughts* are given a concrete presence through the comparison with the *Hornets*. The simile establishes a negative tone and the modifiers *deadly* and *arm'd* develop it, with the verbs *rush* and *thronging* suggesting the intensity of Samson's feeling of entrapment. The reader is then driven on by the enjambement to a recognition of Samson's changed state. The parallel structures, *what once I was, and what am now*, at the end of the sentence are emphatic. The end focus draws attention to the antithesis and prepares the reader for the self-searching that will lead Samson back to God.

The final section, in which Samson destroys the temple (ll.1596–1758), killing both himself and many of the Philistines, provides a fitting conclusion to the opening passage. The modifiers *patient* and *undaunted* suggest that he has reached some kind of inner peace. This is reinforced by his stance when brought to the pillars: he stands *as one who pray'd/Or some great matter in his mind revolv'd*.

His heroic act is commented upon explicitly by the Chorus – it is both *dearly bought revenge* and *glorious*; Samson is *self-kill'd*, but *victorious*. The antithetical language draws attention to the difference between the physical and the spiritual. The image of the phoenix risen from its grave becomes the symbol for Samson's ability to rise above his entrapment. His physical limitations (blindness and bodily weakness) are juxtaposed with his spiritual potential symbolised by the modifier *inward* and the abstract noun *virtue*. The negative connotations of words such as *Despis'd* and *extinguish't* in the first lines are replaced by words associated with fire and light. The verb *illuminated*, the modifier *fiery* and the noun *flame* give Samson's inner life added power and provide a concrete image of his rediscovered faith.

Our recognition of Samson as hero is made explicit by the final words of Manoa, his father (ll.1709–11). At this point, Samson's spiritual journey is complete: he has moved from the despair of the opening to an acceptance of

God's will. The repetition of *Samson* and of *heroicly/Heroic* places him firmly at the centre of the epic. In the opening speeches of the poem, the syntax mirrors Samson's state of mind: long sentences with their parenthetical clauses (ll.12–22), rhetorical questions (ll.23–29/30–36), interjections (ll.36/52/67/68/80) and the exclamatory tone (ll.36–8/52/65–7) are indicative of his despair. By the end of the poem, however, the certainty of Manoa's words and his persuasive rhetoric reinforces our understanding that this was *a death so noble* (l.1724).

Milton and the English poetic tradition

Milton's work is closely linked to his life. Inevitably, his prose pamphlets more explicitly present his personal views, but his poetry also offers readers an insight into his view of the world. His writing reflects his religious beliefs and often mirrors the doubts and fears he had about the social and political state of his country, and about his own blindness.

In the nineteenth century, critical response to Milton ranked him alongside Shakespeare as a key figure in the development of English literature. More recently, however, he has been seen in a less positive light. Some would argue that his convoluted style and his love of Latinate expressions prevented the development of the natural speech rhythms used by the Metaphysical poets. He moved away from their conversational tone and their explicit use of personal experience towards a more reserved and solemn style. Although modern readers may not have the same belief structure as the Puritanical Milton, his works remain fascinating for the way in which he represents familiar material in a new and challenging way.

Activity 10.3

What do the language and structure of this extract from *Paradise Lost* (Book I, ll.84–124) reveal about Satan?

You may like to consider: the focus and organisation of the content; the language; the imagery; and the style.

1	If thou beest he; but O how fall'n! how chang'd
	From him, who in the happy realms of light
	Cloth'd with transcendent brightness didst outshine
	Myriads though bright: if he whom mutual league,
5	United thoughts and counsels, equal hope
	And hazard in the glorious enterprise,
	Join'd with me once, now misery hath join'd
	In equal ruin: into what pit thou seest
	From what highth fall'n, so much the stronger prov'd
10	He with his thunder: and till then who knew
	The force of those dire arms? yet not for those,

Nor what the potent victor in his rage
Can else inflict, do I repent or change,
Though chang'd in outward lustre; that fix'd mind
15 And high disdain, from sense of injur'd merit,
That with the mightiest rais'd me to contend,
And to the fierce contention brought along
Innumerable force to spirits arm'd
That durst dislike his reign, and me preferring,
20 His utmost power with adverse power oppos'd
In dubious battle on the plains of heav'n,
And shook his throne. What though the field be lost?
All is not lost; th' unconquerable will,
And study of revenge, immortal hate,
25 And courage never to submit or yield:
And what is else not to be overcome?
That glory never shall his wrath or might
Extort from me. To bow and sue for grace
With suppliant knee, and deify his power
30 Who from the terror of this arm so late
Doubted his empire, that were low indeed,
That were an ignominy and shame beneath
This downfall; since by fate the strength of gods
And this empyreal substance cannot fail,
35 Since through experience of this great event
In arms not worse, in foresight much advanc'd,
We may with more successful hope resolve
To wage by force or guile eternal war
Irreconcileable, to our grand foe,
40 Who now triumphs, and in th' excess of joy
Sole reigning holds the tyranny of heav'n.

Commentary

The organisation of the content immediately tells the reader something about the tension that exists in the characterisation of Satan. In the opening eight lines, he recognises Beëlzebub lying beside him and comments on his changed state. Satan's concern suggests that he is able to understand the suffering of others, but he quickly moves from an awareness of Beëlzebub to a concentration on himself (ll.8–11). He appears to recognise God's power, but refuses to accept His superiority. Where the opening led us to believe that perhaps Satan has understood his mistake, the tone of the following section (ll.11–22) is clearly unrepentant – he is defiant and refuses to accept defeat. His rhetoric is true 'fighting talk' and we explicitly see his obstinacy and arrogance.

The language varies as Satan's focus changes, allowing Milton to convey a breadth of character and making Satan more complex than the personified Evil of the medieval morality tradition. His innate understanding of Beëlzebub in the opening and his familiar use of *thou* encourage us to respond positively. The modifier *transcendent* and the verb *outshine* (l.3) suggest that Satan is able to appreciate Beëlzebub's qualities, and this is reinforced by the lexical set of words (*mutual*, 1.4; *United, equal* 1.5) that creates a parallel between them. References to *light* (1.2), *transcendent brightness* (1.3) and *bright* (1.4) are juxtaposed with *present misery* (1.7) and *ruin* (1.8), creating a contrast between past glory and present degradation.

Similarly, Satan's rebellion is portrayed positively. The abstract nouns *league* (1.4), *thoughts, counsels* (1.4) and the noun phrase *glorious enterprise* (1.6) all suggest that the uprising has been based on democratic debate and considered action. The positive connotations imply that the action was noble and necessary, but references to God as *the stronger* (1.9) and the use of a rhetorical question (ll.10–11) seem to indicate that, in spite of the nobility of his cause, Satan has recognised his error: he has accepted a power greater than his own.

The use of the contrastive conjunction *Yet* (1.11) explicitly changes the tone of the speech, introducing the reader to another side of Satan's character. Phrases such as *fixed mind* (1.14), *high disdain* and *injured merit* (1.15) reflect his high self-opinion. From this point on, the reader is aware of his arrogance: the juxtaposition of Satan's changed *outward lustre* (1.14) with his unceasing belief that he is right suggests an obstinacy in his nature, while the prepositional phrases *in foresight much advanced* (1.36) and *with more successful hope* (1.37) suggest his blind determination.

References to God as *the potent Victor* (1.12) and *the mightiest* (1.16) are ambiguous: rather than a recognition of a superior power, they are Satan's attempt to glorify his rebellion. The nouns *rage* (1.12), *reign* (1.19) *wrath* and *might* (1.27) and the verb *Extort* (1.28) enhance this by developing an image of God as a tyrant who needs to be restrained. The image is made explicit with phrases such as *grand Foe* (1.39), *Sole reigning* and *the tyranny of heaven* (1.41). The speech builds to a climax as Satan's language becomes more emotive – he is the hero who has lost all in an attempt to challenge an unjustifiable ruler.

Satan's refusal to accept defeat seems honourable. Abstract nouns (*will*, 1.23; *revenge, hate*, 1.24; *courage*, 1.25) make him seem dignified, while the modifiers *unconquerable* (1.23) and *immortal* (1.24) point to his ability to sustain his sense of self even in the face of defeat. Verbs such as *submit, yield* (1.25), *bow, sue* (1.28) and the modifier *suppliant* (1.29) are linked directly to *low* (1.31), *ignominy* and *shame* (1.32), suggesting that acceptance of defeat would be humiliating. Satan firmly consigns God to the role of dictator, while presenting himself as the hero, an underdog who will triumph by *force or guile* (1.38). Yet in failing to recognise God's omnipotence, Satan has clearly not learnt from the *great event* (1.35).

Such lexical choices allow Satan to glorify his intentions and end his speech on a high note. The emotive nature of the argument encourages the reader to accept his interpretation of the situation, yet the dramatic irony is clear – as readers, we are aware of the limitations of Satan's understanding of the situation. The paradox lies in the fact that we know from the Scriptures that God represents good and Satan represents evil.

The style is equally important in making Satan's argument credible. The broken syntax of the opening line reflects Satan's initial horror at the changed Beëlzebub. The lack of composure suggested by the incomplete sentence *If thou beest he* and the two exclamations *how fallen!* and *how changed*, however, is quickly replaced by carefully crafted rhetoric. The tripling of *league, thoughts* and *counsels* and the parallel structure *equal hope/And hazard* (ll.4–5) suggest a return to self-control. These, along with the repetition of *joined* (l.7) and *equal* (ll.5,8), reinforce our sense of a Satan who is able to consciously craft language to win the support of others. After the long complex sentences (ll.1–11; 11–22), the question (l.22) and the emphatic *All is not lost* (l.23) mark an important transition. From this point on, Satan grows in self-confidence. He no longer seems aware of his audience, but revels in the glorification of his own character.

The visual image of the supplicant bowing before his master precedes the main clause *that were low indeed* (l.31), which allows Satan to create a symbol of submission only to destroy it. While the parallel main clauses *that were low . . ./That were an ignominy and shame* (ll.31–2) are emphatic, the anaphoric reference summarising the detail of the image allows Satan to dismiss the idea peremptorily. His confident declaration of intent follows: *We may . . . resolve/To wage . . . eternal war* (ll.37–8). We are forced to wait for the main verb (*resolve*) which gains additional weight in its position at the end of the line. The tentative nature of the modal verb (*may*), however, undermines the statement and the parenthetical phrases *with more successful hope* and *by force or guile* then seem like self-persuasion – Satan is trying to convince himself of the ease with which his revenge can be executed.

Despite the fact that readers know the biblical tradition associating Satan with evil, his arguments seem logical and emotive because of the symmetry of his words. Parallel structures give a sense of balance and reason to his argument: *repent or change* (l.13); *fixed mind/And high disdain* (ll.14–15); *Unconquerable will/And study of revenge* (ll.23–4); *immortal hate,/And courage* (ll.24–5). Parenthesis (*from sense of injured merit*, l.15) allows him to justify the action he has taken as if by chance. It places Satan in the right and therefore casts God once more in the role of tyrant. We are lulled into a sense of security by the patterning, but Milton requires us to be wary of Satan's apparent logic and the subjectivity of his speech.

The character of Satan is far more complex than that of the figure in the Bible. Milton forces the reader to assess the nature of a hero and the nature of good and evil by presenting us with an individual who is made up of both positive and negative qualities. With his Puritanical background, there can be no doubt that Milton wanted the reader to identify God as the force of good and Satan as the representation of evil. The central character in *Paradise Lost*, however, engages the reader because of his weaknesses – he is, like man, an imperfect sinner and in that sense encourages sympathy. It is ultimately his inability to recognise God as the source of all grace that prevents Satan from finding salvation – and it is this that Milton wanted his seventeenth-century audience to recognise.

Restoration poetry

The Restoration period can be characterised by its return to order after the disorder of the years leading up to the reinstatement of the monarchy. Similarly, the literature after 1660 reflects this in its balanced style and its interest in the intellect rather than the imagination. Poetry developed a public voice – the content dealt with society and politics rather than the Metaphysicals' focus on individual experience and Milton's personal interest in religion. The Restoration poets therefore chose an elegant style that was marked by its artificiality and its avoidance of excess.

John Dryden (1631–1700)

Dryden is perhaps the most well known of the Restoration poets and he borrowed from both the preceding poetic traditions. From Spenser and Milton, he inherited an interest in classical texts, using biblical and classical references to give his writing dignity, and adopting their Latinate diction and complex syntax. From the Metaphysical poets, he inherited the metaphysical conceit – replacing their ingenious comparisons with more logical ones. The result was a distinctive style of writing that was to influence many of the poets who followed him. In the eighteenth century, Samuel Johnson wrote of Dryden:

> There was . . . before the time of Dryden no poetical diction, no system of words, at once refined from the grossness of domestic use, and free from the harshness of terms appropriate to particular arts.

He was interested in philosophical and political questions and much of his poetry deals with contemporary events in the form of satire. Other poems addressed to fellow-writers reveal his critical principles.

Dryden studied the work of John Tillotson (1630–94), a member of the Royal Society who became Archbishop of Canterbury, whose sermons were recognised for their plainness and clarity. The matter-of-fact tone of Tillotson's work, his belief in the importance of correct grammar, and his lucid development of ideas were to influence Dryden's work. His style is marked by its balance and sense of order, its illustrative similes, effective modifiers, and witty arguments.

He is commonly associated with the heroic couplet (a pair of rhymed lines using iambic pentameter). Used by Chaucer in the Middle English period, it was adopted by Dryden and given a new sophistication. He is often described as establishing the school of English poetry which was to produce Alexander Pope (1688–1744) and Oliver Goldsmith (?1730–74) in the eighteenth century.

His work can be seen in five distinct sections. His early poems (1660–7) were often panegyrics (a speech or poem in praise of an individual or institution). In works like 'His Highness Oliver, Lord Protector' (1559), 'His Sacred Majesty Charles the Second' (1661) and *Annus Mirabilis* (1666), Dryden's style was formed. In his second period (1663–85), he wrote 22 dramas. The first were based on French models and used rhyme; his later works, like *All For Love* (1678), used blank verse.

The third period saw Dryden as a critic (1668–84), writing pieces to defend his own literary practice. Essays such as *Of Dramatick Poesie* (1668) and *A Defence of an Essay* (1668) and various prefaces justified the technical approaches he adopted. He focused on a range of critical issues: the use of the heroic couplet in drama, the special nature of Restoration literature and the role of the writer.

In his fourth period (1678–85), Dryden wrote political satires. *Absalom and Achitophel* (1681), *The Medall* (1682) and *Macflecknoe* (1682) all originated in the political differences of the day. Between 1665 and 1687, Dryden also wrote two poems on religious issues: *Religio Laici* (1682) was a defence of the Church of England inspired by the Popish plot; *The Hind and the Panther* (1687) marked Dryden's conversion to Roman Catholicism and is a defence of the Church of Rome. The last 20 years of his life (1680–1700) constitute Dryden's fifth period. During this time, his work was very varied, but translations formed the greater part of his writing. He translated Greek and Latin poetry and paraphrased the tales of Boccaccio and Chaucer in *The Fables* (1700).

For Dryden, satire was an important means of conveying current social experience in verse. In *Absalom and Achitophel*, he places a contemporary rebellion in a biblical past. The analogy allows him to give an insight into the Whig campaign for Protestant succession: the biblical story of Absalom's rebellion against King David becomes a parallel to the Whig campaign. It is controversial because it suggests that the Whigs' actions were actually directed against the King.

For modern readers, it is necessary to know something about the political situation of the time. In 1663, Charles II acknowledged his illegitimate son James Scott and made him Duke of Monmouth. The English Protestant leaders tried to force the King to exclude his Catholic brother James, Duke of York, from the succession in favour of Monmouth, who was supported as the heir to the throne by the leader of the Whigs, the Earl of Shaftesbury. The King, however, chose his brother as successor and banished Monmouth from England.

At the death of King Charles in 1685, Monmouth returned to England to claim the Crown. When James II became king, Monmouth thought he could rally the Protestant cause against the Catholic James and win the throne for himself. James, however, had not been king for long, and support for Monmouth was not widespread. While achieving some initial success, he was defeated at the Battle of Sedgemoor, in Somerset, captured and executed for treason along with hundreds of his followers.

This historical background provides the basis for Dryden's satire, while the biblical analogy gives him a way to write about events as they are unfolding – although he was careful not to mirror contemporary events too closely. The characters in *Absalom and Achitophel* represent real individuals: Achitophel is Shaftesbury, Absalom is Monmouth, and David is Charles II. Dryden's sympathies clearly lie with King Charles II and James, Duke of York, and against supporters of the Protestant succession and their leader, the Earl of Shaftesbury.

Dryden's support of Charles is clear in the dignified language and style he chooses. The biblical analogy underpins this since Dryden can be sure that his readers will come to the text with the appropriate preconceptions about David. He is represented as a divine king – he rules with divine right and he recreates his maker's image. In Dryden's hands, Charles's sexual exploits become examples of his warmth and creativity rather than evidence that he is failing to serve the state. Such qualities are directly contrasted with the sterile energies of Absalom, who is presented as a dupe rather than as a vicious rebel, and Achitophel, who is seen as a figure of force whose vitality is misplaced.

Dryden reinforces our sense of David/Charles as a strong king through his ability to maintain control in difficult circumstances, and to act when it is necessary to assert his kingship. He is *The godlike David* whose words are inspired by heaven. The language and style of his speech (e.g. ll.939–50) reinforce this:

rhymed couplets give an air of dignity which is enhanced by parallel structures (*My wrongs . . . my revenge . . .; So willing . . ./So much . . .*); words such as *mercy*, *forgive*, *clemency* build up an image of a generous individual. The repetition of *native* suggests these are his instinctive qualities, and his understanding of king-ship is explicit: they are *the public pillars of the state,/Born to sustain and prop the nation's weight* (ll. 953–4).

Absalom and Achitophel provide a contrast to David in that they create disor-der where he brings order. Achitophel/Shaftesbury is at the poem's centre. He is a real threat to David because he is capable – his positive energies, however, are misdirected and he ends up destroying rather than creating. He is like Milton's Satan – both characters challenge authority and corrupt others; both overturn order. The description of Achitophel is dramatic. Modifiers such as *false*, *close* and *crooked* are juxtaposed with *Sagacious* and *bold* (ll.150–3), drawing attention both to his heroic and unheroic qualities. Dryden's presentation of Shaftesbury suggests that the Whigs' campaign for liberty and individual rights was no more than a desire for a lawless and chaotic state, yet he also implies that Achitophel is to some extent driven by fate and this makes him seem tragic.

Similarly, Absalom/Monmouth is given some heroic attributes: the juxtaposi-tion of *virtue* and *royal* with *fame, honour* and *praise* illustrates the two sides of his character. He represents youthful ambition, but his flaw lies in the fact that he is gullible because of his desire to be great (ll.309–14). Dryden ensures that the portrait is not entirely negative by using words such as *youth* and *Unwarily* that suggest Absalom is naïve rather than wicked, and by using the passive voice in phrases like *was led, [was] Made* and *[was] debauched* to imply that someone is lead-ing him astray.

Dryden ensures that we have some sympathy for Absalom through narrator comment (ll.479–82): he is *unblamed of life, Not stained with cruelty, nor puffed with pride*. If he had been *higher placed* in social position, or *not so high*, his life would have been very different. As King Charles's illegitimate son, Monmouth is presented as neither truly 'royal' nor one of the ordinary populace and it is this discrepancy that Achitophel can exploit. Absalom therefore becomes the dupe who is persuaded to act by the skilful Achitophel. Words such as *drunk* and *debauched* and the repetition of the adverb *too* suggesting excess (ll.309–12) rein-force the feeling that his youth has been corrupted.

Dryden thus characterises the foolishness of the king's bastard son without suggesting that he is completely responsible for his actions. His choice of a verb like *struggled* and the parallel structures of *Half loath* and *half consenting* create the image of a man who does not easily agree with Achitophel's arguments (ll.313–25). This is reinforced by Absalom's recognition of the divine right of kings who rule *with unquestioned right* as *The faith's defender, mankind's delight* and *observant of the laws*. The fact that he is referring not to kings in general, but specif-ically to his father encourages us to have some sympathy with his position. The use of direct speech underpins this – by giving Absalom a voice, Dryden can emphasise the distance between his two characters.

The positive connotations of the modifiers used by Absalom to describe his father (*Good, gracious, just; Mild, easy, humble*) enable Dryden to express both his own support for Charles II and Absalom's potential for good. The style enhances the characterisation: the open-endedness of the asyndetic lists and the balance of the parallel structures suggests an understanding that is both logical and sincere.

The political in-fighting of the Restoration period was extremely complex and by using a familiar story, Dryden has simplified the historical reality. This allows him to celebrate the reinstatement of order by a firm ruler, while also recognising the fragility of the peace. The poem focuses on the rebellion and does not attempt to deal with the actual outcome of events, so Dryden breaks away from the biblical story before the death of Absalom and leaves the poem as a warning of potential disaster.

Dryden chose the mock-heroic form for his epic poem. This allowed him to imitate the classic models of Latin and Greek epic while dealing with ordinary rather than heroic individuals. The style is still formal and elevated, but the tone is satiric because Absalom and Achitophel are not seen as worthy protagonists. Their actions are not heroic and Dryden can draw attention to this by suggesting that the mock-heroic is the only possible form in a corrupt age.

The range of Dryden's literary output is great and he is well known as a playwright and critic as well as a poet. For many, however, his greatest achievements lie in the field of satire where he chose the mock-heroic as his medium. Rather than undermining his subject with outright ridicule, Dryden uses metaphor, comparison and allusion to undercut pretension. His contribution to the English poetic tradition can be seen in his use of the heroic couplet, which, in his hands, became so effective a means of satire that Swift, Pope and Johnson were to use no other form.

The sixteenth and seventeenth centuries and the English poetic tradition

The poetry of the sixteenth and seventeenth centuries reflects the growing strength of the English poetic tradition. It is a period of great individual writers such as Spenser, Milton and Dryden, but also of groups of writers adopting the same genres and using the same conventions. Sidney and Spenser, influenced by the humanist school, wrote verse that demonstrated their interest in the nature of art and the perfection of form. Shakespeare's sonnets explored the potential drama of the sonnet form, taking as its focus the real rather than the ideal in its treatment of love.

John Donne moved poetry in a new direction, replacing Elizabethan lyricism with a striking and original voice, contemporary images, and challenging conceits. While not fitting neatly into a specific school, Milton was to draw on a range of traditions. Moving away from the spoken voice of the Metaphysical poets, he reintroduced a formal structure and classical diction to English poetry. In the humanist tradition, he wrote poetry that engaged the reader in an argument. Dryden, writing during the Restoration period, moved away from Milton's religious debate to poetry that dealt with issues of the real world. His style was transparent and his tone elegant.

By the end of the seventeenth century, English poetry was varied and sophisticated. While poetic tradition associated with the heightened style of Spenser led
to the artificial diction criticised by Wordsworth in his 1800 Preface to the *Lyrical
Ballads*, the Metaphysical poets were to have an ongoing influence. In the twentieth century, the metrical variety of their versification, their feeling for the
rhythms of the spoken voice and their traditionally unpoetic diction were pushed
to new extremes.

■ У I I Poetry of the eighteenth century

The eighteenth century is associated with the desire for order, and the need to establish standardising systems in all fields of life: politics, economics, social organisation, culture, language and literature. It can be seen, for instance, in the ways in which the eighteenth-century explorers tried to 'map' out the world. Because of this belief in the importance of order and pattern, it is often called the **Age of Reason and Logic**, or the **Augustan Age**. It replaced the individualism of the Renaissance with a belief that there was only one form of correctness, which should be a model for everyone to follow.

Politically, the country was stable, with 26 years of peace from 1713 to 1739. Despite the struggle for power between the Whigs and Tories, the long, peaceful administration of Sir Robert Walpole (1721–42) marked a new mood with the virtual disappearance of political agitation. Towards the end of the century, however, the consensus began to fall apart, with the middle classes increasingly feeling that they were being excluded from the process of decision-making. The political interest aroused by key figures like John Wilkes (1727–97), with his emphasis on the importance of free speech, drew attention to middle-class demands for parliamentary reform. It prepared the way for the constitutional changes of 1783 and others that were to follow in the nineteenth century.

The economy was good and the period is marked by a commercial revolution that laid the ground for mass industrial growth in the nineteenth century. There was a marked increase in the number of towns, industries and manufacturers; inventions in the fields of agriculture and textiles helped to keep pace with the demands of a growing population. The first mail coach (1784) improved communications; and the development of steam engines like James Watt's (1763) prepared the way for accessible travel.

Religion was now predominantly Protestant, and the fierce religious hostilities of the sixteenth and seventeenth centuries subsided. The Methodist John Wesley (1703–91) and his followers, however, brought a new kind of religious zeal. Methodism emphasised the concepts of salvation for all who had faith and for all who did good works. In the late 1730s, Wesley delivered open-air sermons after having been refused permission to preach in the parishes. In these mass sermons, the audience were asked to open their hearts to God so that they could attain the state of 'grace' and be saved. The traditional Church feared the enthusiasm and strict devotion of the Methodists and by 1795 they were separate from the Church of England. A further division occurred within the Methodists themselves – the

Calvinist Methodists doubted the Wesleyan concept of salvation. They believed that God had elected the 'chosen' and that only they would reach Heaven regardless of their faith or good works.

The literary context

During the eighteenth century, the growth of commerce had a significant effect on the development of a bourgeois culture. Patronage began to decline as authors turned to a mass readership prepared to subscribe in advance. Despite this, the Court still provided patrons: George III (1760–89) himself gave a pension to Doctor Johnson and patronised John Zoffany (1733–1810), a portrait painter. Many writers still believed it was essential to have the support of a great 'name' and dedications were common.

Writers continued to hold government posts: their influence was useful and writers such as Daniel Defoe (1660–1731), Jonathan Swift (1667–1745), Edmund Burke (1729–97) and Edward Gibbon (1737–94) held a variety of roles. Some, like Richard Steele (1672–1729) and Joseph Addison (1672–1719), were politicians; others, like Doctor Johnson, were involved with questions of current interest or, like David Hume (1711–76), worked on key diplomatic missions.

Clubs for the middle classes also emerged: political and intellectual groups founded the Whig Kit-Cat Club and the Tory Cocoa-tree Club. Later the Literary Club (1763–83) was founded by Doctor Johnson and the painter Joshua Reynolds (1732–92). Its members consisted of contemporary literary figures including Oliver Goldsmith (?1730–74), James Boswell (1740–95), Burke and Gibbon. Theatre continued to thrive, attended now by professional and business men rather than the Court and the aristocracy, who preferred the fashionable opera. Walpole's Playhouse Licensing Act (1737) attempted to regulate the profession, but failed. Instead even larger theatres drew increasingly large audiences, and the first playhouses opened in the provinces. The Royal Academy (1768) was founded by the Crown architect Sir William Chambers (1726–96) and other artists, with Sir Joshua Reynolds as its president until 1790. It organised annual exhibitions of the work of contemporary artists and established a school of art.

After the 'Great Age of Drama' during the sixteenth and seventeenth centuries, the eighteenth century is perhaps best known for the emergence of the novel as a distinct genre in the English literary tradition. Other prose writings also blossomed in the form of journals and essays. Steele founded the *Tatler* (1709–11), published three times a week with news, essays, drama criticism and political satire; and, with Addison, he produced the *Spectator* (1711) which was modelled on the *Tatler*, but avoided political content, claiming independence from both Whigs and Tories. Its essays provided stimulus for essayists and critical writers and it formed the model for modern literary journals. Lending libraries made their first appearance in 1725, and all major collections were brought together in the British Museum in 1754.

The Augustans

The term **Augustan** derives from the period of literary achievement during the rule of the Roman Emperor Augustus (27BC–AD14) when the great poets Virgil, Horace and Ovid flourished. Writers of the eighteenth century such as Alexander Pope, Joseph Addison, Richard Steele and Jonathan Swift admired and imitated their Latin predecessors, seeing in their own desire for order and pattern a parallel with the classical world. They were thus to become known as the Augustans.

Poetry of the period is marked by a restraint of feeling and a correctness of expression. Poets were governed by rules and conventions and the result is verse which appears artificial because of its conformity to set patterns. John Dryden had established the heroic couplet, but Pope was to perfect the form, which was to become the standard measure for poetry, its parallels and antitheses used as a weapon in mockery. Poets were to continue using the heroic couplet, and in the early nineteenth century it was also to become a vehicle for ethical reflection.

The oral, vernacular traditions of earlier periods had been replaced by an emphasis on the classics and Augustan verse drew on these as a source for translation, imitation, and allusion. The eighteenth-century audience was cultivated and writers could expect them to understand literary references, to recognise shades of meaning and changes of tone. After the imaginative Elizabethan era, the desire to entertain was replaced by a belief that poetry should correct and teach.

Fear of political and social rebellion led to a search for order and this can be seen in the literature of the period. Where seventeenth-century Metaphysical verse focuses on personal issues of love and relationships, Augustan verse focuses on ethics and society – its manners, morals and corruptions. Poetry was seen as an opportunity to correct society's failings through its emphasis on decorum and moderation. Its representation of a society in disorder is powerful and, having attacked its failings, it offers an alternative in the positive values it upholds.

The period's interest in the intellect and order can be seen in the poetic diction. The prestige of science with its technically precise language tended to undermine the value of poetic imagery and diction. Instead, the Augustan poets aimed for restraint and control. Despite this, the best verse is marked by its skilful easy rhymes and its elegance. Adaptations to the iambic pentameter are used to give flexibility and to highlight semantically important words.

The English poetic tradition in the eighteenth century is characterised by two dominant strands: **Alexander Pope** and the heroic couplet; and the reflective and elegiac writing of **James Thomson** and **Thomas Gray**. The political ballads of Defoe, the satirical verse of Swift, and the social satire of Pope's *The Dunciad* follow in the tradition of the Restoration mock-heroic verse.

Alexander Pope (1688–1744)

Pope was a Catholic and, because he was unwilling to renounce his religion, he was refused the vote, a place at university and entrance to the professions. In addition to these social limitations on his life, an illness in his teenage years had caused physical restrictions and in *Epistle to Arbuthnot* (1735), he refers to *this long Disease, my Life*. Despite this, he was known for the keenness of his mind: much of his writing reveals his interest in the relationship between the inner and outer life, and between the individual and the state.

He was a member of the 'Scriblerus Club' with John Gay (1685–1732), Dr Arbuthnot (1667–1735), Thomas Parnell (1679–1718) and Jonathan Swift. They met to plan satirical projects – one of which was the compilation of *The Memoirs of Martinus Scriblerus*. It was to be a satire on the excesses in contemporary science, culture and learning, with the central character, Martinus, assigned the role of pedant. Although initiated by the group, it was Pope who developed the idea, publishing it in his *Prose Works* (1741). He also used Martinus Scriblerus as the author of the preface and some of the footnotes in *The Dunciad* (1728–43).

Pope was very much of his age and followed in the tradition of Dryden. As a professional writer, he chose independence rather than patronage and his translation of Homer's *Iliad* as a six-volume subscription (1715–20) established him as the leading literary figure of the day, and brought him financial prosperity. Much of his success lay in his judgement of what was appropriate for his audience, managing to speak both to the particular addressee of a poem and to the wider public audience simultaneously.

The content of his work is wide ranging, but where the seventeenth-century Metaphysical poets were interested in God and man's relationship with Him, Pope was interested only in 'Man'. His work is based on human observation – he considers human nature, friendship, social and political morality, and corruption. The didactic poem *Essay on Criticism* (1711), written in heroic couplets, marks the turning point in Pope's career with his definition of true wit:

> True wit is nature to advantage dressed,
> What oft was thought, but ne'er so well expressed;
> Something whose truth convinced at sight we find,
> That gives us back the image of our mind.   (ll.297–300)

This was followed with the poem *Windsor Forest* (1712) that focused on the Peace of Utrecht signed in October 1711. It praises Queen Anne for bringing an end to the war, and implicitly criticises William III whose invasion of England had brought an end to the reign of James II. It is a more personal poem than the later satiric work and focuses on the unity that can emerge from discord.

With *The Rape of the Lock* (1714), Pope satirises the fashionable world of his day, aiming to laugh two families into unity after a trivial quarrel. His skill lies in his ability to move between two parallel worlds: the epic and the real. In juxtaposing the sublime world of classical epic with the trivial present, he forces readers to reassess: the trivial present, which has falsely assumed importance, is placed alongside the 'great' world of the gods in order to draw attention to its insignificance. This is reinforced in the grand diction that is used for trivial events like pouring coffee and playing cards. Satire of a more bitter kind is found in *The Dunciad* (1728–43) that attacks individuals who had offended Pope – mostly minor writers of the day. He creates a grotesque world of caricatures that become symbols of the moral and intellectual decay he believed marked his age. The humour of *The Rape of the Lock* is replaced by a more ruthless tone. Where characters like Belinda, the Baron and Sir Plume in the earlier work are seen as insignificant alongside their epic counterparts, the unworthy characters of *The Dunciad* are inflated to epic status.

Pope's translations of Homer's *Iliad* (1715–20) and *Odyssey* (1725–6) recreated the classic epics in a form appropriate for an eighteenth-century audience. The Augustan art of 'imitation' also appeared as echoes of the classics in original works: Pope evokes Homer and Virgil in *The Dunciad* and Ovid's heroic epistles in *Eloisa to Abelard* (1717). The latter poem is interesting in its use of the dramatic monologue form – it focuses on the feelings of a woman who has been separated from her lover and forced to forswear her love against her will. It displays none of the complexity of character introduced to the form by Robert Browning (1812–89) in the Victorian period, but is successful in portraying a woman's emotional suffering, and in contrasting spontaneous passion with the controlled religious environment of the convent to which Eloisa has retired.

In the 1730s, Pope published his *Moral Essays*, a group of four discursive poems that comment on human life and manners, and *Essay on Man* (1733–4) that considers the human condition in general. In these works, he attacked contemporary corruption from a personal standpoint, ending *The Essay on Man* with an image of self-love as a pebble that makes ripples and becomes love for all humanity. The final line reinforces the need to understand ourselves in order to improve society:

> And all our knowledge is, OURSELVES TO KNOW.

Pope is well known for his technical skill. His use of the heroic couplet is flexible and effective. Because it is a restrictive form, it intensifies and compresses thought. He uses the pattern in its standard form, but, in many lines, the iambic weak-strong pattern is altered for semantic effect – the altered rhythm draws attention to key concepts.

> 1 Others | for *lan* | *guage* all | their care | express,
>   And val | ue books, | as wo | men men, | for dress . . .
>   Words are | like leaves; | and where | they most | abound,
>   Much fruit | of sense | beneath | is rare | ly found . . .
> 5 But true | expre | ssion, like | th'unchan | ging sun,
>   Clears, and | improves | what'er | it shines | upon . . .
>
> *An Essay on Criticism* (ll.5–16)

Most lines here use the weak-strong iambic pattern in each of the five feet. However, there are three points at which the first iambic foot is replaced by a trochee (ll.1, 3, 6). The effect is to throw the stress on to key words in the initial position. The pronoun *Others* marks a new development in the argument. It suggests that the critics who concentrate all their energies on language are failing to appreciate the nature of *true expression*. The noun *Words* marks the movement away from discussion of language in general to a specific element. The verb *Clears* highlights the benefits of *true expression* for which all writers should be striving. It creates a contrast with the obscurity created by unnecessary verbosity.

Pope uses natural similes to reinforce the point he is making. The concrete image of abundant *leaves* under which there is little *fruit* conveys the idea that an excessively wordy piece of writing will often lack any real meaning. Similarly, the image of *th'unchanging sun* that *Clears* and *improves* creates a visual model for the writer to follow – *true expression* is something that does not change with fashion, illuminating rather than obscuring meaning. The purpose of the figurative language is to engage the reader actively in the abstract discussion. It brings the argument to life with everyday observations that will be meaningful to all readers. Pope's variations in the metrical patterns have a similar effect.

Other techniques such as phrasing and the use of the caesura can divide the lines into two balanced halves, or consciously undermine the balance. In the following extract from *Windsor Forest*, Pope underpins the general meaning of the poem as a whole through his style as well as the content.

> 1   Here hills and vales, the woodland and the plain,
>   Here earth and water seem to strive again,
>   Not chaos-like together crushed and bruised,
>   But, as the world, harmoniously confused:
> 5   Where order in variety we see,
>   And where, though all things differ, all agree.   (ll.12–17)

The rhyming couplets establish the basic structure, but this is reinforced by the stylistic patterning. The parallel structures *hills and vales* and *the woodland and the plain* create the sense of balance that Pope sees in the landscape. This is stressed by the metrical emphasis on Nŏt chá | ŏs-líke, where the first foot is a spondee rather than iambic, and by the oxymoron *harmoniously confused*. An initial and medial caesura alter the balance of the line, throwing weight onto this paradoxical phrase. A similar effect is created in the final line where parenthesis delays the final phrase *all agree*. In addition to the phrasing that divides the lines and throws emphasis on to key words or phrases, the use of antithesis provides another layer of patterning. Words like *order/variety* and *differ/agree* are integral to the semantics of this poem about war and peace.

The use of the mock heroic allows Pope to satirise contemporary society and, in scaling down the epic world of Homer and Virgil to a level of domestic trivia, he can rely on his audience recognising the parallels and contrasts. Thus in *The Rape of the Lock*, the arming of the hero becomes the making-up of Belinda (Canto I, 121–48); the epic voyage becomes a boat-trip on the Thames (Canto II, 1–52); heroic sports become a card game (Canto III, 25–100); dangerous exploits become the formality of tea (Canto III, 105–20); and mortal combat becomes a domestic tiff (Canto V, 75–112). The reader is immersed in the inner world of polite society, with only a cursory awareness of the 'real' outer world.

> 1   Meanwhile, declining from the noon of day,
>   The sun obliquely shoots his burning ray;
>   The hungry judges soon the sentence sign,
>   And wretches hang that jurymen may dine;

| 5 | The merchant from th'Exchange returns in peace, |
| | And the long labours of the toilet cease. (Canto III, 19–24) |

Pope's reminder that life continues outside Belinda's boudoir implicitly suggests that the world we are seeing is superficial, focusing on its own trivia rather than the real decisions of the outer world. The spondee (*Meanwhile*) marks the change of perspective, and the metrical variety of the final line underpins the mock-heroic tone since it gives an undeserved grandeur to Belinda's activities.

Activity 11.1

Discuss the stylistic techniques Pope uses to develop the mock-heroic tone in this extract from *The Rape of the Lock* (Canto I, 121–45).

You may like to think about: the content and themes, the language and tone, the rhetorical devices, and the metre.

1	And now, unveiled, the toilet stands displayed,
	Each silver vase in mystic order laid.
	First, robed in white, the nymph intent adores,
	With head uncovered, the cosmetic powers.
5	A heavenly image in the glass appears,
	To that she bends, to that her eyes she rears;
	Th'inferior priestess, at her altar's side,
	Trembling, begins the sacred rites of pride.
	Unnumbered treasures ope at once, and here
10	The various offerings of the world appear;
	From each she nicely culls with curious toil,
	And decks the goddess with the glittering spoil.
	This casket India's glowing gems unlocks,
	And all Arabia breathes from yonder box.
15	The tortoise here and elephant unite,
	Transformed to combs, the speckled, and the white.
	Here files of pins extend their shining rows,
	Puffs, powders, patches, bibles, billet-doux.
	Now awful beauty puts on all its arms;
20	The fair each moment rises in her charms,
	Repairs her smiles, awakens every grace,
	And calls forth all the wonders of her face;
	Sees by degrees a purer blush arise,
	And keener lightnings quicken in her eyes.

Commentary

As a parody of the epic, Belinda sits at her dressing table to 'arm' herself for 'battle' just as a classical hero would prepare himself for physical conflict – in reality, she is doing no more than preparing herself for the social event at Hampton Court.

Pope's use of the mock heroic reminds the reader that the world of the poem is one of superficial appearance.

The language creates the mood of a traditional epic in its references to things divine that exist beyond the normal world. Phrases such as *mystic order* (1.2), *cosmetic power* (1.4) and *heavenly image* (1.5) transform the everyday world of the boudoir into something of extraordinary potency. This is reinforced with the lexical set of words related to religion: *priestess, altar* (1.7), *sacred rites* (1.8) and *goddess* (1.12). The reality of a dressing table covered with jars, bottles, *combs* (1.16), *pins* (1.17) and *puffs* (1.18) is transformed to a place of worship. The *silver vase* (1.2), *unnumbered treasures* (1.9), *various offerings of the world* (1.10) and *glittering spoil* (1.12) recreate the ordinary world with the elevated diction of an epic. References to *India* (1.13) and *Arabia* (1.14), to the *tortoise* and the *elephant* (1.15), add to this mood of dignity with their connotations of mystery and romance.

The verb *adores* (1.3) exaggerates the tone by reminding us that the whole experience is too intense. Belinda becomes Narcissus regarding herself in the mirror in a way that is egotistic and self-elevating. It draws attention to the underlying theme – that appearance is superficial and that society places too great an emphasis upon it. This is developed in the image of the dressing table as an altar where worship of God is replaced by worship of beauty. Even the beauty is false, however, since it is created from the cosmetics – the use of the verb *decks* (1.12) reinforces this with its connotations of display and decoration. Modifiers such as *glittering* (1.12), *glowing* (1.13) and *shining* (1.17) add to the image of adornment. The present participles help to build a sense of movement as Belinda is transformed from the ordinary dreaming girl of the opening to the hero ready to do battle. The use of the oxymoron *awful beauty* (1.19) is the climax of the incident – beauty will be her weapon.

Pope uses juxtaposition to create the mock-heroic mood: the patterning is formal and rhetorical and this contrasts with the unremarkable nature of the occasion. The juxtaposition of the words in the phrase *curious toil* (1.11) is an integral part of the mock heroic. Although the connotations of *toil* are appropriate to the epic hero's labours and tests, here, the pre-modifier undermines the suggestion of hard work. Pope's tongue-in-cheek use of *curious* acts as a marker and guides reader interpretation of the whole occasion.

Antithesis can be seen in the direct opposition of words within phrases. Pope post-modifies the noun phrase *sacred rites* with the prepositional phrase *of pride* (1.8). This explicitly draws attention to the misplaced values of the society he is satirising – insignificant things assume too great a value. The antithesis of *sacred* and *pride* highlights personal vanity in a context where the diction reminds us of a more spiritual love of God. The irony of the *sacred rites* is also seen in the description of the *pins* (1.17) lined up like an army and in the listing that builds to an ironic anticlimax.

Other devices reinforce the underlying discrepancy between appearance and reality. Parenthesis (ll.1,3) throws stress onto key words and phrases and delays the main clause. In the first example, the reader has to wait for the main clause, *the toilet stands displayed*. The use of an initial position co-ordinator (*And*) and fronted adverbial (*now*) creates an air of suspense, while the connotations of *unveiled* with its sense of revelation create a dramatic mood. Parallelism builds a sense of order, suggesting that the occasion is one of dignity and importance. The balance created by lines that divide neatly into two halves (ll.4, 7) and by co-ordinated phrases like the *tortoise . . . and elephant* (l.15) and *the speckled, and the white* (l.16), however, is satiric since Pope is elevating a daily occurrence to one of epic proportions.

The pompous triviality of the alliteration in the ***Puffs, powders, patches*** (l.18) draws attention to the mock-heroic tone. This is reinforced by the offhand reference to the *bibles* that have lost their true significance amongst the cosmetics that will transform Belinda, and to the *billet-doux* reminding us of the true motivations of her transformation. The asyndetic list with its strong initial plosives moves towards an anticlimax in keeping with the mock-heroic style. The process of metamorphosis is conveyed through the listing of present tense verbs: *puts on* (l.19), *rises* (l.20), *repairs, awakens* (l.21) and *calls forth* (l.22). These are juxtaposed with *all the wonders of her face* (l.22) and *the purer blush* (l.23) – despite the fact that they have connotations of natural grace and beauty, we are aware that the Belinda at the end of Canto I has been 'created'.

Alterations to the metrical patterns allow Pope to develop his mock-heroic tone in the form as well as the content and style – changes to the standard iambic pentameter highlight words and phrases of importance to the underlying themes. In several places the initial foot is spondaic rather than iambic (ll.12, 18). The use of a spondee slows the pace of the verse, making the tone solemn and dignified. This stateliness is ironic, seeming more appropriate for the grandeur of true epic than for Pope's mock heroic. The first example draws attention to the 'recreation' of Belinda, with the two stresses emphasising the initial position co-ordinator and the verb *decks*. The second example marks the beginning of the ironic list of the clutter on Belinda's dressing table (l.18). The two strong stresses alter the rhythm and thus surprise the reader into a more active recognition of the false values that are at the heart of the poem's world. In other places (ll.8, 23), the first foot is trochaic: *Trembling . . .* and *Sees by. . . .* Again the change of pattern makes the reader aware that something of significance is happening – the foregrounded present participle suggests the power of the process which is about to take place; the present tense verb marks the point of change at which the transformation is complete.

The main theme of the extract is transformation; the emphasis is on what can be seen – on appearance. Lexical sets of verbs like *decks* (l.12), *Transformed* (l.15) and *Repairs . . . awakens* (l.21) and the prepositional phrase *by degrees* (l.23) create a sense of the process. Underlying the description is a suggestion that the occasion is trivial and that Belinda's natural beauty is finally *awful* (l.19) something to be wondered at rather than honoured.

The patterning of the verse is formal and grand in the tradition of epics, but the content is insignificant. The mock heroic tone is developed through the discrepancy between the epic style and the domestic process which takes place. Despite Pope's use of satire, the poem is not vicious. Instead he aims to laugh the divided families, the Petres and the Fermors, into unity again. The poem is almost in the tradition of the comedy of manners in its revelations of folly in society and the symbolic 'rape' (the snipping of Belinda's lock of hair) is indicative of the foolish society that places too high a value on external things.

The reflective tradition

Counter to Pope's school, poets such as James Thomson (1700–48), Thomas Gray (1716–71) and William Cowper (1731–1800) attempted to broaden the poetic tradition, replacing the satirical mood with a reflective one. They drew on nature as a link to the human values that had been lost in urban and court life. Observations of the natural world, however, were less important than the reflection they stimulated – in the 'Age of Reason', general reflection was seen as a way of bringing meaning to particular incidents.

Despite preparing the way for Romanticism, the eighteenth-century school was distinct from the nineteenth-century movement in one important way: where the Romantic poets emphasised the individuality of their experience, the eighteenth-century poets united reader and poet in a collective contemplation of nature. In addition, while the Romantics drew attention to their power in recording visual experience, the eighteenth-century poets were more interested in praising the contentment of rural life and solitude. The style of their writing is elegant, combining both classical allusions and diction with colloquial vocabulary and a lively pace.

In the Miltonic tradition, **Thomson** uses blank verse in *Winter* (1725) and *The Seasons* (1730), setting a model that would later be used by **Cowper** who was to influence Wordsworth. Cowper's subject is the country rather than the town, and the natural world that provides inspiration for his poetic ideas. Observations of the weather and scenery led him to reflect on the human condition. Wordsworth praised his poetry for its new images of the natural world, but both the Romantics and the Victorians disliked the artificiality of his diction.

Gray's poetry also draws on the Miltonic tradition, using the elegiac stanza and other lyrical techniques rather than the heroic couplet. *Elegy Written in a Country Church-Yard* (1751) was possibly written for the death of a friend and it represents a clear sense of contemporary intellectual and emotional attitudes. Starting with the local landscape, it moves to reflection – meditating on such universal themes as mortality, humility and contentment. The movement between visual image and thought is subtle and the poem can be seen as the climax of the Augustan reflective tradition.

The Augustans and the English poetic tradition

Pope's literary achievements are clear: his use of autobiography as a means of conveying personal moral and artistic views; his delicate use of the heroic couplet; and his amusing adaptations of contemporary figures and the classics. Poets including Dr Johnson and Oliver Goldsmith were to follow in Pope's tradition. Johnson was also a satirist, a moral judge of his times as can be seen in poems like *London* (1738) and *The Vanity of Human Wishes* (1749). Like Pope, he too reveals something of himself and uses the formal tone of the classics. Goldsmith's *The Deserted Village* (1770) has much of Pope's regular and antithetical style, but also a sense of nostalgia and pathos that is absent in Pope; he too uses the heroic couplet, and gives it a final touch of grace. George Crabbe (1754–1832) is a part of the same school, but introduces a strain of realism adapted from Defoe's work. His debt to Pope is clear in poems like *The Village* (1783).

There was, however, to be a critical reaction against Pope: poetry moved away from 'reason' towards romance and legends; it moved away from rules and conventions towards a freer association between form and content; and it moved away from the classics as a source. William Cowper was to dissociate himself from poetry that was *a mere mechanic art* where *every warbler has the tune by heart*; the Romantic poets accused Pope of being too artificial; and the Victorian poets, Matthew Arnold for instance, believed that he wrote no more than glorified prose.

The reflective tradition with its pre-Romantic sensibilities was to begin the movement from the public and social to the private and personal. Thomson's *The Seasons* was to be one of the most popular of English poems and it is significant in the development of English poetry because it offers an alternative to the civilised urbanity of Pope – the Romantic poets saw Thomson as the first poet since Milton to represent nature in a distinctive way. His verse was to encourage the development of topographical poetry (defined by Dr Johnson as *local poetry, of which the fundamental object is some particular landscape . . . with the addition of . . . historical retrospection or incidental meditation*), and to contribute to the eighteenth-century interest in the picturesque and the landscape.

Edmund Burke's treatise *A Philosophical Enquiry into the Origin of our Ideas of the Sublime and Beautiful* (1757) was another text that was to influence the poets of the late-eighteenth century. Their interest in the sublime, an idea associated with religious awe, vastness, natural magnificence and strong emotion, was preparing the ground for the nineteenth-century nature poets.

■ ᴍ 12 Poetry of the nineteenth century

In the early part of the nineteenth century, the Age of Reason with its emphasis on the imitation of classical models was replaced by Romanticism, the 'age of the individual'. The French Revolution of 1789 had disrupted the aristocratic tradition that allowed a ruling elite to dictate society's organisation. Fear of similar changes in Britain meant that many who had been indifferent to religion suddenly saw it as an alternative to the democratic and revolutionary ideas threatening the status quo.

The Chartist movement in the 1830s and 1840s sought change through petitions. They campaigned for an extension of the franchise, secret ballots, annual elections, payment of MPs, no property qualifications for MPs and equal electoral districts. Despite the fact that their work had no direct effect on Parliament, it reflected the desire for change seen in the Acts of 1832, 1867 and 1884 that reformed the organisation of politics. Other social changes also mirrored the mood of the early part of the nineteenth century: the Apprentices Act (1802) limited the hours of labour; the Factory Acts (1833, 1844, 1847 and 1850) addressed the issues of child labour and the length of hours under-18s should work.

The reign of Victoria (1837–1901) imposed an artificial unity over a period that was marked by change and resistance. The declining power of the Crown was balanced by parliamentary acts which sought to improve the life of ordinary people through social reform: the Public Health Act (1875) was designed to improve sanitation; the Food and Drugs Act (1875) tightened the law on the contamination of food; the Education Act (1876) created committees to compel school attendance. From 1868, meetings of the National Federation of Trade Unions were annual; while unions had begun life as pressure groups for industrial reform, from the 1890s their function was political.

It was an age unmatched at that time for economic growth. Industrialisation and increasing urbanisation changed the whole British way of life. More people were now able to take advantage of cultural developments: the printing of the first cheap newspapers (1816); the introduction of cheap postage (1840); improved travel with the creation of the railway and the steamboat. The spirit of the age was captured in the Great Exhibition (1851) in Crystal Palace that reflected changes in science, industry and commerce.

Religion was also affected as social change led to increasing secularisation. But the transition from faith to scepticism was not easy and the literature of the period is often marked by a personal despair caused by spiritual doubt. The conflict between belief and lack of faith was also reflected in the controversy caused by the publication of Darwin's *The Origin of Species* (1859). Despite this, the middle classes ruled their lives with values that were directly linked to Christianity, with the Bible at its centre. Their belief in high moral principles such as duty and earnestness created a façade of respectability which often concealed dubious practices and double standards. By the end of the century, people were beginning to question traditional Victorian concepts, and this was to prepare the way for the twentieth century, an age less confident and more prepared to accept diversity.

The literary context

The creation of a mass public readership, the introduction of compulsory education in the 1870s and the spread of the vote changed the face of Intellectualism. Literary criticism and the periodical essay emerged as distinctive forms with the writers Charles Lamb, William Hazlitt, John Ruskin and Algernon Swinburne making significant contributions to the discussion of literature and other art forms. The study of the past led to an interest in records and texts, and many of these were restored by the scholars of the time. Up to the 1850s, philosophical, economic and scientific arguments had been written for ordinary people in non-technical publications such as the *Edinburgh Review* (1802–30s) and the *Fortnightly Review* (1865); after the 1880s, increasing specialisation made such subjects more technical and less accessible to the non-specialist. Despite this, many of the great thinkers of the Victorian period such as J.S. Mill (1806–73), Charles Dickens (1812–70) and Benjamin Disraeli (1804–81) did not attend university. The spirit of inquiry which epitomised the age welcomed the contributions of amateurs if they could present valuable knowledge to further an understanding of life and man's place in it.

The French Revolution was to affect English literature quite significantly, becoming symbolic of humanity's hopes for peace and unity. Rather than encouraging compliance through religious belief, writers adopted the aspirations at the heart of the French experience. New ideas and emotions were also introduced by German romantic ballads and the work of Goethe and Schiller. After experimentation with political ideas, many writers then turned to poetry, using their inner struggle to find meaning in the world as their subject matter.

Romanticism was to emerge as a response to the ordered 'Age of Reason'. It can be identified by its focus on the individual and his experience; the power of the imagination; the transfer of political frustrations to art; and the revolution in taste that it represented. The Augustan classical culture was undermined and replaced by a new set of literary ideals: the past was now of interest for its own sake; ordinary people rather than the elite of society provided appropriate material; and plainness of expression marked a move away from the formality of classical convention.

There are two distinct strands in the poetic tradition of the nineteenth century: first the **Romantic movement**, and, from the late 1830s, the **Victorian poets** who turned away from the principles of Romanticism. William Blake was to prepare the way for change, bridging the gap between the satirical 'age of Reason' and the personal 'Age of the Individual' when Romantic poets such as William Wordsworth, Lord George Byron and Percy Bysshe Shelley, and romantic novelists like Sir Walter Scott (1771–1832) adopted a new style for their work. They chose freedom of expression and saw the individual as a source of emotions which were common to all humanity. The second edition of Wordsworth and Coleridge's *Lyrical Ballads* (1800) made a conscious declaration about this new movement in poetry.

John Keats was to mark a movement away from the Romantic interest in evoking mood to the Victorian spirit of intellectual inquiry. His polished style was to be developed in the work of poets like Tennyson. Finally, with Gerard Manley Hopkins and Thomas Hardy, English poetry was to begin its journey towards the twentieth century with its interest in craftsmanship and experimentation.

The Romantics

In the last decades of the eighteenth century, there was a reaction against the order and discipline of the 'Age of Reason'. The attitudes emerging were to prepare the ground for Romanticism: there was a new interest in the imagination and in personal feeling; a revival of romantic literature from the Elizabethan period; and a fascination with the concept of 'childhood'. The work of Jean-Jacques Rousseau (1712–78) drew attention to social and political issues, and analysed contemporary manners and ideas; the French Revolution emphasised the importance of freedom; and eighteenth-century impersonality was replaced with a reassertion of the individual.

William Blake (1757–1827)

William Blake can be seen to represent the break with the restrictive conventions of the eighteenth century – its political philosophy, its social and religious expectations, and its rules of versification. The content of his work reveals his attitude of revolt against authority; the style demonstrates his rejection of both the satiric and the reflective Augustan traditions.

Twentieth-century interpretations of Blake recognise him as an independent thinker whose work reflects his attempts to resist the orthodoxies of the age. His criticism is original and his engravings and etchings demonstrate his desire to do more than just mirror the human body in a two-dimensional form. He condemned the conventional painting of the period because of its superficiality, aiming to capture the spirit of life in his own engravings. The plates that accompany his poems are a complex mix of image and text in which he aims to reveal the *eternal lineaments* of truth. In writing about his professional work as an artist, he describes his engravings as nothing but *mere drudgery*. His attitude to his illustrations for his own work, however, is quite different – he uses the image of a blacksmith to portray the poet as a man of creativity and prophetic power. In the 1850s, the Pre-Raphaelites discovered his work and their school of painting was directly influenced by Blake's style.

As a poet, Blake focuses on human experience, searching for understanding and evaluating the complexity of life: he is the questioning individual, the seer *Who present, past and future sees* (Introduction to *Songs of Experience*). Much of his later work is obscure because of the intensity of his personal mythology. The first signs of a personal system emerged in *Songs of Innocence* (1789) and *The Book of Thel* (1789), but in works like *The Book of Urizen* (1794), *Europe, a Prophecy* (1794), *The Song of Los* (1795) and *The Four Zoas* (1797–1804) the private vision can alienate readers.

As a poet and as a man Blake was isolated in the 'Age of Reason'. His attempts to escape from the conventions of eighteenth-century verse, from the repressive Puritan interpretation of Christianity and the materialist approach to life marked him out as a maverick in a time of conformity. In addition to this, because his work was published with elaborate plates, copies were expensive and editions were limited. This inevitably restricted the kind of audience he reached and his work found no sympathetic readership during his life. His last years were passed in obscurity and he received little financial reward for a lifetime of unique work – by this time, however, others were beginning to think as he did.

Blake was original in his outlook and he questioned rather than accepted received wisdom, morality and institutional religion. His work was a means of recording his thoughts and he often elaborated upon the idea of individual responses to life. In *The Everlasting Gospel* (c.1818), he wrote:

> Both read the Bible day and night,
> But thou read'st black where I read white.　　　　(a,13–14)

The sense that two people can interpret the same material in quite antithetical ways is central to an understanding of Blake's work. Because he was not willing to accept the interpretation of life upheld by the 'Age of Reason', he found freedom from the restrictions of the period in his own vision: *I must Create a System, or be enslav'd by another Man's* . . . (*Jerusalem*, 1804–20, Plate 10, l.20)

As a poet, he fulfils the role of 'seer' and much of his writing is aphoristic – it is a concise statement of his personal principles, the record of his own system. In *The Marriage of Heaven and Hell* (c.1790–3), for instance, he attacks both society and Christian systems of thought and belief:

Prisons are built with stones of Law, Brothels with bricks of Religion.　　(Plate 8, l.1)

His physical images of *Prisons* and *Brothels* become symbols for the restrictions of society that he rejects. The juxtaposition of the concrete nouns *stones* and *bricks* and the abstract nouns *Law* and *Religion* allows Blake to question the inflexible 'man-made' systems that organise society and morality. The parallelism of the line gives the argument a sense of logic, underpinning the reason of Blake's viewpoint. He becomes the prophet who can offer another vision of life – he says in *Jerusalem* (Plate 10, l.21) his *business is to Create*. He recognises the hostility with which his ideas will be met, however, and builds a counterattack into the verse since *What is now proved was once only imagined*. Although his 'imaginings' may also one day be proved, his interest lies not in persuading others to his own point of view, but in uniting those who already think as he does.

The Augustan Age believed in control and much of the literature of the period is characterised by conventions that dictated rules of style and form. Blake's work is clearly a product of its age and yet it also challenges the restrictions placed upon art and poetry. His poetry, prose and engravings represent both eighteenth-century intellect and the expression of emotion that came to be associated with the Romantic movement. His cosmic belief system, for instance, is the product of a disciplined intellect, yet he saw emotion as the key to life. Above all, he believed that the intellect and the emotions were not separate and antithetical entities:

> For a Tear is an Intellectual thing,
> And a Sigh is the Sword of an Angel King,
> And the bitter groan of a Martyr's woe
> Is an Arrow from the Almightie's bow.
>
> *Jerusalem*, Plate 52, ll.25–8

The argument here clearly links expressions of emotion (*tear, Sigh, groan*) with the intellect: the modifier *intellectual* explicitly draws attention to the fusion of thought and feeling; the links developed between emotion and the symbolic *Sword* and *Arrow* are implicit. By associating the abstract nouns *Sigh* and *groan* with the concrete *Sword* and *Arrow*, Blake seems to suggest that expressions of feelings have a direct effect on our world. Where the 'Age of Reason' saw emotion as a weakness, as evidence of a lack of control, Blake recognised its role in defining the individual.

During the period that Blake was writing *Jerusalem*, he addressed the same issue in another work, the prose essay *A Vision of the Last Judgement* (1810):

> Men are admitted into Heaven not because they have curbed & govern'd their Passions or have No Passions, but because they have Cultivated their Understandings. The Treasures of Heaven are Not negations of Passion, but Realities of Intellect, from which all the Passions Emanate Uncurbed in their Eternal Glory.
>
> From the *Note-book*, p. 87

He identifies *the Passions* as an integral part of the *Intellect*, thus uniting feeling and thought in a way that prepares the ground for the Romantic poets. While the verbs *curbed* and *govern'd* are typical of eighteenth-century attitudes, his use of *Cultivated* suggests a more consciously individualistic approach. His viewpoint is given authority by his use of religious lexis like *Heaven* and *Eternal Glory* – by associating feelings with traditional Biblical language, he can imply that in neglecting them we are neglecting our spiritual life. The style is rhetorical, using antithetical oppositions to persuade the reader: verbs like *curbed*, and phrases like *no Passions/negations of Passions* are set against *the Passions Emanate Uncurbed*. The formal tone and logical pattern of the argument allow Blake to present a noncon-formist view in a conventional way – while the content challenges eighteenth-century attitudes, the style does not.

Blake's belief in the individual led him away from accepted interpretations of history and religion. In his passion for freedom and his revolt against convention, he turned away from classicism towards a more personal view of contemporary history. His writing is always grounded in reality – in a letter to Dr Trusler (23

August 1799), he says: *I see Every thing I paint In This World, but Everybody does not see alike*. His poems also draw on the world around him – although not always in a way which we immediately recognise. The *Songs of Experience* (1789–94) recreate a world of poverty and despair in contemporary London; *The French Revolution* (1791) and *America: A Prophecy* (1793) are revolutionary works revealing Blake's response to real events. He saw the revolutions as a symbol for the destruction of Augustan order and hoped that a similar belief in the need for freedom would emerge in England. In reading these poems, we are aware of the poet's personal vision – where the outcome of the French (1789–99) and American (1775–83) Revolutions disillusioned many of the Romantic poets, turning them towards conservatism, Blake instead creates a more individual vision of freedom.

Blake's response to the institution of eighteenth-century religion is similar. In his prose work, *The Marriage of Heaven and Hell*, he challenges the simple dualism of good versus evil at the heart of church teaching:

> I care not whether a Man is Good or Evil; all that I care
> Is whether he is a Wise Man or a Fool. Go! put off Holiness;
> And put on Intellect.   (*Jerusalem*, Plate 91, ll.55–7)

For Blake, even religion is an intellectual act that must be active rather than passive. The submissiveness that he believed the Church required of its congregation was antithetical to the marriage of love and energy he saw as the foundation of active belief. He sees imagination at the heart of Man's relationship with God – thus, writing becomes a spiritual act. For Blake, God is man-created and represents the creative and spiritual force within us all.

Blake's belief in the importance of childhood and the subconscious processes of the mind also sets him firmly in the Romantic school. He treats the child as a real individual whose open outlook on society has not yet been restricted by the limitations of adult conformity. Children's capacity for imagination enables them to *see a World in a grain of sand, Heaven in a wild flower* and to *Hold Infinity in the palm of [their] hand* ('Auguries of Innocence', ll.1–4, from *The Pickering Manuscript*, c.1803). In the child's ability to see beyond the surface value of things, he found a similar viewpoint to his own: where adults are afraid to move outside convention and received wisdom, children view the world with an innocence and simplicity. The power of his imagination is the source of Blake's challenge to society – through it he could deny the restrictions and classifications of conventional minds and eyes.

The form of Blake's verse also marks a movement away from the neo-classicism of the Augustan Age. The poems rarely take any established form, but the patterning within the overall framework is always precise. Despite the fact that his work can be obscure because of the intensity of his personal vision, Blake is very disciplined in his approach to form and style. He sees a link between *Art* (feeling) and *Science* (intellect) because both disciplines have to approach their subject in the same way. The poet, like the scientist, is the questioning individual who uses his work as a record of his search for understanding – and the outcome must be made up of *minutely organised Particulars* if it is to be of lasting value.

For the Augustan poets, language was a functional tool; for the Romantics, it was a part of the creative process, a material to be moulded and shaped. Blake marks the beginning of the Romantic tradition – he is the blacksmith forging verse from the raw material of life as he saw it. In *Jerusalem*, Los with his hammers and furnaces, wiping the sweat from his brow, is an appropriate representation of the creative process for Blake.

His first work is imitative, mainly made up of lyrics and ballads. The language is simple and direct, taking its lead from popular songs and the London streets. Other linguistic influence can be traced to Shakespeare's verse, the Bible and to the news-reports of the French and American Revolutions. The spontaneity of the language, however, is matched by a discipline that prevents the tone becoming sentimental.

The rhythms often reflect the patterns of speech and Blake draws on ballad metres to capture natural cadences. He is also influenced by the patterns of the Bible and by the power of incantation. The clarity of his short lines and phrases is juxtaposed with the depth of his symbols, which are quite unlike anything used by his contemporaries. Where Donne uses a symbol as an analogy, as a means of clarifying an idea through reference to something similar, Blake's poems themselves become symbols. The complexity of the associations requires the reader to look beyond the concrete representations of the poem to a more abstract level. His use of compression adds to the intensity of the meaning – readers must engage actively with the text if they wish to understand Blake's message. The juxtaposition of the apparent simplicity of his writing with the complexity of meaning marks Blake's individual voice at the end of the eighteenth century.

After the lyrical blank verse of the *Poetical Sketches* (1783), Blake turned to the metre of English songs and hymns for *The Songs of Innocence and Experience* (1795). For the prophetic books he was writing at this time, he chose free verse and this suggests that he intentionally chose a more traditional form for the *Songs*, allowing him to put complex ideas into a simple structure.

Blake believed that *without Contraries* [there] *is no progression* and the subtitle to the *Songs* explicitly directs the reader to the connections existing between the two cycles. Together they show *the two contrary states of the human soul* – Blake saw innocence and experience as unavoidable stages in the cycle of life.

In the *Songs of Innocence* (1789), the symbols are traditional – lambs and shepherds from the Bible, watched over by God. Childhood itself is a state of innocence, but it is also symbolic of a state of mind which can be attained by anyone. The contrary state of mind is represented by *The Songs of Experience* (1794) in which materialism has corrupted the freshness of outlook apparent in the first collection. The state of experience becomes a test of innocence, a necessary part of spiritual development.

The symbols are now more elusive as Blake moves away from traditional images towards a more personal system of representation – the violence of the tiger and the wilting of the sick rose. Where traditional images are used, they have a new meaning. In 'Infant Sorrow', for instance, birth is no longer romantic: verbs like *groan'd* and *wept* mark the arrival of the new life; the baby is now like a *fiend*; and the world is *dangerous*. The second stanza then epitomises the revolt that Blake believed was the only way to find meaning in a mechanistic society. Words like *Struggling* and *Striving against* describe the battle for freedom – on one level, literally against the *swadling bands*, but on another, symbolic of Blake's struggle against eighteenth-century convention. The final couplet mirrors the surface acceptance that conceals the inner revolt:

> Bound and weary I thought best
> To sulk upon my mother's breast.

The poems often exist in parallel forms allowing Blake to develop his antithetical approach: 'The Divine Image' from *Songs of Innocence* is juxtaposed with 'The Human Abstract'; 'The Ecchoing Green' is juxtaposed with 'The Garden of Love'.

The basic issues remain the same from *Songs of Experience* and *The Marriage of Heaven and* Hell to *A Vision of the Last Judgement* (1810) and *Jerusalem*, but Blake's style changes. The later verse becomes more obscure as his personal imagery and symbolism develops. Although mirroring traditional mythologies of creation and redemption, he creates his own figures in the prophetic books to portray his personal vision of the world's corruption and possible salvation. The rhythms are altered by the use of long free verse lines with occasional rhyme. Lyricism replaces the terseness of much of the early verse and the simplicity of style is replaced by a more rhetorical approach. His work stands out from his contemporaries' for its combination of linguistic craftsmanship, complex ideas and powerful symbolism. Its failing is that at times it is too personal and too remote from its readers.

For Blake, poetry was a process in which the intellect and the emotions played a part. His distinctive symbolism enables him to combine the two elements in a balance quite unlike other poets of the period. Much of his work focuses on self-analysis as he searches for a pattern or order in life, and the symbolism is an attempt to find a way to express the tensions existing both within himself and within society – where his understanding is still incomplete, his verse tends to be obscure. His themes address issues such as the balance of intellect versus emotion, the relationship between power and authority, the limitations of accepted morality, and the importance of forgiveness.

Critical response to Blake has been varied: in the eighteenth century, he was on the fringes of society with no sympathetic audience, but by the early nineteenth century, Wordsworth recognised that his work was of critical interest. For the Victorian Ruskin, Blake's work represented the product of a *great and wise* mind – even if there was also evidence to suggest that it may have been a *diseased and wild* mind. The publication of the W.M. Rossetti edition of Blake's poems (1874) established him as a lyric poet of note; in the last years of the nineteenth century, Yeats's memoir and interpretation of Blake's mythology (1893) identified him as a poet of great originality. He was to be a dominant influence on the poets of the twentieth century.

Activity 12.1

> **Explore the differences between the two poems titled 'The Nurse's Song' and suggest Blake's reasons for them.**
>
> You should think about: the tone, language, structure and form.

The Nurse's Song

1 When the voices of children are heard on the green
 And laughing is heard on the hill,
 My heart is at rest within my breast
  And everything else is still.

5 'Then come home, my children, the sun is gone down
 'And the dews of night arise;
 'Come, come, leave off play, and let us away
 'Till the morning appears in the skies.'

 'No, no, let us play, for it is yet day
10 'And we cannot go to sleep;
 'Besides, in the sky the little birds fly
 'And the hills are all cover'd with sheep.'

 'Well, well, go & play till the light fades away
 'And then go home to bed.'
15 The little ones leaped & shouted & laugh'd
  And all the hills ecchoed.   *Songs of Innocence*

The Nurse's Song

 When the voices of children are heard on the green
 And whisp'rings are in the dale,
 The days of my youth rise fresh in my mind,
20 My face turns green and pale.

 Then come home, my children, the sun is gone down,
 And the dews of night arise;
 Your spring & your day are wasted in play,
 And your winter and night in disguise. *Songs of Experience*

Commentary

In both poems, the setting is pastoral with references to *green* (1.1), *hill* (1.2) and *dale* (1.18), but the tone of each poem is quite different. Where the first voice speaks of love and happiness, the second speaks of bitterness and envy. This is conveyed through the antithetical language. The first poem is full of positive words such as *the voices of children* (1.1) and *laughing* (1.2); in the second, the language is transformed – laughter becomes *whisp'rings* (1.18), the verbs *leaped*, *shouted* and *laugh'd* (1.15) are replaced by *wasted* (1.23). The creativity of 'play' in the first poem is replaced by restrictions that limit the life of the imagination.

The speakers in each case are also presented antithetically. The first poem is a dialogue in which a compromise is reached between the nurse and children – two voices are heard and the mood is one of co-operation. The adult is identified by reference to her *heart* (1.3), which is *at rest*. This is in direct opposition to the speaker in the second poem – a monologue. The description of the internal *heart* (symbolic of feeling) is replaced by an external description of *face* (1.20), suggesting an alienation from true feeling. The negative image is reinforced in Blake's use of the traditional image of envy in the words *green* and *pale*. The poem represents the bitterness of the adult divorced from the state of childhood (symbolic of creativity and imagination).

The repetition of lines (ll.1/17, 5/21, 6/22) creates an immediate visual bond between the two poems, allowing Blake to suggest that innocence and experience are both part of the cycle of life. The antithesis, however, suggests that they represent quite different responses to life. The natural world and the children of the first poem are united in the echoes that resound from the hills (ll.15–16), while in the second poem, the natural world is recreated only in the figurative language. Instead of creating a background for the children's play, seasonal images of *spring* (l.23) and *winter* (l.24) do no more than convey a sense of time passing and the pointlessness of life.

Although the form and structure are simple, the intensity of meaning is typical of Blake's approach. Throughout the *Songs*, he juxtaposes antithetical images (truth/pretence, natural/unnatural life, happiness/repression, purity/corruption) to reveal the contrast between a life of imagination and one of imprisonment and submission. In these two poems, the form underpins the meaning. In the first, the joyful innocence of the children is mirrored in the alternate rhyme (ll.2/4, 6/8, 10/12, 14/16); in the second, the lack of rhyme is indicative of the disillusioned speaker. Where the inset lines (ll.4, 16) highlight the positive tone of the *Songs of Innocence*, the inset line (l.20) in the second poem is symbolic of 'experience'.

Wordsworth, Coleridge and the principles of Romanticism

Where Blake represented the changing feelings at the end of the eighteenth century on the fringes of society, the Romantics challenged the impersonal 'Age of Reason' in a more popular way. Changes in society's attitudes to religion, to the experience of the individual, and to personal feelings prepared the way for literature in which emotion and the imagination were given free reign. Despite this, Romanticism was never accepted in the same way that Classicism had been.

The emphasis was on the internal world of the poet: the outward perspective of the Augustan period (focusing on society) was replaced by an inward perspective (focusing on the self). The Romantic poets accused Pope of writing with his head (reason) and not his heart (emotion): he was concerned only with morality and the 'right' way to live; his tone was impersonal and satiric; and his style was too highly crafted and balanced. For them, order was no longer found in God and the Bible, but in the natural world and in the poet's imagination – the very act of creation revealed life's pattern.

Although establishing a new tradition in English poetry, Romanticism has some direct links with eighteenth-century poetry. While rejecting Pope and the heroic couplet, the Romantic poets were, to some extent, influenced by the reflective poetic tradition. Where the poets Gray and Thomson created a rural world that was too perfect, however, they sought to find poetry in the real world. The reflective poets were sentimental, their characters were stereotypes, and their language was artificial; the Romantics aimed to create a poetic tradition that went beyond such limitations. Although William Wordsworth and Samuel Taylor Coleridge (1772–1834) had been introduced to Blake's writings in the last decade of the eighteenth century, he was not well known. Nevertheless, their approach to childhood, the individual, imagination and the emotions developed what Blake had begun.

The focus for the Romantic movement lay in the publication of the *Lyrical Ballads* (1798) by Wordsworth and Coleridge. It marks a change in thought at the end of the century: because people had been separated from nature by the rational principles of the 'Age of Reason', poets like Wordsworth and Coleridge looked for truth and meaning in the natural world; because reason and impersonality had alienated man from his feelings, they valued the emotions as a means of reconnecting man with his inner life. The poems rejected the heroic couplet in favour of blank verse and a traditional ballad form; they chose simple rather than artificial language; and focused on ordinary people. Wordsworth said in his 'Preface' to the 1800 edition of *The Lyrical Ballads*:

> The principal object . . . proposed in these Poems was to choose incidents and situations from common life, and to relate or describe them, throughout, as far as possible in a selection of language really used by men . . .

While Coleridge's contributions were to be *directed towards persons and characters supernatural or at least romantic*, Wordsworth was *to give the charm of novelty to things of everyday*. The initial critical response was hostile, but the collection was to change the face of English poetry.

In his 'Preface', Wordsworth clearly establishes his poetic aims – it is a literary document that explicitly records his ideas about poetry. For him, the function of art is to write about things *not as they are, but as they appear*. The poet must draw on his *senses* and *passions* in order to reach below the surface of things to a deeper understanding. He clearly suggests that, as one who sees more than ordinary people, the poet has an obligation to reveal, using the noun *duty* to emphasise this sense of obligation. Blake's representation of the poet as prophet, however, is not the role model that Wordsworth follows. Instead, he sees the poet as an ordinary man with a greater awareness of life: he is

> a man speaking to men; a man . . . endowed with a more lively sensibility, more enthusiasm and tenderness, who has a greater knowledge of human nature, and a more comprehensive soul . . . a man . . . who rejoices more than other men in the spirit of life that is in him.

Above all, the poet must be someone who is closely in touch with his passions and who is able to express what he thinks and feels – the power of his imagination will enable him to reformulate the world through the process of creativity. Wordsworth writes of the poet's ability to transform the ordinary world with *a certain colouring of the imagination* that will give *an unusual aspect* to the things we take for granted around us.

The process of creation is also described and Wordsworth creates a direct link between memory and poetry. Poetry is:

> the spontaneous overflow of powerful feelings: it takes its origin from emotion recollected in tranquillity: the emotion is contemplated till, by a species of reaction, the tranquillity gradually disappears, and an emotion, kindred to that which was before the subject of contemplation, is gradually produced, and does itself actually exist in the mind.

The repetition of *feelings* and *emotion* in Wordsworth's description of the process is crucial to the Romantic movement. Equally, modifiers like *spontaneous* and *powerful* and the noun *overflow* draw attention to the intensity of the creative experience. For the Romantic poets, a moment of *tranquillity* in which a memory is recalled will lead to the recreation of a particular time or place. The experience is intensified by the power of feeling and often leads to a revelation of some kind. For this reason, the poems are often called epiphanies – almost spiritual experiences in which ordinary life is intensified and an underlying meaning is revealed.

The 'Preface' also addresses the nature of poetic language. Wordsworth's aim was to introduce a new freshness and directness into English poetry, uniting thought and feeling rather than drawing on the intellect. The poet must recognise that he is writing not *for his own gratification*, but *for men*. He must therefore choose language that is appropriate, he must *express himself as other men express themselves*. The focus of the poems is *Humble and rustic life* and Wordsworth expresses a belief that rural people speak *a plainer and more emphatic language*. He therefore adopts a *purified* form of their language because they *convey their feelings and notions in simple and unelaborated expressions*. For him the language is more meaningful than the artificial poetic diction of the eighteenth-century poets:

> . . . such a language, arising out of repeated experience and regular feelings, is a more permanent, and a far more philosophical language, than that which is frequently substituted for it by Poets, who think that they are conferring honour upon themselves and their art, in proportion as they separate themselves from the sympathies of men, and indulge in arbitrary and capricious habits of expression, in order to furnish food for fickle tastes, and fickle appetites, of their own creation.

Wordsworth's attack on the poetic traditions of his predecessors is clear. With negative words such as *indulge, capricious* and *fickle*, he suggests that they have an inflated opinion of their own worth. This is reinforced by phrases like *conferring honour on themselves* and *separate themselves from the sympathies of men*. This extract establishes the mission-like intensity of the 'Preface' in its determination to move away from the English poetic tradition of Pope and his followers, and from the moralising pastoral of the reflective poets.

The metre of eighteenth-century verse is also challenged. Where poetic diction makes it *arbitrary* and *subject to infinite caprices*, the poems of the *Lyrical Ballads* use a metre that is *regular and uniform*, and *obeys certain laws*. The regularity and simplicity of the ballad metre makes the poems accessible to all readers. It can *heighten and improve the pleasure* of reading because its predictability allows both reader and poet to concentrate on *the passion* of a poem without distraction.

Coleridge, like Wordsworth, also made clear statements about his views on poetry in a text called *Biographia Literaria* (1817). For him, the poet *brings the whole soul of man into activity* through the power of his imagination. This *synthetic and magical power* can be see in:

> . . . the balance or reconciliation of opposite or discordant qualities: of sameness, with difference; of the general, with the concrete; the idea, with the image; the individual, with the representative; the sense of novelty and freshness, with old and familiar objects; a more than usual state of emotion, with more than usual order;

judgement ever awake and steady self-possession, with enthusiasm and feeling profound or vehement; and while it blends and harmonizes the natural and the artificial, still subordinates art to nature.

The antithetical lexis and phrases in this extract reveal Coleridge's belief that the poet must combine all faculties through the power of imagination – the key lies in a balance of opposites. Imagination is *the SOUL that is everywhere, and in each*; it is the force through which the poet can mould everything into *one graceful and intelligent whole*.

His comments on language reinforce the sense of poetry as a deliberate and conscious process. By thinking about the meaning of words on two levels (both the *correspondent object* and *all the associations which it recalls*), the poet can intensify the poetic experience. For Coleridge, the poetic process is made up of both the visionary and the technical – it involves the heart (feelings and emotions) and the head (reason and logic).

William Wordsworth (1770–1850)

As a young man **William Wordsworth** was a rebel, questioning political, religious, literary and emotional conventions. He developed personal beliefs linked directly to what he saw and experienced. His rejection of established religion freed him from the restrictions of the eighteenth-century church and allowed him to develop his own kind of spirituality – a belief in the omnipresent spirit of the natural world. Similarly in his poetry, he rejected the commonplace ideas, sentimental tones and artificial language of eighteenth-century poetry, developing his own personal subject matter, language and style.

He was acquainted with many of the key literary figures of his day and was also influenced by the work of the philosopher Rousseau, adapting his political theories to suit his own individualistic view of life and society. Most important in his development was the meeting with Samuel Taylor Coleridge in 1795. It was to mark the beginning of a very productive partnership in which the two men stimulated each other in their exchange of views on politics and literature.

Wordsworth's poetic career is clearly divided into two periods. The best poetry was written during the period of his radical beliefs. By the end of his life, he had become a model citizen, a respectable churchgoer who conformed rather than rebelled and, for many critics, the work produced after 1810 was mediocre. The change in his political beliefs and his loss of faith in social progress and equality seem to have marked the end of his career as a poet.

His first work is imitative. *An Evening Walk* and *Descriptive Sketches* (1793) are very much a product of their times. Despite this, Wordsworth's challenge to eighteenth-century poetic conventions is implicitly there in the original images, the distinctive language use, and the presentation of nature in a real rather than symbolic way. In *Lyrical Ballads*, however, changes in metre, the use of simple language, a conversational tone and the focus on people rather than on landscapes mark a conscious movement away from the Augustan model.

The collection is clearly experimental and not every poem in it is successful – poems such as *We Are Seven, Simon Lee* and *The Thorn*, for instance, have been criticised for the childlike simplicity of their style. The one poem that stands out from the rest and indicates the ways in which Wordsworth was to move beyond his bold statement of poetic principles is *Tintern Abbey*. It presents Wordsworth as a nature poet who finds a common bond between the natural world and the inner self. It stands apart from the rest of the ballads and lyrics in the collection because of its elevated language, complex syntax and its link to Wordsworth's personal life.

With the autobiographical work, *The Prelude* (written 1799–1805, published posthumously 1850), Wordsworth develops the techniques that had marked *Tintern Abbey* out from the rest of the *Lyrical Ballads*. He again uses memory as a source of inspiration, and intertwines particular incidents and scenes with reflective, abstract thought. It is a private poem in the form of an epistle, or verse-letter, in which Wordsworth attempts to trace the development of his mind. External events and places, particular people, and passages considering the workings of the subconscious are brought together in Wordsworth's quest for inner understanding. The process of remembering is not always systematic, but the first ten books take the reader through his life chronologically: his infancy and school days; his student days in Cambridge; his final summer vacation; his trip to the Alps; his experience of London; and his time in France during the Revolution. The last three books are no longer chronological, but instead are an attempt to explain the story of his life. He writes about the people who have influenced his development (his sister, his wife and above all the poet Coleridge) and about the growth of his mind. For him, *spots of time* in our memories have a *vivifying virtue* that:

> . . . enables us to mount
> When high, more high, and lifts us up when fallen.

Such memories are *scatter'd everywhere* and are full of a *beneficent influence*. By combining memory and reflection, Wordsworth ensures that the poem is not just a record of external events, but a journey through the poet's mind and imagination.

The Prelude moves away from the traditional subject matter of earlier autobiographical writing. Up to this point, autobiographies often had a religious content – their story was based on conversion and personal religious experience. Wordsworth, however, chose to tell the story of his life. His purpose was to trace the growth of his mind by writing about the things that had influenced his development, so the poem is both personal and philosophical. For Wordsworth, the poem became a quest for understanding. It led him finally to an acceptance of who he was and what made him who he was.

In 1807, a collection of his most individual famous poems was published in *Poems in Two Volumes*. The dominant influence here is that of Dorothy Wordsworth, his sister, and her ability to observe the smaller details of nature. Poems like *The Solitary Reaper*, *The Daffodils* and *My heart leaps up when I behold* reflect a new view of the natural world – it is now comforting and pleasurable where it had been grand and formidable. Other successful poems published in these volumes include *Resolution and Independence* (or *The Leech Gatherer*), *Ode to Duty* and *Ode on the Intimations of Immortality from Recollections of Early Childhood*. Their mood is one of resignation and they regret the loss of inspiration and spontaneous feeling which characterised the earlier poems. Stylistically, they reveal some of the weaknesses that were to mar the verse of Wordsworth's last years when he was to produce conventional poems that contained the kind of versification of which he was so critical as a young man. This change was to be summarised by Hazlitt in *The Spirit of the Age* where Wordsworth's later philosophical poems are described as

> . . . a departure from, a dereliction of, his first principles. They are classical and courtly. They are polished in style, without being gaudy; dignified in subject, without affectation. They seem to have been composed not in a cottage at Grasmere, but among the half-inspired groves and stately recollections of Coleorton.

A close study of Wordsworth's greatest poems will show that he was a skilled craftsman who moved beyond the principles stated in the 1800 *Preface*. Having documented his basic challenge to the poetic tradition he inherited, he was then free to develop a style of poetry that was spontaneous and personal without being simplistic. Critical response to his verse has been varied. The second-generation Romantic poets, Percy Bysshe Shelley and Byron, wrote mocking parodies ridiculing the simplicity of his verse. Shelley had sympathised with Wordsworth's early outlook and his criticism is largely governed by his indignation at Wordsworth's renunciation of freedom. In *Peter Bell the Third* (1819), he directly parodies Wordsworth's poem *Peter Bell* (1798) and attacks him for his loss of faith in the radical cause. For Shelley, Wordsworth's later poems are *simple, the ghosts of what they were* and *dull, beyond all conception dull*.

Wordsworth 'the nature poet' was extremely popular with writers like Matthew Arnold and J.S. Mill, who took little notice of his early work, concentrating instead on the last great poems. By focusing on his presentation of nature as a transcendent force, they found certainty in a time of spiritual doubt. For them, his work was an escape from the mechanistic world of the Industrial Revolution. Others, including Robert Browning (1812–89), continued to criticise the poetry because of Wordsworth's abandonment of his radical beliefs.

The dominant Victorian view of Wordsworth as a nature poet was carried into the twentieth century, accompanied by a decrease in critical popularity at a time when Romanticism was not favoured. More recently, critics have focused on the psychological insights, the social attitudes and the inner conflicts that his poems reveal. The nineteenth-century interest in the later individual poems has therefore been replaced by analysis of the early verse.

Activity 12.2

Explore the literary and linguistic techniques Wordsworth uses to convey his state of mind in the following extract from *The Prelude* (Book 1, ll.357–400).

You may like to think about: the nature of autobiography, the presentation of the natural world, the language and style, the imagery and other poetic features.

1 One summer evening (led by her) I found
A little boat tied to a willow tree
Within a rocky cave, its usual home.
Straight I unloosed her chain, and stepping in
5 Pushed from the shore. It was an act of stealth
And troubled pleasure, nor without the voice
Of mountain-echoes did my boat move on;
Leaving behind her still, on either side,
Small circles glittering idly in the moon,
10 Until they melted all into one track
Of sparkling light. But now, like one who rows,
Proud of his skill, to reach a chosen point
With an unswerving line, I fixed my view
Upon the summit of a craggy ridge,
15 The horizon's utmost boundary; for above
Was nothing but the stars, and the grey sky.
She was an elfin pinnace: lustily
I dipped my oars into the silent lake,
And, as I rose upon the stroke, my boat
20 Went heaving through the water like a swan;
When, from behind that craggy steep till then
The horizon's bound, a huge peak, black and huge,
As if with voluntary power instinct
Upreared its head. I struck and struck again,

25 And growing still in stature the grim shape
Towered up between me and the stars, and still,
For so it seemed, with purpose of its own
And measured motion like a living thing,
Strode after me. With trembling oars I turned,
30 And through the silent water stole my way
Back to the covert of the willow tree;
There in her mooring-place I left my bark, –
And through the meadows homeward went, in grave
And serious mood; but after I had seen
35 That spectacle, for many days, my brain
Worked with a dim and undetermined sense
Of unknown modes of being; o'er my thoughts
There hung a darkness, call it solitude
Or blank desertion. No familiar shapes
40 Remained, no pleasant images of trees,
Of sea or sky, no colours of green fields;
But huge and mighty forms, that do not live
Like living men, moved slowly through the mind
By day, and were a trouble to my dreams.

Commentary

In this extract, Wordsworth relives a childhood memory with an intensity that brings it to life: the adult poet is suddenly a boy once more, experiencing the joy and terror of the experience all over again. The recreation of a childhood experience and the adult's reflection upon its significance is typical of autobiography. What makes this distinctive of the Romantic vision, however, is the power of the imagination to recreate a moment in time, and the child's instinctive sensitivity to his environment. Together these enable Wordsworth to convey his changing state of mind.

As he recalls the experience, the natural world becomes both a backdrop to the memory and a symbol of morality. The adult Wordsworth creates a link between the external landscape and the inner self: it allows him to explore his state of mind, and reflect on the power of a particular event to influence the development of an individual. His recreation of a particular moment in time, his understanding of the importance of individual experience and the inner life, and the power of the emotions he communicates are typical of the Romantic vision.

Wordsworth's focus on the natural world is also typical of the Romantic movement. For the Romantic poets, nature can be a positive force (a comforter, giving pleasure, and marking the point at which internal and external worlds meet), but it can also be negative (grand and austere, standing in judgement over man). These two responses link directly to the concept of the sublime and the beautiful. In the eighteenth century, these terms were defined by Edmund Burke (1729–97) in his treatise *Philosophical Enquiry into the Origin of our Ideas of the Sublime and Beautiful* (1757): while the 'beautiful' is associated with delicacy, smallness and light, the 'sublime' is associated with power, darkness, vastness and isolation. In this extract, Wordsworth draws on both concepts: the natural world is first beautiful and then terrifying as the young boy's guilty conscience indirectly assigns it to the role of judge.

The language and style of the poem help Wordsworth to recreate the intensity of the experience, and to reflect on its effect on him. The diction is powerful with lexical sets of words building up a concrete image of the natural world. While noun phrases like *a willow tree* (l.2), *a rocky cave* (l.3) and *the shore* (l.5) develop our sense of the physical background, modifiers create the mood. At first, we are aware of the atmosphere of exhilaration. Wordsworth conveys his state of mind implicitly through references to light: the positive connotations of *glittering* (l.9) and *sparkling* (l.11) reflect the boy's excitement and pleasure. Similarly, the foregrounded *Proud* (l.12) draws attention to his confidence.

The positive mood is undermined by the introduction of modifiers with negative connotations. The mood is now one of fear and this is conveyed by adjectives like *craggy, huge, black* and *grim* (ll.21–2, 25). The verb modifier *trembling* (l.29) and the verb *stole* (l.30) replace the boy's earlier confidence with an awareness of his insignificance. The final stage of the transformation lies in Wordsworth's description of the boy's feelings of guilt. The language is now marked by its austere mood: the co-ordinated modifiers *grave/And serious* (ll.33–4), *dim and undetermined* (l.36), and the abstract nouns *darkness* and *solitude* (ll.38) set the conclusion apart from the mood of the opening.

Wordsworth uses antithesis to draw attention to the boy's changing state of mind. Words like *glittering/sparkling* are set against *bleak/black*; *dipped* is set against *struck*; *unswerving/fixed* against *trembling*. Opposition is also built into the oxymorons *troubled pleasure* (l.6) and *lustily . . . dipped* (ll.17–18), allowing the adult poet to prepare us for the movement between pleasure, fear and guilt. The careful patterning of lexis helps to divide the extract into two distinct halves around a pivotal line (l.21), in which the foregrounded subordinate clause (*When . . .*) delays the dramatic main clause (*a huge peak . . ./Upreared its head*).

Wordsworth changes the word order and uses parenthesis to direct attention to important words and phrases. He conveys the boy's excitement, for instance, by putting the adverbial *Straight* (l.4) in the initial position; he uses parenthesis (ll.11–13) to dramatise the moment at which the young Wordsworth takes control. The foregrounded *But now* and the delayed main clause (*I fixed my view . . .*) along with the certainty of the lexis (*chosen point, unswerving line* and *fixed*) mark a new mood. Despite the boy's confidence, however, Wordsworth is already preparing us for a change: the modifier *craggy* begins the transformation from a natural world of beauty to one of sublime fear. While the *horizon's utmost boundary* may at present be providing the boy with a sense of security, protecting him from a recognition of the world's vastness, the natural world will soon become judge of his *act of stealth* (l.5).

Repetition also helps to convey mood by building the boy's sense of panic (l.24) and by emphasising the power of the natural world (ll.14/21, 22). The use of negatives helps develop the contrast between the opening and closing of the extract, building to a climax which emphasises the haunting quality of the natural world in the young boy's dreams (ll.39–41). Lexical sets of words like *brain* (l.35), *thoughts* (l.37), *mind* (l.43) and *dreams* (l.44) in the final section of the extract mark the movement from the external to the internal world – Wordsworth has tried to record the workings of the boy's imagination, making this more than just an account of an autobiographical incident.

The imagery enhances the remembered moment, making the experience both more personal and more intense. The metaphor of the boat as an *elfin pinnace* (l.17) marks the height of the boy's confidence; it is a magical transformation indicative of the power of his imagination. The mature poet, however, prepares us for the destruction of this vision: the juxtaposition of *lustily* and *dipped* (ll.17–18), and the opposition created between the verb *heaving* and the simile *like a swan* (l.20) create a tension between the child's perception and the poet's retrospective understanding. It is in keeping with the antithesis running through the extract: the external world versus the inner life; pleasure versus guilt; confidence versus fear; the sublime versus the beautiful; the adult versus the child.

The personification of the *huge peak* (ll.22–4, 25–8) brings these oppositions to a climax. It conveys the child's sense of nature as an austere and unforgiving judge, which is in direct contrast to the delicacy of the simile and metaphors in the first half of the poem. Where the vision of his boat represented a magical world of good, the personified peak is terrifying.

The metre mirrors the natural rhythms of speech and Wordsworth's use of blank verse is flexible. Metrical variation throws stress onto key words, replacing the normal iambic pattern with a substitute foot. For example, key lines open with a trochee or spondee to underpin the content and mark points of contrast. The trochaic foot *Leáviňg* (l.8) highlights the movement of the boat as the consecutive weak stresses mirror the lapping motion of the water; the initial strong beat on *Próud* (l.12) emphasises the boy's state of mind. The spondee *Stráight Í* (l.4) mirrors the growing excitement of the boy and the immediacy of his actions; the emphatic

Stróde áf | tĕr mĕ (1.29) endows the towering peak with a certainty and purpose that terrifies the boy.

Lord George Byron (1788–1824) and Percy Bysshe Shelley (1792–1822)

The life of **Lord George Byron** is well documented: his physical deformity; his rejection of the moral conventions of the time; his wild and extravagant ways; his belief in liberty. He was a rebel who was both loved for his determination to outdo his critics, and abhorred for his licentious behaviour and his incestuous relationship with his half-sister. He left England in 1816 as his debts grew, and was never to return again.

Byron was a man in conflict with his world and much of his poetry reflects this. He conveys his feelings of isolation vividly in *Childe Harold's Pilgrimage* (1812–17) through the repetition of the line *I have not loved the world, nor the world me* (Canto III, 113/114) and in his emotive description of his detachment:

> I stood
> Among them, but not of them; in a shroud
> Of thoughts which were not their thoughts . . .   (Canto III, 113)

Byron was a very productive poet and his manuscripts reveal the kinds of revisions he made as he composed – couplets, for instance, were frequently reworked in order to achieve a forceful ending to a stanza. His overall approach to editing his work, however, seems to have been somewhat haphazard with little attempt to control the publication of less effective poems. This means that not all his published work was successful and critics were often ruthless with the weaknesses they found.

Byron's early work shows him as an outsider on the fringes of literary society, but he was to win public acclaim within five years. His first collection, *Hours of Idleness* (1807), was not well received: an attack by a Scottish Reviewer led to the publication of Byron's satirical attack on reviewers and the first-generation Romantics, *English Bards and Scottish Reviewers*. His distaste for Wordsworth and Coleridge is clear:

> Let simple Wordsworth chime his childish verse,
> And brother Coleridge lull the babe at nurse . . .   (ll.917–18)

The use of the heroic couplet and pointed wit in the style of Pope made Byron's rhetorical satire very effective, but it was not until the publication of the first two cantos of *Childe Harold's Pilgrimage* (1812) that he became popular. The poem is based on his experiences as a traveller, reflecting his love of Greece and his hatred of the Turkish oppressors against whom the Greek fight for independence was directed. He uses a Spenserian stanza and combines descriptions of the landscape with passages focusing on the impression it had made on him.

Byron's popularity grew with the publication of his verse narratives in 1813. *The Giaour*, *The Bride of Abydos*, *The Corsair* and *Lara* are all melodramatic tales full of gloomy passions, wild adventures and the exotic, making Sir Walter Scott's (1771–1832) verse romances seem tame by comparison. At the heart of Byron's poems lies a projection of himself as the Byronic hero: a rebel, darkly handsome, mysterious and misanthropic. The poems are dramatic narratives in which the Byronic hero wanders through various places, facing challenges and overcoming obstacles. Despite the strength of the stories, however, at times the style is careless.

The mature work is marked by the publication of *Beppo* (1817), *Don Juan* (1818–21) and *The Vision of the Last Judgement* (1822), serio-comic poems that combine ironic and lyrical tones. Byron uses ottava rima, a flexible 8-line iambic stanza rhyming abababcc. It allows a degree of technical freedom well suited to the swiftly changing moods and paces of the verse. The style is perfected in *Don Juan* on which Byron's modern reputation is based – it is both a *comedy of the passions* and a *satire on the abuses of the present state of society*.

The extravagance of Juan's adventures is juxtaposed with digressions in which Byron attacks society. The conversational style of the narration is juxtaposed with elevated tones for reflection, and flippant tones for the satire. Byron's skill lies in his ability to combine critical comment with melodrama and the ridiculous.

The verse often lacks originality in its diction and choice of metaphor, yet Byron's awareness of this allows him to use his limitations as subject matter in their own right. In the following extract from *Don Juan* (Canto XIII, 36–7), rather than editing and developing a more original image, Byron exposes his failings for his readers' amusement.

1   But Adeline was not indifferent: for
         (*Now* for a common-place!) beneath the snow,
     As a volcano holds the lava more
         Within – *et cœtera*. Shall I go on? – No,
5   I hate to hunt down a tired metaphor,
         So let the often-used volcano go.
     Poor thing! How frequently, by me and others,
     It hath been stirr'd up till its smoke quite smothers!

     I'll have another figure in a trice: –
10   What say you to a bottle of champagne?
     Frozen into a very vinous ice,
         Which leaves few drops of that immortal rain,
     Yet in the very centre, past all price,
         About a liquid glassful will remain;
15   And this is stronger than the strongest grape
     Could e'er express in its expended shape . . .

The ironic tone here engages the reader, creating a familiarity which is appealing. The conversational tone of the self-deprecation is entertaining: the use of parenthesis and the italicised <u>Now</u> (l.2) demonstrate the poet's willingness to reveal his weaknesses through a wry humour; the reference to having *another figure in a trice* (l.9) suggests that the poet is no more than a technical magician with a bag of linguistic tricks. The self-mockery reduces the poet to the level of his readers – the Romantic representation of the poet as a seer and visionary who feels more strongly than other men is replaced by a matter-of-factness suggesting that the poet is engaged in practical labour.

The irony is underpinned by the replacement of the *tired metaphor* (l.5) of the *volcano* and its *lava* (l.3) with an image which is powerful and original. Although the poet implies that his task is simple, the new metaphor he introduces is far from mundane. The direct address to the reader, *What say you to a bottle of champagne?* (l.10), belies its sophistication. Phrases like *vinous ice* (l.11), *immortal rain* (l.12) and *a liquid glassful* (l.14) convey the exquisite nature of the beauty who is cold on the outside, but passionate on the inside, *in the very centre*. The value of this unseen passion is then underlined by the references to *few drops* (l.12) and *past all price* (l.13), and the use of the comparative *stronger* and the superlative *strongest* (l.15). Having begun with a self-criticism for his own inadequacies as a poet, Byron ends with an image that engages the reader through its novelty and precision.

Some critics see characteristic flaws in Byron's verse; he was not a careful craftsman. His diction is often too grandiose and in places he loses his sense of stylistic balance in the heat of the moment. Despite this, in his best verse, his strengths outweigh any weaknesses in lexis and style. At its best, his language is dramatic, colourful and forthright; his style is varied; and he has a good ear for the nuances of tone and rhythm. He combines the conversational and colloquial with the stylised and the rhetorical; witty humour with perceptive revelations; and precise external observations with a lucid understanding of society's hidden inner life. The strong sense of Byron emerging from the verse and his awareness of the reader create a personal relationship and develop a familiarity that brings his stories to life.

Although Byron admired the Augustan poets Dryden and Pope and attacked the Romantics Wordsworth and Coleridge, he is directly associated with the development of Romanticism in its second stage. His love of liberty and his hatred for oppression, his love for the power of the natural world, and his intensity represent the continuation of Romantic principles established by the earlier poets. In his later work, however, he synthesises the Augustan principles of control with a Romantic sensibility – the result is a new kind of satire. His use of the serio-comic verse form is distinctive, but his unique contribution lies in the creation of a Romantic 'self', the Byronic hero whose flippant manner and heroic pose are a mask for his true feelings. This anti-hero was to become a model for literature, described by Thomas Macaulay (1800–59) as:

a man proud, moody, cynical, with defiance on his brow, and misery in his heart, a scorner of his kind, implacable in revenge, yet capable of deep and strong affection.

The life of **Percy Bysshe Shelley** is marked by his belief in the equality of men and by his vision of the perfectibility of people – in *Queen Mab* (1813), he wrote that *every heart contains perfection's germ* (V, l.147). He rejected traditional institutions like the Church and education as a means of improvement, seeing them as the creations of a ruling elite who wished to control the masses. While at Oxford University, he challenged the authorities to a debate on his heretical views after writing a pamphlet called *The Necessity of Atheism*. He was a sceptic in religion and a rebel in politics, and his views are expressed consciously in his poems. In *Queen Mab* (VII, ll.43–5), for instance, he attacks contemporary religion for its hypocrisy, clearly revealing in his lexical choices his distaste for a ruling elite who he believed exploited ordinary people and ruled through fear rather than love:

> Earth groans beneath religion's iron age,
> And priests dare babble of a God of peace,
> Even whilst their hands are red with guiltless blood . . .

Despite considerable public disapproval at his behaviour in his private life and his rejection of such contemporary institutions as the Church, at the heart of Shelley's poetry lies a very personal moral framework.

Shelley's distinctive worldview was shaped by political, philosophical and literary influences. In a practical way, the French Revolution governed his life, shaping his attitudes just as it had done for Wordsworth and Coleridge. It was symbolic of change – a reaction against the status quo represented by past traditions, customs and institutions such as education and the Church. It reflected Shelley's antagonistic attitude to the past and to convention, while symbolising his belief in the potential of the future.

His relationship with the philosopher William Godwin (1756–1836) was to shape his moral outlook – in Godwin's *Enquiry Concerning Political Justice* (1793), Shelley found the belief that *Man is perfectible, or in other words susceptible of perpetual improvement*. Although he did not use the ideas explicitly in his verse, echoes of Godwin's Utopian dreams can be found in Shelley's idealism.

The Swiss philosopher Rousseau was also influential. Shelley identified with his ideas about the natural world as a teacher removed from the corruption of civilisation. Rousseau also believed in the importance of 'feeling' lessons, of learning through our sensibilities, and the Romantic poets all believed in the power of Nature to reveal the true self. Shelley represents it in his poems as a backdrop against which self-analysis and introspection can reveal the source of true feelings.

Perhaps the most important intellectual and spiritual influence on Shelley's poetry can be seen in Plato's representation of nature as a spirit form of what exists in eternity. For him, wisdom and knowledge will lead to another world existing beyond the physical world of the present. Similarly, Shelley believed that the physical world is *a shadow of the dream* that is waiting to be found in the world of ideas.

In this extract from *Adonais* (1821), an elegy written on the death of Keats, Shelley expresses these beliefs through his use of figurative language.

> Heaven's light forever shines, Earth's shadows fly;
> Life, like a dome of many-coloured glass,
> Stains the white radiance of Eternity,
> Until Death tramples it to fragments.   (Stanza 52, ll.461–4)

The opposition between *Earth* and *Heaven* mirrors Shelley's belief in Plato's juxtaposition of the real world and the world of ideas. This is reinforced by the juxtaposition of *light/shines* with *shadows*. The sense of the physical world as a dull copy of the parallel world of thought is developed in the opposition of *many-coloured* and *white radiance* – the connotations of the verb *Stains* underpin the suggestion that we are blinded by the superficial beauty of our surroundings without recognising that a more distinct vision exists beyond it. With the final duality of *Life* and *Death*, Shelley develops his belief in the transitory nature of worldly beauty. Words like *fly*, *tramples* and *fragments* are linked to Earth, while the adverb *forever* represents the immortality of thought.

Although influenced by the classical tradition, it is the literature of the Romantic movement which governs the spirit of Shelley's work. He admired Wordsworth's earlier poetry, identifying with his hopes for the regeneration of society and his belief in the sympathy between man and nature. Wordsworth's influence can be seen in Shelley's natural descriptions, particularly in poems such as 'Hymn to Intellectual Beauty' (1816) and 'Mont Blanc' (1816). He saw in Byron's poetry a depth of understanding of human emotion that he felt he could not equal, and he loved the wildness of Gothic novels with their sublime treatment of the natural world.

A record of Shelley's views on poetry can be found in *A Defence of Poetry* (written 1821, published 1840). In this prose work, he attacks utilitarianism, arguing that poetry is the most powerful way of teaching morality, and that the creative imagination is the best way to awaken our sense of *the hidden beauty of the world*. For Shelley, poetry is *the expression of the imagination* – it is the process in which the mind acts on thoughts *so as to colour them with its own light*, making *familiar objects be as if they were not familiar*. He writes of the moment of creation where the mind is like *a fading coal* which *awakens to a transitory brightness*. Words like *inconstant*, *fades* and *changes* reinforce the sense that the moment of inspiration is ephemeral – and only after that moment of uncontrollable power can the poet consciously begin to organise and arrange his material.

To make his abstract argument clearer, Shelley uses concrete images, often drawn from the natural world. He explains the function of art using images of an acorn and a fountain to convey the infinite nature of poetry:

> . . . it is as the first acorn, which contained all oaks potentially. Veil after veil may be undrawn, and the inmost naked beauty of the meaning never exposed. A great poem is a fountain for ever overflowing with the waters of wisdom and delight; and after one person and one age has exhausted all its divine effluence which their peculiar relations enable them to share, another and yet another succeeds, and new relations are ever developed, the source of an unforeseen and an unconceived delight.

In understanding that each age reads new meaning into great literature, Shelley demonstrates the maturity of his reflections. For him, the poet *not only beholds intensely the present as it is*, but also *beholds the future in the present*. Thus the role of the poet is a prophetic one: great poets are at once *authors of language, institutors of laws, founders of civil society* and *inventors of the arts of life*; poems are *the image of life expressed in its eternal truth*.

The content of Shelley's poems is often intense because it records his emotions. His vision leads him into an ideal world, but inevitably ends with a sense of his own powerlessness. In *Alastor* (1816), the first poem to bring him public notice, the hero is pure and uncorrupted, led by his idealistic imagination to find a living representation of his vision. He is destroyed by his failure and thus stands as a symbol of Shelley's own vision and failed idealism.

Because he is dealing with abstracts (beauty, love, evil, tyranny, liberty), Shelley's verse can be abstruse. By using imagery from the natural world, by focusing on shape and colour, however, he brings the intangible concepts to life. Certain symbols recur and references to streams, clouds, moons, eagles, veils and lyres or Aeolian harps are common. A natural event or a thing – a skylark's song, the west wind – becomes the basis for the emotion or thought it inspired – sadness at the loss of youth, contemplation of the role of the poet. His observations are more than just physical descriptions since they reflect his understanding of the natural world and his ability to transform it. Like the first-generation Romantic poets Wordsworth and Coleridge, he uses the natural world to convey states of mind and as a backdrop to philosophical debate: he both records and reveals.

The language is startling. Shelley uses words to express his mood, viewpoint and the process of his thought, as well as accurately recreating the natural world. His knowledge of scientific, geological and geographic processes underpins his awareness of the beautiful and the sublime in the natural landscape. To fulfil its prophetic role, Shelley believed that the language of poetry should be figurative, able to reveal *the before unapprehended relations of things*, the world of thought existing just beyond the physical world. He sought to make us see things anew after they have been *annihilated in our minds by the recurrence of impressions blunted by reiteration*. Although not a religious poet in the traditional sense, his poems had moral messages at their hearts and he hoped that his verse would reveal the spirit in the world.

The early poem *Queen Mab* (1813) is an intellectual record of a young man's beliefs, focusing on the corruption of people by institutions and conventional morality. There are already signs, however, of Shelley's Romantic leanings in the magical dream-like atmosphere. Poems such as *The Revolt of Islam* (1818), 'The Cloud' and 'The Sensitive Plant' (1820) and the lyrical drama *Prometheus Unbound* (1820) were to translate his beliefs into visions of utopian society.

Shelley's shorter lyrics, including 'Ode to the West Wind' (1819), 'To a Skylark', 'The Cloud' and 'The Sensitive Plant' (1820), form the basis of his popular reputation. These are more controlled than some of the longer poems and reveal the power of Shelley's imagination more successfully. Where much of his work is marked by a mood of self-pity, the shorter lyrics combine self-concern with pathetic fallacy, a strong rhythm and visual language, lifting them above pathos. Intellectual thought is an integral part of the emotional state and the poems move beyond the physical environment: the natural world is transformed, existing alongside the world of dreams and visions. Despite his awareness that the poet cannot reveal 'truth' because of the limitations of language, Shelley's poems represent his attempt to do so. The imagery combines concrete reality with symbol – the skylark is both a real bird, and a symbol of truth and perfection.

Shelley uses traditional poetic forms (odes, elegies, lyrics), drawing on both classical and contemporary sources. Imitation of the lyric was at its height in the Elizabethan period, but during the seventeenth and eighteenth centuries, poets used it to express their thoughts and feelings. In Shelley's hands, the lyric form becomes the medium through which he can convey the struggle to reveal his inner self.

During his lifetime, Shelley's poetry was not widely known – he found it difficult to get poems accepted for publication in England. His poetry was too subjective for public taste and he was generally criticised for his atheistic views, his subversive politics and his personal immorality. Nineteenth-century criticism tended to balance the qualities of his style against the insubstantial focus of the content.

The high point of Shelley's reputation lies between 1895 and 1920. He was admired by Thomas Hardy, and George Bernard Shaw (1856–1950) derived his religious beliefs from Shelley's views. William Butler Yeats described *Prometheus Unbound* as *a sacred book* and called *A Defence of Poetry* the *profoundest essay on the foundation of poetry in English*. Later criticism avoided judgement based on the 'style versus content' debate, many choosing instead to see Shelley as a minor poet.

As the Romantic poets lost favour, Shelley's concentration on feeling and his belief in the perfectibility of man was unpopular; his political views seemed dated and the intensity of his sensibilities alienated readers. Twentieth-century critics were no longer prepared to respond to texts at the level of feeling rather than intellect, and disliked Shelley's visionary representation of the world – F.R. Leavis (1895–1978) criticised him for his weak grasp of the actual and W.H. Auden (1907–73) for never looking at or listening to anything but ideas. Stylistically, he was criticised for over-elaborate language, repetitive diction, incomplete sentences, excessively convoluted figurative language and rhythms which were too polished. More recently, critics have recognised Shelley's strengths: although tending to abstraction, self-pity and excessive rhetoric, his work is also original, intelligent and idealistic.

John Keats (1795–1821)

John Keats died from tuberculosis just before his twenty-fifth birthday. His writing career spans the three years between the publication of his first poem, a sonnet 'O Solitude', in 1816 and his decision to commit himself to poetry, and the composition of his last poems in 1819. During 1820, he was too ill to do more than revise his last collection of poems for publication. Despite the shortness of his life, Keats experimented widely with a range of forms and styles – his letters trace the emergence of an increasingly disciplined approach to poetry. He saw technical control, richness of expression and the power of physical experience as the essential elements of true poetry. His comments on the creative power of the imagination were to link him directly to the Romantic movement, while his interest in the music of verse was to place him as a precursor to the Victorians.

The dominant influences on Keats are to be found in the writers he chose to read. From Homer, Spenser, Shakespeare, Milton and Dryden, he discovered the ways in which a poet can both create imaginary worlds and provide insights into the human condition. In drawing on such writers, he rejected the objective craftsmanship of the Augustan tradition and opted instead for elevated language and subjective experience. The influence of Wordsworth can be seen in Keats's view of the natural world as a mirror of our state of mind, but also in his belief in the musicality of poetry. In describing the *sweet music* of poetry ('Sleep and Poetry'), some critics think Keats is praising the melodies of Wordsworth's verse as opposed to the artistry of the Augustans.

Just as Wordsworth's *Prelude* and Coleridge's *Biographia Literaria* had recorded their poetic philosophies, so too Keats's letters provide a useful commentary on his thoughts about the nature of poetry. He rejects the concept of didactic verse since it has *a palpable design* on readers. For him, poetry should instead be:

> great and unobtrusive, a thing which enters into one's soul, and does not startle it or amaze it with itself but with its subject . . .
>
> (Letter to John Hamilton Reynolds, 1818)

In another letter (to John Taylor, 1818), Keats states that a poem should *surprise by a fine excess and not by Singularity*; that the reader should see in it *a wording of his own highest thoughts*, that it should *appear almost a Remembrance*. He believes that *What the imagination seizes as Beauty must be truth*. In writing of poetic inspiration, Keats uses words like *elevation, mounted* and *high*, suggesting the way in which the poet rises above the real, reaching a heightened sensibility on the *Wings of Imagination*. He describes writing poetry as a spiritual experience, using religious language to convey the intensity of the poetic process.

The intensity of the experience also lies in the poet's ability to participate in things existing outside himself. Keats was to write of his own ability to watch a sparrow outside his window and to *take part in its existence and pick about the gravel*. He was interested in the insight such experience could provide, but not in rationalising it. In a letter to his brothers George and Thomas (1817), he described his concept of *negative capability* – a state of mind that he believed marked out great writers like Shakespeare. For Keats, *negative capability* is

> when a man is capable of being in uncertainties, mysteries, doubts, without any irritable reaching after fact and reason.

In other words, a poet had to be receptive to the things around him, accepting the insights that the creative process brought without searching for reasons. By engaging with a particular object or moment, Keats can thus rise above the ordinary to reveal an underlying meaning with which readers can identify. His imagery evokes a typically Romantic sensibility, but alongside this he develops a mood of intellectual inquiry that moves beyond the self-absorption of the earlier Romantic poets.

Because of the short period during which Keats wrote poetry, critics have been able to analyse the emergence of his distinctive style: the range of his experimentation with different forms, the growing sophistication of his diction and the power of his imagery. The early death of his father (1804) and mother (1810) affected him deeply and in his poetry the dominant themes are linked to the impermanence of beauty and the fragility of happiness. Seeing personal experience as the means of understanding the self and society, he challenges the conventions of traditional religion and explores human experience and the tension existing between the real and the ideal.

The content of the poetry can be divided into three main categories: the mythological poems (*Endymion* 1817, *Hyperion* 1820, 'Lamia' 1820); the mystery narratives ('Isabella', 'The Eve of St Agnes', 'La Belle Dame Sans Merci' 1819); and the odes ('On a Grecian Urn', 'To a Nightingale', 'To Autumn', 'On Melancholy', 'On Indolence', 'To Psyche' 1819) for which he is most well known. In addition, he wrote numerous sonnets, ballads, epistles and other poems, not all of which were published during his lifetime.

The most successful of his mythological pieces, 'Lamia', explores the conflict between life and art through the figure of Lycius, a young man who is open to the charms of magic, but who is unable to face reality. Keats wrote to his brother that the poem had *a sort of fire in it*, believing that it would appeal to a public readership with a taste for exotic tales of mystery. The poem is in places marked by a lack of clarity, but Keats makes the heroic couplet of Pope and Dryden distinctively his own by using it in a more open way to mirror his interest in the tension between the real and the ideal.

In the narrative poems, Keats addresses the complexity of human life by creating a strong sense of character and place, and by dramatising an autobiographical moment or personal experience. Characters, such as the Knight of 'La Belle Dame', for instance, recall a particular occasion in their lives, and it is their response to this experience that forms the heart of the poem. As readers, we cannot be sure about the 'truth' of the tale, but the narrative framework allows Keats to explore the workings of the human mind.

Four of the five most famous odes were written in a three-week period between April and May 1819, marking the highpoint of Keats's short career. They reveal his response to a particular experience: he explores moods and contradictory feelings. Structurally, each one follows a distinctive pattern: the poet first identifies with an object that will take him beyond the world of flux; the distancing process begins to break down; and the poet finally returns to the mutable world and the inescapability of the human condition. The objects that Keats addresses become symbols for the thought process: through the nightingale, he addresses the nature of human transience; through the Grecian urn, the everlasting but static nature of Art. Despite the poet's desire to escape through the objects, the poems simultaneously revel in the world through their direct appeals to the senses.

The ode allows Keats to develop a single idea over several stanzas – often the relationship between the ideal of eternal lifeless art and the imperfection of experience. 'Ode to Autumn' is regarded by many as the height of Keats's poetic development: the imagery is rich and sensuous; the language combines both the precise and the suggestive; the rhythms are skilfully measured; and the detached tone takes it beyond the recreation of a personal experience to a recognition of the nature of life with which the reader can identify.

The language of the early poems can be repetitious and unoriginal. The rhetorical and archaic nature of the diction, however, can give an air of authority to the role of the poet, and the recurrence of religious lexis suggests the intensity of the creative process. Later poems use elevated language to draw attention to the ability of poetry to rise above the ordinary. The complexity of the odes, with their difficult ideas and detailed arguments, requires wide-ranging diction to communicate the themes.

Where the imagery of Keats's earlier work is conventional, in the later poems it is rich, allowing the reader to identify with objects through sense impressions. The images are designed to evoke an intense response, appealing to the senses through tactile language choices. In such expressions as *the touch of scent*, he uses synaesthesia – an appeal to more than one sense simultaneously.

In early poems like 'Sleep and Poetry', there is already evidence of the metrical and sound patterns that were to become Keats's hallmark. Metrical variation throws stress onto key concepts, and recurring vowel sounds intensify the effect of the syllabic stresses by creating tight links between words.

$$\acute{\text{O}} \text{ Po} \mid \acute{\text{e}}\text{sy} \mid \text{f}\acute{\text{o}}\text{r th}\breve{\text{ee}} \mid \breve{\text{I}} \text{ hol}\acute{\text{d}} \mid \acute{\text{m}}\text{y pen} \qquad\qquad (\text{l.47})$$

Here the three assonantal rhymes (**O**, *Poesy*, h**o**ld) and the two assonantal rhymes (*poesy*, *thee*) are all marked by stresses. The combination of these poetic devices allows Keats to heighten the intensity of his plea for poetic inspiration.

The complexity of the imagery in the later poems is paralleled by an increased control in the versification. Keats was particularly interested in *the principle of Melody in verse* and in *the management of open* [long] *and close* [short] *vowels*. He used interacting patterns of assonance and stress with accents falling on the long vowels. He saw this as an improvement on the forced rhymes and lack of fluency that he believed marked his earlier composition *Endymion*. The elaborate sound patterning of the Odes marks the beginning of the assonantal tradition in English poetry.

The form of Keats's poems changed considerably as he moved from imitation to a distinctive personal versification. Unlike the earlier Romantics, he did not need to establish new conventions, but his poetry is consciously experimental in its matching of form and content. 'Sleep and Poetry' uses Pope's heroic couplet as a model, but often breaks the fluency of the couplet by creating a caesura at the end of the first line, and by using enjambement between the end of the second line and the beginning of the next one.

> 1   Should I rather kneel
> Upon some mountain-top until I feel
> A glowing splendour round about me hung,
> And echo back the voice of thine own tongue?   (ll.49–52)

In this extract from the poem, the enjambement leading from the end of the first couplet to the beginning of the next (ll.2–3) drives the reader onto the focus – *A glowing splendour*. The caesura at the end of the third line creates the opposite effect since it forces the reader to pause – the verb *hung* with its connotations of something suspended, detached, and the stress of its end focus is thus reinforced by the structure.

Keats also experimented with traditional verse forms and stanza length. By combining features of the Shakespearean and Petrarchan sonnet, and by drawing on the influence of the 10-line stanzas of eighteenth-century odes, he created a distinctive verse form. It is made up of one alternate rhyming quatrain abab and the Petrarchan sestet cdecde. He uses this versification in 'Ode to a

Nightingale' and 'Ode to Melancholy', but variations can be seen in 'Ode to a Grecian Urn' (ababcdedce), in the 9-line Spenserian stanza of 'The Eve of St. Agnes' (ababbcbcc), the alternating rhymes of the 10-line stanza in 'Ode to Psyche', and in the 11-line stanza of 'To Autumn' (ababcdedcce or ababcdecdde).

The themes of Keats's poems are familiar: love, death, failure, poetry, art and nature. The common thread running through these is his keen awareness that everything must change. Sometimes he attempts to transcend the changing world through his visionary imagination, but often he comes to an understanding and an acceptance of the transient nature of existence. A conflict between these two views leads to a series of tensions and contrasts in both content and style as he explores the human condition. For Keats, pleasure and pain, love and death, dream and reality are the essence of the poetic imagination. He does not resolve these juxtapositions, but exposes them. Recurring themes reflect his interest in ideas: he was against explicit philosophising like Wordsworth's, but returned again and again to topics such as the nature of life, truth and the role of poetry.

Critical response to Keats identifies him as one of the principal figures in the Romantic movement. His contemporaries, however, did not always understand him: he was attacked in the *Quarterly Review* for publishing work that was half-formed and shapeless, and in *Blackwood's Magazine* for his association with the radical views of Leigh Hunt (1784–1859). Keats himself was aware of the weaknesses in his early work: he saw himself *hovering . . . between an exquisite sense of the luxurious and a love for Philosophy.*

The power of his work was recognised by Lord Jeffrey (1773–1850), founder of *The Edinburgh Review*, who saw it as *impossible to resist the intoxication or shut our hearts to the enchantment.* In the years after his death, he was to be heralded by Tennyson as the greatest poet of the nineteenth century, and praised by Matthew Arnold for his *intellectual and spiritual passion* for beauty. He identified a *quality of sensuousness* in Keats's poems, but also a harder edge – the *flint and iron in him.* In the twentieth century, Keats has continued to interest critics and readers despite anti-Romantic reaction. His mastery of language and phrase, and his ability to convey actual sensations in original images are qualities that have given his work lasting appeal.

Activity 12.3

Explore the ways in which Keats presents and develops his ideas in 'Ode to a Nightingale'.

You may like to think about: the language and mood; changes in tone; the imagery; grammatical and rhetorical features; the themes; and the versification (sound patterning, metre, caesura, rhyme).

Ode to a Nightingale

I

1   My heart aches, and a drowsy numbness pains
     My sense, as though of hemlock I had drunk,
  Or emptied some dull opiate to the drains
     One minute past, and Lethe-wards had sunk:
5   'Tis not through envy of thy happy lot,
     But being too happy in thine happiness –
       That thou, light-wingèd Dryad of the trees,
        In some melodious plot
     Of beechen green, and shadows numberless,
10   Singest of summer in full-throated ease.

II

  O, for a draught of vintage! that hath been
     Cooled a long age in the deep-delvèd earth,
  Tasting of Flora and the country green,
     Dance, and Provençal song, and sunburnt mirth!
15 O for a beaker full of the warm South,
     Full of the true, the blushful Hippocrene,
       With beaded bubbles winking at the brim,
        And purple-stainèd mouth,
     That I might drink, and leave the world unseen,
20   And with thee fade away into the forest dim –

III

  Fade far away, dissolve, and quite forget
     What thou among the leaves hast never known,
  The weariness, the fever, and the fret
     Here, where men sit and hear each other groan:
25 Where palsy shakes a few, sad, last grey hairs,
     Where youth grows pale, and spectre-thin, and dies;
       Where but to think is to be full of sorrow
        And leaden-eyed despairs;
     Where Beauty cannot keep her lustrous eyes,
30   Or new Love pine at them beyond to-morrow.

IV

  Away! away! for I will fly to thee,
     Not charioted by Bacchus and his pards,
  But on the viewless wings of Poesy,
     Though the dull brain perplexes and retards.
35 Already with thee! tender is the night,
     And haply the Queen-Moon is on her throne,
       Clustered around by all her starry Fays;
        But here there is no light,
     Save what from heaven is with the breezes blown
40   Through verdurous glooms and winding mossy ways.

V

  I cannot see what flowers are at my feet,
     Nor what soft incense hangs upon the boughs,
  But, in embalmèd darkness, guess each sweet
     Wherewith the seasonable month endows

45 The grass, the thicket, and the fruit-tree wild –
    White hawthorn, and the pastoral eglantine;
     Fast fading violets covered up in leaves;
      And mid-May's eldest child,
    The coming musk-rose, full of dewy wine,
50   The murmurous haunt of flies on summer eves.

   VI
  Darkling I listen; and, for many a time
    I have been half in love with easeful Death,
  Called him soft names in many a musèd rhyme,
    To take into the air my quiet breath;
55 Now more than ever seems it rich to die,
    To cease upon the midnight with no pain,
     While thou art pouring forth thy soul abroad
      In such an ecstasy!
    Still wouldst thou sing, and I have ears in vain –
60   To thy high requiem become a sod.

   VII
  Thou wast not born for death, immortal Bird!
    No hungry generations tread thee down;
  The voice I hear this passing night was heard
    In ancient days by emperor and clown:
65 Perhaps the self-same song that found a path
    Through the sad heart of Ruth, when, sick for home,
     She stood in tears amid the alien corn;
      The same that oft-times hath
    Charmed magic casements, opening on the foam
70   Of perilous seas, in faery lands forlorn.

   VIII
  Forlorn! the very word is like a bell
    To toll me back from thee to my sole self!
  Adieu! the fancy cannot cheat so well
    As she is famed to do, deceiving elf.
75 Adieu! adieu! thy plaintive anthem fades
    Past the near meadows, over the still stream,
     Up the hill-side; and now 'tis buried deep
      In the next valley-glades:
    Was it a vision, or a waking dream?
80   Fled is that music – Do I wake or sleep?

Commentary

In classical literature, the nightingale has negative associations, but for the Romantics it is a symbol of beauty and perfection: its song is seen as a source of inspiration because it creates in the poet a mood of meditative reflection. In Keats's ode, the bird enables him to escape from human suffering. It becomes a model for its species and, as such, is immortal – although the poet will die, such birds will never stop singing. This and other classical references allow Keats to explore the central paradox of the poem: the world of imagination may provide an escape from the bitterness of reality, but it also, by contrast, makes that reality harder to bear.

Keats uses images to develop this theme, contrasting man and bird, mortal and immortal, the real and the ideal. Although he focuses on images of perfection, the underlying mood draws attention to the fact that we live in an imperfect world. The familiar address to the bird (*thy*, *thou*) heightens our sense of the poet's yearning.

In the first stanza, Keats describes the painful happiness he feels at the beauty of the nightingale's song, and his desire to escape the physical world. The stanza is clearly divided into two opposing halves: the drug-induced stupor of the opening lines is replaced by the richness of language associated with growth and fertility. The contrast emphasises the distance between the world-weary poet and the joyous bird. The language is antithetical, setting verbs (*aches*, *pains*, l.1) and modifiers (*drowsy* l.1, *dull* l.3) against the positive connotations of *light-wingèd* (l.7), *melodious* (l.8), *beechen green* (l.9), *summer* and *full-throated* (l.10). The change in direction is marked by the caesura at the end of line 5, and, in the following line, by the emphatic contrastive conjunction *But* in the initial position and the spondaic foot.

By contrast, the movement of the second stanza is initially back towards worldly things like the *draught of vintage* (l.11) with its *beaded bubbles winking at the brim* (l.17): the drink will lead the poet towards the oblivion he desires so that he can leave the world *unseen* (l.19) and *fade away* (l.20). The natural language is developed here through the classical references to *Flora* (l.13), the goddess of flowers in classical mythology, and *Hippocrene* (l.16), the fountain on Mount Helicon in Greece sacred to the Muses. These and the richness of the Mediterranean references to *Provençal* and *the warm South* intensify the poet's yearning for escape. The longing created by the repeated interjection *O* (ll.11, 15), the rich long vowel sounds (*Cooled*, *deep*, *Flora*, *green*, and so on), and the assonantal rhyme (*sunburnt mirth; fade away*) convey the poet's blissful state of mind as he listens to the nightingale's song.

By running the final sentence of stanza II into stanza III, and by repeating *fade . . . away*, Keats can emphasise the contrast between the idyllic world of the nightingale's song and the bitterness of reality. The juxtaposition of the poet's happiness at this moment and the suffering of the world in general marks a turning point: the language is now negative. References to illness (*weariness*, *fever*, *fret* l.23, *palsy* l.25) and death underpin the themes of mortality and mutability (the fading of beauty; the ephemeral nature of love), with modifiers like *sad* (l.25), *pale*, *spectre-thin* (l.26), *leaden-eyed* (l.28) reinforcing the mood of sorrow. The visual image of the bird hidden *among the leaves* (l.22) becomes a symbol – it represents the distance between the nightingale's perfection and the imperfection of human life.

The fourth stanza bridges the gap between the real and the ideal, with poetry (*the viewless wings of Poesy*, l.33) rather than drink (*charioted by Bacchus and his pards*, l.32) as a means of escape. The certainty of the modal *will* (l.31) and the emphatic minor sentence *Already with thee!* (l.35) marks the poet's transition as he moves from the world of suffering towards the nightingale's blissful ignorance.

The language in the second half of the stanza is positive: references to light (*Queen-Moon* 1.36, *starry* 1.37) illuminate the poet's experience even though there is *no light* (1.37) beneath the rich foliage. The positive connotations of *tender* (1.35) and *heaven* (1.39), the regal image of the moon and her subjects, and the richness of the modifiers *verdurous* (1.40) and *mossy* (1.40) establish a new tone.

The physical darkness of the next three stanzas enables the poet to choose the unreal rather than the real. There is a powerful sense of freedom – only at the end of stanza VII with the introduction of the modifier *forlorn* is the reader aware of the possibility that the escape will be transient, and unfulfilling. The language in stanza V is elevated, giving the vision an intensity that draws the reader into Keats's world. The images create a rich atmosphere that appeals to our sense of smell – the darkness intensifies the poet's awareness of his environment through a sense other than sight. The smells Keats describes have a dense almost tangible quality.

The listing of natural elements like *grass, thicket, fruit-tree* (1.45), *White hawthorn, eglantine* (1.46), *violets* (1.47) and *musk-rose* (1.49) helps to create a strong sense of the physical environment. The modifiers *soft* (1.42), *embalmed* (1.43), *seasonable* (1.44), *dewy* (1.49) and *murmurous* (1.50) then suggest a delicacy that is appropriate for the intensity of the poet's vision. We almost hear the nightingale's song in the music of the verse: the richness of the assonance (*embalmed darkness*; *coming musk*) and the recurring long vowel sounds (*flowers/boughs, feet/seasonable, fading/May*). As darkness makes the sense of sight ineffective, the sense of hearing and the power of the imagination take precedence. Even at this stage in the poem, however, the negative connotations of some words are indicative of the failure that will accompany the end of the vision of perfection. The transience of the natural world is suggested by the modifiers *Fast fading* (1.47), *coming* (1.49); the connotations of *embalmèd* (1.3) specifically conjure up images of death and stasis.

In stanza VI, the positive and negative strands of the poem come together: listening to the perfection of the nightingale's song, the poet feels that this would be the perfect moment to die. The words linked to death have none of the painful connotations of the language in stanza III: the modifiers *easeful* (1.52), *soft* (1.53) and *quiet* (1.54) present death as a fitting climax to the poet's vision. Phrases such as *rich to die* (1.55) and *with no pain* (1.56) place death within a new context. The religious connotations of *soul* (1.57) and *high requiem* (1.60) and the intensity of the phrases *pouring forth* and *In such an ecstasy* (1.57–8) reinforce this – death is now a welcoming rather than a threatening experience. Even the poet's recognition that he will be no longer able to hear the song, which will continue after his death, does not affect the perfection of the moment.

In direct contrast to the transience of human life, Keats introduces the image of the *immortal Bird* (1.61) in the seventh stanza. The references to the different kinds of places in which nightingales have sung enhance our sense of permanence: its *voice* has been heard by *emperor and clown* (1.64), by the biblical *Ruth* (1.66), and before *casements* (1.69) in strange and wild locations. Words like *Charmed* and *magic* (1.19) reinforce our sense of the song as something that has the power to bewitch the poet, transporting him beyond the physical world of suffering to *faery lands* (1.70). The vision is broken, however, by the modifier *forlorn* (l.70). It is first used to describe the isolation of the places in which the nightingale may sing, but its tone and connotations change the mood. Its repetition at the start of Stanza VIII marks the end of the escape and the inevitable return to the physical world.

In the final stanza, the rhetoric and music of the poetry die away as poet and reader are forced to face reality. The caesura is used to fragment lines, mirroring the disruption of the poet's vision. Exclamations like *Forlorn!* and *Adieu!* (ll.71, 73, 75), and divisions after the second foot (ll.75, 77) create a sense of metrical imbalance that is a parallel to the poet's state of mind. Where the caesura lies in the medial position (ll.79–80), Keats uses the imperative mood to highlight the confusion and disillusion as reality returns.

The new mood of dissatisfaction is reinforced by words such as *toll* (l.72), *anthem* (l.75) and *buried* (l.77) with their connotations of death. The music of earlier stanzas is replaced by a more sonorous tone. Long vowels slow the pace of the verse (*toll/sole*, l.72; *plaintive/fades*, l.25) and plosives (*bell/toll/back/deceiving/buried/deep*) give a harder edge to the tone. In addition, the presence of the natural world is no longer as powerful. References to *meadows, stream* (l.76), *hill-side* (l.77) and *valley-glades* (l.78) are not intensified by positive modifiers. Instead, adverbs like *Past, over* (l.76) and *Up* (l.77) convey a sense of movement as the bird retreats into the distance. The transient nature of the moment of inspiration is introduced through the verb *Fled* (l.80), and reinforced through the personification of imagination as a *deceiving elf* (l.74) and the verb *cheat* (l.73). The lexis suggests that believing escape is possible is futile – the poet no longer even distinguishes between *vision* and *waking dream* (l.29), between the states of wakefulness and sleep. He is left at the end with a sense of failure: having lost himself in a moment of happiness, the poet is now forced to recognise the world of suffering even more intensely.

The poem is a record of a developing mood – its onset, rise to a climax, and its dying away as Keats attempts to capture the moment of inspiration and interpret it for his readers. He becomes the medium through which the physical sensation of ecstasy is communicated so that readers can experience the perfection of the moment. The imagery is powerful: it combines sense impressions so that the wine tastes of the green countryside, the light is blown by the breezes, and the incense is so heavy that, were it not for the darkness, it could be seen. The poet dominates the poem and effectively immerses us in the intensity of his vision.

The Romantic poets and the English poetic tradition

It is only in retrospect that the poets of the early nineteenth century have been identified as a coherent group – the first- and second-generation Romantic poets did not regard themselves as a movement during their lifetime. For critics, however, there are defining features that mark them as a distinctive stage in the English poetic tradition: they were to change the face of English poetry dramatically. The 'Age of Reason' became the 'Age of Imagination'; the importance of individual experience and everyday language began to bring poetry closer to the ordinary reader; the use of the first person was an accepted medium, now serious and reflective rather than ironic; and the source of poetry lay in the spontaneous rather than in the crafted and artificial.

The work of Coleridge and Wordsworth was to establish the spirit of Romanticism in nineteenth-century literature and can be seen as a turning point in the history of English poetry. For the main part, Byron's verse does not add anything new, but it was to provide an alternative to the English scenes portrayed by Wordsworth and Coleridge, and the Scottish scenes of Scott. The strong emotions, dark moods and exotic landscape made him popular with readers, despite the fact that he was frequently attacked by critics. Shelley may not have had the discipline of Wordsworth's critical exploration of experience or the depth of Wordsworth's mature reflection, but his poetry reflects the importance of the personal in Romantic verse and his understanding of the relationship between form, style and subject.

Keats was detached from literary circles of his day, yet his focus on feelings as opposed to Augustan reason, on the personal rather than the social, is indicative of the Romantic movement. He is the least typical of the Romantic poets because his realism distances him from the literary conventions of the time, but his interest in the individual, his use of a personal voice, the diversity of his content and his ideas on the imagination are typically Romantic.

The Victorians

The Victorian period was a time of rapid industrial growth, social unrest and scientific discovery. As a result of the changes taking place, new ideas and theories emerged, challenging accepted and received beliefs. The tone of much Victorian poetry reflects this – it is marked by religious doubt, personal despair and a general uncertainty about life and the human condition.

During the period, such poets as **Elizabeth Barrett Browning** (1806–61), **Lord Tennyson** (1809–92), **Robert Browning** and the **Pre-Raphaelites** were to develop the Romantic traditions of their predecessors, but without the certainty found in Wordsworth and Keats. Instead, Victorian verse shows a greater awareness of the complexity of life and its lack of cohesion. While writers such as Lewis Carroll (1832–98) and Edward Lear (1812–88) exploited the comic possibilities of verse, most Victorian poetry is marked by the moral earnestness that was typical of the period's attitude to life. Despite the seriousness of the moral values underpinning much of the verse, the best poetry is notable for its visual and melodic qualities.

Poetry and the role of the poet

Like the Romantic poets, the Victorians developed both formal and informal written records of their poetic principles. Debate revolved around the importance of poetry as a guide for humanity, the nature of 'good' poetry, and the balance of objectivity and subjectivity.

In an essay entitled *The Study of Poetry*, Matthew Arnold considered the **role of poetry** and its historical development. For him, poetry was *immense* because it offered stability in a time of rapid change.

There is not a creed which is not shaken, not an accredited dogma which is not shown to be questionable, not a received tradition which does not threaten to dissolve. Our religion has materialised itself in the fact, in the supposed fact; it has attached its emotion to the fact, and now the fact is failing it. But for poetry the idea is everything . . .

Where facts could be questioned and challenged, Arnold believed the ideas of the best poetry could not because they dealt directly with the human condition and were therefore immutable. Having identified poetry as a point of stability in a world of change, he believed it should be put to *higher uses* – he saw it as having the potential *to interpret life for us, to console us, to sustain us*. Only the *best poetry*, however, could serve as a guide for humanity, and Arnold clearly established his own criteria for verse with *a power of forming, sustaining, and delighting us, as nothing else can*.

While agreeing with much of Wordsworth's poetic theory, Arnold was critical of the Romantic poets in general because of what he saw as defects in form and style – while the content of their poetry aimed to *interpret life*, the technical features were not marked by *high beauty, worth and power*. For him, the Greek classics offered the best model. He saw in poets like Aristotle the potential for *higher truth* and *higher seriousness* in poetic content, and an understanding of the importance of the *diction* and *movement* of a poem.

The debate about the **nature of 'good' poetry** was focused around antithetical terms like didactic versus pure, reflection versus sensation, objective versus subjective. The philosopher J.S. Mill (1806–73) believed that to achieve the status of *a very great poet* a writer also had to be *a great philosopher*. Yet he distinguished between the objective poet whose main goal was didactic and the subjective poet who had *Feeling* as the source of his inspiration. For Mill, a true poet *pours forth the overflowing of his feelings*, while the thoughts that those feelings suggest *are floated promiscuously along the stream* (*Two Kinds of Poetry*, 1833) – the poet's ideas are *subordinate to the course of his emotions*.

For Elizabeth Barrett Browning, poetry was also about 'feeling'. In her poem *Aurora Leigh* (1856), she explored her **view of the artist**.

> 1   The artist's part is both to be and do,
>   Transfixing with a special, central power
>   The flat experience of the common man,
>   And turning outward, with a sudden wrench,
> 5   Half agony, half ecstasy, the thing
>   He feels the inmost, – never felt the less
>   Because he sings it.   (ll.366–73)

This extract clearly suggests that for Barrett Browning the process of writing is intense. With the parallel structures in apposition, *Half agony, half ecstasy*, she draws attention to the duality of the process, which is both positive and negative. Similarly the use of the stative verb *be* alongside the dynamic verb *do* develops our awareness of this polarity: the poet must be both passive, receptive to the world around her, and active, involved in the physical act of creation. Words such as the modifier *special* and the verbs *Transfixing* and *sings* are placed in opposition to the phrase *The flat experience of the common man*: the unique process of poetic creation is seen to transform ordinary life, which is identified by modifiers like *flat* and *common*.

The images are reminiscent of birth where the language of *agony* and *ecstasy* conveys both the physical pain and the romance of the personal experience. It is mirrored in the juxtaposition of *outward* and *inmost*, and in the use of the noun *wrench* that suggests both a physical and mental tearing part. Above all, the poet is one who *feels* and this is the *special, central power* enabling her to rise above the mundane.

Robert Browning distinguished between **objective poetry** that aimed to *reproduce things external*, and **subjective poetry** that focused on *not what man sees, but what God sees* (*Essay on Shelley*, 1852). He saw Shakespeare as representative of the former and Shelley as a poet who looked beyond the surface to a vision of what lay beneath. In the dramatic monologue form, Browning combined both approaches and readers must be wary of what is literal and what is figurative. The poems establish a particular subjective point of view which appears to be objective concrete evidence for a given case, the 'truth': Bishop Blougram's case for his religion ('Bishop Blougram's Apology'); the duke's case in support of his new marriage ('My Last Duchess'); Fra Lippo Lippi's case for his 'unsaintlike' paintings ('Fra Lippo Lippi'). Yet such a reading is misleading since Browning's verse centres upon a recognition that poetry is an art, that it is consciously rhetorical.

The poems therefore provide no declaration of an absolute truth. The facts in each poem are not objective, but represent a viewpoint that is limited and distorted by a particular person in a particular time and place. Nothing has a single meaning – the facts and stance of the speaker are constantly changing. Readers must recognise the complex response required from them in which both sympathy and moral judgement play a part. Browning's long work *The Ring and the Book* (1868–9) is often seen to represent his most successful use of both the objective and subjective styles.

Matthew Arnold also engaged in the debate about objective and subjective poetry, attacking what he saw as the subjectivity of contemporary verse in his 'Preface' (*Poems*, 1833). His second collection (*Poems, Second Series*, 1855) marked a conscious attempt to escape from subjectivity. The relationship between Arnold and his readers is both more direct and more intimate than Browning's: Arnold's poems record the nature of experience in a more detached way, revealing his understanding of himself and his society without Browning's self-conscious subjectivity. Similarly, poems such as Tennyson's *In Memoriam* are recorded in an open and direct style despite the fact that they use personal observations as their starting point.

The content

In his essay 'On Some of the Characteristics of Modern Poetry' (1831), Arthur Henry Hallam wrote:

> Art is a lofty tree, and may shoot up far beyond our grasp, but its roots are in daily life and experience. Every bosom contains the elements of those complex emotions

which the artist feels, and every head can, to a certain extent, go over in itself the process of their combination, so as to understand his expressions and sympathise with his state.

The image of the opening sentence establishes the main point of Hallam's argument. Figuratively, the poet is linked directly to the dynamic verb (*shoot*), while the reader is associated with stative verbs like *are* and *contains*. This clearly differentiates between the two – while poets can actively transform experience, the reader can do no more than passively live life. The juxtaposition of *lofty* and *daily* reinforces the sense of poetry as elevated above the mundane. Yet the poet and the reader have a common bond in the feelings and emotions they experience. It is thus in daily life that the *roots*, the source and inspiration of poetry, are found: although the poet *feels*, the reader can *understand* and *sympathise*.

Hallam's belief that poetry should deal with the **human condition** occurs in the work of other Victorian writers. Arnold wrote of *the great human affections* and the *elementary feelings* that are *independent of time* as the source of great poetry. Their strength lies in the fact that they are *permanent* and therefore meaningful beyond the limitations of a particular period. Similarly, the poet and critic Arthur Hugh Clough (1819–61) wrote that poetry should deal with *general wants, ordinary feelings, the obvious rather than the rare facts of human nature*; that it should *attempt to convert into beauty and thankfulness . . . the actual palpable things with which our every-day life is concerned*. The modifiers *general, ordinary, obvious, actual, palpable* and *every-day* underpin Clough's argument – the emphasis, he believed, should be on *the facts of human nature* since such things are timeless, transcending the physical world and leading to an understanding of the human condition.

Many poets also sought to convey a sense of the **spirit of their age**. Tennyson's verse, for instance, explores the religious doubt affecting society. He was not inspired by the kind of revolutionary fervour associated with the French Revolution, nor did he challenge convention as Wordsworth, Shelley and Byron had done, but his poems address the nature of living with a faith that is based in fear versus living with scientific knowledge that replaces fear, but offers no hope. Despite his rejection of religion, however, Tennyson's poems reflect the morals of Christianity and we see a conclusion to his struggle to achieve a faith that will conquer death in 'Crossing the Bar'. After the wildness of 'Locksley Hall' and the despondence of 'Locksley Hall Sixty Years After', Tennyson seemed to replace doubt and fear with certainty and acceptance.

In contrast to the doubt marking Tennyson's spiritual path, much of Christina Rossetti's (1830–94) religious verse is a traditional expression of devotion, often drawing on the structure and resonance of hymns and prayers. At a time when traditional belief was being challenged, Rossetti's religion was disciplined and orthodox – her verse is full of certainties where Browning and Tennyson consciously explore ambiguities.

The doubt in Rossetti's poems revolves around her own feelings of personal inadequacy rather than the general sense of uncertainty indicative of most Victorian verse. The poem 'Up-Hill', for instance, suggests that faith can still be strong even in a time of doubt.

> Shall I find comfort, travel-sore and weak?
> Of labour you shall find the sum.
> Will there be beds for me and all who seek?
> Yea, beds for all who come.   (ll.13–16)

The image of the *road* that winds *up-hill all the way* is traditional in representing life, but for Rossetti in this poem, it specifically represents the spiritual path. While recognising the hardships of the 'journey' (life/the spiritual path) in words like *travel-sore*, *weak* and *labour*, Rossetti's religious conviction can be seen in the use of complete adjacency pairs – her questions are answered; the doubt of the interrogative mood is balanced by the certainty of the declarative. The image of the *beds* develops the sense of faith as a condition of security and fulfilment.

As well as writing about the human condition and the spirit of the age, Victorian poetry often sought inspiration in the **past**. Historical references enabled poets to draw analogies; historical settings brought the past to life and provided a symbolic background. Both as a central and peripheral subject, the past was used as the basis for a commentary on the present age and its values, on the human condition in general.

For Matthew Arnold, the past was both a source of inspiration and a guide. In his 'Preface' (1853), he quoted a critic writing for *The Spectator* who said that if a poet was to *really fix the public attention*, he would have to *leave the exhausted past, and draw his subjects from matters of present import, and therefore both of interest and novelty*. Arnold denounced this, believing that clear ideals for poetry are established in both the classics (particularly the Greeks) and the moderns who draw on the classics (Goethe and Wordsworth). Study of the classics, he believed, would make modern writers aware of the *noble simplicity*, and the *unity and profoundness of the moral impression* of the great poets of the past. This in turn would make them look beyond the *spirit of the passing time* to something more lasting.

Tennyson drew on the past for his *Idylls of the King* (published as a complete sequence, 1891) where details of the architecture are used symbolically to represent the past. The Pre-Raphaelite poets used the past as an analogue for the present. Although playing an important visual part in both the art and verse of the movement, its purpose was more than just decorative since it represented moral judgements that the poets believed were significant for contemporary society.

Robert Browning's 'Love Among the Ruins' uses the past more explicitly, juxtaposing past and present to explore physical and psychological differences. He develops a sequence of antithetical images: the open land which is now grazed by sheep was *the site once of a city great and gay* (l.7); the young lovers meet in the *turret whence the charioteers caught soul/For the goal* (ll.57–8); the *king looked* where the girl *looks now, breathless, dumb/Till I come* (ll.59–60). The resonance of the past intensifies the meaning of the lovers' meeting in the present.

Most of Christina Rossetti's verse avoided current events and contemporary issues as subject matter, and the love lyrics, for which she is perhaps now most well known, were set in the past. She balanced her subject matter, however, with her use of the modern colloquial idiom of her time, allowing her to avoid the insipid mood that Elizabeth Barrett Browning felt characterised much of the verse of the period. Her subject matter does not directly recreate the past in any particular period, but references, descriptions and images distance it from the contemporary. In 'A Birthday', for instance, the description of the *dais of silk and down* could have been taken straight from the medieval detail of a Pre-Raphaelite painting; the sonnet sequence *Monna Innominata* reflects the love-conventions of Dante and Petrarch, each one beginning with a quotation taken from their work; 'The Prince's Progress' is a medieval tale of hope; and 'Goblin Market' contains medieval imagery.

Other poets chose a poetic content grounded in the **present**, seeing in their own time a rich source of inspiration. In *Aurora Leigh* (1856), Barrett Browning challenged her contemporaries, arguing that *this live throbbing age*, the present, should be the subject of poetry. She believed that poetry drawing on the heroic myths of the past was as lifeless as the characters it aimed to recreate. Her challenge was made more controversial since she was using a female voice to explore her beliefs.

> 1   I do distrust the poet who discerns
>   No character or glory in his times,
>   And trundles back his soul in five hundred years,
>   Past moat and drawbridge, into a castle court,
> 5   To sing – oh, not of lizard or of toad
>   Alive i'the ditch there, – 'twere excusable,
>   But of some black chief, half knight, half sheep-lifter,
>   Some beauteous dame, half chattel and half queen,
>   As dead as must be, for the greater part,
> 10   The poems made on their chivalric bones . . .

She uses a lexical set of medieval words including *moat, drawbridge, castle court, knight* and *dame* to create a stereotypical portrait of the times that she represents by the modifier *dead* – to write of the *lizard* and *toad* would be better because it would be *alive* and 'real'.

The use of the verb *trundles* marks Barrett Browning's ironic stance clearly, setting the tone of the extract. The parallel structures (ll.7–8) imply that contemporary poetry merely glorifies the past, overlaying a mythical meaning that elevates the ordinary to the extraordinary. This is reinforced by the ironic antithesis of nouns: the chief is both a *knight* and a *sheep-lifter* and the dame is both a *chattel* and a *queen*. Barrett Browning goes on to describe Victorian society using verbs like *brawls, cheats, maddens, calculates* and *aspires*. Despite their negative connotations, however, she sees them as representative of a subject matter that is alive and vibrant rather than dead.

The poetry of escape and the 'individual moment'

In an attempt to transcend the doubt of the age, the Victorian poets followed in the tradition of Keats and the Pre-Raphaelites, using the **imagination as a means of escape**. They used symbols as a means of expressing a personal and private world, moving from the limitations of reality into an ideal dream vision. As in

Keats's 'To a Nightingale', however, the poet's escape is always transient, and return to the real world is marked by disillusionment – even when the dream world itself has been marred by imperfection.

In poems like 'The Lotos-Eaters' and 'Mariana', Tennyson retreats into a dream world, trying to convey to his reader just what it would be like to escape from the realities of the Victorian age. Using the Spenserian stanza, he creates a rich scene as a backdrop to 'The Lotos-Eaters', yet there is an ambiguity created in the kinds of words he chooses. Modifiers like the verbs *gleaming* and *sunset-flush'd*, and the adjectives *red*, *yellow* and *rosy* create a positive atmosphere, but these are juxtaposed with the adjectives *languid*, *weary* and *slumbrous*, the verb modifiers *slow-dropping* and *wavering*, and the verb *linger'd*. This antithesis prepares the reader for the seductive atmosphere of the poem where responsibilities can become dreams. The repetitive patterning of the stanza form is symbolic of the bewitching mood of the land, but also of the sense of entrapment that inevitably accompanies any renunciation of personal freedom, however apparently beneficial. This theme is also played out in the diction: Tennyson chooses verb modifiers like *charmed* and *enchanted*, yet these are placed in opposition to the repetition of the adjective *weary*.

For Robert Browning, religion, love and art are potentially transcendent, allowing the individual to rise above physical circumstances. The escape can only ever be momentary, however, and most of his poems end in a sense of failure. Ironically, it is ultimately this failure of the vision that leads man to Browning's personal God. As he writes in *Fifine at the Fair*, it is *through the fleeting* that man is urged on to *reach at length 'God, man, or both together mixed.'*

In 'Andrea del Sarto', Browning considers the nature of perfection through a speaker who is a painter. He has achieved artistic perfection, yet he recognises that other artists less technically perfect have earned greater success. The poem is based on a sequence of contrasts: del Sarto's desire for ideal love versus his empty sordid relationship; art versus commercialism; heart versus face; his present life in which *A common greyness silvers everything* versus his golden youth. At the heart of the poem lies a basic irony – once perfection has been reached, it is lost. Despite the technical perfection of his work, therefore, Andrea del Sarto's paintings are dead: *All is silver-grey/Placid and perfect with my art.*

For Browning, the essence of success is to *strive to do, and agonise to do,/And fail in doing*. The artist must have limitless dreams that he struggles to attain – he can transcend the limitations of physical life through his vision even in failure. The speaker in the poem recognises his own position, but continues to deceive himself: expressions of regret are followed by hollow affirmations of his worth and, in a last attempt at self-deception, he says that he *regret*[s] *little* and *would change less still*.

In this poem and in many others, Browning has focused on the failure of 'perfection' to raise the individual beyond the *fetters* of his life. Underlying the theme of escape, is an interest in psychology – he analysed states of mind by tracing the thoughts and moods of an **individual at a particular moment in time**. He is interested in the conflicts and contrasts within the central character rather than in the drama of the situation. 'A Death in the Desert', for instance, could be at first sight a testimony of the life of Christ from the mouth of the last person who saw him. It is, however, the account of an individual, a personal analysis of the truth of the miracles and the divinity of Christ. It is ambiguously objective: the speaker is both the source of information, and the medium through which it is interpreted. The poem is therefore both subjective (a personal experience) and objective (an apparently detached account).

It is characteristic of Browning's poetry that the content focuses on what Saint John has learned when facing death, rather than what he could relate first-hand of Christ. The main concern is not Saint John's transcendence in death as Christ's disciple, but his discovery of the folly of dying while believing in the invincibility of the 'truths' he had preached in life.

> '. . . man knows partly but conceives beside,
> 'Creeps ever on from fancies to the fact,
> 'And in this striving, this converting air
> 'Into a solid he may grasp and use,
> 'Finds progress, man's distinctive mark alone,
> 'Not God's, and not the beasts'   (ll.582–7)

The juxtaposition of *fancies/fact* and *air/solid* epitomises the source of 'doubt' at the heart of the Victorian period as 'faith' and 'absolute truth' were challenged by scientific, industrial and cultural advances. Through the character of Saint John, Browning portrays 'truth' as a living, changing quantity. We see him moving towards a personal understanding of what has taken place through a process of self-realisation. Just as Arnold believed it was necessary to rise above *stock notions and habits*, so too did Browning – for him, life was a series of tests through which man must move in order to reach beyond a conventional understanding of 'truth'.

In *Fifine at the Fair* (1872), Browning once again deals with an individual moment represented by a figure who limits and distorts what may appear to be fact. Don Juan, like the Duke in 'My Last Duchess', endeavours to make a case for an apparently immoral position – the argument for infidelity within a marital relationship. The poem creates tension between sympathy and morality, and readers are encouraged to suspend judgement as they become immersed in the experience of the poem itself, knowing all the time that they are not being presented with an objective truth, but with a particular perspective.

The subject matter of Browning's poems focuses on a flash of light that momentarily illuminates an experience, *putting the infinite within the finite*. They reflect many of the typical themes of the period: the questioning of the nature of 'truth'; the dramatisation of the individual's attempt to escape; and a consideration of religion, love and art as possible vehicles for transcendence.

The dramatic monologue

The form of a poem can highlight the kind of relationship the poet desires to create with the reader. Perhaps the most distinctive structure of the period is the **dramatic monologue**, a form much used by Robert Browning. It represents the distillation of a crucial moment of human experience, focusing on a particular occasion that becomes a revelation of an almost religious nature as the speaker tries to transcend the finite.

After years of trying to write a successful play, Browning found that the dramatic monologue allowed him to dramatise the human condition in poetry. His monologues are concerned with situations, episodes of lives that are still in the process of developing. They focus on examples of self-occupied men and women as they attempt to overcome the limitations of their physical lives. The sequence of individuals represented in the two volumes of *Men and Women* (1855) demonstrates Browning's most successful use of the form, while *The Ring and the Book* provides an example of the way in which dramatic monologues can be used to create a detailed, multilayered narrative. In this long work, ten versions of a single murder provide various points of view, encouraging readers to consider the relativity of truth.

Browning's dramatic monologues combine both the subjective and the objective. They explore *the truth broken into prismatic hues* – that is, 'truth' as it is seen by particular individuals, broken down into its component parts. Readers must be prepared for the shifting of meaning as different poetic voices speak. They must be aware of the speaker's concrete environment (the physical experience of the recorded moment) and the momentary private illumination that takes place within it. We must engage with the speaker's point of view through the physical details with which we are presented, while simultaneously judging the limitations and distortions of what appears to be objective 'truth'.

In 'My Last Duchess', the reader is instantly aware of the physical background: the gallery of paintings, the curtain covering the picture of the Duchess, the details of the portrait. But the speaking voice does more than draw attention to his environment – his monologue also reveals the nature of his personality. Repeated references to *that spot/Of joy, the faint/Half-flush that dies along her throat, the approving speech,/Or blush* suggest the obsessional nature of the Duke and his desire to possess. His speech requires acceptance of his role and actions from the listener and the rhetorical question, *Who'd stoop to blame/This sort of trifling?* explicitly seeks approval.

Yet Browning makes sure that the reader cannot easily sympathise with the Duke. His personal arrogance can be seen in his false sense of self-importance – he values such insignificant things as wealth, possessions and titles rather than life – and in his sense of superiority (*I choose/Never to stoop*). To underpin this, Browning juxtaposes the Duke's *favour* with *The bough of cherries . . ./Broke in the orchard*; the Duke's *gift of a nine-hundred-years-old name* with *anybody's gift*; and the smile *Whene'er* [he] *passed her* with *Much the same smile* given to any passer-by. The antithetical pattern undermines the confident self-assertion of his tone, leaving the reader to recognise the disequilibrium between what he wishes his listener to believe and what his words actually reveal.

Stylistically, Browning also ensures that readers feel no empathy with the Duke. The brevity of the simple sentences (ll.45–6) marks the matter-of-fact tone with which he talks of the murder of his wife, clearly conveying his lack of feeling. By using the emphatic adverbial *Then* in the initial position, Browning draws attention to the incident as though it were no more than a time marker, a point of change in his life. The euphemistic reference to *all smiles stopped together* reinforces this. It attempts to remove the reality of the act by focusing on something (her smile) that has become no more than a symbol for her life – the Duchess is no more than a *piece of wonder* hanging on the wall alongside statues like that of *Neptune . . ./Taming a sea-horse*.

The ultimate dark irony of the poem lies in the realisation that the listener is an envoy for *The Count*, coming to talk about the details of the Duke's proposed marriage to the Count's daughter. The Duke already treats his intended wife as an object to be possessed – references to *munificence, dowry* and *object* set the monetary context despite the fact that words like *fair* and *avowed* could be used in a quite different tone to convey emotion.

Browning uses the form, tone and language of the dramatic monologue to make readers aware of the ambiguity of 'truth'. The Duke's language is reasonable, his tone matter-of-fact, and yet beneath the surface readers should be aware of the distortions in the version of life he presents. Taken at face value, it is possible to miss the implicit reference to the Duchess's death, but readers of Browning must be prepared to doubt the voice of objective truth just as the Victorians were forced to doubt religious, social and cultural truths.

Style

Where the language of Romantic poetry tended to be decorative, the **style** of Victorian verse was often more formal, and experimentation with rhythm and metre was common. Much of Elizabeth Barrett Browning's work is marked by an economy of expression and an intensity of feeling as she attempts to create a new language for conveying emotion. This is particularly evident in the Shelleyan imagery of *Sonnets from the Portuguese* (1850) and the prosodic experiments in poems like *Aurora Leigh* (1857). Popular during her lifetime, her current critical reputation is based on her linguistic and metrical innovations.

Tennyson was sometimes criticised for his concentration on the technical features of rhyme, rhythm and metrical patterns at the expense of content and meaning. Yet he too was an experimenter, searching for an appropriate poetic medium for his age. The publication of *In Memoriam* (1850) marked a stylistic change in his approach: the octosyllabic lines arranged in rhyming quatrains forced a greater discipline on Tennyson's usually loose style. The tight structure and the close link between style and language reflected a movement away from the lyricism of Tennyson's earlier verse towards something more direct and disciplined.

With *Maud and Other Poems* (1855), he was to use a variety of metrical forms, in particular a variation of blank verse which was distinctively his own, where words are grouped by the number of accents rather than the number of syllables. Each section of the poem uses different metrical patterns, mirroring the different *phases of passion* of the hero who is driven into madness by the death of his lover. Part I concludes on a note of bitter irony as the hero imagines being woken from *an earthy bed* to greet Maud, with Part II as the grim realisation of this prophecy: the duel with Maud's brother, the hero's madness and his belief that he is dead and buried.

In the extract below (Part II, V.I. ll.1–13), we see a disordered world through the eyes of a disordered individual. The hero's earlier fulfilment in loving Maud and being loved is replaced by the madness that follows her death – he is here still immersed in *the fiery furnace* of his passion and beyond the reaches of reason. Tennyson therefore creates a nightmare world where life and death are intermingled in a ghostly vision of something that is neither life nor death. The unnamed lover, who believes that he is dead, longs for escape through death. In the underlying image of the crossroad, we have, perhaps, an allusion to the traditional place of burial for those who took their own lives.

Maud

```
 1   Dead, long dead,
     Long dead!
     And my heart is a handful of dust,
     And the wheels go over my head,
 5   And my bones are shaken with pain,
     For into a shallow grave they are thrust,
     Only a yard beneath the street,
     And the hoofs of the horses beat, beat,
     The hoofs of the horses beat,
10   Beat into my scalp and my brain,
     With never an end to the stream of passing feet,
     Driving, hurrying, marrying, burying,
     Clamour and rumble, and ringing and clatter . . .
```

To convey the duality between life and death, tension is created between the lexical sets of concrete nouns relating to the body of the hero (*heart, head, bone, scalp, brain*) and the environment (*wheels, street, hoofs, horses, feet*). It reflects the conflict that exists between the physical world and the *shallow grave*; between the 'self' of the hero and the 'other' of the world which he imagines going on above him. The repetition of *dead* and *beat* develops the ambiguous relationship between life and death both in the monotony of the monosyllabic rhythm and in the creation of a world which can only be heard and not seen. The morbid vision with which the reader is presented and the linguistic patterns Tennyson creates link directly to the hero's state of madness.

The structural features are equally important in defining the vision of madness. The emphatic exclamations at the opening and the varying line lengths that follow build up an atmosphere of imbalance. This is reinforced by the repetition of the co-ordinator *And* in the initial position, making the actions seem simultaneous and inescapable. The cyclic effect is developed in Tennyson's use of: repeated words at the end of one line and the beginning of the next; present participles with their connotations of ongoing activity; and asyndetic listing that drives the rhythm inevitably onwards. The parallel phrases of the last line then intensify the moment. The balance created by the syndetic co-ordination and the onomatopoeic nature of the nouns heighten our sense of the hero's entrapment – he sees nothing, but feels and hears with an unbearable acuteness.

The metrical patterns vary widely as Tennyson recreates the hero's emotional state. He uses the iambic pattern (ll.7, 9); the anapaest (ll.3–5, 8); the spondee (ll.1–2); the dactyl (l.13); and the weak-strong-weak amphibrach (ll.6, 11). In many cases the patterns are combined within a single line:

The hoofs I oǐ thĕ hor I seš beat,
Beat īntŏ I mў scalp I an̆d mў brain,

The ever-changing patterns mirror the unstable mood of the hero whose vision of living-death has a nightmare quality of intensity. This unpredictable metrical pattern is reinforced by the irregular pattern of the rhyme (aabacbdddcdef).

Maud has been described as a *monodrama*, a play in which there is only one character, yet, in the successive phases of the hero's passions, we are presented with a series of portraits that require Tennyson to experiment with style and form. In this extract, he characterises the hero vividly, communicating his state of mind by dramatising his response to experience.

The Victorians and the English poetic tradition

Critical response to the Victorian poets has often concentrated on them as a reaction against the Romantic movement: craftsmanship replacing personal intensity; doubt replacing certainty; and the use of a first person narrator replacing autobiographical revelation. There is more to the verse written of the period, however. Poets worked in many genres and metrical forms, reflecting social, religious and scientific changes in their subject matter and their relationship with their readers.

Despite universal popularity, Tennyson has been criticised for the emptiness of his subject matter and his ornate style: in 1870, the *National Review* described his verse as the *poetry of the drawing room*; and in the twentieth century, many readers and critics saw his work as too idealistic and out of touch with reality, too bound by Victorian morality and attitudes, with no real sense of originality. W.H. Auden, however, recognised that *his genius was lyrical*, and T.S. Eliot described him as *the great master of metric as well as of melancholia . . . [with] the finest ear of any English poet.*

More recently, there has been a revival of interest in his longer poems: 'Locksley Hall', 'The Princess' and 'Enoch Arden'. Although his subject matter marks him as a product of his age rather than as an original thinker, Tennyson's contribution to the English poetic tradition lies in his mastery of poetic techniques and his understanding of the musicality of the language.

Browning never achieved the commercial success of Tennyson during his lifetime, but his analysis of human motives and impulses sets his poetry apart from other Victorian verse that does no more than reflect the spirit of the age. His verse is notable for its complex interweaving of abstract ideas and specific detail, and its manipulation of metre and rhythm.

He has been criticised for his difficult subject matter, his obscure diction and the harshness of his versification – the publication of *Sordello* (1840) clouded his reputation for years. Yet in his best work critics now recognise: the power of his condensed expression; the originality of his imagery; the skill in his realisation of character; the insight of his dramatic recreation of particular moments and experiences; and his understanding of human nature. For the ordinary reader, *Men and Women* continues to be popular, but most of his other work is now read primarily by academics because of its obscurity and complex philosophical stance.

Critics also acknowledge Christina Rossetti's technical virtuosity. Her style is marked by the use of short irregularly rhymed lines and formal language. She is perhaps most well known for her adaptation of Skeltonics – the hopping, jumping metre used by Skelton (1460–1529). Her use of the form, however, raised it from the status of comic doggerel to that of high poetry.

Like Browning, Arnold never appealed to a wide-ranging contemporary public readership as Tennyson did. He was, however, well aware of his personal strengths as a poet. In a letter to his mother, he wrote:

> My poems represent, on the whole, the main movement of the mind of the last quarter of a century . . . It might be fairly urged that I have less poetical sentiment than Tennyson; and less intellectual vigour and abundance than Browning; yet because I have perhaps more of a fusion of the two than either of them, and have more regularly applied that fusion to the main line of modern development, I am likely enough to have my turn, as they have had theirs.

Critics recognise his success in the intensity of feeling he conveys, in the restraint of his utterance, and in the control of his diction. Both his verse and his prose are marked by the antithetical attitudes of the age – a spiritual longing and an intellectual strength. Although twentieth-century readers cannot identify with all his attitudes and beliefs, it is still possible to value his integrity and his desire to search for the truth.

Activity 12.4

Explore the ways in which Arnold conveys something of the spirit of his age in 'Dover Beach'.

You may like to think about: the ideas, the diction, the style, the imagery, and the poetic features.

Dover Beach

1	The sea is calm to-night.
	The tide is full, the moon lies fair
	Upon the straits; – on the French coast the light
	Gleams and is gone; the cliffs of England stand,
5	Glimmering and vast, out in the tranquil bay.
	Come to the window, sweet is the night-air!
	Only, from the long line of spray
	Where the sea meets the moon-blanch'd land,
	Listen! You hear the grating roar
10	Of pebbles which the waves draw back, and fling,
	At their return, up the high strand,
	Begin, and cease, and then again begin,
	With tremulous cadence slow, and bring
	The eternal note of sadness in.

15   Sophocles long ago
      Heard it on the Ægean, and it brought
      Into his mind the turbid ebb and flow
      Of human misery; we
      Find also in the sound a thought,
20   Hearing it by this distant northern sea.

      The Sea of Faith
      Was once, too, at the full, and round earth's shore
      Lay like the folds of a bright girdle furl'd.
      But now I only hear
25   Its melancholy, long, withdrawing roar,
      Retreating, to the breath
      Of the night-wind, down the vast edges drear
      And naked shingles of the world.

      Ah, love, let us be true
30   To one another! for the world, which seems
      To lie before us like a land of dreams,
      So various, so beautiful, so new,
      Hath really neither joy, nor love, nor light,
      Nor certitude, nor peace, nor help for pain;
35   And we are here as on a darkling plain
      Swept with confused alarms of struggle and flight,
      Where ignorant armies clash by night.

Commentary

Arnold's poem clearly conveys something of the age's religious doubt and his personal sense of disillusionment, yet the opening scene is apparently idyllic. The use of present tense verbs and the patterning of the simple clauses (ll.1–3) immerses us immediately in a concrete world where we have a clear sense of time and place. Positive modifiers (*calm, fair, sweet, tranquil*) and references to light (*Gleams, Glimmering*) establish an uplifting mood, and the image of the *cliffs of England* seems symbolic of stability and permanence. The use of trochaic feet in a predominantly iambic poem reinforces this sense that all is right with the world: an initial stress falls on both *Gléams* and *Glímmĕrĭ́ng* adding to their semantic importance within the opening lines.

The tone is intimate as Arnold changes grammatical mood, using the imperative *Come* (l.6) to engage an unseen observer. It is at this point that we become aware of the detachment of the poet and his companion from the scene before them: they are inside, separated from the landscape by the window. It is the first indication that things may not be what they seem. The turning point is then clearly marked by the conjunction *Only* (l.7) – an informal and intimate expression indicating a contrast between what has been said and what is to follow. It is both separated from the rest of the line by a caesura and has a trochaic rather than iambic stress pattern. It is also the beginning of the first complex sentence, mirroring the fact that the poem's ideas are about to become more complicated. We are forced to wait for the imperative main clause (*Listen . . .*) because of the fronted adverbials (*from . . ./Where* . . .) and this is the first suggestion of doubt and uncertainty in the poem.

The language also now changes as positive modifiers are replaced by the negative connotations of *moon-blanch'd* (l.8) and *grating* (l.9), and stative verbs (*is, stand*) are replaced by dynamic verbs like *fling* (l.10). The sea becomes a symbol of all that is wrong with the human condition: beneath its calm surface an endless movement is concealed. Recurring long vowels (*spray/grating/waves; sea/meets; roar/draw*) and sibilance mirror the sounds of the sea in its inescapable cycle.

The poem's underlying uncertainty is mirrored in the disruption of the rhythm as the caesura divides lines unevenly: after the first foot (*Listen!* l.9); after the first and second foot (*Begin, and cease* l.12); and before the last foot (*and fling* l.10; *and bring* l.13). The broken rhythm, the antithesis of *Begin/cease*, and the repetition of *begin* at the opening and close of the line all mark not only the ebb and flow of the sea, but also an end to the vision of perfection with which the poem opened. Arnold's use of the modifier *tremulous* (l.13) and the noun phrase *The eternal note of sadness* (l.14) marks the climax towards which the first stanza has been moving.

The second stanza moves from the immediate present to the distant past as Arnold draws on the knowledge of others to help him understand his feelings about the present. He has moved from pleasure in the visual scene before him, to doubt about what lies beneath its surface and the language is now explicitly negative (*turbid* l.17, *misery* l.18). In seeing a parallel between himself and *Sophocles*, Arnold is recognising the eternal nature of his doubts – the uncertainty that marks his age is an enduring feature of man's relationship with his world; it is typical of the human condition. Having established this link, Arnold uses a caesura at the end of line 18 to distinguish between Sophocles listening to the sea *long ago* (l.15) and his own experience in the present. Past tense verbs therefore are replaced with the present tense and we are grounded once more in the immediate moment – the sound of the sea becomes the stimulus for *thought*, preparing us for the metaphorical sea of the following stanza.

The two metaphors for faith – a *Sea* (l.21) encircling the whole country, and *the folds of a bright girdle* (l.23) – suggest something omnipresent, embracing and protecting. Yet the use of past tense verbs sets these positive images at a distance from the present. This is reinforced by the use of the adverbs *once* (l.22), *now* (l.24) and the contrastive conjunction *But* in the initial position (l.24): where the literal sea before them is enduring, the figurative sea of faith is inconstant. Arnold underpins this with the consecutive stresses of two spondaic feet: *But now | Í on | lỹ*, and the movement away from positive modifiers (*full* l.22, *bright* l.23) to the negative *melancholy* (l.25), *drear* (l.27) and *naked* (l.28).

The sense of something changing is reinforced by the verbs *withdrawing* (l.5) and *Retreating* (l.6) which develop the image of the *Sea of Faith* as it moves away from the *earth's shore* (l.2) – the use of present participles creates a sense of the ongoing process. Since the withdrawal is not yet complete, the poem becomes a plea for action in an age marked by its faithlessness and disillusion: the bleakness of a faithless age could be prevented.

It is this plea that is developed in the final stanza. In a personal address using the familiar vocative *love* (l.29), Arnold seeks escape from the *drear* and *naked* world in a relationship based on truth. The literal landscape seen in the first stanza becomes no more than a *land of dreams* (l.31) – the tentative verb *seems* (l.30) reminds us that we should not be misled by appearances. The reality is quite different: the three positive adjective phrases intensified by *so* (l.32) are placed in direct opposition to the accumulative asyndetic negative phrases (ll.33–4). As the list builds to its climax with the repetition of the negative conjunction *Nor*, the poet's disillusion is balanced by the commitment he and his lover can make to each other.

The use of the co-ordinating conjunction *And* in the initial position (l.35) slows the pace of the final lines in which Arnold summarises the condition of society in the metaphor of the *darkling plain*. The language is explicitly negative: society is symbolised by the modifiers *darkling* (l.35) and *confused* (l.36), humanity by *ignorant* (l.37); nouns like *struggle* and *flight*, and verbs like *Swept* and *clash* (ll.36–7) are set against the tranquil tone of the first stanza. Despite the final image of chaos and despair, the togetherness represented by the inclusive first person *we* (l.35) and our sense that the poet and his lover are quite separate from the chaos and confusion suggest that their relationship, perhaps, can offer some hope in a deceptive world.

In 'The Scholar-Gipsy', Arnold writes that he has been born into an *iron-time/Of doubts, disputes, distractions, fears*. Although the general mood here is one of weariness, disenchantment and futility, however, Arnold attempts to resist such feelings.

Gerard Manley Hopkins (1844–89)

The early work of **Gerard Manley Hopkins** is quite conventional, but by the 1870s he was voicing a dissatisfaction with poets like Tennyson whose verse he described as artificial. He began to experiment with rhyme schemes and metres, and developed a distinctive diction that set him apart from other Victorian poets. With the completion of *The Wreck of the Deutschland* (1876), he brought his personal theory of poetry to a climax – it was strikingly different from the verse of his contemporaries and was refused publication in a Jesuit journal because it was considered too difficult for readers. None of his poetry was published until 1918 when his close friend Robert Bridges (1844–1930), a poet and essayist, produced *Poems*. Having believed the public was not yet ready for the challenge of Hopkins's poetry, Bridges had waited for 19 years after Hopkins's death before publishing the edition. Although initially greeted with surprise, the poems soon won critical acclaim in the 1920s and 30s for their technical innovation and their perceptive commentary on the failings of industrial society with its poverty, pollution and inequalities.

Hopkins stands as a link between the poetry of the nineteenth and twentieth centuries – he draws on the conventions of Romantic and Victorian poetry, and moves beyond their limitations. His verse uses the keen perception of the Romantics, but he makes no attempt to copy their methods; his themes are typically Victorian (religion, beauty, transience, the 'spirit of the age'), but the sensitivity of his language in such poems as 'Binsey Poplars', 'Felix Randal' and 'The

Caged Skylark' is unequalled in Victorian poetry. Where the Pre-Raphaelites drew on religious emotions for their aesthetic value, Hopkins uses his faith as a means of exposing a deeper meaning in the real world. The technical inventiveness, the intense observations of both the inner and outer world, and the energy of his work, on the other hand, link him directly to the twentieth century, separating him from the highly polished Victorian verse where thought and feeling are often unconnected.

Influences

Two religious influences are important in understanding Hopkins's poetry and his view of the world. **St Ignatius Loyola** (1491–1556), a sixteenth-century founder of the Jesuit order, provided a spiritual guide for Hopkins throughout his life. He believed that nature was created to help man praise God, and this belief helped to free Hopkins from a fear that his poetry was no more than a personal indulgence. In writing about the natural world, he was torn by a feeling that his love of nature and of physical beauty would lead him away from his devotion to God. In recognising St Ignatius's view of Nature as a means of praising God and His creation, however, Hopkins could see his poetry as a celebration of God.

The other crucial figure in Hopkins's life can be seen in the medieval philosopher and theologian **Duns Scotus** (1265–1308) who believed in the distinctive nature of everything, the unique qualities by which each thing can be recognised. This reinforced Hopkins's own belief that there was an underlying unity to the world, ultimately pointing to God as the creator. In addition, Scotus valued the senses as a means of gaining knowledge, and Hopkins saw this as a validation of his own love of the physical world. In experiencing the world through his senses, he could still honour God because his observations led to a greater understanding of the world and God's relationship to it.

Literary influences can be seen in Hopkins's interest in the rhythms of Old English alliterative verse, in the chorus rhythms of classical plays, and in the Welsh bardic tradition of **cynghanedd** (sound patterning in Welsh poetry – particularly alliteration and internal rhyme) which Hopkins called 'consonantal chimes'. His mystical vision of the world is reminiscent of Milton's portrayal of a controlled universe.

Attitudes to poetry

Hopkins's attitude to the poetry of his age was often critical. In his correspondence with the poet R.W. Dixon (1833–1900), he describes the *strictly poetical insight and inspiration* of contemporary poetry as *finer perhaps than the Greeks*. Yet he saw the rhetoric as *inadequate – seldom first rate, mostly only sufficient, sometimes even below par*. As well as his technical criticisms, he attacked what he saw as a separation of reason and thought. He believed Keats, for instance, had lost touch with *great causes, as liberty and religion*, and concerned himself with *impressions instead of thoughts*. For Hopkins, great poetry had to unite the two – the poet, by nature a dreamer and a sensualist, had to raise himself to greatness by addressing great causes. Equally, external structure and subject matter had to be interwoven to form an intricate whole, which reflected the complex unity of the world.

The poetic theories that Hopkins revealed in his correspondence and journals clearly mark out his vision of life both as a poet and as a priest. Religion, nature and poetry become inextricably linked in a personal recognition of God in the natural world. The detail of his observations can be seen in his journals and these reflect the complexity of his vision. The description of a sunset, for instance, becomes an insight into the inner nature of life. Hopkins the poet and Hopkins the priest are bound inescapably together in a revelation of the spiritual nature of all things. He recognised the obscurity that could arise from such intensity, but believed that it was an inevitable result of his poetic principles and spiritual outlook.

Particular terms recur in Hopkins's discussion of his work – coinages which he created to explain his theories – and these help readers come to terms with the complexities and technical innovations of his verse. He used the word **inscape** to refer to the design or pattern of things. References to it occur frequently in his letters, but rarely in his poems since they represent inscape in practice. Detailed observations of the natural world led him to a consideration of what is unique about his particular subject. Underpinning this, however, is a recognition of its place in the larger pattern of life – its similarity to other things, its inner essence. The inscape of nature becomes a visionary and ecstatic experience connected to God's presence in the world, which allows Hopkins to demonstrate his belief in the distinctive nature of all living things and in God's constancy.

Directly linked to inscape, the inward shape and pattern of things, is **instress** – the natural energy or stress of inscape. For Hopkins, instress represents the *sensation of inscape*, an illumination of or insight into the underlying order of creation. It is a fusion of thought and feeling, revealing the *beauty of inscape* that is *buried away from simple people*. The object of Hopkins's poetry is no longer merely a representation of the thing seen, but a revelation of the process of seeing.

Language and structure

Hopkins was sensitive to the flexibility of language and he used it in ways quite different from other nineteenth-century poets, stretching it to its limits. In this, he can be seen as a precursor of the experimental twentieth-century poets even though his content is clearly a product of his age.

The diction provides an insight into Hopkins as a poet: it reflects his distinctive point of view and reveals an underlying tension between his creative impulse and his spiritual belief. The words he chooses to convey an experience are often personal coinages: he creates compound nouns and modifiers, and uses many verbal nouns. Alongside polysyllabic Greek and Latin words, he also draws on everyday language (current idiom, provincialisms, and words that appealed directly to the senses). For Hopkins, this gave his poems an immediacy – it was evidence that the English language was living and changing, that it was flexible and adaptable. In his *Journals and Papers*, he said that poetry was: *speech framed to be heard for its own sake and interest even over and above the interest of meaning.*

Hopkins's powerful sense of pattern and order in life is integral to the syntax of his verse, and the structure of his poems is therefore equally distinctive. He stretches the grammatical relationship between words and phrases to its limit, controlling the reader's response by regulating the order in which impressions are received. He inverts word order, omits function words and draws on the accents of the speaking voice.

Hopkins often uses the sonnet, drawing on the Petrarchan form consisting of an octave and a sestet. The turning point or volta at the sestet allows him to change pace, mood and direction. He extended the convention, however, because he wanted greater depth: the addition of a coda created what critics refer to as the **caudate sonnet**; and experimentation with rhythm made the lines longer and heavier.

Wishing to move beyond the traditional rhythms of 2- or 3-syllable feet and one main stress (what he called an *alternating* or *running rhythm*), Hopkins adopted **sprung rhythm**. This has a varying number of syllables in each line while keeping a fixed number of stresses. He also used monosyllables, the paeon (one stressed and three unstressed syllables that can appear in a variety of patterns – called the first, second, third or fourth paeon according to the position of the stress), and treated the spondee as a normal English foot. Although the lines are inevitably of different lengths, the fixed number of stresses gives a sense of balance, and where the stresses occur in close proximity, the result is dramatic. Hopkins described it as: *the nearest to the rhythm of prose, that is the nature and natural rhythm of speech.* He felt that the alternation of weak/strong syllables was quite unlike real speech – his versification, however, provided freedom within a framework and brought metrical patterns closer to ordinary language use. He did not confine rhythmic patterns within the boundaries of a line and used consecutive stresses without the interruption of weak syllables.

Rhyme schemes provide the cohesion for Hopkins's verse by forging links between the language and the structure. In addition to the traditional end rhyme, he draws on assonance, alliteration, internal rhyme and onomatopoeia. From the Welsh language poetic tradition, he adopts cynghanedd to create an underlying framework of sound associations. For Hopkins, the unity created by the interaction of such poetic devices mirrored the interrelatedness of the world itself.

The content

The **content** of Hopkins's poems reflects both his awareness of his age and his own personal vision. The poem 'Tom's Garland' shows Hopkins's sense of the social conditions endured by workers in the Victorian period. It is the closest he got to writing a political poem – none of the usual religious overtones are present, instead he focuses on those at the bottom of the social hierarchy.

The opening presents the portrait of a working man *garlanded with squat and surly steel* (the steel studs on the soles of his boots) who is given dignity by his work. This image of the nobility of the working man is typical of the age and can be seen in the prose writing of Thomas Carlyle and John Ruskin. The force of Hopkins's vision, however, differs from his contemporaries because of the intensely personal way in which he records his views.

Hopkins was not revolutionary in his approach to the masses, believing that they benefited from *ease of mind* and *absence of care*. He shows, however, an understanding of the deprivations suffered by those without work. Since they are denied the chance to use both *mind* and *mainstrength*, their lives are without meaning – physical deprivation is inevitably accompanied by psychological deprivation. In 'Tom's Garland', Hopkins is not the social humanitarian who desires political change, but the poet-priest who records the horrors he sees in an age that has lost sight of the Christian belief of equality and justice. The unemployed are presented as individuals who are *no one, nowhere*; they are reduced to a subhuman condition by expressions like *Hangdog* and *manwolf*, and in the description of them as *packs* which *infest the age*.

Ultimately what sets Hopkins apart from his contemporaries is his personal vision. It is a view of life that is essentially Christian since he believed that *Man was created to praise*. His poetry is inspired by what he sees as God's presence in the world and the result is a revelation that he believes will benefit everyone. He described inspiration as the force which

> . . . lifts the receiver from one cleave of being to another and to a vital act in Christ: this is truly God's finger touching the very vein of personality which nothing else can reach . . .

Hopkins's whole being is alert to minute details – the poems may appear to be an external observation of nature, but they lead to a vision of creation. As poet-priest, his senses are sharpened, revealing a world ablaze with energy, colour and pattern.

Hopkins's personal vision can be seen in poems like *The Wreck of the Deutschland*. The poem is full of the same kind of detailed observations of the natural world found in other nineteenth-century poems, but Hopkins is not interested in subjective experience or escapism – for him, the beauty of the world is Christ's means of appealing to humanity. The scene is set within the energy and vitality of a storm at sea, and it is this that frames the profound spiritual act at the heart of the poem.

Death is seen to be all around for we are *rooted in earth – Dust!* (stanza 11). In the image of the man *handy and brave* (stanza 16) Hopkins shows that alone we can do nothing – for the faithful, however, the outcome is heavenly reward. The ode ends where it began, focusing on God, but there is now more joy. The tone is heightened and the final image is of Christ as the rising sun, *the crimson-cresseted east* (stanza 35), the source of all renewal.

In other poems, Hopkins brings his awareness of the age and his personal vision together. 'The Sea and the Skylark', for instance, juxtaposes the purity of the natural world (octave) with the squalor of urban life (sestet): the images of the *tide that ramps against the shore* and the skylark's *rash-fresh re-winded new-skeined score* are contrasted with the *shallow and frail town*. In sentiments very much of his age, Hopkins uses modifiers like *sordid* and *turbid* to create a negative image of the time, and *pure* to describe the natural world. In the sestet, he portrays a society where spiritual values have been passed over and humanity is no longer *life's pride* – they have *lost that cheer and charm of earth's past prime*. Instead, repetitions of *make/making* and *break/breaking* suggest that man's life no longer has meaning. While the sea and the skylark are *too old to end*, man is moving quickly towards his *last dust* and *first slime*; while the lowest creatures possess regenerative features and soar skyward, man's life has become purposeless and is now indistinguishable from the drudgery of physical labour.

Hopkins's spiritual view of the world is perhaps the most significant influence on the content. He observes what is around him intently, producing minutely realised portraits of individuals who become representative of particular 'types', or recreating places or moments in the natural world that lead towards a vision of God. The sentiments underpinning the poems are usually conventional – it is in the poetic approach that Hopkins reaches far beyond the achievements of his contemporaries.

The poetic reality of Hopkins's principles can be seen in a poem such as 'The Windhover' where a detailed observation of the bird leads beyond its physical presence to a recognition of its spiritual significance. Although the natural description is reminiscent of the Romantic poets, Hopkins reaches heights of intensity that had not been achieved by his contemporaries.

Hopkins and the English poetic tradition

Despite the fact that his content rarely moves beyond the experience of the Victorian age, Hopkins is often seen as the first 'modern' poet – he forms the bridge between the verse of the nineteenth and twentieth centuries. After an initial period of conventional writing, he modified and expanded poetic conventions, creating a new style that would suit his personal vision. The novelty of his diction and metre, his concern for 'inscape' in language, and his fusion of thought and form set him apart from his contemporaries. His approach means that the poems can often be obscure and this did not suit his contemporary audience. Dr Hake, a critic writing at the time, said: *Poetry that is perfect poetry ought never to subject any tolerable intellect to the necessity of searching for its meaning.* By contrast, a modernist approach believes in the active reader who must work to find meaning. In *Who killed Cock Robin?* (1921), the writer Sir Osbert Sitwell, an ardent supporter of modernist poets like Ezra Pound and T.S. Eliot, wrote: *Poetry cannot be entirely the work of the poet. It must be or should be in part the conception of the reader.* Such opposing standpoints mark the difference between Victorian and modern literature and, in terms of his style, Hopkins is clearly 'modern'. The triumph of his achievement can be seen in the way in which he enlivened poetic language and modified traditional poetic rhythm; blended sound and meaning; integrated vision and theory; combined the personal and the universal; and gave a new depth to religious debate.

Activity 12.6

Explore the linguistic, structural and poetic techniques Hopkins uses to communicate his ideas to the reader in 'The Windhover'.

You may like to think about: the presentation of the bird and its environment, the underlying ideas, the language, the structure, and the poetic features.

The Windhover
To Christ our Lord

1   I caught this morning morning's minion, king-
      dom of daylight's dauphin, dapple-dawn-drawn Falcon, in his riding
      Of the rolling level underneath him steady air, and striding
    High there, how he rung upon the rein of a wimpling wing
5   In his ecstasy! then off, off forth on swing,
      As a skate's heel sweeps smooth on a bow-bend: the hurl and gliding
      Rebuffed the big wind. My heart in hiding
    Stirred for a bird, – the achieve of, the mastery of the thing!

    Brute beauty and valour and act, oh, air, pride, plume, here
10   Buckle! AND the fire that breaks from thee then, a billion
    Times told lovelier, more dangerous. O my chevalier!

      No wonder of it: shéer plód makes plough down sillion
    Shine, and blue-bleak embers, ah my dear,
      Fall, gall themselves, and gash gold-vermilion.

Commentary

The poem focuses on a detailed observation of the bird in its natural environment, but beyond this lies a revelation which exposes the divine in the ordinary world: *the achieve of, the mastery of the thing!* (l.8). For Hopkins, the uniqueness of the falcon (inscape) becomes a symbol of the design and pattern of life, of God's creation. Although the poet's heart is *in hiding* (l.7), the sight of the bird's flight is illuminating since it leads him to God – the subtitle of the poem is *To Christ our Lord*. The use of the verb *Stirred* (l.8) marks the sensation of the experience (instress); it links the natural energy of the bird's flight with the process it inspires. As the bird and the poet almost become one, the poem's celebration of God's creation is complete.

The diction of the poem is typical of Hopkins as he stretches language to its limits. Formal words from Latin/French origins such as *chevalier* (l.11) and *vermilion* (l.14) exist alongside archaisms like *sillion* (furrow, l.13), technical terms from falconry or riding like *rung on a rein* (l.4) and personal coinages like the compound phrases *dapple-dawn-drawn* (l.2) and *bow-bend* (l.6). The verbal nouns *his riding* (l.2) and *the hurl and gliding* (l.5), and the verb modifiers *the rolling level* (l.3) and *a wimpling wing* (l.4) all add to the sense of movement that is at the heart of the octave. They reflect the power of the bird, which is explicit in the dynamic verbs *striding* (l.3) and *rebuffed* (l.7).

The bird's uniqueness is reiterated by the sequence of abstract nouns at the beginning of the sestet: *beauty, valour, pride* (l.9). These sum up the bird's qualities, but simultaneously mark the poet's recognition of the world's worth. As the bird swoops towards the earth, the revelation occurs: the verb *Buckle!* (l.10) is the pivot of the poem, linking the celebration of the bird's physical uniqueness (the octave) with an understanding of God in the mundane world (the sestet). The multiplicity of its meaning is typical of Hopkins's complexity – the bird is 'ready for action' as it swoops on its downward path; the physical world 'bends' as its hidden life is revealed; and the two halves of the poem are 'clasped' or 'brought together', leading to the apostrophe *O my chevalier!* (l.11), which unites the bird and God in a harmonious whole. The bird actually becomes an ideal towards which we must move if we are to emulate Christ.

The powerful images underpin the revelation by presenting ordinary things in a unique way. The tedium of ploughing which is *sheer plod* (l.12) is uplifted by the description of the furrow as the mud is turned – the verb *Shine* (l.13) is unexpected, encouraging the reader to understand the poet's surprise and celebration of the bird and its revelation of God in the world. The description of the dying embers flaring as they fall (ll.13–14) may be more traditional, but Hopkins's lexical choices make the image seem original. By prefacing his images with the elliptical sentence *No wonder of it* (l.12), Hopkins suggests that the spiritual understanding he has gained is there for all who can open their hearts to it – even hearts *in hiding* may be *Stirred*. In each case, an opening out reveals an inner significance.

The structure of the poem is carefully balanced around the verb *Buckle!* Hopkins controls the impressions that the reader receives: first the physical beauty of the falcon in flight, and then the poet's response to that beauty on a larger scale, and a recognition of God's presence in the pattern of the world as a whole. Other techniques to focus reader attention can be seen in the division of the noun *king-/dom* (ll.1–2) in order to place emphasis on the first syllable of the noun, and in the use of capitalisation (l.10).

The sonnet form is Petrarchan, rhyming abbaabba in the octave and cdcdcd in the sestet. The scheme is made more complex by the similarity of the a/b rhymes – although they all end with the -*ing* sound, lines 1, 4, 5 and 8 are masculine one-syllable rhymes, while lines 2, 3, 6 and 7 are feminine two-syllable rhymes. Other poetic features like alliteration in the compound modifier **blue-bleak** (l.13), internal rhyme in **Fall, gall** (l.14), and Hopkins's use of cynghanned (*dauphin . . . dawn-drawn*, l.2; *wimpling wing*, l.4; *Brute beauty*, l.9) add to the resonance of the poem. The sound carries the reader along in the intensity of the poet's vision and the whole experience becomes almost transcendental. The cohesive patterns become a mirror for the unity Hopkins sees in God's creation.

The opening line of the poem uses an iambic pattern:

Ĭ caúght | thĭs mór | nĭng mór | nĭng's mín | ĭŏn kíng-

The traditional nature of this rhythm reflects the poet's calm state of mind as he first sights the falcon. As the experience intensifies, however, the metrical patterns become more diverse – stress can follow stress with no intermediary weak syllables. The result is dramatic, mirroring the power of Hopkins's vision:

. . . thĕn óff, | óff fórth | ŏn swíng . . .   (l.5)

In the sestet, the rhythmic flexibility continues as Hopkins moves towards the climax of the poem – the revelation of God in the world.

. . . Brúte beáu | tў ănd vál | oŭr ănd áct, | ŏh áir, | príde, plúme, | hĕre
Búckle!   (ll.9–10)

For Hopkins, the pattern of the poem as well as the sight of the falcon are evidence of inscape – the intricate interweaving of words, metre, rhyme and alliteration become symbolic of God's creation. The emphatic use of spondees in the last line (*Fáll, gáll* and *gásh góld-*) adds to the dignity of the moment. It develops a final mood of certainty which is in direct contrast to the mundanity of the opening.

Hopkins uses the metrical stresses in his sprung rhythm to 'point' to key words. It is a very personal system and can be difficult to scan. In 'The Windhover', there are five main metrical stresses per line with hanging or outriding feet that are not counted in the metre, but contribute to the rhythmic effects. He describes these 'outriders' in his 'Preface' to *Poems* (1918):

> . . . two, or three slack syllables added to a foot and not counted in the nominal scanning. They are so called because they seem to hang below the line or ride forward or backward from it in another dimension than the line itself.

Marking the outriders on his manuscript, he identified *dauphin, Falcon* (l.2), *rolling, him* (l.3), *heel* (l.6), *achieve of* (l.8), *lovelier, dangerous* (l.11) and *of it* (l.12). They are often followed by a brief pause that adds to the effect by reinforcing the importance of the word.

The sprung rhythm mirrors the flexible patterns of speech. A varying number of weak syllables make up each foot, outriders provide extra weight, and stress follows stress in close succession. The end result is reminiscent of impassioned speech – the tone is sincere and there is a strong sense of the poet's personal involvement in his topic. Hopkins also uses the paeon in a variety of patterns to create variety and mirror the fluidity of the bird's flight.

> . . . High there, how he . . .   (l.4) . . . the mastery of . . .   (l.8)
> . . . dom of daylight's . . . (l.2)

The difficulty in scanning Hopkins's verse lies in the fact that it is possible to interpret the metrical pattern in a poem like 'The Windhover' in a number of ways. The flexibility and the links Hopkins develops between metre and meaning, however, are its strength.

▪ ˅ 13 Poetry of the twentieth century

For some historians, the twentieth century represents a time of underlying continuity for Britain despite the periods of war and the dramatic technological and scientific advances. They see 'modifications' to the traditions of the country rather than fundamental changes. Where other European countries have been forced into new directions by revolutions, occupations or liberations, Britain has retained established patterns and procedures. For other historians, key social, technological and moral changes have fundamentally altered the British outlook, creating a society that is quite different from that of the austere nineteenth century. Whichever perspective you adopt, there are notable events that distinctively shape twentieth-century Britain.

The years of Edward VII's reign (1901–10) seemed to be calm and settled, but political strife at the time was bitter. The Labour Movement was growing in strength, women were fighting for emancipation, Parliament was trying to limit the power of the House of Lords, and Europe was approaching war. When George V came to the throne (1910–36), the mood of unrest was no longer concealed and the monarchy had become little more than a figurehead for the country.

By August 1914, all the European powers were mobilised and the start of war was imminent. Most of the fighting in the First World War took place in the trenches and, although these had been built to protect the troops from machine-gun fire, severe rain left them waterlogged and disease-ridden. The loss of life in the 1914–18 war was horrific: Britain lost 60,000 troops in the first day of the battle of the Somme. By the time Germany surrendered in 1918, 10 million men had been killed and 20 million wounded. For many, the First World War became a symbol of the futility and senselessness of war.

Between 1919 and 1939, much work was needed to overcome a Europe crippled by war. It was a time of unrest, and nationalism swept through Europe: in Germany, Adolf Hitler and the Nationalist Socialist Party sought popularity by creating much-needed jobs in the armed forces and the munitions; in Italy, Mussolini rose to power promising to raise Italy's prestige in Europe; and in Spain, the conflict between the Republicans and the Nationalists resulted in a civil war lasting three years. Italy and Germany expanded their role in Europe by supporting the Spanish Nationalists, but Britain and France failed to help the Republicans. This, along with Japanese economic growth threatening the stability of the Far East, created the context for the Second World War.

It was to have even more devastating and wider-reaching effects than the First World War. By its end in 1945, the horror of what had taken place could be seen as a whole. At least 30 million people had been killed (over half of whom were Russians), another 21 million had been uprooted from their homes, and Jews had been collected up and taken to the concentration camps where they were tortured and murdered. The victorious countries had to face the problem of how to repatriate those who had fled from invading armies, those who had been sent to concentration camps, and those taken to Germany as enforced labour.

In the post-war years, as a ruined Europe was reconstructed, a new tension emerged – the East and West stockpiled nuclear weapons in a strategic struggle to be the potential winner of a nuclear war. It was to become known as the 'Cold War'. Not until the appointment of Gorbachev as the leader of the USSR in 1985 was there any evidence of a real change in East–West relations. Individual republics of the Soviet Union began to demand their independence and, in 1991, the USSR ceased to exist. The disintegration of communist rule in Eastern Europe was to lead to the reunification of Germany, and in November 1989, the Berlin Wall came down. The country was formally reunified in October 1990.

Although many elements of the traditional British way of life remained constant, some changes in society significantly altered our culture. Britain's development as a genuinely multiracial society was crucial in redefining the nature of what it means to be British as society was enriched by a diversity of religious and cultural beliefs, modes of speech, customs and dress. Equally, the movement to gain women the vote was important in its recognition of women's changing role in society. Subsequent changes in attitudes to sexuality, marriage, pregnancy, female employment and women's legal status were to continue the process.

Consumerism and the availability of cheaper goods in the 1950s were also to affect culture. Manufacturers found new markets in the heightened self-consciouness of the young who distanced themselves from the traditional, wanting things that were 'new' and 'different'. The 1960s were to develop this culture of the young, adding a mood of irreverence, ridicule and rebellion. Conventional judgements based on dress and to some extent on speech were challenged as a common youth culture of vitality and originality emerged.

Above all, the twentieth century has been an era of technological change. Cinemas first appeared in towns between the wars offering British culture access to Hollywood romantic escapism. After the war, however, the cinemas were themselves to be affected by the wider availability of television. As more people had access to radio and television, aural and visual modes of mass communication replaced the previous dominance of the written word. By the end of the twentieth century, the development of the internet and email had revolutionised communication and the spread of information.

The literary context

The twentieth century marks a dramatic point in the history of English literature. In all the arts, there was a movement towards exploring and making sense of an increasingly bewildering world. The shared values of the nineteenth century were replaced by disparate and often secular beliefs; traditional literary forms no longer seemed appropriate for discussing a fractured society; and the artist had lost confidence in his ability to control the world around him.

At the end of the nineteenth century, the Decadent poets, inspired by French poets like Baudelaire (1821–67) and Verlaine (1844–96), were interested in the nature of individual experience. They wrote about the meaninglessness of life, juxtaposing this with the intensity of experience itself. The tone was often melancholic and the context urban. The poetry of the pre-war years, by contrast, was pastoral, romantic and patriotic, until the horror and chaos of the First World War inspired verse that was notable for its biting impact and its immediacy.

Post-war, as the country struggled to make sense of what had happened, poets such as T.S. Eliot led the **Modernist movement** with its emphasis on experimentation and the impersonality of the artist. It was a movement notable for its internationalism, drawing its influences from a range of European artistic traditions. The Modernists consciously moved away from the traditional sequential development of narrative and verse structures, from conventional literary diction, and from the established values of artistic practice. In breaking away from long-established rules and conventions, Modernism created new aesthetic perceptions – it looked at the world in a different way and reassessed man's position in the universe.

The modernists' belief in existence as something active rather than passive found its roots in **Existentialism**. In the nineteenth century, the Danish philosopher and theologian Kierkegaard (1813–55) had written extensively about the nature of human character and motivation, the concept of individual free choice, and the rejection of religious and social conventions that engulf the individual consciousness and prevent real choice. This kind of focus was to be central in the work of the Existentialists. They were to be influenced by Kierkegaard's belief in the 'freedom to choose' as both a positive and negative force.

The work of the French Existentialist writer John-Paul Sartre (1905–80) was of particular interest to the Modernists. Sartre saw man as born into a void where he has the choice either to remain in a passive existence and a semiconscious state, or to become consciously aware of himself. Consciousness, however, is not easy because of the anguish that accompanies it, bringing a sense of the absurdity of experience and despair. For Sartre, such suffering was evidence of an active existence since it led to personal choice and was therefore the way out of the void.

This kind of approach can be seen in the Modernist interest in the condition of humanity, in their place and function in the world, and in their relationship (or more commonly their non-relationship) with God. Life is represented as absurd and meaningless: man is trapped in the uncontrollable spiralling of time, and the individual is in constant conflict between his own personal needs and the desire to belong.

Modernist literature tends to be intensely subjective, reflecting the impact of: Sigmund Freud (1856–1939) and his work on psychology, in particular *The Interpretation of Dreams* (1899); and Sir James George Frazer (1854–1941) and his work on anthropology (the study of human beliefs and institutions), in particular *The Golden Bough* (1890–1915). Interest in the way the mind works led to experimentation with style and form. Writers sought ways to record the unpredictable and elusive thought patterns of the individual, and the emergence of the 'stream of consciousness' technique at this time marked a change in the nature of characterisation – the inner life of the mind replaced the conventional focus on external appearance and behaviour.

The **Expressionist** movement was most influential in Germany in the early twentieth century, but was also to have an effect on British Modernism. The term Expressionism was first used by the French painter Julien-Auguste Hervé in 1901 to distinguish his paintings from those of the Impressionist school – in his work, he aimed to move beyond a direct representation of external reality. Expressionist art conveys a highly personal vision of the world, using images, evocative colours and patterns, and the distortion of traditional design to express emotion. 'The Scream' by Edvard Munch (1863–1944) is typical in its use of a vivid and disturbing image, violent colours and emotional symbolism.

In literature, Expressionist writers created a highly idiosyncratic view of life. In poetry, sound and colour effects, the use of synaesthesia (the mixing of senses) and the break with traditional poetic form are distinctive. Although predominantly a European movement, evidence of Expressionism is recognised in British writers including T.S. Eliot (parts of *The Waste Land*) and James Joyce (the Nighttown episode of *Ulysses*).

It is important to recognise that some critics argue against the existence of Modernism as a distinctive movement. They believe that there has been no significant cultural shift since the beginning of the nineteenth century, and that the literature produced in the 1920s is primarily an extension of Romanticism. Rather than a new approach to literature, it represents an intensification and extension of existing literary traditions. For others, the widely disparate approaches and the lack of a distinctive identifiable style also prevent 'Modernism' qualifying as a discrete movement.

Although the **poets of the 1930s** admired Eliot as the founder of modern poetry, many wished to move away from his elitist approach, bringing poetry back to ordinary readers. They believed in the importance of intellectual ideas, but wanted to create poems that were accessible. Their wider aim was political rather than spiritual – to ensure social and educational unity for all. In spite of their underlying differences, however, it was Eliot who got them published and, stylistically, they are often seen as part of Eliot's poetic tradition.

The key poets falling into this category are C. Day Lewis, John Betjeman, Louis MacNeice, W.H. Auden, and Stephen Spender. These men and their contemporaries lived in a time of increasing social tension: significant events such as the First World War, the General Strike (1926) and the 1930s Depression shaped their view of the world. They believed in political change which would replace interest in the individual with an awareness of the common need, and saw social uprising as the means by which society could be cleansed of its selfishness. Their verse was didactic in tone, and expressed a belief in the political message of Socialism. For some critics, the poetry is flawed because of its emphasis on the poet's function as a propagandist. Social observations are at times lacking in depth, and the poets can seem more interested in making their statement than in showing a genuine commitment to it.

The prospect of another world war brought the political poetry of the 1930s to an end. The **poetry of the 1940s** represented a reaction against the social content and didactic style that characterised the work of Auden and his followers. The poetry of argument was replaced by a more Romantic style of verse in which emotions and the imagination were dominant rather than the intellect. It marked a period in the English poetic tradition often described by critics as Neo-Romantic. Two poets in particular can be seen to represent this reaction against the poetry of the 30s: Edith Sitwell and Dylan Thomas, with his striking imagery and experimental approach to language.

Where the First World War had produced a remarkable body of poetry reflecting the experiences of individual poets, the Second World War tends to be remembered for specific poems. While the earlier poets are remembered for their war poetry, the later generation treated war as one of a range of subjects and are therefore less easily defined as 'war poets'. The horror of war expressed in the work of Owen and Sassoon is, on the whole, replaced by a new approach. Where poets like Owen had felt the need to destroy the *old lie*, that it was good and fitting to die for your country, the poets of the 1940s believed that it was no longer considered an 'honour' to fight. The forceful language and sense of immediacy is replaced by a more reflective tone and a more personal approach. The persistent raging of Owen's verse is replaced by an underlying mood of doomed acceptance.

The **poetry of the 1950s** marked another change of direction as poets moved away from both Modernism and Neo-Romanticism. The focus turned instead towards rational intelligence and skilled craftsmanship, emphasising the academic rather than the personal and Romantic. Traditional poetic forms, wit and a sardonic tone were recurring features of the poetry, with poets believing that the social conscience of the 1930s and the loose fashionable writing of the 1940s were no longer appropriate in modern Britain.

The **poetry of the 1960s** offered a new approach: a rejection of Modernism's emphasis on purity of form and technique, and the self-conscious use of artifice and contrasting styles. It was a time when poetry gained a wide audience: poetry readings were very popular and the *Penguin Modern Poets* series published energetic new poetic voices in affordable volumes. Volume 10, *The Mersey Sound*, brought together the Liverpool Poets – Adrian Henri, Roger McGough and Brian Patten – whose work was to introduce poetry to a new and younger audience. Their ongoing popularity is based on the wide range of their content and style, and their belief that poetry should be for enjoyment.

As the twentieth century moved towards its end, poets such as Seamus Heaney and Andrew Motion were to re-establish the importance of narrative and autobiographical verse. Perhaps the most significant change, however, can be seen in the number of female poets now recognised as making an important contribution to the English poetic tradition. Gillian Clarke, Wendy Cope, Carol Ann Duffy and Jackie Kay are just some of the key poets publishing exciting volumes of verse that reflect their personal experiences, the changing world in which they live, and their distinctive poetic voices.

For the poets of the twenty-first century, critical opinion is not fixed because there can be no conclusive retrospective judgement as there can be for a long-dead poet. Some modern poets dislike what they see as the rigidity of literary criticism in its attempts to 'deconstruct' poems, reducing them to the 'bricks and mortar' from which they were put together. It is therefore important to recognise that poems exist as meaningful texts with which the reader forms a relationship – analysis is what takes place on later readings as we try to understand the way in which a poem creates its effects.

Thomas Hardy (1840–1928)

Thomas Hardy had written poetry throughout his life, but it was only with his rejection of the novel form after the publication of *Jude the Obscure* (1895), that he was to concentrate on verse. The first volume, *Wessex Poems*, was published in 1898 and after another seven volumes, the *Collected Poems* appeared in 1930, containing over 900 poems. At the time, his poetry did not gain much popularity – both critics and readers were wary of a man who had abandoned a literary form in which he had excelled. Retrospectively, however, he was to be recognised as a significant figure in the poetic tradition of the twentieth century, influencing such poets as John Betjeman and Philip Larkin.

The literary context

The Edwardian age in literature was one of conservatism. The Empire was seen as a source of pride, the countryside was symbolic of traditional national values, and the aristocratic household and its social gatherings were seen as representative of all that was good about life in the first decades of the century. Below the surface, however, it was an age of considerable change and retrospectively can be seen as a period of prosperity and luxury for the privileged before the catastrophic upheavals of the First World War.

Edwardian poets such as Henry Newbolt (1862–1938) and Alfred Noyes (1880–1959) were interested in Britain as a whole rather than in the individual experience represented by the Decadent poets. They saw themselves as representatives of general British attitudes to morality and religion. Poems like Newbolt's 'Drake's Drum' still see Britain at the heart of the world, ignoring changes in its worldwide status. The confidence of this collective viewpoint mirrors the certainties of the Victorian age and retrospectively seems misplaced in an age of rapid change. Similarly their reliance on traditional poetic forms and diction, their emphasis on imperial adventuring, and their sentimental view of a rural England defies the reality of the world around them.

Rudyard Kipling (1865–1936) was also a patriotic representative of the British Empire. Unlike many of the Edwardian poets, however, he still continues to be read – the poems 'If', 'The Ballad of East and West' and 'Recessional', and his tales for children, *The Jungle Book* (1894) and *Just So Stories* (1902) in particular. His poetry was popular at the time because he was seen as giving a voice to the ordinary people who would otherwise have gone unheard. His use of a commonplace narrator meant that the attitudes he conveyed were representative of middle England. Despite this popularity, the colonial content of his work was increasingly to be seen as jingoistic. While contemporary writers like Henry James, W.B. Yeats and T.S Eliot admired Kipling's work for its skilful adaptation of the ballad form, its fluent versification, and its use of colloquial speech, in a rapidly changing world they felt uneasy about the moral standpoint and attitudes at the heart of the poems.

Georgian poetry was to displace the work of the Edwardian poets. At first, it was seen to represent a positive move away from the overornate and didactic work of Newbolt and Noyes towards something more realistic. Their emphasis on the Empire and the aristocratic way of life was replaced by uncontroversial everyday subjects: childhood and old age; love; nature and the animal world; sleep. Five volumes edited by Edward Marsh were produced between 1912 and 1922, including poems by A.E. Housman (1859–1936), W.H. Davies (1871–1940), Walter de la Mare (1873–1956), John Masefield (1878–1967) and Edward Thomas (1878–1917).

Georgian poetry cannot really be described as a coherent movement, but the anthologies contained poems that were recognisably similar in style. The early volumes were influential because of the freshness of their poetic vision and their straightforward approach to diction and form. The language is often archaic and multiple adjectives are used to create a subjective viewpoint that colours the poet's presentation of the world – the observations of society tend to be direct and tangible, reflections of a 'known' and coherent world which was to seem increasingly distant from the chaos of post-war Europe.

Some critics believe that the work of poets like John Masefield and Walter de la Mare sometimes lacked vitality. While it was approachable and direct, technically skilful, and unpretentious, it did not mark anything new in the English literary tradition. What is important perhaps is the fact that ordinary people enjoyed reading their work – poetry had been brought to the general public. Its popularity can be judged by the sales figures for the anthologies – the first volume sold 15,000 copies.

Although writing at the same time, **Thomas Hardy** stands apart from the Edwardian and Georgian traditions. While Housman, Masefield and de la Mare had drawn on the natural world as a source of inspiration, the harsh reality of Hardy's poetry and its metrical inventiveness set his work apart.

In some ways, Hardy was clearly of the age of Browning and Swinburne, and yet we know that he corresponded with Ezra Pound and read Eliot's *Prufrock* with great interest when it was published in 1917. His poetry is typically Victorian in its attitude to life and in its structure, but the tone befits the twentieth century in its unsentimental outspokenness and its awareness of the ironies of love and life in general. He followed Wordsworth in his desire to write in a language that mirrored the patterns of speech, but experimented with rhythm and stress. His themes reflected both his love of the natural world and his awareness of man's struggle to survive in an indifferent world.

The content

Often the subject matter of Hardy's poems does not conform to what was expected of a Victorian poet and it is not therefore surprising that he found it extremely difficult to get his poetry published in the 1860s. Much of what he wrote is very personal and the subject matter tends to have some bearing on his own private experiences. 'The Voice', for instance, was written in December 1912 after the death of Hardy's first wife, Emma Gifford.

In his poems, Hardy addresses themes of mutability and death; betrayal and broken fidelities; the fragility of the individual in an alien universe; the self versus nature. Having lost his faith in 1865, he searches for an alternative to conventional religion with its *tribal god, man-shaped, fiery-faced and tyrannous*. He portrays man as isolated in a vast hostile world where it is impossible to know 'truth' absolutely. Seasonal laments, journeys and birds recur as symbols in his vision of a world in crisis.

Hardy's poems are often accounts of subjective fleeting impressions that record a personal response to life – he described poetry as *emotion put into measure*. He deals in fragments that are incomplete and unexplained. Critical interest has focused on the relationship between these 'fragments' and Hardy's own life, but the personal allusions can be very difficult to interpret. Part of the problem of deciphering the subject matter of the poems lies in the fact that Hardy reshapes truth. Many of his poems are monologues and it is difficult to be sure whether or not Hardy is himself the speaker because he uses the first person to express a variety of viewpoints both personal and objective. He is a skilful storyteller, interweaving a fictional version of reality with hard fact. 'A Sunday Morning Tragedy' (1902), for instance, deals with a social issue – seduction and abortion – using a traditional ballad stanza and archaic diction. It is a poem in which Hardy looks outward to the world around him, just as he does in the poems that recall an identifiable individual, or a general experience.

What makes Hardy's verse stand out is the personal voice emerging from the lexical and syntactical choices. He rejects nineteenth-century fluidity and creates instead a very personal idiom – the language and grammar are idiosyncratic as Hardy attempts to capture the irregular patterns of spontaneous speech. Despite the personal content and language, however, the tone is restrained and unsentimental. In 'Ah, Are You Digging on My Grave?', for instance, he adopts the sparse and direct tone of a ballad. The simple language, unsentimental tone and the absence of any commentary create a feeling of immediacy as the dead woman converses with her dog. The themes of betrayal and inconstancy are typical of Hardy's pessimistic view of life, as is the sense of the absurd underpinning the dialogue.

Language, structure and style

Perhaps more important than pinning down the autobiographical nature of the poems' content is our recognition that Hardy was doing something quite different from other contemporary poets. Although the range of his themes tends to be narrow, his handling of metre, language and tone is skilful, and his approach to his subject matter is distinctive.

The language of the poems is a living language marked by its use of idiom, its natural rhythms, spontaneity and informality. Lexical choices can surprise us, seeming awkward and conspicuous, but close reading can almost always identify a linguistic reason for the choice. Hardy's manuscripts show evidence of the conscious manipulation of language that went on during the drafting process, and the roughness of his style is a deliberate means of revealing the inner self.

In Hardy's rejection of the Victorian tradition of poetic diction, we can see links with the Modernist movement. Latinate words appear alongside dialect, archaisms and coinages, the conversational alongside a personal poetic language.

He was interested in etymology and in creating layers of meaning – the words he chooses are intended to create certain effects and are always directly linked to the meaning. His experimentation is not always successful because it can seem too self-conscious at times, but at its best form, metre and language are inextricably linked to meaning.

Hardy drew on a wide range of poetic genres including lyrics, ballads ('The Darkling Thrush'), elegies ('Last Words to a Dumb Friend'), narrative poems, dramatic monologues, sonnets, epigrams and pastiches. Similarly varied is his experimentation with metrical and stanzaic form. Hardy represents the climax of the syllabic tradition before the Modernist emphasis on freedom from metrical patterning. His versification is more varied than any other English poet. He takes the traditional orderly metres of the Latin and Greek classics and adds to them a sense of the rhythms of speech. The link between form and meaning is crucial: broken, irregular rhythms are used to reflect a sense of man's vulnerability; fast rhythms are used to convey excitement and shape experience. Underpinning this variety, the regularity of tone and the individual use of language create a sense of cohesion throughout the vast body of Hardy's verse.

At its best, Hardy's experimentation with stanza form, rhyme and metre results in a complex interweaving of structural and semantic elements. By juxtaposing content with an unexpected metrical pattern or rhyme scheme, Hardy can challenge the reader, forcing them to reconsider the nature of versification and diction.

Thomas Hardy and the English poetic tradition

During his lifetime, Hardy wrote more than 1000 short poems. The quality is variable and because he was unselective in his publication, not all the poems are successful. Despite this, it was the poetry rather than the fiction that he valued. He wrote in 1915 that he wished critics to *treat [his] verse . . . as [his]* **essential** *writings, and [his] prose as [his]* **accidental**, *rather than the reverse*. After a period without recognition, his critical reputation has established him as one of the key figures in the English literary tradition.

Contemporary criticism tended to be negative, focusing on what was seen as an awkwardness of style. He was praised, however, by fellow poets such as Siegfried Sassoon, Walter de la Mare and Robert Graves; the 1950s poets of the Movement were to see him as an integral part of the English tradition. Larkin described him as a source of inspiration in his honesty, his avoidance of the grand, and his refusal to make great claims for the power of poetry.

Retrospectively, Hardy perhaps seems more Victorian than Modern. He had no intellectual, political or aesthetic beliefs to expound – his verse is, instead, a reflection of particular places, moods and occasions. Like Hopkins, he is a transitional poet: late Romantic in his approach to nature and his desire to use the language of everyday communication; a precursor of Modernism in his experimentation with diction, structure and style. His contribution to the English poetic tradition lies in his distinctive voice and personal vision.

Activity 13.1

> **How does Hardy use language and structure to communicate his ideas in 'The Voice'?**
>
> You may like to think about: the form, metre, lexical choice, grammar and other poetic features.

The Voice

1   Woman much missed, how you call to me, call to me,
     Saying that now you are not as you were
     When you had changed from the one who was all to me,
     But as at first, when our day was fair.

5   Can it be you that I hear? Let me view you, then,
     Standing as when I drew near to the town
     Where you would wait for me: yes, as I knew you then,
     Even to the original air-blue gown!

     Or is it only the breeze, in its listlessness
10   Travelling across the wet mead to me here,
     You being ever dissolved to wan wistlessness,
     Heard no more again far or near?

       Thus I; faltering forward,
       Leaves around me falling,
15   Wind oozing thin through the thorn from norward,
       And the woman calling.

Commentary

'The Voice' is the first poem in a sequence, *The Haunter*, in which Hardy questions whether he can hear his dead wife's voice. The *town* (l.6) is probably Boscastle where he first met Emma Gifford. They were married in 1874, but it was not to be an easy union. Despite this, her death in 1912 was to be the stimulus for some of Hardy's most moving verse.

    The first three stanzas of the poem are similar in form – each group of four lines establishes a lilting ballad-like mood through their rhythmic regularity and rhyme (abab). The fourth stanza, however, is quite different. After the song-like rhythms of the previous lines which enhance the yearning quality of the poem, the final stanza is harsh – a return to the reality of the woman's absence. The shorter lines and less fluid syntax disrupt the equilibrium established by the first three stanzas.

    This change in pattern is reinforced by Hardy's metrical choices. He uses the expansive dactylic strong-weak-weak stress pattern (ll.1–12) to create the song-like rhythms of his hopefulness.

       Woman much | missed, how you | call to me, | call to me,
       Saying that | now you are | not as you | were

The abstraction of the 'voice' is given a physical presence by the homely and almost jaunty rhythmic pattern. The change of mood in the final stanza is reinforced by a change in metrical pattern as well as in the form. Hardy prepares us for this by irregularity of the metre in line 12.

> Heárd nŏo I móre ă I gáin fár I ŏr néar?

The change is further highlighted by the use of the unmelodious spondee *Thús Í* in which two stresses emphasise the poet's sudden awareness of the present and of his loneliness. The rest of the stanza is dominated by the heavier trochaic strong-weak pattern instead of the delicate dactylic.

> Fálteriňg I forwărd,
> Leáves ă I róund mĕe I fálliňg,
> Wínd ŏo I ziňg thín I thróugh thĕe I thórn frŏm I nórwărd,
> Aňd thĕe I wómăn I cálliňg.

Hardy tends to be very precise in sustaining rhythmic patterns throughout a poem and therefore this metrical variation can be seen to have a direct function in communicating his mood of despair.

The lexical choices help to create the contrast between illusion and reality. Everyday language is juxtaposed with Hardy's disruption of the collocation 'sky-blue'. By creating the coinage *air-blue* (1.8), he draws attention to the mystical nature of this experience. It may appear to be ordinary – seeing his lover waiting for him as he approaches the town – but we are reminded that this is the vision of a man yearning for his dead lover. It is a poem dominated by the senses: we see the woman's figure, we hear her voice, and feel the breeze bringing the poet back to reality. A change of tone can be identified in stanza 3 with the use of the lexis *listlessness* (1.9) and *wistlessness* (1.11) with their strong feminine rhyme. The positive symbolism of the *air-blue gown* (1.8) is replaced by the negative associations of the *wet mead* (1.10) and the verb *dissolved* (1.11) as the vision fades away.

The poet's consciousness of the present moment is striking in the final stanza. He can no longer hide behind the comfort of his vision and the emphasis is on the here-and-now: *Leaves . . . falling* (1.14), *Wind oozing* (1.12). The use of present participles emphasises the sudden movement of time after the almost static epiphany of the first three stanzas. The autumnal mood becomes symbolic of the poet's state of mind and the use of the tentative verb *faltering* (1.13) draws attention to his vulnerability. This is reinforced by the final line of the poem: it echoes both the title and the first line, drawing us back into the inevitable cycle of the poet's mourning. The use of the co-ordinating conjunction *And* in the initial position and the present participle *calling* (1.16) underpin this sense of an inescapable cycle.

Other patterns can be seen to develop our sense of the poem as cyclical. The rhyme scheme (abab) becomes almost claustrophobic in its use of not just a similar sound, but of the same word or final syllables in the longer first and third lines of each stanza: *call to* and *all to me* (ll.1/2); *then* (ll.5/7); *listlessness* and *wistlessness* (ll.9/11). The sense of entrapment created by this kind of repetition is juxtaposed with the lightness of the dactylic stress pattern, underlining the central tension between appearance and reality. The closed world of the vision is further intensified by Hardy's use of internal rhyme: *view/you* (l.5), *knew/you* (l.7), *mead/me/here* (l.10), *dissolved/wistlessness* (l.11), *oozing/through* and *thorn/norward* (l.15). The assonance adds to the sonorous, doleful appeal of the poem. Other sound patterns such as the sibilance of the third stanza and the alliteration of the fricative *f-* and *th-* in the final stanza seem to be part of the harshness of the autumnal environment that impinges upon the poet's attempts to hear the 'voice' that calls to him.

Grammatical patterns also play a significant part in helping Hardy to convey his state of mind to the reader. The opening vocative *Woman much missed* is emotive since it immediately establishes the mood of absence. Tension is then created by the juxtaposition of the past participle *missed* with the present tense *call*, preparing us for the interplay of vision and reality. The complete syntactic structures of the first stanzas reflect Hardy's immersion in the vision of his dead lover. Only in the use of questions (l.5, ll.9–12) are we aware of an alternative reality in which the voice of the woman may be no more than the breeze. The final stanza, by contrast, is made up of incomplete grammatical structures. The emphatic verbless clause *Thus I* (l.13) draws attention away from the vision of the woman and back to the poet, alone against an autumnal landscape. The sense of unrest is portrayed through the use of non-finite clauses in which present participles create a sense of ongoing movement to which there is no conclusion. The reader is left with an image of disruption in which harsh reality has reimposed itself, dispelling the momentary relief found in the vision of the dead woman.

The War poets

With the First World War came a new breed of poets who aimed to reflect the horror of their experiences in an immediate and realistic way. Trench warfare in particular and the chaos of war in general were the source of poems of indignation and disgust. The high death rate and the horrific conditions suffered by those fighting in the trenches meant that the concept of 'heroic sacrifice' in service to one's country became meaningless. Patriotic poetry was therefore replaced with verse that was to symbolise the futility of the war, protesting against the waste of life and forcing readers to engage emotionally with reality.

Rupert Brooke (1887–1915)

Rupert Brooke had established a reputation with his work published in the first Georgian anthologies, but his five 'War Sonnets' (1915) brought him even greater acclaim – he was seen as the nation's poet of war. He welcomed the war and his poetry is patriotic. Death in battle is presented in a detached and impersonal way: it is a noble and dignified sacrifice rather than a threatening or horrific experience. In 'The Soldier', he distances thoughts of death with his use of the hypothetical *If* in the opening line, making the prospect seem remote.

> If I should die, think only this of me:
>   That there's some corner of a foreign field
> That is forever England. There shall be
>   In that rich earth a richer dust conceal'd . . .   (ll.1–4)

The poem then considers what death in battle will mean – not in real, but in symbolic terms as the soldier's body becomes a symbol for England. Despite the use of a first person narrator, the sense of a personal story is lost in the glory of dying for one's country. Brooke's use of the first person personal pronouns *I* and *me* does not extend beyond the first line, with the remainder of the poem personifying England. The 'individual' becomes first *A body of England* and then no more than *A pulse in the eternal mind*.

The use of the comparative *richer* in the extract here suggests the greater value of the 'English man' whose decaying corpse enriches the *foreign* land. Such a viewpoint is clearly sentimental and fails to recognise the gruesome reality of the war experience for many soldiers. A fellow poet, Charles Hamilton Sorley (1895–1915) was to write of Brook's war sonnets: *he has clothed his attitude in fine words; but he has taken the sentimental attitude*. Inevitably such poetry is very different from that written by poets such as Siegfried Sassoon and Wilfred Owen, but it is important to recognise that Brooke's personal experience of the war was in fact very different: while Sassoon and Owen were in the trenches, Brooke was in the navy. He was therefore removed from the grim reality of life in the trenches that was to produce such bitter commentaries on the futility of war.

It is for pre-war poems like 'The Old Vicarage, Granchester' that Brooke is now best remembered. He is clearly influenced by A.E. Housman and uses the English country life as a symbol of heaven. The tone is predominantly nostalgic and sentimental, but there is an ironic undercurrent of wit that takes the poem beyond the achievements of some of his contemporary Georgian writers. Other poems such as 'A Channel Passage' reflect an interest in experimentation that might have seen his work move towards Modernism had he survived the war.

Siegfried Sassoon (1886–1967)

Quite different from the war poems of Brooke were the biting satirical commentaries of **Siegfried Sassoon**. Where Brooke dealt with an illusory symbolic war, Sassoon wrote of the realities of officialdom, physical conditions and patriotism. His 'A Soldier's Declaration' made in July 1917 was a conscious challenge to the authorities – he claimed that the war was being *deliberately prolonged by those who have the power to end it* and attacked the failure of the general public at home to recognise the true horror of the conditions in the trenches. His friend Robert Graves managed to persuade the War Office that there should be no disciplinary action and that Sassoon should be sent to Craiglockhart hospital to recover from a 'severe mental breakdown' – Sassoon's time at Craiglockhart and the relationship he established with the army psychologist W.H.R. Rivers forms the central narration in Pat Barker's novel *Regeneration* (1991).

Sassoon's poetry did not immediately find an accepting audience – Rupert Brooke's nostalgic patriotism was far more palatable. The bitter tone and the depth of feeling at the heart of Sassoon's poems alienated both the general public and those in charge. He attacked figures of authority in 'The General' where innocent soldiers are the victims not of the enemy, but of the *incompetent swine* who organise and plan the battles. The colloquial tone, direct speech and everyday language enhance the poem's sense of reality. By naming *Harry* and *Jack* and using a first person narrative, Sassoon individualises the soldiers while distancing us from authority with the use of the impersonal title *The General*. His use of the inclusive *we* reinforces our sense of distance between the troops and their officers. The poem is a damning indictment of a system that professes to value its soldiers while making no more than token gestures towards them.

Sassoon's poems are vivid and brutal in their sense of reality. His contempt for leaders and for the pious platitudes of dying with dignity for one's country are balanced with a genuine compassion for the men alongside whom he served. The poignancy of poems like 'Everyone Sang' written on Armistice Day and 'Does it Matter?' contemplating the nature of life after the war for the wounded 'heroes', is as disturbing as the most vivid of his trench poems. One of the few poets to survive the war, Sassoon's later work was to be more inward-looking and more experimental in technique.

Wilfred Owen (1893–1918)

For some critics, **Wilfred Owen** was the most individual and best of the war poets. He had met Sassoon at Craiglockhart hospital and had shown him his verse; Sassoon had encouraged him, helping him to revise poems like 'Anthem for Doomed Youth'. The best of Owen's poems were to be written in an intensely creative period from summer 1917 to autumn 1918. Only five were published in his lifetime – the rest appeared in 1920 in an edition arranged by Sassoon.

Owen's earliest work shows the influence of Keats in its decorative style, but his experiences in the trenches were to move his verse towards a stark and powerful realism. The observations are disturbing and the underlying attack on society and its attitudes consistent. For him, the war was a tragedy and beneath the surface disgust lies a pity and compassion that raises the poems above simple propaganda. He sees the violence around him as a symbol of the human condition and the best of his work stands as a universal commentary on man's inhumanity to man.

Readers do not forget the images of Owen's verse. The haunting descriptions of the Western Front in 'The Show' portray a *sad land*

> Gray, cratered like the moon with hollow woe,
> And pitted with great pocks and scabs of plague.   (ll.3–5)

The scene may be presented in the form of a vision, but its reality is inescapable. The image of the soldiers from a distance looking like *thin caterpillars* leaving *slimy paths* as they *writhed and shrivelled* in ditches is horrifying, just as descriptions of soldiers *Bent double, like old beggars under sacks* in 'Dolce et Decorum Est' and the bayonet blade *keen with hunger of blood . . . famishing for flesh* in 'Arms and the Boy' are dismaying.

Owen's lexical choices are an integral part of his powerful images. With the verb *cursed* and the compound modifier *blood-shod* in 'Dolce et Decorum Est', he can bring the hardships of the soldiers to life. By contrast, the language of 'Futility' is used to create a mood of poignancy – a recognition of the finality of death away from the chaos and bloodshed. A contrast is developed between *the seeds* and *the clays of a cold star* that can be awakened by the sun, and the dead soldier *so dear achieved . . . Full nerved – still warm* who is *too hard to stir*.

At the heart of his poems lies a tension between content and style: in his subject matter, he is an 'evangelist', aiming to reveal the truth to those at home; in his technique, he is experimental. The two halves are not always balanced, but in a poem like 'Anthem for Doomed Youth', he combines the two strands powerfully.

The War poets and the English poetic tradition

For some critics, the significance of war poetry lies in its value as a historical document rather than in its contribution to the mainstream tradition of English poetry. It is seen as a personal record that fails to take account of the totality of the situation; a genre in which poetic technique is subordinate to subject matter. Certainly Owen's poetry finds its source in personal experience, in his horror at the waste of life and in his disgust at the conditions in which the men were expected to survive. Yet there is more to his verse than the message: Owen created a technique of half-rhymes or consonance and harsh dissonant sound effects; he is a master of the striking and memorable image; and his lexical choices are powerful. His work was to influence the English poets of the 1930s.

Other poets of the war period were to have wider appeal because their work was not restricted to the subject of the war alone. The work of **Isaac Rosenberg** (1890–1918) is known for the strength of individual lines, but the overall effect can be strained because of a tendency to overwrite. The language can be awkward in places and grammatical inversions can seem inappropriate. In the poem 'Dead Man's Dump', however, Rosenberg is at his best.

Edward Thomas (1878–1917) began writing during the war and turned to poetry from prose after encouragement from his friend the American poet Robert Frost (1874–1963). His subject matter is rarely the war and many of his poems focus on an exploration of the self through symbolic references to the natural world and the English countryside. He is fascinated by the past, describing landscapes and places haunted with the ghosts of previous occupants. His awareness of a sense of loss is both public and private. In the poem 'Blenheim Oranges', loss is seen in terms both of the past of an old house now empty and lifeless, and of the present war that turns *young men to dung*. Where he does deal more directly with the war, his focus is on the disruption and violation of the self.

By contrast, the poetry of **Robert Graves** (1895–1985) is enigmatic and intellectual. Having moved away from his early association with Georgian poetry, Graves was to become increasingly individual in his approach. His war poetry does not rank among the best, but his autobiographical prose work *Goodbye to All That* was interesting for its experimental approach. Critics vary in their judgements about Graves's place in the English poetic tradition, but he has produced a vast body of work that is widely varied in form and always distinctive in its attitude to life. At his best, he moves between real experiences and the mythical, between the individual and the universal.

Activity 13.2

> ### Discuss the links between diction, style, form and meaning in Wilfred Owen's 'Anthem for Doomed Youth'.
>
> You may like to think about: poetic form, grammatical mood, language, tone, sound patterning and imagery

Anthem for Doomed Youth

1   What passing-bells for these who die as cattle?
      Only the monstrous anger of the guns.
      Only the stuttering rifles' rapid rattle
    Can patter out their hasty orisons.
5   No mockeries for them from prayers or bells,
      Nor any voice of mourning save the choirs,
    The shrill, demented choirs of wailing shells;
      And bugles calling for them from sad shires.

    What candles may be held to speed them all?
10   Not in the hands of boys, but in their eyes
    Shall shine the holy glimmers of good-byes.
      The pallor of girls' brows shall be their pall;
    Their flowers the tenderness of silent minds,
    And each slow dusk a drawing-down of blinds.

Commentary

Owen has chosen to use a sonnet to give his argument a tightly structured form. There is a tension between the horror of his subject matter and the orderly pattern of the sonnet – it forces readers to face the difference between the reality of the trenches and the mediated version provided by the authorities. Owen's use of the traditional iambic pentameter mirrors the rise-and-fall of the spoken voice and its regularity is in direct opposition to the chaos of the poem's subject.

Owen adapts the English or Shakespearean sonnet, combining the octave and sestet of the Petrarchan form with the basic pattern of the Shakespearean rhyme scheme. The traditional Shakespearean quatrains and couplet (abab cdcd efef gg) become an octave and sestet (ababcdcd effegg). While the octave develops vivid images of the violence of the front, the sestet marks a change of mood, focusing on the quiet rituals of home.

Beyond the tight structure of the sonnet form, the change of grammatical mood at the beginning of each stanza allows Owen to structure his argument. He addresses two consciously different scenes (the front; home life) both of which allow him to come to the same conclusion. By immediately engaging readers through his use of the interrogative, he can encourage them to feel as he does – accepting the reality of the war as revealed in his descriptions rather than the myth. In the remainder of the stanza, Owen tries to answer the question he has posed. We are aware of the anger of his first question and it is clear that he feels the tribute paid to dead soldiers is insufficient. The second question intensifies his belief that people do not understand the nature of these deaths as he looks at the way the community responds to their loss through ritual.

The language is powerful, interweaving the lexical fields of battle and religion. Words like *die* (l.1), *guns* (l.2), *rifles* (l.3) and *shells* (l.7) are juxtaposed with *passing-bells* (l.1), *orisons* (l.4), *prayers, bells* (l.5), *choirs* (ll.6,7), *candles* (l.9) and *pall* (l.12). Owen's approach, however, is not traditional. By creating a direct link between the two sets he undermines the value of spiritual comforts: the *guns* (l.2) and *rifles* (l.3) deliver the soldiers' only *orisons* (l.4); the *shells* (l.7) are their only *choirs* (ll.6–7). Where we might have expected the religious lexis to offer hope in a time of despair, it is in fact no more than a bitter mockery of the sacrifices being made. From the violence of the first stanza, we move to the meaningless rituals of those at home and Owen seems to use the juxtaposition of the two scenes to reinforce his point.

The tone is created through Owen's choice of modifiers. In the octave, the emphasis is on the noise and chaos of the battlefield. Words such as *monstrous* (l.2), *stuttering* (l.3), *shrill, demented* (l.7) and *wailing* (l.7) heighten our awareness of the physical scene. The mood is one of anger and yet Owen simultaneously develops a feeling of pity and compassion for the men trapped in this hell. The final line of the octave prepares us for a change in mood – the haunting reference to the *bugles calling* and the use of the modifier *sad* (l.8) mark a turning point. The sestet is silent where the first stanza was overwhelmed by the noise of battle; the opening tone of anger becomes an implicit statement about the futility of such deaths. These distinctions are, however, deceptive. Although the ritualistic scene may appear peaceful after the nightmarish qualities of stanza 1, pain and horror are still present in the inner lives of those who have lost someone. The emphasis is now on visual images – the speechlessness of mourning. For Owen, it is not the outward show of public rituals, the candles and flowers, that is meaningful, but inner reflection. The look in the eyes of the boys (ll.10–11), the *pallor* of the girls' faces (l.12), their *silent minds* (l.13) stand as the most fitting tribute to the sacrifices made.

The power of Owen's vision of the battlefield lies in his ability to bring the scene to life through his imagery. He uses personification to animate the weapons of destruction: the abstract noun *anger* (l.2) is linked to the guns; the verb modifier *stuttering* (l.3) and the verb *patter* (l.4) describe the rifles; the verb modifier *wailing* and the noun *choirs* (ll.6–7) describe the shells. While the inanimate is given life, the soldiers are reduced to *cattle* (l.1) – their humanity is lost in the squalor of their surroundings and the inevitability of their slaughter. Through this ironic juxtaposition of the animate and inanimate, Owen is able to emphasise the meaninglessness and indignity of the soldiers' deaths.

The references to *prayers, bells* and other religious images are symbolic and Owen uses them to undermine the expectations of the reader. As representations of the spiritual they are meaningless and this is summarised in the abstract noun *mockeries* (l.5). Similarly the symbolic *candles* (l.9), *flowers* (l.13) and the *drawing-down of blinds* (l.14) are no more than gestures in a public mourning which bears no relation to individual experience. The traditional hopes of an afterlife seem hollow in the light of the sacrifice of life in the trenches – Owen substitutes a private humanism for society's Christianity, where individual memories will last long after the ceremonial rituals have been forgotten.

The sound qualities of the poem are distinctive. The harsh alliterative *rifles' rapid rattle* (l.3) and repeated sibilance at the end of stanza 1 (ll.5–8) are suitably dissonant, mirroring the noise and chaos of the battlefield. Alongside this, the use of assonance reinforces the mood of pity. The sonorous *Nor . . . mourning* (l.6) and *silent minds* (l.13) are internal rhymes befitting the ritualistic tone of the second stanza.

The title encapsulates the juxtaposition at the heart of the poem: it is an *Anthem*, a song of praise often based on a passage from the Bible; and yet it is for *Doomed Youth*, for the young soldiers who go unknowingly to their deaths. The inevitability of their end hangs over the reader who is forced to recognise the needless sacrifice being made. For Owen the 'anthem' lies not in a religious cele-bration of the afterlife, but in a conscious recognition of the waste of life and in the personal memorials of individual families.

W.B. Yeats (1865–1939)

It could be said that the poetic obscurity associated with Modernism began with **Yeats**. The complex systems underlying his verse, the personal symbolism, and the distinctive use of legendary and contemporary Irish references can be alienat-ing for readers. His language, however, can engage through its lyricism and beauty. While much Modernist verse is staccato and disjointed, Yeats aimed for an overall fluency and cohesion that is uncommon in Modern poetry.

The literary context

The nineteenth-century French Symbolist movement was to influence Modernism as a whole, and Yeats in particular. Reacting against the objectivity of the Realist and Naturalist traditions, Symbolism placed its emphasis on sugges-tion and evocation, and avoided direct description. Symbols were used to assimi-late sound, sense and colour, to condense experience into a concentrated form, and to interweave the material and the spiritual worlds – interest in the occult and mystical writings was central to the Symbolist movement. For Symbolist writers and artists, form was more important than content. They were fascinated by the musical properties of language: words were chosen for the power of their sound and rhythm.

In *The Symbolist Movement in Literature* (1899), Arthur Symons (1865–1945) was to introduce Symbolism to England. He described Symbolist literature as *a kind of religion, with all the duties and responsibilities of the sacred ritual* and for many read-ers the private and personal nature of the symbols used made it exclusive and elite. The nineteenth-century French poets Stéphane Mallarmé (1842–98), Paul Verlaine (1844–96) and Arthur Rimbaud (1854–91) were to influence twentieth-century Modernists. Having adopted the Symbolist style, however, both Yeats and Eliot were later to return to poetic diction that was more representative of the speech of their time.

The development of Yeats's verse

Yeats's early work is marked by an Arcadian and pastoral mood. The style is often languorous and Yeats retreats to an ideal landscape, a mythical world divorced from the realities of our own. *The Wanderings of Oisin* (1889) sets the tone for much of his work at this time and introduces the private symbols and signs that were to be his trademark.

Wind Among the Reeds (1899) revealed Yeats as an assured craftsman interested in the lyric and the symbolic. Many of the poems focus on crossed love and dying passion. While firmly grounded in the physical, Yeats was moving towards a more metaphysical view of life. In 'He Wishes his Beloved were dead', images of the lover's hair become entwined *About the stars and moon and sun*; in 'He Wishes for the Cloths of Heaven', the physical image of *cloths* is bound up with the meta-physical *heavens* and *light*. The combination of the two reflects the movement in the poems towards a heavenly paradise even while the poet is marked by earthly anguish.

Yeats's research into mythology and the occult at this time is apparent in the kinds of references he makes. He published extensive notes with the poems to indicate his source material in Irish legends. The symbolism is increasingly complex, the tone is often marked by melancholy, and the style is hauntingly lyrical.

In the Seven Woods (1903) marks a change in style. In the time between publi-cation of *Wind Among the Reeds* and the *Seven Woods* volume, Yeats had concen-trated on drama. He now felt that his poetry needed a harder edge. When he returned to verse, therefore, his style was less lyrical, reflecting his new interest in a leaner and more speech-like approach as he moved away from a 'Celtic Twilight' towards the real world of Ireland and his personal life.

Responsibilities (1914) marks a distinctive point in Yeats's poetic career and crit-ics often describe it as a major change in direction. There is a growing interest in the physical as well as the soul, myths are used to awaken a *hope to live*, and Yeats pronounced that he would now be *walking naked* ('A Coat'), abandoning the *embroideries/Out of old mythologies*. As other writers adopted the romanticism of his earlier 'Celtic Twilight' phase, Yeats sought to distance himself from it. His style becomes increasingly public in its approach and his subject matter focuses on his disillusionment with Irish politicians and patrons. In his epilogue, Yeats defended the things in which he believed (the psychic, pride in his family, admi-ration for Lady Gregory, his love for Maud Gomme, and his belief in his own work); he ended with an attack on those who saw *all [his] priceless things* as *but a post the passing dogs defile*.

Yeats's marriage in 1917 to Georgie Hyde-Lees was to have a significant effect on his verse. The automatic writing undertaken by his wife prompted Yeats to formalise his own system of the patterns underlying reality. *A Vision*, first published in 1925 and rewritten in its final form in 1937, represented Yeats's metaphor for the interdependence of all things. Its influence can be seen in the 1917 volume *The Wild Swans at Coole* in which he attempts to explain its central image.

Two years later in *Michael Robartes and the Dancer* (1921), Yeats again explores the ideas of *A Vision* alongside personal matters arising from public events (the 1916 Easter Rising and the subsequent troubles). The central themes focus on private happiness juxtaposed with national and international crises, and the potential social chaos that could result.

This juxtaposition of personal and public continues in *The Tower* (1928) where events of the civil war become symbols for the potential disintegration of Western society. Alongside the political poems, he writes about events in his own life, about friendship and love. His personal success (international recognition, the award of the Nobel Prize for literature) is balanced by the bitterness of his tone, which marks his fear of the increased violence he saw in the world, and of the approaching ruin and decay he believed inevitable. The physical world of his poems at this time is often violent, symbolised by storms, damaged trees and loosening masonry.

The Winding Stair (1933) focuses more exclusively on the private and on an acceptance of life – the image of the 'winding stair' is symbolic of Yeats's gyres, which organise and provide the underlying pattern to life. The collection works in opposition to *The Tower* and the two volumes need to be considered together. Yeats's new-found interest in rebirth and life can be seen in the appearance of two new symbols: his Japanese sword and the silk in which it is wrapped.

In 1935, *A Full Moon in March* was published. Yeats was not happy with the collection as a whole, but believed that particular poems were successful. Continuing ill-health led to an operation in 1934 and a renewed energy for writing – Yeats felt that he was at last creative again. Two new collections mark this creative outburst: *New Poems* (1938) and *Last Poems* (1939) in which he reviews his life and speculates on the nature of death; addresses the nature of the poet; returns to political themes; and tries to bring a final order to his work. What makes the poems distinctive is their recognition that the best we can do in life is to see the meaninglessness of the underlying patterns. The style combines characteristics of the traditional ballad with conventional lyrics.

Yeats's approach to writing

Yeats often used his prose diary as a starting point for his poetry, reworking prose statements into verse. The process was arduous, involving multiple drafts in which he experimented with various combinations of words. In the long term, he aimed to create a coherent body of work, an organic collection, which reflected his life interests, his personal system of symbols, and his growing stylistic maturity, so he wrote and rewrote everything to ensure that it fitted into the overall structure. Poems were revised, volumes were rearranged, and some poems were deleted from the collected works.

Chronological order was less important to Yeats than thematic and stylistic concerns, and before his death, he had intended to write a final essay explaining his private philosophy of life. As he recorded in a letter to Lady Elizabeth Pelham, it was to be the fitting end to his life's work. Although he had completed his final revision of the poems, however, he was to die before he finished his definitive essay.

Because of Yeats's approach to his work, readers can use events in his life, his letters, essays, and his speculations on philosophy and the cosmos as an interpretative framework. They become a guiding backdrop against which the poems can be read. In addition, his use of recurring themes and images provides a structure that leads us through the poems. Despite their difficulty, the illusion of order Yeats creates is reassuring: through his carefully worked and ordered texts, we can find layers of meaning that consistently point towards his central concerns.

Yeats believed that the poet's strength lay in the personal, but that he should be wary of sentimentality. In revising his earlier verse, he attempted to moderate the romantic language that came to be associated with the 'Celtic Twilight'; his theory of the 'mask' enabled him to present his inner 'self', his personal life, to the reader without becoming too subjective. It became the means by which Yeats could objectify the personal, linking the power of private experience to the universality of general truth. The mask could be adopted from history or mythology, but should always be the antithesis of the poet. Yeats's own mask allowed him to produce in his work: *something hard and cold, some articulation of the Image, which is the opposite of all that I am in my daily life* . . . The tension existing between the external mask and the inner self lies at the heart of the poetry – Yeats's style and persona are deliberately adopted as a technique to shape his art.

He believed that the poet must be prepared to sacrifice the perfect life, choosing to live in the real world with all its imperfections rather than aiming for *A heavenly mansion* ('The Choice'). He saw the actual experience of living as a fundamental part of the creative process, shaping the poet and leaving its mark. He addresses this in 'The Choice' where he chooses *raging in the dark*, and in 'Vacillation' where he disregards the offer of heavenly perfection and follows *Homer . . . and his unchristened heart*. The poet's reward of immortality is found in his creativity, in the poems that will live beyond him.

For Yeats, poetry is more than just a record of an emotional experience. It is rather a complex intertwining of images, rhythms and sounds; a symbolic representation of a particular moment that would otherwise be inexpressible. It is important that the poet aims to record his thoughts *in as nearly as possible the language [he] thought them in, as though in a letter to a friend*. He sees everything rooted in the earth, and from this rootedness in the physical comes the epiphany, the moment of understanding in which random experiences become meaningful. For Yeats, a specific event is *a thing never known again*, a unique moment in which the poet can find a transcendent purpose.

Yeats's beliefs

Yeats's interest in Irish culture and traditions underlies all his work, providing cohesion and supporting his belief in a unity of culture. Through his use of heroic figures and Irish folklore, he hoped to encourage familiarity with legends and awaken interest in Ireland's history. There are recurring figures in his poems: *the Sidhe*, the fairy folk; *Maeve*, the fairy queen buried in Sligo; *Niamh*, who led Oisin on a chase; *Aengus*, the master of love who carries a hazel rod and has four birds about his head; the valiant *Cuchulain*, the nephew of Conchubar, the cunning king of Ulster; *Fergus*, the heroic fighter and lover. These become symbols in Yeats's verse for the heroic Ireland of the past, a land quite different from the Ireland Yeats now believed was approaching a cataclysmic end.

The key lies in the oppositions of light and dark, chaos and order. For Yeats, at the heart of existence lies tension: between body and soul, flesh and spirit, love and hate, good and evil, dream and reality. In a world of change, an understanding of the relationship between these is crucial – good is meaningless without evil, love is unsatisfying if it does not include the physical as well as the spiritual. In moments of insight we can see this and even chaos is then underpinned by order.

A similar tension underpins Yeats's attitude to the arts. While believing in the importance of the aristocratic class as patrons and intellectual leaders, he also saw the disenfranchised beggar as a source of artistic inspiration. Representing the rejection of restrictive middle-class values, and the promotion of 'real' language and the raw energy of life, Yeats saw in the beggar material to be shaped by the artist.

Although Yeats accepted the miracles of the Christian faith, he did not believe that Christianity could reveal the hidden pattern of life. He also disliked its tendency to reject the personal – something he saw as crucial to the artist. His life was, however, inextricably linked to the spiritual, and his belief in magic and the occult was central.

Rejecting traditional systems of belief, he created his own complex vision in which the physical world is paralleled by an active spiritual world that influences our lives and is the source of the underlying pattern in the chaos of modern life. The system that Yeats developed in *A Vision* is helpful in understanding many of his poems since he often uses it symbolically. Yeats represented his ideas diagrammatically as two interlocking cones that he called Gyres. While the *Primary gyre* is basically physical, the *Antithetical gyre* is primarily spiritual. It is crucial to Yeats's theory that they are interlocked and that each affects the other to varying degrees. They are, for Yeats, *stylistic arrangements of experience* representing central juxtapositions in life: moon/sun, spiritual/physical, emotions/facts, the artist/moral man, the objective/the subjective. The age, the individual and the nation are made up of such antithetical elements and the system allowed Yeats to find pattern underlying everything.

He refined this system in his metaphor of the Great Wheel divided by 28 spokes that represented distinct phases of the moon, basic personality types, incarnations of man, phases of a single life, and the historical cycle. Antithetical elements face each other on the wheel, symbolising the opposing forces at the heart of life. One revolution takes approximately 2000 years and ends in chaos followed by an age quite different from the last.

Content and themes

The wide-ranging content of Yeats's verse reflects the breadth of his interests and reading. The interrelationship between politics, the occult, history, mythology, and his own personal life forms the basis for poetic reflections that seek to redefine life and its meaning. References to mythological figures, to classical writers, to historical events, and to both Eastern and Western religions shape the poetic language he uses. His aim was to evoke a distinctive emotional response in his reader through a content that is rooted in the physical here-and-now and yet speculates about the mystical 'other' world.

Because of the **personal or autobiographical** content of Yeats's poetry, it is useful to know something about his life and the people who were important to him. In the poem 'Friends' (*Responsibilities*), Yeats honours the

> Three women that have wrought
> What joy is in my days   (ll.2–3)

He establishes their place in his life, and their role in helping him to define his 'self'. His literary discussions with Olivia Shakespear are remembered in the reference to the interactions between *Mind and delighted mind*; Lady Gregory is praised for the way in which she changed Yeats, leaving him able to *live/Labouring in ecstasy*; and the *eagle look* of Maud Gomme can still stir his *heart's root*, making him *shake from head to foot*.

Poems relating to Lady Gregory frequently combine Yeats's personal gratitude to her with a celebration of her role as a patron of the arts. He uses the Coole estate and its surrounding landscape as a physical backdrop against which reflective meditations can be played out – the seven woods of the title poem in *In the Seven Woods*; the wild swans in the lake at Coole Park; and Yeats's Ballylee tower. In 'Coole Park, 1929' (*The Winding Stair*), he honours the *dance-like glory that those walls begot* under the guidance of *a woman's powerful character*. He uses the concept of five very different visitors all interested in the arts to emphasise the range of Lady Gregory's influence. The final image of the ruined house is juxtaposed with the *laurelled head* of Lady Gregory, who Yeats believes should be remembered in a *moment's memory* for her work.

The poems linked to Maud Gomme, a passionate nationalist whom Yeats had loved and courted unsuccessfully for more than thirteen years, tend to be love poems. Despite the often almost colloquial tone, she is deified: in 'A Woman Homer Sung' (*The Green Helmet and Other Poems*, 1910), Yeats determines to paint her portrait to immortalise her; in 'No Second Troy' (*The Green Helmet and Other Poems*), she is seen as the unparalleled mythological Helen.

In the collection of poems *A Man Young and Old* (*The Tower*), Yeats considers love as it is experienced by the young and the old. The first four poems represent young love. Maud Gomme is the cold lady, the moon goddess, who drives away her lovers after draining them, just as the light of the moon diminishes the stars. The *mermaid* of poem III is Diana Vernon, a name Yeats borrowed from Scott's *Rob Roy* for his unpublished autobiography to conceal the identity of Olivia Shakespear. The juxtaposition of verbs like *laughed* with *drown* and the oxymoron *cruel happiness* mirror the nature of their relationship. The next poems, by contrast, are those of the old man reflecting on lost opportunities, culminating in poem XI, which represents a freedom from youthful memories as the old man moves towards an acceptance of death.

In the same volume, 'The Gift of Harun Al-Rashid' celebrates Yeats's relationship with his wife as an ideal in which love is no longer an obsession. The poem works as an allegory charting the nature of the marriage and the automatic writing that was to form the basis for *A Vision*. Where in the eighth poem of *A Man Young and Old*, Yeats described his love of Maud Gomme as *a blossoming*, he now describes his relationship with Georgie Hyde Lees as one that can

> Shake more blossom from an autumnal chill
> Than all my bursting springtime knew.   ('The Gift', ll.111–12)

As a general topic, **love** is treated in a variety of ways. Some poems are celebratory and Yeats offers his lover gifts: of rhymes in 'He gives his Beloved certain Rhymes' (*The Wind Among the Reeds*); of his dreams in 'He wishes for the Cloths of Heaven' (*The Wind Among the Reeds*). In others, he marks the changing or passing of love: 'Never Give all the Heart' (*In the Seven Woods*); 'Broken Dreams' (*The Wild Swans at Coole*). The 'Crazy Jane' poems (*Words for Music Perhaps*, 1932), on the other hand, deal with physical love.

Yeats also deals with **universal subjects** in his poetry: life and death, the sacrifice of youth, old age. These ideas all come together in the poems focusing on the death of Robert Gregory, Lady Gregory's son, who was killed in action on the Italian front in 1918. The content of 'In Memory of Major Robert Gregory' (*The Wild Swans at Coole*) is very personal, but Yeats moves beyond the individual death to a general consideration of the death of young heroes. Robert Gregory becomes a symbol for the waste of youth's potential as Yeats catalogues his dead friends and their qualities. The repetition of *Soldier, scholar, horseman* celebrates Gregory's life, while the power of the last line leaves only silence as a possible response to such a waste of life.

Yeats also addresses contemplation of his own survival in a world where young men like Robert Gregory die – the emphasis is on the **wisdom of old age**, something Robert Gregory will never be given the opportunity to experience. In 'The Tower', Yeats addresses what it means to be old, when *Decrepit age* has become *A sort of battered kettle at the heel*. In such poems as 'The Wheel', 'Youth and Age' and 'The New Faces', Yeats suggests that with old age comes an acceptance of death, a *longing for the tomb* ('The Wheel'), when *night can outbalance day* ('The New Face').

As well as using personal references to reflect on the nature of life, Yeats also draws on the **political**. He sees Ireland as a nation troubled by the violence of events in its contemporary history. Many of the poems in *Responsibilities* reveal a Yeats disillusioned with politics and politicians – his hopes for an Ireland united politically and culturally had come to nothing. The poem written after the Easter Rising in Dublin, 'Easter 1916' (*Michael Robartes and the Dancer*), is an account of Yeats's reaction to the 5-day occupation of Dublin by the Irish Republican Brotherhood. As a result, 15 of the leaders were sentenced and executed. It became a symbol for Yeats of the violence of the age, and of Ireland's failure to achieve political and cultural unity

In *The Tower*, after 'Sailing to Byzantium', there are a sequence of poems dealing with the Irish troubles. 'Meditations in Time of Civil War' and 'Nineteen Hundred and Nineteen' focus on the political violence taking place in Ireland at the time Yeats was writing. After the signing of the Anglo-Irish treaty in London (December 1921), and its acceptance by the Irish parliament (January 1922), the Republicans led by Eamon de Valera (1882–1975) refused to accept the treaty and civil war broke out. 'Meditations in Time of Civil War', considers both past and present violence. The tone is marked by the repetition of *bitter* and *bitterness* in the first section ('Ancestral Houses'). Images of *loosening masonry*, of empty houses and the *dead young soldier in his blood* in section VI ('The Stare's Nest by My Window'), remind us of the dreadful uncertainties of war.

For Yeats, the age is clearly one of **violence and destruction** and this is another subject that recurs in the content of his poetry. His vision of the future is played out in 'The Second Coming' (*Michael Robartes and the Dancer*). It marks the end of Yeats's 2000-year cycle and, as the gyres reverse, prophesies the birth of a new and even more violent age. The language of the poem is negative: *ceremony* is juxtaposed with *anarchy*; the repetition of the passive *is loosed* suggests an unidentified and uncontrollable power overwhelming civilisation; and the *revelation* of the *Second Coming* is ironic. As he writes in 'Meru' (*A Full Moon in March*), civilisation is but *hooped together . . . under the semblance of peace*. The apparent order of society is a *manifold illusion* that is soon broken to reveal the *desolation of reality*.

Yeats's poems often address the **nature of the poet** and the **art of poetry** as a subject. 'A Coat' (*Responsibilities*) deals with the way in which the public world can imitate and corrupt a poet's *song*, wearing it and believing *they'd wrought it*. 'The Scholars' (*The Wild Swans at Coole*) distinguishes between the passionate young men who *tossing on their beds/Rhymed out in love's despair* and the dispassionate *Old learned, respectable* scholars who *edit and annotate*.

Underlying all the autobiographical, political and literary references is Yeats's belief in the **pattern underlying life**. His symbolic gyres represent the opposition at the heart of life and human nature – an opposition he saw as fundamental to existence. In 'The Phases of the Moon' (*The Wild Swans of Coole*), Aherne and Robartes discuss the characteristics of the phases Yeats had outlined in *A Vision*. 'Byzantium' (*The Winding Stair*) focuses on the 'dreaming back' that takes place in Yeats's system when an individual is freed from the reincarnations of life. His images of the golden bird of *changeless metal* and of the dance that drives away *all complexities of fury* represent the moment at which the confusions of human life can be overcome.

The thematic structure of Yeats's poetry is closely linked to the kind of subject matter he addresses. The themes of youth, age and death are broached through autobiographical material relating to key moments in Yeats's life. The theme of violence and the search for an underlying order can be seen in the focus on politics, the nature of the age Yeats was living in, and in poetic explanations of the systems he had created to explain reality and its hidden patterns. The theme of the poet and poetry is tackled through poems addressing the arts and art patronage, the nature of the poetic process and the role of the poet in society. Often these themes do not occur in isolation but co-exist, and it is important to understand the ways in which they interrelate.

Different themes dominate in different volumes and although the poems are not always placed chronologically in terms of the date they were written, their location is an indication of Yeats's interests at the time. *The Wild Swans of Coole* and the collections before it focus on themes of **youth**, **love**, **age and ageing**, **death**, **time** and the apparently **illusory pattern in life**. In the title poem, the juxtaposition of the ageing Yeats with the swans whose *hearts have not grown old* is central. The swans are *Unwearied still* and become symbols of the eternal. The repetition of *still* in the noun phrases *still sky* and *still water* links them directly to the elemental: they are of the earth (*water*) and therefore mortal, and yet they are of the ethereal (*sky*) and therefore immortal. The use of a verb like *wheeling* and a noun like *rings* links their existence to the pattern of eternity established in Yeats's system of gyres. The questions he reflects on here become increasingly common in his work.

The volumes from *Michael Robartes and the Dancer* to *A Full Moon in March* are dominated by the themes of **violence and the search for order**. They reflect Yeats's despair at the violence and disorder he saw around him and his explication of the pattern underlying reality. The recurring strand can be seen in his juxtaposition of personal happiness (his marriage, the birth of his children, and literary recognition) with what he saw as uncontrollable violence. Increasingly he was to see modern Ireland as *no country for old men* ('Sailing to Byzantium', *The Tower*). The disorder of civil war and Yeats's alienation as the prophet are represented in 'Meditations in Time of Civil War'. The war imagery is dominated by negative language: adjectives such as *empty, violent, desolate*; abstract nouns like *violence, adversity, aimlessness, uncertainty*. The intensity builds towards Section VII where the compound modifiers *rage-driven, rage-tormented, and rage-hungry* reinforce the horror of what is happening.

Yeats is isolated in the middle of the *indifferent multitude*, aware of *the Coming Emptiness*. The values of artistic order that he upholds are represented by the *changeless sword* and the *changeless work of art*. These are, however, unable to overcome the chaos. In 'Parnell's Funeral' (*A Full Moon in March*), disorder similarly overcomes a political hero who is destroyed by *popular rage*. He too is an isolated man in an Ireland dominated by *the contagion of the throng*.

In the *Last Poems*, Yeats concentrates on **art and the artist** and the **pattern** that can be found even in chaos. 'The Gyres' introduces the dominant theme: the certainty that the gyres will be reversed. This can be seen in the emphatic use of the modal *shall* and in the juxtaposition of *numb nightmare* and *Rejoice!* The artist is now a spectator, able to observe and shape events – and thus able to control them despite the disorder. Similar themes are developed in 'Lapis Lazuli': the cyclical rise and fall of civilisations; the sense that an age is coming to an end; and the victory of art and philosophy over chaos. The artist is represented as a 'creator', confident in his knowledge of the cycle.

> All things fall and are built again,
> And those that build them again are gay.   (ll.35–6)

When he can reach beyond modern degeneration to the underlying pattern that his art reveals, he is distanced from reality and its instability. In recognising the inner unchanging light, the *magnanimity of light* as he calls it in 'A Bronze Head', the artist can rise above external changes.

Style

The style of Yeats's work also changes from volume to volume. Read chronologically, it is possible to see the ways in which he was experimenting. In his earliest work, the language is often romantic and haunting, dominated by Irish folklore. Later reworkings aimed to make his language more natural. By the publication of *In the Seven Woods*, his stated aim was to *bring a less dream-burdened will* to his verse. This can be seen in the more matter-of-fact diction and his movement towards the conversational. The transitional volume *The Green Helmet and Other Poems* shows Yeats's verse being stripped of all decorative language, and drawing on everyday conversation as a unifying register. By using a common language, he hoped to ensure a wide circulation for his sometimes abstruse theories.

The tone is directly linked to the kind of language Yeats uses. The dramatised conversation first appearing in poems like 'Adam's Curse' was to be a characteristic form to which he returned again and again: 'Beggar to Beggar Cried' (*Responsibilities*), 'The Phases of the Moon' (*The Wild Swans at Coole*), the 'Crazy Jane' poems (*Words for Music Perhaps*), 'Parting' (*A Woman Young and Old*), 'The Man and the Echo (*Last Poems*).

In other poems, the conversational tone engages the reader in a kind of dialogue. This can be seen in the introduction to 'In Memory of Major Robert Gregory' (*The Wild Swans at Coole*) where Yeats considers the nature of friendship, or in 'In Memory of Eva Gore-Booth and Con Markiewicz' (*The Winding Stair*) where we are almost invited to eavesdrop upon the scene. His last poem 'Under Ben Bulben' uses the same kind of easy conversational diction – it is an elegy for his own death, defining his convictions and recording his epitaph.

Yeats's use of the mask can distance him from his content, making the tone more objective and avoiding sentimentality. It allows him to put his personal material into a more public form by using a symbolic antithetical self. He first began to experiment and to use the term 'mask' in his writings between 1900 and 1910. It functions on a number of levels: as a social front, as a defence against the world, or as a heroic ideal self. He was to define the concept in *A Vision* as *the image of what we wish to become*, the opposite, or anti-self.

'Ego Dominus Tuus' (*The Wild Swans at Coole*) is directly concerned with the mask. Two characters debate the nature of 'self' and the modern world: *Hic* is *primary* man; *Ille* is *antithetical* man. While *Hic* is objective, associated with the body and the moon, *Ille* is subjective, associated with the soul and the sun. Their quests are quite different: *Hic* searches for *[him]self and not an image*; *Ille* searches for his opposite in *an image* – the antithetical mask that will lead him to an understanding of his true nature. He knows that when he finds *the mysterious one* who is *indeed [his] double*, his *anti-self*, he will find *All that [he] seek[s]*.

Yeats uses linguistic patterning to reinforce his message. Recurring words, parallel structures and refrains provide cohesion and underpin the thematic structure. In the early volume *Wind Among the Reeds*, he is already experimenting with balanced phrases, repetition and sentence structure. 'He remembers Forgotten Beauty', for instance, is constructed of one long compound-complex sentence. The main clauses . . . *I press/My heart* . . . *And* . . ./*I hear* relating to Yeats' actions in the present are embedded in a sequence of phrases and subordinate clauses remembering past beauty. The language is romantic, recreating a medieval world of *jewelled crowns, kings* and *armies*. Alongside this, is the world of fairytales created with noun phrases such as *love-tales, dreaming ladies, white Beauty*. The sequence of pre- and post-modified noun phrases in the first half of the poem (*the loveliness/That . . ., The jewelled crowns that . . ., The love-tales wrought . . ., The roses that . . ., The dew-cold lilies [that] . . .*) intensifies the first image of the beauty of Yeats's lover through comparisons with the past.

The second half, describing the lover's *pale breast and lingering hand*, is more haunting and this is created through the linguistic patterning, perhaps reminiscent of the structure of fairytales. Repetition of the compound modifier *dream-heavy* sets the tone, while the repetition of *sigh/sighing* and *kiss* reinforces the content and the links with romance. The parallel structures *flame on flame, deep on deep, Throne over throne* give the poem an air of order and suggest the contentment of the lover at this point in time.

Refrains and functional repetition are common in Yeats's work. While adding to the lyrical qualities of the verse, they also underpin meaning by highlighting key concepts and words. In *The Wild Swans at Coole*, for instance, echoes of phrases recur from poem to poem, marking his interest in age and his consciousness of the effects of time. In 'The Living Beauty' and 'A Song', refrains like *O heart, we are old* and *the heart grows old* remind us of such themes. The repetition used in 'An Irish Airman Foresees his Death' creates a monotonous rhythm mirroring, perhaps, the inevitability of what is about to happen. Exact repetition of such clauses as *Those that I . . . I do not . . .* and the phrases *waste of breath/A waste of breath* are reinforced by echoed words scattered throughout the poem (*fight, clouds, years, waste, balanced/balance*). The linguistic patterning underpins the meaning, allowing Yeats to reinforce the climactic parallelism of the final line where *this life* is juxtaposed so bleakly with *this death*.

Metrical patterns also play an important part in the patterning of Yeats's verse. In a poem like 'The Second Coming', changes in the basic iambic pattern are used to underpin the meaning. The two dactylic feet in the opening line draw attention to Yeats's idea of the historical cycle he sees coming to its end in the poem.

Tŭrnĭng ănd | túrnĭng ĭn | thĕ wíde | nĭng gýre.

Similarly, the use of a spondee in the middle of a line emphasises the collapse of order and authority in an unstable and violent age.

Thĕ blóod | -dímmed tíde | ĭs loósed, | ănd éve | rŷwhére . . .

The metrical change in the final line places emphasis upon the verb *Slouches* in the initial position. Its connotations are crucial in terms of the meaning of the poem: it enhances the concept of the *rough beast*, and develops the contrast between the birth of Christ and this *Second Coming*.

Ănd whát | roúgh beást, | ĭts hóur | cŏme roúnd | ăt lást,
Sloúchĕs tŏ | wárds Bĕthlĕ | hém tŏ bĕ | bórn?   (ll.21–2)

The change here from iambic pentameter to dactylic trimeter with the additional stress at the end of the line slows the pace and adds to the fearful anticipation of the coming age.

Imagery and symbolism

Yeats uses recurring images to underpin his themes. They provide internal cohesion by reinforcing the external framework of verse form, rhyme and rhythm. In addition, they link poems within a volume by providing a common thread between sometimes disparate work. The images are directly linked to the physical – particularly the natural world. They give the ordinary and obvious an importance that heightens our awareness of experience. Yeats once described himself as *the last of the Romantics*, and despite his very 'modern' approach to poetry, his link with the nineteenth-century poets is clear.

The use of images as a symbolic representation of his message, however, links Yeats with the French symbolists. His poems are often representative of a moment in time and the symbols within them can be linked to a number of possible meanings on both a literal and an associative level. The reader must be active, therefore, considering the range of possibilities and their effect on the poems' meanings. Although he often provides glosses, Yeats believed that the *meaning may be different for everyone*, and that a poet should avoid interpreting his work so that he did not *limit its suggestibility*.

Although the images and symbols change as Yeats's work progresses, some remain constant. Images of trees and birds appear throughout the work, while others like the sea and water become less important. In the later work, architectural images are used to underpin the thematic structure and to mirror the nature of the age. The study of magic also gives him an inexhaustible supply of images that was later to be supplemented by his own work *A Vision*.

In *The Wind Among the Reeds*, Yeats establishes imagery that will recur in his later work. Here, the dominant references are to **water**, which Yeats was to describe as: . . . *everywhere the signature of the fruitfulness of the body, and of the fruitfulness of dreams*. Drawing on elemental forces, he sees the sea as an image of life itself: *a symbol of the drifting indefinite bitterness of life*; and the wind as *a symbol of vague desires and hopes*.

The middle period is marked by a change of tone. In 'All Things Can Tempt me', Yeats writes of the way in which he wishes his verse to change. The poetic process should no longer be a song sung *with such airs*, but an *accustomed toil* marked by verse that is *Colder and dumber and deafer than a fish*. The imagery of the poems during this period is no longer romantic, but **elemental**, **classical** and **visionary**.

The same images recur, but they seem less positive. In 'Red Hanrahan's Song about Ireland' (*In the Seven Woods*), the modifiers *bitter*, *black* and *wet* are used to represent the wind that blows over a sorrowful Ireland. In 'The Coming of Wisdom with Time' (*The Green Helmet and other Poems*), the *leaves and flowers* of the tree are now symbolic of the youth that must die. Just as the poet must *wither* into old age, so too will the *leaves and flowers* fade, leaving only the *root* as *one* and unchanging. The root becomes symbolic of *truth* – the knowledge of mortality.

The image of the **mask** appears at this time in 'The Mask' (*The Green Helmet and Other Poems*). It was to have an ongoing influence on Yeats and can be linked to his interest in the theatrical as a source of images. In 'Never Give all the heart' (*In the Seven Woods*), he had already explored the idea of the lover playing a part and 'The Mask' develops this.

In *Responsibilities*, recurring images are accompanied by an increasing interest in the **visionary**. Birds are again present as symbols of freedom and immortality. We see them in 'The Cold Heaven' as *delighting* in their medium – they create like artists and their songs communicate with God. 'The Magi' introduces a new key symbol through the image of the Magi *In their stiff, painted clothes*. It is the first poem in which Yeats was to convey the ideas that would later form the basis of *A Vision*. The cyclical pattern of history and Yeats's belief that the Christian revelation was not final are evident in the embedded language patterns. Adverb phrases like *as at all times* and *once more*, the parallelism of *Appear and disappear*, and the functional repetition of *And all their . . .* become external markers of the cyclical pattern represented in the content.

In the later period, Yeats's work is increasingly focused on the concepts underlying *A Vision*. Recurring images like those of the bird still appear, but their meaning is broadened. In 'The Hawk' (*The Wild Swans at Coole*), for instance, each stanza is voiced by a different figure so that three viewpoints combine to make the hawk a symbol. On a basic level, it is representative of the practical life and the freedom associated with birds in earlier poems. Yeats's final stanza, however, addresses the hawk as a symbol of the difficulties the artist encounters living in the world. The swans of the title poem are reminiscent of those in 'The Cold Heaven' – they are representatives of immortality *wheeling in great broken rings*, *Unwearied* and ageless.

A new image – the **dancer** – is used in 'The Double Vision of Michael Robartes' to symbolise the artist's vision of order in a chaotic world. Underpinning the poem are references to Yeats's lunar phases: in the first section, *the old moon is vanished from the sky* in Phase 1; in the second, *the moon's light* is *at its fifteenth night*; and in Section III, we are *caught between the pull/ of the dark moon and the full*. The first stage is symbolic of a physical life in a disordered world where everything is *Constrained, arraigned, baffled, bent and unbent*; the second is representative of the life of the soul in a vision of elemental order where the girl has *outdanced thought* and *Body perfection brought*; the third stage presents the human world of inescapable opposition where understanding can only be momentary. The dance becomes symbolic of the moment at which soul overcomes body, and the mundane is replaced by vision.

The content in *Michael Robartes and the Dancer* is often **political** and in a poem like 'Easter 1916' Yeats uses natural images (*a stone, the living stream*) to represent the central juxtaposition of constancy versus change. After the Easter Rising, Yeats believed that everything had been changed by the violence and that *A terrible beauty [had been]born*. The repeated oxymoron is symbolic of the martyrdom of the leaders shot by the British – they may have transformed Ireland by their actions, but they had also created something terrifying.

The central image of change has a different field of reference in the third stanza. While the repetition of the verb *changed* and the use of synonyms like *transformed* have ambiguous connotations in stanzas 1–2, the image of the unchanging stone in the stream in the third stanza appears to suggest inner strength and single-mindedness. It is symbolic of the way in which the nationalists' focus, their *one purpose alone*, has disturbed the course of life. Its static, unchangeable nature, however, is deceptive as the carefully patterned long complex sentence of the stanza indicates. The nature of life itself is mirrored in the sentence structure and in the repetition of the phrase *minute by minute*, which emphasises the contrast between the *living stream* and the *hearts . . ./Enchanted to stone*. The natural world is seen to be full of movement and part of the natural flux of life. It is linked to dynamic present tense verbs (*slides*, *plashes*, *dive*, *call*) that build to the climax of the simple clause *they live*, while the stone remains unmoving and unmoved by all that goes on around it.

The final stanza once again focuses on the stone: while *Hearts . . ./Enchanted to a stone* suggests a state that can be reversed, the *sacrifice* that *Can make a stone of the heart* seems to be symbolic of a permanent condition. The language clearly implies that the nationalists' intentions are good (*We know their dream*; *excess of love*), but these positives are set against the ambiguous verbs (*dreamed*; *bewildered*) and the repetition of *dead/died*. Their single-minded purpose has ultimately reduced them to feelingless, bitter representatives of a political principle that is detached from the living and therefore from the human capacity to feel.

In *The Tower*, the dominant images are symbolic of sterility, but references to towers, trees, birds and dancers recur. The first poem 'Sailing to Byzantium' sets the tone: the imagery juxtaposes the natural physical world with the concept of old age. Despite our awareness of life and its power in the listing of *The young . . . birds . . . salmon-falls, mackerel-crowded seas*, the overriding emphasis is upon the cycle that will inevitably bring death. References to *dying generations* and the tripling of *begotten, born, and dies* underpin Yeats's emphasis on the tension between life and death.

Beyond the tension of this *sensual music*, however, Yeats sees a constancy in *Monuments of unageing intellect*. *Byzantium* is used as a symbol of an ideal world where the intellectual, aesthetic and practical lives are part of one integrated culture. References to the *aged man* as *a paltry thing/A tattered coat upon a stick* are replaced by descriptions of artistic beauty – the repetition of *gold* and *golden* emphasises artistic perfection. The knowledge of mortality is replaced by *the artifice of eternity*, the beauty of art overcomes the passage of time, and the soul is more important than the body. The final image is of a bird *Of hammered gold and gold enamelling*, singing *Of what is past, or passing, or to come*. As a symbol of immortality, it represents unchanging perfection since it is *out of nature* and distinct from the *dying generations*; as a symbol of consolation, however, it is artificial and emotionless. The complexity of the poem lies in this duality – although art is perfect and beautiful, it can never really be a substitute for life.

Other new symbols appear in this volume: the **tower** rooted in earth and yet pointing to the skies – references to 'monuments' as symbols of the past are also common; and the **sword** and its covering of silk representative of the unchanging nature of art in a transient world.

The Winding Stair functions as a companion volume to *The Tower* and this can be seen in the kind of images Yeats chooses. Where images of sterility recur in the earlier collection, *The Winding Stair* draws on images of sexuality and regeneration. The symbolism is cohesive and references to the natural world are linked to reflections on life. In 'Coole Park and Ballylee 1931', images of water, trees, and the white swans form the physical backdrop against which Yeats can reflect on death, creativity, the past, and the kind of literature he and his friends believed in. The underground stream running between the Ballylee tower and the Coole estate becomes a symbol, an *emblem*, for the soul on its journey through life from darkness to light; the *mounting swan* is a symbol for the soul which *sails into the sight/And in the morning's gone*; and the *ancestral trees* and *gardens rich in memory* are symbolic of the rich aristocratic past of Coole.

The sword as a symbol of vitality and changeless life appears again in 'A Dialogue of Self and Soul' along with a new image – the **winding stairs** – used by Yeats to symbolise escape from life towards the afterlife promised at the end of the soul's journey through the opposing gyres.

In 'Byzantium', Yeats draws on the same images used in 'Sailing to Byzantium', but they are now in reverse order. Leaving behind the world of flesh and blood, *The fury and the mire of human veins*, in stanza 1, the images focus on first the *Miracle* golden bird (stanza 3), then the flames of purgatory (stanza 4) and finally the spirits crossing the sea (stanza 5). It is a poem about the making of images and Yeats symbolises the process of creativity as a *dance/An agony of trance* in which the confusions of life, *blood-begotten*, become the source of inspiration.

While drawing on the images and symbols of the earlier work, *Last Poems* uses distinctive images of climbing to represent the movement towards self-fulfilment and the freedom from life's oppositions. In 'Lapis Lazuli', the Chinamen of the final stanza climb towards their goal, *the little half-way house*, from which they can contemplate the *tragic scene* of the world; in 'High Talk', the speaker looks down on the world from his high stilts. Many of the last poems such as 'The Gyres', 'A Model for the Laureate' and 'The Old Stone Cross' reflect on the nature of life and modern degradation. Recurring images of darkness and the mysterious world of dreams are common ('The Wild Old Wicked Man', 'To Dorothy Wellesley' and 'The Statues').

Structure

For Yeats, the power of a poem was created through the interaction and arrangement of its elements, and constant revision enabled him to ensure that such structural organisation functioned across his work as a whole.

Despite the laborious process of drafting, writing and revising, Yeats desired his verse to have an *accidental look* that concealed the precision with which each poem and each volume was structured. Recurring images and the underlying focus on the framework of *A Vision* provided an internal structure for individual poems, while Yeats's interest in Blake's antithetical *Songs of Innocence and Experience* provided an overall structure for many of the volumes. It gave Yeats a method for linking groups of lyrics and reinforced his belief in the opposing forces underpinning life.

Often the poems within a volume are arranged in a distinctive way so that their order influences the way in which the reader understands them. *The Green Helmet and Other Poems* opens with two public poems, which frame the following sequence of very personal conversational works. *Responsibilities* uses the title as its key to the structure and this can be seen clearly in Yeats's own working plan for the volume. He opens with 'Pardon, Old Fathers' and 'The Grey Rock' addressing the idea of *Supernatural responsibilities*; moves to *social responsibilities* in poems about the Lane pictures and the riots associated with performances of Synge's *The Playboy of the Western World*; addresses *The function of irresponsibility* in the 'beggar' poems; considers *Personal responsibilities* in 'Friends' and the poems addressing Maud Gomme and her daughter Iseult; and concludes with *Aesthetic responsibilities* in supernatural poems like 'The Magi' and poems like 'A Coat' where he addresses the nature of literature.

The Wild Swans at Coole uses a group of personal poems about the death of Lady Gregory's son as a preface to observations on old age and a formal elegy on a young man's death. A group of 'mask' poems then consider love and death, and the volume concludes with six poems directly linked to Yeats's visionary system. The movement from death to life, and the patterns underlying death and life dictate the overall framework. Yeats's conscious organisation of his work can be seen in the fact that he omitted some poems written at the time because they did not fit into the structure he had established for the volume.

Sometimes the overriding structure extends beyond the boundaries of one volume. In writing *The Winding Stair*, Yeats was consciously providing a counterbalance to his previous volume *The Tower*. Each volume develops an opposing point of view: where the poems of *The Tower* tend to be political and pessimistic, the poems of *The Winding Stair* tend to be aesthetic and optimistic. The group of poems titled *A Woman Young and Old* (*The Winding Stair*) are to be read as an antidote to *A Man Young and Old* (*The Tower*). While the tone of the first more public volume tends to be marked by bitterness and disillusion, the later more personal volume tends to be reflective, ending with a final affirmation and acceptance of life.

In addition to this external framework, many of Yeats's poems are themselves intricately structured. He uses a range of forms. 'Leda and the Swan' (*The Tower*), for instance, is a sonnet using an octave and a sestet to juxtapose the shift in emotions. In the first two quatrains, Leda is vulnerable and terrified while Zeus is passionate; in the sestet, Leda is *caught up* in the moment while Zeus is *indifferent*. This inverted pattern is reinforced by the metre where the predominantly iambic pattern is disrupted by anapaestic feet at key points:

> Above | the stag | gĕrinğ girl, | hĕr thighs | cǎressed . . .
> Thĕ fea | thĕred glo | rỹ from | hĕr loos | eñninğ thighs . . .
> Before | the ĭn diff | ĕreñt beak | could let | hĕr drop.   (ll.2/6/14)

Some poems adopt the form of conversations using either the conventional marking of direct speech ('The Mask', *The Green Helmet*) or the conventions of the playscript ('The Phases of the Moon', *The Wild Swans at Coole*). Others use rhyming couplets – 'Why Should Not Old Men be Mad?' (*Last Poems*) juxtaposes the unpredictability of life with the tight ordered patterning of the rhyme. 'Coole Park and Ballylee' (*The Winding Stair*) uses ottava rima, 8-line stanzas traditionally rhyming ababbcc, but adapted by Yeats to follow a pattern of ababacdd.

For some critics, Yeats's elegies are the best written this century: 'In Memory of Major Robert Gregory' celebrates the young man's skills and mourns his untimely death; 'All Souls Night' celebrates three friends from Yeats's youth; 'The Municipal Gallery Revisited' pays tribute to memorable individuals.

Beneath the apparent simplicity of Yeats's poetry lies a recognition of the complexity underlying life – oppositions and intricate patterns provide the complex structure that mirrors our passage through Yeats's interlocking gyres. His skill lies in the juxtaposition of this complexity with his use of the language that *comes most naturally when we soliloquise.*

Yeats and the English poetic tradition

Critics easily categorised Yeats's early work as Celtic and mystical. Not all were aware, however, of the significance of the new style emerging with the publication of *Responsibilities* in 1914. Ezra Pound's review of the new volume clearly identified the movement towards a greater realism in both content and style, and his comments mark a key point in the criticism of Yeats's work.

After his death in 1939, there was a growing critical interest in his poetry. In particular, critics began to explore the relationship between his life and his art, but there was also interest in his use of the occult, politics, classical references and symbolism. On the whole, critical response is mainly positive, recognising his position as a key figure in the developments of Modern poetry in the first half of the twentieth century.

His use of Irish traditional material and his own private symbols can make the poems difficult to read, but Yeats himself provided glosses of his references and sources, and critics have elaborated upon these. While knowing something of Yeats's life can help readers, a chronological approach to reading his work is perhaps equally important since the emergence and reiteration of key references and images illuminates his central themes and their development.

Activity 13.3

What do we learn about Yeats's view of the world in 'Meru' (from 'Supernatural Songs', *A Full Moon in March*), and how does he communicate his ideas to the reader?

You may like to think about: the poem's context and its ideas, the poetic form, the rhythm and metre, the language, the sentence structure, the use of patterning and the images.

Meru
1   Civilisation is hooped together, brought
     Under a rule, under the semblance of peace
     By manifold illusion; but man's life is thought,
     And he, despite his terror, cannot cease

5   Ravening through century after century,
     Ravening, raging, and uprooting that he may come
     Into the desolation of reality:
     Egypt and Greece, good-bye, and good-bye, Rome!
     Hermits upon Mount Meru or Everest,
10   Caverned in night under the drifted snow,
     Or where that snow and winter's dreadful blast
     Beat down upon their naked bodies, know
     That day brings round the night, that before dawn
     His glory and his monuments are gone.

Commentary

The context in which this poem was written tells us much about the way that Yeats was thinking about the world in the 1930s. In 1931, he had made the acquaintance of an Indian Swami, Shri Purohit, and learnt much about Eastern philosophy. He was particularly interested in the concept of the individual 'self' who is responsible for the creation of the past and the future through personal action; and in the quest for self-knowledge that came in the highest moments of consciousness as the individual detaches himself from action and therefore knows his true identity. Just as an Indian holy man will attempt to divest himself of everything that impedes his journey towards self-knowledge, so for Yeats, the poet cuts away all that is inessential in his quest to find the source of reality.

In following the objectives of Eastern philosophy, Yeats sought, at this time, to create *impersonal poetry* that would be *sweet & exultant, a sort of European* Geeta, *or rather my* Geeta *not doctrine but song*. The result was a group of philosophical poems written in 1933 and 1934. 'Meru' is the twelfth poem in the sequence where Yeats abandons conventional morality and attitudes as he searches for an alternative pattern underpinning reality.

The subject matter and themes are typical of many of Yeats's poems as he tries to unravel what he sees as the complexities of modern life and searches for a pattern to bring order to the chaos. Although 'Meru' is a lyrical poem, it explores the world of violence Yeats sees around him, and tries to understand its origins. Recognising that man is driven by *thought*, he sees conflict as inevitable in the Western world and thus turns to an alternative. He displaces *Civilisation* and its organised systems of thought in favour of the life of the holy man who is at one with his environment and who recognises the ephemeral nature of the material world.

The use of the sonnet form is effective in bringing a tight structure to control and define the philosophical thought at the heart of the poem. Yeats uses the Shakespearean sonnet to shape his ideas and bring them to a climax in the final couplet. Where the first eight lines define the nature of civilisation governed by Western principles of thought, the following four lines define the alternative; the couplet then provides a climax in summarising the ultimate knowledge that comes with the highest moments of consciousness.

The end rhyme is typically Shakespearean in that it defines three quatrains and a couplet within the 14-line structure: abab cdcd efef gg. Yeats, however, does not divide the ideas of his first two quatrains into two distinctly different units, but creates a continuity that is mirrored in the run-on lines (ll.4–5): man, driven by his desire to 'know', cannot be stopped from creating chaos. This sense of restlessness and the destruction it causes is also conveyed by Yeats's use of the caesura. Rather than balancing the lines in two equal halves, Yeats either divides them unequally (ll.1–3) or uses more than one caesura (ll.4, 6). This reinforces the sense of disturbance created by the imagery.

The metrical patterns are similarly disrupted. Most lines have five stresses and are decasyllabic, but changes to this enable Yeats to draw attention to key concepts. The first lines, for instance, use mainly dactyls and trochees to emphasise the strong visual image with which the poem begins.

Cíviliš | atiŏn iš | hoóped tŏ | géthĕr | broúght
Undĕ̌r | ă rulé | undĕ̌r thĕ̌e | sémblaňce ŏf | peáce   (ll.1–2)

In other cases, spondees provide consecutive stresses on mán's lífe (l.3), Moúnt Merŭ̌ (l.9) and Beát doẃn (l.12), highlighting for the reader lexical items of semantic importance. The lilting iambics of the final two lines, on the other hand, suggest the peace that comes with Yeats's recognition of the true nature of things.

The language is crucial to the poem's effect. The opening lines are dominated by abstract nouns that characterise its philosophical nature: *Civilisation* (l.1), *rule, peace* (l.2), *semblance, illusion* (l.3), *thought* (l.4), *terror* (l.5), *desolation, reality* (l.7). Distinct lexical sets emerge that underpin the point Yeats is making: nouns with connotations of control and harmony (*Civilisation/rule/peace/thought*) are juxtaposed with nouns that have negative connotations (*terror/desolation*). The two groups are held in a tenuous relationship by man's self-deception (*semblance/illusion*). This tentative grasp of reality is reinforced by the dynamic verbs *Ravening* (ll.5–6), *raging* and *uprooting* (l.6), which underpin the destructive rather than the harmonious lexical set. Yeats's use of present participles with their sense of ongoing action, the negative verb phrase *cannot cease* (l.4) and the prepositional phrase *through century after century* (l.5) emphasise the chaos of the modern world as Yeats sees it.

By contrast, the second half of the poem deals with the concrete and physical. Nouns like *Hermits* (l.9), *snow* (ll.10–11) and *bodies* (l.12) change the focus: the pace slows down and abstract *thought* is replaced by the elemental and natural. Where action in the first part of the poem is dictated by the directionless frenzy of man, here it is predictable and cyclical. The elements are portrayed as brutal in the noun phrase *winter's dreadful blast* (l.11) and the phrasal verb *Beat down* (l.12), but the holy men have achieved an understanding that comes from stillness and acceptance. The dynamic verb (*Beat down*) describes the movement of the natural world, not the hermits, who are linked only to the stative verb *know* (l.12). Their state of knowledge is directly linked to a detachment from the world of activity – they have reached a consciousness that extends beyond the individual self.

Yeats uses the grammatical structure of 'Meru' to underpin the meaning in a number of ways. The division of the sonnet into two distinct halves is mirrored in the two sentences of the poem. The first compound-complex sentence (ll.1–8) begins with the emphatic simple clause *Civilisation is hooped together* with its connotations of something bound into a shape that it could not hold independently. The passive voice (*is hooped . . . [is] brought/Under . . . [is brought] under . . .*) here is effective since it foregrounds the object of the sentence (*Civilisation*) and delays the subject, which appears as 'by + agent' at the end (*By manifold illusion*). This delay allows Yeats to create an image of order and control that he can then undermine, thus drawing attention to the central theme: man's activity is meaningless and the systems that order his life are illusory.

His argument is carefully structured through a sequence of clauses. The asyndetic listing of the three passive clauses (ll.1–2) suggests the thinly disguised disorder that will eventually overwhelm man's seemingly regulated life, but it is the contrastive conjunction (*but*, l.3) that consciously disturbs the uneasy balance of the opening. This potential for disorder is then intensified by the co-ordinating conjunction (*And*, l.4) and the following non-finite clauses (*Ravening . . ./ Ravening, raging, and uprooting*, ll.5–6). The first section of the poem builds to a climax with the exclamative minor sentence *Egypt and Greece, good-bye, and good-bye, Rome!* marking the poet's rejection of Western systems of thought.

The second complex sentence focuses our attention on an alternative: the wisdom of the East. Again Yeats manipulates the word order by separating the subject (*Hermits*, l.9) from the verb (*know*, l.12) with a sequence of adverbials of place (*upon Mount Meru or Everest* l.9, *under the drifted snow* l.10, *Where that snow . . . bodies* ll.11–12) and time (*Caverned in night*, l.10). When we finally reach the verb (l.12), its passivity is in direct contrast to the drama of the scene that has been created. The use of the present tense gives the poem a sense of immediacy that adds to the importance of the final two noun clauses (*That day . . . that before dawn . . .*, ll.13–14) in which Yeats professes the knowledge that he believes we should all recognise.

The poem ends with a grammatical ambiguity that reinforces its central theme. The possessive determiner *His* in the final line could be seen as an anaphoric reference to the main noun of the previous line (*day*, l.13), or it could be seen in a wider sense as a reference to 'man' at the beginning of the poem. In either case, it is a recognition of the ephemeral nature of life: either the metaphorical *glory* and *monuments* of day are concealed by night's darkness (*before dawn*); or the physical representations of civilisation are illusory and, as such, are symbolic of the meaninglessness of man's life. Perhaps Yeats intended shades of both interpretations to colour our reading of the poem – certainly we are left with an emphatic end where the certainty of the verbs (*brings/are gone*) reinforces the axiomatic nature of the 'truths' he reveals.

The imagery of the poem is both literal and figurative. The metaphor of the barrel with which the poem opens is immediately suggestive of a man-made creation that in staying together defies natural forces. This is underpinned by the tentative nature of the nouns *semblance* and *illusion* (ll.2–3). It is an image symbolic of impermanence, which prepares us for the negative images of man's literal (physical) and metaphorical (mental) *uprooting* – a fruitless activity that leads him no closer to *the desolation of reality* (l.7). As a 'thinking' animal, man is doomed to error because he continues to search in the world of things, which are by their very nature ephemeral, and fails to recognise the inescapable pattern of human events.

Many of the images are symbolic and Yeats uses them to underpin his central theme. *Egypt*, *Greece* and *Rome* (l.8) are symbolic of the ancient civilisations that are the source of Western thought. Reminiscent of his image of the barrel, Yeats sees them as a group of disparate cultures that have been bound indiscriminately together. *Mount Meru* and *Everest* (l.9) are symbolic of spiritual and physical achievement. Where Everest is the world's tallest mountain and therefore a physical challenge, Mount Meru is a mythical Hindu mountain of spiritual realisation. The physical and spiritual are brought together in the image of the hermits exposed on the mountain: their passive physical endurance opens their minds to spiritual understanding. In their acceptance of the elements, they are instinctively aware of the pattern underlying life – the chaotic cyclical activity of the natural world. The image of elemental chaos has replaced Yeats's earlier belief in an ordered universe; he now sees God in the chaos underlying all order and pattern.

This thematic pattern can be seen in the linguistic and syntactical patterning of the poem. Parallel phrases (*Under . . . under . . .*, l.2), repetition (*Ravening* ll.6–7, *good-bye* l.8, *snow* ll.1–2), patterning (*century after century* l.5, *That day . . . that before dawn . . .* l.13) and recurring sounds (*Civilisation is hooped together*; *Ravening, raging*) underpin the poet's quest for order. The tight structure controls his response and reinforces his message.

Just after the First World War, Yeats wrote 'The Second Coming' reflecting the chaos of the post-war period. It is a poem of violence and fear as *Mere anarchy is loosed upon the world* and *The ceremony of innocence is drowned* (ll.4–6). He transforms St John's vision of the coming of the anti-Christ into a fearful Doomsday beast that *Slouches towards Bethlehem to be born* – Christian values of love and innocence have been overwhelmed by the tide of violence, and Yeats sees no hope for the future. 'Meru', written in 1934, reflects a very different state of mind. In this poem, Yeats suggests that there is hope if man can stop his frenzied activity for long enough to find a higher consciousness. It is perhaps, ironic, that only five years later, there was to be another world war, evidence that man has not learnt from past events, that he *cannot cease/Ravening . . ./Ravening, raging, and uprooting*.

T. S. Eliot (1888–1965)

Thomas Stearns Eliot is another key figure in the English Modernist poetic tradition. His innovative style and influential critical essays helped to establish new attitudes to literature. They drew attention to tradition, the importance of continuity, and the role of objectivity. In rejecting the poetic values of the previous century, Eliot, along with Yeats and Pound, was to set new poetic standards.

The literary context

At the beginning of the twentieth century in Britain, **Georgian** poets such as John Masefield, W.H. Davies, Edward Thomas and Walter de la Mare continued to use the pastoral subjects and methods of the nineteenth-century Romantics. *Wheels*, an anti-Georgian magazine produced by the Sitwells between 1916 and 1921, encouraged Modernist writers to challenge what they saw as the anachronistic and inappropriate writing of the Georgian poets whose work failed to reflect the dramatic changes in thinking that marked the onset of the Modern period.

Eliot was very interested in the work of the **French Symbolists** who believed it was impossible to use conventional language to convey sensations as we actually experience them. Instead, the poet needed to create a special language of symbols that could suggest the vague, fleeting nature of experience to the reader. Where direct statement or description failed to represent real experience, they believed that a succession of images could convey a true sense of consciousness.

For Eliot, the Symbolists had transformed the poetry of France and he saw their methods as a means of rejuvenating British verse. He therefore drew on key features of French Symbolism in his own poetry. Like Baudelaire, he used the more sordid side of urban life as the source of his content; like Laforgue, he experimented with *vers libre* and the dramatic monologue form.

Imagism was perhaps one of the most important developments in poetry in the early years of the century. Although contemporaries of the Georgians, the Imagists' aims were very different: like the Symbolists they were looking for new ways to encapsulate experience. It was a revolt against Romanticism and the sentimentality the Imagists believed was characteristic of much Romantic verse.

For the Imagists, English poetry had reached a low point and the emergence of Imagism marked a rebellion against the recycling of stale traditions. The poetry published under the name of 'Imagism' is not all of a first-rate quality and it does not always conform to the ideals represented by the Imagists in their manifestoes, but it does reflect the interest in literary form and technique that was to shape the Modernist movement.

Ezra Pound (1885–1972) has historical significance in literary tradition as the main figure in the Imagist movement. He believed in the power of a poem as a word picture with which the reader must actively engage in order to interpret implicit messages – emotional, intellectual and imaginative. In an Imagist poem, he said, the poet: *is trying to record the precise instant when a thing outward and objective transforms itself, or darts into a thing inward and subjective*. For the Imagists, the connection between the physical scene or moment and the image marked a crucial point of understanding: the link established revealed the physical world in a new light.

Imagism can be recognised by its literal approach to the world. The poets aimed to be objective and direct, focusing on the concrete rather than the abstract, avoiding sentimentality, and moving away from moralising and any kind of reflection, towards the physical. An Imagist poem will often focus on a single concentrated moment, bypassing any need for narrative. In 'Oread' by H.D., for instance, the six lines revolve exclusively around a vivid portrayal of the sea. We observe the scene from the viewpoint of the rocks and the poet condenses the description of the sea into the moment at which it towers above them. This enables her to convey the grandeur and power of the sea within the limitations of a single image.

The poems are usually short with lines organised around musical rather than metrical rhythms and patterns. The language is concise; modifiers are used with discretion; such literary devices as similes and symbols are avoided; and there is a strong sense of the spoken voice. Influenced by the French Symbolists, the Imagist poets developed *vers libre* as an open form in which they were free to explore their poetic inspiration. They avoided conventional metrical patterns, seeing these as unnecessarily restrictive. In the traditional Japanese tanka (a verse form of 31 syllables in lines of 5, 7, 5, 7, 7 syllables) and haiku forms, however, the Imagists saw a method that reflected their own interest in a powerfully focused image. They imitated these classical forms, seeking to reproduce their lyricism and powerful images. In the poem 'Autumn' by Amy Lowell, the mood and intensity mirror the universality of the traditional Japanese forms. Beneath the physical description of the autumn leaves lies an implicit understanding of the passage of time.

Most important of all were the images. These had to be hard, clear, and based in the concrete world; they had to avoid abstraction and carry no explicit symbolic value; they had to be evocative, conveying a fresh look at something commonplace. Ezra Pound wrote in 'A Few Don'ts by an Imagiste' (1913) that an image *presents an intellectual and emotional complex in an instant of time*. It allows the poet to remain impersonal while creating a distinctive view of the world in which the image becomes the thing it describes.

In 'The Skaters' by John Gould Fletcher, for instance, the image of a bird dominates the description and the skaters seem like land-bound birds as they almost fly over the frozen river.

> Black swallows swooping or gliding
> In a flurry of entangled loops and curves;
> The skaters skim over the frozen river.
> And the grinding click of their skates as they impinge upon the surface,
> Is like the brushing together of thin wing-tips of silver.

The movement of the birds becomes integral to our understanding of the movement of the skaters. Present participles functioning as post-modifying non-finite clauses (*swooping and gliding*), as a pre-modifier (*grinding*) and as a verbal noun (*the brushing*) enhance the sense of activity. This is intensified by the present tense verbs (*skim, Is, impinge*) which bring the scene to life as we read. The enjambement and the use of the co-ordinating conjunction *And* in the initial position add to the sense of continuous motion.

The image is very physical, appealing to our senses as well as our intellect – readers must first consciously link the flight of the swallows to the patterns made on the ice by the skates, and must then immerse themselves in the tactile and aural sensations of the moment. The poet has intensified the experience by heightening our awareness: the external scene has been transformed by the image of the swallows and we are left with a distinctive vision, a new way of looking at the world.

Imagism was to influence the English poetic tradition in a variety of ways: the poets Basil Bunting and William Carlos Williams in the 1920s adopted the objectivism of the Imagists; e.e. cummings developed their interest in the physical, working on the shape of poems on the page; D.H. Lawrence explored the possibilities offered by *vers libre*. Eliot's theory of the 'objective correlative', in which sets of objects, situations or chains of events become a formula for emotion, can be seen to have its roots in the Imagist concentration on a single image as representative of a meaningful experience.

The poetry of T.S. Eliot is dominated by strong images, and the influence of Pound and the Imagist movement on his work is clear. He uses common speech and is often conversational in tone; he attempts to convey the essence of life; and the content represents actual contemporary life rather than an escape from the grinding nature of reality. Eliot's images, however, function in a different way – they are <u>used</u> rather than presented, often taking on a symbolic significance.

The development of Eliot's verse

Between 1909 and 1911, Eliot was to write the first of *Selected Poems*: 'Preludes', 'Portrait of a Lady', 'The Love Song of Alfred J. Prufrock' and 'Rhapsody on a Windy Night'. They demonstrate his interest in French symbolism and the ironic self-disparaging verse of Laforgue, and the flexible blank verse of the Metaphysical poets and Jacobean drama. These early poems and those written up to 1915 in Boston, Europe and during his first year in England mark the boundaries of what critics call his first period. They are based on observations of people, social behaviour and urban landscapes; the tone is often one of disillusion and irony.

In his second period, the French poems and those often known as the 'Quatrain poems' written between 1916 and 1919 show the influence of Pound. Society is now represented as corrupt and selfish; the tone is harsher and more satirical; and the form is more precise and economic. The poetry of 1919–25 is known as the 'poetry of despair'. In this third stage, Eliot broadens his vision of society, focusing on the breakdown of standards and attitudes which had previously ordered life. While the tone is bleak, there is a sense of potential hope underpinning the despair; the form is increasingly compressed, making the verse seem fragmented.

The publication of *The Waste Land* in 1922 was to mark both critical acclaim and public bewilderment. It was seen by many as a defiant rejection of traditional literary ideals. Readers were disconcerted by the wide-ranging literary references and the often colloquial style; they were confused by the obscurity. What emerged, however, was an awareness of Eliot's view of contemporary civilisation and his attempt to reflect this in the style as well as in the content. Disparate images suggest the chaos Eliot saw in the post-war world; ancient myths re-enacted in a modern urban setting highlight the disintegration of traditional values; and the bitter ironic tone underpins his yearning for spirituality in a faithless age.

The turning point comes in the fourth stage – the Christian work of the late twenties and thirties. In these poems, Eliot is searching for a way to communicate his Christian beliefs, making more explicit the underlying spirituality of the earlier poems. In 1927, he was confirmed in the Church of England and his work takes a noticeably different direction from this point. While *The Hollow Men* (1925) marks a spiritual low point in which the speaker represents a state of despair and emptiness, *Ash Wednesday* (1930) reflects the path of spiritual progress. There is no emphatic assertion of belief, but Eliot addresses the need to believe and the nature of the struggle towards faith.

The publication of the *Four Quartets* (1943) brought his work to a climax. Written between 1935 and 1942, Eliot believed it was his greatest poetic achievement. Where the work of the thirties is explicitly religious, *Four Quartets* deals with the religious ideas of incarnation, time and eternity, and the nature of spiritual insight in general. Eliot interweaves earlier features such as the portrayal of urban desolation with more universal themes. The underlying message suggests that while recognising the meaninglessness of twentieth-century life and the harshness of existence, it is still possible to have faith and hope.

Eliot's approach to poetry

For Eliot, the role of the poet was to bring order to the *irregular, fragmentary* experience of life, *transmuting ideas into sensations* and *amalgamating disparate experience*. This belief was to make many of his poems into a sequence of cinematic images representing his own particular view of the world.

He believed that poets should find ways to express emotion implicitly without using a romantic outpouring of feelings or sentimentality. The result was his statement on the objective correlative:

> The only way of expressing emotion in the form of art is by finding an 'objective correlative', in other words, a set of objects, a situation, a chain of events which shall be the formula of that particular emotion; such that when the external facts, which must terminate in sensory experience, are given, the emotion is immediately evoked.

This means that images from the memory are used to evoke a particular scene or occasion, a mood or feeling. They have a symbolic function since they are representative of a certain emotion. Eliot's theory of the objective correlative ensures that even the most abstract poetry has a concrete basis – he praised John Donne for his ability to treat a *thought* like an *experience*, and his theory enables him to communicate emotion through physical images.

In addition, Eliot avoids self-pity and sentimentality through impersonality and irony. He believed that the poet should not reveal his personality in his writing. For him, the process should be one of *continual self-sacrifice, continual extinction of the personality*. Poetry is not *the turning loose of emotion*, but *an escape from emotion*; it is not *the expression of personality*, but *an escape from personality*. His approach was a reaction against the nineteenth-century Romantic movement which emphasised the importance of the individual and emotion. For Eliot, the poet must aim to appeal to the mind rather than to the emotions since the *intellectual* rather than the *reflective* poet produced the best verse.

Content and themes

The meaning of Eliot's verse can be difficult to pin down – it makes great demands upon the reader. It is no longer possible to rely on narrative structure, instead we must recognise the significance of sequences of images, repeated words, recurring themes and allusions. In an age of breakdown and collapse, Eliot believed that the poetic response had to be complex – poetry did not have to be immediately understood and meaning would be different for each reader.

He saw **ordinary urban life** as a valuable source of material and used close observation as a means of revealing the human condition as it appeared to him. The result is a kind of verse that he hoped would be read by the public at large – verse that created an intensity of vision by appealing to the senses. In the sequence of poems titled 'Preludes', for instance, we are presented with cinematic observations that reveal a view of urban society directly linked to Baudelaire, who saw the *poetical possibilities* of the *more sordid aspects of the modern metropolis*. Eliot focused on the effects of industrialisation, on the monotony of the urban land-scape, and on the people living in anonymous bedsits isolated from their communities. In a faithless world, he saw sin and despair as the necessary precursors to the grace that would illuminate the soul. Only in the moment of understanding could individuals be drawn out of their nothingness so that their essence could be revealed.

The **human condition** was central to Eliot's presentation of twentieth-century life. The individuals in his poems are detached, without bonds to a living spiritual community, and therefore despairing. There is an inevitability about their lives because they are outsiders, rootless and lacking in direction. In 'The Love Song of J. Alfred Prufrock' and the 'Sweeney' poems, we see individuals searching for a pattern, for something that will give them fixity, something that will order their lives. While seeing them as distinctive characters, it is important simultaneously to recognise their role as representative figures, as symbols for the state of modern man.

The physical world of 'Prufrock' is the urban streets. Modifiers like *half-deserted*, *restless* and *tedious* suggest the disorder of modern life. This is reinforced by the monotony of the repetitious structure and the patterning of the language. Recurring emphatic phrases (*there will be time . . .; I have known . . .*) work in opposition to the doubt created by the unanswered and unanswerable *overwhelming question*.

The content is firmly based in the real and sordid world. Complex noun phrases such as *one-night cheap hotels/And sawdust restaurants, The yellow smoke that rubs its muzzle on the window-panes, the pools that stand in drains* and *the soot that falls from chimneys* are cinematic, creating a real physical world. This back-drop is placed in opposition to the universal questions Prufrock must address: love, the meaning of life and the need for action. He must move beyond the trivi-alities of life represented by the *necktie, rich and modest*, by *coffee spoons* and *tea and cakes and ices*.

The poem is a representation of what it feels like to be Prufrock in a world where it is *impossible to say just what [you] mean* and thus the tone is marked by failure. The repeated use of the modal *would* implicitly reveals Prufrock's inability to act – he has not *bitten off the matter with a smile*, he has not *squeezed the universe into a ball*.

References to detached body parts (*face, hands, voices, eyes, arms*) intensify the loss of humanity by reducing individuals to fragments. Similarly Prufrock sees himself in terms of his *bald spot*, his *arms and legs* and his clothes; in terms of the *face* he must *prepare* for society. He is disconnected from his inner self and the image of him viewed from above on the stairs becomes an objective correlative for the division of self that prevents meaningful action in modern society. Nothing is complete and these unconnected symbols become representative of the human condition as Eliot sees it.

Eliot chose to use the dramatic monologue form to reveal the inner life of Prufrock, and adopted Laforgue's tone of ironic cynicism. Potential for change lies at the heart of the episode, but Prufrock, a true representative of a sterile society, cannot act. The possibility for action is dramatised through Eliot's changing moods and time scales. The poem opens with the emphatic imperative *Let us go*, but the certainty is soon replaced by the repetition of the modal *will* with its connotations of possible future action. Further doubt is introduced with the use of the interrogative mood: *Do I dare/Disturb the universe?*; . . . *how should I presume?*; *Then how should I begin . . .?* The modal *should* with its tentative connotations emphasises the doubt about Prufrock's intended action. With the replacement of *should/shall* with *would*, we realise that the moment for action has passed: Prufrock is now contemplating what could have been rather than what will be. He does not analyse himself, but by looking closely at the language Eliot uses we can see directly what it is like to be Prufrock.

The imagery is distinctive. The lightly ironic social images are symbolic of the ennui underlying twentieth-century society. Life is *measured out . . . with coffee spoons*; social expectation dictates the kind of clothes worn (the fashionably combed hair; the cuffs on the bottom of the trousers; the *rich and modest* necktie with its *simple pin*); and recurring references to *toast and tea*, to *tea and cakes and ices*, and to *the cups, the marmalade, the tea,/. . . the porcelain* reflect the inevitability of the human condition. The conversation is meaningless small talk – the *voices dying with a dying fall* provide a permanent backdrop to Prufrock's monologue, but no real communication takes place. While he is unable to communicate, however, Eliot describes the streets, using a modifier like *muttering* and a simile comparing them to *a tedious argument/Of insidious intent*. Prufrock's failure to communicate becomes a running thread in the poem with repetition of *That is not what I meant at all* emphasising his detachment from those around him.

The poem creates a portrait of someone who has failed to make a relationship – not just with the unnamed woman, but with society as a whole. It is significant that after the appearance of *Love* in the title, it is conspicuously absent. The poem is a paradox – Prufrock's love song is a failure to make a declaration of love. He is ill-adapted to urban life and this is conveyed in Eliot's use of synecdoche: he should have been *a pair of ragged claws*, immersed in a *silent* world. The metaphor is both subhuman and reductive – in symbolic terms, it represents the fragmentation of Prufrock. He has a social 'mask', a front, and life will continue in its inevitable cycle of social occasions and meaningless talk, but he will also continue to fail as a human being, establishing no relationships and experiencing no intimacy. The poem ends with the vision of the mermaids into which he can escape until voices from the real world attempt to engage him. Eliot's use of the verb *drown* is symbolic of Prufrock's relationship with the real world in which he struggles to face the *overwhelming question*.

Eliot's use of **allusions** can be difficult for the reader. He draws extensively on a wide range of references to create complex patterns of meaning. A quotation from Dante in the epigraph to 'The Love Song of J. Alfred Prufrock' sets the tone for the poem and prepares us for the suffering of Prufrock in his personal hell. Other references are literary (*Hamlet*), or biblical (John the Baptist; Lazarus). They function thematically as a cohesive thread, but also help to give us an insight into the mind of Prufrock. In *The Waste Land*, the allusions help to give the poem its fragmentary feel, creating stylistic and typographical variations. Biblical and classical references, cultural and spiritual allusions and literary quotations, however, also create cohesion since they reveal the common concerns of humanity in both the past and the present.

The allusions and quotations are an integral part of Eliot's approach. The *heap of broken images* (*The Waste Land*, I) not only reflects the disintegration he saw in twentieth-century society, but also, paradoxically, provides meaning. The *fragments [he has] shored against [his] ruin* (*The Waste Land*, V) create a common bond between the past and the present, instilling hope and suggesting a way forward.

The **themes** in 'Prufrock', 'Sweeney Among the Nightingales' and *The Waste Land* focus on the state of society and the human condition, on inaction and detachment. In the second half of his career, in later poems like 'Journey of the Magi' and *Four Quartets*, the themes are less negative, considering renunciation, resurrection and questions of spirituality.

Eliot's thematic **criticism of society** can be seen in the lexis he chooses. In the *Four Quartets*, for instance, he replaces the traditional image of morning as a time of freshness and new beginnings with a sense of stagnant inevitability: he describes *the uncertain hour before morning/Near the ending of interminable night* ('Little Gidding', II), using the recurring modifier *dead* to set the tone. Similarly, in 'Preludes', modifiers like *stale*, *sawdust-trampled* and *muddy* (II) reflect more than just the literal street scene – they become symbolic of the state of mind of the inhabitants. Repeated references to the *soul* in the poems written before the late 1920s are ironic within the irreligious society portrayed. The emphasis is on both physical and moral decay, and the style as well as the content reflects this. The poems are made up of a *heap of broken images* and the fragmentation is symbolic of the theme of disillusion.

Time is another theme that allows Eliot to focus on the state of society. His representation of modern life as monotonous, spiritually empty and fragmented is set against allusions to past life. Some references glorify individuals from the past, juxtaposing their purpose and ultimate constancy with modern man's aimlessness: John the Baptist with his head *(grown slightly bald) brought in upon a platter*, *Lazarus* and *Prince Hamlet* in 'Prufrock'. Others reflect time as a cycle of repetition in which nothing ever changes: the allusions to Middleton's *Women Beware Women* – a play exploring lust, manipulation and deceit – portrays a world of sterile relationships (*The Waste Land*, II) no different from those of Albert and Lil, or the typist and *the young man carbuncular* (*The Waste Land*, III).

In the later work such as *Four Quartets*, time becomes representative of an eternal now: the present is seen to be made up of all events that have preceded it, and to form the basis of all that is to come. Time is therefore no longer linear, but a constant process of change ('Burnt Norton', ll.1–5). Thematically, Eliot establishes time as a state of permanent change so that he can then search for a point of contrast: *the still point of the turning world* ('Burnt Norton', II/IV). Where the detachment of the earlier poems is escapist, the distance from the movement of time here is visionary. It allows the individual a momentary understanding of the pattern of life. For most of us, however, such a vision is unattainable – we are *time-ridden* (III), *empty of meaning* (III). Eliot's use of the verb *whirled* (III) reminds us of the chaotic image of existence in 'Gerontion' as the gull fights against the wind, and the image of *the whirling plover* in *Ash Wednesday* (VI). For most of us, part of the *twittering world* ('Burnt Norton', III), we will never rise above the meaninglessness of life. Time has become a patterned sequence in which only the calm, desireless love of God will offer an opportunity to rise above earthly disorder.

Although much of the early poetry is dominated by themes of despair and disillusion, the theme of **hope** can be traced. In poems like 'Prufrock' and 'Preludes', escape is offered through a fantasy world that can momentarily replace the harsh reality of twentieth-century life. The imagery is cinematic: Prufrock retreats into the world of the sea where he will stay until *human voices* wake him and he will *drown*; the dozing woman in 'Preludes III' replaces external reality with a life of the imagination – typically, no romantic world of perfection, but a *thousand sordid images* that *flickered against the ceiling*. Eliot suggests that in neither vision can the participant escape since the dream world is no more than a reflection of the sordid suffering of everyday life. Hope without spirituality is therefore seen as yet another one of the *masquerades/That time resumes* ('Preludes' II).

In *The Waste Land*, the sterility of the land is symbolic of life without faith – the quest at the heart of the poem is for water. Despite the dereliction and suffering, the meaningless relationships and pointless journeys, however, there is a hint of the hope that can be found in spirituality. In 'The Burial of the Dead', Eliot's modifiers function on a symbolic as well as a literal level: the description of the desert as *stony, broken, dead*, and *dry* is indicative of the faithless lives of the people who appear in the poem. The unrelenting journey through the desert is intensified by the listing of adverbial clauses of place *where the sun beats,/And the dead tree gives no shelter . . .*, by the elliptical nature of the clauses (the verb *gives* is omitted), and by the initial position conjunction *And*. Even at this point, however, there is a reference to *the shadow* that could offer relief from the wasteland. The use of the imperative *Come in* makes explicit the opportunity for man to turn to God, the chance to see *something different*. The biblical allusion to Isaiah with its images of destruction and desolation and its offer of *the shade of a great rock in a weary land* underpin Eliot's concept of hope – in the land of death, however, the opportunity for salvation is ignored.

In the title of section III, 'The Fire Sermon', Eliot offers another kind of hope. His evocation of Buddha is appropriate at this point in the poem where lust and physical passion dominate. In the sermon, Buddha tells his followers that the human senses and all that they perceive are burning: the fire of lust, anger and ignorance are bound up with earthly concerns of birth, death, grief, misery and despair. Only in studying the scriptures can man rise above the world of passion to free himself from the cycle of birth, death and rebirth. Fire thus becomes a symbol for all that separates man from his God – the asyndetic repetition of the present participle at the end of Part III emphasises our immersion in a world of passion and our distance from God. No one notices the burning because the time for spiritual redemption has not yet come.

A similar effect can be seen in *The Four Quartets* where the *dove* brings fire – an overwhelming positive force of divine love ('Little Gidding', IV.1–4). It is symbolic of a terrifying spiritual power beyond humanity, to which we must surrender. The fire as a symbol is ambiguous, representative of both damnation (*despair*) or purification (*hope*). Eliot emphasises, however, that we do have a choice (IV.6–7) and this is what the poem ends with. The images of *exploration/exploring* (V.27–8) and the journey (V.29–33) lead us to the certainty of the modal verb *shall* (V.44) and the unity of two powerful images: *the tongue of flames . . . in-folded/Into the crowned knot of fire* (divine love, V.45–6) and *the rose* (human love, V.47).

Eliot sees hope in terms of Eastern as well as Christian frames of reference. In *The Waste Land*, for instance, he uses both St Augustine (354–430) and the Buddha as symbols for our potential to move beyond the sterility of twentieth-century life towards something more meaningful. Both led lives of pleasure before deciding to follow a spiritual path and the quotation taken from Augustine's *Confessions* suggests the importance of experiencing the world and its pleasures before understanding the nature of spirituality: *To Carthage then I came*. The over-laying of Christian and Buddhist ideas in the final lines of this section marks the most explicit reference to salvation in *The Waste Land*. The lack of punctuation, the spacing of lines and the use of the final hanging present participle *burning*, however, suggest that the people of London are not yet ready to recognise the sterility of their lives.

In the final section, hope is offered in reference to Christ's resurrection (*Who is the third who walks always beside you?*) and to the Fisher King. In addition, the reference to the Indian holy book the *Upanishad* in both the title of the section, 'What the Thunder Said', and in the last lines allows Eliot to establish a foundation for better living: *Datta* (give), *Dayadhvam* (be compassionate) and *Damyata* (restrain yourselves). Although not adopted by the inhabitants of the wasteland, these are virtues at the heart of all major religions and therefore offer a route out of the desolation for those who are ready. Eliot suggests no easy solutions – the themes of his poetry analyse the nature of twentieth-century life as he saw it and attempt to find connections that may help the *humble people* (*The Waste Land*, III) of his poem make connections.

Style

Eliot saw many of his contemporaries continuing to use the stylistic techniques of the Romantics, which he believed to be worn out and lacking in vitality. The French Symbolists, on the other hand, offered Eliot a new approach both in their content (urban life) and in their form (*vers libre*). From the Imagists, he learnt the power of compression and the effect of capturing emotional experience in an image. The result is a style that, although sometimes obscure, attempts to represent twentieth-century life in a new and vibrant way.

In his essay, 'The Metaphysical Poets', he writes of the need for a complex poetic response that is appropriate for an age of breakdown: *The poet must become more and more comprehensive, more allusive, more indirect, in order to force, to dislocate if necessary, language into meaning.* He moves beyond a comfortable narrative sequence to a collection of fragments which reflect the disintegration he saw around him. The words he chooses are 'unpoetic'; the tone is often conversational; repetition and inverted or elliptical sentence structures are used to reflect the mundanity of life; alliteration, internal rhyme and assonance enhance the mood.

The **diction** of Eliot's poetry moves away from the traditional. Like the Metaphysical poet Donne and the Romantic Wordsworth before him, he turned to the language of everyday to replace what he saw as the artificial, traditional diction of poetry. In spite of his focus on the concrete, Eliot's poetry can be obscure – the accumulation of disparate images, the unusual combination of words, and the elliptical syntax force the reader to work hard. All words are crucial to our understanding, however, for Eliot aimed to use only what was *essential to the sense* of a poem.

The **tone** reflects Eliot's attitude to life and the role of the artist. He believed that the poet should seek impersonality, and he therefore hides behind a mask of irony, using characters like Prufrock to convey his personal view of the world. The aim is to achieve complete objectivity, preventing the content of the verse from becoming self-pitying and sentimental. The poetic form of the dramatic monologue and the symbolism of the objective correlative allow Eliot to achieve this distance.

In 'Preludes', for instance, we are aware of an unnamed and detached observer focusing us on key details of an urban scene. The use of the noun phrase *your feet* (I) reinforces this: the observer distances himself with the use of the second person possessive determiner instead of the first; humanity is reduced to no more than a body part in the head word *feet*. By contrast the street is animated – the complex noun phrase *The conscience of a blackened street* (IV) and the post-modified adjective phrase *Impatient to assume the world* create a sense of the dominating presence of the street in a society where people are dehumanised. The introduction of the first person pronoun and the emotive verb *moved* suggest that Eliot is conveying a more personal response to the world around him. To avoid accusations of sentimentality or pity, however, this is juxtaposed with the coarse imperative clause *Wipe your hand across your mouth* and the cynical use of the verb *laugh*. The sequence of images in 'Preludes' becomes an objective correlative for the futility of modern life. Eliot's stylistic techniques thus become a distinctive cover for the depth of his feeling.

In 'Prufrock', the ironic tone of the title immediately establishes the context for failure: the love song is never sung and Prufrock fails to live up to the grandeur of his title. The imagery is used as a means of representing the triviality of Prufrock's life and his lack of self-esteem – both are symbolic not just of Prufrock and his society, however, but of twentieth-century society and its inhabitants. Through these techniques and through the allusions that indirectly comment on the present by reference to the past, Eliot is able to present his personal views without directly engaging in a personal expression of them.

We are always aware of Eliot's views underlying the observations of a poem, but he ensures that they can rarely be directly connected with him. A sequence of poems like 'Landscapes' may seem more personal: they are lyrical; the mood is contemplative rather than cynical; the content is rural rather than urban; the absence of allusion makes them seem more like a direct expression of personal attitudes. Despite this, Eliot described them as exercises and this immediately makes even these poems seem impersonal. His critical writing clearly establishes his aims in writing poetry and his verse clearly communicates his views, and yet, ironically, the reader does not really have any sense of the man himself in the writing.

Imagery and symbolism

The overall effect of Eliot's poetry is cinematic because of the way he puts together sequences of pictures. Fragments are overlaid in a montage to create a distinctive impression of a particular scene. The kind of **images** he chooses and the order in which he presents them reflect Eliot's attitude or viewpoint.

Eliot believed that images played a crucial role in revealing the meaning of a poem, however complex its content might appear on first reading. The reader must allow the images to *fall into his memory without questioning the reasonableness of each* so that at the end of a poem, *a total effect is produced*. Apparently random images function together, giving a poem an underlying cohesion that concentrates the reader's mind.

The images become **symbols** for Eliot's state of mind, representing his personal view of twentieth-century life. By recognising key images and understanding their symbolic function, it is therefore possible to move towards an understanding of Eliot's attitude towards life. The images become an objective correlative for his disillusion – his subject is the human condition, but it is explored indirectly through the physical images that he chooses. Emotion is replaced with a sequence of images that depersonalise the message and give it a concrete visual life.

In broad terms, the first half of Eliot's work focuses on the state of society and the human condition. The images are of urban life (the sordid city, its tainted inhabitants and their material lives); they convey a sense of social desolation, withdrawal and paralysis. The second half deals more directly with man's spiritual needs and the search for enlightenment. The imagery here is more explicitly religious, drawing on images of nature and Christianity – the dying of the old life and the rebirth of the new. These later images tend to be less shocking: the biting realism of the earlier work is replaced by a more dream-like, contemplative quality.

Eliot's imagery is often striking and he is clearly influenced by the complex conceits of the Metaphysical poets. Like them, he uses conventional images in a startling way and creates new ones by linking unexpected things. In 'Prufrock', for instance, the opening simile of the *patient etherised upon a table* sets the tone for the images that follow. It is an image of paralysis, symbolic of the passivity of Prufrock in his role as lover. Other images suggest Prufrock's feeling of exposure: he is like a trapped insect *sprawling on a pin*; the *magic lantern* displays his internal turmoil (*nerves*) publicly *on a screen* as he tries to *say just what [he] mean[s]*. Such images force us to reconsider everyday things: street lights beat *like a fatalistic drum*, doors open *like a grin* ('Rhapsody on a Windy Night'); souls are *stretc across the skies* or are *trampled by insistent feet* ('Preludes', IV); the song of the nightingales is no longer linked to romance but to imminent catastrophe ('Sweeney among the Nightingales'). Such images convey Eliot's sense of a world in crisis, of a society no longer able to understand the immaterial world that absorbed earlier writers like Webster and Donne.

Urban images are used to convey Eliot's sense of the rootlessness of modern life. Individuals are portrayed as exiles, outsiders in a social vacuum where no one can make relationships. Descriptions of smoke and fog in poems such as 'Prufrock', 'Portrait of a Lady' and 'Preludes' are indicative of confusion and detachment. While modifiers like *burnt-out/grimy* ('Preludes', I) convey the physical scene, personification animates the fog ('Prufrock'), making it seem more threatening and purposeful. The images become symbolic for the inertia Eliot sees around him in a spiritually empty society.

References to city streets are also common and Eliot frequently personifies them. Long complex noun phrases like *The muttering retreats/Of restless nights, Streets that follow like a tedious argument/Of insidious* ('Prufrock') and *The conscience of a blackened street* ('Preludes', IV) create a threatening atmosphere in which the inanimate streets are more active than the paralysed humans that inhabit them.

Natural images are often sterile. The memory of the *twisted branch upon the beach* and the *sunless dry geraniums* in 'Rhapsody on a Windy Night' contribute to the mood of futility and desolation. In 'Sweeney Among the Nightingales', references to *the stormy moon, the shrunken seas*, and to *Death* and the symbolic *Raven* create an appropriate background for Eliot's portrait of Sweeney and the two women.

Other recurring references can be seen in images of detached **body parts**: *The eyes* ('Prufrock'; *The Hollow Men*), *your feet* ('Preludes', I), *The broken fingernails of dirty hands* (*The Waste Land*, III), *Six hands at an open door dicing for pieces of silver* ('Journey of the Magi'). The depersonalisation is an essential part of Eliot's portrait of twentieth-century society – people are no longer in touch with themselves, they have lost sight of God. In many examples, the complexity of the noun phrases allows Eliot to reinforce his message: modifiers like *broken* and *dirty* establish the tone; post-modifying non-finite clauses like *dicing for pieces of silver* symbolise the godlessness of the age.

In the later work, images are more positive. The barren waterless land of *The Waste Land* and *the dead land* of *The Hollow Men* are replaced by something more fertile. In *Ash Wednesday*, for instance, there is an awareness of something quite distinct from the everyday world of ambition and desire. It may not be easily attainable, but it is there, just beyond our temporal world – a place where *trees flower, and springs flow* (I). The dynamic present tense verbs give life to this other world even while the negatives (*do not think . . . shall not know . . . cannot drink*) deny the speaker entrance to it. In part II, death becomes the means of achieving a pure life detached from mortal existence: the speaker is *dissembled* by the leopards, but the images are not gruesome. The juxtaposition of adjective phrases *Calm/distressed* and *Torn/most whole* and the image of the bright bones symbolise the movement away from the earthly world of base desire towards purity and selflessness. The stark images of *the whiteness of bones* represent humanity reduced to nothingness, detached from the need to exist – natural images of fertility, the *single Rose* and the *Garden/Where all love ends*, offer an alternative. This is reinforced in part III with the description of *the hawthorn blossom* and the *pasture scene*.

References to the **sea** are equally important to Eliot. In 'Prufrock', the poem ends with a haunting image of *the mermaids* who are *riding seaward*. The sea offers an alternative reality to Prufrock, a place of escape where he will no longer be faced with his own inability to communicate. The language Eliot uses creates a vision that is quite contrary to the real world of the poem: repetition of words (*waves, white, blown/blows*, assonance (*riding, white; Combing/blown; sea-girls/wreathed/seaweed*) and changes in metrical pattern all highlight the distance between this world of dreams and the real world from which Prufrock yearns to escape.

> I´havĕ I séen thĕm I ri´din̆g I séaward I on̆ thĕ I wa´ves
> Co´mbin̆g thĕ I whi´te ha´ir I ŏf thĕ wa´ves I blo´wn ba´ck
> When thĕ I wind blo´ws I thĕ wa´t I ĕr white I an̆d bla´ck   (ll.126–8)

Other sea images can be found in 'Gerontion' where the final description of the *Gull against the wind* flying *in the windy straits/Of Belle Isle* or *running on the Horn* becomes symbolic of mankind *whirled* chaotically into *fractured atoms*. The poetic vision of the sea in 'Prufrock' as an image of escape is replaced by a recognition of its destructive power – symbolic of man's struggle to live in a godless society. In Part IV of *The Waste Land*, Phlebas is reborn as he enters *the whirlpool* and moves beyond a life of *profit and loss*. At the end of *Ash Wednesday*, the sea becomes a symbol of all that is tempting in human life. The repetition of the modifier *lost* in the noun phrases *the lost sea voices* and *the lost sea smell* emphasises the difficulty in abandoning the physical world and its pleasures: the *white sails* become symbolic of the temptations that draw the speaker back to life. The strength of this temptation is underpinned by the repeated subordinate clause at the start of part VI (*Although I do not . . .*) and by the speaker's longing to learn *peace* even when confronted by the sea. The prayer-like structure of repeated imperatives *Suffer us not . . .* and *Teach us . . .* along with the repetition of the prepositional phrase *among these rocks* draws attention to the *time of tension between dying and birth*, the struggle for the speaker to look beyond the physical to the spiritual.

Images based on **classical mythology** are also common. Eliot uses them as references to intensify the effect of his verse, building layers of intertextuality that create contrasts between the past and present. He encourages readers to draw on their knowledge of past writers in order to understand the deficiencies of the present and to recognise ways in which society could regain its sense of direction.

The Waste Land is full of textual references and images that both illuminate the paucity of twentieth-century life and offer an alternative. The references to Virgil's Dido and Aeneas and Shakespeare's Cleopatra in 'A Game of Chess' are symbolic of desertion and abandonment; the image of Philomel from Ovid's *Metamorphoses* with her tongue cut out and the voice of a nightingale to proclaim the wrong done to her is symbolic of the brutality of the world Eliot sees around him. By avoiding the traditional image of beauty associated with the nightingale, Eliot challenges the reader, denying them the comfort of recognisable and palatable images.

In 'What the Thunder Said', the image of the Fisher King with the *arid plain* behind him and the sea in front recalls the pre-Christian story of the sick king whose lands are desolate, awaiting the questing knight who will restore his lands to prosperity. Here, the Fisher King's inertia becomes symbolic of the sterility of twentieth-century society and its need for regeneration. He may have reached water after the barrenness of the poem, but there is no certainty in its presence – the poem's conclusion is appropriately ambiguous. The use of the interrogative mood and the tentative modal verb *Shall* is indicative of the lack of certainty in the conclusion.

Implicitly linked to the image of the Fisher King is that of the **journey**. It is symbolic of the process of learning and self-discovery that must accompany the rebirth of a decaying society. Eliot uses journeys in the present to structure his verse: in *The Waste Land*, the reader travels through post-First World War London and each location (London Bridge, the churches, the Thames, the banks of the canal) has both a literal and a symbolic significance. They represent both the physical and spiritual dereliction of Eliot's time. We are also introduced to individuals who travel: Marie's need to escape is seen in her trips abroad as she attempts to flee the natural seasonal cycle ('The Burial of the Dead'); the rich lady's carriage trips reflect the pointlessness of her existence ('A Game of Chess'); Prufrock keeps moving around in an attempt to avoid facing the reality of his situation. In each case, the individual is aware that something is lacking in life and that there is a need for something more – their restlessness, however, is symbolic of their failure to recognise the real solution to their problems.

The image of the **quest** is directly linked to this and Eliot uses the idea of a purposeful journey with a goal to represent the search for spirituality. In particular, it becomes linked with the search for the 'lost father'. *The Waste Land* is full of references to this: the allusion to Ferdinand's search for his father on the magical island of Shakespeare's *The Tempest* (I.48; III.191–2); the description of Christ's last night in the Garden of Gethsemane, the disciples' journey to Emmaus and the arrival at the decayed Chapel Perilous with its last test, the temptation of despair (V.322–6/359–65/385–90). In each case, something could be achieved – the potential for spiritual fulfilment is apparent.

These two images (the physical journey and the spiritual quest) come together in 'Journey of the Magi' where the hardship of the physical journey mirrors the personal sacrifices required by spiritual redemption. The monologue effectively dramatises the monotony of the literal journey through repetition of the initial position conjunction *And*, modifiers like *hostile* and *unfriendly*, verbs like *regretted*, and juxtapositions of present hardships with what has been left behind. Although the spiritual goal is achieved at the end of this journey, the moment of recognition is underplayed by Eliot's choice of the predicative adjective *satisfactory*. In addition, the use of parenthesis in the simple sentence delays the subject complement making it seem even more of an anticlimax when we complete the clause: *it was (you may say) satisfactory*. The journey towards spirituality is ambiguous because it involves personal sacrifice. For the speaker in the poem, the birth of Christ therefore becomes synonymous with death as well as life.

Poetic form

Although Eliot could use traditional verse structures skilfully, as seen in his *Old Possum's Book of Practical Cats*, much of his verse is free verse – there may be rhymes, rhythms and stanzas but they do not conform to a regular pattern. The poetic form is, however, organic, giving shape to the content and underpinning meaning. For Eliot, a society distanced from its God and bound up with corruption and disillusion could not be described in rhyming couplets or balanced stanzas. He chose instead the irregularity of verse freed from conventional rigid forms to characterise the broken and chaotic world around him.

Eliot uses the **dramatic monologue** to characterise individuals like Prufrock and Gerontion. The form has a dual function: it allows him to give a direct insight into a character, but simultaneously acts as a mask. He can thus externalise an aspect of himself and represent a particular way of looking at experience without becoming subjective.

The poems focus on a critical moment, looking into the minds of particular characters and recording the process of their 'thinking aloud': Prufrock is about to declare his love; one of the magi assesses the significance of his journey. The poems thus represent the characters' attempts to order their lives, to impose a pattern on the randomness of experience, to find meaning in an artificial world. In the earlier works, the desire to change is unsuccessful and Eliot's ironic tone is distinctive – Prufrock's love song, for instance, is never sung and he retreats from his failure into the comfort of *the chambers of the sea*. In 'The Journey of the Magi', the old man reflects on life and addresses the paradox of experience, but for him there is acceptance and understanding as he awaits death and the rebirth that will accompany it.

Although the poetic forms Eliot chooses are irregular, he draws on **musical structures** to develop his ideas. Titles are often reminiscent of music: a love song, a prelude, a rhapsody, a quartet. The rhythms and sounds are fluid; repetitions of words and phrases function like refrains or choruses; and disrupted syntax creates pauses or drives the reader on.

Eliot and the English poetic tradition

Eliot was a poet with a strong sense of his own time and with deep religious convictions. This has not, however, affected his continuing popularity or his critical status. He believed that good verse could survive changes in attitude and even the *complete extinction of interest in the issues with which the poet was passionately concerned*. This is clearly the case with his own writing: it is closely tied up with a particular world view and yet modern readers can continue to find relevance in its vision.

His verse is complex and at times obscure, and for contemporary readers both the content and style were bewildering. He wrote of *dirty gutters* and *cigarettes*, describing everyday life in everyday language, shocking some readers by the unconventionality of his approach. Many contemporary critics objected to Eliot's allusive style – some saw his borrowings as mere plagiarism, while others believed it to be no more than an ostentatious display of his learning. He was also accused of parody and inferior imitation, and of unnecessary obscurity.

Eliot, however, clearly distinguished between different kinds of borrowings:

while immature poets *imitate*, mature poets *steal*, and bad poets *deface what they take*, the good poet will create something *better, or at least different*, he will [*weld*] *his theft into a whole of feeling which is unique, utterly different from that from which it was torn*. This is what we see in Eliot's work: a blending of implicit references, direct quotations and symbolic allusions that are used to distance the poet from his personal attitudes and impressions.

There are two distinct critical responses to Eliot's work: for many of his contemporaries, his verse was obscure and unmetrical; for others, he is the first great Modernist and representative of a new kind of society. In addition, his critical writing was significant in the development of the English literary tradition. Together F.R. Leavis and Eliot can be seen as the founders of modern academic literary criticism. Eliot not only created a critical vocabulary with terms like *objective correlative* and *the dissociation of sensibility*, but also brought a precision to the art of critical writing.

His contribution to the English poetic tradition is significant. Along with Pound and other experimental writers, he challenged the literary conventions of the nineteenth century, changing the subject matter and the language of poetry. Eliot was no longer a *man speaking to men* as Wordsworth was, but a manipulator and creator of words and patterns. He was prominent in the development of artistic symbols as representations of the sensibility of the time, and consciously moved away from the sentimentality of much Victorian verse, replacing emotional outpourings with detachment.

Initially, his verse alienated the ordinary reader, but the First World War was to alter public perception: idealism was replaced by realism, and poetry was no longer seen as a comfortable literary form reflecting only the most palatable elements of life. Against this backdrop, Eliot's verse was seen as evidence that poetic traditions were being revitalised – his conversational speech rhythms were to influence the poets of the 1930s who adopted a colloquial style, although their approach was far less obscure.

Poets such as Dylan Thomas in the 1940s were to move away from the detachment of Eliot's work, replacing his impersonality with a personal engagement that was reminiscent of the Romantics, and, by the 1960s, his reputation was in decline. His position as a highbrow elitist did not fit comfortably with a changing society where poetry sought to gain mass popularity. In spite of this, Eliot is still recognised as a unique force, bringing to poetry an intellectuality that challenged readers and revitalised English poetry.

Activity 13.4

> **Discuss the literary and linguistic approaches Eliot uses to portray the city and convey his ideas in this extract from 'The Burial of the Dead' (*The Waste Land*, I, II.60–76).**
>
> You may like to think about: the content, language, grammar, poetic features, imagery and allusions.

<pre>
1   Unreal City,
           Under the brown fog of a winter dawn,
           A crowd flowed over London Bridge, so many,
           I had not thought death had undone so many.
5   Sighs, short and infrequent, were exhaled,
           And each man fixed his eyes before his feet.
           Flowed up the hill and down King William Street,
           To where Saint Mary Woolnoth kept the hours
           With a dead sound on the final stroke of nine.
10   There I saw one I knew, and stopped him crying: 'Stetson!
           'You who were with me in the ships at Mylae!
           'That corpse you planted last year in your garden,
           'Has it begun to sprout? Will it bloom this year?
           'Or has the sudden frost disturbed its bed?
15   'O keep the Dog far hence, that's friend to men,
           'Or with his nails he'll dig it up again!
           'You! hypocrite lecteur! – mon semblable, – mon frère!'
</pre>

Commentary

The content of the poem is typically urban and its concrete references to *London Bridge* (l.3), *King William Street* (l.7) and *Saint Mary Woolnoth* (l.8) clearly establish a real scene. Eliot is therefore interested in creating a sense of contemporary city life through close observation. In the second half of the extract, however, he moves beyond the confines of a recognisable reality to something almost surreal. The juxtaposition of the two sections challenges readers' complacency, forcing them to reconsider the nature of twentieth-century life. By linking disparate experiences in this way, Eliot ensures that his verse is not comfortable – readers are jolted out of their security into a new world of degeneracy and disillusion.

The language Eliot chooses reinforces the mood he aims to create. He avoids traditionally poetic diction in favour of an everyday language that communicates his vision of the human condition. The connotations of words are important: traditionally, dawn is associated with a fresh start, with rebirth and yet here it is a time for despair rather than hope. Its position at the end of a complex noun phrase and its pre-modification by the noun *winter* undermine its positive connotations. The repetition of the verb *flowed* (ll.3, 7) suggests a lack of conscious intention in the movements of the crowd: people are denied their individuality; they become no more than mindless cogs in the machine of the city. This is reinforced by the verb *fixed* (l.6) that enhances the lifelessness of the people heading for work.

It is an *Unreal* (l.1) city and Eliot implicitly suggests that the inhabitants are no more than the living dead in his reference to *death* (l.4). Modifiers reinforce the underlying tone of despair: the use of *dead* (l.9) to pre-modify the sound of the bell seems appropriate in this world of living ghosts; the use of *hypocrite* (modifying the direct reference to the reader, l.17) forces us to recognise our own failings in the light of the urban society Eliot portrays.

The direct speech in the second half of the extract adopts the structures of spontaneous spoken language. Sentences are loosely structured (ll.11–12) and the interrogative mood predominates (ll.11–13). The fact that there are no responses is typical of the scene of lifeless mechanisation created in the first part of the extract – adjacency pairs are incomplete: the vocatives do not attract the attention of Stetson (ll.10–11); the questions remain unanswered (ll.12–14). General references to *A crowd* and *each man* are replaced by the direct use of a proper noun *Stetson*, but even this does not induce an individual response from the mass. The almost surrealistic content adds to our sense of displacement.

The grammatical structure is often incomplete or disrupted to reflect the fragmentation of society. The foregrounding of the post-modified noun phrase *Unreal City,/Under the brown fog of a winter dawn* (ll.1–2) delays the main clause and establishes a negative atmosphere. The parenthetical co-ordinated adjective phrase *short and infrequent* (l.5) also disrupts the clause structure, and, alongside Eliot's use of the passive voice (*were exhaled*), reinforces our sense of the passivity of the people. By omitting the prepositional phrase 'by + agent', Eliot removes any conscious personal response from the workers. This feeling of passivity is intensified by the omission of the subject before *Flowed* (l.7), which draws the reader back to the first reference to the crowd (l.3) and makes the vision of mindlessness seem inescapable.

After the longer sentences of the first half, the questions of the second change the pace. The enjambement (ll.8–9) can be contrasted with the strong end stop on lines ending with a question mark or exclamation (ll.10–11, 13–15). It is the speaker, however, the unnamed participant, who is active and the change in pace is thus deceptive since it does not break the monotony and mindlessness of the first half.

The poetic form mirrors the content, with Eliot's use of free verse as a fitting reflection of his uncomfortable representation of life. The traditional iambic foot is juxtaposed with lines where the metre is disrupted. The direct speech, for instance, is dominated by the weak-strong stress pattern and this creates a sense of logic and order that is in direct opposition to the surrealistic quality of the content:

'Ŏr hás | thĕ súd | dĕn fróst | dĭstúrbed | ĭts bed?

The opening, however, in its creation of a disturbing vision, frequently changes stress patterns and thus prevents the reader from drifting into the security of a recognised rhythm:

Undĕr thĕ | brówn fóg | ŏf ă wín | tĕr dáwn   (l.61)

Similarly, the sound patterning does not create a sense of a coherent whole. End rhymes (*many/many, feet/Street, garden/men*) are infrequent, reflecting a feeling that there are no easy solutions or neat conclusions to this vision of the human condition. The use of assonance (*flowed/over/so*) adds to the monotony of the journey over the bridge – the long vowel sounds enhance the tedium of the workers' lives.

The images are typical of Eliot's verse. They draw on experiences the reader will recognise: the city, going to work, daily routine. Within the context of his work, however, they become an objective correlative for his view of twentieth-century life. The lexical choices and grammatical structures underpin the visual detail, making the reader more aware of social desolation and the isolation of individuals. The paralysis of their lives is evident in the image of their apparently unconscious movements; the dereliction of the city is ever-present in the images of death and despair; and the meaninglessness of life is conveyed in the image of the journey without apparent goal or purpose.

The use of allusions also plays a part in portraying Eliot's views. In the opening lines, the city is described in terms reminiscent of Baudelaire's Paris and Dante's hell – life is hollow and sterile and people are like ghosts. Eliot thus demonstrates that his vision of twentieth-century life is not just a problem for London but is endemic to mankind. Other references are classical, allowing Eliot to suggest contrasts between the past and present. *Mylae* is the name of the battle in 260BC where the Romans and the Carthaginians fought to see who should control trade in the Mediterranean. By linking its name with *Stetson*, he is able to suggest that mankind does not change, and that all wars ultimately are the same. The *corpse* is reminiscent of the Egyptian myth in which Osiris, after being brutally murdered, was buried by his wife in various places across Egypt. Each year, grain was planted at the holy sites of his burial and when they grew, people believed in the resurrection of Osiris in the life of the new crops.

The themes are closely linked with the kind of images Eliot chooses. His criticism of twentieth-century life is clear in the negative representation of the human condition. There is little hope in this extract to alleviate the despair. The reference to the church, *Saint Mary Woolnoth*, offers no salvation to the lifeless people since it no longer stands as a symbol of man's link with the spiritual world. Its function has been reduced to that of keeping *the hours*. The image of resurrection perhaps suggests the underlying hope that Eliot's later poems were to make more explicit. In the world of death portrayed here, however, there are no answers to the questions and we do not know whether the positive connotations of *sprout* and *bloom* (l.72) will be fulfilled.

Eliot has used a montage of images to act on his reader. The fragments (descriptions of people, bits of conversation, references to real places, quotations) become representations of a modern life that is characterised by spiritual deprivation. The emphasis is on death rather than life, on the failure of communication, and on the inability of man to break out from the cycle of despair.

Dylan Thomas (1914–53)

When *18 Poems* was published in 1934, it established a characteristic voice that was to set the verse of **Dylan Thomas** apart from his contemporaries. Certain features were to recur: the use of refrains to create cohesive threads running through the poems; a powerful rhythm and rhyme that gave the verse a tight structure; a heightened tone; and the creation of an organic relationship between the natural and human worlds. It marked a return to personal poetry and the intensity of a private vision in what was to be described as a Neo-Romantic tradition.

The literary context

Although the poets of the 1930s admired Eliot as the founder of modern poetry, they wished to move away from his elitist approach, bringing poetry back to ordinary readers. They believed in the importance of intellectual ideas and their tone was didactic. They also wanted, however, to create poems that were accessible: the content dealt with everyday things and the language was commonplace.

Within the poetic movement of the 1930s, **W.H. Auden** (1907–73) clearly emerges as the leader. Of particular importance is his ongoing belief that people did want to read poetry and that it could be used to change society. To reach as wide an audience as possible with his political message, he therefore often used popular light verse as an accessible medium. At his best, Auden focuses on the here-and-now, reflecting on what it is to be human with an intensity that brings the moment to life. His imagery and metrical control are impressive, but, for some critics, his stark juxtaposition of light forms with serious content is a weakness.

Although overshadowed by Auden's reputation in the 30s and 40s, **Louis MacNeice** (1907–63) is perhaps the poet who is still most widely read: the range of his work is impressive and it is often anthologised. He writes about ordinary things, focusing on the world around him and dealing with everyday experiences in an intense and visionary way. He takes a simple observation or moment in time and explores the experience, revealing a symbolic layer beneath the surface as he searches for order and meaning. For critics, the strength of MacNeice's verse lies in this ability to observe something ordinary and recreate it as a meaningful experience. Stylistically, the use of assonance, internal rhyme and ballad-like repetition characterises his writing.

John Betjeman (1906–84) is a controversial figure – one of the best-known and best-selling English poets, and yet often seen as the creator of trite and superficial verse. Closer reading of the poems, however, reveals a witty and satiric interpretation of contemporary life, and he is now recognised as a valid social commentator of his time. What strikes the reader first is the humorous tone of the poems, but beneath this there is often an underlying melancholy. The light verse exterior conceals an inner understanding of life: in 'Slough' and 'Executive', modern attitudes to town development are satirised; in 'In Westminster Abbey', self-centred attitudes to prayer and war are exposed; and in 'On a Portrait of a Deaf Man', he questions the easy truths of the afterlife.

The content of Betjeman's verse is based firmly in everyday life. He is a close observer of visual details, recording the sights, smells and sounds of life as it passes his characters by. We see the *the slippery third path,/Trodden away with gym-shoes* ('Pot Pourri from a Surrey Garden'), we smell the *mushroomy, pine-woody, evergreen smells* ('A Subaltern's Love-song'), and we hear the chauffeurs *Crunching over private gravel* ('Indoor games near Newbury') and the *clocks ticking/Over thick carpets with a deadened force* ('Death of King George V'). He is a writer of topographical poetry with a predilection for *suburbs and gaslights and Pont Street and Gothic Revival churches and mineral railways, provincial towns and garden cities*. As well as conveying a strong visual image of the places he records in his verse, his attitude to modern towns and their architecture is clear.

Many of the poems use the dramatic monologue form in which the voice of the speaker is distinctive. The lovers of 'Pot Pourri from a Surrey Garden' and 'A Subaltern's Love-song' clearly express their feelings for Pam the *great big mountainous sports girl* ('Pot Pourri'), and Miss Joan Hunter Dunn *With the tilt of her nose and the chime of her voice,/And the scent of her wrap, and the words never said* ('Subaltern's Love-song'). The poems are humorous and their use of detail makes the girls seem larger than life – they are not idealised in the tradition of English love poetry. Beyond the comedy, however, Betjeman has given a voice to ordinary speakers using ordinary language to celebrate their love. The use of the dramatic monologue and the first person voice in 'Executive' has a harsher purpose. We are no longer in the comfortable world of Pam and Miss Joan Hunter Dunn, but in the company of an ambitious businessman. The underlying tone is satiric and the speaker ironically undermines his own case as he speaks. The repetition of the first person pronoun here is indicative of the self-centred and arrogant nature of the *young executive* whose role is to *integrate the current export drive*.

By contrast, the poems where Betjeman uses the third person have a poignancy of distant observation. 'Devonshire Street W.1' and 'Death in Leamington' leave the reader as a detached observer of a touching moment: in the first case, a confirmation of terminal illness, and in the second a suicide. The use of pronouns (*he/she/her*) and possessive determiners (*his/her*) distances the reader and makes the occasion in each poem seem more disturbing.

The language of the poems is firmly grounded in the ordinary. Betjeman uses everyday expressions and avoids the traditionally poetic in his portrait of the world around him. The tone is often conversational – in 'Executive' we are literally overhearing a conversation and the parenthetical *you know, No soda, please, just plain* and *with respect* remind us there is an unseen listener. In this particular poem, Betjeman captures the business jargon of the speaker with the noun phrases *the firm's Cortina, the current export drive, vital off-the-record work* and *my other hat*; the adjective phrase *viable*; the adverb phrase *transport-wise*; and the verbs *acquire* and *integrate*. The use of colloquialisms like *bird* (for girlfriend) and overused sentence adverbs like the disjuncts *Essentially* and *basically* reveal the speaker as an ordinary man. His self-importance, however, is seen in his need to use French expressions such as *maîtres d'hôtel* and *savoir faire*, and the proper nouns *Slimline brief-case* and *Aston Martin*.

In the 1950s and 60s, Betjeman's work was considered inconsequential, lacking in depth and substance. Although he has not always had a high critical standing, however, he has always had admirers of note: Philip Larkin saw him as the best English poet writing. His verse has always been and continues to be very popular. It follows in the tradition of the playful wit of Cowper (1731–1800) and the gentle satire of Hood (1799–1845), rather than the Modernism of Yeats and Eliot. The humour and approachable diction make it accessible for a wide audience, but this does not detract from the technical skill of the writing. Betjeman's eye for visual detail, his satiric view of his society, and the poignancy of his feelings for suffering individuals give the poems a biting edge that is missed by some readers.

While Dylan Thomas's verse shares some features with his contemporaries, he was clearly distancing himself from the poetic traditions of the 1930s. Where Betjeman, Macneice and Auden were concerned with events at home (poverty, unemployment, the effects of industrialisation) and abroad (the Spanish Civil War, the rise of Fascism), Thomas's verse shows little awareness of the social, political and industrial period in which it was written. Where the poetry of the 1930s is unemotional and intellectual, Thomas appeals to the emotions at a primitive and elemental level.

Thomas's approach to poetry

When asked about his *theory of poetry* Thomas wrote: *Really I haven't got one.*

> I like things that are difficult to write and difficult to understand; I like 'redeeming the contraries' with secretive images; I like contradicting my images, saying two things at once in one word, four in two words and one in six. But what I like isn't a theory . . .

Although claiming he had no theory, however, Thomas had very strong ideas about poetry. He saw it as a disciplined craft rather than an outpouring of feelings, believing that a poem should look like a poem on the page and sound like poetry – not like an overheard conversation.

In a review in the *Daily Worker*, Stephen Spender (1909–95) had described Thomas's poetry as being *turned on like a tap*, with *no beginning nor end, shape, or intelligent and intelligible control*. Thomas was to counter this criticism in a letter to Henry Treece (16 May 1938). He described his poems as *formed . . . watertight compartments*, juxtaposing the verb *flow* and the adjective *hewn* to emphasise the difference between his consciously crafted work and the outpourings of other poets for whom form is less important.

Some saw the influence of Surrealism in Thomas's writing, but his laborious approach to the crafting of poems was quite unlike the 'automatic' writing of many of the Surrealists. Certainly, he explored a world that existed beneath the surface of everyday life, but where the Surrealists were driven by a desire to reveal the secrets of the self in order to understand life, Thomas's vision was very personal – he was not guided by a manifesto, nor was he seeking to make socio-political comments.

Thomas's conception of the poet's function and his religious attitude to experience are essentially Romantic. The poet is a prophet or seer who reveals the world in a new light through the power of his poetic imagination. His vision may be unfamiliar and the powerful expression of his emotions may make the poetry obscure. His work is the product of the subconscious, finding its source in the heart rather than the head. Thomas, however, distances himself from traditional Romantic poets such as Wordsworth, believing his verse to be *chockful of clichés* and *ridiculous inversions of speech and thought*. Thomas's complaint was that Wordsworth did not *feel* what he described – he was *the verbose, the humourless, the platitudinary reporter of Nature in her dullest moods* (Letter to Pamela Hansford Johnson, 15 October 1933). Instead, he saw himself in the Romantic and mystical tradition of Blake, *but so far behind him that only the wings on his heels are in sight.* We can see evidence of Blake's influence in Thomas's distinctive sense of self, his vision of the mysticism of the natural world, and in the emotion that underpins the poems.

The content of his poems tends to be evocative and descriptive rather than narrative, which can make it difficult for the reader because revelation rather than explanation lies at the heart of the poetic process. When accused of writing 'difficult' poems, Thomas claimed he would feel it dishonest to write only poems that were *simple* and *unambiguous*. He wanted readers to try and unravel the meaning *by thinking and feeling* about a poem, avoiding making judgements based on *preconceived standards*, and reading and rereading – preferably aloud – in order to become familiar with the poet's *standards, codes of appreciation* and *aura* (Letter to Pamela Hansford Johnson, early November 1933).

Thomas's love of words is apparent in all of his writing. Like Mallarmé, he believed that words rather than ideas should come first and his work is marked by its music and its linguistic experimentation. There are, however, examples of lucid and controlled writing in the letters and in poems like 'Paper and Sticks' or 'Hunchback in the Park', and there is clear evidence of his laborious writing practices. This suggests that where the language seems obscure, it is the result of conscious manipulation rather than carelessness. Some critics see his anomalous position as an Anglo-Welsh writer as the source of his linguistic creativity – without a language he could rightfully call his own, he attempted to forge something distinctive.

The sound of the poems is perhaps what first strikes a listener. Recurring consonant and vowel sounds, internal and end rhyme, and strong rhythms form the basis for the elaborate patterning at the heart of the stanza structure. In common with Welsh language poetry, Thomas uses complex verbal patterns to express his vision of the world. The combination of alliteration and sibilance in *Herons, steeple stemmed, bless* ('Poem on his Birthday'), for instance, not only draws attention to the heron within the literal landscape, but prepares us for its elevation to the role of priest. The religious connotations of the words and their cohesive sound quality intensify the line, emphasising Thomas's religious attitude to experience.

In 'On no work of words', a poem about the difficulties of writing, Thomas consciously draws on both negative and positive meanings of words in order to convey the ambiguity of his situation. The central contrast is developed in the first stanza: the productivity of the natural world, conveyed by the noun phrase *the bloody/Belly of the rich year* with its connotations of fertility and birth, is directly contrasted with Thomas's own *three lean months*. Paradoxically, the contemplation of his failure to write creates a powerful poem. The punning on the verb phrase *take to task* is central to this: as an informal verb phrase, it stands as a self-criticism of Thomas's failure to write; but he is also taking on his *craft* as a *task* in a new attempt to create a poem.

The inventiveness in this poem is striking. Words with financial connotations (*rich, purse, pounds, currencies, expensive*) work on two levels, juxtaposing the richness of the natural world with the poverty of Thomas's *three lean months*. The image is underpinned by the infinitives (*To take to give, To lift to leave, To surrender . . . to pay, to burn or return*) marking the reciprocal bond that should exist between nature's creation and man. Collocations like *gift of the gab* and the colloquial connotations of *lift* (steal) exist alongside religious lexis (*manna, heaven*). The result is a poem in which Thomas celebrates the fertility of the natural world and considers man's choices in relation to this creativity. He can *burn or return* nature's gifts, surrendering to death or *Puffing the pounds of manna up through the dew to heaven*. In creating his poem, Thomas is returning nature's gift of life.

Content and themes

Thomas writes of people ('The Hunchback in the Park'), of intimate experiences like getting his daughter to sleep ('In Country Sleep') or the moment of birth ('If my head hurt a hair's foot'), of particular events of the war ('Among those Killed in the Dawn Raid was a Man aged a Hundred'; 'Ceremony after a Fire Raid'), and topical issues ('The hand that signed the paper'). His poems deal with the nature of the artist, imagination, everyday occurrences, childhood, life and death – his themes are universal.

Thomas often draws on **ordinary events** as the source for his poems, but through a process of transformation, they take on new meaning. The poet intensifies experience and things we take for granted are distorted – they become symbols, connecting elements of life that had previously seemed disparate. In 'Over Sir John's Hill', for instance, the ordinary scene of the bay becomes a universal backdrop as Thomas reveals the complex pattern of life and death at the centre of all existence. Within the symbolism of the poem, the hawk becomes the executioner, and the heron the priest. The lexical choices transform the natural scene: noun phrases like *a hoisted cloud, fiery tyburn, the noosed hawk* and *a black cap* of *jack-/Daws*, and verbs like *hangs* and *gallows* develop the metaphor of the hangman. The imagery is of a court of execution and Thomas uses it to present us with a landscape inescapably marked by the adult poet's awareness of death.

The violence of *the hawk on fire* is juxtaposed with the dignity of *the fishing holy stalking heron* that *bows his tilted headstone*. Poet and heron become one in their grieving for *the blithe birds*, and the repetition of the compound phrase *The heron and I* and the pronoun *We* emphasises the importance of the vision. The poem becomes an elegy for the acceptance of death in life, but as the vision, the moment of understanding, fades, a mood of sadness replaces the ecstasy.

The language of death is linked to both the heron and the hawk, yet their presentation in the poem is quite different. The dynamic verbs *Crashes* and *crack* suggest the power and strength of the hawk, but the verbs linked to the heron are different. The dignity of the verb *bows* is given more status by the adverb *slowly*; the dynamic verb *stabs* is mediated by the noun phrase *the elegiac fisherbird* with its connotations of mourning. While the hawk is portrayed as a non-thinking instinctive killer, Thomas suggests the heron responds in a human manner. Verbs like *grieve* and *hymning*, noun phrases like *the fishing holy stalking heron* and *his tilted headstone*, and references to his ability to *tell-tale the knelled/Guilt* raise the heron above the natural world. Yet the heron, like the hawk and the sparrows, is also a part of the landscape and paradoxically, by the end of the poem, the reader senses the distance between the poet and the heron. After the complicity implied by the pronouns and compound noun phrases, we ultimately see the heron as an allegory for what it is to be human and aware of your own mortality.

The plea to God in stanza 4 (*God . . ./Have mercy on,/God . . . save*) is replaced by a resignation that shows an understanding of the inevitability of death. The final stanza ends on a quieter note (*no green cocks of hens/Shout/Now*) as the poet accepts, not the Christian belief in resurrection, but an emphatic awareness of our own mortality. References to *the lunge of night* and *this time-shaken stone* remind us that we are bound by time and thus mortal. The heron *Makes all the music*, but it is the poet who understands – he <u>hears</u> *the tune of the slow,/Wear-willow river* – and the mood of acceptance is marked by his attempt to record (*grave*) his vision.

Thomas uses the **natural world** in two distinct ways in his poetry: the concrete representation of the physical world around him can be seen in the poems firmly embedded in the Welsh landscape, where the natural world becomes the back-drop to personal reflections on death and writing; and the symbolic representa-tion where elements of the natural world are drawn together to reveal the organic pattern underpinning life. Both approaches are distinctive in the way that they combine the physical and the abstract, using a moment of revelation in which the poet is united with the natural world to explore the nature of existence.

Thomas's presentation of the natural world is quite different from that evoked in the poetry of Wordsworth. Where the Romantics bring a landscape to life through their description of its physical properties and the spirit that these embody, Thomas reflects on the processes at the very heart of the natural world.

The kind of **transformation of the landscape** at the heart of 'Over Sir John's Hill' is a recurring theme in Thomas's poetry. He tries to reveal the inner life of the natural world and to reach a unity with it. In such poems as 'A Refusal to Mourn the Death, by Fire, of a Child in London', 'Poem in October' and 'Especially when the October Wind', he feels at one with the world he is describing. In the two 'October' poems, the concrete nature of the landscape is linked to abstract ideas: in 'Poem in October', Thomas contemplates the loss of childhood innocence and the inevitability of the movement towards death; in 'Especially when the October Wind', he meditates on the nature of language, revealing the interconnections that exist between physical things and words.

While the 'October' poems are representations of personal experience, 'A Refusal to Mourn' is a more public poem. It uses the natural world in a different way – the landscape is no longer the specific background to Thomas's country walks, but the symbolic natural world of the organic cycle. The poem was written to mark the death of a girl killed in wartime bombing raids on London. Often crit-icised for appearing to ignore the effects of the war on life, Thomas's sense of moral outrage here is clear. His response is not explicit because his approach to poetry is so different from the poets of the thirties – the poem is a personal rather than a public declaration. What Thomas does is to celebrate the natural cycle of which the girl will become a part – only in the very last moments of all existence will he mourn death.

Our sense of the natural world is bound up in references to the cycle of life and death. Nouns like *bird, beast, flower, sea, water, corn* and *valley* in the first two stan-zas establish our sense of pattern in a world that is being destroyed by man. The noun phrases are long and complex and their accumulative effect drives the reader on to the final line: *After the first death, there is no other*. The biblical allusion is clear, but this elegy is not written in the Christian tradition. Instead there is a pantheistic feel to Thomas's view of death as a part of life – both are represented as an integral part of the organic process.

In the first stanza of the poem, for instance, the compound noun phrase *the mankind making/Bird beast and flower/Fathering and all humbling darkness* establishes a link between the human, animal and plant worlds. Everything is seen to come from darkness and, in Thomas's scheme of things, will return to the darkness of *the last light breaking*. The use of present participle pre-modifiers (*making, Fathering, humbling*) develops a sense of process that is symbolic of the cycle. The effect is intensified because Thomas uses nouns like 'father' and adjectives like 'humble' as the source of his present participles, ensuring that all humanity is drawn in to the inevitability of the life-death process.

The poem is an elegy in which the expression of grief is controlled by the tightness of the structure. The patterning of the syntax and the sound contributes to the apparent impersonality of 'A Refusal to Mourn'. This is reinforced by the overall formality: the mood of this requiem for a lost child seems marked by an absence of grief. Thomas is not refusing to mourn, however, but delaying it. The juxtaposition of the adjective *still* with the present participle post-modifier *tumbling* marks the point at which mourning will be appropriate. The tone is, in fact, celebratory: the third stanza recognises humanity's responsibility for the child's death in the noun phrase *The mankind of her going*, but he refuses to add to this by further 'blasphemy'.

Where the language of the first stanzas is firmly embedded in the natural world, stanza 3 moves towards a more abstract diction: *majesty, truth, innocence* and *youth*. The sentiments are not Christian, however, despite the final stanza's reference to *the first death* – the resurrection here is a natural rather than a spiritual one. The final stanza then returns us to the natural world and Thomas's celebration of the inevitable process where the child has become a part of something much greater, she is *Deep with the first dead, Robed in the long friends*. The language is comforting: the connotations of the nouns *friends* and *mother* are positive, representing not what she has left behind, but what she has been reunited with. This is the consolation Thomas offers: the child is not alone, but has become a part of an organic process in which life and death are inextricably bound together. The adjectives *dark* and *Secret* remind us that this pattern in nature is often unrecognised, while the noun phrase *the unmourning water* becomes symbolic of the attitude we should adopt to death.

Thomas is poet as priest, revealing and celebrating the process of life and death. The accumulative effect of the syntax imitates the natural cycle, drawing the reader in and uniting meaning and form. The poem becomes a pantheistic celebration of life and death in which Thomas sees a time when mourning will be irrelevant because sadness will no longer be our response to death.

Although he is sometimes seen as an escapist poet who failed to face the horrors of war, **death** appears as the central theme in several of Thomas's poems. He shows little belief in the comfort of a Christian afterlife, but uses biblical allusions to underpin his vision of resurrection in the organic cycle, in which death is seen to bring new life through the process of decomposition and fertilisation of the soil. The early poem 'And death shall have no dominion' and the late one 'Poem on his Birthday' both broach the complex ideas of the afterlife in terms of a union with the natural world.

In 'A Refusal to Mourn', death is approached in an impersonal way, and the tone in 'And death shall have no dominion' is equally public and declamatory. It is a poem that celebrates opposites as a part of a single unified process. Juxtapositions of *mad/sane, sink/rise* and *lovers . . . lost/love . . . not* reflect the positive and negative forces of the lifecycle. Man and the natural world become one and the lexical choices of the poem mirror this. The *Dead men naked* will no longer experience life physically – they will not hear the *gulls cry at their ears* or the *waves break loud on the seashores*. Instead, they will become part of the life force. The dynamic verbs *hammer* and *break* reflect this new existence that will end only when *the sun breaks down.*

Like 'A Refusal to Mourn', the poem is an emphatic declaration of the unity of life and death in the organic process. The poet's authority is conveyed in the repetition of the modal negative verb phrase *shall have no* at the beginning and end of each stanza. The connotations of certainty implicit in the modal verb and the frequency of end-stopped lines give the argument of the poem its weight. Thomas can perhaps rely on his readers to recognise the biblical allusions, but their field of reference here is not Christian. For him, religious belief dies with the believer – *Faith in their hands shall snap in two* – while the organic cycle goes on. The poem therefore challenges traditional belief structures and offers an alternative perspective.

This is the earliest of Thomas's poems celebrating the organic cycle – man and the natural world are united in the face of death which thus no longer has the power to terrify. The emphatic *they shall be one* in the second line explicitly establishes the theme that is then developed through the lexical choices and the rhetorical patterning. To convey his attitude to death, Thomas manipulates familiar language patterns, forcing the reader to reconsider things in a new light. He disrupts familiar collocations such as 'man in the moon' and 'the west wind (*the man in the wind and the west moon*) and reworks clichés, euphemisms for death – 'pushing up the daisies' becomes *hammer through daisies*.

The biblical tone of the repeated line *And death shall have no dominion* is ironic in the context of Thomas's attitude to death. The poem is a triumphant statement of death's insignificance in the face of a greater force – it should not be feared because it is merely another stage in the cycle of existence. While Thomas clearly recognises the end of the individual's physical life, his treatment of death takes place in a wider context. Distanced from the individual, it is presented against a backdrop of the natural world's eternal life and thus becomes less threatening.

Other poems using death as a central idea in the content take a different viewpoint. In 'After the Funeral (In memory of Ann Jones)', addressed to his aunt, and 'Do not go gentle into that good night', addressed to his father, Thomas faces death in a closer context – it touches him more personally and the mood is no longer calm or accepting. In these very personal contexts, there is no understanding in the face of death.

'Do not go gentle' protests against the inevitability of death with language that is forcible and emotive. Using the villanelle, Thomas is forced to control his grief within a restrictive pattern of rhyme and repetition. The tightness of the formal structure is juxtaposed with a personal tone; a rhetorical imperative mood is offset by the development of a logical argument as Thomas attempts to move away from the personal towards the presentation of an objective case.

Dynamic verbs like *burn, rave* and *rage* are addressed directly to his father in an emotive plea that he should defy death, and the use of the imperatives (*Do not go; Rage, rage; Curse, bless*) adds force to this. Only the first and final stanzas, however, are addressed to Thomas's father explicitly. The other stanzas broaden the plea by considering death in a range of contexts, addressing *wise men, Good men, Wild men* and *Grave men*. This movement towards a logical consideration of death is underpinned by the return to the declarative mood, so that the same dynamic verbs, *Do not go* and *Rage*, are now part of a statement rather than a command. This balance between personal rhetoric and general argument lies at the heart of the poem, creating a controlled and balanced emotion and avoiding the overtly sentimental.

The language reflects the central opposition between life and death. Juxtapositions of *dark/lightning, sang/grieved, Grave/gay, curse/bless* underpin Thomas's plea for defiance in the face of death, reminding us that at the moment of death, life is still present. The lexical set of words associated with light is used to enhance this idea: the verbs *burn* and *blaze*, the noun phases *the sun in flight* and *meteors*, and the adjective *bright* and the verb modifier *blinding* create a positive mood despite the references to death. The meaning of words and phases is often ambiguous, allowing Thomas to create layers of meaning. The *Grave men*, for instance, are both serious and at the point of death; *gentle* is both an adverb 'gently' and a reference to Thomas's father, a 'gentle man', tamed by his illness. References to death are euphemistic – the prepositional phases *into that good night, at close of day* and *at their end*; the noun phrases *the dying of the light* and *the last wave*; the noun clause *(that) dark is right* – keeping the harsh reality of death at a distance. It is here symbolic of a lack of fulfilment and the refrains are like incantations urging Thomas's father to fight against the inevitable.

Childhood is another recurring theme that is central to Thomas's work. He recreates a child's view of the world by distilling memories of his own experiences, focusing on a state of innocence that is quite unconscious of the passage of time. He represents it as a golden age of creativity and sensitivity, of oneness with the natural world. It becomes a symbol for the condition an artist must enter in order to create. The imagination, therefore, becomes analogous to the experience of childhood; the artist, in essence, must become a child again if he is to recreate the world around him in poetic form. The child's openness to experience and freedom from preconceptions lie at the heart of the poetic experience.

The imaginative act becomes a moment of transformation when the world is seen through the freshness of the child's eyes. Because the poet's senses are heightened and the child's sense of wonder is reinstated, language is intensified as Thomas sees beneath the surface of ordinary things to discover the nature of existence. What begins as a recollection of childhood experience becomes something transcendent – the poem becomes an analogue for the essential truth of things. It is a very subjective experience and although Thomas begins as the child, the poems inevitably end with a feeling of the poet as priest, shaping the world and revealing its secrets for the reader.

In a poem like 'After the Funeral', we are given a sense of the experience from the child's perspective – we see the *desolate boy* who remembers the time spent at Fernhill, his aunt's farm. This image is overlaid with our sense of the mature poet, *Ann's bard*, able to create a memorial from his words, *this skyward statue*. This dual time scale merges so that we are not aware of the moment at which the child becomes the man, but we instinctively feel the movement from the concrete physical observations of the opening to the emphatic initial position *But* that begins the epitaph for his aunt.

Thomas uses childhood as a particular way of seeing and experiencing the world. In 'Poem in October', for instance, he contrasts the adult and child viewpoints so that the poem becomes more than just a nostalgic yearning for youth. The specific events (the poet's walk on his birthday and looking down on the town where he lives) provide the stimulus for an exploration of human and natural life.

The first stanza establishes the sounds of the natural world that *beckon* the poet while the rest of the human world is asleep. The *still sleeping town* is juxtaposed with the references to the *water praying* and the *call of seagull and rook*, enhancing the 'livingness' of the natural world. This is reinforced by the religious connotations of words like *heron/Priested* and *praying* which give the external world a spiritual significance and prepare the reader for the transformation of the natural world that will take place.

The autumnal mood is evident in Thomas's choice of the modifier *rainy*. The gloomy connotations set the tone of the poem and this is reinforced by the representation of life as an inevitable movement towards death – it is his *thirtieth year to heaven*. The modifiers in the third stanza, however, mark a change in mood as Thomas is affected by the 'livingness' of the natural world. We know from the title that it is October, but the noun phase *A springful of larks*, the description of the October sun as *Summery* and the use of the modifiers *fond* and *sweet* reflect a new perception of the world. Where the clause *the rain wringing/Wind blow cold* reflects Thomas's earlier perception of the morning, the adverb *suddenly* records the moment of change. This is reinforced by the prepositional phase *In the wood faraway under me* as the poet begins to move towards a state of ecstasy in which he soars above the human world.

In this heightened state, Thomas can perceive the world as he did in childhood – a change marked by the verb modifier *altered* and the adverb *again* indicating a return to a lost world of the *wonder of summer*. The pleasure of the child is reflected in the listing of *apples/Pears and red currants* and in the image of the Garden of Eden. Noun phases like *the parables/Of sun light* and *the legends of the green chapels* intricately interweave religious imagery of innocence with natural references to the physical landscape and suggestions of imaginative creativity. The combination of these mirrors the poet's transformation from distant observer to spontaneous celebrant.

The integration of adult and child is completed in the opposition of *his/my/mine* in the penultimate stanza where the present autumnal world is transformed by *the twice told fields of infancy*. The climactic noun phrase *the truth of his joy* is given an emphatic position at the end of the line. Its significance becomes clear when the verb *whispered* is transformed into *sang* – the boy's vision, *the mystery*, has been recreated and the adverb *still* in the initial position stresses the importance of this recognition. For Thomas, the grey autumn day has acquired new meaning, and even though the vision fades and the town is once more *leaved with October blood*, the intensity is sustained. The language is ecstatic: the noun phases *the true/Joy of the long dead child* and *my heart's truth* and the repetition of the celebratory verb *sang/sung* reflect the artist's exaltation.

The contrast of line lengths, the use of enjambement and a tight rhyme scheme add to the reader's sense of a pattern underlying life. There is no fixed number of stresses per line, but the regularity of the syllabic pattern maintains a rapidity of movement through the stanzas. Each one is made up of a loosely structured compound-complex sentence that gives the poem what Thomas described *as a lovely slow lyrical movement.*

What we see in this poem is a breakdown of the barriers existing between the poet and the natural world and this is achieved through the recreation of the child's view of experience. The poet's outpouring of feelings colours the way we view the landscape and, in a kind of pathetic fallacy, poet and landscape become one. Even though this cannot be sustained, the use of the celebratory interjection *O* and the modal verb *may* in the final lines create a sense of hope that was absent at the beginning of the poem.

One other significant thematic area in Thomas's poetry is his interest in the **artist and his art**. As we have already seen, many of the poems address the nature of the artist and his function implicitly: we see the 'poet as priest' celebrating his oneness with the natural world; we see the artist reaching an ecstatic vision through a recollection of childhood memories. Other poems, however, deal more explicitly with the process of writing.

A poem like 'How shall my animal' may at first seem quite distant from the concept of the poet and his art, but beneath the animal imagery lies a discussion about the way in which experience is transferred to the page. In the first two stanzas, Thomas uses the interrogative mood to formulate a rhetorical question *How shall . . .?*, expressing his doubts about the creative process. He cannot see how 'experience' will *Endure burial under the spelling wall*. The noun phrases *the spelling wall* and *The invoked, shrouding veil* reflect his feeling that the technicalities of the process and the poet's inability to explain will inevitably result in the poem's failure. Concrete images are used to give a physicality to an otherwise abstract theme. We see poetry as a craft – Thomas has *a living skein* with which he will *angle* and *Trace out* his words. Verbs like *lie shorn, Lops* and *Clips* in the final stanza, however, remind us of the imperfections of the process as the poetic *gesture of breath* is drained of life by the poet's *wrackspiked maiden mouth*. The harsh consonantal sounds and the inexperience conveyed by the modifier *maiden* emphasise the failure, which is reinforced by the brutal and restrictive verbs (*Nailed, clasp, clap . . . down, lops, clips short*).

The running image of sculpture in the final stanza is one to which Thomas returns in 'After the Funeral'. The lexical choices (*carved, stone, hewn*) reflect the hard physical process of creation – an idea which is reiterated in 'In my Craft or Sullen Art' where we see Thomas as the Romantic poet whose interest lies not in fame, but in revealing the inner life and interpreting the mysteries of life. He is the poet as outsider, a distant observer who comments on, but who does not participate in life. The juxtaposition of *craft* (the learnt skill) and *art* (the spontaneous outpouring of feelings) lies at the heart of his debate. Verbs like *Exercised* and *labour* are symbolic of the intensity of poetic creation and the repetition of *rages/raging* underpins this. The traditional Romantic diction of *the moon, lovers, nightingales* and *psalms* is juxtaposed with the representation of the 'craft' of poetry. The poem may celebrate the process of creation, but the modifier *sullen* is indicative of Thomas's relationship with his muse. While the lyricism of the poem suggests the poet's romantic, spontaneous response to life, its tight structure reflects the conscientious craftsman who works at his masterpiece. The rhyme scheme, rhythm and syntactical structure *Not for . . . or . . . nor*, as well as the content, thus become an integral part of Thomas's statement of artistic intent.

Images and symbols

Thomas's use of images contributes to the distinctive nature of his verse – the striking effects of modifiers and the unexpected combinations of words are immediately noticeable. His originality can make the meaning obscure, but where the images work the effects are dramatic.

Many of the letters exchanged by Thomas and Pamela Hansford Johnson include interesting discussion of the poetry they sent to each other for critical comment. In a letter dated early November 1933, Thomas addresses the nature of the images that she has been using in her poetry. His comments are illuminating because of the light they throw on his own approach to imagery.

> The image is smart and cheap; it falls too easily on the paper. And the attitude behind it is wrong, relying too much on a quick, admittedly vivid, visual impression, instead of upon a mentally digested experience. It is written from the mind's eye, not even from the mind's ear, for the sounds are unintentionally ugly. You have seized on a glimpse of what you wanted to express, and not on the still, slow scrutiny.

This extract helps readers of Thomas's work to understand what he was trying to achieve in his imagery. Although a *visual impression* is a part of the overall effect, an image should enable the reader to move beyond this to the *mentally digested experience* that underpins it. In other words, Thomas's imagery has evolved as a result of his experience of the world and his attitudes to it. The images form the *single thread of action* in a poem – they may have a strong visual impact, but they also function as part of the underlying framework of ideas. Each one represents Thomas's *still, slow scrutiny* of life and in unravelling its layers we may come closer to the meaning of his poems.

We have already seen in Thomas's choice of themes that the natural world plays a crucial part in his worldview and many of the images he creates find their source in **nature**. Descriptions of *the crabbing sun* ('Especially when the October Wind') and *the mustardseed sun* ('Poem on his Birthday') create strong visual images by using unfamiliar modifiers. The verb modifier *crabbing* is indicative of the autumnal mood of the poem and representative of the poet's crab-like shadow; the compounding of the two nouns 'mustard' and 'seed' creates a visual impression, surprising the reader with its unexpected contrast of size (sun/mustard seed). In both contexts, the image also functions as part of the framework of ideas: in 'Especially when the October Wind', a poem linking language and things, the sun is named and the gap between the word and the reality is bridged; in 'Poem on his Birthday', the modifier suggests the insignificance of the sun in comparison to the vastness of the process of life and death as a whole.

In 'Fern Hill', images of the sun fulfil a similar dual function: they contribute to the visual impression of the poem and underpin its themes. Noun phrases like *the sun that is young once only* (l.12) and *the sun born over and over* (l.39) are an integral part of the celebration of the child's oneness with the natural world around him. They also develop the theme of childhood innocence and reinforce the adult's awareness of mortality.

Thomas also draws on **biblical** images to enable readers to make links between the familiar and the unfamiliar. Although he draws increasingly on Christian imagery as a source for his verse, he is not a Christian poet in the traditional sense of the word. A note at the beginning of *Collected Poems* (1952) records that Thomas was writing his poems *for the love of Man and in praise of God*. This may seem to suggest that Thomas, like Gerard Manley Hopkins, was celebrating the presence of God in the natural world. His qualification *and I'd be a damn fool if they weren't*, however, points to the underlying ambiguity. As Thomas himself said, the poems were written *in praise of God's world by a man who doesn't believe in God*.

The religious language and imagery of his verse, therefore, is not traditionally Christian, but is used to underpin Thomas's view of the world. While some poems such as 'Out of the Pit' and 'No Man Believes' deal with the concept of God and religious belief directly, most religious images are used for their implicit associations. Thomas makes references to heaven, Adam, Christ, the Holy Ghost and the Garden of Eden, using their links to innocence, the resurrection, and immortality through salvation.

The poem 'This bread I break' uses the symbols of the Holy Communion in an unconventional way: the symbolic bread and wine are seen in relation to the oat and the vine they once were. The negative connotations of verbs such as *laid . . . low*, *broke* and *pulled . . . down* reflect man's destruction of the natural world. They can be juxtaposed with the positive language associated with the oat and the vine in their natural setting: the abstract noun *joy* and the adjective *merry*. Thomas adopts the style and tone of the Holy Communion to give his poem weight, using the religious images to explore an idea from an unusual perspective.

Perhaps most common is the way in which he combines natural and religious imagery – he sacramentalises the landscape, endowing it with spiritual meaning through the language he chooses. Noun phrases like *the heron/Priested shore*, *the parables/Of sun light* and *the legends of the green chapels* in 'Poem in October' highlight Thomas's view of the landscape as spiritual, and his communion with it takes on a religious tone. In 'Fern Hill', he describes *the holy stream*, *the fields of praise* and *the lamb white days*. The overlaying of religious and natural lexis colours our view of the child's vision of the world. This is reinforced by the description of the morning as *Adam and maiden* – Thomas disrupts the collocation 'Adam and Eve', bringing a freshness to the world he describes and reinforcing the mood of innocence untouched by experience.

The complicated sonnet sequence 'Altarwise by owl-light' and 'Vision and Prayer' uses explicit religious imagery. The *gentleman of wounds* ('Altarwise') and *the turbulent new born* with *his torrid crown* ('Vision and Prayer') are both references to Christ and each poem addresses the relationship between man and God. The poems reflect Thomas's attitude to religion – it is an integral part of him, a natural and direct process rather than a philosophical idea. He is not, like Eliot, an overtly religious poet, but he has, like the Romantics, a religious attitude to experience. This is represented in his verse in images of the unifying life force at the heart of all existence.

The imagery with its implicit symbolic function can be very personal and therefore difficult for readers to unravel. Thomas's approach is subjective and the compression of images can be intense as he attempts to go beneath the surface of life, stretching language to its limits in the process. His aim, although perhaps not always successful, is to use imagery to bring all *thought or action . . . onto a physical level*. In 'Poet: 1935', he uses the physical image of flowers to represent the nature of the poet's craft: the poet makes his images *dance, cut capers/Choreographed on paper*, drops them *into their prison with a slack sound* when their symbolic function is complete, and creates *Fresh images* to develop his strand of thought. The flower imagery gives the reader a strong visual picture and fits neatly into the seasonal theme of the poem, but there is still a symbolic complexity that readers must overcome. Where the imagery is at its most intense and abstruse, an awareness of Thomas's general themes can help readers to approach the underlying meaning.

Poetic form

In a letter to Pamela Hansford Johnson (15 October 1933), Thomas was to write that a verse should *find its own form,* that *the structure should rise out of the words and the expression of them*. He argued against the imposition of a particular form by the poet, aiming for something more organic that he believed would reveal something new about life.

His earliest poems tend to be more traditional, using patterns of metre and stanza structure that are familiar. In *Eighteen Poems* (1934) and *Twenty-Five Poems* (1936), the iambic foot is common. A poem like 'The force that through the green fuse drives the flower', for instance, with its four 5-lined stanzas and final couplet uses an iambic metre to add an air of authority to the statement it is making about the unity of life. Thomas reduces the human body to a machine-like status and personalises the natural world as he explores the structure of things and tentatively gropes towards meaning. The solemnity of the structure is reinforced by the rhyme pattern (ababa aa) and the recurring 10-syllable line with a short 4-syllable line at the centre of each stanza. The effect is to add weight to the argument: the tone is sonorous, the language is rhetorical, and the structure reflects the cyclical nature of the force Thomas describes.

Thomas becomes the 'poet as priest' with the poem as an incantation celebrating, not the glory of God, but the impersonal force at the centre of life that can both destroy and create. Even as he reveals the world, he does not attempt to explain it because he is *dumb* and knows that the vision will soon fade.

In later work, Thomas became more interested in syllabic poetry, where the number of syllables per line is more significant than the number of weak or strong stresses. He did not quite abandon traditional metrical patterns, but he tended to use them less frequently. The syllabic approach to verse structure gave Thomas greater flexibility while still requiring great discipline. 'Poem in October' is a tightly structured syllabic poem in which each stanza is made up of 9, 12, 9, 3, 5, 12, 12, 5, 3, 9 syllables. Thomas's close adherence to this syllabic sequence makes a distinctive visual pattern on the page. Initially, many critics saw this poem as an example of free verse, failing to appreciate the tightness of the syllabic patterning. Its conscious rhythm, however, underpins the movement of the verse and ties together the vision of autumn. The pattern is reinforced by the distinctive rhyme scheme in which Thomas draws on repeated vowel sounds within words containing different consonants – in stanza 1 *heaven* rhymes with *heron, beckon, second*; *wood* rhymes with *rook* and *foot*; and *shore* with *wall* and *forth*. The pattern in each stanza is not always exact, but the effect of the three recurring rhymes is cohesive.

It is important to remember that Thomas saw poetry as part of an organic process in which content and form were inextricably linked – the shape of a poem on the page, its sound, and its rhythm all contribute to the meaning. When Thomas chooses a complex traditional form like the villanelle in 'Do not go gentle', therefore, we know that the form is significant in our interpretation of the meaning of the poem: he uses the tight structure of repeated lines and two recurring rhymes to control his grief.

Style

Thomas's use of language and syntax is distinctive. His style is heightened and rhetorical, reflecting a strong individual response to the experiences he records. Particularly in the early work, the syntactical complexity and personal nature of the metaphors can cause obscurity. In the later work, the poet's presence and the descriptive sense of place help the reader to overcome difficulties with abstract ideas and style.

Just as his manipulation of poetic form and devices is painstaking, so too is his crafting of the words themselves. This is borne out by comments in his letters about the *many painful hours spent over the smoothing and removing of the creakiness of conflict* from his poems (Letter to T. S. Eliot, November 1933). Thomas loved words and although the language of the poems is not difficult in itself, he seems to use words in ways that make them appear unfamiliar. He places them in unexpected contexts, combines them in unusual ways, and coins new expressions. He believed it was the poet's job to take overused words and to recreate them, *to smooth away the lines of [their] dissipation and to put [them] on the market again, fresh and virgin* (letter to Pamela Hansford Johnson, 15 October 1933). He disrupts our expectations by forcing us to reconsider what we often take for granted. Familiar expressions are altered and descriptions associated with one thing are transferred to another.

Lexical sets focus Thomas's topics and develop the metaphors. In 'The spire cranes', for instance, two groups of words dominate the diction: those associated with stone (*statue, stone, carved*) and those associated with music (*Chimes, music, note, songs, voice, bells*). These two groups form the basis for Thomas's exploration of the creative process. He describes crafted poems whose technical perfection denies them life, and 'living' poems that make contact with real experience and thus communicate with their readers. Verb phrases like *does not let* and *jump back* associated with the first lexical set suggest a failure to connect, while verbs like *plunge* and *fly* indicate a productive process. The difficulty lies in interpreting the metaphors: the *spire* is the poet, and the *birds* are the poems. Studying the lexical sets in a poem can help to reveal the ideas that are represented by the literal words.

Modifiers are also significant in understanding Thomas's poems. Noun phrases tend to be long and the modification will often develop the central theme. 'In the White Giant's Thigh' celebrates the power of life in the face of death as Thomas walks on a *high chalk hill*, where the figure of a huge giant is carved. As a symbol of fertility, it is representative of life in a place marked by the burial of childless women – *barren as boulders women* who *lie longing still/To labour and love*. The poem is grounded by its noun phrases with their striking use of modification – they create a powerful sequence of images linking the human (*their moonshade/Petticoats galed high*; *a bloom of wayside brides*), the natural (*the pitching cloud*; *the after milking moonlight*), and the religious (*The scurrying, furred small friars*; *the thistle aisles*). The modification forges links between the different layers, placing unexpected words in conjunction and thus engaging the reader in a new and exciting view of the world. The combination of words focuses on celebration of the life force, immersing us in a vision of activity where even *the daughters of darkness* are characterised by the dynamic verb *flame* and the time adverb *still*.

Unusual expressions help to make Thomas's work memorable. As can be seen in 'In the White Giant's Thigh', Thomas uses words in unexpected ways (*a hedgerow of joys*; *a torch of foxes*) and disrupts collocations (*ducked and draked white lake* – adapted from the game 'ducks and drakes', in which flat stones are skipped across the water). Similarly in 'Once it was the colour of saying', Thomas explores the language and style of his early verse which he sees as steeped in the excesses of romance. He describes *the colour of saying* (suggesting a use of language that is more interested in verbal delight than in meaning) that has *soaked [his] table*. The imagery is dominated by references to water (*a capsized field*; *The gentle sea-slides of saying*; *the charmingly drowned*) and these reflect what Thomas sees as his failure to address his subject matter effectively, to communicate with his reader. The poem explores the poet's attitude to language – he believes his *saying shall be [his] undoing* and yet, paradoxically, we recognise in Thomas's linguistic originality the richness of his verse and the freshness of his vision.

The **syntax**, too, is pushed to the limit: word order is inverted; sentence elements are separated; and the relationship between clauses can be confusing. Thomas distorts everyday events to present them to us in a new light and this means that he distorts grammar too. The poems can, therefore, seem very difficult because they do not conform to customary patterns. Thomas refuted claims that he was an experimentalist, claiming that he wrote in the only way he could – his poetry was not the result of *theorising but of pure incapability to express [his] needless tortuities in any other way*.

Thomas writes long complex sentences, often delaying the subject, main verb or object. In 'Refusal to mourn', for instance, the sequence of modifiers describing *darkness* separates the opening emphatic *Never* from its inverted subject and predicator *Shall I let pray*. The conjunction *until* and its related subordinate clause draw attention to the time when all living things will have returned to their original state, thus marking the time when mourning will be appropriate. The complexity of the syntax is integral to the meaning of the poem, mirroring the natural cycle that Thomas believes unites life and death.

Other distinctive features can be seen in the use of **inverted word order**. The emphatic *nothing I cared* ('Fern Hill') draws attention to the child's innocent physical pleasure in life by foregrounding the negative *nothing*. **Disrupted collocations** reflect Thomas's love of word play and his interest in challenging the reader's conception of the world. The well-known *Once below a time* ('Fern Hill') implicitly undermines the child's vision by reminding the reader of the adult poet's awareness of mortality – we are all bound by time.

Dylan Thomas and the English poetic tradition

Although there may be a number of poems that continue to cause critical debate, where language and meaning are hard to connect, where readers struggle to relate to the central idea or conceit, Thomas does achieve something distinctive in his verse. He is remembered as the first poet who was both popular and enigmatic, and he contributes something new to the English poetic tradition. His individual view of the world is typically Romantic and he is the leading figure in the Neo-Romantic poetry of the 1940s.

A change in direction in Thomas's career is often seen to lie in 1938. At this point, he began to reflect on his earlier work, reining in the exuberance of his youth. For the most part, the poetry written after this date tends to be more accessible. Images are familiar; a generalised sense of nature is often replaced by a clear focus on a specific place; and the syntactical patterns are less distorted and therefore less challenging. The later poems are more immediately approachable, but their themes tend to be less optimistic. Written during the war years, they combine a celebration of childhood innocence with an unavoidable recognition of mortality.

Critical response is mainly positive, praising the power of his rhetoric and his linguistic innovation. During his lifetime, he was admired as a charismatic reader of his own verse and an engaging personality. His first volumes in the 1930s attracted the attention of the critics; and the final volumes *Deaths and Entrances* (1946), containing some of his most well-known work, *In Country Sleep* (1952), and *Collected Poems* (1953) were well received by both critics and readers.

In his best poems, a personal voice, a distinctive diction, and a disrupted syntax are interwoven to create verse that strikes a chord with readers. Recordings of Thomas reading his own poems make it, perhaps, more easy to understand the dramatic effect both his life and death had upon the literary world: he engaged with his audience in such a way that he brought his poetry to life and, even as we struggle towards meaning, we can be roused by the sound and emotion of the words we hear.

Thomas is widely recognised as a conscientious craftsman with a love of words and structures. He uses language distinctively, shapes the poem on the page consciously, and manipulates poetic form skilfully. Although the intensity of the images and symbols, and the complexity of the syntax can make the poetry seem incomprehensible, in most cases, it is possible to reach an understanding of the underlying meaning. The language, structure and style are inextricably linked to the meaning – underlying the apparent disorder is a tightly worked and personal view of the world.

For some, however, his work is deliberately obscure, uncontrolled and self-indulgent. It attempts to do with language something that is impossible, and therefore fails. Thomas's critics would argue that the poems reflect no more than an outpouring of uncontrolled feelings. They see in his work distorted language, cliché, and an elitism that excludes readers. The lack of order and Thomas's excessive interest in the sound of words become obstacles to meaning.

Thomas is seen as the antithesis of Eliot and the 1930s poets: his style is essentially Romantic where his predecessors are of the realist school; his language is stretched to its limits where Eliot and Auden choose the language of everyday conversation. Their intellectualism is replaced by Thomas' emotionalism; their focus on the urban by Thomas's immersion in the natural world. He follows in the tradition of Hopkins, searching for a language that will enable him to reveal the world in a new light.

Activity 13.5

Explore the ways in which Thomas creates the child's voice in 'Fern Hill' and develops a contrast between this and the adult's view of the world.

You may like to think about: the style, the lexical choices, the syntax and the imagery.

Fern Hill

1   Now as I was young and easy under the apple boughs
     About the lilting house and happy as the grass was green,
          The night above the dingle starry,
               Time let me hail and climb
5   Golden in the heydays of his eyes,
     And honoured among wagons I was prince of the apple towns
     And once below a time I lordly had the trees and leaves
          Trail with daisies and barley
               Down the rivers of the windfall light.

10   And as I was green and carefree, famous among the barns
     About the happy yard and singing as the farm was home,
          In the sun that is young once only,
               Time let me play and be
          Golden in the mercy of his means,
15   And green and golden I was huntsman and herdsman, the calves
     Sang to my horn, the foxes on the hills barked clear and cold,
          And the Sabbath rang slowly
               In the pebbles of the holy streams.

All the sun long it was running, it was lovely, the hay
20   Fields high as the house, the tunes from the chimneys, it was air
          And playing, lovely and watery
              And fire green as grass.
          And nightly under the simple stars
          As I rode to sleep the owls were bearing the farm away,
25   All the moon long I heard, blessed among stables, the nightjars
          Flying with the ricks and the horses
              Flashing into the dark.

      And then to awake, and the farm, like a wanderer white
      With the dew, come back, the cock on his shoulder: it was all
30   Shining, it was Adam and maiden,
              The sky gathered again
          And the sun grew round that very day.
      So it must have been after the birth of the simple light
      In the first, spinning place, the spellbound horses walking warm
35   Out of the whinnying green stable
              On to the fields of praise.

      And honoured among foxes and pheasants by the gay house
      Under the new made clouds and happy as the heart was long,
          In the sun born over and over,
40   I ran my heedless ways,
          My wishes raced through the house high hay
      And nothing I cared, at my sky blue trades, that time allows
      In all his tuneful turning so few and such morning songs
          Before the children green and golden
45   Follow him out of grace,

      Nothing I cared, in the lamb white days, that time would take me
      Up to the swallow thronged loft by the shadow of my hand,
          In the moon that is always rising.
              Nor that riding to sleep
50   I should hear him fly with the high fields
      And wake to the farm forever fled from the childless land.
      Oh as I was young and easy in the mercy of his means,
          Time held me green and dying
              Though I sang in my chains like the sea.

Commentary

This poem captures the remembered sights and sounds of childhood experience in a sequence of strong visual images. In essence, it is autobiographical since Thomas is writing about a real place, but it moves beyond a straightforward recollection of past events to an exploration of innocence and experience. Memories may be the starting point, but ultimately they become subsumed in the vision of childhood that Thomas recreates. We are not presented with a narrative, but with an ecstatic epiphany in which the natural world and the child become one.

Thomas consciously uses language and structure to create the world of the child. Although we are, at times, aware of the mature adult reflecting on life, the reader is carried along by the exuberance of the child's voice. The physical sense of the natural world is strong: concrete nouns such as *apple boughs* (1.1), *dingle* (1.3), *trees and leaves* (1.7), *streams* (1.18), *Fields* (1.20) and *ricks* (1.26) set the background against which Thomas will address the idea of mortality. In addition, references to the farm (*barns* 1.10, *yard, home* 1.11, *chimneys* 1.20, *stables* 1.25) establish the real world that is transformed in the child's vision.

The noun phrases colour our perception of the farm and its locality. Where the nouns taken in isolation are neutral in their connotations, the modification that Thomas uses is evocative. The farmyard, for instance, takes on the mood of the child – the noun phrases the *happy yard* (1.11) and *the gay house* (1.37) are representative of the way in which the child sees his environment. The transferred epithets (*happy/gay*) become more meaningful in their new context than they would have been linked directly to the child. In other noun phrases, the natural world is given a spirituality that reflects the child's innocence and purity: *the pebbles of the holy stream* (1.18) and *the fields of praise* (1.36). The magical atmosphere also becomes a part of the natural world: the noun phrases *the spinning place* and *the spellbound horses* (1.34) combine the idea of new creation with the elements of the landscape.

The child's imagination dominates the scene; the world of imaginative play recreates the landscape through the child's eyes. There are lexical sets of words related to a fairytale world: the child is *prince of the apple towns* (1.6); he is *huntsman and herdsman* (1.15). The repetition of the verb *honoured* (ll.6/37) functioning as a modifier and the adjective phrase *famous* reinforce our sense of the child's power in his own world – he is the leader, the creator, the lord of all he sees. Another lexical set can be found in the recurrence of words linked to music. The verb modifier *lilting* (1.2), the dynamic verbs *singing* (1.11), *sang* (ll.16/54) and *rang* (1.17), the reference to the huntsman's *horn* (1.16) and the noun phrases *the tunes from the chimney* (1.20), *his tuneful turning* and *such morning songs* (1.43) all contribute to the mood of ecstasy running through the poem. The activity of the child is also seen in the way that he goes to sleep. Thomas's use of the dynamic verbs *rode* (1.24) and *riding* (1.49) make even an inactive process energetic. The child's voice marks the very nature of the experience, colouring our view of the world with which we are presented.

The adjective phrases are striking in their creation of a child's viewpoint. Thomas takes collocations and disrupts them in order to reinforce our sense of the newness of the world through the child's eyes. Expressions like 'free and easy' become *young and easy* (ll.1/52), emphasising the child's innocence. This is reinforced by the repetition of the adjective *green*: *green and carefree* (1.10); *green and golden* (ll.15/44); *green and dying* (1.52). Its connotations of youth and inexperience contribute to the central theme of the poem.

While the use of compound adjective phrases gives the vision a sense of balance, asyndetic listing mirrors the child's exuberance. In describing the day, Thomas uses a sequence of complements (ll.19–22) to create a sense of the child's physical pleasure in the natural world. The use of commas rather than conjunctions recreates the child's breathless excitement. The unco-ordinated simple clauses *it was running, it was lovely* (1.19) are followed by the unco-ordinated complex noun phrases *the hay/Fields high as the house* and *the tunes from the chimneys* (ll.19–20). The repetition of *it was* (l.20) and the sequence of complements – the compound noun phrase *air/And playing* and the compound adjective phrase *lovely and watery* (ll.20–1) – increase the pace and heighten our sense of the freshness of the experience. A similar effect is achieved with the asyndetic simple sentences *it was all/Shining, it was Adam and maiden* (ll.29–30). Here the emphasis is on the newness of the world each day for the child and the absence of co-ordinators reinforces this.

The recurrence of co-ordinating conjunctions in the initial position intensifies the child's excitement. The frequency with which lines begin with *And* ensures that we do not forget this is a child's viewpoint – it mirrors a feature of child language development when the child suddenly becomes aware of the power of speech and the infinite possibilities it offers.

Inverted word order allows Thomas to place emphasis upon key words. Adjective phrases like *honoured among wagons* (l.6), *green and golden* (l.15) and *honoured among foxes and pheasants* (l.37) are given emphasis by their position: they occur before the subject and thus become the focus of the sentence. In other instances, negatives are used in the initial position to reinforce the difference between the child and adult viewpoints. The repetition of the clause *nothing I cared* (ll.42/46) is dismissive in its ignorance of mortality.

The contrast between the adult and child perceptions of the world is made clear in the frequent references to time throughout the poem. The first line opens with the adverb *Now* in the initial position. This conveys a sense of immediacy that is interestingly juxtaposed with the past tense verb *was*. The conflict created in this way is central to the theme of the poem – a past time of innocence and joy is recreated by an adult now aware of his own mortality. Noun phrases like *night* (l.3) and *the sun that is young once only* (l.12), and clauses like *I rode to sleep* (l.24) and *the sun grew round* (l.32) draw attention to the cyclical nature of time. The initial position prepositional phrases *All the sun long* (l.19) and *all the moon long* (l.25) suggest the child's lack of awareness of the passage of time – there is no sense of urgency; there will always be enough time. This is underpinned by the adverb *slowly* (l.17) reflecting the child's unhurried delight in the natural world. Thomas draws attention to our subjection to time, however, in the disrupted collocation *once below a time* (l.7). By using a pattern with which all his readers will be familiar, he both enhances the imaginative fairytale world of the child and hints at our inescapable end. By replacing the adverb 'upon' with *below*, Thomas reinforces the power of time to control us.

The personification of time gives Thomas's exploration of his temporal theme a concrete basis. Time is represented as a facilitator – verbs like *let* (ll.4/13) and *allows* (l.42) with their connotations of 'permission granted' draw attention to his power. His absence from the third and fourth stanzas reflects the child's blissful state of ignorance; the reader is aware only of the child's activity and excitement. By the final stanzas, however, the adult's sense of mortality is beginning to intrude upon the exaltation of the child's vision. The verbs now change – the expansive possibility of the earlier verbs linked to time are replaced with the certainty of the modal verb *would* (l.46). Despite the unavoidable suggestion that life is not infinite, time is still presented in a positive light – the verb *take* (l.46) and the prepositional phrase *by the shadow of my hand* (l.47) suggest an almost paternal figure. This is reinforced by the use of the verb *held* in the final lines. The connotations are ambiguous: we are *dying* and we are *in . . . chains* (ll.53–4), but time is seen to support us in our journey towards death. The suggestions of entrapment are balanced by the repetition of the prepositional phrase *the mercy of his means* (ll.14/52). Thus while the adjective *heedless* (l.40) and the prepositional phrase *in the lamb white days* (l.46) are representative of the child's viewpoint, the final lines reflect the adult's emphatic affirmation of life.

The imagery of the poem underpins the lexical and syntactical choices Thomas makes. The natural world is presented through the child's fairytale world – images of the apple trees as *towns* (l.6) and the child as *huntsman and herdsman* (l.15) help to create the visual image of a child at play. Other images reflect the physical perspective of the child: high on the wagon he can decorate the trees with *daisies and barley* (l.8); the hay is as *high as the house* (l.20) and becomes *the house high hay* (l.41).

The religious images sacramentalise the landscape. Each morning is like the first birth of the world and Thomas's disruption of the collocation 'Adam and Eve' reflects its newness. The verb modifier *Shining* (l.30), the compound phrase *Adam and maiden* and the description of the world *white/With the dew* (ll.28–9) uses connotations of an Eden-like paradise to describe the world the child inhabits. The adult's distance from this world of energy is suggested by the reflective clause *So it must have been after the birth of the simple light* (l.33).

By contrast, the image of the *swallow thronged loft* (l.47) is representative of the adult world of mortality. The reference to the *shadow* (l.47) of the child's hand with its connotations of death is juxtaposed with the image of the *moon that is always rising* (l.48). Thus even when the child's vision is fading and the adult awareness of time is dominant, Thomas uses images that reflect the cycle of life in a positive way. The final lines with their image of *chains* and their explicit reference to *dying* (l.53) are balanced by the celebratory interjection *O* (l.52) and the assertive verb *sang*. The simile of the sea with its connotations of immortality is a fitting end to the poem. After an emphasis on the child's view of the world, we recognise the poet's ability to rise above mortality, preserving in his vision of childhood the freshness and vitality of life.

Neo-Romanticism and its alternatives

As a lyrical poet, Dylan Thomas was standing against the pull of his contemporaries towards a real and urban poetry. While his use of metre was not innovative, and while he had no explicit intellectual theory about poetry, his exploration of the potential of words has left its mark – his style has been imitated by many.

The New Apocalypse

Just before the onset of the Second World War, poets including Vernon Watkins (1906–67), Norman MacCaig (1910–96), George Barker (1913–91) and Nicholas

Moore (1918–86) were published in an anthology of verse entitled *The New Apocalypse: an anthology of criticism, poems and stories* (1939). The name was linked to D.H. Lawrence's *Apocalypse* (1931), a non-fiction work exploring man's disconnectedness from his world. The poets of the New Apocalypse were opposed to the rationalism of the 1930s poets, choosing instead the Surrealist movement as their inspiration. They followed in the neo-Romantic tradition of Dylan Thomas, emphasising the importance of feeling rather than thought. Reacting to what they saw as Auden's intellectual classicism, their verse is characterised by biblical symbolism, surreal imagery, and fragmentation. Dreams and the subconscious were seen as a source of inspiration and the disintegration of society was reflected in their disconnected style.

The critical reputation of the poetry associated with this movement tends to be negative. The work is criticised for its obscurity and technical looseness – for many, it does not contribute anything of significance to the English poetic tradition. Some of the poets associated with the movement in the 1940s consciously moved away from its characteristic style to produce work that is markedly different: MacCaig wrote of his *long haul towards lucidity* as he left behind the excesses of the New Apocalypse movement.

Alternatives to Neo-Romanticism

Edwin Muir (1887–1959) and **Kathleen Raine** (1908–2003) are Scottish poets producing work in the 1940s that is quite different from the work of Dylan Thomas and his imitators. Both found inspiration in the Scottish landscape and portrayed the natural world as a source of vitality. Their focus is on ordinary events, but these take on an almost mythological or universal significance – personal incidents are represented as symbols for common experience. Unlike Thomas, however, their vision of the world is not distorted as they search for meaning.

While the diction of their poems is often ordinary, the images can be powerful. Rhythm and rhyme are used traditionally and recurring syntactical patterns are sometimes used to produce an almost incantatory tone. Their poems tend to be more approachable than Thomas's on first reading because language is not stretched to its limit. Where Dylan Thomas's poems can seem obscure because of the intensity of the imagery and the compression of style, Raine's work is less threatening. The language is familiar, the imagery is kept to a minimum, and the elliptical style does not impede understanding. This in essence represents the difference between the poets who were writing in the neo-Romantic tradition and those like Muir and Raine who chose a different approach.

The verse of Edwin Muir is also grounded in the here-and-now. He uses familiar language in recognisable contexts, his style is unobtrusive, and his images are approachable. It was the deliberately unassuming quality of his style that appealed to the Movement poets of the 1950s.

The content of his poems is familiar: living in a wartime world ('The Horses'), death ('The Child Dying'), suburban life ('Suburban Dream'), and the passage of time ('Merlin'). Muir focuses on specific details, but at the end of many of his poems, there is an expansive mood that broadens the perspective and makes his theme universal. At the end of 'The Horses', for instance, the parallel simple clauses of the final line suggest a hope for the future that is absent in the rest of the poem: *Our life is changed; their coming our beginning.* This is reinforced by the juxtaposition of the possessive determiners *our* and *their,* and the verbal nouns *coming* and *beginning.* These mark the point of change in a world that was previously *Curled blindly in impenetrable sorrow.* In 'Merlin', the repeated use of incomplete adjacency pairs mirrors the open-ended nature of the poet's underlying question: can we ever regain our innocence? The biblical references to *Adam* and *the apple on the tree* are reinforced in the final lines by the fairytale images of *The sleeping bride* and *Time locked in his tower.* These are all symbols for an innocence that has been lost and the poem thus becomes a commentary on the modern world.

Muir's use of the first person personalises his subject matter. In 'The Killing', the crucifixion is presented from the viewpoint of *a stranger.* The descriptions are objective, observed from a point of detachment; the language is matter-of-fact. Verbal nouns like *the writhings* and *the moanings* seem to distance the reader from the personal suffering they represent; the noun phrase *the ceremonial preparation* is euphemistic, concealing the horror of the process with a sense of formal ritual. The drama of the occasion is conveyed without emotion – asyndetic listing describes the sequence of events: *The scourging, nailing . . ./Erection*; parallel clauses mark the passage of time: *The sun revolved, the shadow wheeled,/The evening fell.* The final stanza explicitly records the response of the *stranger*: the interrogative mood of the final lines offers no answers, but suggests that the experience has touched the speaker. Muir's use of the image of the journey brings the dying *Son of God, this outlandish deity,* and the unengaged observer together in a more concrete way – while one is passing on a literal journey, the other is, metaphorically, *walking in the park of death.*

Unlike Dylan Thomas, Muir uses images that are powerful in their simplicity. While Thomas aims to recreate the intensity of the child's world through his distinctive language and syntax, Muir chooses simple and emotive language. He conveys a child's freshness of vision through the directness of his approach – underlying this, we are aware of the adult's understanding. In 'The Child Dying', for instance, the imagery is firmly based in the real world, yet there is a visionary quality that raises it above the everyday. It is a sensitive and moving poem about a difficult subject, addressing universal themes of life and death in a very personal way. Where Thomas's 'Do not go gentle' rages against death, this poem searches for an understanding that will bring acceptance.

Both Muir and Raine stand apart in the 1940s as writers outside the predominant neo-Romantic tradition. Their approach to life is recognisable; the events they write about are familiar; and the language they use does not alienate the reader. Unlike Dylan Thomas, they do not fulfil the role of 'poet as priest', or 'poet as seer' – they are instead individuals viewing a familiar world in a way that makes us reconsider the ordinary without losing sight of the world we know. Some critics cite their everyday diction and unchallenging style as evidence of their limitations, but the symbolism that endows personal events with a universal significance makes their poetry interesting. Muir's work in particular is published in a range of anthologies and continues to be read and enjoyed.

At the end of the 1940s, another poet was also writing verse that was quite different from the emotional and experimental approach of the neo-Romantic poets like Dylan Thomas and his imitators: where Dylan Thomas's vision is transcendental, **R.S. Thomas** (1913–2000) is concerned with the harsh reality of life. Born in Cardiff and ordained in 1936, his working life as a clergyman was spent in remote Welsh rural parishes where he found the inspiration for much of his poetry.

The tone of R.S. Thomas's poetry is often desolate and harsh, reflecting the kind of life he saw his parishioners experiencing. He combines indignation with grim honesty, and he has become particularly well known for his creation of a personal and bleak pastoral poetry. The effect of reading his verse, however, is not depressing since Thomas is ultimately inspired rather than disillusioned by what he finds in the world around him. In 'A Poet' (*Destinations*, 1985), Thomas describes the duality of the poet: who with *Disgust tempered by an exquisite/charity* must *[wrap] life's claws/in purest linen.*

His aim was for simplicity, for a kind of retelling of ordinary events that would recreate the freshness and intensity of the original experience in words that were familiar, lucid and precise. Unlike Dylan Thomas, he believed that the power of the poet lay not in revealing a hidden underworld that ordinary people could not see and did not understand, but in using carefully chosen ordinary words to broaden the reader's experience of life. For R.S. Thomas, the focus is frequently on Wales and the natural environment, on his experiences as a clergyman in a rural community, and his awareness of the godlessness of his age. He uses language drawn directly from these fields to portray, for a predominantly urban society, something of the essence of Wales and the rural way of life.

As an Anglo-Welsh writer, Thomas saw Celtic writers in Ireland such as Yeats, Synge and Joyce, and Dylan Thomas in Wales, feeding and enriching the English literary tradition. He believed the context in which literature is written is just as important as the individuality of the writer and his personal interests – the Welsh background in which he was producing his verse, therefore, is a significant force, defining and guiding his poetry. Although almost all his creative writing has been composed in English, Thomas clearly engages with the Welsh life and there is a running thread of interest in Welsh culture (the language, the religious values, the tradition of the Welsh chapels, the landscape, the national identity). At the heart of his poetry lies an exploration of what it is to be Welsh in an increasingly urban and materialistic world, where life as a whole is losing sight of traditional values and beliefs.

Self-questioning and an underlying search for a truth about life are indicative of Thomas's response to the age in which he was living. This is reflected too in the thematic conflicts at the heart of the poems: tension is created between appearance and reality, doubt and faith, outsiders and insiders, life and death, the rural and the urban. His poetry is an attempt to explore the nature of experience, to expose hypocrisy by revealing the harsh reality of life, and to make a connection with his readers.

The popularity of *Song at the Year's Turning: Poems 1942–54* (1955) established Thomas's reputation as a leading Anglo-Welsh poet. He went on to publish many volumes of verse until his death in 2000. Critics praise him for his unobtrusive style, his striking images, his refusal to romanticise life, and his honesty. He is recognised as a major poet in both the English and Welsh traditions for his distinctive style and subject matter.

Activity 13.6

> **How does Raine use language and style to communicate her ideas about the creative process in 'Invocation'?**
>
> You may like to think about: the content, the diction, the grammatical structure and mood, the rhetorical devices

Invocation

1   There is a poem on the way,
     there is a poem all round me,
     the poem is in the near future,
     the poem is in the upper air
5   above the foggy atmosphere
     it hovers, a spirit
     that I would make incarnate.
     Let my body sweat
     let snakes torment my breast
10   my eyes be blind, ears deaf, hands distraught
     mouth parched, uterus cut out,
     belly slashed, back lashed,
     tongue slivered into thongs of leather
     rain stones inserted in my breasts,
15   head severed,

     if only lips may speak,
     if only the god will come.

Commentary

The language is ordinary in this poem, but the effects that are created heighten experience, making it a powerful vision of what it is like to write a poem. The repetition of the noun phrase *a poem* (1.1) clearly establishes the topic and the image of *a spirit/that I would incarnate* (ll.6–7) gives the creative process a physical presence – the poet can make ethereal ideas concrete by recording them. There is, however, something more: the religious undertones of the adjective *incarnate* (1.7) and the noun *the god* (1.17) make the process of writing a spiritual experience. It is a process marked by uncertainty as is made clear by the juxtaposition of the repeated *There is a poem . . .* with the hypothetical *Let my body . . ./if only . . ./if only. . . .* Until the idea is given a solid presence on the page, the poet is helpless, able to do no more than plead with her muse. The connotations of the verb *hovers* (1.6) are significant here since the 'idea' is not yet realised in any concrete form.

The use of asyndetic listing and the patterning of the clause elements (ll.1–4) suggest a mood of urgency – the reader is driven on to the end of the loosely structured sentence where the uncertainty of the modal verb *would* (l.7) is juxtaposed with the certainty of the recurring *is*. The underlying doubt about the conception of this poem is then reinforced by the sequence of prepositional phrases (*on the way, all round me, in the near future, in the upper air, above the foggy atmosphere*) – in each phrase, it becomes more intangible. In language reminiscent of birth, the first phrase suggests the poem's proximity: it is *on the way* (l.1); the second phrase is also hopeful for the poem is *all round* (l.2). The final three phrases, however, mark its retreat into the distance: the noun phrase *the near future* (l.3) removes its conception from the present moment implied by *on the way* to some indefinable time; the modifiers *upper* (l.4) and *foggy* and the preposition *above* (l.5) suggest both physical distance and obscurity.

The declarative mood of the first section of the poem (ll.1–7) is replaced by the imperative mood *Let . . .* as the poet pleads with the muse. Asyndetic listing and an elliptical style are again used to drive the reader on as the poet's requests become increasingly violent. Verbs like *cut out* (l.11), *slashed, lashed* (l.12), *slivered* (l.13) and *severed* (l.15) reflect the sacrifice the poet is prepared to make for the creation of her poem. Internal rhyme (*eyes/blind, slashed/lashed, head/severed*) adds to the intensity and the pace is only reduced with the line break between stanzas. The hypothetical *if only . . .* (ll.16–17) and the tentative modal verbs *may* and *will* bring the poem to an uncertain end.

While the diction of the poem does not challenge the reader, Raine has used a tightly patterned structure to draw us into the process of creation. The effect is incantatory – the repetition is spell-like and the mood ethereal. The images may be unsettling and we may be left with a sense of the physical hardships of writing, but, paradoxically, a poem has been created.

Philip Larkin (1922–85)

Philip Larkin was one of the central poets of the Movement, a group of poets in the 1950s who believed that intelligence and skilled craftsmanship rather than the personal were the source of true poetry. Larkin's verse perhaps most closely reflects the underlying principles holding the disparate group together. The cool tone, tight form and intellectual approach of his work are typical of the verse associated with the period – quite distinct from the romantic and emotional excesses of the 1940s poets. He is in many ways typical of the 'angry young man' of the 1950s, alienated from the past and the present, dissatisfied with tradition, and irreverent.

The literary context

In the 1950s, English poets moved away from both Modernism and neo-Romanticism. They doubted the value of traditional myths and classical literary references, aiming instead to root their poems in the everyday and to use a language that was not removed from ordinary people. Their antiromantic and sardonic tone was indicative of their desire to challenge tradition. Grouped together by the literary editor of the *Spectator*, J.D. Scott, in 1954, the poets of the period, many of whom worked in the universities, became known collectively as the Movement.

The poets Donald Davie, Philip Larkin, Elizabeth Jennings and Thom Gunn were all associated with the Movement, and were represented in Robert Conquest's anthology *New Lines* (1956). In the introduction, Conquest described them as a loose group of poets who shared a common interest in avoiding *bad principles* and promoting *rational structure and comprehensible language*. It was a poetry that brought together *the whole man, intellect, emotions, sense and all*. By 1957, however, many of the poets associated with the Movement had distanced themselves from it – the poet, critic and novelist John Wain, one of its contributors, believed its work was done.

Although initially identified with the Movement, **Elizabeth Jennings** (1926–2001) is a more personal poet than many of her contemporaries, avoiding the sardonic detachment typical of 1950s verse. Faith rather than irony was to be her distinguishing feature, and later works were to have a confessional theme as she explored her mental breakdown and subsequent hospital treatment. Critics have not always been positive in their assessment of her poetry – she has been criticised for the narrowness of her range, her lack of selectivity in publishing the mediocre as well as the effective poems, and for the looseness of some of her writing. Despite this, her best poems can be recognised by their tightly woven structure, their distinctive use of language, and their striking images.

In the poem 'One Flesh', Jennings juxtaposes lexical sets to convey her sense of changing relationships: the adjectives *cool* and *cold*, and the abstract noun *Chastity* are representative of the parents who have apparently grown apart; the concrete noun *fire* and the abstract noun *passion*, on the other hand, represent a past that underpins the relationship. Thus, although the poem is dominated by the language of distance (*apart, separate, hardly ever touch, strangely apart*), there is a sense that beneath their physical separation lies something unseen: they are *strangely close together*. The image of *Silence* conveyed by the simile *like a thread to hold/And not wind in* becomes a symbol for something that time cannot affect.

The images in Jennings's poetry encourage the reader to think about everyday things in a new way. In 'My Grandmother', for instance, she appeals to our senses in an image that is olfactory rather than visual: *The smell of absences where shadows come/That can't be polished*. The figurative link established between the nouns *smell, absence* and *shadows* moves the reader beyond the literal objects kept by Jennings's grandmother to an awareness of the power of memory and the past life associated with old things. In 'The Clown III', Jennings uses another physical image to convey something abstract: *loneliness [walking] tightropes in your breast*. Drawing on the lexis of the circus, the literal image of the tightrope earlier in the poem becomes figurative: the abstract noun *loneliness* is given a physical presence by its association with the metaphorical *tightropes*. The image allows Jennings to explore a traditional literary theme – the conflict between the external world of appearances and the inner life of feeling – in a distinctive way.

The development of Larkin's work

Larkin's earliest poems in the anthology *Poetry from Oxford in Wartime* (1944) and in his first volume *The North Ship* (1945) were influenced by Yeats. Unlike the cool detachment of the later verse, these early poems are marked by an uncharacteristically rhetorical style and rhapsodic tone. At this time, however, Larkin was more interested in the novel form, focusing his energies on the writing of *Jill* (1946) and *A Girl in Winter* (1947). While Oxford friends Kingsley Amis and John Wain already admired Larkin's work, critical interest was minimal.

After funding the publication of *XX Poems* (1951) himself and following his failure to finish his third novel, Larkin began to focus on verse and produced his first serious poems. By the mid-1950s, he was established as a significant new voice, reacting against what were seen as the excesses of the neo-Romantics and the naïve political enthusiasms of Auden, Spender and the poets of the 1930s. With the publication of *The Less Deceived* (1955), and his inclusion in Robert Conquest's 'Movement' anthology, *New Lines*, he was recognised as a noteworthy poet in the English tradition of Hardy and Edward Thomas. The restraint of his style, his use of colloquial, everyday language and his focus on everyday details of life were to become trademark features of his verse. Two other major volumes followed: *The Whitsun Weddings* (1964), a satiric commentary on twentieth-century life full of melancholy urban and suburban landscapes, and marked by a stoic wit; and *High Windows* (1974), a distinctive combination of contemporary speech rhythms and elegant metrical patterns.

While admiring the work of D.H. Lawrence and Virginia Woolf, Larkin essentially disliked the obscurity, elitism, and poetic impersonality of the Modernist tradition. He avoided Modernist experimentation, preferring traditional metrical forms and lucidity rather than obscurity. Rejecting contemporary literary fashion, he sought instead to write poetry that could be read by the average reader. Despite this, however, it is possible to see some Modernist influences in Larkin's verse. The minimal style of 'Going' suggests the sparsity associated with the Imagist movement: the brevity, lack of rhyme, concrete imagery, and abrupt sentence structures are typical of Imagism. It is a poem on death in which Larkin creates thought-provoking images out of familiar materials. 'Absences' borrows from the symbolist tradition, using a description of rain falling on a restless sea as a dispassionate symbol for the transcendent power of a landscape in which the poet plays no part. It is in the tradition of the sublime ode in which the poet celebrates God's presence in the natural world, or, for the non-Christian poet, the power of the imagination. Larkin's scene, however, is a recognition of a self-less oblivion in which the poet is a passive observer of the seascape.

Attitudes to poetry

At Oxford University, Larkin disliked the traditional focus on Old and Middle English verse because he disputed the value of literary classics. He was to write of his rejection of *tradition* and the *common myth-kitty* on which writers could draw, seeing casual allusions in poems to the classics as no more than a means of avoiding *the writer's duty to be original*. He does not, however, always observe his principled dislike of allusions to other texts: in 'Toads', the reference to Shakespeare's *The Tempest* is clear in the lines *the stuff/That dreams are made on*.

For Larkin, a poem is a verbal device that can be used to *preserve an experience indefinitely by reproducing it in whoever read[s] the poem*. He has no didactic or political purpose, but sees the process of writing as a *mental 'clenching' that crystallises a pattern and keeps it still while you draw it*. He writes to retain the things he has seen, experienced, or felt using two kinds of stimulus: *How beautiful that is* or *How true that is*. These two sources of poetic inspiration reflect the two kinds of poems he writes – *the beautiful and the true*. His subject matter is everyday life because, as Kingsley Amis wrote in the 1955 manifestoes for D.J. Enright's *Poets of the 1950s*, readers no longer want poems about: *philosophers or paintings or novelists or art galleries or mythology or foreign cities or other poems*.

While aiming to write about ordinary things for the ordinary reader, however, his response to the 'average' reader is ambiguous. Although distancing himself from the erudition of many Modernist writers, Larkin also disliked the popular response to novels by writers like Lawrence and Woolf. In his letters, he expressed contempt for those who knew nothing of *the consuming delight of genius* and *the candleflame purity of art*.

Content and themes

The content of Larkin's verse is firmly linked to the urban world of the 1950s and 60s. He draws on the emerging middle-class consciousness as a prism through which to see the world, focusing on the false hope of commercialism; the uncertainty of the future; the alienation of the individual; and the disillusion of unfulfilled dreams. His themes are directly linked to the kind of world he observes and his personal response to it. Everything is rooted in the familiar, the everyday, and yet Larkin rises above this to reach an understanding of life – we may find some of his judgements socially unacceptable in the twenty-first century, but we recognise the importance of questioning rather than accepting life.

He is often described as a **sardonic commentator** on the social and cultural changes taking place. He observes the world around him precisely, but from a distance. Despite his detachment and apparent lack of personal involvement, however, Larkin is a compassionate observer. His ironic commentary is not nihilistic: his images may reveal the banality of urban life and his language may suggest an underlying disapproval, but the tone is ultimately objective as he rejects romantic myths and reduces things we take for granted to their essential elements. The wry poetic voice strips away layers of illusion to reveal the ritual underpinning ordinary events. His tone is not affirmative, but the reader is often left with something worthwhile: in 'Church-Going', for instance, the church is *not worth stopping for* and yet Larkin juxtaposes this with *Yet stop I did* – because, ultimately, he recognises that we will always find within ourselves *A hunger . . . to be more serious*.

Some of Larkin's poems find their source in his **personal relationships**, tracing his state of mind and reflecting on the way life and art can be at odds. His engagement to Ruth Bowman, a young woman he had first met as a schoolgirl when he was working in the Wellington Library, is addressed in 'Deceptions' and 'If, My Darling'; 'No Road', 'To My Wife' and 'Marriages' were written in the months after his separation from Bowman; and 'Long roots moor summer to our side of earth' reflects on his feelings on the day Winifred Arnott, a trainee in the Belfast University Library with whom Larkin had formed a strong attachment, married.

For the most part, Larkin avoided explicitly **political themes** in his verse in line with his belief that poetry should not be didactic and should not _do things_. There are two exceptions to this: in 'When the Russian tanks roll westward' and 'Homage to a Government'. These poems reflect his instinctive feelings rather than a considered understanding of political situations and he was himself aware that he had engaged with something beyond his terms of reference. He clearly did not think about politics in any serious way and often resorted to the blustering extremism of his father's right-wing beliefs.

Larkin is a keen **observer** of people and places; his poems are full of recognisable individuals and landscapes. He is a realist presenting the world as he sees it with no apparent desire to change what he observes. The tone is characterised by a dry cynical humour and a self-critical honesty as he deconstructs romantic visions of love and weddings, childhood and escapist dreams. He refuses to take things at face value and strips away illusions, questioning rather than accepting universal truths.

The poems are dominated by a strong sense of **place and time**. They reproduce the urban landscape with concrete details of the city centre ('Here'); sprawling urban estates ('Afternoons'); and the industrial ('Dockery and Son'). The language is bleak: the modifiers _raw_, _cheap_ and _grim_ ('Here'), the verbs _fading_ and _ruining_ ('Afternoons'), and the abstract nouns _nothing_, _boredom_ and _fear_ ('Dockery and Son') convey the mood of disillusion Larkin sees as typical of the modern age. Juxtaposed with this is a vision of the natural world, a place of expansive freedom that is quite at odds with the imprisonment of the city.

In poems such as 'At Grass' and 'Here', the rural world is harmonious where the urban is chaotic; it is uncontrollable where the city is man-made; and it is tranquil, quite separate from the illusions, fears and doubts of industrial life. The language is different too, reflecting Larkin's movement away from entrapment towards a vision of freedom and isolation.

Just as important in reading Larkin is an understanding of the way he portrays the **individual** and the **'crowd'**. Although he creates personal portraits of people like 'Mr Bleaney' and 'Dockery and Son', ultimately Larkin is more interested in the way such individuals represent the mass of humanity. He believes that people are not really distinctive because they are all yearning for the same thing. They are all trapped by their environment, deceived by commercialism, and alienated from the real world by their pursuit of the ideal. In some poems, Larkin's representation of the impersonal 'crowd' is emphasised by his use of general plural nouns such as _residents_, or by indefinite noun phrases such as _A cut-price crowd_ ('Here'); in others, individuals are defined by their role as _Young mothers_ and _husbands_, for instance ('Afternoons'); and in others, the crowd is depersonalised as a _Giant whispering and coughing_ in which an individual's face is lost _among all those faces_ ('Broadcast'). Larkin suggests that our belief in our own individuality is an illusion since we all live in a commercial society that encourages us to define ourselves through acquisition.

By focusing on representative details, Larkin can create the sense of an individual who is both recognisably different from the reader, and yet frighteningly familiar. This unwilling recognition lies at the heart of Larkin's poetic vision – both poet and reader are forced towards self-knowledge as their illusion of superiority is subtly eroded. In 'Mr Bleaney', for example, the reader is introduced to the character through the casual utterances of the landlady and the detached observations of the poet. The tone is primarily conversational and our sense of Mr Bleaney emerges almost indirectly. The first three stanzas are dominated by the landlady's urbane chatter and this moves smoothly into the poet's acceptance of the room (stanzas 3–5) after his emphatic simple sentence *'I'll take it.'* The language of the two final stanzas, however, is quite different. The concrete nouns (*curtains, window, garden, bed, chair*) and literal modifiers (*thin, frayed, upright, sixty-watt*) are replaced by more figurative language. Noun phrases like *the frigid wind/Tousling the clouds* suggest a change in the speaker's intentions: he is no longer observing the room or Mr Bleaney's routines, but reflecting on the nature of life itself. The distance between the dismissive poet and the bleak Mr Bleaney has narrowed, and in reflecting on the meaninglessness of Mr Bleaney's life, the poet is forced to recognise the nature of his own illusions.

Larkin marks the change in tone by moving away from the shorter sentences of the first five stanzas to a single long, complicated sentence and a more literary style. The compound-complex clause moves from the fronted co-ordinating conjunction *But* through a sequence of subordinate clauses to the main clause *I don't know*. In forcing the reader to wait for the completion of the sentence, the poet's lack of certainty is reinforced – we move with the speaker towards an unwilling recognition of his similarity with the late Mr Bleaney. Larkin's portrait of a lonely life thus becomes more than just an individual character sketch – both the poet and the reader are forced to recognise the poem as a representation of twentieth-century life in which pathos is substituted by horror at the moment of recognition.

Larkin's **vision of the age** is reductive. He deflates expectations and undermines accepted interpretations of ordinary events: weddings in 'Whitsun Weddings'; the happiness of communal living in 'Reasons for Attendance' and 'Dry-Point'; the desire to escape from the routine of work in 'Toads'. The reader is not, however, left with nothing – instead, at the end of the poem, there is a feeling that Larkin has stripped away our illusions so that we can better recognise the essence of his subject. In 'Lines on a Young Lady's Photograph Album', for instance, he juxtaposes the unchanging, potentially perfect nature of a photograph with the unpredictability of real life. The running image of the first two stanzas suggests that photographs are delicacies to be consumed: verbs like *choke* and *hungers*, noun phrases like *Too much confectionery* and *such nutritious images*, and the adjective phrase *too rich* suggest that the perfection is desirable and yet overwhelming. The fourth stanza, however, marks a change in tone as Larkin moves away from the specific moment to a more general reflection on the art of photography. The juxtaposition of the adjective *Faithful* and the verb modifier *disappointing* represent the heart of his argument: the *candour* of the camera's lens mirrors life as it is and *will not censor blemishes*. While the girl in the photographs is *Unvariably lovely*, the distance between her static image and her real-life presence increases. The comparative adjective phrase *Smaller and clearer* draws attention to this discrepancy and underpins Larkin's reflection on the gap between reality and desire.

The realisation is not, however, entirely negative. Although Larkin's reflection on the nature of time and memory (stanzas 6–8) is marked by negative lexis like the verbs *lacerate, Contract* and *mourn* and the abstract nouns *exclusion* and *grief,* the tone in the final stanza changes. The positive connotations of the adjectives *calm* and *dry,* and the noun *heaven* suggest there is something of worth in the photographs. Although the frozen moments are irrecoverable and the poet is distanced from them by his absence, the images are perfect and unaffected by the transitory nature of life.

Larkin's reductive view of life is influenced by his attitudes to **commercialism** and **advertising**. In several poems, he uses images of advertising to explore the discrepancy between our ideals and reality – as in his treatment of the 'crowd', we see individuals lost in the overwhelming fantasies that offer us unachievable perfection. In 'Essential Beauty', for instance, the grinding routine of everyday life is juxtaposed with static images *Of how life should be.* Larkin juxtaposes the grim urban reality of *graves, slums, the gutter* and *the rained-on streets and squares* with the images *In frames as large as rooms.* The emphasis is on the inescapability of the pictures – the post-modifying relative clause *that face all ways* and the verbs *Block, Screen* and *cover* emphasise the way advertising obscures the harshness of real life.

The first stanza is dominated by concrete nouns: *loaves, custard, motor-oil, salmon, knife, butter, milk.* They focus the reader's attention on the inescapable images that dictate the nature of the ideal. The modifiers *giant, silver, golden, deep* and *radiant* intensify the representation of the ideal – their positive connotations create a sense of perfection that is not attainable in real life. This is enhanced by the pastoral metaphor of the pictures as *sharply-pictured groves* and the recurrence of rural images that suggest good health and prosperity. The sentence structure reinforces our sense of the ideal: the fronted prepositional phrase *In frames . . .* delays the main clause and mirrors the dominating presence of the images; the inversion of the subject *(these sharply-pictured groves/Of how life should be)* and the verb *(shine)* allows Larkin to place emphasis on *shine* with its connotations of brightness; and the positioning of the adverb *Perpetually* at the beginning of a line reinforces the ongoing power of the images.

The second stanza marks a change in tone as Larkin begins to make the contrast between the ideal and the real explicit. The repetition of the adjective *pure* is balanced by Larkin's use of the adjective *imperfect,* juxtaposing the perfect world of the advertisements with reality of life where *nothing's made/As new or washed as clean.* The negative comparison leads Larkin towards a more cutting contrast in which the advertisement's *white-clothed ones from tennis-clubs* are juxtaposed with the reality of *the boy puking his heart out.* The indefinite pronoun *ones* adds a mock grandeur to the description of the men wealthy enough to join the tennis club, while the simple noun phrase *the boy* and the colloquial *puking his heart out* links him to the harshness of real life. Similarly, the noun phrases *dark raftered pubs* and *the Gents* reinforce the difference between the romantic images on the billboards and sordid reality. The following portraits of *the pensioner* and the *dying smokers* continue this mood: buying a certain more expensive brand of tea does not improve the old man's life, and the vision of the unnamed and unfocused *she* is hypothetical – the negatives *no match lit up* and *nor drag brought near* emphasise the illusory nature of this ideal woman.

Directly linked to this puncturing of illusions is Larkin's interest in the **contemporary way of life**. His overriding vision of the age's materialism and illusive ideals is made more specific as he explores the nature of routine and the ways in which it imprisons us. In 'Toads', Larkin considers the merits of breaking free from routine and, paradoxically, the intrinsic freedom in being tied by routine and able to dream of escape. The poem takes the form of a debate in which the speaker attempts to convince himself of the unnecessary burden of work. The language is negative: the metaphor of the *toad* and the connotations of the verbs *Squat* and *soils*, and the noun phrase *its sickening poison* establish an oppressive tone. The conversational feel of the poem engages the reader directly in the argument and Larkin's use of the interrogative mood (*Why should I . . .?; Can't I . . .?*), exclamatory minor sentences (*Just for paying a few bills!*), and the italicised imperative (*Stuff your pension!*) create a sense of the speaker's exasperation.

The argument for escaping routine, however, is undercut by the language Larkin uses. The asyndetic listing and alliteration of *Lecturers, lispers,/Losels, loblolly-men, louts* suggests an underlying uncertainty in the speaker's justification of a life without routine. Similarly, modifiers with negative connotations imply that the lifestyle he is supposedly promoting is not entirely satisfactory. Adjectives like *bare*, *unspeakable* and *skinny* undermine the ideal of people who *live on their wits* and *up lanes*.

The implicit sense that this is not the way to live becomes explicit in the sixth stanza. Larkin's use of the subjunctive *were I* marks a turning point as the speaker recognises that he is not going to distance himself from a life of routine. The recognition, however, does not suggest that the speaker has failed – rather, he has understood the true nature of life. The colloquial verb *blarney* and the syndetic listing of *The fame and the girl and the money* identify the illusory nature of the ideal. The simple noun phrases represent success in a stereotypical way and the repetition of the conjunction emphasises their meaninglessness. The complexity of the final stanza brings the argument to a conclusion: an understanding that within the security of routine, it is comforting to yearn for freedom.

As well as addressing the dull routines that govern our lives and the illusory dreams that remain firmly beyond reach, Larkin's verse sometimes considers **occasional moments of happiness** that can surprise us. In 'Wedding-wind', for instance, we are presented with a newly wed woman's joy. Although we are also aware of her fears, Larkin captures her joy in a sequence of natural images that make her love seem universal. In other poems, Larkin explores what is for him the ultimate goal: *desire of oblivion* ('Wants'). While life is dissatisfying and dreams are illusory, oblivion, *the wish to be alone*, is the true escape from suffering. The structure of 'Wants' emphasises the monotony of life: the repetition of the adverb *However* and the prepositional phrases *Beyond . . .* and *beneath . . .*, and the noun phrases mirroring the mundane trivialities of everyday life suggest a mood of disillusion. The framing of the stanzas with recycled lines and the use of the caesura to highlight the central noun phrases in each case, however, focus attention on Larkin's poetic 'truth'. Life is oppressive and, other than in transitory moments of happiness, we must seek satisfaction in an oblivion that recognises the need for isolation and ultimately annihilation.

Relationships are equally problematic in Larkin's verse: just as the escape from routine is illusory, so is the likelihood of a fulfilling relationship. Dreams of romantic love, sexual satisfaction and emotional identification are short-lived in the face of reality. Relationships as well as work, he suggests, are governed by routines and patterns of behaviour. In 'Love Songs in Age', love is the *much-mentioned brilliance* that is meant to *solve, and satisfy, to set unchangeably in order.* The love songs may have survived, but the reality of love for the widow is very different. The final line emphasises its failure in the two negative clauses: *It had not done so then, and could not now.* The caesura draws attention to the adverbs *then/now* and thus suggests love is no more than an illusion.

There are a few poems in which Larkin adopts a slightly more optimistic tone. 'Whitsun Weddings' may at first appear to be typically dismissive of the wedding parties: *girls/In parodies of fashion, fathers with broad belts* and *mothers loud and fat.* The use of plural nouns with no determiners identifies these individuals as 'types', representative of life in general and the tone is critical. Yet Larkin's detached sardonic observations give way to a final image of fertility that suggests these lives are now at a turning point – there is no sense that love will solve all, but the verb *swelled* and the metaphor of the arrows falling *out of sight* suggest the potential for future growth.

Larkin's treatment of **religion** is ambiguous. In a material age, he sees faith in God as an ever-diminishing force in our lives, and yet he affirms the importance of faith in life itself. A belief in man's essential dignity and decency overrides the general move towards cynicism and despair. In 'Church Going', perhaps Larkin's most anthologised poem, he begins with a concrete experience that leads him to a reflective assessment of the *hunger* in people *to be more serious.*

The light-hearted chatty tone of the first two stanzas appropriately reflects the casual manner in which the speaker observes the church. His distance from the church and its religious significance is apparent in his use of the colloquial *brass and stuff* and the non-subject specific *the holy end* to refer to the altar. Yet the poet's response is surprisingly conventional – although apparently dismissive, he feels the need to make some gesture, taking off his bicycle clips because he has no hat.

The passivity of the first stanza is replaced in the second by the poet's activity, but the movement from observation to participation is not a direct acceptance of all that the church stands for. The emotive verb *snigger* is as much an indication of the poet's mood as of the echoes he creates, and the verb modifier *hectoring* with its negative connotations of insolence and bullying suggests the poet's attitude to the verses he reads.

In typical Larkin style, however, there are no easy conclusions to be reached. The fronted conjunction *Yet* at the beginning of the third stanza marks a change in direction. Concrete observations are replaced by reflections, and colloquialisms by a more rhetorical style – the language of the final stanza emphasises the conclusion to Larkin's meditation. The abstract nouns *compulsions, destinies* and *hunger* are in direct contrast to the concrete nouns of the opening, drawing attention to the reflective tone and endowing man's life with relevance.

For Larkin, the church, or *this cross of ground*, becomes a place in which it is *proper to grow wise* – the emphasis is not on conventional spiritual enlightenment, but on an awareness of the value of life. In a commercial age where possession has replaced the need to believe and the church has been reduced to a *shape less recognisable each week*, Larkin offers an alternative that restores meaning to life. He does not yearn for the *ghostly silt* of divine faith, but recognises the need for affirmation in a time of disillusion.

What emerges from reading a range of Larkin's poems is the underlying thematic pattern that gives cohesion to his work as a whole. He invariably takes something (a concept, place or character) and reduces it to a recognisable convention or type. From this, he engages in a process of reflection that results in the revelation of the essential element of his focus. Although his process is reductive, the outcome is usually marked by a mood of acceptance.

Poetic voice and style

While the verse of Modernists such as Yeats and Eliot is anchored by their particular personal myths, Larkin has no unifying ideology to interpret the world and his content is therefore varied and at times contradictory. It is in the voice and style that we find uniformity.

Through the distinctive, unifying **voice** that emerges from Larkin's poems, we are exposed to his view of the world and his response to the diversity of experience. He is wary of human pretensions and his poems expose affectation and hypocrisy: he explodes cultural myths about weddings, pre-1914 innocence and post-1960 permissiveness. His personæ are numerous – the nonchalant bachelor ('Reasons for Attendance'), the failed womaniser ('Wild Oats'), the newly married woman ('Wedding-Wind'), the ironic detached observer ('Whitsun Weddings').

Some critics believe it is unhelpful to see each speaker in the first person poems as an imaginative creation quite distinct from Larkin himself. For them, the poems are often a personal expression of Larkin's mood at a particular moment in time, a dramatisation of his more or less ironic view on life. In this sense, the poems become an argument in which the poet must defend his position and, as the focus shifts, so too does the mood. The relationship between the speaker in the poems and the poet is complex: it is too limiting to see them as the result of either an imaginative creation, or an autobiographical experience. Instead, readers must be prepared to recognise their originality as the product of an individual who sees the world in a distinctive way.

The speakers of the poems engage the reader by sharing their thoughts and feelings, expressing a truth about life in the twentieth century and about themselves. The tone is conversational and the language familiar, fixing the exchange firmly in the real world. Often the poems resemble a dramatic monologue in which the speaker's internal dialogue reveals what lies beneath the surface ('Self's the Man'). In others, an implied participant is directly addressed and the internal dialogue is accompanied by vocalised utterances ('Mr Bleaney', 'Lines on a Young Lady's Photograph Album').

The conversational tone of the poems, however, is deceptively inclusive. On closer reading, the speakers always seem isolated and out of place. Their questioning invariably leads to a personal revelation that they have tried to evade:

self-deception is exposed, and the gap between illusion and reality has to be faced. We need to recognise the underlying irony to appreciate the revelation, identifying Larkin's skilful variations in diction as the speakers move towards understanding.

Larkin's verse is recognisable by the economy and precision of its **style**. He is skilful at combining the dispassionate, impersonal tone of classical literature with Romanticism's feeling for humanity, while avoiding any tendency towards sentimentality with his sombre wit and grounded language.

Dispensing with literary allusion, Larkin creates his own distinctive diction. It can shock, delight and challenge our accepted view of the world with its verbal surprises. Words are positioned so that the reader is forced to notice them; the boundaries of word classes are blurred; and noun phrases are stretched to breaking point. He creates an original tone by combining wit, elegiac seriousness and colloquial idiom in such a way that the reader must always remain alert to subtle changes. The underlying principle is one of logic: he develops an argument and guides reader response through the stylistic choices he makes.

The **lexical choice** is the reader's guide to the subtleties of Larkin's changes in direction. His use of contemporary language and unpoetical colloquial idiom is set against formal, literary and archaic expressions, marking the movement from concrete observations to abstract reflections. A recurring pattern emerges: everyday, conversational language is used to introduce the focus – the here-and-now; as the visual is replaced by meditation on a theme, the language becomes more elevated.

Noun phrases and the pre- and post-modification they contain are distinctive in both the lexical choice and structure. In 'At Grass', the descriptive opening records the scene literally, using mostly minimal noun phrases: *The eye, them, wind, tail and mane* and *one*. These create a sense of the natural scene, the observer and the observed in a very general way. Where the noun phrases contain modification, Larkin can move away from his neutral description towards a more reflective interpretation of the scene. The pre- and post-modified noun phrase *the cold shade they shelter in* seems to carry undertones of death both in the adjective *cold* and in the head noun with its connotations of the classical underworld. The two consecutive metrical stresses on *cóld sháde* and the alliteration of *shade/shelter* add to the significance of the phrase as a whole. Similarly, the post-modified parenthetical noun phrase *The other seeming to look on* begins to develop the reader's sense of distance between the horses and the observer. While the first lines emphasise the physical distance, this noun phrase draws attention to the psychological and emotional distance – the present participle *seeming* implies a human interpretation of the moment that is unrelated to the experience of the animals themselves. This is reinforced in the penultimate stanza by the simple sentence *They shake their heads*. The human gesture of negation is superimposed on the horses' simple physical act, apparently in response to the interrogative of the preceding line.

In the second stanza, the noun phrase *Two dozen distances* effectively combines the connotations of physical and psychological distance that have underpinned the first stanza. Playing with the racing jargon 'over the distance', Larkin creates an opposition between the abstract plural noun *distances* and the precise pre-modification (*Two dozen*). The distance is both literal (the length of the race) and figurative (the gulf that separates the horses from humanity). The co-ordinated lists of noun phrases in the second and third stanzas develop this theme by emphasising the distance between the human experience of the races and that of the horses. Simple noun phrases like *Silks . . ./Numbers and parasols* and the modified *faint afternoons/Of Cups and Stakes and Handicaps, Squadrons of empty cars* and *littered grass* create a sense of the occasion that is exclusively human and alien. It is from this that the horses have escaped to become *anonymous*. The striking noun phrase *the unmolesting fields* reinforces our sense of their escape into freedom away from *The starting-gates, the crowds and cries*.

The repetition of the simple noun phrase *their names* again reminds us of Larkin's theme of distance. In the human world, the names live on memorialised, *Almanacked*; in the field the anonymous horses *stand at ease*, having *slipped their names*. Larkin's distinctive verbal skill is evident in the way he manipulates his lexical choice for effect: he creates a verb from the noun in his fronted past participle *Almanacked*; adapts the collocation of 'slipped their bridles'; reminds us this is a human viewpoint with his tentative verb phrase *must be*; and uses the transferred epithet *curious* and the humanising verb *prophesies*, strangely isolated with its lack of a grammatical object, to describe the stopwatch rather than the spectators. This kind of linguistic creativity is typical of Larkin's approach and demonstrates the stylistic challenges of his work.

Larkin's ease with the language of **ordinary speech** is perhaps his most widely recognised technique – in particular his use of 'bad language'. Lines like *they fuck you up, your mum and dad* ('This be the Verse') are often anthologised in books of quotations and are quoted in diverse situations. People who take exception to this kind of use of expletives often do not recognise the skill with which Larkin moves between registers and fits his obscenities into tight patterns of rhyme and metre. The effect of mixing poetic and demotic registers is dramatic and Larkin consciously mixes linguistic extremes to underpin the focus or theme of his poems. In 'Toads', for example, the juxtaposition of the colloquial idiomatic *Stuff your pension!* with the allusion to Shakespeare's *the stuff/That dreams are made on* skilfully manipulates register and plays with the meaning of words. The effect is comic: the repetition of 'stuff' as a colloquial verb and as a non-specific poetic noun undermines the fantasy of escaping from work; the allusion to Shakespeare's play sets classical beauty against the squalor of twentieth-century urban life.

Larkin's games with language are a central part of his work and in reading the poems, we need to be aware of the techniques he uses. In 'A Study of Reading Habits', for instance, he moves between a number of registers: familiar conversational clichés (*getting my nose in a book*); the ideal world of popular fiction (*deal out the old right hook, dirty dogs*); and dismissive expletives (*Get stewed; a load of crap*). The movement between registers in this poem marks the transition from boyhood immersion in a fantasy world to adult realisation that reality is quite different. The language is not judgemental but matter-of-fact: it mirrors the reader's changing interests in fiction. Beginning with the language of comic book heroes in stanza 1, it moves through Gothic images of vampires in stanza 2, and ends with the Western. The title's apparent gravity is undercut by the ironic final line written by the respected librarian. Larkin is playing games with language and the creation of a persona – the sentiments are not his own, but there is a gratifying satisfaction in the poem's challenge to authority.

Other linguistic features to observe include Larkin's use of negation and unexpected words. His poetry is of the real world and either avoids or undermines the ideal. The use of **negatives** is therefore common. In 'Nothing to be Said', the title and its repetition in the final line frame Larkin's discussion of life as a process of *slow dying*; in 'Love Songs in Age', the final line *It had not done so then, and could not now* emphasises that love will never provide solutions to life's problems; and in 'MCMXIV', the repetition of *Never such innocence* suggests the impossibility of human dreams of idealism. His choice of **unexpected words** forces the reader to remain alert to the lexical choice and its effects. In 'At Grass', the noun phrase *the unmolesting fields* uses a surprising verb modifier to draw attention to the race-horses' escape from human harassment. The choice of the almost archaic verb *strewn* to describe the children in 'Ambulances' is distinctive, suggesting a casualness that is in direct contrast to the purposefulness of the passing ambulance.

Larkin's use of **puns and clichés** is also notable. He takes collocations with which his reader will be familiar and disrupts them – the clichés of 'The Poetry of Departure' and 'A Study of Reading Habits' are deflated to distance the reader from the ideals of the world of fiction and film. In 'I Remember, I Remember', Larkin's satire on childhood, traditional clichés are mocked. The *splendid family* is one he *never ran to when [he] got depressed*; his childhood has been *unspent*; and the inverted cliché of the final line *'Nothing, like something, happens anywhere'* with its ironic use of quotation marks undermines the myth of childhood innocence and bliss.

The puns are equally telling. In 'At Grass', Larkin's use of the verb *distresses* works at a number of levels: it is a literal description of the movement of the horses' tails and manes in the wind; it puns on the 'tresses' of their manes; and implies a semantic link to the emotions of the animals. Larkin does not require his reader to isolate any one of these meanings – they all co-exist, contributing to the complexity of the poem as a whole.

In discussing any Larkin poem, the **grammatical structures** are central to an understanding of the effects he is trying to create. The sentence type, changes in grammatical mood and the use of foregrounding are means by which he guides reader response. Sentences frequently run over lines and from one stanza to the next ('Toads Revisited'); pauses are used to mark the development of a theme ('Love Songs in Age'); foregrounded non-finite clauses force the reader to wait for grammatical and semantic completion ('Here'); interrogatives remain unanswered ('Toads') or are dismissed ('Church Going').

Imagery

The **imagery** of Larkin's verse is perhaps on first glance quite minimal – his colloquial use of language, his concrete focus on the real world, and the precision of his style seem at odds with a figurative use of language. While he may not draw on traditional poetic images, however, his poems are full of individual and striking comparisons that illuminate the reader's understanding of the world he portrays.

Larkin's work is dominated by the industrial and commercial world of the twentieth century: images of advertising hoardings, urban housing and urban landscapes recur. He often provides us with a wide vista – rather than focusing on a particular place, the reader is drawn into a journey, sometimes literal, in which the images create a powerful physical sense of the landscape. As observers, we rely on Larkin's long and complex noun phrase structures to pinpoint key details of the scene. In 'Whitsun Weddings', for instance, the long noun phrases with their pre- and post-modification create images of the passing landscape. Urban streets (*the backs of houses, a street/Of blinding windscreens*) are replaced by the rural (*The river's level drifting breadth*), then by the industrial (*Canals with floatings of industrial froth*), and finally by the metropolitan (*walls of blackened moss*). The detail is precise, evoking distinctive features of the scene. Within the context of the poem and its themes, such images are symbolic of Larkin's attitudes and the kind of world he represents.

All poets use these noun constructions to recreate their view of the world; what is distinctive to Larkin is his use of striking images that reflect his individual viewpoint. Typical of his original approach are the description of memories plaguing the horses *like flies* ('At Grass'), or the ambulance *Closed like a confessional* ('Ambulances'). Such comparisons strike a chord with the reader, casting new light on ordinary things. The noun phrase *Luminously-peopled air* ('Here'), for instance, hints at the paradoxical sense of past generations of which we may be aware in a state of solitariness: the compound-modifier gives an ethereal concrete quality to the abstract air. The image of London at the end of 'Whitsun Weddings' as *postal districts packed like squares of wheat* juxtaposes urban and rural in a simile suggesting the richness of city life. This prepares the reader for the final simile of *an arrow-shower/Sent out of sight, somewhere becoming rain* with its connotations of hope for the future, fertility and potential fulfilment. There is an underlying ambiguity, however, for although the lexis is positive (the fecund connotations of a verb like *swelled* and the noun *rain*), the 'arrow' is also a symbol of conflict. The verb *aimed*, the post-modified adjective phrase *ready to be loosed* and the abstract noun *power* remind the reader of a less harmonious context. This allows Larkin to balance the potential sentimentality of his theme with a realism that is typical of his style.

While in most poems the images emerge in the course of Larkin's representation of a landscape or the people who inhabit it, there are some poems in which a central image dominates, functioning as a symbol and illuminating the theme. The metaphor of 'Toads' and 'Toads Revisited', for instance, has a physical presence through the lexical choice (*Squat; its sickening poison; Its hunkers*) and a symbolic function in its representation of work. In 'Water', Larkin's use of imagery is predominantly symbolic. In the tradition of the nineteenth-century French Symbolist poets, he is more interested in the symbolic associations of water than with the physical element itself. Traditional religious associations (purification/rebirth) become the basis for a new belief system – Larkin's use of the non-finite verb *To construct* suggests his need to believe in something other than the established religions. The language of the church (*litany; devout; congregate*) is directly linked to water (*sousing; drench; A glass of water*). The symbolism is intense and the images original. With the final image of light refracted through water, Larkin removes spirituality from the bricks and mortar of the church and finds it instead in the power of the natural world. The raised glass becomes an act of homage in which the poet recognises and honours the timelessness of the elements in a world of ephemeral desires and transitory pleasures.

Poetic form

While drawing on recognised traditional poetic structures and devices, Larkin does not create 'traditional' poems. He may use recognisable stanza structures and a familiar iambic metre, but he offsets such regularity with the grammatical complexity of his long and carefully punctuated sentences.

He borrows from traditional structures, then adapts and customises them to match his verbal dexterity, using rhyme, metre and enjambement to free his poems from the tightness of traditional poetic structures. Enjambement is used to run not only from line to line, but from stanza to stanza, thus creating an intricate link between the structure on the page and the meaning. The rhyme scheme can be unusual and Larkin often draws on discordant or half-rhymes to reflect the uncertainty of modern life. At the heart of his poetry, there is a tension between the formality of convention and the freedom with which he adapts it.

The 9-line Spenserian stanzas of 'Church Going', for instance, use half-rhyme, changes in metrical pattern and run-on lines between stanzas to move the poem from description to reflection. The neatness of the iambic pentameter is disrupted in places to emphasise keywords or ideas. In stanza 1, the change from iambic to trochaic marks the poet's observations as he begins to look around. The emphasis is on the tedious similarity between this church and any other, but the change in metre prepares the reader for the fact that this visit will move beyond the physical sameness to a recognition of the power of the *tense, musty, unignorable silence*.

> Ano̕ | the̕r chu̕rch: | ma̕ttin̕g, | se̕ats, an̕d | sto̕ne,
> An̕d li̕ | ttle̕ boo̕ks; | spra̕wlin̕gs | of̕ flo̕ | we̕rs, cu̕t
> Fo̕r Sun̕ | da̕y, bro̕wn | is̕h n'ow

The trochaic feet disrupt the easy harmony of the lilting iambic and thus make this visit seem special. Similarly, Larkin's use of the spondee draws attention to key phrases: *ble̕nt ai̕r*.

In 'Whitsun Weddings', the poetic form also underpins meaning. The regularity of the 10-line stanzas with their tightly organised rhyme scheme helps to create a sense of inevitability – the journey, *this frail/Travelling coincidence*, will move to its conclusion and the travellers will depart to continue their lives. There is, however, a tension underlying the certainty: the neatness of the abab rhyme is counterbalanced by the less obvious cdecde; and the short second line disturbs the harmony of the predominantly decasyllabic rhythm. By offsetting the end of sentences and the end of lines, Larkin creates a similar effect: the first two stanzas establish the context and the narrator viewpoint, each ending neatly with an end-stopped line – the conclusion of a grammatical sentence; the following stanzas use run-on lines, avoiding the natural pause between each one. This creates a driving rhythm that both mirrors the physical journey and forces the reader towards the final ambiguous image.

Other interesting patterns can be seen in the changing rhyme patterns of 'Vers de Société' where the neat couplets of the first and last stanzas are replaced by a changing pattern in the middle four stanzas (abbcca abccba abbcac). In addition, the language juxtaposes the poetic with the vernacular, and the rhythm counterbalances mainly decasyllabic lines with a short disruptive line. This denies the reader the security of a recognisable and consistent pattern, and is in keeping with Larkin's honest exploration of age, loneliness and death.

In discussing Larkin's verse, it is important to be aware of the technical choices he makes to underpin meaning. Sound patterning (end rhyme and internal rhyme) contributes to the precision of his writing and enhances the mood: the consistent alternate rhymes of 'Mr Bleaney' add to our awareness of the tedium of life both for the dead Mr Bleaney and the speaker; the half-rhymes of 'Toads Revisited' can seem discordant, reflecting the mood of endurance that marks the piece; the internal rhyme of *Till wind distresses tail and mane* ('At Grass') highlights the overlaying of human emotions on the oblivious horses. Metrical patterning is dominated by the lilting iambic reminiscent of spontaneous speech, but changes draw attention to key words and phrases, disrupt our expectations, and underpin thematic juxtapositions.

Larkin and the English poetic tradition

Larkin is recognised for his individual viewpoint on contemporary life: the content is firmly grounded in the real world, the tone is self-mocking, and the attitudes are distinctive. Detached cynical observations are accompanied by an underlying compassion for humanity; a dislike of pretentiousness is balanced by a recognition of the value of the mundane. Stylistically, Larkin juxtaposes elegantly phrased poetic diction and the vernacular; he subverts traditional poetic forms with ingenious adaptations.

Critical opinion is divided, however, on his contribution to the English poetic tradition. For many, he is one of the two most important English poets since the war (the other being Ted Hughes). His contribution to the Movement is seen as significant and his work is described as broadening the expression of English life in verse. The complexity and verbal dexterity of his poems and the individuality of his vision make him an important figure in the literary tradition despite the fact that he did not engage in critical debate about his own writing or the nature of poetry in general.

For others, Larkin is a minor poet because of the limited range of his work: the recurring tone of defeatism, the consistently reductive view of emotion, and the narrowness of the content. In returning to common themes and subjects, he is criticised for failing to challenge his readers, for failing to face the real horrors of a post-war society, and for upholding acceptance rather than opposition. Even critics who see Larkin's work in this light, however, recognise a number of significant poems that contribute to the body of English verse as a whole: the control of 'No Road', the stylistic skill of 'Here' and 'The Whitsun Weddings', and the toughness of the best poems in *High Windows*.

Debate about Larkin's style revolves around his lack of interest in experimenting and developing new approaches. After the Modernist innovative approach to writing earlier in the century, Larkin's consistency has been seen by some critics as a sign of his unwillingness to change – another sign of his parochialism and conservatism. Those who see him as a major English poet, however, see his mastery of style and verbal dexterity as evidence of his greatness: he had evolved a distinctive and effective approach that required no modification. After the dramatic changes of the Modernist period, Larkin's verse is seen to mark a period of consolidation in the English poetic tradition.

Critics have read Larkin's poems in a variety of ways, but he always disassociated himself from such readings: 'Church Going' was not the work of a 'religious' poet; 'Sunny Prestatyn' was not the work of a 'moral' poet; 'MCMXIV' was not the work of a 'reactionary' poet. Larkin was not didactic and had no interest in changing or influencing his readers. What his poems give us is a snapshot of a particular individual's view of contemporary life. It is for this personal viewpoint and for the particular stylistic features of his work that he will be remembered. His reputation rests on what the critic Peter Levi describes as *85 perfect poems*.

Activity 13.7

Explore the way in which Larkin uses language and grammatical structure in 'Here' to describe the journey he takes and to convey its significance.

You may like to think about: noun phrases and modifiers, sentence structure and organisation, listing, fronted conjunctions, and any other features you find interesting.

Here

1   Swerving east, from rich industrial shadows
     And traffic all night north; swerving through fields
     Too thin and thistled to be called meadows,
     And now and then a harsh-named halt, that shields
5   Workmen at dawn; swerving to solitude
     Of skies and scarecrows, haystacks, hares and pheasants,
     And the widening river's slow presence,
     The piled gold clouds, the shining gull-marked mud,

     Gathers to the surprise of a large town:
10 Here domes and statues, spires and cranes cluster
     Beside grain-scattered streets, barge-crowded water,
     And residents from raw estates, brought down
     The dead straight miles by stealing flat-faced trolleys,
     Push through plate-glass swing doors to their desires –
15 Cheap suits, red kitchen-ware, sharp shoes, iced lollies,
     Electric mixers, toasters, washers, driers –

A cut-price crowd, urban yet simple, dwelling
Where only salesmen and relations come
Within a terminate and fishy-smelling
20   Pastoral of ships up streets, the slave museum,
Tattoo-shops, consulates, grim head-scarfed wives;
And out beyond its mortgaged half-built edges
Fast-shadowed wheat-fields, running high as hedges,
Isolate villages, where removed lives

25   Loneliness clarifies. Here silence stands
Like heat. Here leaves unnoticed thicken,
Hidden weeds flower, neglected waters quicken,
Luminously-peopled air ascends;
And past the poppies bluish neutral distance
30   Ends the land suddenly beyond a beach
Of shapes and shingle. Here is unfenced existence:
Facing the sun, untalkative, out of reach.

Commentary

The grammatical structure of 'Here' is a good example of the way in which Larkin exerts a very precise control over his material. The poem describes a journey to the north-east coast of England through different locations. Noun phrases like *rich industrial shadows/And traffic* (ll.1–2), *the surprise of a large town* (l.9), *fast-shadowed wheat-fields* (l.23), *isolate villages* (l.24) and *a beach/Of shapes and shingle* (ll.30–1) mark the transition from urban to rural landscapes. The freedom of the structure allows Larkin to create a sense of the chaotic urban world on the page: run-on lines mirror the journey, driving the reader relentlessly towards the final stanza and the first full stop; parenthesis (ll.15–16, 17) stretches grammatical structure to its limit, mirroring the entrapment of modern life; and syndetic (ll.6, 10) and asyndetic listing (ll.15–16, 20–1) vary the pace.

Stanza 1 portrays a landscape empty of people as the poet travels through the night. By using the present participle *Swerving* (ll.1,2,5), Larkin is able to suggest something of the ongoing movement of his journey – there is a feeling of immediacy and the reader is thrown directly into the experience. Larkin observes the scene in a detached way and the stanza is dominated by concrete nouns (*fields* l.2, *halt* l.5, *skies, scarecrows, haystacks, hares, pheasants* l.6) that convey what he sees. The few modifiers are negative (*thin, thistled* l.3), suggesting the paucity of the landscape. As the journey takes the poet away from the *rich industrial shadows/And traffic* (ll.1–2) and towards *solitude* (l.5), however, the final noun phrases of stanza 1 are rich in their imagery. The positive connotations of the language (*gold, shining* l.8) and the extensive pre- and post-modification change the mood of the poem: we sense the poet's pleasure as dawn reveals a landscape untouched by man. Where the other natural features are merely listed, the river assumes a *slow presence* (l.7) that brings life to the scene. Similarly the mud has been transformed by the dawn sun and the pre-modifier *gull-marked* reminds us of the natural inhabitants of the landscape.

The repetition of long vowel sounds (*widening, slow, piled, gold, clouds, shining,* ll.7–8) and the consecutive stresses (*The piled gold clouds*) slow the pace as we move towards the first finite verb *Gathers* (l.9) in the initial position, divided from its subject (*the widening river's slow presence*) by the parenthetical noun phrases (*The piled gold clouds, the shining gull-marked mud*, l.8). The effect is disruptive and, although the colon at the end of the line provides a brief respite, the reader is immediately drawn back into the restlessness of the poet and the world around him.

In the noun phrase *the surprise of a large town* (l.9), Larkin again forges links between meaning and form: the abstract noun *surprise* functions as the head of the phrase and we have to wait for the concrete noun *town* in the post-modification. The fore-grounded adverbial (*Here*) then establishes a sense of arrival before the journey once again picks up speed. We are overwhelmed with concrete nouns associated with the town (*domes, statues, spires, cranes, streets*) and with the infinite purchasing choices of an urban, materialist society (*suits, kitchen-ware, shoes, iced lollies, Electric mixers, toasters, washers, driers*, ll.15–16). The list of products is symbolic of the materialism that governs our response to life, but their potential for providing satisfaction is undermined by the judgemental modifiers (*cheap/sharp*) that reflect Larkin's attitude, and the exclusively material connotations of the abstract noun *desires* (l.14). There is no hope here of self-fulfilment and enlightenment. In this context, individuals are subsumed within the group: they are *residents from raw estates* (l.12) or part of *A cut-price crowd* (l.17).

While the compound phrases (*domes and statues, spires and cranes*), the medial caesura, and the connotations of the verb *cluster* (l.10) create a sense of entrapment, the grammatical structure of stanzas 2 and 3 suggests something of the frenetic pace of urban life. The reader has to work hard to link subject and predicator (*residents . . ./Push; wheat-fields . . ./Isolate*) in the midst of a multitude of details. Adverbials (*Beside . . ., through . . ., out beyond . . .*), non-finite clauses (*brought down . . ., dwelling . . ., running . . .*), parenthesis (ll.15–16) and asyndetic listing (ll.11.15–16, 20–1) overwhelm us with information and a sense of the chaotic meaninglessness of life.

Only with the final relative clause *where removed lives/Loneliness clarifies* does the frantic pace slow down. The change from concrete to abstract language, the rhyme of *lives/clarifies* and the emphatic end focus on the verb suggest a change in direction – we are now presented with an alternative to the urban life of materialism. This is reinforced by the clarity of the simple sentence that follows: *Here silence stands/Like heat.* After the entanglement of the previous long compound-complex structure, the emphatic fronted adverbial and the inactivity implied by the present tense verb mark a new tone.

Verb modifiers like *unnoticed* (l.26), *Hidden, neglected* (l.27) and *unfenced* (l.31) suggest a life that exists beyond human restrictions. Within the context of the poem, their connotations are positive rather than negative since they represent the opportunity for reflection away from the distractions of the town. Similarly, abstract nouns such as *Loneliness, silence* (l.25) and *existence* (l.31) move the reader beyond the concrete to a heightened sense of life's meaning. While the poet's physical journey has taken him from the urban to the rural, his psychological journey has taken him from chaos and routine to emptiness and oblivion.

To enhance the reader's sense of arrival, Larkin repeats the fronted adverbial

Here (ll.25–6, 31), creating a feeling of completion. This is reinforced by his use of simple clauses: *leaves . . . thicken, . . . weeds flower, . . . waters quicken, . . . air ascends;/And . . . bluish neutral distance /Ends . . . ll.26–30*). These suggest a simplicity that was absent from the chaotic urban life. The verbs (*thicken, flower, quicken, ascends*, ll.25–28) are dynamic and Larkin's use of the simple present tense adds to our sense of the immediacy and clarity of the vision he shares.

The conclusive use of the co-ordinating conjunction (*And*, l.29) and the verb in the initial position (*Ends*, l.30) on two consecutive lines draws attention to an openness that is both physical and symbolic. The following emphatic simple clause, *Here is unfenced existence*, reinforces our sense of arrival and Larkin's thematic celebration of isolation. The non-finite clause *Facing the sun*, the adjective phrase *untalkative* and the adverb phrase *out of reach* (l.32) relate both to the implied observer and to *unfenced existence* itself – the ambiguity emphasises the impersonal oblivion offered by the natural world. Here, 'nothingness' is a positive since it is an escape from the materialism of the urban world.

Larkin has used language and grammatical structure to communicate both the physical and the psychological experience of his journey. While the concrete language conveys the literal elements of the landscape, the modifers and the organisation of the sentences suggest the poet's attitude. The poem thus simultaneously recreates the changing landscape and functions as a symbol for the poet's quest for a psychological and emotional freedom to be found in the natural world of the final stanza.

Ted Hughes (1930–98)

The publication of *The Hawk in the Rain* (1957) was to launch a new poet into the public consciousness. **Ted Hughes**'s first volume represented a criticism of the lack of vitality in post-war English society and contemporary English poetry. He was reacting to a poetic generation who had wanted to render everything casual and everyday in the language of conversation.

The literary context

The poetry of Ted Hughes represents an implicit challenge to the dominant poetic temperament of the time. Where the poets of the Movement had been interested in urban life and the urban landscape, Hughes was to turn to the natural world. His poetry explores the brutal energy of life and the landscape in language that is more intense and more physical than the urbane conversational tone of Larkin.

The hard edge to Hughes's verse can be linked to his interest in the post-war Eastern European poets: Vasko Popa (1922–91), Zbigniew Herbert (1924–98), Miroslav Holub (1923–98) and János Pilinszky (1921–81). Their work reflects the difficult times in which it was composed: the language is concise and unpoetic because they are striving to express the inexpressible. Like Hughes, these poets take nothing for granted, questioning all art that aims to beautify and console, subverting myths, and doubting both God and life itself.

Hughes also identified with D.H. Lawrence who was writing in the mining communities of Nottinghamshire, quite apart from the literary and cultural elite. Hughes responded to Lawrence's use of free verse as opposed to Eliot's use of fragments and allusions, and to his exploration of the natural world and the otherness that lies beyond the surface of things. In *Birds, Beasts and Flowers* (1923), Lawrence had created a new kind of poem and his anthropomorphic vision was to influence Hughes's early work.

The work of Dylan Thomas was another stimulus: Hughes saw Thomas as a challenge to the 1930s political verse and the 1950s suburban verse that dominated contemporary English poetry. The totally comprehensible everyday language and experiences of poets like Auden and Larkin were countered by Thomas's style and content, which forced the reader to see things in a new way. Hughes was to describe Thomas's work as a *holy book*, identifying with his search for a deeper sense of human life running beneath the superficial and the artificial.

Amongst the 1950s poets, **Thom Gunn** (1929–2004) is recognised as the writer with whom Hughes has most in common. Originally associated with the Movement, Gunn has clearly emerged as a poet whose work forms a bridge between the controlled and elegant poetry of Larkin and the violent energy and intensity of Hughes.

Critical opinion has not always recognised Gunn's place in the development of the English poetic tradition, but current critical thought tends to rank him alongside Philip Larkin and Ted Hughes as one of the most distinguished poets of his generation. His verse is marked by a linguistic precision and syntactical control that is indicative of his wit – an intellectual shrewdness that challenges convention and undercuts received opinions. In addition, his experimentations with syllabics and the exactness of his diction reflect his biting rather than lyrical view of the world.

The poetry of Thom Gunn tends to avoid the personal – it deals with life on a larger scale, focusing on the nature of the individual and free will. His vision of the world is nihilistic: there is a ferocity and violence that some critics find difficult. He celebrates men of action, and recurring images of movement reflect his interest in the way we attempt to make our lives meaningful. In 'On the Move', subtitled '*Man, you gotta Go*', he describes the perpetual motion in which the individual becomes both *hurler and the hurled*. The choice of verbs such as *joins* and *choosing* emphasises the importance of free will, and the repetition of the adverbials *always toward, toward* establishes the idea of a goal towards which the movement is directed. Gunn concludes the poem with a juxtaposition: although *Reaching no absolute*, we are *always nearer by not keeping still*. The importance of movement is reinforced by his use of dynamic verbs *(spurts; throws; burst away)*, verb pre- and post-modifiers (*The blue jay scuffling*; *the wheeling swallows*), and nouns with connotations of movement (*the gust of birds*; *a flight of birds*; *movement*).

A similar emphasis on movement can be seen in a poem with a very different mood and pace. Where 'On the Move' is an urban poem, dominated by images of machines, man-made roads and manufacturing, 'Considering the Snail' addresses the power of the snail – its tenacity in laboriously following its path. Verbs like *pushes*, *moves* and *hunts* may be less dramatic, but they still reflect

Gunn's fascination with motion. His use of the present tense gives a sense of immediacy, intensifying the snail's progress; abstract nouns (*power, purpose*) invest an apparently insignificant animal with importance; and the parallel noun phrases *the slow passion* and *that deliberate progress* make its movements seem symbolic of some underlying meaning despite the fact that it *know[s] nothing*. Where the men in 'On the Move' *manufacture both machine and soul*, the snail moves instinctively *in a wood of desire, drenched . . ./with purpose*; man is *self-defined* ('On the Move') while the snail is driven by less conscious inner forces. Both, however, are seen by Gunn to be in pursuit of a goal that is an integral part of their lives.

Gunn's work is perhaps best seen as a balancing of the techniques and approaches associated with the Movement and the American 1950s Beat poets. His anti-Romantic images and tone of detachment mirror the writing of the English Movement poets, while the energy of his verse, its violence and its interest in the individual's struggle against centralised authority reflect the work of the American Beat poets.

His first volume, *Fighting Terms* (1954), established Gunn as one of the most interesting poets of the age. He took traditional topics and explored them in an untraditional way – love is presented as a struggle; accepted views of life are replaced by uncertainty; startling images are used to deconstruct traditional concepts. In the poem 'Human Condition', the recurring image of the fog becomes symbolic of the confusion and uncertainty felt by the poets of the 1950s. Gunn writes of the need to *find out the limitations/Of mind and universe* and his poems can be seen as his attempt to search for meaning in a time when *much is unknowable*. Even the punctuation reflects this mood of discord. In the final lines of 'Human Condition', for instance, Gunn disrupts the natural grammatical rhythm of a simple sentence through his use of the caesura:

Ĭ séek, Ι tŏ bˊreak, Ι mў ́span.

The rhythmic fluency associated with the weak-strong stress pattern is set against the disruption of the grammatical units – the object, the non-finite clause 'to break my span', is separated from the subject and verb (*I seek*) by a comma, and is itself broken into two discrete parts.

The style is economic, and the violence and energy of Gunn's poems marks him out as a precursor of poets like Ted Hughes. Recurring themes address the nature of existence, self-sufficiency, the power of individual will, and the importance of movement as a means of expressing value. He rejects tradition and passivity in preference for active participation and an anti-Romantic view of life.

The development of Hughes's verse

The much lauded *The Hawk in the Rain* (1957) was to establish Hughes's characteristic imagination. It is a volume marked by the strong aural qualities of the language – its guttural consonants and harsh plosives are indicative of the physical nature of the verse. Hughes addresses reality no longer as something known, but as something uncertain and indefinable. The tone is rebellious and there is a powerful sense of the unconscious and primitive. In the second volume, *Lupercal* (1960), Hughes emerged as a mature poet. Although not ground-breaking, the volume contains many of the animal poems for which Hughes is best known, and introduces themes that were to recur (the destructive nature of modern materialism; the importance of the inner life; the vital energy of the natural world).

Critical interest in these first two volumes was significant, leading to a general recognition of Hughes as one of the major poets of his generation. There was, however, concern about the violence of the content and language, and the intensity that some critics felt led to obscurity.

Wodwo (1967), an experimental volume, was to consolidate the success of *Lupercal*. Made up of 5 prose stories, a play and 40 poems, it continued to focus on animals and the natural world. As Hughes made his challenge to the poetic tradition more explicit, critical debate began to revolve around the incomprehensibility of the text. The publication of *Crow* (1970) did nothing to pacify those who found his verse difficult, but it was to remain one of Hughes's most enduring volumes. Retelling the legends of creation and birth through the vision of a mocking and predatory crow, Hughes challenges received wisdom. The tone is bleak and bitter as the central protagonist attacks traditional beliefs and ridicules a tyrannical God. Crow is not, however, a totally heroic figure: his response to events and his actions are limited, particularly when he must face the true nature of reality.

Collaboration with the American artist Leonard Baskin was to result in *Cave Birds* (1978), seen by some critics as containing some of Hughes's finest work. It was first presented publicly in performance at Ilkley Literature Festival (May 1975) and then broadcast on BBC Radio 3. The poems are accompanied by Baskin's drawings – most of which were done before the poems were written. Beyond a response to a particular picture, however, the poems chart the transformation of a 'persona' who undergoes a process of change in self, in attitudes, and in awareness of life.

Gaudete (1977) reflects Hughes's enduring interest in mythology. Drawing on the success of his earlier short stories, it is experimental. Like *Crow*, this volume is bleak in outlook, presenting humanity engaged in a life that is little more than meaningful than a cosmic joke. This was followed in 1979 by *Moortown*, based on Hughes's experiences working on a farm, and *Elmet*, a sequence of poems accompanying photographs by Fay Godwin of the Calder Valley, west of Halifax. After the extreme vision of life in his last three works, *Moortown* and *Remains of Elmet* are melancholy in tone as Hughes celebrates the landscape and explores an idiosyncratic sense of what it is to be English. They mark an attempt by Hughes to capture a region that he had seen changing and believed was now dying.

Hughes was made Poet Laureate in 1984 and did much to give poetry a public voice. Many critics, however, feel that the verse written as Laureate (*Rain-Charm for the Duchy and Other Laureate Poems*, 1992) is less likely to be remembered for its literary qualities than his earlier work. In 1998, he was to win the £10,000 Forward Poetry Prize for his poetic memoir *Birthday Letters* and the Whitbread Prize for *Tales from Ovid* (1997). The 83-poem collection *Birthday Letters* deals explicitly with Hughes's relationship with the poet Sylvia Plath. It sold 10,000 hardback copies in less than a year in Britain alone and was immediately hailed as a masterpiece. It is a work of anguish, tenderness and sincerity, quite different from the poems for which he is well known. The publication of *Selected Poems 1957–94* (1995) had given rise to a critical summing-up, but *Birthday Letters* caused both readers and critics to reassess Hughes's life's work: the combination of poetic control and emotional range mark this as the work of a poet at the height of his powers.

Hughes's approach to poetry

For Hughes, the poet is an observer who perceives the inner life and the energy existing beneath the surface of things. It is his role to explore rather than to suggest, to tentatively reveal the unconscious in a medium that is, paradoxically, linked to consciousness. The poems, however, do more than reveal something of a specific animal, place or experience at a particular moment in time. Beginning with something concrete and specific, Hughes moves towards the general and universal. Although his bleak tone, dark sense of humour and uncompromising approach are to be found in other contemporary literature (Joseph Heller's *Catch-22*, 1961; Kurt Vonnegut's *Slaughterhouse Five*, 1969), ultimately, Hughes's verse represents an affirmation rather than a negation of life. In the process of poetry, common beliefs are rediscovered as the poetic imagination unifies the outer world of objects and the inner world of the self.

The poet is a *keeper of the dreams*, who, like the shaman, can transcend the physical world to reveal something. He must try to *catch those elusive or shadowy thoughts, collect them together* and *hold them still so we can get a really good look at them*. The abstract process is made concrete for us in Hughes's poem 'The Thought-Fox' where the poet explores the intensity of the moment of creation.

Hughes, nature and the inner life

Hughes's poetry challenges accepted poetic and cultural attitudes. Often described as violent both in the subject matter and the language, Hughes consistently denied such claims, arguing that his poems were *not about violence but vitality*. He believed that animals are vital rather than violent because they are *so much more completely controlled than men*. For Hughes, the so-called violence of the natural world was quite different from that in the human world: true violence is the inhumanity of man to man, and this he condemned passionately in the poems 'Crow's Account of the Battle', 'Wilfred Owen's Photographs' and 'Crow's Account of St. George'.

He accepted that in writing poems about the natural world, the subject matter often could be described as *ugly*, but believed that all *true poems* had to face tragedy and make *great complete statements of the world*. In this context, poetry then becomes a *biological healing process*, which:

> seizes on what is depressing and destructive in life and lifts it into a realm where it becomes healing and energising – or it tries to do. That is what it is always setting out to. And to reach that final mood of release and elation is the whole driving force of writing . . .

During his study of anthropology at Cambridge, Hughes had read much about the role of poetry in primitive societies and had immersed himself in their folklore and mythology. He was particularly interested in animism – a recognition of the spirit life immanent in all elements of the natural world. He saw in the primitive societies' focus on the inner life and the animal world an alternative to the materialistic commercialism of the twentieth century.

He was to be a long-term critic of contemporary Western culture, which he saw as governed by sensationalism – we see disasters and admire our real and cinematic heroes without engaging emotionally or intellectually with the event that has taken place. Equally, he avoided the black-and-white dialectic of Christianity, preferring instead to explore the grey area that exists in any judgement of good and evil, guilt and innocence, knowledge and ignorance.

Hughes's interest in the inner life, the subconscious and the animal world also finds its source in his knowledge of shamanism. Just as a shaman moves beyond a consciousness of ordinary reality to the realms of the spirit world, so Hughes attempts to reveal something of the life that lies beneath surface reality through the language and structure of his verse. For Hughes, the shaman's journey beyond everyday experience to a deeper level is similar to the poetic process of creation in which the poet becomes a 'seer' revealing the nature of existence. Like the shaman, he draws on myths to explain his inner experiences and visions.

Content and themes

Hughes's verse deals with the physical and the natural, the self and the subconscious, the personal and the universal. His poems often begin with a still point, a close focus on an animal or part of the landscape. Attention to specific detail is balanced by an awareness of life going on in a wider sense. His verse explores the relationship between man and the natural world as he searches for what lies beyond consciousness. Nature is both 'other', quite apart from man, and an integral part of the lifecycle to which we are all subject. Hughes's poems therefore exist on two levels. At a physical and literal level, we see him recreating a specific scene, moment in time or idea, using analogy to bring abstractions to life. He then goes beyond this, revealing something about life and the way we perceive it, challenging received wisdom, and forcing his readers to rediscover truths.

At their very best, the animal poems dramatise the conflict between knowledge and ignorance – Hughes moves beyond a straightforward representation of animals as a natural life force to be envied or emulated to a study of our perception of consciousness. He is also interested in people, studying our reactions in moments of crisis. His landscapes are sometimes inhabited and we see, increasingly, the importance of the personal. His verse draws on the landscape of his childhood, his experiences as a farmer, on his own beliefs. He was not to address explicitly personal subjects until his last volume, *Birthday Letters*, in which he focuses on his first meeting with Sylvia Plath, their love, their marriage and its breakdown, and Plath's death.

The raw energy of nature is a recurring theme in Hughes's work as he searches for a means to recreate the world of things in a meaningful way. The **landscape** is animated by a sense of process and becomes the backdrop to man's metaphysical quest for understanding. Hughes explores the landscape's natural rhythms and observes how man interacts with nature. In 'A Wind Flashes the Grass', Hughes sees man *listening for below words,/Meanings that will not part from the rock*. The poem appeals to our sense of sight and sound: while modifiers (*blackly, gloomy, darkly*) create the atmosphere, it is the descriptions of sound (*the tree's cry, the incomprehensible cry/From the boughs, The stirrings of their twigs*) that lead us to an understanding that the trees are *the oracle of the earth*.

In 'Pennines in April', the natural world is inspirational. The sturdy dependability of the hills is conveyed in noun phrases like *mass behind mass* and *Those barrellings of strength*, but Hughes is interested in their symbolic value. He draws an analogy between the mountainous landscape of the Pennines and the sea: the juxtaposition of the hypothetical subjunctive (*If this country were . . .*) and the parenthesis (*that is solid rock/Deeper than any sea*) makes the comparison explicit. The language of movement associated with sea (*heaving, rolling, gliding*) is then overlaid on the static landscape so that the *locked land* becomes active. The focus is on the way in which the hills raise life skyward. The present participle *hoisting*, the repetition of the adverb *upwards/upward*, and the image of surfing suggest the creative power of the natural world. The opposition created between the present participles *heaving/hauling* and *carrying* defines the antithetical relationship between man and nature. Where the larks seem an integral part of this creativity, man is detached: the act of imagination has to be dragged from him while the birds' flight is instinctive.

Closely linked to Hughes's study of the landscape is his interest in **animals**. In his portraits of the hawk, the pike, the otter, and in the raw, vivid approach to nature in *Wolfwatching* (1989), he presents the violent predatory and destructive face of the natural world. His approach is not moral, but he sees in the instinctive life force of nature, in the instinctive desire for survival, something that we cannot deny in our own civilised existence. The poems have two distinct strands: an exploration of the creative and destructive force underpinning life; and the poet's search of human consciousness for links between the human and animal worlds.

In 'Pike', we see something of man's relationship with nature – man is insignificant, haunted by the age and size of the ancient fish in the *Stilled legendary depth*. A boyhood memory of fishing becomes the stimulus for the poet's expression of awe at the beauty and ferocity of the pike.

The elliptical style of the first three lines enables Hughes to focus on the pikes' physical perfection: he uses adjective phrases to draw attention to their size (*three inches long*) and their colouring (*green tigering the gold*), and noun phrases to communicate their essential nature (*Killers from the egg: the malevolent aged grin*). He juxtaposes the abstract nouns *delicacy* and *horror* to emphasise both their perfection and their predatory relationship with their environment – an environment characterised by modifiers like *Gloom* and *black*, where the emphasis is on a subterranean existence suggested by adverbs like *under* and *upwards*.

Even when extracted from their pond and isolated *behind glass*, however, their instinctive nature governs their behaviour – the fish lead *A life subdued to its instrument*. This is the natural world of predation and the final present participle *watching* leaves the child narrator of the poem *with the hair frozen on [his] head*, a potential victim to *the dream/Darkness beneath night's darkness had freed*.

The final stanzas of 'Pike' remind us that Hughes's animal and landscape poems are firmly rooted in his own life and experience in the world of South Yorkshire. In 'Sheep', we see a somewhat different tone, but the poet's personal connection with the content is equally strong. Here, rather than the muscular strength and energy of the poems 'An Otter' and 'Pike', we are presented with a sheep's despair for her *vanished lamb*.

The attention to detail recreates the scene vividly. The lamb was *only half the proper size* with a cry that was *wrong*; its hindlegs *Cowered in under its lumped spine*; its hips *leaned towards/Its shoulders for support*. The physical observations are practical in their assessment of deformity, but in the description of the lamb's cry and its eyes, we see a poignant recognition of the creature's fate. Its cry is *human . . . a despairing human smooth*, and its eyes are *sad and defeated . . . pinched, pathetic*. The modifiers move beyond observation to empathy and, in this, the poem is quite unlike those that communicate an implicit reverence for the evolutionary perfection of nature's predators.

The language here is of everyday communication – the lamb *wasn't right* and *hadn't the gumption to feed*; the imagery is often domestic: his legs are like *a loose bundle/ Of firewood* and his coat is a *cardigan*. The effect is intensified by Hughes's movement between the neutral third person pronoun *it* and possessive determiner *its*, and the more human *he/his*, giving the lamb individuality and worth. Yet Hughes lifts this poem beyond the particular incident to something more universal. He has catalogued the lamb's physical deformities, but it is not these that lead to its death. Ultimately, its death can be traced to its lack of will to live – a *difficulty/Much more urgent and important* than its physical limitations. Born with a will that is *deformed* like its body, the lamb fails to *thrive*. Concrete language is replaced by the abstract as Hughes reaches the climax of the poem.

> Death was more interesting to him.
> Life could not get his attention. (ll.44–5)

The final images develop this antithesis of life and death. Positive references to *a warm summer night* and *the blossom* are juxtaposed with the mother's *crying* and the *oceanic* wind, as the lamb dies with *the yellow birth-mucus* still in its wool coat.

It is a poem of acceptance rather than rage, of gentleness rather than violence. It shows how Hughes moves from the specific to the general in his quest for understanding, recognising the importance of the vital life force that underpins so many of his nature poems. It may contain images that disturb the reader, but they are not sensational. In reading a poem about the birth of a lamb that he had to slaughter gruesomely to save the mother ('February 17', *Moortown Diary*), a member of the audience rebuked Hughes, calling it 'a disgusting piece of horror writing'. Hughes argued that his attention to detail was a crucial part of the poetic process: . . . *we either have a will to examine what happens, or we have a will to evade it*. For Hughes, evasion is the response of modern man who does not wish to accept responsibility for his relationship with the world around him; examination, on the other hand, offers both understanding and the potential for the *biological healing process* of poetry.

Hughes's treatment of the natural world, inevitably, explores the tension between the vital force of life and death. His preoccupation with **death** is physical and real – he vividly portrays the way in which bodies decay. In 'Coming down through Somerset', Hughes describes the death of a badger, balancing its beauty with the inevitability of its decay. Death is represented as an inescapable stage in which the inner self and the external world will be united.

In 'Stations', Hughes engages readers with the inevitability of their own deaths as he moves from the general (third person) to the personal and direct (second person). While he draws on the traditional associations of the Catholic 'Stations of the Cross', the poem also mirrors the Sufi stages on the road to annihilation. The pathos of Sections I–III, with their emphasis on the vulnerability and meaninglessness of the body, is replaced by an acceptance of death's inevitability in Section IV:

> Whether you say it, think it, know it
> Or not, it happens, it happens . . .   (ll.27–8)

We are left with the striking image of physical destruction: a head severed by a train, *with its vocabulary useless*, lying amongst *the flogged plantains*.

A similar attitude is explored in 'The Green Wolf', where Hughes addresses the ending of life and the beginning of death. The description of a man dying from a stroke focuses on physical detail as *The dark bloodclot moves in*. The tone is again one of passive acceptance:

> You watch [death] approaching, but you cannot fear it   (l.10)

The enjambement in the final stanzas drives the reader on as the individual self is submerged in the universal (ll.16–21). The cyclical repetition of the noun phrases and the asyndetic listing immerse the reader in the collective life of the natural world. In the final line, the combination of the natural (*dew/nightfall*) with the distinctively human (*scarves/wet hair*) symbolises the inevitable oneness that Hughes believes comes with death.

When focusing on animal death, we see Hughes equally detached. In 'View of a Pig', death is seen without the dignity of ritual or the decorations of ceremony. The attention to physical detail is precise and removes all emotion from the poet's response. The monosyllabic diction and the short, often simple, sentences emphasise the lifelessness of the pig. It is more than dead (*less than lifeless, further off, Too dead*); it is neither dignified nor *a figure of fun*. The concrete language (*trotters, thick pink bulk, gash*) is set against the abstract (*remorse, dignity, pity*), but ultimately we are left with activity rather than contemplation. The dynamic verbs *scald/scour* and the bland domestic simile of scrubbing the doorstep leave us not with the poignancy of death, but the continuation of life.

While asserting that death was part of the natural cycle, however, in his personal life it was less easy to respond to death in a detached and emotionless way – perhaps because the deaths were not part of a natural process. The suicides of his first wife, Sylvia Plath, in 1963, and then the woman for whom he left Plath, Assia Wevill, in 1969 – also the year in which his mother was to die – were to have a long-term effect. The tone of his fourth collection, *Crow*, was to be marked by these tragedies.

As Hughes faced his own death from cancer, he returned to his relationship with Plath, replacing the mythology that had grown up with an emotional and personal analysis. In 'Fingers' (*Birthday Letters*), Plath is immortalised not in a public memorial, but in her *daughter's/Fingers that remember [her] fingers* in everything they do. The language of the poem is dynamic and vital; it ends with an image of religious reverence quite unlike the domestic simile of 'View of a Pig'. Here the biblical resonance of *obey and honour* and the metaphorical reference to the Roman households gods (*Lares and Penates*) suggest the continuation of life after death in a more personal and emotive symbol.

The final image of 'The Dogs Are Eating Your Mother' (*Birthday Letters*) is more reminiscent of the earlier work where the inner life and the external world become one. Using symbols reminiscent of Tibetan and early Egyptian cultures, Hughes describes what may appear to be a very brutal process. Tibetan sky burials leave the dead body open to the elements so that the sacred vultures can consume the physical and free the spirit for its journey. A similar process occurred in the early Zorastrian religion where the vultures, known as 'compassionate purifiers' would reduce the physical body to nothingness. So in the poem, the vultures, characterised by the compound modifier *bone-crushing*, will free Plath's spirit so that it can be *take[n]back into the sun*. For the ancient Egyptians, the scarab, or dung beetle, was sacred because it mimicked the passage of the sun across the sky in its own struggle to roll balls of dung containing its eggs. The hatching of the young was symbolic of new life emerging from the earth – the image of the poem is therefore clearly one of regeneration.

Hughes is interested in our sense of self, the **consciousness** that separates us from the natural world. While skylarks are *Conscience perfect* ('Skylarks', VI), their behaviour is instinctive, they are *shot through the crested head/With the command, Not die/But climb/Climb/Sing* (II). The caged jaguar appears unaware of his imprisonment, driven as he is by the instinctive. Although grounded in the physical, the poem 'The Jaguar' moves beyond observations to a tentative exploration of the boundaries of perception, and the relationship between our experience and our understanding of the world. The language of the final lines is expansive: *world/horizons* are placed in opposition to *cage* – where we see entrapment, the animal sees only *the wilderness of freedom*.

'Second Glance at a Jaguar' undermines the potential for freedom of spirit suggested in 'The Jaguar', but Hughes still presents mechanistic and instinctive behaviour rather than consciousness. The animal's deformed body is no more than an *engine shoving . . . forward*, ruled by an internal ungovernable force that *keep[s] his rage brightening*. The rosette markings on his fur become symbolically the spurred rosettes goading the bull in a bullfight, and the indelible signs of a murderer (*cain-brands*).

It is in some of the *Crow* poems that Hughes explores consciousness most explicitly: we see the imperfect anthropomorphic Crow reaching tentatively towards an understanding of himself and his place in the order of things. Unlike the other animals in Hughes's poems, Crow acquires a human status as he searches for self-understanding, questioning his relationship with his creator and the world around him.

In 'Crow on the Beach', Crow's heightened awareness leads him to a transitory

knowledge of his limitations. His inability to communicate with the sea undermines his self-importance; he realises that the natural world is not dependent
upon him. This need for humility is replayed in 'Crow and the Sea' where Crow
must face his own insignificance. The structure of the poem reflects the stages of
Crow's journey: the patterning of verb + object (*tried ignoring . . ., tried talking . . .,
tried sympathy . . ., tried hating . . ., tried just being . . .*) and the repetition of the
contrastive conjunction *But . . .* at the beginning of alternate lines emphasise
Crow's failure. All his attempts at communication are meaningless and Crow
becomes a helplessly inadequate observer of the reality existing outside himself.
The similes (*like a scrutty dry rabbit-dropping on the windy cliff; like a water-drop off a
hot stove*) draw attention to this.

The emphatic end of the poem is ironic. The isolated adverb *Finally* and the
emphatic verb phrases *turned/marched*, no longer made tentative by the inclusion
of 'tried', suggest a conclusive moment has been reached. This firmness, however,
is undercut by the ineffectual nature of Crow's action: he attempts to turn his
back on the sea, failing to recognise that it is inescapable. Hughes emphasises this
in his image of death – like the *crucified man*, Crow is motionless, unable to make
contact with the flow of life and unable to escape his condition.

In Hughes's exploration of consciousness, he suggests that we must be able to
feel guilt, express horror, show humility in the face of our limitations, and respect
both the self and the wider world. The final poems in the *Crow* collection demonstrate this. 'How Water Began to Play' is a conceptual climax to the sequence; it
marks the movement from Crow's self-deception towards an awareness that
emphasises the importance of basic human values.

The yearning conveyed by the repetition of the short line *Water wanted to live*
is set against the suffering implied by the dynamic verbs (*burned, crumpled*) and
the pathos of the repeated clause *it came weeping back*. The cyclical structure
moves each time to an antithetical anti-climax: the positive desire for life is
subsumed by the desire for death (*it wanted to die*).

The final three lines of the poem stand separated from the inescapable cycle of
the first two stanzas. They represent first humility, then recognition, and finally
acceptance. Water, with *no weeping left*, leaves behind self-deception and recognises that it is fundamental to the life process, it lies *at the bottom of all things*. The
balanced parallelism of the final line symbolises the climax towards which *Crow*
has been moving: the connotations of *clear* imply not only the elemental purity
of water, but also its self-knowledge.

Hughes represents the struggle towards consciousness as a painful process.
Stripped of our self-deceptions, we are ready to understand our place in the
greater scheme of things and the ultimate absurdity of existence. The celebratory
tone of the final *Crow* poem, 'Littleblood', replaces Crow's questions with
certainty, his arrogance with knowledge, and his raucous cry with song.

Religion is another recurring theme, closely related to Hughes's interest in
consciousness. He saw religion and mythology as the structures we use to explain
the world and, in this sense, Christianity is no more than *another provisional myth
of man's relationship with the creator and the world of spirit* (*London Magazine*, 1971).
More important in the context of his verse is an understanding of the point at
which spirit and body become one.

In *Crow*, Hughes challenges the received wisdom of Christianity as he explores a new version of creation – the creation of Crow. The parody of the Old Testament genealogy in 'Lineage' moves from the natural and animal (*Eye, Wing, Bone, Granite, Violet*) to the human (*Guitar, Sweat*). Hughes's God is man-made – created by *Adam* and *Mary*, and creator of *Nothing*. In challenging the biblical position of God as creator of everything, Hughes emphasises that the God of his poems is human: *the man-created, broken-down, corrupt despot of a ramshackle religion* (*London Magazine*, 1971). Crow, created from nothing, is born into the real world of *the nest's filth*. The negative image of the nest and the strong emphasis on Crow's desire for survival (*Screaming for Blood/Grubs, crusts/Anything*) sets the tone for the volume.

A number of the poems subvert Christian traditions. Like 'Theology' (*Wodwo*), 'A Childish Prank' alludes to the familiar Christian account of man's creation and fall from grace. The passive and incompetent God, driven to sleep by the problems of creation, allows Crow to substitute animal lust in place of the soul to bring the *inert* bodies of man and woman to life. To understand the humour of the poem and the ironic relationship between body and soul, Hughes relies on the reader's knowledge of the *provisional myth* on which he draws: Crow now becomes creator, amusing himself with no more than a *childish prank*. The cartoon-like image of man being *dragged across the grass* and woman waking up *to see him coming* works in comic opposition to the Edenic context, allowing Hughes to challenge the concept of religion as absolute truth.

Hughes uses the language of religion, myth and science in his poems, intertwining them to create a discursive tone. He embraces variety rather than adhering to a single code and the breadth of the allusions adds to the intensity of his work. He draws on the Buddhist doctrine of *The Tibetan Book of the Dead* in 'Examination at the Womb-Door' (*Crow*); he attacks scientific determinism in 'Crow's Account of the Battle'; he challenges the concept of the self-sufficient hero in 'Crow's Account of St George'. Crow himself is a direct descendant of the North American 'Trickster' myths. These tell of a semi-divine creature that is driven out of society for breaking its taboos and sets off on a journey that leads to absurd and often violent adventures.

Hughes is drawn to satire because of its lucid and direct undermining of what is held sacred. He combines the comic, the fantastic and the absurd in a form that is uncompromising and thought-provoking. It is subversive, allowing Hughes to challenge accepted attitudes and beliefs.

Many of Hughes's poems draw on **personal experience** in a general way, allowing him to understand something about life and the world around him. Some draw on the Yorkshire landscape of his childhood; others begin with a particular occasion or experience that provides a stimulus. Hughes then uses the concrete incident as a point from which he can move towards the universal. A visit to a zoo becomes an exploration of the power of the mind over the body ('A Jaguar'); finding it difficult to write a poem leads to a recognition of the creative process ('The Thought-Fox'); seeing a dead pig sets thoughts of life against the nothingness of death ('View of a Pig'); a childhood experience of fishing forms the basis for a contemplation of the power of the natural world and the perfection of evolutionary design ('Pike'); finding a jawbone on the shoreline becomes a celebration of natural energy and violence ('Relic').

At times, Hughes draws on more private events. 'Full Moon and Little Frieda', for instance, is a poem about his small daughter. He takes an ordinary event – the child's innocent wonder at the moon – and makes something extraordinary and original from it. The intensity of the imagery and the power of the last two lines elevate the poem beyond an autobiographical moment.

Hughes's last volume, *Birthday Letters*, takes the 'private moment' to even greater heights: poems about his relationship with Plath reveal a private side. He no longer moves from specific to general, from personal to universal, but explores an inner world of intensity and raw emotion. The tone is often marked by anguish, but always accompanied by tenderness.

He describes his first meeting with Plath ('St Botolph's'), her fears ('The Machine'), their marriage ('A Pink Wool Knitted Dress'), and their friendship with Assia Wevill, who was to become Hughes's lover ('Dreamers'). Having tried to avoid personal attention from the media and the literary establishment all his life, *Birthday Letters* represents a return to the instinctive and passionate tone of his early work, but this time with no attempt to immerse the autobiographical in the wider context of life. Distant from the earlier satire, it is a heartfelt collection in which Hughes, facing death himself, explores matters of great personal significance. He once said that writing was about *trying to take fuller possession of the reality of your life* and in these poems, as many critics saw it, we see a man attempting to make peace with himself.

Images and symbols

Hughes's verse is dominated by strong and often unexpected images that create cohesion both within a particular poem and within the wider context of his work as a whole. The natural world, religion, mythology and the commonplace provide the basis for the imagery, but Hughes's eye for detail and his ability to bring disparate things together makes us see the world around us in a new light.

Natural imagery dominates Hughes's work, both literal and figurative. His attention to visual detail, however, is not Wordsworthian in its precision. Instead, Hughes transforms the natural world. Reflections in a pond become *the floating woods* ('Pike') as the world retreats into insubstantiality and the boy's dreams become the stuff of life. The literal countryside walls that Hughes celebrates in 'Walls' become, figuratively, the language of the landscape.

Hughes's imagery also finds links between the animal and the human. The anthropomorphic Crow is consciously human in his struggle to understand life – his birth ('A Kill') is recognisably human rather than bird-like. The *malevolent aged grin* of the pike ('Pike') seems to give the fish an almost human consciousness of its instinctive nature. Thistles become Icelandic warriors whose sons *Stiff with weapons* will avenge their death ('Thistles'). A snowdrop appears to have a conscious sense of purpose as she *pursues her ends,/Brutal as the stars of this month/Her pale head heavy as metal* ('Snowdrop'). Yet the thrushes are defined by their difference to man: they are *poised*, *triggered*, primed for action, having

> No indolent procrastinations and no yawning stares.
> No sighs or head-scratchings. ('Thrushes' ll.6–7)

While man is lost on self-indulgence and his imaginings, the birds are *streamlined*, created without *any doubt to pluck at [them]*.

In 'The Thought-Fox', Hughes uses natural imagery to make an abstract concept (composing a poem) concrete. The poem represents a thought that comes to life on the poet's page like a wild animal appearing silently in a forest clearing. The opening stanzas are marked by loneliness and emptiness, by a blankness that is not ultimately depressing because of the suggestive nature of the imagery. While *the clock's loneliness* and the *blank page*, symbolic of the poet's world, are negative, the metaphor of the abstract *moment* as a *midnight . . . forest* and the sense that *something else is alive* replace negativity with a mood of potential. Our anticipation is fulfilled in the arrival of Hughes's muse in the form of a metaphorical fox. The image is vivid and a sense of tentative movement replaces the immobility of the first stanzas. The description of the fox is reminiscent of Hughes's animal poetry in the attention to detail. The adverbs chart its progress: first *delicately* and *warily*, then *brilliantly* and *concentratedly*, it leads us towards the moment of creation.

In the final stanza, the metaphor becomes explicit in the bringing together of the powerful noun phrases *a sudden sharp hot stink of fox* and *the dark hole of the head*. As the poem comes full circle, we end where we began: the window is still *starless*, the clock still *ticks*, but *The page is printed*.

We recognise in Hughes's imagery his distinctive way of looking at the world – we see things anew through his eyes. In 'The Owl' (*Birthday Letters*), he attempts to understand another person's viewpoint, using imagery to communicate Plath's view of a world that was to her *foreign*. We are prepared for this by another poem in the collection, 'The Machine', in which Hughes quotes metaphors that Plath herself wrote. Her images of *A huge dark machine* and *The grinding indifferent/Millstone of circumstance* are ominous, characterised by the fear and oppression she felt. We therefore understand when in 'The Owl' *Plain hedge hawthorns* are transformed into *peculiar aliens* and *common mallards* become *artefacts of unearthliness*. The central image of the poem, towards which all Hughes's observations move, is the camera that reproduces reality without making a connection or understanding – so too for Plath, *Recording reflections [she] could not fathom*.

The effect of the imagery in Hughes's poems is to communicate meaning in a very physical way. It is a means of elevating the ordinary to a symbolic level and in Hughes's best work we see the power of his imagination to recreate the world.

Poetic form

Hughes used the short lyric form in his early work and he also did much to contribute to a revival of the dramatic monologue in the 1960s. As a Modernist poet, however, Hughes chose free verse rather than tightly structured traditional poetic forms as a suitable medium for his exploration of a chaotic and often violent world. The disjointed and fragmentary approach of many of the *Crow* poems, for instance, was a direct response to the age in which they were written.

The underlying narrative, whether it be autobiographical, fictional or mythical, provides a cohesive framework even in Hughes's most complicated poems. He enables us to relate to the text at the level of imagination, even when we may be challenged by the grammatical structures and ideas. The *Crow* sequence, for instance, offers us a central protagonist with whom we can engage despite his limitations – or, perhaps, because of them – and a sequence of events.

When reading Hughes's verse, the visual image of the poem on the page is important and there is always a direct link between the layout and the meaning. We need to be aware of the irregularity of line length, the structure of stanzas and their arrangement on the page, the spacing of lines, the use of enjambement or end-stopped lines, the cyclical use of words, phrases and lines, and the way in which sound patterning creates cohesion.

Style

The style of Hughes's poems, like his imagery, is distinctive – the publication of *Hawk in the Rain* in 1957 was to mark the appearance of a new poetic voice quite at odds with the ordered verse of Hughes's contemporaries. Language is stretched to its limits because it is used symbolically to redefine meaning in a world where meaning and truth are perceived as shifting rather than absolute. Pared down to its barest form, it is quite unlike the traditional poetic language of pre-Modernist verse.

The diction is simple, often drawing on the vernacular. Its intensity comes from the way in which Hughes brings together unlikely elements, changes word classes, and creates new words or language patterns. His verse represents an attempt to challenge our expectations, to get close to the nature of existence and the essence of language. Pronouns shift as Hughes alters perspectives and unbalances the traditional expressive function of the lyric ('The Executioner'); nouns take the form of verbs (*Something **magnets** and **furnaces***, 'Incompatibilities'); adjectives take the form of verbs (***crimsoning** into the barbs*, 'Macaw and Little Miss'); verbs are often energetic, establishing the tone and driving the poem forward (*heaving*, *Hoisting*, *burst*, *topple*, 'Pennines in April').

The tone is directly related to the diction and the austere style Hughes found in the work of the Eastern European poets he admired. The often aggressive language and the sometimes nihilistic view of existence means the poems can, on first reading, seem very bleak, unemotional and detached. The rough consonantal sounds and the sometimes abrupt poetic voice, however, are balanced by the energy of the verse and the warmth of a colloquial and vernacular language. In many poems, Hughes's underlying humour also lightens the nihilism.

The style is often rhetorical as Hughes uses rhythm and repetition in a manner reminiscent of incantation. Similarly, he employs antithetical words in a dialectal opposition that explores the tension in life between dark/light, good/evil, spirit/material things, creation/destruction. Word order is often manipulated to delay the main clause or to emphasise key words and phrases; sentences are often long and complex. Hughes moves between registers, juxtaposing the colloquial with the scientific, the religious with the coarse, the journalistic with the poetic. The result is a complex mix that allows Hughes to exploit the links between language, style and meaning to the full.

Ted Hughes and the English poetic tradition

At a time when English verse was dominated by the ironic, urban middlebrow tone of the Movement, the publication of *The Hawk in the Rain* in 1957 was momentous. Hughes's vernacular and his emphasis on the physicality of the natural world was to change the face of English poetry. By the 1960s, Hughes had secured his position as one of the major poets of the twentieth century.

Hughes's influence on his contemporaries is significant. While there was to be much derivative verse emulating Hughes's approach to the natural world, critics have also found creative links between the work of Hughes and that of R.S. Thomas (*H'm*) and Seamus Heaney (*Death of a Naturalist*).

Critics recognise in Hughes's best work his ability to ground universal themes firmly in everyday experiences; his stylistic craftsmanship; his striking diction and powerful imagery; his narrative skill; and the range of his imagination. While for some his reputation as a poet was to decline during the 1980s after his appointment as Poet Laureate, the lyrical and impassioned *Birthday Letters* was to strike a new chord.

Hughes is sometimes criticised for obscurity, and for a carelessness in composition. He perhaps demonstrates a less controlled mastery of technique than Thom Gunn and Philip Larkin, but his experimental approach is more challenging, and he binds form and meaning in a complex relationship. Others dislike what they see as a reductive approach that reduces life to no more than a quest for survival at a basic physical level. Looking at his poetry as a whole, however, it is difficult to accept this as his only level of engagement with life.

Hughes is a poet who feels life intensely, who faces its hardships realistically, and yet still has a sense of wonder and an ability to see its comic possibilities. His power as a modern mythmaker has been compared with that of Yeats, Blake and Milton; and he gave English poetry a new style that was more appropriate for the second half of the twentieth century. Focusing on the landscape and its inhabitants, on specific incidents and personal relationships, and on the universal and contemporary, his verse will endure.

Activity 13.8

How does Hughes communicate his feelings in 'Red', the final poem in *Birthday Letters*?

You may like to think about: the language, the imagery, the sentence structure, the rhetorical and poetic features, and the form.

Red

1   Red was your colour.
If not red, then white. But red
Was what you wrapped around you.
Blood-red. Was it blood?

5   Was it red-ochre, for warming the dead?
Haematite° to make immortal   *a valuable iron ore,*
The precious heirloom bones, the family bones.   *often red*

When you had your way finally
Our room was red. A judgement chamber.

10   Shut casket for gems. The carpet of blood
Patterned with darkenings, congealments.
The curtains – ruby corduroy blood,
Sheer blood-falls from ceiling to floor.
The cushions the same. The same

15   Raw carmine along the window-seat.
A throbbing cell. Aztec altar – temple.

Only the bookshelves escaped into whiteness.

And outside the window
Poppies thin and wrinkle-frail

20   As the skin on blood.
Salvias, that your father named you after,
Like blood lobbing from a gash,
And roses, the heart's last gouts,
Catastrophic, arterial, doomed.

25   Your velvet long full skirt, a swathe of blood,
A lavish burgundy.
Your lips a dipped, deep crimson.

You revelled in red.
I felt it raw – like the crisp gauze edges

30   Of a stiffening wound. I could touch
The open vein in it, the crusted gleam.

Everything you painted you painted white
Then splashed it with roses, defeated it,
Leaned over it, dripping roses,

35   Weeping roses, and more roses,
Then sometimes, among them, a little bluebird.

Blue was better for you. Blue was wings.
Kingfisher blue silks from San Francisco
Folded your pregnancy

40   In crucible caresses.
Blue was your kindly spirit – not a ghoul
But electrified, a guardian, thoughtful.

In the pit of red
You hid from the bone-clinic whiteness.

But the jewel you lost was blue.

Commentary

As the final poem, 'Red' provides a symbolic climax to the collection, expressing Hughes's feelings, his version of events, through powerful imagery. The direct address (*you/your*) makes it a very personal poem – the poet is speaking directly to Plath, seeking understanding as he himself faces death. The reader becomes a bystander, a detached observer of a private communication.

The opening line of the poem is emphatic: the simple sentence *Red was your colour* uses the declarative mood to make a clear statement of fact. The confidence of this statement, however, is undermined by the following line where the hypothetical *If . . .* and the contrastive conjunction *But . . .* (l.2) contradict the certainty of the first line. The tension between the two colours is apparent immediately, but Hughes chooses to explore the power of red. The protective verb *wrapped* (l.3) suggests its positive qualities, but these are tempered by the imagery of blood.

The move to an interrogative mood (ll.4–5) reflects the poet's uncertainty as he attempts to understand the instinctive nature of another person. The juxtaposition of death (*warming the dead*, l.5) and life (*to make immortal*, l.6) in the imagery of *red-ochre* and *Haematite* prepares us for the stark contrasts developed in the following stanzas.

The poem both conjures up vivid physical images based in day-to-day life and immerses us in the powerful emotions surrounding these ordinary events. Drawing on the rich connotations associated with colour, Hughes explores literal events (the painting of a room, the colour of a skirt) and their psychological significance. The result is very intense, communicating Hughes's private feelings within a carefully controlled structure. The strongly visual element of the poem engages the reader at a concrete level, making the complex emotions more accessible.

The concrete nouns *room* (l.9), *carpet* (l.10), *curtains* (l.12), *cushions* (l.14), *window-seat* (l.15) and *bookshelves* (l.17) provide a physical background. We are struck by the everyday nature of this world where people choose colour schemes and decorate their homes. The intensity is conveyed in the symbolic images that Hughes sets alongside the literal. The room painted red becomes *A judgement chamber* (l.9), a *Shut casket for gems* (l.10). The images go beyond the physical detail, suggesting something of the relationship, of Plath's view of the world. The connotations are claustrophobic – the beauty of the gems is shut away, leaving instead an image of imprisonment that reinforces the symbolic confinement and guilt implied by the *judgement chamber*.

The patterned carpet becomes nightmarish in its association with blood. While blood-red can be used to describe a certain quality and intensity of red, here the metaphor *The carpet of blood* (l.10) is ominous. The mood is intensified by the striking nouns *darkenings, congealments* with their implicit suggestion of blood spilt in violence. As the style becomes increasingly elliptical, the mood becomes more claustrophobic – we are trapped within the context of this room. The noun phrases describing the curtains reinforce the imagery of blood. The intensity of colour (*ruby corduroy blood*, l.12) is matched by the excess (*Sheer blood falls*, l.13) – it is a suffocating room from which there is no escape.

The second stanza moves towards its climax in the striking images of its conclusion. The sentence structure is fragmented, leaving only the noun phrases *A throb-*

bing cell, Aztec-altar and *temple* (l.16). The verb modifier *throbbing* with its suggestion of both life (the living pulse) and pain is reinforced by the reference to the *Aztec-altar* – an early South American culture known for the splendour of its art and ceremonial rituals and the horror of its blood-letting sacrifices. It is therefore an emotive conclusion to a description of a room that has become prison and sacrificial altar.

The blood imagery continues in the fourth stanza, focusing now on Plath rather than the room she has created in her own image. The fact that we are still inside looking out reinforces the sense of imprisonment established in the second stanza, but the language now implies weakness and fragility rather than suffocating excess. The modifiers *thin and wrinkle-frail* (l.19) describing the poppies are linked directly to Plath. The redness of the *Salvias* (l.21), after which she has been named, and the *roses* (l.23) is associated with wounds in the simile *Like blood lobbing from a gash* (l.22) and the metaphor *the heart's last gouts* (l.23). The sound patterning intensifies the semantic effects: the cumbersome medial plosives in *lobbing* and the internal rhyme of *heart's last* seem to turn the poem inwards, mirroring the suffocation of the second stanza.

A climax is again reached in the final line where the asyndetic listing of the three modifiers (l.24) suggests that the poet and his lover are trapped in some inescapable cycle. Hughes develops the imagery of blood-letting that has run through the stanza: the life-giving connotations of *arterial* are undermined by the negative *Catastrophic* and *doomed*.

The focus moves back into the room as Hughes addresses Plath in stanza 5. The rich imagery of the *velvet long full skirt* of *lavish burgundy* (ll.25–6) is undercut by the metaphor Hughes uses. The noun phrase *a swathe of blood* (l.25) develops the overwhelming excess of stanza 2 and the blood-letting of stanza 4. The imagery of blood is brought to a head in the simile *like the crisp gauze edges/Of a stiffening wound* (ll.29–30). The suggestion of a physical wound that has been implicit in the blood imagery is now explicit. It communicates Hughes's feelings in a vivid and painful way, representing their relationship as an experience of intensity and pain. The image of the *stiffening wound* with its *crusted gleam* (ll.30–1) is redolent of the healing scab that can be so easily opened. It gives a very physical quality to the vulnerability of their love.

The tension between the poet and Plath is emphasised by their different responses. The simple emphatic sentence *You revelled in red* (l.28) is set against *I felt it raw* (l.29): where Hughes is aware only of the figurative wound, Plath luxuriates in the colour's richness. The antithesis of these sentences draws the two strands of the imagery together, binding the luxurious sense of excess and the life-threatening wound together in an uneasy partnership. The tension in the relationship is mirrored within Plath herself in the opposition Hughes sees in her use of red and white (ll.1–2, 32–3) – she overlays the tranquillity of white with red roses. The verbs in stanza 6 suggest the overwhelming power of the red (*defeated/Leaned over*) and its excess (*dripping, roses . . . and more roses*). The personified *weeping roses* become symbols of both the beauty and the pain that characterises their love.

The change in direction in the final line of stanza 6 suggests the potential for something existing between the two symbolic extremes of white and red. The balance of the medial caesura (ll.34–5) is replaced by the fragmented minor sentence with its movement towards a symbol of hope. The fronted adverbials

(*Then sometimes, among them*) delay the noun phrase *a little bluebird*, giving it added importance at the end of the line, and the initial spondee and trochees are replaced by a lilting iambic metre.

Thén so′me ∣ tim′es, ă ∣ m′ong thěm, ∣ ăli ∣ ttlě b′lue ∣ bi′rd.

This marks a change in mood as Hughes contemplates another side to Plath.

The language is now warm and positive, symbolic of life-giving rather than blood-letting. Hughes's viewpoint is clear in the opening simple sentence, the comparative *better* (l.37) suggesting what could have been. The bird imagery (*wings* l.37, *Kingfisher blue* l.38), with its connotations of flight and freedom, releases the poem from the intensity of its vision of blood; the nurturing image of pregnancy conveyed by the protective verb *folded* (l.39) and the noun *caresses* (l.40) establishes the positive mood. It is reinforced by the metaphorical noun phrases *your kindly spirit* and *a guardian* (l.42). The juxtaposition of the modifiers *electrified* and *thoughtful* suggests that this alternative state of mind is not a passive emptiness, but a constructive blend of the highly charged (*electrified*) and the reflective (*thoughtful*) – it balances the antithesis of the earlier stanzas.

The final three lines confirm this. The juxtaposition of *the pit of red* and *the bone-clinic whiteness* (ll.43–4) suggests the two extremes of Plath's response to the world. The connotations of *pit* symbolise the fearful depths into which Plath can sink, while the compound modifier *bone-clinic* strikes us with its starkness. In the final line, the fronted conjunction offers an alternative in the metaphor of the *jewel* (l.45). Hughes's choice of the verb *lost*, however, undercuts its potential value, leaving us with a mood of sadness at the possibilities that have not been fulfilled.

The fragmented sentence structure, the intensity of the noun phrases and the recurring lexis (*red/blood/white/blue*) contribute to the powerful statement made by the poem. The predominance of noun phrases freezes the images Hughes creates, focusing attention on both the literal and the figurative significance of the imagery. The patterning of sound within the lines (*casket/carpet* l.10, *falls/floor* l.13, *throbbing/altar* l.16) enhances the sense of enclosure communicated by the poem's diction and structure. The isolated line *Only the bookshelves* . . . (l.17), on the other hand, stands out not only in its contrasting colour and its use of the verb *escaped*, but also in its hissing sibilance. The sequence of strong plosives (*blood lobbing* . . . *gash* . . . *gouts* . . . *catastrophe* . . . *doomed*) builds the poem to a climax of potential despair; the vivid image of Plath that follows then stands as a reminder of the power of her attraction, culminating in the alliterative plosives and internal rhyme of *Your lips a dipped, deep crimson* (l.27).

The poem is a very private account of Hughes's relationship with Plath. Beginning with the symbolism of red, Hughes focuses first on their shared room, then on the view outside and finally on Plath herself. In many ways, the imagery is traditional: the red of passion and intensity is set against the cold restraint of white. Reminiscent of Brontë's *Jane Eyre*, the red room of the poem can be seen as a female symbol of creativity, and rebellion against a male-dominated world. The red is certainly passionate and vibrant, but it is also suffocating and over-whelming for the male poet. The symbolic whiteness of the bookshelves (l.17), representative of cool-headed intellectualism, offers an alternative, but it is also another extreme in which restraint and repression limit the spirit for passion. What Hughes communicates in his portrait of Plath is the extreme intensity of her existence – neither she nor their relationship can exist in the calm of the middle ground.

'Red' is a heartfelt poem in which Hughes expresses his own view. The language is passionate, but not judgemental. He uses imagery to explore, retrospectively, the complexity of a relationship that, in many ways, has become public property.

Women poets 1960–90

Traditionally seen as an 'elite' genre read by the few, poetry has been the territory of male poets and male critics. While there are some notable exceptions, it has not always been easy for women poets to find publishers willing to print their work. The male-dominated academic poetry of the Augustan Age may have been replaced by the subjectivity of the Romantics with their emphasis on the personal and confessional, but mainstream English poetry offered few opportunities for women.

Within the context of this book, it has been necessary to highlight key points in the development of the English poetic tradition, and this has been, on the whole, a male-dominated journey. This section is a recognition of the contribution made by women poets to the English poetic tradition at the end of the twentieth century. Where they may have been unheard voices, they have now directly affected the development of English poetry, and this is both a celebration of their range and diversity, and an acknowledgement of their critical status.

The emergence of a strong women's tradition

In the last decades of the twentieth century, perhaps the most significant development can be seen in the emergence of a strong women's tradition. Having been denied access to the mainstream for centuries, women poets began to find increasing opportunities for publication, bringing their work into general readership for the first time. Where literary tradition had represented them as passive objects – the subject matter of poetry – they now took up their rightful position as participants. Like the Romantic poets, they aimed to give a voice to those who had no voice, and to use the language of ordinary people.

As with all poetry, we see the desire to communicate and make sense of things as a major concern of the women poets of this period. A dominant theme is the relationship between the self (internal) and society, culture and politics (external). Where the Romantic lyric claimed to be a true representation of subjective experience recovered through memory and made objective through language, modern women poets no longer saw the self as a source of universal truth. Identity was no longer seen as a fixed quantity that could be isolated and used to determine who we are. Instead, as Queer theory was to suggest in the 1990s (based on *Gender Troubles*, 1990, by Judith Butler), it can be reinvented; it becomes a performance in which we can redefine ourselves, according to the audience, purpose and context of our interactions. The nature of identity in women's poetry therefore becomes an area of exploration rather than explication. A poem may speak to readers who have a common experience, but the emphasis is on the difficulty of 'knowing', the instability of 'truth' and the uncertainty of 'meaning'.

What unites these disparate poets is not the emergence of particular 'schools' of poetry, but a belief in the imagination's power to transform. Some critics have seen a likeness between the transformative power of ritual oral verse traditions and the women poets of the late-twentieth century. Communities like the Native Indians of North America use their female-dominated ritual verse to heal and induce visionary trances; the process of women's poetry is also redemptive in giving the silent a voice, in making sense of personal experience, and in recreating our understanding of the 'self'. It is transformative in its reworking of male versions of history and literature (retelling of historical events and fairytales from a female point of view), in its reinterpretation of traditional images (the 'woman as flower'), and in its integration of figures and motifs from other cultures.

In the last decades of the twentieth century, women poets have been responsible for moving the English poetic tradition in a new direction. They have placed the 'female' at the centre of a male-dominated literary genre, and have brought female issues and female points of view to the heart of the mainstream. This is not to say, however, that their concerns are limited by gender – they have cast new light on subjects by reworking the old and repositioning the female self in relation to society as a whole.

Single-gender anthologies

In 1962, *The New Poetry* edited by A. Alvarez offered readers an anthology of contemporary British poetry. It was an exclusively male collection that showed no awareness of the contributions of contemporary women poets. A revised volume published in 1966 included an American section with poems by Sylvia Plath and Anne Sexton, but there were still no British women poets. It was a situation that the 1970s were to remedy with the publication of single-gender anthologies that would change the status of women poets and their work.

Initially, an interest in 'lost voices' led to the publication of *The World Split Open: Women Poets 1552–1950* edited by Louise Bernikow (The Women's Press, 1974) in which such recognisable names as the nineteenth-century poets Charlotte and Emily Brontë, Elizabeth Barrett Browning and Christina Rossetti were set alongside the seventeenth-century Aphra Behn (1640–89) and the twentieth-century Kathleen Raine. This volume was to prepare the way for the important collection *One Foot on the Mountain: An Anthology of British Feminist Poetry 1969–1979* edited by Lilian Mohin, which was to assert the place of women poets in the English poetic tradition. Its symbolic title was indicative of the upward struggle women poets were to encounter in their journey towards critical and public recognition.

This volume was to mark the launch of a number of single-gender collections in the 1980s: *Bread and Roses: Women's Poetry of the Nineteenth and Twentieth*

Centuries (ed. Diana Scott, Virago 1982); *Making for the Open: The Chatto Book of Post-Feminist Poetry 1964–1984* (ed. Carol Rumens, 1985); *The Faber Book of Twentieth Century Women's Poetry* (ed. Fleur Adcock, 1987). Such collections were considered necessary because mixed-gender anthologies still did not reflect the strength and range of contemporary women poets.

Critics identify the appearance of these volumes with the rise of feminism and the increasing awareness that women could play a part in socialist politics. It was a context that gave women the impetus to take their writing seriously. Believing that to some extent it was male anthologists who were responsible for denying them access to the mainstream, they aimed to publish themselves in women-run presses such as the Women's Press and Virago, and in the feminist magazines *Spare Rib*, *Red Rag* and *Writing Women*. At the same time, writing collectives encouraged black women to share their common experiences, resulting in poetry that spoke to a specific audience on themes such as anger, isolation, hurt, motherhood and black identity. The focus was on a political exploration of women's experience: their sexuality and the female body, the relationship between the female 'self' and literary and cultural traditions.

Although it was clearly the feminist movement that had encouraged women's writing and publication in the 1970s and 80s, a division was to emerge between those who saw themselves within this feminist tradition and those who wished to set themselves apart from it. In the 1990s, Queer theory was to suggest that feminism had merely reinforced the binary opposition between male and female, limiting the possibilities for a particular person to define herself as an individual. It saw the definition of a 'group' on the basis of one shared characteristic as misleading: defining poets in terms of their sex, their 'male-ness' or 'female-ness', fails to take account of all the other elements of their individuality, and of the fact that 'gender' is not a fixed attribute, but fluid and variable.

In her introduction to the 1985 volume *Making For the Open*, the poet Carol Rumens was to suggest that much of the women's poetry published in the 1970s promoted the feminist cause at the expense of more traditional women poets. She saw her selection as an opportunity to recognise a new stage in women's poetry: quality rather than 'message' was the basis for inclusion, with the emphasis on *verbal intensity* and each poem's *integrity as art*. The result, she believed, encouraged an acceptance of women's poetry as a serious medium that placed women poets on an equal footing with their male counterparts.

Both this volume and *The Faber Book of Twentieth Century Women's Poetry* edited by Fleur Adcock offered readers a very different selection from the earlier small-press collections. Their aim was to promote women poets as an integral part of the mainstream, focusing on their contribution to the poetic tradition rather than on their gender. Poetry was seen as distinct from politics and representative of life in general; the viewpoint universal rather than 'female'. For some, however, the volumes did not offer a sufficiently challenging version of contemporary women's poetry: they were, instead, safe, accessible and frequently lacking intensity.

These different attitudes to the collections of the 1970s and 80s were reflected in debate about what it meant to be a 'woman poet'. The single-gender volumes did initially ensure critical and public attention, but there were to be significant doubts about the long-term value of such an approach to publishing women's poetry. While the need to actively promote their work was seen as paramount, tension surrounded the terms used: was there a difference between being a 'poet' and a 'woman poet'?

To some, the concept of gender was irrelevant in the critical arena – they believed that the epithet 'woman poet' suggested limitations in content, appeal and quality. They felt that defining poetry in terms of its 'female-ness' would suggest that it lacked objectivity, and immersed itself in subjects that were exclusively the domain of women and therefore of no significance to the mainstream poetic tradition. Elizabeth Bishop (1911–79) and others like Sheenagh Pugh (1950–) and Anne Stevenson (1933–) were to describe themselves as 'poets', disliking the implication that 'women poets' were an amorphous group who could be collected together en masse, as they saw it, because they had little individual value. Their aim was to be treated as part of the central poetic tradition and to be given serious critical attention. Bishop, who limited the reproduction of her poems in single-gender collections, was to write that although gender inevitably plays a part in creation, *art is art* and the separation of literature, music and painting into *two sexes* does no more than *emphasize values in them that are not art*.

With the onset of the 1990s, an increasing number of women poets were to be recognised within the mainstream and included in mixed-gender anthologies. Their work was available; public performances were popular; and their voices were heard. There was still concern, however, that they were not awarded the same critical or academic attention as their male peers. In the introduction to the Bloodaxe volume of women's poetry, *Making for Planet Alice* (1997), Maura Dooley argued that rather than being divisive, creating a slipstream, a counter-culture for women's poetry, single-gender collections had a specific function at the end of the twentieth century. They drew attention to the diversity and range of individual poets; created the context for a critical perspective to emerge; and offered opportunities to exciting new voices. It was generally recognised, however, that such volumes had to be seen within the wider context of the mainstream poetry if the poets were to attain recognition within the English poetic tradition.

The groundbreakers

Women poets, like their male counterparts, describe the influence of traditional poets of the literary canon including Chaucer, Shakespeare, the Metaphysicals, Blake and the Romantics, Tennyson, Gerard Manley Hopkins and Seamus Heaney. There are also, however, notable links between the emergence of the 1970s women's tradition and the groundbreaking work of earlier twentieth-century women poets such as the Americans Elizabeth Bishop and Sylvia Plath and the British Stevie Smith (1902–71) and Elizabeth Jennings.

Both Bishop and Jennings were outspoken advocates against a separate women's tradition, believing in the importance of integration into the mainstream on the basis of critical judgement. Where Bishop's work is detached, objective and observational, meditating on details of places, journeys and movement, Jennings writes of suffering, loneliness and friendship; where Bishop's style is colloquial with a strong sense of the spoken voice, Jennings's expression is tightly controlled. Although initially associated with the Movement because of her inclusion in Robert Conquest's anthology *New Lines* (1956), Jennings's work lacks the ironic detachment common to many of the Movement poets such as Philip Larkin. The tone of her poetry is far more personal and spiritual with all the intensity of a confessional. Despite differences in content, style and voice, however, Bishop and Jennings were both outsiders actively challenging predominantly male poetic traditions: Jennings as a 'sacred' poet and Bishop as a poet of place and travel.

Stevie Smith, in the tradition of Edith Sitwell's poetic experiments in language and sound, can be identified by her distinctive voice. She wrote witty caustic verse, often illustrating it with her own particular style of comic drawings. The nursery-rhyme rhythms and structure often conceal an underlying complexity: the poet becomes an analytical observer of the ordinariness of life. The much anthologised 'Not Waving but Drowning' is typical of Smith's work. The opposition created between the tightly controlled structure, the mainly monosyllabic diction and the ironic detachment of the speaking voice results in a poem that is both cartoon-like and philosophical. The surreal visual image of *the dead man* as he lies *moaning* and the colloquial vocative *Poor chap* do not prepare us for the seriousness of the climax in the final lines. This enhances the poignancy of our sudden understanding in the penultimate line that he has been 'drowning' in life.

In the 1960s, Smith was to find a new and younger audience for her work. She was an accomplished reader and, in the growing area of 'performance' poetry, she was to become extremely popular for her distinctive public readings and recordings. In bringing her quirky verse to a wider audience, she was to prepare the way for the women poets of the 1970s and 80s. In addition, her non-traditional style and apparently simple diction were to prepare the way for women poets to find their own voice.

Sylvia Plath (1932–63)

Perhaps most important of all in the emergence of a strong women's tradition is the work of Sylvia Plath in the 1960s. She was to be an important precursor to contemporary women poets because of her challenge to the role and nature of women as they are defined by society. Her work is a constant process of self-definition, in which the very act of writing becomes proof of her identity, and the refusal of publishers to print her work becomes an act of self-negation. It is important to remember that few of Plath's *Ariel* poems and none of the more challenging poems for which she is now most well known were accepted for magazine publication during her lifetime even though she regularly sent off poems to literary editors. At the heart of this process lies her need for approval: only when she is accepted as a poet can she be accepted as a whole and valuable human being. Her verse therefore becomes, ironically, both the means of salvation (the opportunity for Plath to lift herself beyond despair through the process of creation) and the cause of her self-doubt.

Much is known of Plath's biography from media coverage, books like Anne Stevenson's *Bitter Fame: A Life of Sylvia Plath* (1989) and the poetic novel *Ted and*

Sylvia by Emma Tennant (2001), and from Plath's fundamentally autobiographical novel *The Bell Jar* (1963). Invariably details of her relationship with Ted Hughes and her mental health problems are used to interpret her verse, yet it is also important to be aware of the significance of the historical and social context in which she was writing. Women tended to be defined by their role within the home: they were responsible for domestic chores, household management and childcare; they were also expected to be subservient to their husbands, fulfilling the needs of the 'providers' often at the expense of their own. In addition, there was limited general understanding of mental health problems – Plath was isolated, coping with the depression and self-doubt that characterised her life. In the wider world, the Cold War and the stockpiling of nuclear weapons cast a shadow over the lives of many – both Hughes and Plath attended meetings of the Campaign for Nuclear Disarmament – and the political climate clearly affected Plath's response to the world around her.

In the poems 'Daddy', 'Lady Lazarus' and Getting There' (*Ariel*, 1965), we are aware of a fragmented post-war Europe in which death dominates. The language is of war, violence and destruction: references to Jews, Nazis, swastikas and Fascists, images of *Legs, arms piled outside/The tent of unending cries* ('Getting There') and *The boot in the face* ('Daddy'), and the repetition of words linked to death, killing and burial are disturbing, making reading the poetry an uneasy experience. Plath seems fascinated by the destruction of identity and the facelessness of individuals who are reduced to nothing only to rise again defiant: she may be *featureless*, she may be reduced to *nothing* and yet she will rise again *Out of the ash* ('Lady Lazarus'). In many of the *Ariel* poems, Plath seems to create a character who stands as a mythic representation of herself as she works through the anger and hurt in her own life – she was to write in 'Stings' (*Ariel*), *I/Have a self to recover.* The poems are therefore aggressive and challenging, offering the women poets of the next generation a model who categorically refused to conform to the role society assigned her as a woman and as a female poet.

Where the representation of 'self' is central in *Ariel* as a means of responding to personal social and historical contexts, in *Winter Trees* (1971), Plath was to move towards a less personal and more detached exploration of a fragmented world. Her vision is apocalyptic: in 'Mary's Song', the domestic fire in which the *Sunday lamb cracks in its fat* becomes the fire *Melting the tallow heretics*, the Jews, whose *thick palls* float suffocatingly above us. The Holocaust becomes a symbol of not one specific historical event, but of the world itself, and the poem ends with the emotive image of the innocent children who will inevitably be consumed by the world's cruelty. The menacing image of the people with *torsos of steel/Winged elbows and eyeholes* ('Brasilia') becomes representative of the dehumanisation, the inability to feel that Plath saw as indicative of the world around her.

Some poems deal directly with specific events: 'Thalidomide' (*Winter Trees*) is a poem about the abnormal development of the foetus caused by thalidomide, a drug to prevent morning sickness in pregnancy; 'The Courage of Shutting Up' (*Winter Trees*) addresses the Burma crisis and the principles of colonisation and cultural independence. In most poems, however, it is general feelings evoked by the political, social and cultural context that pervade her work. Plath herself said that her poems were 'shaped' by such fears rather than being explicitly about them. She chose to write about the bleakness of a landscape, about the process of creativity, the *hurt and wonder* of love, or the growth of her child in the womb.

Many of the poems have a personal basis: Plath writes of the landscape around her house ('Elm', 'Letter in November', The Moon and the Yew Tree', *Ariel*), of her attempts to keep bees ('The Bee Meeting', 'The Arrival of the Bee Box', *Ariel*), of picking blackberries ('Blackberrying', *Crossing the Water*, 1971). Underlying all these poems, however, there is a horror at the ultimate meaninglessness of the world. Where 'Blackberrying' at first seems to be a vivid account of a personal experience in which time and place are evocatively recreated, we realise on second reading that it is in fact a poem in which Plath is once again exploring her tenuous link with life. The tone of despair is set in the haunting repetitions (*nothing, nothing; protesting, protesting; Beating and beating*), in the language of excess (*Blackberries/Big as the ball of my thumb; fat/With blue-red juices*) and in the images of blood, flies and emptiness. Rather than pleasure, the mood is one of dread.

Even in the poems of motherhood and those celebrating her children, we are aware of the inner landscape of fear that can so easily overwhelm Plath. The mother-figure appears in many of the early poems as an ambiguous and unpredictable character capable of devouring and annihilating, the source of death and darkness. In 'Moonrise' (*The Colossus*, 1960), Lucina is the *bony mother* who labours *Among the socketed white stars*; she is representative of the whiteness of death that can overcome the pain of living. The use of symbolic colours (red for life; white for death) gives this poem a haunting mood: the emphasis is on Plath's state of mind as she sits in a cemetery, contemplating death in life. In 'Frog Autumn' (*The Colossus*), the personified waning summer is a *cold-blooded mother*; in 'I Want, I Want' (*The Colossus*), the *Open-mouthed* baby with his *milkless lip* goes unsatisfied by his mother; in 'The Disquieting Muses' (*The Colossus*), the daughter expresses her anger, blaming her mother for her inability to prepare her child for life. The emphasis is on pain, absence and failure.

While Plath's best known poems tend to focus on illness, suffering and death, those written to her children offer an alternative mood of tenderness and affection. They often express a momentary exhilaration with life that is absent in much of her work. The emotional attachment evident in 'Nick and the Candlestick' (*Ariel*) and 'By Candlelight' (*Winter Trees*) as Plath watches over her child by night, for instance, keeps the fearful inner landscape at bay. While the language in the first half of 'Nick and the Candlestick' is negative with images of *Black bat airs*, *Cold homicides*, a *vice of knives* and a *piranha*, the yellow light of the candle *hearten[s]*. The final stanzas then focus on the beauty of her sleeping child – the images are now of blood that *blooms clean*, of *roses*, *soft rugs* and *stars*. The tone of the final three stanzas is reminiscent of Antony's passionate *Let Rome in Tiber melt . . .* in Shakespeare's *Antony and Cleopatra*: Plath's emphatic imperatives (*Let the stars/Plummet; Let the mercuric/Atoms . . . drip*) build towards a climax in which the baby becomes a certainty in a world of darkness and destruction – the poem was written at the time of the Cuban Missile Crisis. The tension of the real world is juxtaposed with the certainty of Plath's 'feeling'; the personal and domestic can temporarily keep the sense of imminent disaster under control. The declarative *You are the one/Solid* and the authoritative statement of the final line suggest that, at least for a time, Plath has found a constant in her life – it is a certainty echoed in the relationship between child and mother revealed in 'By Candlelight'.

In the poems exploring creativity, on the other hand, Plath is far less secure. For her, artistic creation is a religious act: in 'Sculptor' (*The Colossus*), a poem dedicated to the sculptor Leonard Baskin, Plath describes his hands as *priestlier/Than priest's hands*. Similarly, the writer is a creator responsible for *an ordering, a reforming, a relearning and reloving of people and the world as they are and as they might be*. Her identity is securely bound up with the process of creation and when the writing process fails, Plath's sense of self is undermined. This can be seen in a poem like 'Words' (*Ariel*), where the ambiguity of the language conveys both the destructive and the nurturing power of words. The image of words as *Axes* suggests their power, yet the gentle connotations of the dynamic verb *strokes*, the resonance of the verb *rings*, the repetition of *echoes* and the simile of the horses undermine the destructive nature of the image. In the final stanza, however, the poet realises that ultimately words are *dry and riderless*, they are no more than *indefatigable hoofbeats* that cannot sustain her.

'Stillborn' (*Crossing the Water*) represents an even greater threat to Plath's stability – despite the connotations of the title, the poem is not related to childbirth, but to the creation of poems that *do not live*. The images of embryos in formaldehyde whose *lungs won't fill* and whose *hearts won't start*, even though they are *proper in shape and number and every part* are chilling. The mother who is *near dead with distraction* is the poet, struggling to create and yet failing to produce the works of art that will live beyond the page. In 'Barren Woman' (originally titled 'Small Hours', *Crossing the Water*), we see the poet's creativity reabsorbed because it is unrecognised – without attention, without publishers and readers, the poet is helpless.

The voice in Plath's poems is often the poet herself, observing from a distance her own sense of powerlessness in a world that is terrifying. The sense of dislocation distances the poet from her 'self' and the result is a tone of ironic impersonal detachment – often despairing as she approaches extreme states of mind, but also at times witty. She writes about tulips, elm trees, her experiences as a wife, daughter and mother, her suicide attempts, but the process does not help her to gain control and there is therefore always an undercurrent of terror. The emphasis is on the impossibility of escaping your personal, social and historical background.

Because Plath's poetry represents her search for herself, the poetry has its own frame of reference. Its associations and images, its recurring patterns and haunting repetitions are indicative of the way that Plath saw and related to the world around her. Dominating images are of death, miscarriage, failure, excess and pain; the ordinary, the domestic and the natural world become threatening. The images have a symbolic function, breaking through the surfaces of appearance and shocking us into recognising deeper levels of meaning.

Plath's poems do not always make easy reading and we cannot expect to fathom their depths immediately – they are complex personal responses to a changing and fragmentary world. Critics sometimes cite an apparent lack of control in her writing, seeing it as a weakness or self-indulgence, but it is also indicative of her particular viewpoint of life. We have to read closely and be prepared to work for understanding. These poems exist as one individual's response to post-war life, but, in the process of creation, they also acquire a symbolic universal significance as Plath struggles to find a means of communicating with her readers.

At the time of Plath's suicide, her reputation as a significant twentieth-century poet was growing and a place in the mainstream literary tradition seemed inevitable. Her first collection, *The Colossus*, had caused great interest, but the posthumous publication of *Ariel* was to establish her critical standing. She is now seen by many as one of the best mid-twentieth-century poets writing in English. As a precursor to the women poets of the 1970s and 80s, Plath represented the possibilities for women both to break free of the images of femininity imposed upon them, and to be taken seriously by a patriarchal literary tradition.

As readers, we sense a compulsive search for meaning as Plath attempts to put together a fragmented experience. Through the content and style, she seeks to convey a new way of seeing the world, to balance the inner landscape of fear that coloured her experience of the world with the pleasure and freedom she found in the process of 'creating'. Her voice is distinctive – she refuses to accept the silence expected of the suffering woman.

Women poets of the 1970s and 1980s

In the early 1970s, the best known women poets representing English poetry were U.A. Fanthorpe (1929–), Elaine Feinstein (1930–), Jenny Joseph (1932–), Anne Stevenson (1933–) and Fleur Adcock (1934–). They were, however, little known outside Britain. Where contemporary American poets such as Adrienne Rich (1929–), Marge Piercy (1936–) and Alice Walker (1944–) were well known and taught at American universities and colleges, the British women poets were still on the margins of the poetic tradition. Critical accounts of post-war English poetry tended to deal with them cursorily, if at all.

The 1970s poets asserted their rights through poems that consciously expressed something about what it meant to be female. Personal experience was used as a basis for work that would unite reader and poet in a recognition of the female situation: work, friendships, domesticity, abortion, childbirth, sex, motherhood and the nature of identity provided rich sources of material. Seen within the wider contexts of history, society and culture, the individual's experience becomes the tool by which the poet can raise awareness.

Poetry was used to give women a social significance within a patriarchal society, continuing the trend that can be seen to have its beginning in the work of Sylvia Plath. The poets adopted a content, language and voice that distinguished them from the male tradition. Although they made no claim to a distinctively feminine language, they did aim to write poetry that was recognisably different, poetry in which inventive voices, rhythms, syntax and structure made readers conscious of something new in the English poetic tradition.

In the 1980s, the diversity of women poets was becoming increasingly evident as the reading public and the critical world began to recognise their contribution to the English poetic tradition. Gillian Clarke (1937–), Carol Rumens (1944–), Eavan Boland (1944–), Wendy Cope (1945–), Selima Hill (1945–), Liz Lochhead (1947–), Grace Nichols (1950–), Jo Shapcott (1953–) and Carol Ann Duffy (1955–)

began to move women's poetry in a new direction. Some consciously avoided 'women's subjects' and the traditionally feminine areas of 'emotions' and 'sensitivity'; they moved away from the central focus on personal experience as a means of challenging society and its expectations.

For this generation of poets, the exploration of language and its relationship with our identity became a dominant theme. In the creative process, language and syntax were at times pushed to the limits and this sometimes resulted in problems of accessibility for the reader. Poems that used personal experience as the basis for their exploration of language and identity, however, offered critiques of society, gender and culture that were simultaneously accessible and thought-provoking.

The search for an appropriate voice

The women poets of the 1970s and 80s consciously separated themselves from the poetic tradition of 'woman as object' by placing the emphasis on their power of action rather than passivity. Poetry became, for them, a predominantly social medium in which the poet was aware of her future audience. The private act of writing therefore assumed a wider public importance – the underlying purpose was the desire to communicate, to make sense of things. Taking its raw material from women's lives, the poetic process involved a reflective response that universalised the initial experience.

At the heart of the poetry of this period, we see a common search for an appropriate voice through which the poet can communicate with her audience. Using traditional poetic conventions of form and structure to support the reader, the poets challenged received wisdoms through the diverse voices and viewpoints that they employed. While few can be described as experimental in their approach, their verse nevertheless demonstrated their interest in sculpting words and syntax, in finding patterns and connections, and in creating strong visual images.

The poets were to adopt a communal role, speaking out for those who had no voice or who were less articulate. As 'communicators', they were to use language to reconstruct different viewpoints, and we see in their work a range of registers and voices that reveal women's experiences as mothers, lovers, daughters; as representatives of a particular culture, race or geographical area; and as females in a patriarchal society. As readers, therefore, we need to think about who is telling the tale, how it is being told and what the language tells us.

Crucial to the range of voices that emerge from the women's poetry of this period are the cultural, geographical and linguistic backgrounds from which the poets come. Jackie Kay (1961–) is a poet for whom 'voice' is an essential part of her writing. As a child of an unknown white mother and a Nigerian father, adopted by Scots parents and raised in Glasgow, she is fascinated by identity. In her 1991 volume *The Adoption Papers*, she explores the nature of personal and family identity within the wider context of national and cultural identity. Three distinct voices, used both separately and interwoven, form the basis for the poems: the adopted child, the natural mother and the adoptive mother. In 'The Seed', for instance, the adopted child, now pregnant herself, imagines the pain of the situation: the pain of the mother who must give up her child; the pain of the child in coming to terms with her mother's choice; and the pain of the adoptive mother who must cope with social workers, the racism experienced by her adopted child and her child's desire to know about her biological mother. The overlaying of the different voices adds to the intensity of the experience; it allows Kay to present multiple viewpoints that recognise the complexity of life.

For Liz Lochhead, her Scottish heritage is an essential part of her identity as a poet. After the radical orthography of Tom Leonard's verse, which captured the regional dialect of the Glasgow working classes in such a way that the words on the page reflected pronunciation, Lochhead chose to write in Standard English. She personalised it, however, by embedding a sense of the spoken voice and sometimes the Scots vernacular within it. The result is a linguistic medium that reflects her experience, and is quite distinct from traditional 'poetic' language. The sense of the poet (or her persona) speaking to her reader is dominant and Lochhead has developed what she describes as 'recitations' rather than poems: verse that is designed to communicate something of contemporary characters and situations, to shed light on things that happen ('Bagpipe Muzak'); verse that combines the modern and the violent, essential world of oral ballads ('Everybody's Mother'); and verse that uses legends and myths, and then transforms them through her use of contemporary female voices ('Beauty & The').

For other poets of Caribbean or Asian descent, there is an even more distinct range of 'Englishes' to choose from. Grace Nichols, Valerie Bloom and Merle Collins (1950–), for instance, combine Standard English with Caribbean dialects, demonstrating the range and strength of expression that they can draw on. The poem 'Language Barrier' by the Jamaican-born poet Valerie Bloom (1956–), who has lived in England since 1979, explores the nature of language difference using a Creole dialect that draws the reader into another way of seeing the world. Bloom begins with an emphatic statement: *Jamaica language sweet yuh know bwoy*. Yet it is a recognition that has only come to the poet in the process of explaining her language to a *foreign frien'* who draws her attention to the fact that *Some tings . . . soun' queer*. It is a poem in which the spoken voice brings the issues to life as the poet considers the nature of a language's sound, meaning and origins. The words on the page may look alien, but when the poem is spoken aloud the unfamiliarity is replaced by recognition.

The work of the Bengali poet Ketaki Dyson (1940–), who writes poetry in both English and Bengali, is coloured by her experience of two cultures and two languages. In her second volume in English, *Spaces I Inhabit* (1983), Dyson explores the nature of language and identity, and the verse is characterised by the richness and variety of its cultural and linguistic fusion. Another Asian poet, Debjani Chatterjee (1952–), writes of her subversion of the English language as she mines *rebellious corridors of sound*, and of the *treasures of other traditions* that she brings to the poems she writes ('To The English Language').

The distinctive voices emerging from the poems of this period are an integral part of the writing. We must be aware of the language, tone and background of the speaker – whether it is the poet herself or a persona. Only in understanding the relationship between the language and the voice, between the poet and her material, will we understand the poems.

As well as producing work in which a strong voice emerges from the page, the women poets of the 1970s and 80s also followed in the performance tradition of the 1960s poets Roger McGough, Adrian Henri, Adrian Mitchell and Brian Patten. It provided another medium through which the female poets could give a platform to the 'voices' they created. They produced verse that was successful in performance because of the quality of its sound, the relevance of its ironic social and political comment, and the engaging nature of the content.

A specific type of performance poetry can be seen in dub poetry – a genre originating in the practice of West Indian DJs speaking poetry over a background of music, often reggae. It tends to be associated with male poets like Linton Kwesi Johnson and Benjamin Zephaniah, but the female voices of Valerie Bloom and the Jamaican-born Jean Binta Breeze (1956–) have brought a new complexity to the tradition. The use of female voices was to give the black woman a public stance – the poets gave voice to issues of particular relevance to black women and spoke directly to them. They reasserted the genre's political roots in that they, like Johnson and Zephaniah, tackled social and cultural matters in verse that rose above the simplistic doggerel of some of the more popular forms of dub poetry.

The performance tradition associated with women's verse in this period has done much to give poetry a more popular face. The content of poems tends to explore recognisable situations; the style is approachable; and the poets engage directly with their audience. Beyond the 'poetry reading' and the music-orientated dub verse, however, poetry has reached further into everyday life. Jackie Kay, for instance, used verse as the basis for a television documentary. The focus was on the case of a 63-year-old woman sentenced to life imprisonment for killing her husband after suffering years of abuse. Kay used poetic repetitions of the judge's words to represent the restrictions placed upon the woman by the masculine world of the law, and set against this a repetition of the woman's thoughts (*There's no way out, no way out*) to convey her entrapment. The result was a dynamic mix of film and verse that poignantly communicated the woman's situation.

The dramatic monologue

Where the lyric is often based on autobiographical material and is written from a personal point of view allowing the poet to forge a link between the reader and herself, the dramatic monologue creates a different kind of relationship between poet, subject matter and reader. The poet and the 'I' are separate entities; imagination replaces experience; and the viewpoint is 'perceived' rather than personal.

In the dramatic monologues of the 1970s and 80s, women poets used real, fictional, mythical and historical personae as an alternative means of exploring what it meant to be a woman – or at times, a man. While their use of the form appears conventional, they implicitly challenge gender, racial, social and religious expectations through the characters they create. The dramatic monologue becomes a process of interrogation in which the poet deconstructs a moment in time in order to explore the nature of language and identity.

In 'Dorothy Wordsworth' by Jean Earle (1909–), the poet adopts the persona of a real historical person – the Romantic poet William Wordsworth's sister. The poem conveys her inner turmoil as she faces her brother's marriage to Mary Hutchinson, and then comes to terms with the reality of her changed position. The tone is intimate and the style intense as we are given a privileged insight into her sense of self. By contrast, 'Yuppie Considering Life in Her Loft Apartment' by Julie O'Callaghan (1954–), presents us with a fictional character. The unnamed speaker becomes representative of a certain type of person in a certain period. The language is colloquial (*Like I can't handle it*; *Cancel him offa yer floppy disk*; *Ya wanna/come with me*) and indicative of the 1980s with its references to floppy disks and 'Elizabeth Arden'. What we see here is a moment in the life of a particular woman as she faces the departure of her lover: the language is not sentimental or mournful, but pragmatic; the tone is satiric.

Gillian Clarke's monologue 'Overheard in County Sligo' presents us with a very different fictional character in a very different context. The opening two lines of the poem were overheard by Clarke and they are italicised to indicate this.

> *I married a man from County Roscommon*
> *and I live at the back of beyond*

The resulting poem, however, is a fictional account of what may have followed. The woman here considers what she has sacrificed in order to lead the kind of life that society expected her to lead. The simple present tense used to describe her daily routines (*I turn . . .*) and the neat tripling of the infinitives (*to fold . . . to polish . . . to order*) are set in opposition to the use of the 'unreal' past perfective *I had thought to . . .* with its connotations of something that did not happen, and the poignant modal auxiliary *ought to* that emphasises the discrepancy between the reality of her life and her dreams (*I ought to feel I'm a happy woman*). Where O'Callaghan wrote in free verse as an appropriate medium for the kind of life she was exploring, Clarke opts for the more traditional quatrain with its alternate rhyming lines – a contained form in keeping with the way that society has contained and restricted the life of the speaker.

U. A. Fanthorpe in 'Sisyphus' and Elma Mitchell (1919–2000) in 'The Death of Adam' take mythical characters as their starting point. We see Sisyphus, a figure in classical mythology condemned to roll a huge stone uphill for eternity, describing his task and his response to it. The quotation cited from Albert Camus at the beginning of the poem establishes the mood:

> *The struggle itself towards the heights is enough to fill a man's heart. One must imagine Sisyphus happy.*　　　　　　　　　　　　　　The Myth Of Sisyphus

This is not the 'Sisyphean task' of endless and fruitless labour, but an example of the absurdity of life that should not prevent us from fulfilment. The style is conversational and the tone matter-of-fact; the language juxtaposes the concrete reality of the physical relationship between Sisyphus and the stone (*wart, ribby edges*; *Cheek, chin, shoulders, elbow*) with the abstract ideas at the poem's heart (*preoccupations, interest, difficulty, vocation, patience, emotion*). The rhythm, the regularity of the line length, and the frequent use of enjambement mirror the cyclical and perpetual nature of Sisyphus' task.

In Mitchell's poem, we are presented with Eve's dramatic monologue on the death of Adam. Again the tone is conversational, but the structure of the verse is less even – short lines are set against long lines; short minor sentences are set against long compound-complex sentences with parenthesis; the declarative mood is set against the interrogative. Where Sisyphus was characterised by his mood of acceptance, Eve is seen in terms of her questioning. The poem balances the received wisdom of Adam as the creation of a Christian God, *come up from the dust*, with his human reality as he ages: *Withers and wrinkles and shrivels like an apple*. The emphatic syndetic listing represents Adam's vulnerability as a human, but the implicit reminder of the Garden of Eden and the fall from grace embedded in the simile perhaps hints at a reality that could have been quite different. Eve, in this monologue, however, is more than just a byproduct of Adam, *the wife that was part of him*. She assumes an importance through her understanding of the situation and her ability to rationalise. In the final stanza, made up of three questions, Eve raises issues of gender, innocence and experience, and her relationship with the godhead.

Perhaps most well known for her use of the dramatic monologue form is Carol Ann Duffy, who has been praised for taking this traditional form into new ground. She uses it to give her women characters a voice and to challenge accepted ideas of truth and art. In the poems 'Warming Her Pearls' and 'Standing Female Nude', the speakers reveal something of their lives, their positions, their relationships and their inner selves. Just as Robert Browning's dramatic monologues allowed us to see beneath the surface of the words to an inner truth, so too in Duffy's work we see beneath the restrictions imposed upon her characters by their society to an understanding of the speakers as individuals.

In 'Standing Female Nude', we see beyond the external passivity of the artist's model to an inner life of thoughts, which is at times interrupted by the practical instructions of the artist (*Further to the right, do try to be still, Don't talk*). Duffy explores layers of representation and we therefore see the experience from a range of points of view: the poverty-stricken model, who questions the very concept of 'Art'; the artist, who is concerned with *volume, space*; the bourgeoisie who will *coo/at such an image of a river-whore*; and the museum where the painting will be *represented analytically* and the model romanticised.

The language appears to represent the model as an object to be possessed – the artist desires to 'possess' her both physically and through his portrait; the museum will 'possess' the portrait; and the middle class will 'possess' an image that emphasises their difference. In addition, the opening and closing lines refer to the model's payment (*a few francs/Twelve francs*), drawing attention to her status as object. Yet the emphatic declaration of the final line (the simple sentence *It does not look like me.*) becomes a triumphant assertion of self as others attempt to reduce her to the status of object, to a portrait in which the 'self' is subsumed in an interpretation of her individuality. It is a stand against those who desire to diminish her. What emerges from this poem is not a female body made into an object, but the voice of an individual who speaks out and thus reclaims her identity.

Content and themes

The women's poetry of this period is dominated by an interest in the ordinary and everyday as it is experienced by women. It gives a voice to their often invisible and unheard experiences, thus emphasising the validity of their role within a patriarchal society. Through the processes of remembering, reinterpreting and writing, the subjective gains an authority. Domestic matters, childcare, gender and identity issues are given a significance that lifts the content of the poems from personal anecdote to universal social comment.

The poems represent new ways of seeing the world, with the poet as a witness who describes ordinary events that she and the reader can share. Drawing on memories, recounted experiences, observations and the imagination, the poet explores what it means to be a woman. She transforms things we take for granted by balancing opposites: self/society; mother/child; personal/political; male/female; past/present; domestic/wider world. These sometimes contradictory forces are seen as co-existing and lie at the heart of the poetry of the 1970s and 80s. Because it reflects a different view of the world, it requires a new kind of relationship between the poet, the reader and literary tradition.

Many poets start the process of transformation with their own personal experiences. Selima Hill writes of autobiographical incidents in her childhood in 'Chicken Feathers'; Fleur Adcock writes about being a young girl at school in 'Outwood'; Grace Nichols describes women she saw as a child working up to their waists in water in 'Those Women'. While the poems draw on memories to recreate a specific moment in the past, they also function in a wider context. Nichols's recollection becomes the basis for a celebration of the black women who are both physically at ease in their work and sensual. The language emphasises their sexuality (*voluptuous*; *their laughing thighs*) and self-confidence – they are in *their own element*. Adcock's poem uses her personal childhood fears of school to explore the making of a poet: in the detailed observations of the natural world and in the creativity of the child we see the potential from which the adult poet grew. Beginning with an old photograph of her mother, Selima Hill uses a sequence of reminiscences to explore the nature of our relationships with others. The poem's emphasis is on separation and distance: the image of the mother's eyes as *distant stars* and the father's symbolic drawing of a ship *disappearing over a white horizon* communicate this poignantly. The poem's power lies in its ability to create visual images of domestic scenes that have significance for the poet in understanding her parents.

It is this use of the domestic that sets the women's poetry of this period apart – in making the ordinary and small-scale events of daily life into the subject matter of verse, they have elevated the worth of 'women's work'. This can be seen in Vicki Feaver's celebration of her mother's crab apple jelly ('Crab Apple Jelly'), in Gillian Clarke's celebration of polishing brass ('Still Life') and in Carol Rumens's celebration of the working mother who must exist in both the male world *built on money* and *the jugular torrent/of family life* ('Two Women').

Gillian Clarke's long poem 'Letter from a Far Country' is epistolary in form – the poet writes an imaginary letter to the men in women's lives, meditating on the role of women in society. The emphasis is on domestic activity and the verbs are dynamic – Clarke often uses present participles (*counting and listing, harvesting and ordering, numbering and placing*) to draw attention to the ongoing nature of the woman's tasks. Although the men are represented as part of the wider external world, the ones who *close the white gates* to keep women in their place, there is an essential satisfaction in the tone and language of the poem. The images of priests who *fold . . . break bread, share wine*, of harvesting, and of the sea communicate the richness that Clarke finds in the woman's role as provider.

The poem recognises the entrapment of the domestic life with its requirements *To mind things . . . keep. And wait. And pass time*, yet it challenges the *masculine question* that sees no *great works* in a woman's life. It asks us to reconsider the value of a woman's life while, ironically, the 'letter' goes unfinished because the school bells sound to mark the imminent return of the family. The final italicised rhyming quatrains explicitly celebrate the triumph of women's work through a change in grammatical mood – the use of the interrogative to frame a sequence of unanswered hypothetical questions allows the poet to underline the importance of the domestic, nurturing and educative role of the woman.

A focus on childbirth and childrearing is common in women's poetry and is directly linked to this portrayal of the domestic world. Grace Nichols's poem 'In My Name' epitomises the tender relationship between mother and child. The speaker is a black slave directly addressing her unborn child as she begins to give birth. Though society will see the baby as *tainted* because it is born out of wedlock and is of mixed-race parents, the mother sees her child as *perfect*. This opposition between the personal viewpoint of the mother and the judgemental detachment of society is reflected in the imagery. The negative connotations of *bastard* are balanced by the fertility of the natural images (*my seedling/my sea grape*); the clinical *mulatto* is undermined by the mystery of *strange*, and the familiar and diminutive *my little bloodling*. As the poem moves into the imperative mood (*Let the snake . . ./be dumb, Let the centipede writhe and shrivel*), it becomes a triumphant celebration of the child's birth, reaching its climax in the emphatic *For with my blood . . .*, and the imagery of water.

Anne Stevenson's poem 'The Spirit is too Blunt an Instrument' marvels at the perfection of the *intricate/exacting particulars* of the newly born child. Through her use of the imperative (*Observe . . ., Imagine . . .*), she directs us to the physical marvel of the *completed body*, which even at birth *already answers to the brain*. Juxtaposed with the long noun phrases describing the physical perfection of the baby's body, Stevenson draws attention to our *unskilled* passions and sentiments, to *the vagaries of the mind* that create *love and despair and anxiety/and their pain*. The contrast between the concrete and abstract language makes this a meditative poem: the poet both celebrates the baby and reflects on human nature.

The imagery in the poems celebrating motherhood is often natural, balancing the beauty of the baby with the delicacy of nature. In 'Dawn', Jeni Couzyn (1942–) marvels at her baby's *loveliness*: watching the sleeping child becomes a *voyage* as the poet repeatedly studies the baby's perfection. Concrete nouns (*hand, mouth, ear, eye, flesh, back and belly, feet*) are set against beautiful natural images that draw attention to the baby's physical presence: the hand is *a bird poised in mid-air in flight*; the ear *a tiny sea-horse, immortal*. Through the sequence of metaphors, the poet establishes the uniqueness of her sleeping baby; the language is of innocence and purity. In Eavan Boland's 'Night Feed', dawn is the setting for the poet's epiphany: it is the time when we can [*drown*] *our sorrows*, the time at which, in the silence of the world, the mother can be at one with her child before day again brings *The long fall from grace*. For Boland, it is the time when she is *the best* [*she*]*can be*.

A recurring interest in women's issues and in women's attitude to relationships also dominates the poems of the 1970s and 80s. Jean Earle's poem 'Menopause' and Liz Lochhead's poem 'The Abortion', in which the poet emphasises with a cow aborting its foetus, give an insight into distinctively feminine experiences. Jeni Couzyn's poem 'The Message' considers the very different male and female responses to life: men are *rapid pines* that *swarm upwards/jostling for space* where women are characterised by *the circle of light* carried *at the centre of* [*their*] *bodies*.

Such poems place what it means to be a woman at their centre – it becomes acceptable to talk about eroticism, birth, motherhood and love in non-traditional terms. Wendy Cope can parody the Peter and Jane reading scheme books in her poem 'Reading Scheme' – a comic study of an extramarital affair; Grace Nichols can explore the sexuality of a mixed-race relationship in 'Configurations', a sensual poem about identity and physical love; Carol Ann Duffy can subvert the traditional giving of *a red rose or a satin heart* in 'Valentine' to reveal the true nature of love through her image of *an onion . .. a moon wrapped in brown paper*.

The women's poems of this period move beyond a male assertion of the 'self' as a valid poetic voice to an exploration of identity: they consider what it means to be black, Scottish, a writer, a woman. Jackie Kay's dialect poem 'Maw Broon Visits a Therapist' subverts the hierarchy of therapist and patient – we hear only one side of the conversation that is taking place, but Maw Broon appears to be the dominant participant and her strength of character is evident in the richness of her language. She may begin with doubt – she is with the therapist because she *canny hawnle life*, because everything is *awfy* and she is not herself – but as the conversation develops we see that she is resilient and perceptive.

The poem is a poignant statement of what it means to be Maw Broon, of what it means to be a woman defined by a *pinnie* and *heid scarf*. The ambiguity of the final image adds to the poem's complexity. Although the language is negative, the *tatty old rope* becomes a symbol of free choice as the emphatic simple sentences of the last line demonstrate: *I could break. I could jist give in*. Kay's use of the modal verb *could* implies potential for independent action and it is this that Maw Broon finds exciting.

For Moniza Alvi (1954–), identity is an issue of race and culture. Born in Pakistan and brought up in Britain, her poems explore the interaction between two different ways of life and the effect these have had upon her. In her poem 'The Laughing Moon', Alvi sets Pakistan, which *held* [*her*] *and dropped* [*her*] *in the night*, against England, which *Shakily . . . picked* [*her*] *up*. The language of the poem communicates the spontaneity and richness of Pakistan with the stiffness of England. Where Pakistan is associated with colour (*red, green*), England is *grey*; where Pakistan is characterised by dynamic verbs (*crept, threw, spinning*), England is static, characterised by the tentative adverb *Shakily*; where the concrete nouns linked to Pakistan are sensuous and mysterious (*silk, kingfishers and tigers*), those linked to England are practical (*bricks, houses*). We see the poet's excitement at the interaction between these two cultures in the juxtaposition of the *very old* continents and the description of herself as *new and breathing*. The poem is thus a celebration of the richness of Alvi's cultural heritage – the symbolic *laughing moon in its place* becomes a witness to the joys and tensions existing at the heart of Alvi's poetry.

Similar themes about identity and belonging are explored in 'Presents from My Aunts in Pakistan' in which the distant world of Pakistan comes alive in the distinctive clothes and bangles sent by her aunts. The language again is rich and vibrant, creating tension between Alvi's desire for *denim and corduroy*, and her awareness of the beauty of the gifts that represent such a different way of life. Verbs like *marvel* and *admired*, modifiers like *lovely, radiant* and *aflame*, and the richness of the colours reflect her instinctive response to the gifts. She is, however, *half-English, of no fixed nationality*, and this tension within her identity is the source of much of her verse.

As well as exploring the nature of the 'self' in terms of background, race and culture, like Sylvia Plath, many of the women poets of the 1970s and 80s write about writing poetry. Elaine Feinstein's poem 'Muse' describes the process as one of protection and defence – although poetry may seem to be as *powerless as grass*, it is a source of strength in that the poet's *fierce and obstinate centres* are fortified, her sense of identity is reinforced. A similar sense of fulfilment can be found in Elizabeth Jennings's poem 'The Way of Words and Language', where the poet tentatively approaches her content, allowing thoughts to grow until the poet can *unreel* them in a *long-/Travelling, moving everywhere line*. It is a poem in which life is seen through a sequence of images – the emphasis is on transformation and discovery. Only in the final lines as the random ideas become *a song* do we find the assertive simple sentence *'That is mine'*. In the creative process, the poet has found a means of self-validation.

While poems like Anne Stevenson's 'Making Poetry' and 'And even then', explore what poetry is and the nature of the language poets use, Jean 'Binta' Breeze's poem 'I Poet' considers the way in which life experiences make a poet who she is. Written in patois, the poem suggests that *readin* and *lovin* must come before *writin* – immersion in the real world, interaction with other people, and the ability to recognise the validity of one's own experience is the basis for the creation of a poet. Being told she wasn't a poet *well hurt inside*, but the strength of Breeze's character emanates from the certainty of her verse: *I never mind/cause I sey/I was a poet all de time*. The poem is an emphatic declaration of 'self' in that Breeze understands herself and her relationship with the external world: when she writes, she is writing about everyone, about life that is full of *de warmes ting*.

The diversity of women's poetry in this period cannot possibly be addressed fully here, but alongside the ideas and themes that had been the focus of poetry for centuries, women began to write verse about issues that were of particular relevance to themselves. Their underlying aim was to transform the ideal deified image of womanhood by balancing images of the sacred, innocent and pure with real life experiences of domesticity, motherhood and a wider sense of the female 'self'.

Language, style and tone

Where the work of the nineteenth-century American poet Emily Dickinson was experimental in style and language, the poetry of the 1970s and 80s tends not to challenge our expectations. The language is marked by its everyday qualities – it is familiar, accessible and direct. Yet it also has a specific function in that the poets are using ordinary words to claim the value of female experience and liberate their inner selves. The dominant voice is the first person and some poets replace the traditional 'I', which they see as an example of male self-assertion, with *i* to express the tentative nature of their self-representation. This act of conscious manipulation reflects an attempt to establish a place for women poets as distinctive individuals in a male-dominated language.

It is important to consider the relationship between the voice of the poem and the poet. Although frequently autobiographical, the poets also use fictional personae in a variety of historical, social and political contexts to explore their experiences. They move between different registers and tones, exploiting the rich associations and possibilities of language.

In Jean 'Binta' Breeze's poem 'Spring Cleaning', she interweaves the psalm 'The Lord's My Shepherd' with the everyday activity of her character. The unnamed woman's work is conveyed through present participles (*scraping, lifting, drying, mixing*) that suggest the ongoing nature of what she must do. As the poem builds to its climax, we are aware of the ritual quality of her actions: she is dispelling *all de dark spirits*, which are *departing wid de dus*. The integration of the psalm with its traditional archaic verb endings (*leadeth, restoreth*) creates an additional layer of spirituality to the traditional ritual of the woman's springcleaning – the poem becomes both a celebration of ordinary domestic activity and an act of devotion. Breeze writes the poem in a patois that brings a familiar, personal quality to the verse. The lack of traditional punctuation, the variation in line length and the use of enjambement add to this, engaging the reader directly in the experience.

In 'Translating the English, 1989', Carol Ann Duffy also moves between registers in her challenge to the 'official' version of England. The tourist brochure tone of the opening *Welcome to my country!* is set against the vernacular, the language of high culture, nationalism, journalism. The style is dominated by minor sentences, creating a disconcerting and dislocated experience for the reader. The apparently random connections between phrases, however, are designed to force the reader to reconsider: the ideal (*Daffodils. Wordsworth . . .; Shakespeare; Last night of Proms*) is juxtaposed with the real (*the football hooligan; child abuse; rape*) in a process that forces the reader to recognise the exclusion at the heart of our society. The use of first person pronouns (*I/we*) draws us into an unsettling complicity and the traditionally patriotic sentiments of the phrase *my country* become a dubious accolade.

The women poets of this period tend to choose the rhythms of spoken English rather than the strict traditional metrical patterns. The 'beat' of words, their sounds, pitch and pace become a crucial part of the process of communication. The imagery they draw on is equally important: its richness and variety, its sources and associations, reflect on the way in which the poets want us to re-experience the world. The domestic, the natural, the historical, the mythic and the 'here-and-now' become symbols that give an objective structure to subjective experience. They allow the poet to explore the ordinary and the extreme, to challenge and subvert things we take for granted. The process of transformation that takes place lies at the heart of this poetry – it requires the reader to reconsider rather than accept, to question rather than assume.

Women poets and the English poetic tradition

The women poets of the 1970s and 80s bring a new strand to the history of English poetry. They represent a collection of diverse voices rather than a literary school, but their work constitutes a distinct development in the poetic tradition. They have had to find a new language in which to express their ideas and have thus reinterpreted myths, symbols and historical 'truths' so that their readers see them in a new light. The content gives validity to women's experiences – the domestic, the maternal, the ordinary, previously considered 'inappropriate', become legitimate material for poetry. Yet their work also has a political and philosophical relevance: interest in the nature of identity leads them to explore the cultural, social and historical contexts in which women exist, and the effect these have on the female 'self'.

The work of the women's presses and the challenging work of the poets in this period resulted in greater opportunities for women and a greater awareness of what it meant to be a woman. It changed the face of English poetry in that mainstream male poets like Seamus Heaney and Andrew Motion also drew on the everyday, the domestic and the personal as a source of their subject matter. Despite the achievements of the women poets, however, some critics still saw them as marginal because their work was not experimental and did not cover new ground. They were therefore seen by some as less significant than the poets of the accepted male-dominated poetic canon.

Where the growth of feminism had provided an impetus to the recognition of women's poetry, its fall from favour was seen to mark a reciprocal decline in the status of women poets. This has led to the continued publication of single-gender anthologies in an attempt to balance a recognition of the importance of women's work with their need to be a part of the mainstream. To sustain their achievements, they needed to be part of the critical and academic arenas as well as published and read.

Some saw the debate that emerged over the replacement of the Poet Laureate following Ted Hughes's death in October 1998 as evidence that it was still difficult for women poets to establish a public role. The favourites for the post were Andrew Motion and Carol Ann Duffy: while Motion was recognised as a fine lyric poet and biographer, for some Duffy offered an opportunity to break with tradition. She could have been the first woman Laureate and with her reputation for brilliant readings, witty realism and her passion for poetry, many believed that she would have given the public face of poetry a new energy.

The appointment of Motion in May 1999 as Poet Laureate did not mark the end of the debate. The government's decision not to appoint Duffy was met with widespread disbelief in both literary and journalistic circles. She was seen as a popular poetic voice, a supporter of women's rights and a significant influence on the English poetic tradition, and many believed that she had not been appointed because of her sexuality and outspokenness. Where Duffy was non-establishment, insisting that the role of Poet Laureate be thoroughly overhauled and expressing her unwillingness to write poems for the royal family, Motion was a safe choice, an establishment figure who would not cause controversy. For those who supported Duffy, Motion's appointment represented the government's failure to give English poetry a popular public face. Read and enjoyed by critics, students and people who are not conventional 'poetry readers', Duffy, it was believed, could have been a modern-style people's poet who represented a break with the 'elite' male tradition.

Perhaps the ultimate evidence of the success of the women poets at the end of the twentieth century, however, lies in the ongoing richness and variety of women's poetry. As collections like *Making for Planet Alice* (1997) demonstrate, their work is exciting and challenging, both drawing on the work of their predecessors and moving forward in new directions. Readers are buying and enjoying the work of women poets, poetry readings are popular, and students are offered courses of study that focus on women poets. It would seem fair to say, therefore, that the pioneering work of the women poets in the second half of the twentieth century has significantly changed the face of English poetry.

Activity 13.9

Comment in detail on the way Grace Nichols presents the woman in 'Because She Has Come'.

You may like to think about: the language, the sound, the imagery, the sentence structure, the rhetorical and poetical features and the form.

Because She Has Come

1 Because she has come
with geometrical designs
upon her breasts

Because she has borne five children
5 and her belly is criss-crossed
with little tongues of fire

Because she has braided her hair
in the cornrow, twisting it upwards
to show her high inner status

10 Because she has tucked
a bright wrap
about her Nubian brownness

Because she has stained her toes
with the juice of the henna
15 to attract any number of arrant males

Because she has the good sense
to wear a scarab
to protect her heart

Because she has a pearl
20   in the middle
of her lower delta

Give her honour
Give her honour, you fools,
Give her honour.

Commentary

As in many of the poems of Grace Nichols, we see here a celebration of the strength and beauty of black women. It is a poem about black female identity, about what it means to be a black woman. Rather than stereotyping their suffering and the restrictions of their lives, she glorifies them. The woman in this poem attains a godlike status and it is not surprising that in Nichols's spiritual poems, the 'god' figure often has female qualities.

The language of the poem is concrete. Each stanza focuses on a distinctive physical feature (breasts, belly, hair, skin, toes, heart), which builds a strong visual image of the woman. Her dominating presence contributes to her god-like status – she becomes an archetype, an example of womanly perfection. The recurring plosives (*Because, designs, cornrow, twisting, pearl*) add strength to the portrait: the language itself resounds with the woman's poise and self-assurance. The poem is not painting a picture of a commercially acceptable Hollywood-style woman, but a real woman who has the marks of childbirth upon her stomach. The *little tongues of fire* (l.6), however, are not marks of age that need to be purged from the body, but symbols of fulfilment, of a life lived to the full, and of experience.

The images Nichols draws on are varied, reflecting the diversity of this woman. The image of the *geometrical designs* (l.2) on her breasts locates the woman firmly in her cultural background; the image of childbirth reflects her fertility and her role as nurturer; the brightness of the wrap against her *Nubian brownness* (l.2) and her hennaed toes are images of sensuality; the pearl suggests the riches she can offer. All these contribute to the physical beauty of the character Nichols creates, but the image of her cornraked hair functions in another way. While it is an image of physical black beauty, it is also indicative of spiritual beauty – it is symbolic of her *high inner status* (l.9). The one wider reference in the poem that moves beyond the central focus of womanhood is in the description of men as *arrant* (l.15). The negative connotations of the word (a variant of 'errant') serve to elevate the status of the woman further.

The poem is tightly structured: each tercet focuses on a distinctive feature of the woman; each has an image that functions symbolically; and each begins with the subordinating conjunction *Because*. Nichols's use of the subject pronoun *she* without a direct reference to a name makes her portrait archetypal – this is not one particular woman, but a representative of black women in general. This is reinforced by her use of the present perfective (*has come; has borne; Has braided*) with its sense of an action begun in the past and continuing in the present. It is an aspect that emphasises the ongoing relevance of an action: here, it draws attention to the symbolic value of the woman.

The patterning of the language gives the poem a liturgical quality – it becomes a hymn in honour of black women. The foregrounded subordinate clauses (*Because she has . . .*) force us to wait for the main clauses in the final stanza where the poem reaches its climax in the repetition of the imperative *Give*. The abstract noun *honour* (ll.22–4) marks the accumulation of all the images in the previous stanzas; its positive connotations make the implicit god-like status of the woman tangible. She is deserving of respect, veneration, while the reader is addressed with the derogatory vocative *you fools* (l.23). The direct address engages us, ensuring that we recognise our failings in the face of the woman's perfection. The tripling of *Give her honour* brings the poem to an irrefutable conclusion in that it implicitly denies the validity of any other response to the woman.

In her poem 'Of Course When They Ask for Poems About the "Realities" of Black Women', Nichols asserts the variety of black women, and rejects the stereotypes of suffering and downtrodden women. 'Because She has Come', on the other hand, may appear to replace this belief in variety with a single portrait that is representative of a 'type'. Yet this is a poem that challenges negative stereotypes (fixed conventionalised representations), replacing them with an archetype (an original pattern or model). Black women thus become the source of life and its complexity.

Nichols's poem communicates with its readers in a very concrete way, focusing on details that give it a physical presence. The language is direct and ordinary, and it is this down-to-earth quality that makes the poem so powerful. The rhythmic patterning of the structure and style contribute to the effect by creating an almost biblical mood. Taken from *Lazy Thoughts of a Lazy Woman* (1989), it is clearly a poem of its period: it celebrates womanhood, raises the status of black women, and explores the identity of the female 'self'.

▼ 14 Into the twenty-first century

Developments in printing and computer technology have changed the publishing world, making reasonably priced literature of all kinds available to everyone. Poetry still tends to be an elite genre, but public readings and 'performance' poetry are thriving. Schools and universities have writers in residence encouraging young people to express themselves through the medium of verse; newspapers, for example *The Guardian*, have a poetry page that includes commissioned poems, new works and reviews of newly published collections; literary festivals bring readers and poets into contact; the internet gives access to texts and criticisms. All of this breathes life into what had become a genre associated with examination courses and rarefied study.

Poetry in the twenty-first century is a rich and varied genre, with poets working in traditional forms like the sonnet, experimenting with the possibilities of free verse, and creating distinctive voices that will leave their mark on the English poetic tradition. Women poets are no longer sidelined, but exist at the heart of a vibrant culture.

The six poems in this final chapter represent just some of the leading poetic voices of English poetry in the twenty-first century. The discussions accompanying them explore the poets' ideas and the literary and linguistic techniques they have used to communicate them to the reader.

Poems written to mark a public event

The following poems have been written in response to a public event: a solar eclipse ('Everyday Eclipses'), the national announcement of the death of a poet ('R.S.'), and the declaration of war against Iraq ('Regime Change'). In each case, the poet responds at a different level and adopts different linguistic and literary approaches to convey his or her response.

The first poem, 'Everyday Eclipses' (*Everyday Eclipses*, 2002), is written by **Roger McGough** (1937–). Alongside Adrian Henri and Brian Patten, he was first known as one of the 'Liverpool Poets', whose aim was to write poetry for public performance. McGough's work continues to reflect their beliefs that poetry should be popular and anti-academic. The tone is often humorous and the subject matter is of the everyday. McGough has given poetry a human face: his public readings, the appearance of his work in a wide range of anthologies, and his presentation of

Radio 4's 'Poetry Please' programme have introduced his own work and that of other poets to a wide audience.

The second poem, 'R.S.', is written by **Gillian Clarke** (1937–). Born in Cardiff, she is a poet, playwright and translator. Much of her work chronicles everyday happenings in the rural world, but she also explores the domestic, the personal and the traditions of Welsh culture and mythology. She is known for the economy of her style and the power of her images, which are often drawn from the natural world. She teaches creative writing to children and adults, and is the co-founder of the Ty Newydd Writers' Centre in North Wales.

The third poem, 'Regime Change', is written by the current Poet Laureate **Andrew Motion** (1952–). He is a poet, novelist and biographer. His first collection of verse, *The Pleasure Steamers* (1978), showed the influence of Philip Larkin and achieved notable critical acclaim along with his second collection *Secret Narratives* (1983). Where these collections were dominated by narrative poems, his later work was to be more autobiographical. After becoming Poet Laureate in 1999, he was to write many 'public' poems: some are based on events like the Paddington rail crash (5 October 1999), while others support such campaigns as Childline. His aim is to write using *No ornate language; very few obvious tricks* so that readers can see beyond the surface to the hidden depths. His public presence has done much to raise the profile of poetry.

Activity 14.1

> **How do Roger McGough, Gillian Clarke and Andrew Motion communicate their response to the events they describe?**
>
> You may like to think about: the ideas in the poem and the poets' attitude to them; the language; grammatical structure; form; poetic features; and anything else you find of interest

Everyday Eclipses

1   The hamburger flipped across the face of the bun
     The frisbee winning the race against its own shadow
     The cricket ball dropping for six in front of the church clock
     On a golden plate, a host of communion wafers
5   The brown contact lens sliding across the blue iris
     The palming of small change
     Everyday eclipses

     Out of the frying pan, the tossed pancake orbits the Chinese lampshade
     The water bucket echoing into the well, well, well
10   The lifebelt spinning past the open porthole
     The black, snookering the cue ball against the green baize
     The winning putt on the eighteenth
     The tiddlywink twinking toward the tiddly cup
     Everyday eclipses

15   Neck and neck in the hot air balloon race

Holding up her sign, the lollipop lady blots out the belisha beacons
The foaming tankard thumped on to the beer mat
The plug into the plughole
Two thin slices; first salami, then mortadella
20   In the fruit bowl, the orange rolls in front of the peach.
Everyday eclipses another day

Goodbye bald patch, hello yarmulke°   a skullcap worn by Jewish men
A sombrero tossed into the bullring
Leading the parade, the big bass drum.
25   We hear cymbals but cannot see them
One eclipse eclipses another eclipse.
To the cold, white face, the oxygen mask.
But too late

One death eclipses another death
30   The baby's head, the mother's breast
The open O of the mouth seeking the warm O of the nipple
One birth eclipses another birth
Everyday eclipses.

ROGER MCGOUGH, 1999 (as printed in the *Guardian*)

R.S.

For R.S. Thomas (1913–2000)

1   His death
on the midnight news.
Suddenly colder.

Gold September's driven off
5   by something afoot
in the south-west approaches.

God's breathing in space out there
misting the heave of the seas
dark and empty tonight,

10   except for the one frail coracle°   a small oval rowing boat used in
borne out to sea,   Wales, made of skins or tarred or oiled
burning.   canvas stretched on wickerwork

GILLIAN CLARKE, 2000

Regime Change

1   Advancing down the road from Niniveh
Death paused a while and said 'Now listen here.
You see the names of places roundabout?
They're mine now, and I've turned them inside out.
5   Take Eden, further south: at dawn today
I ordered up my troops to tear away
its walls and gates so everyone can see
that gorgeous fruit which dangles from its tree.
You want it, don't you? Go and eat it then,
10   and lick your lips, and pick the same again.

Take Tigris and Euphrates; once they ran
through childhood-coloured slats of sand and sun.
Not any more they don't; I've filled them up
with countless different kinds of human crap.

15   Take Babylon, the palace sprouting flowers
which sweetened empires in their peaceful hours –
I've found a different way to scent the air:
already it's a by-word for despair.
Which leaves Baghdad – the star-tipped minarets,

20   the marble courts and halls, the mirage-heat.
These places, and the ancient things you know,
you won't know soon. I'm working on it now.'

ANDREW MOTION, 2003

Commentary

Each of these poems celebrates an event in a distinctive way. Roger McGough was commissioned to write a poem about the 1999 solar eclipse by *The Guardian* and he chose to focus on the ordinary and everyday in order to highlight the extraordinary and unique nature of life in all its forms. Gillian Clarke marks the death of the poet R.S. Thomas in an elegy that uses natural imagery to communicate her own personal sense of loss and celebrate Thomas's importance as an Anglo-Welsh poet. Andrew Motion wrote his poem in opposition to the war against Iraq (2003–4), believing that the Poet Laureate should be able to express political views even if they are at odds with the establishment. He focuses on the historic past of Iraqi places that are now newsworthy for military manoeuvres rather than for their cultural achievements. Motion read the poem on BBC Radio 4's morning news/magazine programme and it was printed in *The Guardian*.

The subject matter of each poem is very different and the poets respond to their material in very different ways. This means that the tone, language and style are varied – each poem is a distinctive response to the public event it marks and reveals something of the poet as well as the occasion.

Roger McGough's approach in **'Everyday Eclipses'** is characteristic: he chooses to celebrate the eclipses of everyday life in a poem that is both light-hearted and reverent. His ability to transform the everyday, creating something valuable and unique of it, dominates the poem, which is made up of a sequence of ordinary images that imitate the rare event of the solar eclipse. Through his comparisons, McGough therefore elevates the ordinary to the extraordinary.

In the first stanza, the images range from the urban (fast food) to the rural (cricket on the village green). Their effect is intensified because McGough uses a sequence of noun phrases rather than grammatically complete sentences. Most of the noun phrases are post-modified: the head words (*hamburger, frisbee, cricket ball*, ll.1–3) are stressed at the beginning of the line and followed by a non-finite clause (*flipped . . ., winning . . ., dropping . . .*). In each case, the image consists of one surface overlaying another in imitation of the solar eclipse.

While some images are dramatic (*The lifebelt spining past the open porthole*, l.10), others are ecstatic (*The winning putt on the eighteenth*, l.12); some are mundane (*The plug into the plughole*, l.18) and others are emotive (*To the cold, white face, the oxygen mask*, l.27). The pathos of this last image is underlined by the break in the pattern – the following line contains not another noun phrase, but the contrastive conjunction *But* and the adverbial *too late* (l.28).

The poignant image of lost life is in direct contrast to the humour of other images like the *bald patch* concealed by a *yarmulke* (l.22). The conversational *Goodbye . . . hello* structure, the comic connotations of the concealed bald patch, and the use of the *yarmulke* in a non-religious context are delicately funny. The humour of other images such as the *tossed pancake* (l.8) is intensified by McGough's use of a grammatically complete sentence which draws attention to the action of the event. The verb *orbits* reminds us of the astronomical occasion the poem is officially celebrating, but is comic in this context. The connotations of the verb and the juxtaposition of the pancake and *the Chinese lampshade* create a cartoon-like image that is consciously light-hearted.

McGough also plays with language to create a comic tone. The echoes of the *water bucket* (l.9) as it drops into the well are realised on the page by the repetitions *well, well, well* (no doubt performed with a dying tone in public readings). The *tiddlywink* as it moves towards the *tiddly cup* (l.13) is described by the neologism *twinking*. McGough has created his verb by compacting 'tiddlywink' into 't–wink': it is comic in the process of its creation, its internal rhyme (*twinking*), its mirroring of the sounds of the line as a whole, and its implicit links to 'twinkle'.

Having addressed the eclipses of everyday life in a range of tones, McGough brings his poem to an emotive end. The image of death communicated in the penultimate stanza is intensified by the emphatic simple sentence *One death eclipses another death* (l.29). The unmodified noun phrases stand out in stark contrast to the detail of the other noun phrases. The unqualified offsetting of *One death . . . another death* in a neatly balanced sentence seems to offer no hope or escape from the inevitability of mortality.

In the final lines, however, McGough creates images of life. The downbeat tone created by the images of death is replaced by a sense of infinite possibilities. The parallelism of *One death . . . another death* is balanced by two noun phrases: *The baby's head . . . the mother's breast* (l.30). The starkness of the earlier image is counteracted by the delicate balance of the medial caesura, and the internal rhyme (*head/breast*). The visual nature of the image, the sense of life conveyed by the post-modifying present participle *seeking* (l.31), and the parallelism of *The open O of the mouth* and *the warm O of the nipple* bring the poem to a striking end. This is reinforced by the mirroring of lines: *One death eclipses another death* becomes *One birth eclipses another birth* (l.32), and McGough leaves us with life rather than death.

The visual effect of this poem is dramatic since it recreates physical situations that are an integral part of everyday life, and reminds us of this in the refrain at the end of each stanza. While the use of free verse creates an open and conversational rhythm, the tightness of the noun phrases provides an internal structure that controls the images as the poem moves towards its climax.

Although apparently simple in language and structure, the poem ranges widely, transforming things we take for granted by applying the basic principle of the eclipse to everyday events. McGough's ability to move between the matter-of-fact and the comic, the serious and the light-hearted, the essential and the periphery, makes this poem unique. It is a jubilant celebration of life in all its diverse forms – from throwing a frisbee to breastfeeding a child.

Where McGough celebrates life, Gillian Clarke's poem, **'R.S.'**, celebrates a life's work; where he adopts a detached, objective voice, Gillian Clarke's voice is personal, the 3-lined stanzas limiting and containing her sadness. The elliptical style of the first stanza vividly communicates her private response to the death of the poet R.S. Thomas. The simple noun phrase *His death* (l.1) is a striking and bleak opening, with the precision of the prepositional phrase that follows (*on the midnight news*, l.2) immediately setting the poem in time. The factual information is reported in a detached and distant tone, but the adjective phrase *Suddenly colder* (l.3) marks a change. We move from the objective to the subjective – from a state-ment of fact to the poet's reaction. The effect is dramatic in its brevity: the physi-cal change in temperature symbolises an inner emotional response.

The thematic *colder* is developed in the second stanza where the autumnal mood is replaced by something more austere. Clarke's use of the passive voice (*[i]s driven off*, l.4) allows her to foreground the noun phrase *Gold September*. Its posi-tion at the beginning of the line draws attention to its symbolic importance – the autumnal connotations of warmth and light indicative of life before the midnight news are displaced by the negative connotations of the phrasal verb *driven off*. The bleak suggestion of *something afoot/in the south-west approaches* (ll.5–6) reinforces our feeling that a symbolic as well as a literal winter is blowing in from the Atlantic.

The poem is marked by an expanding perspective that takes us from the poet's home (the internal), to the natural world (the external), and finally to the vast-ness of space and the open seas (the universal). The sibilance (ll.7–8) and lilting dactylic make us feel we have reached the emotional climax.

místinğ th̆e | heáve o̓f t̆he | séas

The reference to a seemingly human *breathing* God reminds us of His presence in the world. Just as the sea mists become symbolic of God, the physical motion conveyed by the head noun *heave* (l.8) suggests the unsettling effect of Thomas's death on the natural world. The desolate language (*dark/empty*, l.9) is reminiscent of the wintry tone of the first stanza.

After the conclusive end stop at the end of stanza 2, the enjambement of stan-zas 3–4 drives us on to the preposition *except for* (l.10) with its suggestion of contradiction. What we are ultimately left with is not the gloom and darkness of a winter landscape, but a vivid image of light. Reminiscent of a Viking burial, Clarke's poem ends with an image of a symbolic celebratory ritual: the *one frail coracle*, highlighted by the sequence of stresses that fall on it, is sent out to sea in the style of a Viking chieftian's funeral pyre. Where the Viking ships were symbolic of invasion, wealth and, power, however, the *coracle* is a cultural symbol. Its fragility is both literal, and symbolic of man's mortality and Thomas's creativity. The present participle *burning* (l.12), with its symbolism of light and warmth, casts a new mood over the poem. Instead of sadness and disillusion, we are left with a celebration of Thomas, an implicit recognition of his Welshness and his importance as a leading poet in the twentieth century.

As the poet explores the personal and universal affect of Thomas's death, the style of the poem changes. The fragmented phrases of the first stanza are replaced by a simple sentence in stanza 2 as the poet contemplates the symbolic arrival of winter in the world outside. The poem moves towards its climax in the complex sentence that runs from stanzas 3–4. It is a quiet and restrained poem, a poem of reflection rather than grief.

Andrew Motion's poem is quite different from both McGough's celebration of ordinary life and Clarke's contemplation of a specific death. Where they deal with the everyday, **'Regime Change'** is a political poem that asks us to contemplate the pointlessness of a war that did not have international backing. It approaches its subject matter obliquely: rather than addressing the horrors of war in the forthright tone of the First World War poets with their explicit attention to physical detail, Motion focuses on cultural devastation through a sequence of symbolic references to *Niniveh* (l.1), *Eden* (l.5), the *Tigris and Euphrates* (l.11), *Babylon* (l.15) and to *Baghdad* (l.19) – all formerly part of Mesopotamia, the ancient cultural centre of learning.

For the title, Motion adopts the euphemistic noun phrase *Regime Change* used by the government to make their decision to go to war seem ethical and principled. It is an example of 'doublespeak', of the misleading language use that George Orwell saw as characterising the modern age ('Politics and the English Language', 1946). In its neutrality, the phrase focuses on the abstract concept of a 'regime', rather than on the very physical nature of war. Similarly, the bland connotations of 'change' conceal the horror and destruction that will inevitably follow – the human cost of war.

The title adopts the language of government, the language of authority. In its failure to take account of the human, emotional and psychological price of war, the phrase is typical of a piece of propaganda. By drawing on symbols of civilisation and beauty in his poem, however, Motion clearly distances himself from the attitudes of the establishment. This is a war that divided government ministers, ordinary people and countries. Described as immoral and unethical by those who saw it as a strongarm tactic to protect American interests in Iraq, the poet avoids explicitly political issues and focuses instead on the figurative.

The physical setting of the poem is the ancient land of Mesopotamia, Greek for the 'land between two rivers', now known as Iraq. This was one of the areas in which civilised human societies first developed around 4000BC – people lived in cities; kept written records; and had knowledge of metal technology. The ancient Mesopotamians were pioneers in mathematics and astronomy; they wrote the first poetry – in particular, the epic 'Gilgamesh', probably the world's oldest story, written in cuneiform script on clay tablets that still survive. Motion uses this cultural heritage symbolically to represent human achievement in the face of the unprincipled destruction he believes is about to take place.

The spoken voice of the poem makes its content particularly devastating because it personalises what is being said and makes the threats more ominous. The fact that the opening adverbial delays the subject intensifies this, since it is only in the second line that we realise the identity of the speaker – Death. In the wider context, the use of the present participle *Advancing* (l.1) suggests a military campaign in which Death inevitably will be the only victor. Juxtaposed with the sense of an ongoing and unstoppable movement, the verb *paused* and the adverbial *a while* (l.2) suggest an almost casual attitude that is daunting in the face of the real war on which the poem is commenting.

The colloquial *Now listen here* (l.2) sets an authoritative tone that is reinforced by the use of the imperative mood. Death is therefore immediately established as a figure to be reckoned with. The direct address draws the reader into the conversation, but Death's extended turn leaves no room for dialogue. The colloquial *Take . . .* identifying the introduction of each new symbolic place reinforces the casual arrogance of the poem's voice.

The reference to *Nineveh* (l.1), capital of ancient Assyria, marks the beginning of Death's journey. Known for its great palaces, sculptural reliefs, archives and its great library (which forms the basis for our current knowledge of Mesopotamian history), Death's confident statement of ownership is ominous (l.4). In the role of a personified character, he becomes a military ruler; as a symbolic abstraction, he represents the literal deaths resulting from military conflict.

The military language (*ordered up/troops*, l.6), geographical references (*the names of places roundabout*, l.3, *further south*, l.5) and time markers (*at dawn today*, l.5) contribute to the physical and immediate mood of the poem. The dynamic verbs *turned . . . inside out* (l.4) and *tear away* (l.6) are juxtaposed with the Edenic *gorgeous fruit* (l.8), symbolic of the biblical apple of temptation. The apparent democracy of taking down *wall and gates so everyone can see* (l.7) is undermined by the nature of the speaker who has authorised such action. Death's style is rhetorical, however, and his use of direct address (*You want it*), a persuasive tag (*don't you*) and the emphatic syndetic listing of *Go and eat . . /.and lick . . . and pick* (ll.9–10) urge us on. The sense of excess implied by *again* and the claustrophobic internal rhyme (*lick/lips/pick*) are warnings – eating this fruit is not as innocent as it may seem.

The symbolic value of *Eden* is painfully significant in this context. Representative of the unbroken harmony between God and humankind before the first sin, Death appears to urge us to partake in the violence of his sins. The field of reference here is not specifically religious, but Motion uses it as a symbol of perfection within a context of physical and emotional destruction.

In describing the rivers, *Tigris and Euphrates* (l.11), Motion draws on another symbol of fertility – their seasonal flooding and the creation of irrigation channels enabled the dry plains to be transformed into farmland. Here the juxtaposition of their past purity, symbolised by the nostalgic image of *childhood-coloured slats of sand and sun* (l.12), and their current pollution is indicative of the destructive nature of war. The excess implied by *countless different kinds* (l.14) and the recurring plosives (*countless/different/kinds/crap*) undermine the images of fertility and purity. The negative mood is underpinned by Death's cavalier narrative voice: the colloquial *Not any more they don't* (l.13) and the slang *crap* are representative of his insidious intentions.

The symbol of *Babylon* (l.15) functions in the same way. Known for its legendary Hanging Gardens (*the palace sprouting flowers*), one of the Seven Wonders of the Ancient World, Death replaces beauty with horror. The positive language (*sweetened/peaceful*, l.16) and the sensual description of the scent of flowers are undermined by a different kind of scent – the 'sweet' smell of death, *a by-word for despair* (l.18).

Having followed Death in his journey of destruction, we reach Baghdad – capital of modern Iraq and a centre for political, cultural and trade activities in the ancient world. Motion creates a very visual image of the city's beauty (*the star-tipped minarets/the marble courts and halls*, ll.19–20). The juxtaposition of *you know* and *you won't know soon* (ll.21–2) emphasise the devastating change that is to follow. The poem ends on an ominous note: the colloquial present continuous *[I]'m working on it* (l.22) and the adverb *now* suggest the immediacy of events and their inevitability.

There is no explicit sense of the poet's own voice in this poem since it is dominated by the character of Death, but there can be no doubt about Motion's attitude to the war. The symbolism is emphatic: the physical representation of long-term human achievement communicated by the proper nouns is undermined by the casual attitude to destruction and the colloquial tone of the spoken voice.

On first reading, the poem may seem to underplay the inevitable disaster by avoiding the language of horror and the fragmentation of grammatical structures. Death's monologue is persuasive – he uses rhetoric to engage us in his quest; his tone is confidential; his manner authoritative; his sentences are controlled and grammatically complete. The poem's message, however, is unavoidable. The conversational tone may lull us into a false sense of security, but the antithetical structure and the symbolism ensure that we respond at an ethical as well as an emotional level.

All three poets use imagery to communicate a sense of the occasion they are marking, but the effects are very different. Where McGough's images are indicative of everyday life, Motion's are symbolic of something unique and worthy of preservation; where Clarke's images allow her to respond personally to one specific death, Motion's implicitly lament the deaths of countless individuals and a civilisation that has existed since 3000BC. In each case, the different relationship between the poets and their material affects the tone and style of the verse: McGough's celebration of the ordinary is light-hearted and jubilant; Clarke's contemplation of the loss of an important poet replaces personal shock with a recognition of achievement; Motion's mourning for a nation under attack is both poignant and political.

Poems written to mark a private experience

The following poems have been written in response to a private experience: seeing an unborn child on an ultrasound scan ('Ultrasound'), watching a father near death ('Seeing the Sick'), and expressing love for a partner ('White Writing'). While each poet responds in a different way, the poems all represent a moment of conscious awareness as the poet finds a means to communicate his or her feelings.

The first poem, 'Seeing the Sick' (*Electric Light*, 2001), is written by **Seamus Heaney** (1939–). He began writing poetry in the early 1960s within the context of a poets' workshop led by Philip Hobsbaum, which aimed to give young poets an opportunity to air their work. Heaney's first collection, *Eleven Poems*, was published in 1965, followed by *Death of a Naturalist* (1966), which was to establish his reputation. Awarded the Nobel Prize for Literature in 1995, Heaney's modern English version of *Beowulf* was to win the Whitbread Award as the best book of 1999, and in 2003, he won the Truman Capote Award for Literary Criticism. His work is well known for its use of personal memories, images of Irish heritage and the Irish landscape, and references to the English–Irish and Catholic–Protestant conflict.

The second poem, 'White Writing' (*Feminine Gospels*, 2002), is written by **Carol Ann Duffy** (1955–). She was born in Glasgow, but moved to Stafford at the age of six. She was brought up in a traditional working-class Catholic family, but was later to reject her childhood religion. She became a full-time writer in 1985. Ten years later, she was to receive an OBE and in 2001 a CBE in recognition of her services to literature. Her work explores issues of sexuality, the inadequacy of language, the role of women in a male-dominated society, and love and relationships. She is particularly well known for giving women a strong voice, and for appealing to ordinary readers as well as academics.

The third poem, 'Ultrasound' (*Jizzen*, 1999), is written by **Kathleen Jamie** (1962–). She is a Scottish poet whose work is of Scotland, her own life and beyond. Her style is unrhetorical, but the effect of her verse is striking: the Scots dialect gives it a warmth and personal depth; the everyday diction grounds it firmly in real life; and the powerful imagery engages the reader in her view of the world. Jamie has a real sense of the musicality of words, and her poetry is often lyrical. She consciously manipulates line-breaks and syntax to influence the way readers respond, engaging them with cultural, political and personal issues through the structure and diction.

Activity 14.2

How do Seamus Heaney, Carol Ann Duffy and Kathleen Jamie convey their experiences in these poems?

You may like to think about: the poets' experiences and their attitude to them; the language; grammatical structure; form; poetic features; and anything else you find of interest

Seeing the Sick

1   Anointed and all, my father did remind me
    Of Hopkins's Felix Randal.
                  And then he grew
    (As he would have said himself) 'wee in his clothes' –
5   Spectral, a relict –
                 And seemed to have grown so
    Because of something spectral he'd thrown off,
    The unbelonging, moorland part of him
    That was Northumbrian, the bounden he
10   Who had walked the streets of Hexham at eighteen
    With his stick and task of bringing home the dead
    Body of his uncle by cattle-ferry.

Ghost-drover from the start. Brandisher of keel.

None of your fettled and bright battering sandal.

15   Cowdung coloured tweed and ox-blood leather.

*

The assessor's eye, the tally-keeper's head
For what beasts were on what land in what year . . .
But then that went as well. And all precaution.
His smile a summer half-door opening out
20   And opening in. A reprieving light.
For which the tendered morphine had our thanks.

SEAMUS HEANEY

White Writing

1   No vows written to wed you,
     I write them white,
     my lips on yours,
     light in the soft hours of our married years.

5   No prayers written to bless you,
     I write them white,
     your soul a flame,
     bright in the window of your maiden name.

     No laws written to guard you,
10   I write them white,
     your hand in mine,
     palm against palm, lifeline, heartline.

     No rules written to guide you,
     I write them white,
15   words on the wind,
     traced with a stick where we walk on the sand.

     No news written to tell you,
     I write it white,
     foam on a wave
20   as we lift up our skirts in the sea, wade,

     see last gold sun behind clouds,
     inked water in moonlight.
     No poems written to praise you,
     I write them white.

CAROL ANN DUFFY

Ultrasound
(for Duncan)

1   Oh whistle and I'll come to ye,
     my lad, my wee shilpit ghost
     summonsed from tomorrow.

<pre>
          Second sight,
5   a seer's mothy flicker,
          an inner sprite:

          this is what I see
          with eyes closed;
          a keek-aboot among secrets.

10   If Pandora
          could have scanned
          her dark box,

          and kept it locked –
          this ghoul's skull, punched eyes
15   is tiny Hope's,

          hauled silver-quick
          in a net of sound,
          then, for pity's sake, lowered.
</pre>

KATHLEEN JAMIE

Commentary

Each of these poems addresses a private experience that the poet fixes within a framework of words. Although of personal relevance to the poet, the process of poetry makes each experience universal: they are dealing with birth, death and relationships, and their work therefore has relevance to us all. While not a part of the specific moment, we can identify with the feelings evoked and the rites of passage each poem records. The poems offer us an individual response that can, perhaps, help us to understand events in our own lives.

Seamus Heaney described, in an article written for the Poetry Book Society Bulletin, what he called an *informed consciousness*: a state of mind in which a particular experience or occasion can be relived in a more detached and less personally emotional way. Beginning with a line that may have its source in memory, poets use their *acquired knowledge and understanding* of language, culture and literature to shape their initial response. What we see in these poems is that detached response: the poets can draw on personal experience and create from it something that illuminates everyday events so that we see them in a new light.

While each poet has a similar attitude to their subject matter, they adopt a different style, tone and structure to communicate their experience in a distinctive way. Each poem is a response to a private moment and reveals something of the poet as well as the occasion.

Seamus Heaney's approach in '**Seeing the Sick**' begins with a memory of seeing his father as he approached death (Patrick Heaney died in 1987) and then draws on Gerard Manley Hopkins's poem 'Felix Randal' to order and control his personal response. He skilfully interweaves the literal and the literary in a tribute to the man his father used to be, just as Hopkins remembers the strength and vigour of the dead blacksmith, one of his parishioners.

The allusions can be seen both in a literal borrowing of phrases and in the language and rhythm of the poem as a whole. The title is taken from a noun phrase in Hopkins's poem, but here it functions as a non-finite clause, the present participle suggesting the harrowing process of the sick man's movement towards death. The opening compound phrase *Anointed and all* (l.1) is also borrowed – it marks the Catholic inheritance Heaney shares with Hopkins. In a rite known as unction, those close to death are anointed with oil in the name of Christ while prayers of forgiveness for sins committed in life are said. In 'Felix Randal', the *sweet reprieve and ransom* (communion) is *tendered*; for Heaney's father, the *reprieve* comes with morphine. Heaney's mirroring of the verb *tendered*, however, carries with it the sense of a holy sacrament that brings relief from pain – the morphine gives his father the capacity to transcend the horror of his condition. In Hopkins's poem, the final line leaves us with an image of the blacksmith in his prime and Heaney adapts this in his poem (l.14) to recreate a visual sense of his own father as he was.

Implicit in the formality suggested by the ritual *Anointed and all*, we sense a physical image of Heaney's father laid out on his bed as death approaches. A change of mood in the following lines (ll.3–4) is indicated by the conversational tone of the parenthesis, by the regional diminutive *wee*, and in the use of direct speech. The formality of the Church is thus replaced by the informality of personal knowledge. Heaney manipulates our response using the parenthesis to separate the verb (*grew*) from its complement (*wee*). This leaves the positive connotations of *grew* hanging: the death-like image of the sick man's shrinking body is therefore more shocking when we reach it. The metaphorical references (*Spectral, a relict*) then add an extra dimension – Heaney's father is both ghost-like in his weakened state and a lone survivor of a past age. He has *thrown off/The unbelonging, moorland part of him/That was Northumbrian* (ll.7–9). The sequence of noun phrases (ll.13–15) establishes the nature of the man as he was: the head nouns (*Ghost-**drover**/ **Brandisher***) are derived from verbs and this implicitly conveys the vitality of the young man.

The language is reminiscent of the farmer's life with the modifiers *Cowdung coloured* and *ox-blood* (l.15) used to ground the portrait in a physical reality. What we see is the disappearance of the purposeful, the conscious, until all that is left is *a relict*. The image of Heaney's father *at eighteen* (l.10), *the bounden he* (l.9), is made real in Heaney's attention to detail: the proper noun *Hexham*, the reference to the *stick and task* (l.11), and the journey *by cattle-ferry* (l.12) recreate a moment that is in sharp contrast to the image of the opening lines.

The line alluding to 'Felix Randal' (l.14) works on a number of levels. In Hopkins's poem, it is an image conveying the skill of the farrier's work: the verb *fettle* is a dialect word for 'to make ready' or 'to fix up' and the *sandal* is used figuratively to convey both the grace of *the great grey drayhorse* ('Felix Randal', l.14) and the perfect art of the blacksmith. As a reminder of this, Heaney's line reinforces the portrait of his father as a dynamic and active man of the land. In relation to the following line (l.15), Heaney's description perhaps works literally – the *bright battering sandal* thus becomes an ironic reference to the footwear of the urban man, set in opposition to the rural image of the *ox-blood leather* that characterises Patrick Heaney. We can almost hear the dismissive tone in the conversational lead-in *None of your . . .* (l.15).

Having first created a physical contrast between the image of his father growing *wee* and the image of him as a young man, Heaney then focuses on the disintegration of his mind. The noun phrases (*The assessor's eye/the tally-keeper's head*, l.16) are indicative of what made Patrick Heaney the passionate farmer and cattledealer. The associations are mathematical (*assessor/tally-keeper*) and this refines our image of him as a simple rural man – this is no stereotype, but a portrait of an individual.

The lines are emotive because we see a vibrant man losing his inner self. Where the first section uses physical language, the images in the last lines are emotional. The *smile* is symbolic of Patrick Heaney's condition: the metaphor of the *summer half-door* (l.19) is an image of warmth and light in what could be a very dark poem. For the dying man and those around him, the smile is a symbolic communication: the parallel phrases *opening out* and *opening in* suggest that it is an expression of Patrick's Heaney's true self. The figurative 'door' allows the poet to make emotional contact with his father, and enables his father, momentarily, to exist beyond his present condition. We are left with the image of a dying man, relieved only by the *tendered morphine*, but the darkness of this image is balanced by that of the *smile*, a *reprieving light* that lifts the tone and reminds us of the vibrant young man of the first part of the poem.

The structure of the poem guides us through the different stages of Heaney's portrait of his father. The formal opening with its religious language and conscious link to the Hopkins poem (ll.1–2) is separated from the poignant physical image (ll.3–5) by the inset line and the use of a co-ordinating conjunction in the initial position. Similarly, the image of Patrick Heaney as a dying man is separated from the image of him at eighteen (l.6). The fronted conjunctions bring the process of change to the foreground, drawing our attention to the poignancy of the poem. In the final section, the pace is increased as Heaney focuses on cognitive as well as physical change. The close proximity of the fronted *But then . . . And . . .* (l.18) brings death closer as Patrick Heaney loses his skills. The cumulative phrase *all precaution* implies the end of a process that began when *he grew/. . . wee.*

The complex sentences of the opening section are replaced by fragments as the poet frames his response to an emotional and personal experience. Tightly structured noun phrases functioning as minor sentences (ll.13–7, 19–20) convey images of the past and present in a concise and visual form. Both literal and figurative, they communicate a powerful sense of Heaney's father as a distinctive individual.

The cohesive nature of the verse is intensified by the recurring sound patterns that are reminiscent of Hopkins's 'chiming'. The close repetition of internal rhyme (*Anointed/all, grown/so, Ghost-drover, Cowdung coloured, assessor's/tally, then/went, all precaution*) is lyrical – it makes the poem sing and lifts the mood towards celebration. Similarly, long vowel sounds (*smile, door, opening, out*) allow us to relish the evocative image of the smile that lightens the poem.

At a distance from the pain of the scene, Heaney can recreate the experience from his memories. While recognising the reality of his father's condition, he, like his predecessor, conjures up an image of vitality that exists alongside the poignant description of his present condition. It is this juxtaposition of past and present, of strength and weakness, of reason and oblivion that makes the poem so moving.

Heaney creates something new and original from the general associations and literal fragments he borrows from 'Felix Randal'. They help to make his personal experience universal in recognising that this is a moment we will all have to face. The poem thus becomes not just an individual requiem, but a study of mutability and mortality, and man's capacity to endure.

Where Heaney's poem is about death, Carol Ann Duffy's poem, **'White Writing'**, is about love, a living relationship that is vibrant and real in spite of society's desire to ignore it; where Heaney's poem is made up of fragments, Duffy's is a tightly structured incantation; where Heaney's tone is elegiac, Duffy's is intensely lyrical in the manner of song.

The title of the poem is immediately striking in its suggestion of a communication that cannot be seen: white print on a white page. Only as we read the poem do we understand the wider implications of this – Carol Ann Duffy is exploring the inadequacy of language within the context of society. The emphasis is on the failure of public language, since it provides no acceptable way for the poet to express her love for her partner. The poem therefore becomes a private declaration in which the poet can use the expansive language of poetry to communicate her love. The intensity of the imagery demonstrates the potential of language when it is not restricted by religious, legal and social expectations.

The subject matter sets public and private in opposition as the poet attempts to define the nature of her relationship on two distinct levels. The first line of each stanza grounds the poet's love in the external world of religion (*vows/prayers*, ll.1/5), the law (*laws/rules*, ll.9/13) and the media (*news*, l.17). The use of the emphatic negative in the strong position at the beginning of each first line establishes the derogatory attitudes held by society at that time: prior to the Civil Partnership Act 2004 (implemented from 5 December 2005), single-sex couples could not marry or seek a Church blessing; they were not afforded the same protection by the legal system as mixed couples; and were often stereotyped by the media. It is in this context that the poet seeks to provide a personal and private affirmation of her love. She may not be able to do so in a way recognised by the external world, but she can through the power of the poetic image.

In the second half of each quatrain, the language is positive. It combines the physical and the abstract to emphasise the value of the poet's love. Traditional images (*my lips on yours*, l.3; *your soul a flame*, l.7; *your hand in mine*, l.11) are made unique by the overlaying of another more unexpected image. The poet challenges society's received wisdom: she and her lover may be denied the right to marriage, but their relationship is characterised by the possessive noun phrase *our married years* (l.4) and the delicacy of the language (*light/soft*, l.4, *bright*, l.8). Similarly, the noun phrase *the window of your maiden name* (l.8) reiterates the symbolic change of name denied them.

The image in the third stanza of *palm against palm* (l.12) is reminiscent of Shakespeare's *palm to palm is holy palmers' kiss* (*Romeo and Juliet*, I.v.100) with all its resonance of a holy union. It is made more powerful here by its associations with the physical – literal lines marking the palms – and metaphysical – the implicit suggestion of prophecy in the reference to *lifeline* and *heartline* as prophetic symbols of the rightness of their relationship.

As the poem moves away from the physical presence of the poet's lover, we see a new kind of image emerge. The natural references to *wind* (l.15), *foam/wave* (l.19) provide a concrete background against which we see the poet and her lover, united in a private experience that excludes the world. Their oneness is communicated by the replacement of the singular pronouns *I/you* with inclusive *we*. The experience is ordinary (*words . . ./traced with a stick where we walk on the sand*, ll.15–16; *we lift up our skirts in the sea*, l.20) and the poet thus implicitly draws attention to the fact that their relationship is different from no other, despite what society would like to believe. The use of the present tense (*walk*, l.16, *lift* l.20, *wade/see*, l.21) emphasises the currency of this declaration of love.

The change in the final stanza marks the poem's climax. The traditional romantic images of the setting sun and the moonlight on water colour our reading of the poem as a whole. The images of light (*gold sun*, l.21) and dark (*inked water*, l.22) are set against the central image of white on white. The poet has no need to write poems in praise of her lover for a public audience because it is a private matter: the day-to-day existence of their love is justification enough and Duffy can *write [her poems] white* (l.24).

The lyric qualities of the poem are enhanced by the harmony of its sounds. The internal rhyme of *white/write* and the recurrence of the soft lateral /l/, the approximant /w/ and the voiceless fricative /f/ create a lilting tone that is in keeping with the personal nature of the subject matter. This is underpinned by the form with its refrain and patterned structure, which is reminiscent of incantation or prayer. The rhythmic pattern adds to this effect. The sequence of stresses in the first two feet of each first line contributes to the emphatic point being made.

No vows | written | to wed | you

The lilting iambic of the middle lines softens the negative public statement, replacing an attack on society's limitations with a powerful personal declaration.

I write | them white
my lips | on yours

In the fourth and fifth stanzas, the pattern changes slightly: the third line uses a trochee followed by an iambic foot to highlight the change in imagery from personal to natural.

words on | the wind

The final line of each stanza is more varied; it combines a variety of metrical patterns so that there is a lightness of touch in keeping with the subject matter.

light in the | soft hours | of ou ma | rried years
as we lift | up our skirts | in the sea, | wade

The movement between dactyls, anapaests, iambs and spondees gives the final line a conversational mood that enhances the private and intimate feel of the poem.

This poem is interesting because it is a love poem with a difference – the poet communicates the value of her relationship by negating society's value system and creating a more personal and meaningful one. Many of Carol Ann Duffy's poems are associated with the inability of language to say anything. Here we see the language of religion, law and the media as inadequate, where the language of poetry is rich and intense, able to capture the moment and communicate the unique. In this poem, Duffy makes her words sing and her declaration of love – possibly for her partner the poet Jackie Kay – is marked by its lyric intensity.

Where Heaney faces approaching death in 'Seeing the Sick', Kathleen Jamie's poem, '**Ultrasound**', deals with the onset of life. Both poets, however, reflect the complexity of emotions surrounding the experience they describe. Like Carol Ann Duffy's, Jamie's language is firmly rooted in the everyday and yet still achieves a lyric intensity that heightens the emotions it conveys.

The poem is the first in a sequence published in *Jizzen* that was originally part of a longer work commissioned by BBC Radio 4. Focusing on the ultrasound scan that is a routine part of any pregnancy the poet explores her feelings for the unborn child she sees on the screen, an image produced by rapid sound vibrations that is recognisable for its grey tones and grainy resolution.

The poignant interjection *O Whistle . . .* (1.1) and the familiar *ye* establish an immediate protective relationship between mother and child. Vocatives (*my lad/my wee shilpit ghost*, 1.2) reinforce this with their possessive determiners, the diminutive *wee* and the tenderness of the dialect modifier, making this a consciously intimate poem. We are quite unaware of the hospital context with its machinery and clinical starkness, but are, instead, immersed in a powerful world of magic and prophecy. The connotations of *ghost* (1.2) and *summonsed* (1.3) alongside the suggestion of unearthly prediction in the prepositional phrase *from tomorrow* make this moment intensely personal.

The theme of prophecy continues in stanza 2 in the references to *Second sight* (1.4) and a *seer* (1.5): the ghostly image of the first stanza has become *an inner sprite* (1.6). The use of a colon at the end of the stanza sends the reader directly into the third, where the vision of the *wee shilpit ghost* and the *inner sprite* become not external images on a screen, but internal visions. The anaphoric reference *This* (1.7) internalises the previous stanzas while the Scots dialect (*keek-aboot*, 1.9) and the connotations of *secrets* make the poem a private contemplation, which we are privileged to overhear.

The tone changes in stanza 4 where we move from the real to the figurative. The hypothetical *If . . .* (1.10) and the symbolic reference to *Pandora* (the first woman in Greek mythology, created by Zeus to punish men for the theft of heavenly fire by Prometheus) signify this movement. Pandora's box is the feminine symbol representing unconsciousness when it is closed, but when opened it can unleash a storm of devastation, disease and death upon the world. Here we have the image of the ultrasound (*scanned*, 1.11) applied to Pandora's box – if, like the poet, she could have looked inside and *kept it locked* (1.13), the outcome would have been very different. The poet leaves the hypothetical subordinate clause incomplete and this is resonant of what could have been.

The following image of *the ghoul's skull* (1.14) is ambiguous. It could mirror the familiar and intimate tone of *my wee shilpit ghost*, or it could develop the potential for horror symbolised by Pandora's *dark box* (1.12). The connotations of death implicit in the poet's lexical choice are undermined, however, by the emphatic final line of the stanza. The child may appear almost skeletal on the ultrasound, but the substitution of the possessive noun *Hope's* (1.15) for *ghoul's* undermines the potential for fear. The ellipsis of 'skull' (*Hope's [skull]*), which is understood from the previous line, and the strong end position of the noun return the tone to the intimacy of the opening stanzas. Pregnancy becomes not a Pandora's box of hidden horrors, but a symbol of potential and creativity.

The final stanza reiterates this by bringing the poem full circle. The extended metaphor of fishing encapsulates the process: the dynamic verbs *hauled/lowered* (ll.16–18) reflect the physical activity of fishing, while the post-modification of the noun phrase *a net of sound* (1.17) draws the two disparate processes together. The physical image captured on the screen is *silver-quick* (1.16), its nature reminiscent perhaps of the silvery qualities of mercury ('quicksilver').

While the poem is varied in its rhythms, the effect of certain lines is enhanced by their metrical patterns. The tenderness of the opening line, for instance, is mirrored in the lilting iambic rhythm.

Oh̆ whi | stĭle ańd | I'l̆l come | tŏ you

The change of mood in stanza 4 is then marked by a trochaic metre (*If Păn | dŏră*) and sequences of stresses (*dark box/ghoul's skull/punched eyes*). Such variations are linked to the tone and reflect the poet's state of mind.

The poem moves away from the excitement of seeing the unborn child and the mother's instinctive desire to protect, to a momentary fear of the unknown, and finally to a sense of release as the image is *lowered*. The emotive parenthetical *for pity's sake* (1.18) suggests a relief as the unborn child is returned to darkness; there is an implicit feeling that in observing, we have perhaps intruded.

Although apparently straightforward, this is an intense poem in which the poet engages the reader in her changing moods as she watches her unborn child. The language moves from the intimacy of dialect to the objectivity of a traditional symbol like Pandora. The syntax moves from the heartfelt imperative of the opening compound-complex sentence with its familiar vocatives to the excitement of the second stanza's asyndetic noun phrases; from the underlying fear of the unknown conveyed by the incomplete hypothetical subordinate clause to the final complex sentence that expresses both hope and relief.

The three poems are all very different in their approach, but in each case the poets explore their feelings in an intense and evocative way. Where Seamus Heaney draws on the associations of 'Felix Randal' to frame his response, Carol Ann Duffy uses physical images to override society's negative attitudes, and Kathleen Jamie moves between an internal monologue with her unborn child and figurative images of the unknown world she secretly observes. Although each poem is written in free verse, the structure is an integral part of the meaning as the poets guide us through their changing emotions.

Where next?

The examples here demonstrate just some of the poets writing in the twenty-first century, but there are many more exciting and innovative works to discover. Try looking at the collections from which these poems have been taken and see if you can explore the techniques and approaches used in other works by these poets. Then broaden your range and read work by other contemporary writers. One of the best ways of becoming familiar with the work of a range of poets is by dipping into a modern anthology like *Staying Alive* (Bloodaxe Books). The more poetry you read, the more confident you will become; the more confident you become, the more fulfilling the experience.

Whether you are intending to read for pleasure or study, understanding the approaches a poet can use to communicate ideas and the effects these create is a helpful springboard into the fascinating world of poetry. Poets begin with a feeling, an idea, a visual image, a memory, and create a web of words around it so that we too can engage with their experience. While they are unlikely to 'deconstruct' the process of writing as we do for criticism, it is the mark of a good poem that we can explore its linguistic, structural and literary approaches in order to understand the way it affects us.

While a poem may not be immediately accessible, we can engage with its music and the power of its words before tackling its complexity. Poetry is an emotional as well as an intellectual genre, and if we engage on both levels we will experience the interplay of ideas, language and structures that lies at the heart of the genre. As R.S. Thomas wrote:

> Poetry is that
> which arrives at the intellect
> by way of the heart.

■ ∇ Glossary

This glossary contains a brief definition of the key literary and linguistic words used in this book. Examples are printed in *italics*, with **bold type** to highlight the key term. Following the explanations, there is a diagram to help you use the terms effectively. It displays the terminology visually so that you can clearly see which terms are literary and which linguistic. You could use it alongside a poem as you read, or as a guide to help you use an appropriate critical vocabulary in your essays.

abstract noun
A term used to classify nouns that have no physical or concrete qualities. Abstract nouns refer to ideas, qualities and processes; they convey emotions and states of mind (*consciousness, happiness, misery, despair*).

active voice
A grammatical structure in which the subject is the actor of a sentence.

adjacency pairs
A sequence of utterances that we would expect to have two parts: a question and an answer; a command and a related action in response to it. Adjacency pairs follow each other and are produced by different speakers; they have a logical connection and conform to a predictable pattern.

adjective
A word that defines attributes of a noun (*thy fearful symmetry*) and that can also express contrasts of degree (*weaker/weakest*).

adjective phrase
A phrase which usually has an adjective as its head word and which can function as a complement in a clause. Adjective phrases are described as **predicative** because they follow a copula verb such as *appear, seem, become, be* (*The snow was* **brilliant white***; the tree grew* **taller and taller***; the sky seemed* **dark**). Poets use predicative adjective phrases because the information contained in the phrase is given added weight in its position after the verb.

adverb
A word that describes the action of a verb (*The child laughed* **tentatively**); that can act as an intensifier (**very** *blue*); and that can function as a sentence connector (**Somehow***, the world was different now*).

adverb of degree
Adverbs which modify other words such as adjectives, adverbs and verbs. Adverbs of degree or **intensifiers** grade words on a scale (**very** *bright*; **quite** *quickly*; **completely** *finished*).

adverb phrase	A phrase which usually has an adverb as its head word and which functions as an adverbial in a clause (*stealthily falling*; *perpetually settling*). They qualify the verb by providing information about 'how' the process is carried out.
adverbial	A term to describe words, phrases or clauses that function as adverbs by providing extra information in a sentence about time (when?), place (where?) and manner (how?). They are the most mobile clause element and create different effects according to their position in a sentence (*As the sun rose*, the world, *in a place far away*, awoke WHEN? WHERE? *diffidently*). HOW?
adverbial clause	Subordinate clauses which act as adverbials, answering questions such as 'when?', 'why?', 'what for?'. They begin with subordinating conjunctions (*after, before, if, although, because, where*) and usually go at the end of a clause. Fronted adverbial clauses allow writers to change the emphasis of a sentence by focusing attention on the information contained in the adverbial clause.
alexandrine	A line of verse which has 12 syllables and an iambic rhythm. Also known as iambic hexameter.
allegory	A story in verse or prose with an underlying meaning, which can therefore be read and interpreted at two levels.
alliteration	The repetition of the same sound in the initial position of a sequence of words (*When **cr**ickets **cr**oak and **scr**eech-owls **scr**eak*).
allusion	An implicit reference, which may be to another work or writer, to a person or event. It requires the reader to make a connection between the poem and something outside it.
amphibrach	A unit of poetic metre made up of a stressed syllable with an unstressed syllable before and after it (*de–**PEN**–dent*).
anapaest	A unit of poetic metre made up of two unstressed syllables followed by a stressed syllable. A line of verse using the anapaest has an anapaestic rhythm (*un–a–**LIKE***).
anaphoric reference	A form of referencing in which a pronoun or noun phrase points backwards to something mentioned earlier in the text (*The hawk reared skyward,/**Its** presence a reminder/ Of the living world*).
anticlimax	A sentence or larger piece of text in which the last part does not come to a satisfying conclusion or fulfil our expectations. The tone will often be deflated and the content or ideas undermined. The

effect can be comic as the writer moves from a heightened and elevated style to something more ordinary.

antithesis
A rhetorical device in which thoughts or words are balanced in opposition (*hot/cold*; *positive/negative*).

aphorism
A succinct expression of a general truth.

apostrophe
A literary device in which a thing, a place, an absent person, an idea, or an abstract quality is addressed as if present and able to understand (*O wisdom! You should be with me now*).

approximant
A term used to describe consonants in which the organs of speech (lips, teeth, tongue etc.) approach each other, but do not get close enough to produce a plosive, nasal or fricative (*/l/, /j/*).

archaism
A word or phrase no longer in current use.

aspect
The timescale of the action expressed by a verb, which may be complete or in progress. There are two forms: **progressive** and **perfect**.

assonance
A repetition of the same or similar vowel sounds, usually close together (*Down some profound dull tunnel*).

asyndetic listing
The omission of conjunctions in a list. The effect of this may create a sense of breathless excitement, urgency, overwhelming chaos, or infinite possibilities (*There was no chance to pause; we ran **foolishly, without thought, ignorant of the consequences***).

attributive adjectives
Adjectives that precede the noun in a noun phrase – they are 'attributes' of the noun. As modifiers in a larger phrase structure, attributive adjectives have less emphasis placed upon them than predicative adjectives, which constitute a discrete clause element (***wise** philosophy; a **full-hearted** evensong*).

auxiliary verb
A verb that precedes the lexical verb in a verb phrase. The primary verbs *to have, to be* and *to do* help to construct different timescales, questions and negatives; the modal verbs *can/could, may/might, shall/should, will/would* and *must/ought* give information about mood and attitude (*The child **could have** gone home*).

ballad
A traditional narrative poem originally set to music. It is an oral form dating back to the late Middle Ages.

bilabial
A term used to denote consonants formed with both lips (*/b/, /m/, /p/*).

blank verse
Poetry written with unrhymed five-stress lines, usually with an iambic metre. It is very common in English poetry and is considered to be close to the rhythms of everyday speech.

burlesque
A derisive imitation or 'sending up' of a piece of literature.

cacophony	A term that denotes harsh sounds, usually produced by plosive consonants, short vowels and awkward consonant clusters (*Dry cl**a**shed his harshness in the **i**cy caves/And b**a**rren ch**a**sms*). It is the opposite of euphony.
caesura	A break or pause in a line of poetry, usually dictated by the natural rhythm of the language. Near the beginning, it is called the **initial caesura**; near the middle, the **medial caesura**; and near the end, the **terminal caesura**. The medial caesura is the most common.
caudate sonnet	A form of sonnet in which the normal pattern of 14 lines is modified by one or more codas.
clause	A group of words, usually with a finite (tensed) verb which is structurally larger than a phrase. Clauses may be described as **independent** (main) or **dependent** (subordinate).
climax	The high point of a narrative, poem or list where some kind of crisis, resolution or conclusion is reached.
collocation	Two or more words that frequently occur together as part of a set phrase (*bright and breezy*; *slap and tickle*). Writers can disrupt collocations with which we are familiar for dramatic effect (*Once **below** a time*).
colloquial	Language associated with informal conversation.
complement	A clause element that adds extra information about the subject or object of the clause after a copula verb (*Our hopes of escape were **nothing but dreams***).
complex sentence	A sentence made up of one main and one or more subordinate clauses (***Because** it was so wet, we <u>did not go</u> out, **preferring** to enjoy ourselves indoors*).
compound sentence	A sentence made up of two or more main clauses joined together by a co-ordinating conjunction (*The weather <u>seemed</u> to change suddenly **and** we were <u>caught</u> out in the storm*).
compound-complex sentence	A sentence that contains co-ordination and sub-ordination (***When** the snow covered the land **and** the snow flakes obscured our vision, we <u>knew</u> we were lost*).
concrete noun	A term used to refer to physical things such as people, objects, places, or substances which can be seen, touched, or measured (***garden, poem, room***).
conditional	A subordinate clause that expresses a condition or hypothesis (***If it rains**, we will get wet*) which fills the adverbial site. It may begin with *if, unless, provided that, so long as, on condition that.*
conjunction	A word that links words, phrases and clauses. **Coordinating** conjunctions join elements of equal rank (*the stifling heat **and** the airless room*); **subordinating** conjunctions introduce a subordinate

clause; **although** *the temperature was unpleasant, we continued with our journey*).

connotations	The associations attached to a word in addition to its dictionary definition.
consonance	A repetition of identical consonant sounds before and after different vowels (**crash** – **crush**; **tick** – **tock**).
coordinating conjunction	A word that joins elements of equal rank (*and*, *or*, *but*).
cynghanedd	A Welsh term describing sound patterns (alliteration and internal rhyme) distinctive to Welsh poetry.
dactyl	A unit of poetic metre made up of one stressed syllable followed by two unstressed syllables. A line of verse using the dactyl has a dactylic rhythm (**BEAU**–*ti*–*ful*).
decasyllable	A line of verse of 10 syllables. It forms the basis of the sonnet, the Spenserian stanza, the heroic couplet and blank verse.
delayed main clause	Sometimes the main or independent clause can be moved from its usual position at the front of a sentence. By placing a subordinate clause in the initial position, a poet can influence the order in which the reader receives information. Foregrounding the subordinate clause can give it importance at the front of the sentence, but it can also throw added weight onto the main clause since we have to wait for the completion of the sentence. In order to establish what kind of effect the poet has created, you will need to look at the example in the context of the poem as a whole (*Reaching the edge,/**The cliff fell resplendently***).
demotic	A term used to describe language that is 'of the people'.
determiner	A lexical item that specifies the number and definiteness of a noun (*a, the, some, any, his, our*).
dialect	A language variety marked by distinctive grammar and vocabulary, which is used by a group of speakers (or writers) with common regional or social backgrounds.
dialogue	Language interaction with two or more participants.
diction	The type and range of language used by poets.
didactic	Any literary work which sets out to instruct.
discourse	Any spoken or written language that is longer than a sentence.
doggerel	Poetry that has a loose and irregular pattern, which is often now used to describe poorly constructed verse that has clumsy rhyme, monotonous rhythms and trivial subject matter.
double speak	A term coined by The Plain English Campaign to describe language use that was seen to confuse and

obscure rather than clarify. It is a form of euphemism, which allows unpleasant concepts to be made more palatable: cars don't break down, they *fail to proceed*; we don't have a recession, we have *a period of accelerated negative growth*; we don't kill the opposition in war, we *de-grade* them; we don't accidentally kill soldiers on our own side, they are victims of *friendly fire*.

dramatic monologue A poem in which there is one imaginary speaker addressing an imaginary audience.

dream vision A form of literature extremely popular in the Middle Ages in which the writer goes to sleep in pleasant rural surroundings (often on a May morning) and then sees either real people or personified abstractions. The dream is often expressed as an allegory.

dynamic verb A verb that expresses an action rather than a state and that can be used in the progressive (*fly/flying*; *stumble/stumbling*).

eclogues A short poem, or part of a longer one, that is often a pastoral in the form of a dialogue or soliloquy.

elegy A poem written on the death of a specific person, which will both praise and mourn the loss as the poet attempts to come to terms with his grief.

elision The omission of sounds in spoken or written language.

ellipsis The omission of part of a sentence which can be understood from the context.

elliptical A telegraphic style in which a word or words are left out without affecting the meaning. The omitted words are often grammatical function words or the verb 'to be'. ([The] *Snow* [is] *falling on motionless streets*/ [and is] *Hiding man's taint*).

end focus The arrangement of clause elements so that attention is focused on the end of a sentence (*When the hounds of spring are loose,/And the sun is in the sky/With winter's rains now over,/***Blossom quivers into life***).

end rhyme The echoing of similar sounds at the end of a line of verse (*Forget not yet the tried* **intent**/*Of such a truth as I have* **meant**).

end-stopped A line of verse that concludes with punctuation to mark a natural pause in the grammatical structure. A full stop or a semi-colon mark a strong pause; a comma or a colon create a weaker one (*But as they left the dark'ning heath,/More desperate grew the strife of death*).

enjambement A line of verse which runs into the next line without any grammatical break (*We would sit down and think which way/To walk, and pass our long love's day*).

epiphany	A moment of revelation, in which God's presence in the world is understood. As well as a spiritual state, the epiphany can also reveal an understanding of life in more secular terms.
euphony	A term that denotes pleasing or harmonious sounds, usually produced by long vowels rather than consonants – although laterals can also create a similar effect (*W<u>or</u>d l<u>a</u>st! N<u>ow</u> a lush-kept plush-capped sl<u>oe</u>/Will*).
exclamatory	A tone of emotional expression highlighted by an exclamation mark.
eye rhyme	A rhyme which appears to the eye to be an exact rhyme, but does not, in fact, sound identical (*come/home*).
feminine rhyme	Polysyllabic rhyming words (*hilarious/vicarious*).
figurative language	Language which uses figures of speech (metaphor, simile, personification, symbolism) in order to say one thing in terms of something else, thus allowing the poet to add layers of meaning to a poem. Literal language creates a visual picture (*the fallen leaves covered the ground*); figurative language creates a relationship between something literal and something imagined (*the fallen leaves **carpeted** the ground in **a rich tapestry of colours***).
finite verb	A term used to denote verbs marked for tense (past/present), person (singular/plural) and number (first/second/third).
first person pronoun	A reference that relates directly to the speaker or writer (*I*) or to a group of people including the speaker or writer (*we*).
foregrounding	A change in the sequence of clause elements in order to draw attention to a particular word, phrase or clause (***Without warning**, the tree fell*).
form	The word class and structure of a word (*mountain – a **concrete noun**; splintering – a **present participle verb***).
free verse	Verse with no regular metre or line length, which depends on the natural rhythms of speech and the interplay between stressed and unstressed syllables. Also known as ***vers libre***.
fricative	A term used to describe consonants where the air escapes through a small passage making a hissing sound (*/f/, /v/, /z/, /sh/, /th/*).
fronting	The movement of a clause element other than the subject to the beginning of a sentence in order to throw added weight onto it (***Terrible** it was*).
full rhyme	A rhyme where the recurring sounds are exactly matched (*Of these the false Achitophel was **first**/A name to all succeeding ages **curst***).
future time	A means of referring to things that are happening at a time in the future. In English, there is no future

'tense' because we do not have an inflected verb form to indicate future action. Instead, we use *will* (*I will visit France next year*), *be* + *going* (*I am going to visit France next year*), the present progressive (*We are expecting to visit France next year*) or for future 'certainties', the simple present tense (*It is Friday tomorrow*).

generic	A word or sentence that refers to a class of people or entities (*the old; the French; the poor*).
genre	A type or class of literature (*poetry, drama, novel; tragedy, comedy, satire*), which can be subdivided into smaller groups (*sonnet, ode, ballad*).
grammar	A study of the lexical and structural features of a language. By applying grammatical understanding of the ways in which language works to poetry, it is possible to explore how poets communicate meaning.
grammatical function words	Words like conjunctions (*and, or, but*), prepositions (*in, on, over, through*) and determiners (*the, a, this, some*) which express grammatical relationships.
grammatical mood	Main clauses can have one of three moods: the **declarative** mood is used to make statements; the **imperative** mood is used to give orders and make requests; and the **interrogative** mood is used to ask questions. Changes of mood within a poem can have a significant effect upon the way in which we respond.
half rhyme	A repetition in accented syllables of the final consonant sound, but with no echoing of the vowel sound (*peer/pare*).
heroic couplet	Poetry consisting of rhymed pairs of decasyllabic lines, nearly always in iambic pentameter. It is one of the most common forms in English poetry.
homographs	Words with the same spelling but different meanings (*bow* – a tied ribbon; *bow* – a curtain-call).
homophone	Words with the same pronunciation, but different meanings (*rode/rowed; flour/flower*).
iamb	A unit of poetic metre containing one unstressed syllable followed by a stressed syllable. A line of verse using the iamb has an iambic rhythm (*a–MONG*).
idiom	An expression in which the meaning of the whole conveys more than the meaning of the individual words (*The family were hard up for a long time* – i.e. short of money).
imagery	A descriptive or figurative use of language that appeals to our senses and aims to produce a visual picture, to convey emotions or to suggest ideas. Literal images will often create a physical representation of a particular place, person or experience. Figurative images require the reader to work harder

because the poet uses language in a more complex way: the words on the page are designed to evoke a response that goes beyond the concrete. In order to achieve this, poets use figures of speech that enable them to say one thing in terms of something else.

infinitive
A non-finite verb which is in the base form and often preceded by the preposition *to* (*to burn*, *to frame*).

initial position
The site at the front of a sentence, which usually contains the subject. Clause elements can be moved around, however, so that the initial position is filled by something other than the subject: a complement (*terrible it was*); an object (*the window was broken*); an adverbial (*Dreaming of the future, she sat alone*); predicator (*Sit down now!*). In some instances, a conjunction can also be placed in the initial position (*But this was not the last we were to hear of it*).

inflections
The marking of a grammatical relationship with an affix (*-ing*, *-ed*, *-'s*)

interjection
A word or phrase that has an emotive meaning, which does not play a part in the grammatical structure of a sentence as a whole.

internal rhyme
The recurrence of sounds within a line of poetry (*Ten thousand fleets sweep over thee in vain*).

invocation
An appeal or request for help or inspiration, usually addressed to a muse or deity. It often comes at or near the beginning of a poem.

irony
A way of writing in which what is meant is the opposite of what the words appear to say. Because it allows a writer to deflate, scorn or 'send up' his subject, it is often used by satirists.

juxtaposition
A term used to describe the placing of two different things in close proximity in which the relationship is often one of opposition.

labial
A term used to describe consonants articulated with the lips (/*m*/, /*b*/, /*p*/).

lateral
A term used to describe consonants made by the flow of air around one or both sides of a closure made in the mouth (/*l*/).

lexical choice
The words a poet selects.

lexical set
Groups of words within the diction of a poem that can be classified by their association with each other. They may be taken from a specific register or field (topic area); they may be linked by their similarity or their difference.

lexical verb
A verb conveying an action, an event or state. It is also known as the main verb of a sentence and carries the meaning.

lyric
A poem in which the poet writes about thoughts and feelings. It is often in the form of a song, but

sonnets, odes and elegies are also regarded as 'lyric' poetry

main clause
A clause that is not dependent, makes sense on its own and contains a tensed verb (*Gulls soared confidently above the clifftop*).

manner
The relationship between participants in a language interaction. It can be formal, informal or anywhere in between.

marked theme
A clause element moved to the front of a sentence from its usual position (***Too light** the wind travels/To shake the fallen birch leaves from the fern*). Also known as **fronting** or **foregrounding**.

masculine rhyme
Monosyllabic rhyming words (*old/gold*).

medial position
In the middle of a line of poetry.

metaphor
A figurative device in which two things that are unlike are brought together in an implicit comparison. The poet requires the reader to make an association between the literal and the figurative and a metaphor therefore adds layers of meaning (*The snake's tongue flickered,//A **death-coloured arrow***).

metre
The pattern of stressed and unstressed syllables in a line of verse.

metrical feet
Groups of syllables forming a recognisable poetic unit. Each foot contains a stressed syllable and any unstressed syllables that accompany it. A foot will therefore be iambic, trochaic, anapaestic, dactylic or spondaic.

minor sentence
A sentence that lacks one or more of the clause elements and that often occurs as an unchanging formulaic structure (***O Heart!** Night is a time of sorrow*).

mock heroic
Writing in which the heroic manner of classical epic is adopted to make a trivial subject seem grand, thus satirising the content. It is commonly used in burlesque and parody.

modal verbs
Auxiliary verbs (*can/could, may/might, shall/should, will/would, must/ought*) that mark contrasts in attitude such as obligation, possibility and prediction.

modifier
A linguistic item that specifies or defines the nature of another. Modifiers can be used to describe attributes of a noun; they may take the form of an adjective (*the **spotty** dog*), a verb (*the **snarling** dog; the **beaten** dog*), or a noun (*the **farm** dog*). They can also be used to describe the action of a verb (*the dog snarled **viciously***).

monosyllabic
Having one syllable.

nasal
A term used to describe consonants produced with an open nasal passage, which allows air to escape through the nose as well as the mouth (*/m/, /n/*).

neologism	The creation of a new word from existing lexical items (*a **wannabe***). Also known as **coinage**.
non-finite clause	A clause without a finite verb. In a non-finite clause, the first verb form is either an infinitive with *to* –, a present participle, a past participle, or an infinitive without *to* – (*Tyger! Tyger! **Burning bright**/In the forests of the night*).
non-finite verb	A verb which is not marked for tense, person or number such as present participles (*seeing*), past participles (*seen*) and infinitives (*to see*).
non-standard	Any variety that does not conform to the standard prestige form used as a norm by society.
noun	A word class with a naming function, which can be used as a subject or object in a clause. A **common noun** refers to a general group of objects or concepts and usually has a plural form (*trees, stars; strength, earth*); a **proper noun** refers to the name of a distinctive person, place or other unique reference and is recognisable by the initial capital letter (***New York, Achilles, Tennyson, Death***); a **collective noun** refers to a group of people, animals or things (*government, herd, family*).
noun clause	A subordinate clause which can fill the subject, object or complement site of a clause. They begin with *that* or *what* (*No-one believes **that the earth is flat***).
noun phrase	A phrase which usually has a noun as its head word and which can function as a subject or object in a clause. Poets often use noun phrases because they can contain a lot of descriptive information in a compact form (*The turning **world** that heedless marks the passing **days***).
object	The person or thing that receives the action of the verb (*The sun struck **the water** as it changed its course*).
objective correlative	A literary term used by T.S. Eliot that describes the process of expressing emotion in verse through representation: a set of objects, a situation or a sequence of events become the means by which an emotion can be evoked.
octave	A group of 8 lines of verse, occurring as a stanza form (**ottava rima**) or as the first 8 lines of a Petrarchan sonnet.
octosyllabic lines	A tetrameter line containing 8 syllables and usually consisting of iambic or trochaic feet.
ode	A complex lyric poem with an elevated style and tone, addressed to a person, a thing, or an abstraction. Originally written in praise of its subject, it became a more philosophical poetic form.
onomatopoeia	A term used to denote words that imitate sounds. It is a figure of speech in which the sounds reflect the sense (*crackle, pop, whoosh*).

paeon	A unit of poetic metre containing one stressed and three unstressed syllables. It is known as the first, second, third or fourth paeon according to the position of the stressed syllable.
panegyrics	A speech or poem in praise of an individual, institution or group of people, in which the style is often rhetorical.
parallelism	The use of paired sounds, words or grammatical structures (*O breast that 'twere rapture to sleep on!/O arms that 'twere delicious to feel*).
parenthesis	The use of commas, brackets or dashes around an additional piece of information in a sentence which could be omitted without affecting the grammatical structure. It is often used when a poet wishes to qualify or add to a statement (*The tree rose – **suddenly, elegantly** – from the ground*).
parody	The imitative use of words, style, content and tone of an author in such a way that the original work is made to seem ridiculous. The parody will exaggerate certain traits while creating a close resemblance to the original.
passive voice	A grammatical structure in which the subject and object can change places in order to alter the focus of a sentence. In the passive voice, the object of an active sentence occurs in the subject site followed by *to be + past participle* (*the window **was broken***). The subject of the active sentence can be included following *by* (*the window was broken **by the small boy***).
past participle	A non-finite verb form that can be recognised by its *–ed* ending for regular verbs. Irregular past participles are formed in a number of ways (*write → **written**; stand → **stood**; swim → **swam***). Past participles can occur after an auxiliary verb in the perfect aspect (***has/had fallen***); as a pre-modifier in a noun phrase (*the **fallen** tree*); or in a non-finite clause (***Twisted** by age, the tree shook in the wind*).
past tense	A term to denote verbs that describe something which happened at a definite time in the past. Regular past tense verbs are formed by adding the inflection *–ed* (*twisted*); irregular verbs have a distinct form, often with a spelling change (*bring → brought; go → went*). The past tense is also sometimes used to describe something which is supposed to be happening in the present time (*It's time the government **took** responsibility for their actions*). This is called the unreal use of the past tense because it means that the event or state is not taking place – it is 'imaginary'.
pathetic fallacy	A term used to describe the way in which poets attribute human feelings and actions to the natural

world. It contributes to the mood of a poem by creating striking images.

patterning The use of sounds, words, phrases or clauses in a recognisable sequence to create a sense of balance, logic and control (*I came, I saw, I conquered*).

perfect The perfect or perfective aspect is made up of *to have + past participle* and has two forms: present perfect, describing a past action with present relevance (*the child **has felt** fear*); and past perfect, describing an action completed before a specific time (*the child **had felt** fear*).

persona Originally a mask or false face worn by actors, which has come to denote the 'person' (the *I* character) who speaks or narrates in a poem. The persona provides a mask that separates the poet from the speaking voice of the poem.

personification A literary device in which the non-human or an abstraction is given personality and human qualities (*Courage strode before me, thrusting cowardice behind*).

phrase A group of words that has no finite verb (except for a verb phrase): noun phrase (*the abandoned Earth*); adjective phrase (*more lovely*); verb phrase (*could have been*); adverb phrase (*quite unhappily*).

plosive A term used to denote consonants made by a complete closure of the air passage followed by a sudden release of air (/p/, /b/, /t/, /d/, /k/, /g/).

polysyllabic Having more than one syllable.

possessive A possessive determiner (***my/your/his/her/our/their*** *coat*), a possessive pronoun (*mine/yours/his/hers/ours/ theirs*) or inflection (*'s* or *s'*) signalling possession.

post-modification Phrases or clauses that follow the head word of a phrase and provide extra information (*the angry storm, **raging on its path**; the child **who wandered through the night**; the river **on its ordained path to the sea***).

post-modifying clause Clauses that follow the head word of a noun phrase (*the peacocks **preening in the sun***) or an adjective phrase (*anxious **to please***; *scared **that he'll fall***). They may be non-finite clauses (beginning with a present or past participle, or with an infinitive), relative clauses (beginning with a relative pronoun) or noun clauses (beginning with *that*, which may be omitted).

predicative adjectives Adjectives that follow a copula verb such as *seem, appear, be, become, grew* (*The frost was **spectre-gray**; the town grew **drowsy***). Poets use predicative adjective phrases where they wish to give added emphasis to the adjective.

predicator The verb phrase which fills the verb site of a sentence in a main clause (*Knifelike, he **struck***).

pre-modification	Modifiers that precede the head in a phrase (*The garlanded triple-arched cavern*).
prepositional phrase	A grammatical structure made up of a preposition and a noun phrase (*in the depth*; *over the hill*; *away from the crowd*). They can function as post-modifying phrases or as adverbials. In each case they provide information about place, time and reason.
present participle	A non-finite verb form that can be recognised by its –**ing** ending. Present participles can occur after an auxiliary verb in the progressive aspect (**is/was falling**); as a pre-modifier in a noun phrase (*the **shooting** star*); or in a non-finite clause (*The clouds scudded aimlessly,/**Drifting across the sun and on***).
present tense	A term to denote verbs that describe something which is happening now. Regular present tense verbs are usually in the base form, except for the third person singular which has an –*s* inflection (*I walk*; *he walks*). The verb *to be* is irregular and has three distinct present tense forms (*I **am**, you **are**, she **is***); modal verbs do not take the third person singular inflection.
progressive	An aspect used to describe an event which is in progress. It is made up of *to be + present participle* (*Sweet perfumes **are blowing** on the wind*).
pronoun	Words that can replace a noun phrase (PERSONAL: *I, you, he, she, it, we, they; me, you, him, her, it, us, them;* POSSESSIVE: *mine, yours, his, hers, ours, yours, theirs;* REFLEXIVE: *myself, yourself, himself, herself, itself, ourselves, yourselves, themselves;* DEMONSTRATIVE: *this/these, that/those;* INTERROGATIVE: *who? what?;* RELATIVE: *who, that, which*).
provincialisms	A manner or mode of speech, or way of thinking, peculiar to a particular area, unaffected by the wider context of society.
pyrrhic	A metrical foot consisting of two unstressed syllables.
quatrain	A stanza of 4 lines, rhymed or unrhymed. It is the most common of all stanzaic forms.
relative clause	A clause beginning with a relative pronoun (*which, who, that*), which adds extra information about one of the nouns in the main clause (*The green elm **which has but one bough of gold**/Lets leaves into the grass slip*).
repetition	A rhetorical device that emphasises an idea through reiteration of a word, phrase or clause.
rhetorical devices	Devices such as repetition, listing and parallelism which allow poets to consciously pattern and structure their verse, drawing attention to key ideas and intensifying the tone.
rhyme	The echoing of word endings which agree in vowel and consonant sounds for aesthetic effect or as

part of the structure of the verse. It is a device that intensifies the meaning and binds the lines together. Where there is a definable pattern of rhyme, it is useful to consider the rhyme scheme and its effect.

rhythm
The pattern of stressed and unstressed syllables in language.

rime riche
Rhyming syllables in which accented vowels and the consonants before and after them sound identical. Also known as **identical rhyme** (*bare/bear*).

run-on line
A line of verse which runs into the next line without any grammatical break (*In human hearts what bolder thought can rise/Than man's presumption on to-morrow's dawn?*)

satire
A form of writing in which the follies and vices of society are censured and ridiculed in order to bring contempt and derision upon those who display such behaviour. The underlying aim is to correct. While the target of the satire may be specific, it will also be sufficiently representative to give a universality that is meaningful beyond the original context.

second person pronoun
A reference that relates to the person or people addressed by the speaker or writer (*you*).

semantic field
An area of meaning (for example, *medicine*), which is characterised by common vocabulary (*GP, surgery, tablets, nurse*).

semantics
The study of the meaning of language.

sentence
A grammatical structure made up of one or more clauses. In written language, the beginning is signalled by a capital letter and the end by a full stop. They are made up of a sequence of elements (subject, predicator, object, complement, adverbial) that fulfil different functions.

sestet
A group of 6 lines of verse, occurring as the last six lines of the Petrarchan sonnet.

sibilance
The recurrence of sounds such as /s/ and /sh/, which produce a hissing sound.

simile
A figurative device that takes two things which are essentially similar and makes an explicit comparison between them using words such as 'like', 'as' or 'than' (*The garnets burned,/Fierce **as the** volcano's eye*).

simple sentence
A sentence made up of one main clause (*The sky was blue*).

Skeltonics
A kind of verse named after John Skelton in which short lines, multiple rhyme, alliteration and parallelism create a headlong, 'tumbling' effect.

sonnet
A 14-line verse form, usually in iambic pentameters, with a distinctive rhyme scheme. The Petrarchan sonnet comprises an octave rhyming

	abbaabba and a sestet rhyming cdecde or cdcdcd, or in any combination except a rhyming couplet. The Spenserian sonnet has 3 quatrains and a couplet rhyming abab bcbc cdcd ee; a Shakespearean sonnet also has 3 quatrains and a couplet, rhyming abab cdcd efef gg.
speech turn	The time taken by each speaker in a conversation. Turns may be equal, or one of the participants may dominate.
Spenserian stanza	A stanza of 9 iambic lines, the first eight using pentameters and the last a hexameter or alexandrine. The rhyme scheme follows a distinctive pattern: ababbcbcc. It is named after the sixteenth-century poet Edmund Spenser who invented the form for his long allegorical poem *The Faerie Queene*.
spondee	A unit of poetic metre containing two stressed syllables. A line of verse using the spondee has a spondaic rhythm (*HEED*–*LESS*).
sprung rhythm	A term invented by Gerard Manley Hopkins to describe his own metrical experiments in which he moved away from the traditional iambic 'running' metre. It has feet of between 1 and 4 syllables with any number of extra weak syllables called 'outrides'. For some critics, it is not a distinctive poetic metre, but a kind of free verse in which irregular patterns reflect the natural rhythms of language.
standard English	A term used to describe a prestige form of English, which has been accepted as a norm. It is the variety with which other forms of English are compared. Variations from SE are described as non-standard.
stanza	A group of lines of verse that form the unit structure in a poem. It may be of any number, but 4 is the most common and more than 12 is unusual.
stative verb	A verb that expresses states of being or processes in which there is no obvious action (*seem*, *appear*, *become*).
stream of consciousness	A literary term that describes a writer's attempt to create the workings of the mind on the page. In order to imitate the random nature of thought, the style is elliptical: minor sentences, asyndetic listing and repetition are common. It represents an attempt to suggest the complexity of the human mind and, although the author is still responsible for the crafting of the words on the page, it offered twentieth-century writers a means of addressing the psychology of their characters more explicitly.
stress	The comparative force, length and loudness with which a syllable is pronounced. For instance, we say SY–LLA–BLE rather than SY–LLA–BLE or SY–LLA–BLE.

subject	A noun phrase (and sometimes a clause) that is responsible for the action of the verb (***The day rolled on regardless***).
subjunctive	A grammatical mood which expresses something hypothetical or tentative. It can be recognised by its use of the base form of the verb without a third person *–s* inflection (*I propose that he **leave***); and by the use of *were* instead of *was* (*I wish I **were** at home*). It is no longer used widely, but occurs in formulaic expressions such as *Heaven forbid* and following *if* in structures such as *If I **were** to continue . . .*).
subordinate clause	A clause that cannot stand as a sentence on its own, but needs another clause to complete its meaning. Also known as a **dependent clause**.
subordinating conjunctions	A conjunction used to introduce a subordinate clause (*because, although, while, since, until*).
syllable	A word or part of a word that can be uttered in a single beat. Syllables may be strong (**stressed**) or weak (**unstressed**). Patterns of stressed and unstressed syllables constitute the rhythm of a language (*HUM–ble; i–NNU–me–ra–ble–*).
symbol	A figurative device in which a word or phrase represents something in addition to itself. It does not depend upon a physical likeness since associations and sensory resemblance contribute to the significance of a symbol (***an old man*** could be a symbol for ***wisdom and experience, frailty and vulnerability*** or ***the mortality of humankind***).
syndetic listing	The use of conjunctions to link the items in a list. The effect of this may create a sense of logic and reason, a feeling that things can be controlled and managed, that they are predictable and reassuring (*And there was **light and warmth and companionship and hope***).
synonyms	Different words with the same or nearly the same meaning (*valiant – brave*).
syntax	The grammatical relationships between words in a sentence.
tense	A change in the structure of a verb to signal changes in the timescale. There are two tenses in English: **present** and **past**. The present tense uses the base form of the verb except in the third person singular, which is inflected with an *–s*; it refers to actions in the present time and describes habitual actions. The past tense is formed by adding an *–ed* inflection to regular verbs; it refers to actions or states that have taken place in the past.
tercets	A stanza of 3 lines, often linked by rhyme.
terms of address	A term used to describe the ways in which a poet names characters, indicating something about the

relationship between the poet and his or her creation.

theme   The underlying ideas or concepts at the heart of a work of literature.

third person pronoun   A reference that relates to other people, animals or objects (*he, she, it, they*).

tone   The reflection of the poet's attitude to his or her subject created by the choice of words. It is the equivalent in writing of tone of voice in speech: the tone may be serious or light-hearted; it may be intimate or detached; or formal or informal. It also tells us something about the poet's relationship with the reader.

topic   The thing or person about which something is said in a sentence; the focus of a written or spoken text. Topic management relates to the way in which a writer or speaker organises and develops a topic.

tripling   The use of sounds, words or grammatical structures in patterns of threes (*None other Lamb, none other Name,/None other Hope in heaven or earth or sea*).

trochaic   A unit of poetic metre containing a stressed syllable followed by an unstressed syllable (*SPI–rit*).

turn-taking   The organisation of speakers' contributions in a conversation.

verb   A word that expresses states, actions or processes. They can be marked for tense, aspect, voice and mood.

verbal noun   A noun derived from a verb (***Teaching*** *is hard work;* *the **flattering** of the master is important*) Also known as a gerund.

verb modifier   A verb that functions as a pre-modifier: it may be a present participle (*the **shimmering** river*) or a past participle (*the **fallen** tree*).

verb phrase   A group of verbs consisting of a lexical verb and up to 4 auxiliaries, which fills the site of a predicator in a main clause.

vers libre   A literary term used to describe verse forms that moved away from traditional poetic structure to an emphasis on rhythm and the division of verse into rhythmical units. Metrical patterns, the number of syllables per line and the use of a regular rhyme scheme were abandoned as twentieth-century poets sought to create a very different kind of poetic structure.

villanelle   A poetic form in which there are 5 tercets and a final quatrain. The first and third lines of the first tercet recur alternately in the following stanzas as a refrain and form a final couplet.

vocative   The words used to name or refer to people when talking about them. A vocative will usually be a noun phrase; it is optional and is distinct from the main clause sites (**Fiend**, *you must no further go*).

volta The change in thought or feeling which separates the octave from the sestet in a sonnet.

word class Groups of words with characteristic features (*nouns, adjectives, verbs, determiners, adverbs*).

word order The arrangement of words in a sentence. In poetry, word order can be manipulated in order to meet the requirements of a rhyme scheme or metrical pattern, or to draw attention to important words and phrases.

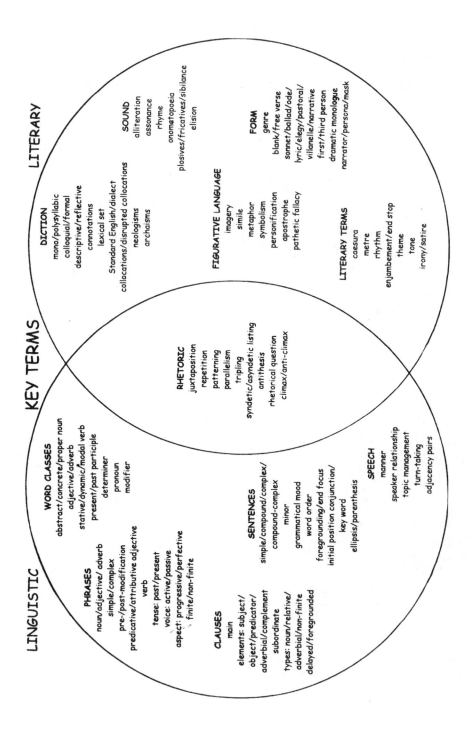

KEY TERMS

LITERARY

DICTION
mono/polysyllabic
colloquial/formal
descriptive/reflective
connotations
lexical set
Standard English/dialect
collocations/disrupted collocations
neologisms
archaisms

SOUND
alliteration
assonance
rhyme
onomatopoeia
plosives/fricatives/sibilance
elision

FIGURATIVE LANGUAGE
imagery
simile
metaphor
symbolism
personification
apostrophe
pathetic fallacy

FORM
genre
blank/free verse
sonnet/ballad/ode/
lyric/elegy/pastoral/
villanelle/narrative
first/third person
dramatic monologue
narrator/persona/mask

LITERARY TERMS
caesura
metre
rhythm
enjambement/end stop
theme
tone
irony/satire

RHETORIC
juxtaposition
repetition
patterning
parallelism
tripling
syndetic/asyndetic listing
antithesis
rhetorical question
climax/anti-climax

LINGUISTIC

WORD CLASSES
abstract/concrete/proper noun
adjective/adverb
stative/dynamic/modal verb
present/past participle
determiner
pronoun
modifier

PHRASES
noun/adjective/ adverb
simple/complex
pre-/post-modification
predicative/attributive adjective
verb
tense: past/present
voice: active/passive
aspect: progressive/perfective
finite/non-finite

SENTENCES
simple/compound/complex/
compound-complex
minor
grammatical mood
word order
foregrounding/end focus
initial position conjunction/
key word
ellipsis/parenthesis

CLAUSES
main
elements: subject/
object/predicator/
adverbial/complement
subordinate
types: noun/relative/
adverbial/non-finite
delayed/foregrounded

SPEECH
manner
speaker relationship
topic management
turn-taking
adjacency pairs

▼ Wider reading
▲

Poetry

Having worked through the examples in this book, you may like to read more by a poet who has caught your interest, or you may wish to read more widely. The following list includes volumes by individual poets as well as anthologies.

Individual poets

Matthew Arnold, *Selected Poems and Prose* (Dent, 1978).
Elizabeth Barrett Browning, *Selected Poems* (Chatto and Windus, 1988).
John Betjeman, *Collected Poems* (John Murray, 2001).
William Blake, *Complete Writings* (Oxford University Press, 1966).
Robert Bridges, *A Choice of Bridges' Verse* (Faber, 1987).
Rupert Brooke, *The Collected Poems* (Sidgwick and Jackson, 1942).
Robert Browning, *Poetical Works 1833–1864* (Oxford University Press, 1970); *The Ring and the Book* (Penguin, 1971).
Byron, *Poetical Works* (Oxford University Press, 1970).
Geoffrey Chaucer, *The Complete Works* (Oxford University Press, 1974).
Gillian Clarke, *Letter from a Far Country* (Carcanet, 1982); *Making the Beds for the Dead* (Carcanet, 2004).
S.T. Coleridge, *Selected Poems* (Heinemann, 1959).
Wendy Cope, *Making Cocoa for Kingsley Amis* (Faber, 1986); *If I Don't Know* (Faber, 2001).
Hart Crane, *Complete Poems* (Bloodaxe Books, 1984).
John Donne, *Selected Poems* (Heinemann, 1974).
John Dryden, *The Oxford Authors* series (Oxford University Press, 1987).
Carol Ann Duffy, *Standing Female Nude* (Anvil Press Poetry, 1985); *The World's Wife* (Picador, 1999); *Feminine Gospels* (Picador, 2002).
Jean Earle, *The Bed of Memory* (Seren, 2001).
T.S. Eliot, *Collected Poems 1909–1962* (Faber, 1974).
Thom Gunn, *Selected Poems 1950–1975* (Faber, 1979); *The Man with Night Sweats* (Faber, 2002).
Seamus Heaney, *Death of a Naturalist* (Faber, 1966); *Seeing Things* (Faber, 1991); *Electric Light* (Faber, 2001).
Gerard Manley Hopkins, *Poems and Prose* (Penguin, 1963).
Ted Hughes, *Wodwo* (Faber, 1971); *Crow* (Faber, 1974); *Birthday Letters* (Faber, 1998).
John Keats, *The Complete Poems* (Penguin, 1977).
William Langland, *The Vision of Piers Plowman* (Dent, 1982).

Philip Larkin, *Whitsun Weddings* (Faber, 1971); *High Windows* (Faber, 1974); *Collected Poems* (Faber, 1988).

D.H. Lawrence, *Birds, Beasts and Flowers* (Poetry First Editions, Penguin, 1923).

Roger McGough, *Melting into the Foreground* (Penguin, 1986); *Blazing Fruit: Selected Poems 1967–1987* (Penguin, 1989); *Everyday Eclipses* (Penguin, 2002).

John Milton, *Paradise Lost* (Macmillan – now Palgrave Macmillan, 1972).

Wilfred Owen, *The Poems of Wilfred Owen* (Chatto and Windus, 1965).

Brian Patten, *Grave Gossip* (Unwin Paperbacks, 1979); *Grinning Jack* (Flamingo, HarperCollins, 1995).

Sylvia Plath, *The Colossus* (Faber, 1960); *Ariel* (Faber, 1965); *Crossing the Water* (Faber, 1971); *Winter Trees* (Faber, 1971).

Poems of the Pearl Manuscript, ed. Andrew and Waldron, *York Medieval Texts* – Gawain and the Green Knight (Arnold, 1951).

Alexander Pope, *Poetical Works* (Oxford University Press, 1966).

Ezra Pound, *Selected Poems* (Faber, 1948).

Christina Rossetti, *Selected Poems* (Bloomsbury Poetry Classics, 1992).

Siegfried Sassoon, *The War Poems* (Faber, 1983).

Percy Bysshe Shelley, *Poetical Works* (Oxford University Press, 1970).

Stevie Smith, *Selected Poems* (Penguin, 1975).

Edmund Spenser, *The Faerie Queene* (Penguin, 1978).

Alfred Lord Tennyson, *Selected Poems* (Oxford University Press), 1973.

Dylan Thomas, *The Poems* (Dent, 1978).

R.S. Thomas, *Collected Poems 1945–1990* (Phoenix Press, 2001).

William Wordsworth, *Poetical Works* (Oxford University Press, 1969); *The Prelude* (Oxford University Press, 1970).

W.B. Yeats, *Selected Poetry* (Pan Classics, 1979).

General anthologies

Neil Astley (ed.), *Staying Alive* (Bloodaxe, 2002); *Being Alive* (Bloodaxe, 2004).

Michael Benton and Peter Benton (eds), *Touchstones 5* (The English Universities Press, 1971).

Thomas Blackburn (ed.), *Gift of Tongues* (Nelson, 1967).

D.J. Brindley (ed.), *The Turning World* (Schofield & Sims, 1968).

Seamus Heaney and Ted Hughes (eds), *The Rattle Bag* (Faber, 1952).

Seamus Heaney and Ted Hughes (eds), *The School Bag* (Faber, 1997).

Period anthologies

Kenneth Allott (ed.), *English Poetry 1918–60* (Penguin, 1962).

Bernard Bergonzi (ed.), *Poetry 1870–1914* (Longman, 1980).

A.A. Evans (ed.), *Victorian Poetry* (University of London Press, 1958).

Michael Hulse, David Kennedy and David Morley (eds), *The New Poetry* (Bloodaxe, 1993).

Philip Larkin (ed.), *The Oxford Book of Twentieth Century English Verse* (Oxford University Press, 1973).

Edna Longley (ed.), *The Bloodaxe Book of 20th Century Poetry* (Bloodaxe, 2000).

Edward Lucie-Smith (ed.), *British Poetry Since 1945* (Penguin, 1970).

George Macbeth (ed.), *Poetry 1900 to 1975* (Longman, 1979).

Robin Skelton (ed.), *Poetry of the Thirties* (Penguin, 1964).

Patrician Thomson (ed.), *Elizabethan Lyrical Poets* (Routledge and Kegan Paul, 1974).

Genre anthologies

A.A. Evans (ed.), *The Poet's Tale: An Anthology of Narrative Verse* (University of London Press, 1957).
Brian Gardner (ed.), *The Terrible Rain: The War Poets 1939–1945* (Methuen, 1966).
Edward B. Germain (ed.), *Surrealist Poetry* (Penguin, 1978).
John Gross (ed.), *The Oxford Book of Comic Verse* (Oxford University Press, 2002).
Matthew Hodgart (ed.), *The Faber Book of Ballads* (Faber, 1965).
Peter Jones (ed.), *Imagist Poetry* (Penguin, 1972).
Robert Nye (ed.), *The Faber Book of Sonnets* (Faber, 1976).
Jon Silkin (ed.), *The Penguin Book of First World War Poetry* (Penguin, 1979).
Lucien Stryk and Takashi Ikemoto (eds and translators), *The Penguin Book of Zen Poetry* (Penguin, 1977).

Women's poetry collections

Fleur Adcock (ed.), *The Faber Book of Twentieth Century Women's Poetry* (Faber, 1987).
Louise Bernikow (ed.), *The World Split Open: Women Poets 1552–1950* (The Women's Press, 1974).
Jennifer Breen (ed.), *Victorian Women Poets 1830–1901* (Dent, 1994).
Jeni Couzyn (ed.), *Singing Down the Bones* (Livewire, The Women's Press, 1989).
Jeni Couzyn (ed.), *The Bloodaxe Book of Contemporary Women Poets* (Bloodaxe, 1985).
Linda France (ed.), *Sixty Women Poets* (Bloodaxe, 1993).
Germaine Greer (ed.), *101 Poems by 101 Women* (Faber, 2001).
Judith Kinsman (ed.), *Six Women Poets* (Oxford University Press, 1992).
Lilian Mohin (ed.), *One Foot on the Mountain: An Anthology of British Feminist Poetry 1969–79* (Onlywomen Press, 1979).
Carol Rumens (ed.), *Making for the Open: The Chatto Book of Post-Feminist Poetry, 1964–1984* (Chatto and Windus, 1985).
Diana Scott (ed.), *Bread and Roses: Women's Poetry of the Nineteenth and Twentieth Centuries* (Virago, 1982).

Critical writing

You may also like to develop your understanding by referring to other critical works. The following list includes books that will support and broaden the ideas introduced in *Mastering Poetry*. Some focus on individual poets, others on literary periods or concepts.

Casebooks (Macmillan – now Palgrave Macmillan).
Macmillan Study Guides (Palgrave Macmillan).
Open Guides to Literature (Open University Press).
Preface Books (Longman).
A Reader's Guide (Thames and Hudson).
Transitions series (Palgrave Macmillan).
Twentieth Century Interpretations (Prentice-Hall).
York Notes Advanced (Longman).

N.F. Blake, *An Introduction to the Language of Literature* (Palgrave Macmillan, 1990).
Tony Curtis, *How to Study Modern Poetry* (Palgrave Macmillan, 1990).

Lindy Miller, *Mastering Practical Criticism* (Palgrave Macmillan, 2001).
John Peck and Martin Coyle, *Practical Criticism* (Palgrave Macmillan, 1984).
Don Shiach, *The Critical Eye: Appreciating Prose and Poetry* (Nelson, 1984).
Jeremy Tambling, *What is Literary Language?* (Open University Press, 1988).

Language study

If you feel that you would like to develop your understanding of grammar and language structures, the following list includes books that will support and add depth to the explanations introduced in *Mastering Poetry*.

David Crystal, *Rediscover Grammar* (Longman, 1988).
Leech, Deuchar, Hoogenraad, *English Grammar for Today* (Palgrave Macmillan, 1984).
Geoffrey Leech, *An A–Z of English Grammar and Usage* (Edward Arnold, 1989).
Sara Thorne, *Mastering Advanced English Language* (Palgrave Macmillan, 1997).

▼ Index

This index has been designed to help you develop your study of poetry. You can use it to track down discussion of a particular poet, poem or genre; or to identify references to key terms. It can also help you to research topics of interest: the way in which different types of grammatical mood can change our relationship with a poem; the semantic effect of present participles; or the way in which poets control reader response through their use of patterning.

Many of the key terms are used throughout the text, making it cumbersome to list all relevant references. Page numbers cited in these cases focus on examples of usage in the activities where the poems are quoted in full. As you read, however, you will be able to collect further examples to broaden your understanding.

Main entries and poems cited in activities are in **bold**.

Donne, John (1572–1631), **144–54, 157,** 170
  'A Feaver', 145–7; 'A Valediction: Forbidding Mourning', 147–8; 'Goodfriday, 1613. Riding Westward', **151–4**; 'Holy Sonnet XIV', 150–1; 'The Flea', 148–50
dramatic monologue, 98, 176, 219, **224–6,** 284, **293,** 356, **374–6**
dream vision, 98, 100, 102, 104, 222, 410
Dryden, John (1631–1700), **167–70**
dub poetry, 374
Duffy, Carol Ann (1955–), 245, 371, 376, 382–3, 395, 403
  'Standing Female Nude', 376; 'Translating the English, 1989', 382; 'Valentine', 379; 'Warming Her Pearls', 376; 'White Writing', 396, **400–2**
dynamic verbs, 44, 46, **51,** 67, 102, 231, 238, 276, 393, 410

eclogues, 136, 410
Edwardian poets, **246**
elegy, 13–14, **38–9, 44–5,** 117, 159, 303–4, 389, 410
Eliot, T.S. (1888–1965), **278–97**
  Ash Wednesday, 281, 286, 290, 291; *Four Quartets*, 282, 285, 287; 'Gerontion', 286; 'Journey of the Magi', 285, 290, 292; 'Preludes', 283, 286, 288, 289–90; 'The Love Song of J. Alfred Prufrock', 23–4, 281, 283–4, 285, 288–9, 291–2, 293, 294–7; *The Waste Land*, 281, 285, 286–7, 290, 291, **294–7**
elliptical, 8, 14, 46, 65, 79, 239, 324, 360, 410
end focus, **66,** 143, 162, 210, 342, 410
end rhyme, *see under* rhyme
end-stopped, 12, **13–14,** 15, 27, 305, 338, 410
enjambement, **14,** 15, 49, 210, 280, 296, 338, 351, 375, 391, 410
  see also run-on lines
epic, **40,** 136, 139, 158, 161, 170, 175, 177, **178–80**
epiphany, 38, 86, 251, 261, 316, 411
euphony, **69**
exclamatory, 14, 163, 331, 411
Existentialism, **243**
Expressionism, **244**
eye rhyme, *see under* rhyme

fabliau, **126,** 127, 130
Fanthorpe, U.A. (1929–), 371, 375
  'Sisyphus', 375

Feinstein, Elaine (1930–), 371
  'Muse', 380
feminine rhyme, *see under* rhyme
figurative language, 15, 33, 47, 50, 64, **74–9,** 124, 206
foot, metrical, **18–19**
foregrounding, **65,** 67–8, 83, 154, 296, 314, 411
  see also under fronting; initial position; marked theme
free verse, **26–7, 29, 30,** 67, 293, 296, 356, 390, 403, 411
fricatives, 15, 46, **70,** 72, 102, 252, 401, 411
fronting, **65,** 411
  see also under foregrounding; initial position; marked theme
full rhyme, *see under* rhyme
future time, **58,** 411–12

Georgian poets, **246–7,** 255, **278–9**
grammar, 48, **55–68,** 313, 412
grammatical mood, **58,** 412
  declarative, 11, 37, 65, 221, 306, 324, 360, 369, 376; imperative, 37, 47, 63, 83, 153–4, 216, 230, 385, 393; interrogative, 11, 154, 257, 284, 296, 331, 360, 376
Gray, Thomas (1716–71), 174
  Elegy Written in a Country Church-Yard, 181
Gunn, Thom (1929–2004), 344–5
  'Considering the Snail', 344–5; 'Human Condition', 345; 'On the Move', 344, 345

haiku, **38,** 280
half rhyme, *see under* rhyme
Hallam, Arthur Henry (1811–33), 219–20
Hardy, Thomas (1840–1928), **246–52**
  'The Voice', **250–2**
Heaney, Seamus (1939–), 245, 394, 403
  'Seeing the Sick', 395–6, **397–400**
Herbert, George (1593–1633), 154–6
  'The Church-Porch, 154–5'; 'The Collar', 155; 'Virtue', 17, 18, 19, 155–6
heroic couplet, 24, 170, 174, 175, 176, 193, 201, 209, 210, 412
heroic verse, **104–7**
hexameter, **18,** 137
Hill, Selima (1945–), 371, 377
  'Chicken Feathers', 377
homographs, **70,** 412
homophones, **70,** 412

Plath, Sylvia (1932–63), **367–71**
'Barren Woman', 370; 'Blackberrying', 369; 'Brasilia', 368; 'By Candlelight', 369; 'Frog Autumn', 369; 'Getting There', 368; 'Lady Lazarus', 368; 'Mary's Song', 368; 'Moonrise', 369; 'Nick and the Candlestick', 369–70; 'Sculptor', 370; 'Stillborn', 370; 'Stings', 368; 'Words', 370
plosives, 22, 44, **70**, 72, 85, 103, 180, 216, 361, 362, 384, 393, 417
poetry,
guide to analysis, 89–91; how to read a poem, 88–9; poetry *vs* prose, 8; what is poetry, 4–5; what makes a poem, 8–9; what writers say about poetry, 6–8
Pope, Alexander (1688–1744), **174–80**
The Rape of the Lock, 175, **177–80**; *Windsor Forest*, 177
Pound, Ezra (1885–1972), 8, 38, 237, 249, 274, 279, 280
'In a station of the Metro', **8**
predicative adjectives, **56**, 57, 292, 417
predicators, **56**, **60**, 83, 313, 342, 417
present participles, *see under* participles
present tense, *see under* tense
progressive, *see under* aspect
pronouns, 418
first person, 47, 82, 85, 153, 288, 381; second person, 47, 63, 76, 153; third person, 64, 299, 350
proper nouns, *see under* nouns
pyrrhic, **72**, 418

quatrain, 29, 32, 36–7, 43, 52, 141, 226, 418
questions, **57**, 252
see also under grammatical mood, interrogatives

Raine, Kathleen (1908–2003), 320–1, 364
'Invocation', **232–4**
reflective tradition, **181**, 182
relative clauses, *see under* clauses
religious verse, **98–100**, **100–4**, 150–1, 151–4, 220–1
devotional poetry, 98, 145; medieval sermon, 126, 180
repetition, 40, 44, 47, **70**, **80** 192, 200, 324, 418
rhetorical devices, **69**, **79–87**, 118, 418
see also listing, patterning, tripling
rhetorical questions, 159, 165, 225

rhyme, **23–4**, **69–73**, 418–19
end, 12, 29, 30, 31, **70**, 71, 74, 275, 301, 410; eye, **70**, 411; full, 23, **70**, 71, 411; feminine, 24, **70**, 251, 411; half, 23, 338, 339, 412; internal, 46, **70**, 72, 74, 97, 239, 252, 361, 393, 399, 413; masculine, 24, 53, **70**, 414
rhythm, 26, 419
falling, **18**, 22; of speech, 19, 20, 25, 145, 171, 294, 326, 381; rising, **17**, 21; *see also* metre
rime riche, **70**, 419
romance, **40**, 97, 104, 116
court, 126, **127–9**, 129–32; *Sir Gawain and the Green Knight,* **107–11**
Romanticism, 181–2, 183, **184–5**, **192–5**, 203, **216–17**, 244
Ross, Alan (1922–2001), 'Embankment Before Snow', **56–7**
Rossetti, Christina (1830–94), 220–1, 221–2, 229
'A Birthday', 81, **83–4**, 222; 'Up-Hill', 220–1
Rousseau, Jean-Jacques (1712–78), 185, 195, 204
run-on lines, **14–15**, 25, 29, 36, 276, 338, 419
see also enjambement

Sassoon, Siegfried (1886–1967), 245, **253–4**
'The General', 254
satire, 14, 115, 124, 126, 129–32, 144, 167–70, 174–6, 354, 419
sentences, 56, **60–5**, **65–8**
complex, **61**, 63, 166, 230, 271, 277, 392, 399, 403, 408; compound, **61**, 63, 408; compound-complex, **62**, 74, 153, 267, 276, 308, 376, 403, 408; minor, 14, 55, **62**, 214, 277, 331, 361, 399, 414; simple, **60–1**, 79, 225, 292, 342, 360, 362, 390, 392, 419
sestet, 12, 32, 419
see also sonnet
Shakespeare, William (1564–1616), 133, **140–4**
'Sonnet LX', **141–3**; 'Sonnet LXXIII', **32–3**
Shelley, Percy Bysshe (1792–1822), 184, **203–7**, **217**
Adonais, 204–5; *Queen Mab*, 203–4, 206
sibilance, 46, 102, 231, 252, 258, 362, 391, 419
Sidney, Sir Philip (1554–86), 135, 170
similes, **35–6**, 63, **75**, 76, 79, 86, 419

Wordsworth, William (1770–1850), 185, 192, 193–4, 195–201, 217
'Composed Upon Westminster Bridge', 84–7; *The Prelude*, 25–6, 196, **197–201**
Wyatt, Sir Thomas (1503–42), 134

Yeats, W.B. (1865–1939), **258–78**
'A Coat', 259, 265; *A Man Young and Old*, 263; 'Byzantium', 265, 272; 'Coole Park, 1929', 262; 'Easter 1916', 264, 270–1; 'Ego Dominus Tuus', 267; 'He Remembers Forgotten Beauty', 267–8; 'In Memory of Major Robert Gregory', 264; 'Lapis Lazuli', 266, 272; 'Leda and the Swan', 273; 'Meditations in Time of Civil War', 265, 266; 'Meru', 265, **274–8**; 'Responsibilities', 262; 'Sailing to Byzantium', 264, 271; 'The Choice', 261; 'The Double Vision of Michael Robartes', 270; 'The Gyres', 262, 266; 'The Second Coming', 265, 268–9; 'The Tower', 264; 'The Wild Swans of Coole', 266; 'Vacillation', 261